English Grammar in Use

A self-study reference and practice book for intermediate students of English

with answers

THIRD EDITION

Raymond Murphy

CAMBRIDGE
UNIVERSITY PRESS

being → know somebody is behaving use for that.

CAMBRIDGE UNIVERSITY PRESS
Cambridge, New York, Melbourne, Madrid, Cape Town, Singapore, São Paulo

Cambridge University Press
The Edinburgh Building, Cambridge CB2 8RU, UK

www.cambridge.org
Information on this title: www.cambridge.org/9780521532891

First published 2004
13th printing 2007

Printed in Singapore by KHL Printing Co Pte Ltd

A catalogue record for this publication is available from the British Library

ISBN 978-0-521-53289-1 Edition with answers
ISBN 978-0-521-53290-7 Edition without answers
ISBN 978-0-521-53762-9 Edition with CD-ROM
ISBN 978-0-521-84311-9 Hardback edition with CD-ROM
ISBN 978-3-12-534086-2 Klett edition with CD-ROM
ISBN 978-3-12-534084-8 Klett edition
ISBN 978-0-521-53760-5 CD-ROM for Windows
ISBN 978-0-521-53761-2 Network CD-ROM

Contents

IF YOU ARE NOT SURE WHICH UNITS YOU NEED TO STUDY, USE THE **STUDY GUIDE** ON PAGE 326.

iii

IF YOU ARE NOT SURE WHICH UNITS YOU NEED TO STUDY, USE THE **STUDY GUIDE** ON PAGE 326.

v

IF YOU ARE NOT SURE WHICH UNITS YOU NEED TO STUDY, USE THE STUDY GUIDE ON PAGE 326.

Thanks

I wrote the original edition of English Grammar in Use when I was a teacher at the Swan School of English, Oxford. I would like to repeat my thanks to my colleagues and students at the school for their help, encouragement and interest at that time.

More recently I would like to thank all the teachers and students I met and who offered their thoughts on the previous edition. It was fun to meet you all and extremely helpful for me.

Regarding the production of this third edition, I am grateful to Alison Sharpe, Liz Driscoll, Jane Mairs and Kamae Design. I would also like to thank Cambridge University Press for permission to access the Cambridge International Corpus.

Thank you also to the following illustrators: Paul Fellows, Gillian Martin, Roger Penwill, Lisa Smith and Simon Williams.

To the student

This book is for students who want help with English grammar. It is written for you to use without a teacher.

The book will be useful for you if you are not sure of the answers to questions like these:
□ What is the difference between *I did* and *I have done*?
□ When do we use *will* for the future?
□ What is the structure after *I wish*?
□ When do we say *used to do* and when do we say *used to doing*?
□ When do we use *the*?
□ What is the difference between *like* and *as*?

These and many other points of English grammar are explained in the book and there are exercises on each point.

Level

The book is intended mainly for *intermediate* students (students who have already studied the basic grammar of English). It concentrates on those structures which intermediate students want to use, but which often cause difficulty. Some advanced students who have problems with grammar will also find the book useful.

The book is *not* suitable for elementary learners.

How the book is organised

There are 145 units in the book. Each unit concentrates on a particular point of grammar. Some problems (for example, the present perfect or the use of *the*) are covered in more than one unit. For a list of units, see the *Contents* at the beginning of the book.

Each unit consists of two facing pages. On the left there are explanations and examples; on the right there are exercises. At the back of the book there is a Key for you to check your answers to the exercises (page 336).

There are also seven *Appendices* at the back of the book (pages 292–301). These include irregular verbs, summaries of verb forms, spelling and American English.

Finally, there is a detailed *Index* at the back of the book (page 373).

How to use the book

The units are *not* in order of difficulty, so it is *not* intended that you work through the book from beginning to end. Every learner has different problems and you should use this book to help you with the grammar that *you* find difficult.

It is suggested that you work in this way:
□ Use the *Contents* and/or *Index* to find which unit deals with the point you are interested in.
□ If you are not sure which units you need to study, use the *Study guide* on page 326.
□ Study the explanations and examples on the left-hand page of the unit you have chosen.
□ Do the exercises on the right-hand page.
□ Check your answers with the *Key*.
□ If your answers are not correct, study the left-hand page again to see what went wrong.

You can of course use the book simply as a reference book without doing the exercises.

Additional exercises

At the back of the book there are *Additional exercises* (pages 302–325). These exercises bring together some of the grammar points from a number of different units. For example, Exercise 16 brings together grammar points from Units 26–36. You can use these exercises for extra practice after you have studied and practised the grammar in the units concerned.

CD Rom

The book is sold with or without a CD Rom. On the CD Rom you will find more exercises on all the units (different from those in the book). There are also 1,700 test questions, and you can use these to make your own tests. The CD Rom can also be bought separately.

To the teacher

English Grammar in Use was written as a self-study grammar book, but teachers may also find it useful as additional course material in cases where further work on grammar is necessary.

The book will probably be most useful at middle- and upper- intermediate levels (where all or nearly all of the material will be relevant), and can serve both as a basis for revision and as a means for practising new structures. It will also be useful for some more advanced students who have problems with grammar and need a book for reference and practice. The book is not intended to be used by elementary learners.

The units are organised in grammatical categories (*Present and past, Articles and nouns, Prepositions* etc.). They are not ordered according to level of difficulty, so the book should not be worked through from beginning to end. It should be used selectively and flexibly in accordance with the grammar syllabus being used and the difficulties students are having.

The book can be used for immediate consolidation or for later revision or remedial work. It might be used by the whole class or by individual students needing extra help. The left-hand pages (explanations and examples) are written for the student to use individually, but they may of course be used by the teacher as a source of ideas and information on which to base a lesson. The student then has the left-hand page as a record of what has been taught and can refer to it in the future. The exercises can be done individually, in class or as homework. Alternatively (and additionally), individual students can be directed to study certain units of the book by themselves if they have particular difficulties not shared by other students in their class. Don't forget the *Additional exercises* at the back of the book (see **To the student**).

The book is sold with or without a CD Rom. This contains further exercises on all the units in the book, as well as a bank of 1,700 test questions from which users can select to compile their own tests. The CD Rom is also available separately.

An edition of *English Grammar in Use* without the *Key* is also available. Some teachers may prefer this for use with their students.

English Grammar in Use *Third Edition*

This is a new edition of *English Grammar in Use*. The differences between this edition and the second edition are:

☐ There are eight new units on phrasal verbs (Units 138–145). There is also a new unit on *wish* (Unit 41). Units 42–81 and 83–137 all have different numbers from the second edition.

☐ Some of the material has been revised or reorganised, and in most units there are minor changes in the examples, explanations and exercises.

☐ The *Additional exercises* have been extended. The new exercises are 14–16, 25, 30–31, and 37–41.

☐ The book has been redesigned with new colour illustrations.

☐ There is a new CD Rom with further exercises to accompany the book.

English Grammar in Use

Present continuous (I am doing)

A Study this example situation:

Sarah is in her car. She is on her way to work.
She **is driving** to work.

This means: she is driving *now*, at the time of speaking.
The action is not finished.

Am/is/are + -ing is the *present continuous*:

I	**am**	(= I'm)	driv**ing**
he/she/it	**is**	(= he's etc.)	work**ing**
we/you/they	**are**	(= we're etc.)	do**ing** etc.

B **I am doing** something = I'm in the middle of doing it; I've started doing it and I haven't finished yet:

- □ Please don't make so much noise. **I'm trying** to work. (*not* I try)
- □ 'Where's Mark?' 'He**'s having** a shower.' (*not* He has a shower)
- □ Let's go out now. It **isn't raining** any more. (*not* It doesn't rain)
- □ (*at a party*) Hello, Jane. **Are** you **enjoying** the party? (*not* Do you enjoy)
- □ What's all that noise? What's **going** on? (= What's happening?)

The action is not necessarily happening at the time of speaking. For example:

Steve is talking to a friend on the phone. He says:

> I'm reading a really good book at the moment. It's about a man who ...

Steve is not reading the book at the time of speaking.
He means that he has started it, but has not finished it yet.
He is in the middle of reading it.

Some more examples:

- □ Kate wants to work in Italy, so she**'s learning** Italian. (but perhaps she isn't learning Italian at the time of speaking)
- □ Some friends of mine **are building** their own house. They hope to finish it next summer.

C You can use the present continuous with **today / this week / this year** etc. (periods around now):

- □ A: You**'re working** hard **today**. (*not* You work hard today)
  B: Yes, I have a lot to do.
- □ The company I work for **isn't doing** so well **this year**.

D We use the present continuous when we talk about changes happening around now, especially with these verbs:

get   change   become   increase   rise   fall   grow   improve   begin   start

- □ **Is** your English **getting** better? (*not* Does your English get better)
- □ The population of the world **is increasing** very fast. (*not* increases)
- □ At first I didn't like my job, but **I'm beginning** to enjoy it now. (*not* I begin)

Exercises

1.1 Complete the sentences with the following verbs in the correct form:

get   happen   look   lose   make   start   stay   try   ~~work~~

1 'You __'re working__ hard today.' 'Yes, I have a lot to do.'
2 I __am looking__ for Christine. Do you know where she is?
3 It __is getting__ dark. Shall I turn on the light?
4 They don't have anywhere to live at the moment. They __are staying__ with friends until they find somewhere.
5 Things are not so good at work. The company __is losing__ money.
6 Have you got an umbrella? It __is starting__ to rain.
7 You __are making__ a lot of noise. Can you be quieter? I __am trying__ to concentrate.
8 Why are all these people here? What __is happening__?

1.2 Put the verb into the correct form. Sometimes you need the negative (**I'm not doing** etc.).

1 Please don't make so much noise. I __'m trying__ (try) to work.
2 Let's go out now. It __isn't raining__ (rain) any more.
3 You can turn off the radio. I __am not listening__ (listen) to it.
4 Kate phoned me last night. She's on holiday in France. She __is having__ (have) a great time and doesn't want to come back.
5 I want to lose weight, so this week I __am not eating__ (eat) lunch.
6 Andrew has just started evening classes. He __is learning__ (learn) German.
7 Paul and Sally have had an argument. They __are not speaking__ (speak) to each other.
8 I __am getting__ (get) tired. I need a rest.
9 Tim __isn't working__ (work) this week. He's on holiday.

1.3 Complete the conversations.

1 A: I saw Brian a few days ago.
  B: Oh, did you? __What's he doing__ these days? (what / he / do)
  A: He's at university.
  B: __What is he studying__? (what / he / study)
  A: Psychology.
  B: __Is he enjoying__ it? (he / enjoy)
  A: Yes, he says it's a very good course.

2 A: Hi, Liz. How __are you getting on__ in your new job? (you / get on)
  B: Not bad. It wasn't so good at first, but __things are getting__ better now. (things / get)
  A: What about Jonathan? Is he OK?
  B: Yes, but __he is not enjoying__ his work at the moment. (he / not / enjoy)
  He's been in the same job for a long time and __he is beginning__ to get bored with it. (he / begin)

1.4 Complete the sentences using the following verbs:

begin   change   get   ~~increase~~   rise

1 The population of the world __is increasing__ very fast.
2 The world __is changing__. Things never stay the same.
3 The situation is already bad and it __is getting__ worse.
4 The cost of living __is rising__. Every year things are more expensive.
5 The weather __is beginning__ to improve. The rain has stopped, and the wind isn't as strong.

Unit 2

Present simple (I do)

A Study this example situation:

Alex is a bus driver, but now he is in bed asleep.
He is not driving a bus. (He is asleep.)

but He **drives** a bus. (He is a bus driver.)

Drive(s)/work(s)/do(es) etc. is the *present simple*:

I/we/you/they **drive/work/do** etc.
he/she/it **drives/works/does** etc.

B We use the present simple to talk about things in general. We use it to say that something happens all the time or repeatedly, or that something is true in general:

- ☐ Nurses **look** after patients in hospitals.
- ☐ I usually **go** away at weekends.
- ☐ The earth **goes** round the sun.
- ☐ The café **opens** at 7.30 in the morning.

Remember:

I work ... *but* **He works ...**   They **teach ...** *but* My sister **teaches ...**

For spelling (**-s** or **-es**), see Appendix 6.

C We use **do/does** to make questions and negative sentences:

do does	I/we/you/they he/she/it	work? drive? do?		I/we/you/they he/she/it	don't doesn't	work drive do

- ☐ I come from Canada. Where **do** you **come** from?
- ☐ I **don't go** away very often.
- ☐ What **does** this word **mean**? (*not* What means this word?)
- ☐ Rice **doesn't grow** in cold climates.

In the following examples, **do** is also the main verb (do you **do** / doesn't **do** etc.):

- ☐ 'What **do** you **do**?' 'I work in a shop.'
- ☐ He's always so lazy. He **doesn't do** anything to help.

D We use the present simple to say how often we do things:

- ☐ I get up at 8 o'clock **every morning**.
- ☐ **How often** do you go to the dentist?
- ☐ Julie **doesn't drink** tea **very often**.
- ☐ Robert usually **goes** away **two or three times a year**.

E I promise / I apologise etc.

Sometimes we do things by saying something. For example, when you *promise* to do something, you can say '**I promise ...**'; when you *suggest* something, you can say '**I suggest ...**':

- ☐ **I promise** I won't be late. (*not* I'm promising)
- ☐ 'What do you **suggest** I do?' '**I suggest** that you ...'

In the same way we say: I **apologise ...** / I **advise ...** / I **insist ...** / I **agree ...** / I **refuse ...** etc.

Present simple and present continuous → Units 3–4   **Present tenses for the future →** Unit 19

Exercises

2.1 Complete the sentences using the following verbs:

> **cause**(s)   **connect**(s)   **drink**(s)   **live**(s)   **open**(s)   ~~**speak**(s)~~   **take**(s)

1 Tanya __speaks__ German very well.
2 I don't often __drinks__ coffee.
3 The swimming pool __opens__ at 7.30 every morning.
4 Bad driving __cause__ many accidents.
5 My parents __lives__ in a very small flat.
6 The Olympic Games __takes__ place every four years.
7 The Panama Canal __connects__ the Atlantic and Pacific oceans.

2.2 Put the verb into the correct form.

1 Julie __doesn't drink__ (not / drink) tea very often.
2 What time __the banks close__ (the banks / close) here?
3 I've got a computer, but I __don't use__ (not / use) it much.
4 'Where __are mum comes__' (Martin / come) from?' 'He's Scottish.'
5 'What __do you do__ (you / do)?' 'I'm an electrician.'
6 It __takes__ (take) me an hour to get to work. How long __does it takes__ (it / take) you?
7 Look at this sentence. What __is this word means__ (this word / mean)?
8 David isn't very fit. He __does not do any__ (not / do) any sport.

2.3 Use the following verbs to complete the sentences. Sometimes you need the negative:

> **believe**   **eat**   **flow**   ~~**go**~~   ~~**grow**~~   **make**   **rise**   **tell**   **translate**

1 The earth __goes__ round the sun.
2 Rice __doesn't grow__ in Britain.
3 The sun .... in the east.
4 Bees .... honey.
5 Vegetarians .... meat.
6 An atheist .... in God.
7 An interpreter .... from one language into another.
8 Liars are people who .... the truth.
9 The River Amazon .... into the Atlantic Ocean.

2.4 You ask Liz questions about herself and her family. Write the questions.

1 You know that Liz plays tennis. You want to know how often. Ask her.
   How often __do you play tennis__ ?
2 Perhaps Liz's sister plays tennis too. You want to know. Ask Liz.
   .... your sister .... ?
3 You know that Liz reads a newspaper every day. You want to know which one. Ask her.
   .... ?
4 You know that Liz's brother works. You want to know what he does. Ask Liz.
   .... ?
5 You know that Liz goes to the cinema a lot. You want to know how often. Ask her.
   .... ?
6 You don't know where Liz's grandparents live. You want to know. Ask Liz.
   .... ?

2.5 Complete using the following:

> **I apologise**   **I insist**   **I promise**   **I recommend**   ~~**I suggest**~~

1 It's a nice day. __I suggest__ we go out for a walk.
2 I won't tell anybody what you said. ....
3 *(in a restaurant)* You must let me pay for the meal. ....
4 .... for what I did. It won't happen again.
5 The new restaurant in Hill Street is very good. .... it.

A Compare:

Present continuous (**I am doing**)	*Present simple* (**I do**)
We use the continuous for things happening at or around the time of speaking. The action is not complete.	We use the simple for things in general or things that happen repeatedly.

I am doing	◄───────── **I do** ─────────►
past *now* *future*	*past* *now* *future*

- □ The water **is boiling**. Can you turn it off?
- □ Listen to those people. What language **are** they **speaking**?
- □ Let's go out. It **isn't raining** now.
- □ 'I'm busy.'   'What **are** you **doing**?'
- □ **I'm getting** hungry. Let's go and eat.
- □ Kate wants to work in Italy, so she's **learning** Italian.
- □ The population of the world **is increasing** very fast.

We use the continuous for *temporary* situations:
- □ **I'm living** with some friends until I find a place of my own.
- □ A: You're **working** hard today.
  B: Yes, I have a lot to do.

See Unit 1 for more information.

- □ Water **boils** at 100 degrees Celsius.
- □ Excuse me, **do** you **speak** English?

- □ It **doesn't rain** very much in summer.
- □ What **do** you usually **do** at weekends?
- □ I always **get** hungry in the afternoon.
- □ Most people **learn** to swim when they are children.
- □ Every day the population of the world **increases** by about 200,000 people.

We use the simple for *permanent* situations:
- □ My parents **live** in London. They have lived there all their lives.
- □ John isn't lazy. He **works** hard most of the time.

See Unit 2 for more information.

B **I always do** and **I'm always doing**

I always do (something) = I do it every time:
- □ I always **go** to work by car. (*not* I'm always going)

'**I'm always doing** something' has a different meaning. For example:

I've lost my pen again. **I'm always losing** things.

I'm always losing things = I lose things very often, perhaps too often, or more often than normal.

Two more examples:
- □ You're **always watching** television. You should do something more active.
  (= You watch television too often)
- □ Tim is never satisfied. He's **always complaining**. (= He complains too much)

Present continuous and simple 2 → Unit 4   Present tenses for the future → Unit 19

Exercises

3.1 Are the <u>underlined</u> verbs right or wrong? Correct them where necessary.

1 Water <u>boils</u> at 100 degrees Celsius. _____ OK _____
2 The water <u>boils</u>. Can you turn it off? _____ is boiling _____ ✓
3 Look! That man <u>tries</u> to open the door of your car. _____ is trying _____
4 Can you hear those people? What <u>do</u> they <u>talk</u> about? _____ are they talking _____
5 The moon <u>goes</u> round the earth in about 27 days. _____ O.K _____
6 I must go now. It <u>gets</u> late. _____ It's getting _____
7 I usually <u>go</u> to work by car. _____ O.K _____
8 'Hurry up! It's time to leave.' 'OK, I <u>come</u>.' _____ am coming _____
9 I hear you've got a new job. How <u>do</u> you <u>get</u> on? _____ are / getting _____
10 Paul is never late. He<u>'s</u> always <u>getting</u> to work on time. _____ gets _____
11 They don't get on well. They<u>'re</u> always <u>arguing</u>. _____ O.K _____

3.2 Put the verb into the correct form, present continuous or present simple.

1 Let's go out. It __isn't raining__ (not / rain) now.
2 Julia is very good at languages. She __speaks__ (speak) four languages very well.
3 Hurry up! Everybody __is waiting__ (wait) for you.
4 'Are you not listening (you / listen) to the radio?' 'No, you can turn it off.'
5 'Do you listen (you / listen) to the radio every day?' 'No, just occasionally.'
6 The River Nile __flows__ (flow) into the Mediterranean.
7 The river __is flowing__ (flow) very fast today – much faster than usual.
8 We usually __grow__ (grow) vegetables in our garden, but this year we __aren't growing__ (not / grow) any.
9 A: How's your English?
  B: Not bad. I think it __is improving__ (improve) slowly.
10 Rachel is in London at the moment. She __is staying__ (stay) at the Park Hotel. She always __stays__ (stay) there when she's in London.
11 Can we stop walking soon? I __am starting__ (start) to feel tired.
12 A: Can you drive?
  B: I __am learning__ (learn). My father __teaches__ (teach) me.
13 Normally I __finish__ (finish) work at five, but this week I __am working__ (work) until six to earn a little more money.
14 My parents __are living__ (live) in Manchester. They were born there and have never lived anywhere else. Where __are your parents living__ (your parents / live)?
15 Sonia __is looking__ (look) for a place to live. She __stays__ (stay) with her sister until she finds somewhere.
16 A: What __is your brother doing__ (your brother / do)?
  B: He's an architect, but he __isn't working__ (not / work) at the moment.
17 (at a party) I usually __enjoy__ (enjoy) parties, but I __am not enjoying__ (not / enjoy) this one very much.

3.3 Finish B's sentences. Use **always –ing**.

1 A: I've lost my pen again.
  B: Not again! __You're always losing your pen__ .
2 A: The car has broken down again.
  B: That car is useless. It __is always breaking the car__ .
3 A: Look! You've made the same mistake again.
  B: Oh no, not again! I __am always making same mistake__ .
4 A: Oh, I've forgotten my glasses again.
  B: Typical! ~~I am always forgetting~~ __You are always forgetting your glasses__ .

Present continuous and present simple 2 (I am doing and I do)

Unit 4

A

We use continuous forms for actions and happenings that have started but not finished (they **are eating** / it **is raining** etc.). Some verbs (for example, **know** and **like**) are not normally used in this way. We don't say 'I am knowing' or 'they are liking'; we say '**I know**', 'they **like**'.

The following verbs are not normally used in the present continuous:

like   love   hate   want   need   prefer
know   realise   suppose   mean   understand   believe   remember
belong   fit   contain   consist   seem

- ☐ I'm hungry. I **want** something to eat. (*not* I'm wanting)
- ☐ **Do** you **understand** what I **mean**?
- ☐ Ann **doesn't seem** very happy at the moment.

B

Think

When **think** means 'believe' or 'have an opinion', we do not use the continuous:
- ☐ I **think** Mary is Canadian, but I'm not sure. (*not* I'm thinking)
- ☐ What **do** you **think** about my plan? (= What is your opinion?)

When **think** means 'consider', the continuous is possible:
- ☐ **I'm thinking** about what happened. I often **think** about it.
- ☐ Nicky **is thinking** of giving up her job. (= she is considering it)

C

He is selfish and **He is being selfish**

He's being = He's behaving / He's acting. Compare:
- ☐ I can't understand why he's **being** so selfish. He isn't usually like that.
  (**being** selfish = behaving selfishly at the moment)
- ☐ He never thinks about other people. He **is** very selfish. (*not* He is being)
  (= He is selfish generally, not only at the moment)

We use **am/is/are being** to say how somebody is *behaving*. It is not usually possible in other sentences:
- ☐ It's hot today. (*not* It is being hot)
- ☐ Sarah **is** very tired. (*not* is being tired)

D

See   hear   smell   taste

We normally use the present simple (not continuous) with these verbs:
- ☐ **Do** you **see** that man over there? (*not* Are you seeing)
- ☐ This room **smells**. Let's open a window.

We often use **can** + see/hear/smell/taste:
- ☐ I **can hear** a strange noise. **Can** you **hear** it?

E

Look   feel

You can use the present simple or continuous to say how somebody looks or feels now:
- ☐ You **look** well today. *or* You're **looking** well today.
- ☐ How **do** you **feel** now? *or* How **are** you **feeling** now?
but
- ☐ I usually **feel** tired in the morning. (*not* I'm usually feeling)

Present continuous and simple 1 → Unit 3   **Have** → Unit 17   **Present tenses for the future** → Unit 19

4.1 Are the <u>underlined</u> verbs right or wrong? Correct them where necessary.

1 Nicky <u>is thinking</u> of giving up her job.   *OK*
2 <u>Are</u> you <u>believing</u> in God?   *believe*
3 <u>I'm feeling</u> hungry. Is there anything to eat?   *ok*
4 This sauce is great. It<u>'s tasting</u> really good.   *tastes*
5 <u>I'm thinking</u> this is your key. Am I right?   *I think*

4.2 Use the words in brackets to make sentences. (You should also study Unit 3 before you do this exercise.)

1 (you / not / seem / very happy today)
You don't seem very happy today.

2 (what / you / do?)
What are you doing?
Be quiet! (I / think)
I am thinking.

3 (who / this umbrella / belong to?)
Who does this umbrella belong to?
I have no idea.

4 (the dinner / smell / good)
The dinner smells good

5 Excuse me. (anybody / sit / there?)
Does anybody sit there?
No, it's free.

6 (these gloves / not / fit / me)
These gloves don't fit me
They're too small.

4.3 Put the verb into the correct form, present continuous or present simple.

1 Are you hungry? __Do you want__ (you / want) something to eat?
2 Don't put the dictionary away. I __am using__ (use) it.
3 Don't put the dictionary away. I __needs__ (need) it.
4 Who is that man? What __does he want__ (he / want)?
5 Who is that man? Why __he is looking__ (he / look) at us?
6 Alan says he's 80 years old, but nobody __believeing__ (believe) him.
7 She told me her name, but I __do not remember__ (not / remember) it now.
8 I __am thinking__ (think) of selling my car. Would you be interested in buying it?
9 I __think__ (think) you should sell your car. You __be not using__ (not / use) it very often.
10 Air __consists__ (consist) mainly of nitrogen and oxygen.

4.4 Complete the sentences using the most suitable form of **be**. Sometimes you must use the simple (am/is/are) and sometimes the continuous is more suitable (am/is/are being).

1 I can't understand why __he's being__ so selfish. He isn't usually like that.
2 Sarah __is be__ very nice to me at the moment. I wonder why.
3 You'll like Debbie when you meet her. She __is being__ very nice.
4 You're usually very patient, so why __are you being__ so unreasonable about waiting ten more minutes?
5 Why isn't Steve at work today? __Steve he is__ ill?

Unit 5

Past simple (I did)

A Study this example:

> Wolfgang Amadeus Mozart was an Austrian musician and composer. He **lived** from 1756 to 1791. He **started** composing at the age of five and **wrote** more than 600 pieces of music. He **was** only 35 years old when he **died**.
>
> **Lived/started/wrote/was/died** are all *past simple*.

B Very often the past simple ends in **-ed** (*regular* verbs):

- ☐ I work in a travel agency now. Before that I **worked** in a department store.
- ☐ We **invited** them to our party, but they **decided** not to come.
- ☐ The police **stopped** me on my way home last night.
- ☐ Laura **passed** her examination because she **studied** very hard.

For spelling (stopped, studied etc.), see Appendix 6.

But many verbs are *irregular*. The past simple does *not* end in **-ed**. For example:

write	→ **wrote**	☐ Mozart **wrote** more than 600 pieces of music.
see	→ **saw**	☐ We **saw** Rose in town a few days ago.
go	→ **went**	☐ I **went** to the cinema three times last week.
shut	→ **shut**	☐ It **was** cold, so I **shut** the window.

For a list of irregular verbs, see Appendix 1.

C In questions and negatives we use **did/didn't** + *infinitive* (**enjoy/see/go** etc.):

I	enjoyed
she	saw
they	went

	you	enjoy?
did	she	see?
	they	go?

I		enjoy
she	**didn't**	see
they		go

- ☐ A: **Did** you **go** out last night?
  B: Yes, I **went** to the cinema, but I **didn't enjoy** the film much.
- ☐ 'When **did** Mr Thomas **die**?' 'About ten years ago.'
- ☐ They **didn't invite** her to the party, so she **didn't go**.
- ☐ '**Did** you **have** time to write the letter?' 'No, I **didn't**.'

In the following examples, **do** is the main verb in the sentence (**did ... do / didn't do**):

- ☐ What **did** you **do** at the weekend? (*not* What did you at the weekend?)
- ☐ I **didn't do** anything. (*not* I didn't anything)

D The past of **be** (**am/is/are**) is **was/were**:

I/he/she/it	**was/wasn't**
we/you/they	**were/weren't**

was	I/he/she/it?
were	we/you/they?

Note that we do not use **did** in negatives and questions with **was/were**:

- ☐ I **was** angry because they **were** late.
- ☐ **Was** the weather good when you **were** on holiday?
- ☐ They **weren't** able to come because they **were** so busy.
- ☐ Did you go out last night or **were** you too tired?

Past simple and past continuous → Unit 6   Past simple and present perfect → Units 12–14

Exercises

5.1 Read what Laura says about a typical working day:

> I usually get up at 7 o'clock and have a big breakfast. I walk to work, which takes me about half an hour. I start work at 8.45. I never have lunch. I finish work at 5 o'clock. I'm always tired when I get home. I usually cook a meal in the evening. I don't usually go out. I go to bed at about 11 o'clock, and I always sleep well.

Laura

Yesterday was a typical working day for Laura. Write what she did or didn't do yesterday.

1 _She got up at 7 o'clock._
2 She _........................._ a big breakfast.
3 She _........................._ .
4 It _........................._ to get to work.
5 _She ...._ at 8.45.
6 _........................._ lunch.
7 _She finished work_ at 5 o'clock.
8 _She ...._ tired when _she got_ home.
9 _She cooked_ a meal yesterday evening.
10 _She did not go_ out yesterday evening.
11 _She went to bed_ at 11 o'clock.
12 _She always slept_ well last night.

5.2 Complete the sentences using the following verbs in the correct form:

buy   catch   cost   fall   hurt   sell   spend   teach   throw   ~~write~~

1 Mozart _wrote_ more than 600 pieces of music.
2 'How did you learn to drive?' 'My father _taught_ me.'
3 We couldn't afford to keep our car, so we _sold_ it.
4 Dave _fell_ down the stairs this morning and _hurt_ his leg.
5 Jim _caught_ the ball to Sue, who _threw_ it.
6 Ann _cost_ a lot of money yesterday. She _bought_ a dress which
   _........................._ £100.

5.3 You ask James about his holiday. Write your questions.

    Hi. How are things?
                          Fine, thanks. I've just had a great holiday.
1 Where _did you go_ ?
                          To the U.S. We went on a trip from San Francisco to Denver.
2 How _did you go_ ? By car?
                          Yes, we hired a car in San Francisco.
3 It's a long way to drive. How long _it was_ ?
                          Two weeks.
4 Where _did you stay_ ? In hotels?
                          Yes, small hotels or motels.
5 _How was weather_ ?
                          Yes, but it was very hot – sometimes too hot.
6 _did you over to_ the Grand Canyon?
                          Of course. It was wonderful.

5.4 Complete the sentences. Put the verb into the correct form, positive or negative.

1 It was warm, so I _took_ off my coat. (take)
2 The film wasn't very good. I _didn't enjoy_ it very much. (enjoy)
3 I knew Sarah was very busy, so I _didn't disturb_ her. (disturb)
4 I was very tired, so I _left_ the party early. (leave)
5 The bed was very uncomfortable. I _didn't sleep_ very well. (sleep)
6 The window was open and a bird _did fly_ into the room. (fly)
7 The hotel wasn't very expensive. It _cost_ very much. (cost)
8 I was in a hurry, so I _didn't have_ time to phone you. (have)
9 It was hard carrying the bags. They _be heavy were_ very heavy. (be)

11

Unit 6

Past continuous (I was doing)

A Study this example situation:

Yesterday Karen and Jim played tennis. They began at 10 o'clock and finished at 11.30.
So, at 10.30 they **were playing** tennis.

They **were playing** = they were in the middle of playing. They had not finished playing.

Was/were -ing is the *past continuous*:

I/he/she/it **was**	playing
we/you/they **were**	doing
	working etc.

B I **was doing** something = I was in the middle of doing something at a certain time. The action or situation had already started before this time, but had not finished:

I started doing	I was doing	I finished doing	
↓	↓	↓	
past		*past*	*now*

- □ This time last year I **was living** in Brazil.
- □ What **were** you **doing** at 10 o'clock last night?
- □ I waved to Helen, but she **wasn't looking**.

C Compare the *past continuous* (I **was doing**) and *past simple* (I **did**):

Past continuous (in the middle of an action)	*Past simple* (complete action)
□ I **was walking** home when I met Dave. (in the middle of an action)	□ I **walked** home after the party last night. (= all the way, completely)
□ Kate **was watching** television when we arrived.	□ Kate **watched** television a lot when she was ill last year.

D We often use the past simple and the past continuous together to say that something happened in the middle of something else:

- □ Matt **phoned** while we **were having** dinner.
- □ It **was raining** when I **got** up.
- □ I **saw** you in the park yesterday. You **were sitting** on the grass and **reading** a book.
- □ I **hurt** my back while I **was working** in the garden.

But we use the past simple to say that one thing happened after another:

- □ I **was walking** along the road when I **saw** Dave. So I **stopped**, and we **had** a chat.

Compare:

□ When Karen arrived, we **were having** dinner. (= we had already started before she arrived)	□ When Karen arrived, we **had** dinner. (= Karen arrived, and then we had dinner)

E Some verbs (for example, **know** and **want**) are not normally used in the continuous (see Unit 4A):

- □ We were good friends. We **knew** each other well. (*not* We were knowing)
- □ I was enjoying the party, but Chris **wanted** to go home. (*not* was wanting)

12

Exercises

6.1 What were you doing at these times? Write sentences as in the examples. The past continuous is not always necessary (see the second example).

1 (at 8 o'clock yesterday evening) _I was having dinner._
2 (at 5 o'clock last Monday) _I was on a bus on my way home._
3 (at 10.15 yesterday morning) _I was in office doing my work_
4 (at 4.30 this morning) _I was wake up was_
5 (at 7.45 yesterday evening) _I was from some_
6 (half an hour ago) _I am breaking my dinner_

6.2 Use your own ideas to complete the sentences. Use the past continuous.

1 Matt phoned while we _were having dinner_ .
2 The doorbell rang while I _was cooking_ .
3 We saw an accident while we _were out to the club_ .
4 Ann fell asleep while she _was hurrying up_ .
5 The television was on, but nobody _was not was watching_ .

6.3 Put the verb into the correct form, past continuous or past simple.

1	2	3

I _saw_ (see) Sue in town yesterday, but she _did out saw_ (not / see) me. She _looked_ (look) the other way.

I _met_ (meet) Tom and Jane at the airport a few weeks ago. They _were going_ (go) to Paris and I _went_ (go) to Rome. We _had_ (have) a chat while we _were waiting_ (wait) for our flights.

I _was cycling_ (cycle) home yesterday when a man _step_ (step) out into the road in front of me. I _was going_ (go) quite fast, but luckily I _did manage_ (manage) to stop in time and _didn't hit_ (not / hit) him.

6.4 Put the verb into the correct form, past continuous or past simple.

1 Jenny _was waiting_ (wait) for me when I _arrived_ (arrive).
2 'What _did you do_ (you / do) at this time yesterday?' 'I was asleep.'
3 '_did you went_ (you / go) out last night?' 'No, I was too tired.'
4 How fast _did you drive_ (you / drive) when the accident _happened_ (happen)?
5 Sam _took_ (take) a photograph of me while I _was not looking_ (not / look).
6 We were in a very difficult position. We _were not any_ (not / know) what to do.
7 I haven't seen Alan for ages. When I last _saw_ (see) him, he _was trying_ (try) to find a job.
8 I _was walking_ (walk) along the street when suddenly I _heard_ (hear) footsteps behind me. Somebody _followed_ (follow) me. I was scared and I _start_ (start) to run.
9 When I was young, I _wanted_ (want) to be a pilot.
10 Last night I _dropped_ (drop) a plate when I _was doing_ (do) the washing up. Fortunately it _did not break_ (not / break).

→ Additional exercise 1 (page 302)

Unit 7 Present perfect 1 (I have done)

A Study this example situation:

Tom is looking for his key. He can't find it.
He **has lost** his key.

He **has lost** his key = He lost it recently, and he still doesn't have it.

Have/has lost is the *present perfect simple*:

I/we/they/you	**have**	(= I've etc.)	finished lost
he/she/it	**has**	(= he's etc.)	done **been** etc.

The present perfect simple is **have/has** + *past participle*. The past participle often ends in **-ed** (finished/decided etc.), but many important verbs are *irregular* (**lost/done/written** etc.).

For a list of irregular verbs, see Appendix 1.

B When we say that 'something **has happened**', this is usually new information:
- ☐ Ow! **I've cut** my finger.
- ☐ The road is closed. There**'s been** (there **has** been) an accident.
- ☐ (*from the news*) Police **have arrested** two men in connection with the robbery.

When we use the present perfect, there is a connection with *now*. The action in the past has a result *now*:
- ☐ 'Where's your key?' 'I don't know. **I've lost** it.' (= I don't have it *now*)
- ☐ He told me his name, but **I've forgotten** it. (= I can't remember it *now*)
- ☐ 'Is Sally here?' 'No, she**'s gone** out.' (= she is out *now*)
- ☐ I can't find my bag. **Have** you **seen** it? (= Do you know where it is *now*?)

C You can use the present perfect with **just, already** and **yet**.

Just = a short time ago:
- ☐ 'Are you hungry?' 'No, **I've just had** lunch.'
- ☐ Hello. **Have** you **just arrived**?

We use **already** to say that something happened sooner than expected:
- ☐ 'Don't forget to send the letter.' '**I've already sent** it.'
- ☐ 'What time is Mark leaving?' 'He**'s already gone**.'

Yet = until now. **Yet** shows that the speaker is expecting something to happen. Use **yet** only in questions and negative sentences:
- ☐ **Has** it **stopped** raining **yet**?
- ☐ I**'ve written** the letter, but I **haven't sent** it **yet**.

D Note the difference between **gone (to)** and **been (to)**:
- ☐ Jim is on holiday. He **has gone to** Italy. (= he is there now or on his way there)
- ☐ Jane is back home now. She **has been to** Italy. (= she has now come back)

Present perfect → Units 8, 11 **Been to** → Units 8A, 126B Present perfect continuous → Units 9–10
Present perfect and past → Units 12–14 **Yet and already** → Unit 111 American English → Appendix 7

Exercises

7.1 Read the situations and write sentences. Use the following verbs:

arrive   break   fall   go up   grow   improve   ~~lose~~

1 Tom is looking for his key. He can't find it.   <u>He has lost his key.</u>
2 Margaret can't walk and her leg is in plaster.   She <u>has</u>
3 Last week the bus fare was 80 pence. Now it is 90.   The bus fare
4 Maria's English wasn't very good. Now it is better.   Her English
5 Dan didn't have a beard before. Now he has a beard.   He
6 This morning I was expecting a letter. Now I have it.   The letter
7 The temperature was 20 degrees. Now it is only 12.   The

7.2 Complete B's sentences. Use the verb in brackets + **just/already/yet**.

	A	B
1	Would you like something to eat?	No, thanks. <u>I've just had lunch.</u> (I / just / have / lunch)
2	Do you know where Julia is?	Yes, ... (I / just / see / her)
3	What time is David leaving?	.... (he / already / leave)
4	What's in the newspaper today?	I don't know. .... (I / not / read / it yet)
5	Is Sue coming to the cinema with us?	No, ... (she / already / see / the film)
6	Are your friends here yet?	Yes, ... (they / just / arrive)
7	What does Tim think about your plan?	.... (we / not / tell / him yet)

7.3 Read the situations and write sentences with **just**, **already** or **yet**.

1 After lunch you go to see a friend at her house. She says, 'Would you like something to eat?'
   You say: No thank you. <u>I've just had lunch</u> . (have lunch)
2 Joe goes out. Five minutes later, the phone rings and the caller says, 'Can I speak to Joe?'
   You say: I'm afraid .... (go out)
3 You are eating in a restaurant. The waiter thinks you have finished and starts to take your
   plate away. You say: Wait a minute! .... (not / finish)
4 You are going to a restaurant tonight. You phone to reserve a table. Later your friend says,
   'Shall I phone to reserve a table.' You say: No, ... (do it)
5 You know that a friend of yours is looking for a place to live. Perhaps she has been successful.
   Ask her. You say: .... ? (find)
6 You are still thinking about where to go for your holiday. A friend asks, 'Where are you going
   for your holiday?' You say: .... (not /decide)
7 Linda went to the bank, but a few minutes ago she returned. Somebody asks, 'Is Linda still at
   the bank?' You say: No, ... (come back)

7.4 Put in **been** or **gone**.

1 Jim is on holiday. He's <u>gone</u> to Italy.
2 Hello! I've just .... to the shops. I've bought lots of things.
3 Alice isn't here at the moment. She's .... to the shop to get a newspaper.
4 Tom has .... out. He'll be back in about an hour.
5 'Are you going to the bank?' 'No, I've already .... to the bank.'

Present perfect 2 (I have done)

A Study this example conversation:

DAVE: **Have** you **travelled** a lot, Jane?
JANE: Yes, **I've been** to lots of places.
DAVE: Really? **Have** you ever **been** to China?
JANE: Yes, **I've been** to China twice.
DAVE: What about India?
JANE: No, I **haven't been** to India.

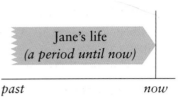

Jane's life
(a period until now)

past   *now*

When we talk about a period of time that continues from the past until now, we use the *present perfect* (**have been** / **have travelled** etc.). Here, Dave and Jane are talking about the places Jane has visited in her life (which is a period that continues until now).

Some more examples:

- □ **Have** you ever **eaten** caviar? (in your life)
- □ **We've** never **had** a car.
- □ '**Have** you **read** *Hamlet*?' 'No, I **haven't read** any of Shakespeare's plays.'
- □ Susan really loves that film. **She's seen** it eight times!
- □ What a boring film! **It's** the most boring film **I've ever seen.**

Been (to) = visited:

- □ **I've** never **been to** China. **Have** you **been** there?

In the following examples too, the speakers are talking about a period that continues until now (**recently** / **in the last few days** / **so far** / **since breakfast** etc.):

- □ **Have** you **heard** from Brian **recently**?
- □ **I've met** a lot of people **in the last few days**.
- □ Everything is going well. We **haven't had** any problems **so far**.
- □ I'm hungry. I **haven't eaten** anything **since breakfast**. (= from breakfast until now)
- □ It's good to see you again. We **haven't seen** each other **for a long time**.

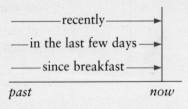

————— recently —————→
——— in the last few days ———→
——— since breakfast ———→

past   *now*

B We use the present perfect with **today** / **this evening** / **this year** etc. when these periods are not finished at the time of speaking (see also Unit 14B):

- □ **I've drunk** four cups of coffee **today**.
- □ **Have** you **had** a holiday **this year** (yet)?
- □ **I haven't seen** Tom **this morning. Have** you?
- □ Rob **hasn't studied** very hard **this term**.

————— today —————→

past   *now*

C We say: It's the (first) time something **has happened**. For example:

- □ Don is having a driving lesson. It's his first one.
  It's the first time he **has driven** a car. (*not* drives)
- *or*   He **has never driven** a car **before**.
- □ Sarah has lost her passport again. This is the second time this **has happened**. (*not* happens)
- □ Bill is phoning his girlfriend again. That's the third time **he's phoned** her **this evening**.

This is the first time
I've **driven** a car.

Present perfect 1 → Unit 7   Present perfect + **for/since** → Units 11–12
Present perfect and past → Units 12–14

Exercises

8.1 You are asking people questions about things they have done. Make questions with **ever** using the words in brackets.

1 (ride / horse?) ___Have you ever ridden a horse?___
2 (be / California?) Have _____
3 (run / marathon?) _____
4 (speak / famous person?) _____
5 (most beautiful place / visit?) What's _____

8.2 Complete B's answers. Some sentences are positive and some negative. Use the following verbs:

be   be   eat   happen   have   ~~meet~~   play   read   see   see   try

	A	B
1	What's Mark's sister like?	I've no idea. __I've never met__ her.
2	How is Diane these days?	I don't know. I _____ her recently.
3	Are you hungry?	Yes. I _____ much today.
4	Can you play chess?	Yes, but _____ for ages.
5	Are you enjoying your holiday?	Yes, it's the best holiday _____ for a long time.
6	What's that book like?	I don't know. _____ it.
7	Is Brussels an interesting place?	I've no idea. _____ there.
8	Mike was late for work again today.	Again? He _____ late every day this week.
9	Do you like caviar?	I don't know. _____ it.
10	I hear your car broke down again yesterday.	Yes, it's the second time _____ this week.
11	Who's that woman by the door?	I don't know. _____ her before.

8.3 Complete the sentences using **today / this year / this term** etc.

1 I saw Tom yesterday, but ___I haven't seen him today___ .
3 I read a newspaper yesterday, but I _____ today.
4 Last year the company made a profit, but this year _____ .
4 Tracy worked hard at school last term, but _____ .
5 It snowed a lot last winter, but _____ .
6 Our football team won a lot of games last season, but we _____ .

8.4 Read the situations and write sentences as shown in the example.

1 Jack is driving a car, but he's very nervous and not sure what to do.
  You ask: ___Have you driven a car before?___
  He says: ___No, this is the first time I've driven a car.___

2 Ben is playing tennis. He's not good at it and he doesn't know the rules.
  You ask: Have _____
  He says: No, this is the first _____

3 Sue is riding a horse. She doesn't look very confident or comfortable.
  You ask: _____
  She says: _____

4 Maria is in London. She has just arrived and it's very new for her.
  You ask: _____
  She says: _____

Present perfect continuous (I have been doing)

A It has been raining

Study this example situation:

Is it raining?
No, but the ground is wet.

It **has been raining**.

Have/has been -ing is the *present perfect continuous*:

I/we/they/you **have** (= I've etc.) he/she/it **has** (= he's etc.)	**been**	doing waiting playing etc.

We use the present perfect continuous for an activity that has recently stopped or just stopped. There is a connection with *now*:

- ☐ You're out of breath. **Have** you **been running**? (= you're out of breath *now*)
- ☐ Paul is very tired. He's **been working** very hard. (= he's tired *now*)
- ☐ Why are your clothes so dirty? What **have** you **been doing**?
- ☐ I've **been talking** to Amanda about the problem and she agrees with me.
- ☐ Where have you been? I've **been looking** for you everywhere.

B It has been raining for two hours.

Study this example situation:

It began raining two hours ago and it is still raining.

How long **has** it **been raining**?
It **has been raining** for two hours.

We use the present perfect continuous in this way with **how long, for ...** and **since ...** . The activity is still happening (as in this example) or has just stopped.

- ☐ **How long have** you **been learning** English? (= you're still learning English)
- ☐ Tim is still watching television. He's **been watching** television **all day**.
- ☐ Where have you been? I've **been looking** for you **for the last half hour**.
- ☐ Chris **hasn't been feeling** well **recently**.

You can use the present prefect continuous for actions repeated over a period of time:

- ☐ Debbie is a very good tennis player. She's **been playing since she was eight**.
- ☐ Every morning they meet in the same café. They've **been going** there **for years**.

C Compare **I am doing** (see Unit 1) and **I have been doing**:

I am doing *present continuous* *now*	**I have been doing** *present perfect continuous* *now*
☐ Don't disturb me now. **I'm working**.	☐ I've **been working** hard. Now I'm going to have a break.
☐ We need an umbrella. It's **raining**.	☐ The ground is wet. It's **been raining**.
☐ Hurry up! We're **waiting**.	☐ We've **been waiting** for an hour.

Present perfect continuous and simple → Units 10–11   Present perfect + for/since → Units 11–12

Exercises

9.1 What have these people been doing or what has been happening?

1 *earlier* *now*

They __'ve been shopping.__

2 *earlier* *now*

She _____

3 *earlier* *now*

They _____

4 *earlier* *now*

He _____

9.2 Write a question for each situation.

1 You meet Paul as he is leaving the swimming pool.
You ask: (you / swim?) __Have you been swimming?__

2 You have just arrived to meet a friend who is waiting for you.
You ask: (you / wait / long?) _____

3 You meet a friend in the street. His face and hands are very dirty.
You ask: (what / you / do?) _____

4 A friend of yours is now working in a shop. You want to know how long.
You ask: (how long / you / work / there?) _____

5 A friend tells you about his job – he sells computers. You want to know how long.
You ask: (how long / you / sell / computers?) _____

9.3 Read the situations and complete the sentences.

1 It's raining. The rain started two hours ago.
It __'s been raining__ for two hours.

2 We are waiting for the bus. We started waiting 20 minutes ago.
We _____ for 20 minutes.

3 I'm learning Spanish. I started classes in December.
I _____ since December.

4 Mary is working in London. She started working there on 18 January.
_____ since 18 January.

5 Our friends always spend their holidays in Italy. They started going there years ago.
_____ for years.

9.4 Put the verb into the present continuous (**I am –ing**) or present perfect continuous
(**I have been –ing**).

1 __Maria has been learning__ (Maria / learn) English for two years.

2 Hello, Tom. _____ (I / look) for you. Where have you been?

3 Why _____ (you / look) at me like that? Stop it!

4 Linda is a teacher. _____ (she / teach) for ten years.

5 _____ (I / think) about what you said and I've decided to take your
advice.

6 'Is Paul on holiday this week?' 'No, _____ (he / work).'

7 Sarah is very tired. _____ (she / work) very hard recently.

A Study this example situation:

Kate's clothes are covered in paint. She **has been painting** the ceiling.	The ceiling was white. Now it is red. She **has painted** the ceiling.
Has been painting is the *present perfect continuous*.	**Has painted** is the *present perfect simple*.
We are interested in the activity. It does not matter whether something has been finished or not. In this example, the activity (painting the ceiling) has not been finished.	Here, the important thing is that something has been finished. **Has painted** is a completed action. We are interested in the result of the activity (the painted ceiling), not the activity itself.

Compare these examples:

□ My hands are very dirty. **I've been repairing** the car.	□ The car is OK again now. **I've repaired** it.
□ Joe **has been eating** too much recently. He should eat less.	□ Somebody **has eaten** all my chocolates. The box is empty.
□ It's nice to see you again. What **have** you **been doing** since we last met?	□ Where's the book I gave you? What **have** you **done** with it?
□ Where have you been? **Have** you **been playing** tennis?	□ **Have** you ever **played** tennis?

B

We use the continuous to say *how long* (for an activity that is still happening):	We use the simple to say *how much*, *how many* or *how many times* (for completed actions):
□ How long **have** you **been reading** that book?	□ How much of that book **have** you **read**?
□ Lisa is still writing letters. She'**s been writing** letters **all day.**	□ Lisa **has written** ten letters today.
□ They'**ve been playing** tennis **since** 2 o'clock.	□ They'**ve played** tennis three times this week.
□ I'm learning Spanish, but I **haven't been learning** it very long.	□ I'm learning Spanish, but I **haven't learnt** very much yet.

C Some verbs (for example, **know/like/believe**) are not normally used in the continuous:

□ I'**ve known** about it for a long time. (*not* I've been knowing)

For a list of these verbs, see Unit 4A. But note that you *can* use **want** and **mean** in the present perfect continuous:

□ I'**ve been meaning** to phone Jane, but I keep forgetting.

Present perfect simple → Units 7–8   Present perfect continuous → Unit 9
Present perfect + for/since → Units 11–12

Exercises

10.1 For each situation, write two sentences using the words in brackets.

1 Tom started reading a book two hours ago. He is still reading it and now he is on page 53.
(read / for two hours) _He has been reading for two hours._
(read / 53 pages so far) _He has read 53 pages so far._

2 Rachel is from Australia. She is travelling round Europe at the moment. She began her trip three months ago.
(travel / for three months) She _has been travelling for three months._
(visit / six countries so far) _She has visited six countries so far._

3 Patrick is a tennis player. He began playing tennis when he was ten years old. This year he is national champion again – for the fourth time.
(win / the national championships / four times) ....
(play / tennis since he was ten) ....

4 When they left college, Lisa and Sue started making films together. They still make films.
(make / five films since they left college) They ....
(make / films since they left college) ....

10.2 For each situation, ask a question using the words in brackets.

1 You have a friend who is learning Arabic. You ask:
(how long / learn / Arabic?) _How long have you been learning Arabic?_

2 You have just arrived to meet a friend. She is waiting for you. You ask:
(wait / long?) Have ....

3 You see somebody fishing by the river. You ask:
(catch / any fish?) ....

4 Some friends of yours are having a party next week. You ask:
(how many people / invite?) ....

5 A friend of yours is a teacher. You ask:
(how long / teach?) ....

6 You meet somebody who is a writer. You ask:
(how many books / write?) ....
(how long / write / books?) ....

7 A friend of yours is saving money to go on holiday. You ask:
(how long / save?) ....
(how much money / save?) ....

10.3 Put the verb into the more suitable form, present perfect simple (**I have done**) or continuous (**I have been doing**).

1 Where have you been? _Have you been playing_ (you / play) tennis?

2 Look! .... (somebody / break) that window.

3 You look tired. .... (you / work) hard?

4 '................................ (you / ever / work) in a factory?' 'No, never.'

5 'Liz is away on holiday.' 'Is she? Where .... (she / go)?

6 My brother is an actor. .... (he / appear) in several films.

7 'Sorry I'm late.' 'That's all right. .... (I / not / wait) long.'

8 'Is it still raining?' 'No, ... (it / stop).'

9 .... (I / lose) my address book. .... (you / see) it?

10 .... (I / read) the book you lent me, but .... (I / not / finish) it yet. It's very interesting.

11 .... (I / read) the book you lent me, so you can have it back now.

A Study this example situation:

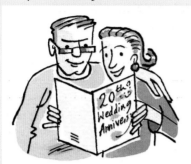

Dan and Jenny are married. They got married exactly 20 years ago, so today is their 20th wedding anniversary.

They **have been** married **for 20 years**.

We say: They **are** married. *(present)*

but **How long have** they **been** married? *(present perfect)*
(*not* How long are they married?)
They **have been** married **for 20 years**.
(*not* They are married for 20 years)

We use the *present perfect* to talk about something that began in the past and still continues now. Compare the *present* and the *present perfect*:

□ Bill **is** in hospital.
but He **has been** in hospital **since Monday**.
(*not* Bill is in hospital since Monday)

□ **Do** you **know** each other well?
but **Have** you **known** each other **for a long time**?
(*not* Do you know)

□ She's **waiting** for somebody.
but She's **been waiting** all morning.

□ **Do** they **have** a car?
but **How long have** they **had** their car?

present

present perfect

now

B **I have known/had/lived** etc. is the *present perfect simple*.
I have been learning / been waiting / been doing etc. is the *present perfect continuous*.

When we ask or say 'how long', the continuous is more usual (see Unit 10):
□ I've **been learning** English **for six months**.
□ It's **been raining** since lunchtime.
□ Richard **has been doing** the same job **for 20 years**.
□ 'How long have you **been driving**?' 'Since I was 17.'

Some verbs (for example, **know/like/believe**) are not normally used in the continuous:
□ How long **have** you **known** Jane? (*not* have you been knowing)
□ I've **had** a pain in my stomach all day. (*not* I've been having)
See also Units 4A and 10C. For **have**, see Unit 17.

C You can use either the present perfect continuous or simple with **live** and **work**:
□ Julia **has been living / has lived** in Paris for a long time.
□ How long **have** you **been working / have** you **worked** here?

But we use the simple (**I've lived / I've done** etc.) with **always**:
□ I've **always lived** in the country. (*not* always been living)

D We say '**I haven't done** something **since/for** ...' (*present perfect simple*):
□ I **haven't seen** Tom since Monday. (= Monday was the last time I saw him)
□ Sue **hasn't phoned** for ages. (= the last time she phoned was ages ago)

Exercises

11.1 Are the <u>underlined</u> verbs right or wrong? Correct them where necessary.

1 Bob is a friend of mine. <u>I know him</u> very well.   _OK_
2 Bob is a friend of mine. <u>I know him</u> for a long time.   _I've known him_
3 Sue and Alan <u>are married</u> since July. ....
4 The weather is awful. <u>It's raining</u> again. ....
5 The weather is awful. <u>It's raining</u> all day. ....
6 I like your house. How long <u>are you living</u> there? ....
7 Gary <u>is working</u> in a shop for the last few months. ....
8 <u>I don't know</u> Tim well. We've only met a few times. ....
9 I gave up drinking coffee. I <u>don't drink</u> it for a year. ....
10 That's a very old bike. How long <u>do you have</u> it? ....

11.2 Read the situations and write questions from the words in brackets.

1 John tells you that his mother is in hospital. You ask him:
(how long / be / in hospital?)   _How long has your mother been in hospital?_
2 You meet a woman who tells you that she teaches English. You ask her:
(how long / teach / English?) ....
3 You know that Jane is a good friend of Caroline's. You ask Jane:
(how long / know / Caroline?) ....
4 Your friend's brother went to Australia some time ago and he's still there. You ask your friend:
(how long / be / in Australia?) ....
5 Tim always wears the same jacket. It's a very old jacket. You ask him:
(how long / have / that jacket?) ....
6 You are talking to a friend about Joe. Joe now works at the airport. You ask your friend:
(how long / work / at the airport?) ....
7 A friend of yours is learning to drive. You ask him:
(how long / learn / to drive?) ....
8 You meet somebody on a plane. She says that she lives in Chicago. You ask her:
(always / live / in Chicago?) ....

11.3 Complete B's answers to A's questions.

	A	B
1	Bill is in hospital, isn't he?	Yes, he _has been_ in hospital since Monday.
2	Do you see Ann very often?	No, I _haven't seen_ her for three months.
3	Is Margaret married?	Yes, she .... married for ten years.
4	Are you waiting for me?	Yes, I .... for the last half hour.
5	You know Linda, don't you?	Yes, we .... each other a long time.
6	Do you still play tennis?	No, I .... tennis for years.
7	Is Jim watching TV?	Yes, he .... TV all evening.
8	Do you watch TV a lot?	No, I .... TV for ages.
9	Have you got a headache?	Yes, I .... a headache all morning.
10	George is never ill, is he?	No, he .... ill since I've known him.
11	Are you feeling ill?	Yes, I .... ill all day.
12	Sue lives in London, doesn't she?	Yes, she .... in London for the last few years.
13	Do you go to the cinema a lot?	No, I .... to the cinema for ages.
14	Would you like to go to New York one day?	Yes, I .... to go to New York. (_use_ **always / want**)

A

We use **for** and **since** to say how long something has been happening.

We use **for** + a period of time (**two hours, six weeks** etc.):

□ I've been waiting **for two hours**.

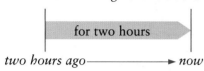

for two hours

two hours ago ——————→ now

for		
two hours	a long time	a week
20 minutes	six months	ages
five days	50 years	years

□ Sally has been working here **for six months**. (*not* since six months)
□ I haven't seen Tom **for three days**. (*not* since three days)

We use **since** + the start of a period (**8 o'clock, Monday, 1999** etc.):

□ I've been waiting **since 8 o'clock**.

since 8 o'clock

8 o'clock ——————→ now

since		
8 o'clock	April	lunchtime
Monday	1985	we arrived
12 May	Christmas	I got up

□ Sally has been working here **since April**. (= from April until now)
□ I haven't seen Tom **since Monday**. (= from Monday until now)

It is possible to leave out **for** (but not usually in negative sentences):
□ They've been married (for) **ten years**. (with or without **for**)
□ They **haven't had** a holiday **for ten years**. (you must use **for**)

We do *not* use for + all ... (all day / all my life etc.):
□ I've lived here **all my life**. (*not* for all my life)

B

Compare **when ... ?** (+ *past simple*) and **how long ... ?** (+ *present perfect*):

A: **When** did it start raining?
B: It started raining   **an hour ago / at 1 o'clock**.

A: **How long** has it been raining?
B: It's been raining   **for an hour / since 1 o'clock**.

A: **When** did Joe and Carol first meet?
B: They first met { **a long time ago.**
{ **when they were at school.**

A: **How long** have they known each other?
B: They've known each other { **for a long time.**
{ **since they were at school.**

C

We say 'It's (a long time / two years etc.) **since** something happened':
□ **It's two years since** I last saw Joe. (= I **haven't seen** Joe for two years)
□ **It's ages since** we went to the cinema. (= We **haven't been** to the cinema for ages)

You can ask 'How long is it since ... ?':
□ **How long is it since** you last saw Joe? (= When did you last see Joe?)
□ **How long is it since** Mrs Hill died? (= When did Mrs Hill die?)

You can also say 'It's been (= It has been) ... since ... ':
□ **It's been** two years since I last saw Joe.

How long have you (been) ... ? → Unit 11

Exercises

12.1 Write **for** or **since**.

1 It's been raining ....*since*.... lunchtime.
2 Sarah has lived in Paris .... 1995.
3 Paul has lived in London .... ten years.
4 I'm tired of waiting. We've been sitting here .... an hour.
5 Kevin has been looking for a job .... he left school.
6 I haven't been to a party .... ages.
7 I wonder where Joe is. I haven't seen him .... last week.
8 Jane is away. She's been away .... Friday.
9 The weather is dry. It hasn't rained .... a few weeks.

12.2 Write questions with **how long** and **when**.

1 It's raining.
(how long?) ....*How long has it been raining?*....
(when?) ....*When did it start raining?*....
2 Kate is learning Japanese.
(how long / learn?) ....
(when / start?) ....
3 I know Simon.
(how long / you / know?) ....
(when / you / first / meet?) ....
4 Rebecca and David are married.
(how long?) ....
(when?) ....

12.3 Read the situations and complete the sentences.

1 It's raining. It's been raining since lunchtime. It ....*started raining*.... at lunchtime.
2 Ann and Sue are friends. They first met years ago. They've ....*known each other for*.... years.
3 Joe is ill. He became ill on Sunday. He has .... Sunday.
4 Joe is ill. He became ill a few days ago. He has .... a few days.
5 Liz is married. She's been married for a year. She got ....
6 You have a headache. It started when you woke up.
I've .... I woke up.
7 Sue has been in Italy for the last three weeks.
She went ....
8 You're working in a hotel. You started six months ago.
I've ....

12.4 Write B's sentences using the words in brackets.

1 A: Do you often go on holiday?
B: (no / five years) ....*No, I haven't had a holiday for five years.*....
2 A: Do you often see Sarah?
B: (no / about a month) No, ...
3 A: Do you often go to the cinema?
B: (no / a long time) ....
4 A: Do you often eat in restaurants?
B: (no / ages) No, I ....

Now write B's answers again. This time use **It's ... since ...** .
5 (1) ....*No, it's five years since I had a holiday.*....
6 (2) No, ...
7 (3) ....
8 (4) No, it's ....

Present perfect and past 1
(I have done and I did)

A Study this example situation:

Tom is looking for his key. He can't find it.

He **has lost** his key. (*present perfect*)

This means that he doesn't have his key *now*.

Ten minutes later:

Now Tom **has found** his key. He has it now.

Has he **lost** his key?   No, he **has found** it.

Did he **lose** his key?   Yes, he **did**.

He **lost** his key (*past simple*)

but now he **has found** it. (*present perfect*)

The present perfect (something **has happened**) is a *present* tense. It always tells us about the situation *now*. 'Tom **has lost** his key' = he doesn't have his key *now* (see Unit 7).

The past simple (something **happened**) tells us only about the *past*. If somebody says 'Tom **lost** his key', this doesn't tell us whether he has the key now or not. It tells us only that he lost his key at some time in the past.

Do *not* use the present perfect if the situation now is different. Compare:
- ☐ They've **gone** away. They'll be back on Friday. (they are away *now*)
  They **went** away, but I think they're back at home now. (*not* They've gone)

- ☐ It **has stopped** raining now, so we don't need the umbrella. (it isn't raining *now*)
  It **stopped** raining for a while, but now it's raining again. (*not* It has stopped)

B You can use the present perfect for new or recent happenings:
- ☐ 'I've **repaired** the TV. It's working OK now.' 'Oh, that's good.'
- ☐ Have you heard the news? Sally **has won** the lottery!

Use the past simple (*not* the present perfect) for things that are not recent or new:
- ☐ Mozart **was** a composer. He **wrote** more than 600 pieces of music.
  (*not* has been … has written)
- ☐ My mother **grew** up in Scotland. (*not* has grown)

Compare:
- ☐ Did you know that somebody **has invented** a new type of washing machine?
- ☐ Who **invented** the telephone? (*not* has invented)

C We use the present perfect to give new information (see Unit 7). But if we continue to talk about it, we normally use the past simple:
- ☐ A: Ow! I've **burnt** myself.
  B: How **did** you **do** that? (*not* have you done)
  A: I **picked** up a hot dish. (*not* have picked)

- ☐ A: Look! Somebody **has spilt** something on the sofa.
  B: Well, it **wasn't** me. I **didn't do** it. (*not* hasn't been … haven't done)

13.1 Complete the sentences using the verbs in brackets. Use the present perfect where possible. Otherwise use the past simple.

1 I can't get in. I **'ve lost** (lose) my key.

2 The office is empty now. Everybody .... (go) home.

3 I meant to call you last night, but I .... (forget).

4 Mary .... (go) to Egypt for a holiday, but she's back home in England now.

5 Are you OK?
Yes, I .... (have) a headache, but I feel fine now.

6 Can you help us? Our car .... (break) down.

13.2 Put the verb into the correct form, present perfect or past simple.

1 It **stopped** raining for a while, but now it's raining again. (stop)
2 The town is very different now. It **has changed** a lot. (change)
3 I did German at school, but I .... most of it now. (forget)
4 The police .... three people, but later they let them go. (arrest)
5 What do you think of my English? Do you think it .... ? (improve)
6 A: Are you still reading the paper?
   B: No, I .... with it. You can have it. (finish)
7 I .... for a job as a tourist guide, but I wasn't successful. (apply)
8 Where's my bike? It .... outside the house, but it's not there now. (be)
9 Look! There's an ambulance over there. There .... an accident. (be)
10 A: Have you heard about Ben? He .... his arm. (break)
   B: Really? How .... that .... ? (happen)
   A: He .... off a ladder. (fall)

13.3 Are the <u>underlined</u> parts of these sentences right or wrong? Correct them where necessary.

1 Do you know about Sue? <u>She's given</u> up her job.   *OK*
2 My mother <u>has grown</u> up in Scotland.   *grew*
3 How many plays <u>has Shakespeare written</u>? ....
4 Ow! <u>I've cut</u> my finger. It's bleeding. ....
5 Drugs <u>have become</u> a big problem everywhere. ....
6 The Chinese <u>have invented</u> paper. ....
7 Where <u>have you been born</u>? ....
8 Mary isn't at home. <u>She's gone</u> shopping. ....
9 Albert Einstein <u>has been</u> the scientist who <u>has developed</u> the theory of relativity. ....

Present perfect and past 2
(I have done and I did)

A

Do not use the present perfect (**I have done**) when you talk about a *finished* time (for example, **yesterday** / **ten minutes ago** / **in 1999** / **when I was a child**). Use a past tense:

- It **was** very cold **yesterday**. (*not* has been)
- Paul and Lucy **arrived ten minutes ago**. (*not* have arrived)
- **Did** you **eat** a lot of sweets **when you were a child**? (*not* have you eaten)
- I **got** home late **last night**. I **was** very tired and **went** straight to bed.

Use the past to ask **When ... ?** or **What time ... ?**:

- **When did** your friends **arrive**? (*not* have ... arrived)
- **What time did** you **finish** work?

Compare:

Present perfect	*Past simple*
□ Tom **has lost** his key. He can't get into the house.	□ Tom **lost** his key **yesterday**. He couldn't get into the house.
□ Is Carla here or **has** she **left**?	□ **When did** Carla **leave**?

B

Compare:

Present perfect (**have done**)
- I've **done** a lot of work **today**.

We use the present perfect for a period of time that continues *until now*. For example: **today** / **this week** / **since 1985**.

Past simple (**did**)
- I **did** a lot of work **yesterday**.

We use the past simple for a *finished* time in the past. For example: **yesterday** / **last week** / **from 1995 to 2001**.

┌*unfinished*┐
today
past　　*now*

┌*finished*┐
yesterday
past　　*now*

- It **hasn't rained this week**.
- **Have** you **seen** Anna **this morning**? (it is still morning)
- **Have** you **seen** Tim **recently**?
- I don't know where Lisa is. I **haven't seen** her. (= I haven't seen her recently)
- We've **been waiting** for an hour. (we are still waiting now)
- Ian lives in London. He **has lived** there for seven years.
- I **have never played** golf. (in my life)
- *It's the last day of your holiday. You say:* It's **been** a really good holiday. I've really **enjoyed** it.

- It **didn't rain last week**.
- **Did** you **see** Anna **this morning**? (it is now afternoon or evening)
- **Did** you **see** Tim **on Sunday**?
- A: **Was** Lisa at the party **on Sunday**? B: I don't think so. I **didn't see** her.
- We **waited** (*or* **were waiting**) for an hour. (we are no longer waiting)
- Ian **lived** in Scotland for ten years. Now he lives in London.
- I **didn't play** golf **last summer**.
- *After you come back from holiday you say:* It **was** a really good holiday. I really **enjoyed** it.

Past simple → Unit 5　Present perfect → Units 7–8　Present perfect and past 1 → Unit 13

Exercises

Unit 14

14.1 Are the <u>underlined</u> parts of these sentences right or wrong? Correct them where necessary.

1 <u>I've lost</u> my key. I can't find it anywhere.   _OK_
2 <u>Have you eaten</u> a lot of sweets when you were a child?   _Did you eat_
3 <u>I've bought</u> a new car. You must come and see it.   ....
4 <u>I've bought</u> a new car last week.   ....
5 Where <u>have you been</u> yesterday evening?   ....
6 Lucy <u>has left</u> school in 1999.   ....
7 I'm looking for Mike. <u>Have you seen</u> him?   ....
8 'Have you been to Paris?' 'Yes, many times.'   ....
9 I'm very hungry. <u>I haven't eaten</u> much today.   ....
10 When <u>has this book been</u> published?   ....

14.2 Make sentences from the words in brackets. Use the present perfect or past simple.

1 (it / not / rain / this week)   _It hasn't rained this week._
2 (the weather / be / cold / recently) The weather ....
3 (it / cold / last week) It ....
4 (I / not / read / a newspaper yesterday) I ....
5 (I / not / read / a newspaper today) ....
6 (Emily / earn / a lot of money / this year) ....
7 (she / not / earn / so much / last year) ....
8 (you / have / a holiday recently?) ....

14.3 Put the verb into the correct form, present perfect or past simple.

1 I don't know where Lisa is. _Have you seen_ (you / see) her?
2 When I .... (get) home last night, I .... (be) very
   tired and I .... (go) straight to bed.
3 A: .... (you / finish) painting the bedroom?
   B: Not yet. I'll finish it tomorrow.
4 George .... (not / be) very well last week.
5 Mr Clark .... (work) in a bank for 15 years. Then he gave it up.
6 Molly lives in Dublin. She .... (live) there all her life.
7 A: .... (you / go) to the cinema last night?
   B: Yes, but it .... (be) a mistake. The film .... (be) awful.
8 My grandfather .... (die) before I was born. I
   .... (never / meet) him.
9 I don't know Carol's husband. I .... (never / meet) him.
10 A: Is Martin here? B: No, he .... (go) out.
    A: When exactly .... (he / go) out? B: About ten minutes ago.
11 A: Where do you live? B: In Boston.
    A: How long .... (you / live) there? B: Five years.
    A: Where .... (you / live) before that? B: In Chicago.
    A: And how long .... (you / live) in Chicago? B: Two years.

14.4 Write sentences about yourself using the ideas in brackets.

1 (something you haven't done today) _I haven't eaten any fruit today._
2 (something you haven't done today) ....
3 (something you didn't do yesterday) ....
4 (something you did yesterday evening) ....
5 (something you haven't done recently) ....
6 (something you've done a lot recently) ....

→ Additional exercises 2–4 (pages 303–04), 14–15 (pages 310–11)

29

Past perfect (I had done)

A Study this example situation:

at 10.30   *at 11.00*

Bye!   Hello!

PAUL   SARAH

Sarah went to a party last week. Paul went to the party too, but they didn't see each other. Paul left the party at 10.30 and Sarah arrived at 11 o'clock. So:

When Sarah arrived at the party, Paul wasn't there.

He **had gone** home.

Had gone is the *past perfect (simple)*:

I/we/they/you he/she/it	**had**	(= I'd etc.) (= he'd etc.)	**gone** **seen** **finished** etc.

The past perfect simple is **had** + *past participle* (**gone/seen/finished** etc).

Sometimes we talk about something that happened in the past:
- ☐ Sarah **arrived** at the party.

This is the starting point of the story. Then, if we want to talk about things that happened *before* this time, we use the past perfect (**had …**):
- ☐ When Sarah arrived at the party, Paul **had** already **gone** home.

Some more examples:
- ☐ When we got home last night, we found that somebody **had broken** into the flat.
- ☐ Karen didn't want to go to the cinema with us because she'**d** already **seen** the film.
- ☐ At first I thought I'**d done** the right thing, but I soon realised that I'**d made** a big mistake.
- ☐ The man sitting next to me on the plane was very nervous. He **hadn't flown** before.
  or … He **had** never **flown** before.

B Compare the *present perfect* (**have seen** etc.) and the *past perfect* (**had seen** etc.):

Present perfect	*Past perfect*
have seen ▶	**had seen** ▶
past *now*	*past* *now*

- ☐ Who is that woman? I've never **seen** her before.
- ☐ We aren't hungry. We've just **had** lunch.
- ☐ The house is dirty. They **haven't cleaned** it for weeks.

- ☐ I didn't know who she was. I'd never **seen** her before. (= before that time)
- ☐ We weren't hungry. We'd just **had** lunch.
- ☐ The house was dirty. They **hadn't cleaned** it for weeks.

C Compare the *past simple* (**left, was** etc.) and the *past perfect* (**had left, had been** etc.):

- ☐ A: Was Tom there when you arrived?
  B: Yes, but he **left** soon afterwards.
- ☐ Kate **wasn't** at home when I phoned. She **was** at her mother's house.

- ☐ A: Was Tom there when you arrived?
  B: No, he **had** already **left**.
- ☐ Kate **had** just **got** home when I phoned. She **had been** at her mother's house.

Past perfect continuous → Unit 16   Irregular verbs (gone/seen etc.) → Appendix 1

Exercises

15.1 Read the situations and write sentences from the words in brackets.

1 You went to Sue's house, but she wasn't there.
(she / go / out) ___She had gone out.___

2 You went back to your home town after many years. It wasn't the same as before.
(it / change / a lot) _____

3 I invited Rachel to the party, but she couldn't come.
(she / arrange / to do something else) _____

4 You went to the cinema last night. You got to the cinema late.
(the film / already / begin) _____

5 It was nice to see Dan again after such a long time.
(I / not / see / him for five years) _____

6 I offered Sue something to eat, but she wasn't hungry.
(she / just / have / breakfast) _____

15.2 For each situation, write a sentence ending with **never ... before**. Use the verb in brackets.

1 The man sitting next to you on the plane was very nervous. It was his first flight.
(fly) ___He'd never flown before.___

2 A woman walked into the room. She was a complete stranger to me.
(see) I _____ before.

3 Sam played tennis yesterday. He wasn't very good at it because it was his first game.
(play) He _____

4 Last year we went to Denmark. It was our first time there.
(be there) We _____

15.3 Use the sentences on the left to complete the paragraphs on the right. These sentences are in the order in which they happened – so (1) happened before (2), (2) before (3) etc. But your paragraph begins with the <u>underlined</u> sentence, so sometimes you need the past perfect.

1 (1) Somebody broke into the office during the night.
(2) <u>We arrived at work in the morning.</u>
(3) We called the police.

We arrived at work in the morning and found that somebody ___had broken___ into the office during the night. So we _____ .

2 (1) Laura went out this morning.
(2) <u>I tried to phone her.</u>
(3) There was no answer.

I tried to phone Laura this morning, but _____ no answer. She _____ out.

3 (1) Jim came back from holiday a few days ago.
(2) <u>I met him the same day.</u>
(3) He looked very well.

I met Jim a few days ago. _____ just _____ holiday. _____ very well.

4 (1) Kevin sent Sally lots of emails.
(2) She never replied to them.
(3) <u>Yesterday he got a phone call from her.</u>
(4) He was very surprised.

Yesterday Kevin _____ from Sally. He _____ very surprised. He _____ lots of emails, but she _____ .

15.4 Put the verb into the correct form, past perfect (**I had done**) or past simple (**I did**).

1 'Was Paul at the party when you arrived?' 'No, he ___had gone___ (go) home.'

2 I felt very tired when I got home, so I _____ (go) straight to bed.

3 The house was very quiet when I got home. Everybody _____ (go) to bed.

4 Sorry I'm late. The car _____ (break) down on my way here.

5 We were driving along the road when we _____ (see) a car which _____ (break) down, so we _____ (stop) to help.

→ Additional exercises 5–8 **(pages 304–07)**

Past perfect continuous (I had been doing)

A Study this example situation:

yesterday morning

Yesterday morning I got up and looked out of the window. The sun was shining, but the ground was very wet.

It **had been raining**.

It was *not* raining when I looked out of the window; the sun was shining. But it **had been** raining before.

Had been -ing is the *past perfect continuous*:

I/we/you/they he/she/it	had	(= I'd etc.) (= he'd etc.)	been	doing working playing etc.

Some more examples:

- □ When the boys came into the house, their clothes were dirty, their hair was untidy and one of them had a black eye. They'**d been fighting**.
- □ I was very tired when I got home. I'**d been working** hard all day.
- □ When I went to Madrid a few years ago, I stayed with a friend of mine. She'**d been living** there only a short time but knew the city very well.

B You can say that something **had been happening** for a period of time before something else happened:

- □ We'**d been playing** tennis for about half an hour when it started to rain heavily.
- □ George went to the doctor last Friday. He **hadn't been feeling** well for some time.

C Compare **have been -ing** (*present perfect continuous*) and **had been -ing** (*past perfect continuous*):

Present perfect continuous

I have been -ing

past   *now*

- □ I hope the bus comes soon. I'**ve been waiting** for 20 minutes. *(before now)*
- □ James is out of breath. He **has been running**.

Past perfect continuous

I had been -ing

past   *now*

- □ At last the bus came. I'**d been waiting** for 20 minutes. *(before the bus came)*
- □ James was out of breath. He **had been running**.

D Compare **was -ing** (*past continuous*) and **had been -ing**:

- □ It **wasn't raining** when we went out. The sun **was shining**. But it **had been raining**, so the ground was wet.
- □ Cathy **was sitting** in an armchair resting. She was tired because she'**d been working** very hard.

E Some verbs (for example, **know** and **like**) are not normally used in the continuous:

- □ We were good friends. We **had known** each other for years. (*not* had been knowing)

For a list of these verbs, see Unit 4A.

Present perfect continuous → Units 9–10   **Past perfect simple** → Unit 15

Exercises

16.1 Read the situations and make sentences from the words in brackets.

1 I was very tired when I arrived home.
(I / work / hard all day) _I'd been working hard all day._

2 The two boys came into the house. They had a football and they were both very tired.
(they / play / football) ....

3 I was disappointed when I had to cancel my holiday.
(I / look / forward to it) ....

4 Ann woke up in the middle of the night. She was frightened and didn't know where she was.
(she / dream) ....

5 When I got home, Tom was sitting in front of the TV. He had just turned it off.
(he / watch / a film) ....

16.2 Read the situations and complete the sentences.

1 We played tennis yesterday. Half an hour after we began playing, it started to rain.
We _had been playing for half an hour_ when _it started to rain_ .

2 I had arranged to meet Tom in a restaurant. I arrived and waited for him. After 20 minutes
I suddenly realised that I was in the wrong restaurant.
I .... for 20 minutes when I ....
.... the wrong restaurant.

3 Sarah got a job in factory. Five years later the factory closed down.
At the time the factory .... , Sarah ....
.... there for five years.

4 I went to a concert last week. The orchestra began playing. After about ten minutes a man in
the audience suddenly started shouting.
The orchestra .... when
....

This time make your own sentence:

5 I began walking along the road. I ....
when ....

16.3 Put the verb into the most suitable form, past continuous (**I was doing**), past perfect
(**I had done**) or past perfect continuous (**I had been doing**).

1 It was very noisy next door. Our neighbours _were having_ (have) a party.

2 We were good friends. We _had known_ (know) each other for years.

3 John and I went for a walk. I had difficulty keeping up with him because he
.... (walk) so fast.

4 Sue was sitting on the ground. She was out of breath. She .... (run).

5 When I arrived, everybody was sitting round the table with their mouths full. They
.... (eat).

6 When I arrived, everybody was sitting round the table and talking. Their mouths were empty,
but their stomachs were full. They .... (eat).

7 Jim was on his hands and knees on the floor. He .... (look) for his
contact lens.

8 When I arrived, Kate .... (wait) for me. She was annoyed with me
because I was late and she .... (wait) for a long time.

9 I was sad when I sold my car. I .... (have) it for a very long time.

10 We were extremely tired at the end of the journey. We .... (travel) for
more than 24 hours.

→ Additional exercises 5–8 (pages 304–07)

Have got and have

A

Have got and **have** (= for possession, relationships, illnesses etc.)

You can use **have got** or **have** (without **got**). There is no difference in meaning:

- ☐ They**'ve got** a new car.   *or*   They **have** a new car.
- ☐ Lisa**'s got** two brothers.   *or*   Lisa **has** two brothers.
- ☐ I**'ve got** a headache.   *or*   I **have** a headache.
- ☐ Our house **has got** a small garden.   *or*   Our house **has** a small garden.
- ☐ He**'s got** a few problems.   *or*   He **has** a few problems.

With these meanings (possession etc.), you cannot use continuous forms (**am having** etc.):

- ☐ We're enjoying our holiday. We**'ve got** / We **have** a nice room in the hotel. (*not* We're having)

For the past we use **had** (without **got**):

- ☐ Lisa **had** long hair when she was a child. (*not* Lisa had got)

B

In questions and negative sentences there are three possible forms:

Have you got any questions?	I **haven't got** any questions.
Do you have any questions?	I **don't have** any questions.
Have you any questions? *(less usual)*	I **haven't** any questions. *(less usual)*
Has she got a car?	She **hasn't got** a car.
Does she have a car?	She **doesn't have** a car.
Has she a car? *(less usual)*	She **hasn't** a car. *(less usual)*

In past questions and negative sentences, we use **did/didn't**:

- ☐ **Did** you **have** a car when you were living in London?
- ☐ I **didn't have** a watch, so I didn't know the time.
- ☐ Lisa **had** long hair, **didn't** she?

C

Have breakfast / have a bath / have a good time etc.

We also use **have** (*but not* have got) for many actions and experiences. For example:

have	**breakfast / dinner / a cup of coffee / something to eat** etc.
	a bath / a shower / a swim / a break / a rest / a party / a holiday
	an accident / an experience / a dream
	a look (at something)
	a chat / a conversation / a discussion (with somebody)
	difficulty / trouble / fun / a good time etc.
	a baby (= give birth to a baby)

Have got is *not* possible in the expressions in the box. Compare:

- ☐ Sometimes I **have** (= eat) a sandwich for my lunch. (*not* I've got)
- *but*   I**'ve got** / I **have** some sandwiches. Would you like one?

You can use continuous forms (**am having** etc.) with the expressions in the box:

- ☐ We're enjoying our holiday. We**'re having** a great time. (*not* We have)
- ☐ Mike **is having** a shower at the moment. He has a shower every day.

In questions and negative sentences we use **do/does/did**:

- ☐ I **don't** usually **have** a big breakfast. (*not* I usually haven't)
- ☐ What time **does** Jenny **have** lunch? (*not* has Jenny lunch)
- ☐ **Did** you **have** difficulty finding a place to live?

Exercises

17.1 Write negative sentences with **have**. Some are present (**can't**) and some are past (**couldn't**).

1 I can't get into the house. (a key) _I haven't got a key._
2 I couldn't read the letter. (my glasses) _I didn't have my glasses._
3 I can't get onto the roof. (a ladder) I ....
4 We couldn't visit the museum. (enough time) We ....
5 He couldn't find his way to our house. (a map) ....
6 She can't pay her bills. (any money) ....
7 I can't go swimming today. (enough energy) ....
8 They couldn't take any photographs. (a camera) ....

17.2 Complete the questions with **have**. Some are present and some are past.

1 Excuse me, _have you got_ a pen I could borrow?
2 Why are you holding your face like that? .... a toothache?
3 .... a lot of toys when you were a child?
4 A: .... the time, please?
   B: Yes, it's ten past seven.
5 I need a stamp for this letter. .... one?
6 When you worked in your last job, ... your own office?
7 A: It started to rain very heavily while I was out.
   B: .... an umbrella?

17.3 Write sentences about yourself. Have you got these things now? Did you have them ten years ago?
Write two sentences each time using **I've got / I haven't got** and **I had / I didn't have**.
(You can also write about your family: **We've got … / We had …** etc.).

	now	*ten years ago*
1 (a car)	_I've got a car._	_I didn't have a car._
2 (a bike)	I	I ....
3 (a mobile phone)	....	....
4 (a dog)	....	....
5 (a guitar)	....	....
6 (long hair)	....	....
7 (a driving licence)	....	....

17.4 Complete the sentences. Use an expression from the list and put the verb into the correct form where necessary.

have a baby	have a break	have a chat	have difficulty	have a good flight
have a look	~~have lunch~~	have a party	have a nice time	have a shower

1 I don't eat much during the day. I never _have lunch_ .
2 David starts work at 8 o'clock and .... at 10.30.
3 We .... last week. It was great – we invited lots of people.
4 Excuse me, can I .... at your newspaper, please?
5 Jim is away on holiday at the moment. I hope he ....
6 I met Ann in the supermarket yesterday. We stopped and ....
7 A: .... finding the book you wanted?
   B: No, I found it OK.
8 Suzanne .... a few weeks ago. It's her second child.
9 A: Why didn't you answer the phone?
   B: I ....
10 *You meet your friend Sally at the airport. She has just arrived. You say:*
   Hi, Sally. How are you? .... ?

A   Study this example situation:

a few years ago

these days

Diane doesn't travel much these days.
She prefers to stay at home.

But she **used to travel** a lot.
She **used to go** away two or three times a year.

She **used to travel** a lot = she travelled a lot regularly in the past, but she doesn't do this any more.

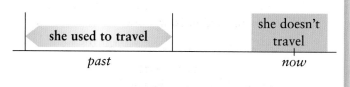

she used to travel		she doesn't travel
past		*now*

B   Something **used to** happen = it happened regularly in the past, but no longer happens:

- [ ] I **used to play** tennis a lot, but I don't play very often now.
- [ ] David **used to spend** a lot of money on clothes. These days he can't afford it.
- [ ] 'Do you go to the cinema much?' 'Not now, but I **used to**.' (= I used to go)

We also use **used to** ... for things that were true, but are not true any more:

- [ ] This building is now a furniture shop. It **used to be** a cinema.
- [ ] I **used to think** Mark was unfriendly, but now I realise he's a very nice person.
- [ ] I've started drinking tea recently. I never **used to like** it before.
- [ ] Nicole **used to have** very long hair when she was a child.

C   'I **used to** do something' is past. There is no present form. You cannot say 'I use to do'.
To talk about the present, use the present simple (I **do**).

Compare:

past	he **used to play**	we **used to live**	there **used to be**
present	he **plays**	we **live**	there **is**

- [ ] We **used to live** in a small village, but now we **live** in London.
- [ ] There **used to be** four cinemas in the town. Now there **is** only one.

D   The normal question form is **did** (you) **use to** ... ?:

- [ ] **Did** you **use to eat** a lot of sweets when you were a child?

The negative form is **didn't use to** ... (**used not to** ... is also possible):

- [ ] I **didn't use to** like him. (*or* I **used not to** like him.)

E   Compare I **used to do** and I **was doing**:

- [ ] I **used to watch** TV a lot. (= I watched TV regularly in the past, but I no longer do this)
- [ ] I **was watching** TV when Mike called. (= I was in the middle of watching TV)

F   Do not confuse I **used to do** and I **am used to doing** (see Unit 61). The structures and meanings are different:

- [ ] I **used to live** alone. (= I lived alone in the past, but I no longer live alone.)
- [ ] I **am** used to **living** alone. (= I live alone, and I don't find it strange or difficult because I've been living alone for some time.)

Past continuous (I was doing) → Unit 6   Would (= used to) → Unit 36
Be/get used to (doing) something → Unit 61

18.1 Complete the sentences with **use(d) to** + a suitable verb.

1 Diane doesn't travel much now. She <u>used to travel</u> a lot, but she prefers to stay at home these days.
2 Liz .... a motorbike, but last year she sold it and bought a car.
3 We came to live in London a few years ago. We .... in Leeds.
4 I rarely eat ice-cream now, but I .... it when I was a child.
5 Jim .... my best friend, but we aren't good friends any longer.
6 It only takes me about 40 minutes to get to work now that the new road is open. It .... more than an hour.
7 There .... a hotel near the airport, but it closed a long time ago.
8 When you lived in New York, ... to the theatre very often?

18.2 Matt changed his life style. He stopped doing some things and started doing other things:

He stopped { studying hard
going to bed early
running three miles every morning

He started { sleeping late
going out in the evening
spending a lot of money

Write sentences about Matt with **used to** and **didn't use to**.

1 <u>He used to study hard.</u>
2 <u>He didn't use to sleep late.</u>
3 ....
4 ....
5 ....
6 ....

18.3 Compare what Karen said five years ago and what she says today:

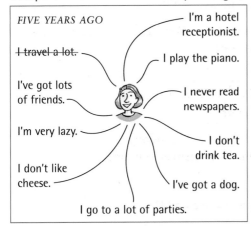

FIVE YEARS AGO
I'm a hotel receptionist.
I travel a lot.
I play the piano.
I've got lots of friends.
I never read newspapers.
I'm very lazy.
I don't drink tea.
I don't like cheese.
I've got a dog.
I go to a lot of parties.

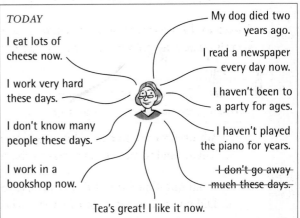

TODAY
My dog died two years ago.
I eat lots of cheese now.
I read a newspaper every day now.
I work very hard these days.
I haven't been to a party for ages.
I don't know many people these days.
I haven't played the piano for years.
I work in a bookshop now.
I don't go away much these days.
Tea's great! I like it now.

Now write sentences about how Karen has changed. Use **used to / didn't use to / never used to** in the first part of your sentence.

1 <u>She used to travel a lot,</u> but <u>she doesn't go away much these days.</u>
2 She used .... but ....
3 .... but ....
4 .... but ....
5 .... but ....
6 .... but ....
7 .... but ....
8 .... but ....
9 .... but ....
10 .... but ....

→ Additional exercise 9 **(page 307)**

Present tenses (I am doing / I do) for the future

A *Present continuous* (**I am doing**) with a future meaning

This is Ben's diary for next week.

He **is playing** tennis on Monday afternoon.
He **is going** to the dentist on Tuesday morning.
He **is having** dinner with Kate on Friday.

In all these examples, Ben has already decided and arranged to do these things.

I'm doing something (tomorrow) = I have already decided and arranged to do it:
- □ A: What **are** you **doing** on Saturday evening? (*not* What do you do)
  B: **I'm going** to the theatre. (*not* I go)
- □ A: What time **is** Cathy **arriving** tomorrow?
  B: Half past ten. **I'm meeting** her at the station.
- □ **I'm not working** tomorrow, so we can go out somewhere.
- □ Ian **isn't playing** football next Saturday. He's hurt his leg.

'**I'm going to** (do)' is also possible in these sentences:
- □ What **are** you **going to do** on Saturday evening?
But the present continuous is more natural for arrangements. See also Unit 20B.

Do not use **will** to talk about what you have arranged to do:
- □ What **are** you **doing** this evening? (*not* What will you do)
- □ Alex **is getting** married next month. (*not* will get)

You can also use the present continuous for an action *just before you begin to do it*. This happens especially with verbs of movement (**go/come/leave** etc.):
- □ I'm tired. **I'm going** to bed now. Goodnight. (*not* I go to bed now)
- □ 'Tina, are you ready yet?'   'Yes, **I'm coming**.' (*not* I come)

B *Present simple* (**I do**) with a future meaning

We use the present simple when we talk about timetables, programmes etc. (for public transport, cinemas etc.):
- □ My train **leaves** at 11.30, so I need to be at the station by 11.15.
- □ What time **does** the film **begin** this evening?
- □ It's Wednesday tomorrow. / Tomorrow **is** Wednesday.

You can use the present simple to talk about people if their plans are fixed like a timetable:
- □ I **start** my new job on Monday.
- □ What time **do** you **finish** work tomorrow?

But the continuous is more usual for personal arrangements:
- □ What time **are** you **meeting** Ann tomorrow? (*not* do you meet)

Compare:

Present continuous	Present simple
□ What time **are you arriving**?	□ What time **does the train arrive**?
□ **I'm going** to the cinema this evening.	□ **The film begins** at 8.15 (this evening).

I'm going to → Units 20, 23   **Will** → Units 21–22   **Present simple after when/if etc.** → Unit 25

Exercises

19.1 A friend of yours is planning to go on holiday soon. You ask her about her plans.
Use the words in brackets to make your questions.

1	(where / go?) _Where are you going?_	Scotland.
2	(how long / go for?)	Ten days.
3	(when / leave?)	Next Friday.
4	(go / alone?)	No, with a friend.
5	(travel / by car?)	No, by train.
6	(where / stay?)	In a hotel.

19.2 Tom wants you to visit him, but you are very busy. Look at your diary for the next few days and explain to him why you can't come.

TOM: Can you come on Monday evening?
YOU: Sorry, but _I'm playing volleyball_ .... (1)
TOM: What about Tuesday evening then?
YOU: No, not Tuesday. I .... (2)
TOM: And Wednesday evening?
YOU: .... (3)
TOM: Well, are you free on Thursday?
YOU: I'm afraid not. .... (4)

19.3 Have you arranged to do anything at these times? Write sentences about yourself.

1 (this evening) _I'm going out this evening._ or _I'm not doing anything this evening._
2 (tomorrow morning) I ....
3 (tomorrow evening) ....
4 (next Sunday) ....
5 (*choose another day or time*) ....

19.4 Put the verb into the more suitable form, present continuous or present simple.

1 I _'m going_ (go) to the cinema this evening.
2 _Does the film begin_ (the film / begin) at 3.30 or 4.30?
3 We .... (have) a party next Saturday. Would you like to come?
4 The art exhibition .... (finish) on 3 May.
5 I .... (not / go) out this evening. I .... (stay) at home.
6 '... (you / do) anything tomorrow morning?' 'No, I'm free. Why?'
7 We .... (go) to a concert tonight. It .... (start) at 7.30.
8 I .... (leave) now. I've come to say goodbye.
9 A: Have you seen Liz recently?
   B: No, but we .... (meet) for lunch next week.
10 *You are on the train to London and you ask another passenger:*
   Excuse me. What time .... (this train / get) to London?
11 *You are talking to Helen:*
   Helen, I .... (go) to the supermarket. .... (you / come) with me?
12 *You and a friend are watching television. You say:*
   I'm bored with this programme. What time .... (it / end)?
13 I .... (not / use) the car this evening, so you can have it.
14 Sue .... (come) to see us tomorrow. She .... (travel) by train and her train .... (arrive) at 10.15.

→ Additional exercises 10–13 (pages 308–10)

(I'm) going to (do)

A

I am going to do something = I have already decided to do it, I intend to do it:

- □ A: **Are** you **going to watch** the late film on TV tonight?
  B: No, **I'm going to have** an early night.
- □ A: I hear Sarah has won some money. What **is** she **going to do** with it?
  B: She**'s going to buy** a new car.
- □ **I'm** just **going to make** a quick phone call. Can you wait for me?
- □ This cheese looks horrible. **I'm not going to eat** it.

B

I am doing and **I am going to do**

We use **I am doing** (*present continuous*) when we say what we have *arranged* to do – for example, arranged to meet somebody, arranged to go somewhere:

- □ What time **are** you **meeting** Ann this evening?
- □ **I'm leaving** tomorrow. I've got my plane ticket.

I am going to do something = I've decided to do it (but perhaps not *arranged* to do it):

- □ 'Your shoes are dirty.' 'Yes, I know. **I'm going to clean** them.' (= I've decided to clean them, but I haven't *arranged* to clean them)
- □ I've decided not to stay here any longer. Tomorrow **I'm going to look** for somewhere else to stay.

Often the difference is very small and either form is possible.

C

You can also say that 'something **is going to happen**' in the future. For example:

The man can't see the wall in front of him.

He **is going to walk** into the wall.

When we say that 'something **is going to happen**', the situation *now* makes this clear. The man is walking towards the wall now, so we can see that he **is going to walk** into it.

situation now　　　　　　　　　*future happening*

Some more examples:

- □ Look at those black clouds! It**'s going to rain.** (the clouds are there now)
- □ I feel terrible. I think **I'm going to be** sick. (I feel terrible now)
- □ The economic situation is bad now and things **are going to get** worse.

D

I was going to (do something) = I intended to do it, but didn't do it:

- □ We **were going to travel** by train, but then we decided to go by car instead.
- □ Peter **was going to do** the exam, but he changed his mind.
- □ I **was** just **going to cross** the road when somebody shouted 'Stop!'

You can say that 'something **was going to happen**' (but didn't happen):

- □ I thought it **was going to rain,** but it didn't.

I am doing for the future → Unit 19A　**I will** and **I'm going to** → Unit 23

Exercises

20.1 Write a question with **going to** for each situation.

1 Your friend has won some money. You ask:
   (what / do with it?) _What are you going to do with it?_

2 Your friend is going to a party tonight. You ask:
   (what / wear?) ....

3 Your friend has just bought a new table. You ask:
   (where / put it?) ....

4 Your friend has decided to have a party. You ask:
   (who / invite?) ....

20.2 Read the situations and complete the dialogues. Use **going to**.

1 You have decided to tidy your room this morning.
   FRIEND: Are you going out this morning?
   YOU: No, _I'm going to tidy my room._

2 You bought a sweater, but it doesn't fit you very well. You have decided to take it back.
   FRIEND: That sweater is too big for you.
   YOU: I know. ....

3 You have been offered a job, but you have decided not to accept it.
   FRIEND: I hear you've been offered a job.
   YOU: That's right, but ....

4 You have to phone Sarah. It's morning now, and you have decided to phone her tonight.
   FRIEND: Have you phoned Sarah yet?
   YOU: No, ...

5 You are in a restaurant. The food is awful and you've decided to complain.
   FRIEND: This food is awful, isn't it?
   YOU: Yes, it's disgusting. ....

20.3 What is going to happen in these situations? Use the words in brackets.

1 There are a lot of black clouds in the sky.
   (rain) _It's going to rain._

2 It is 8.30. Tom is leaving his house. He has to be at work at 8.45, but the journey takes
   30 minutes.
   (late) He ....

3 There is a hole in the bottom of the boat. A lot of water is coming in through the hole.
   (sink) The boat ....

4 Lucy and Chris are driving. There is very little petrol left in the tank. The nearest petrol
   station is a long way away.
   (run out) They ....

20.4 Complete the sentences with **was/were going to** + the following verbs:

   buy   **give up**   **have**   **phone**   **play**   ~~travel~~

1 We _were going to travel_ by train, but then we decided to go by car instead.

2 I .... some new clothes yesterday, but I was very busy and didn't
   have time to go to the shops.

3 Martin and I .... tennis last week, but he was injured.

4 I .... Jane, but I decided to email her instead.

5 A: When I last saw Tim, he .... his job.
   B: That's right, but in the end he decided to stay where he was.

6 We .... a party last week, but some of our friends couldn't come,
   so we cancelled it.

Will/shall 1

A

We use **I'll** (= I will) when we decide to do something at the time of speaking:

- ☐ Oh, I've left the door open. **I'll go** and shut it.
- ☐ 'What would you like to drink?'   '**I'll have** an orange juice, please.'
- ☐ 'Did you phone Lucy?'   'Oh no, I forgot. **I'll phone** her now.'

You cannot use the *present simple* (**I do / I go** etc.) in these sentences:

- ☐ **I'll go** and shut the door. (*not* I go and shut)

We often use **I think I'll ...** and **I don't think I'll ... :**

- ☐ I feel a bit hungry. **I think I'll have** something to eat.
- ☐ **I don't think I'll go** out tonight. I'm too tired.

In spoken English the negative of **will** is usually **won't** (= will not):

- ☐ I can see you're busy, so I **won't stay** long.

B

Do *not* use **will** to talk about what you have already decided or arranged to do (see Units 19–20):

- ☐ **I'm going** on holiday next Saturday. (*not* I'll go)
- ☐ **Are** you **working** tomorrow? (*not* Will you work)

C

We often use **will** in these situations:

Offering to do something
- ☐ That bag looks heavy. **I'll help** you with it. (*not* I help)

Agreeing to do something
- ☐ A: Can you give Tim this book?
  - B: Sure, **I'll give** it to him when I see him this afternoon.

Promising to do something
- ☐ Thanks for lending me the money. **I'll pay** you back on Friday.
- ☐ I **won't tell** anyone what happened. I promise.

Asking somebody to do something (**Will you ... ?**)
- ☐ **Will you** please turn the stereo down? I'm trying to concentrate.

You can use **won't** to say that somebody refuses to do something:

- ☐ I've tried to give her advice, but she **won't listen**.
- ☐ The car **won't start**. (= the car 'refuses' to start)

D

Shall I ... ?   Shall we ... ?

Shall is used mostly in the questions **shall I ... ? / shall we ... ?**

We use **shall I ... ? / shall we ... ?** to ask somebody's opinion (especially in offers or suggestions):

- ☐ **Shall I** open the window? (= Do you want me to open the window?)
- ☐ I've got no money. What **shall I** do? (= What do you suggest?)
- ☐ '**Shall we** go?' 'Just a minute. I'm not ready yet.'
- ☐ Where **shall we** go this evening?

Compare **shall I ... ?** and **will you ... ?**:

- ☐ **Shall I** shut the door? (= Do you want me to shut it?)
- ☐ **Will you** shut the door? (= I want you to shut it)

Will/shall 2 → Unit 22   **I will and I'm going to** → Unit 23   **American English** → Appendix 7

21.1 Complete the sentences with I'll + a suitable verb.

1 I'm too tired to walk home. I think _____I'll take_____ a taxi.

2 'It's cold in this room.' 'Is it? .... on the heating then.'

3 A: We haven't got any milk.

B: Oh, I forgot to buy some. .... and get some now.

4 'Shall I do the washing-up?' 'No, it's all right. .... it later.'

5 'I don't know how to use this computer.' 'OK, ... you.'

6 'Would you like tea or coffee?' '................................ coffee, please.'

7 'Goodbye! Have a nice holiday.' 'Thanks. .... you a postcard.'

8 Thanks for letting me borrow your camera. .... it back to you on Monday, OK?

9 'Are you coming with us?' 'No, I think .... here.'

21.2 Read the situations and write sentences with **I think I'll ...** or **I don't think I'll ...** .

1 It's a bit cold. The window is open and you decide to close it. You say:

I think I'll close the window.

2 You are feeling tired and it's getting late. You decide to go to bed. You say:

I think ....

3 A friend of yours offers you a lift in his car, but you decide to walk. You say:

Thank you, but ....

4 You arranged to play tennis today. Now you decide that you don't want to play. You say:

I don't think ....

5 You were going to go swimming. Now you decide that you don't want to go. You say:

....

21.3 Which is correct? (If necessary, study Units 19–20 first.)

1 'Did you phone Lucy?' 'Oh no, I forgot. ~~I phone~~ / I'll phone her now.' (I'll phone *is correct*)

2 I can't meet you tomorrow. I'm playing / ~~I'll play~~ tennis. (I'm playing *is correct*)

3 'I meet / I'll meet you outside the hotel in half an hour, OK?' 'Yes, that's fine.'

4 'I need some money.' 'OK, I'm lending / I'll lend you some. How much do you need?'

5 I'm having / I'll have a party next Saturday. I hope you can come.

6 'Remember to get a newspaper when you go out.' 'OK. I don't forget / I won't forget.'

7 What time does your train leave / will your train leave tomorrow?

8 I asked Sue what happened, but she doesn't tell / won't tell me.

9 'Are you doing / Will you do anything tomorrow evening?' 'No, I'm free. Why?'

10 I don't want to go out alone. Do you come / Will you come with me?

21.4 What do you say in these situations? Write sentences with **shall I ... ?** or **shall we ... ?**

1 You and a friend want to do something this evening, but you don't know what.

You ask your friend. _What shall we do this evening?_

2 You try on a jacket in a shop. You are not sure whether to buy it or not. You ask a friend for advice. .... it?

3 It's Helen's birthday next week. You want to give her a present, but you don't know what.

You ask a friend for advice.

What ....

4 You and a friend are going on holiday together, but you haven't decided where.

You ask him/her. ....

5 You and a friend are going out. You haven't decided whether to go by car or to walk. You ask him/her. .... or ....

6 Your friend wants you to phone later. You don't know what time to phone. You ask him/her.

....

Will/shall 2

A

We do *not* use **will** to say what somebody has already arranged or decided to do:

- Diane **is working** next week. (*not* Diane will work)
- **Are** you **going to watch** television this evening? (*not* Will you watch)

For '**is working**' and '**Are** you **going to** … ?', see Units 19–20.

But often, when we talk about the future, we are *not* talking about what somebody has decided to do. For example:

Kate is doing an exam next week. Chris and Joe are talking about it.

*Do you think Kate **will pass** the exam?*

CHRIS   JOE

Yes, she'll pass easily.

She'll pass does *not* mean 'she has decided to pass'. Joe is saying what he knows or thinks will happen. He is *predicting* the future.

When we predict a future happening or situation, we use **will/won't**.

Some more examples:

- Jill has been away a long time. When she returns, she'll **find** a lot of changes here.
- 'Where **will** you **be** this time next year?'   'I'll **be** in Japan.'
- That plate is hot. If you touch it, you'll **burn** yourself.
- Tom **won't pass** the exam. He hasn't studied hard enough.
- When **will** you **get** your exam results?

B

We often use **will** ('ll) with:

probably	I'll **probably** be home late tonight.
I expect	I haven't seen Carol today. **I expect** she'll phone this evening.
(I'm) sure	Don't worry about the exam. **I'm sure** you'll pass.
(I) think	Do you **think** Sarah **will** like the present we bought her?
(I) don't think	I **don't think** the exam **will** be very difficult.
I wonder	**I wonder** what **will** happen.

After **I hope**, we generally use the present (**will** is also possible):

- I hope Kate **passes** the exam. (*or* I hope Kate **will pass** …)
- I hope it **doesn't rain** tomorrow.

C

Generally we use **will** to talk about the future, but sometimes we use **will** to talk about *now*. For example:

- Don't phone Ann now. She'll **be** busy. (= she'll be busy *now*)

D

I shall … / we shall …

Normally we use **shall** only with **I** and **we**. You can say:

I shall *or* **I will** (**I'll**)   **we shall** *or* **we will** (**we'll**)
- **I shall** be late this evening. (*or* **I will** be)
- **We shall** probably go to Scotland in the summer. (*or* We **will** probably go)

In spoken English we normally use **I'll** and **we'll**:

- **We'll** probably go to Scotland.

The negative of **shall** is **shall not** or **shan't**:

- **I shan't** be here tomorrow. (*or* I **won't** be)

Do not use **shall** with **he/she/it/you/they**:

- She **will** be very angry. (*not* She shall be)

Will/shall 1 → Unit 21   **I will and I'm going to** → Unit 23   **Will be doing and will have done** → Unit 24
The future → Appendix 3   **American English** → Appendix 7

Exercises

22.1 Which form of the verb is correct (or more natural) in these sente~~nces~~

1 Diane isn't free on Saturday. <u>She'll work / She's working</u>. (She's w~~orking~~
2 <u>I'll go / I'm going</u> to a party tomorrow night. Would you like to co~~me~~
3 I think Jenny <u>will get / is getting</u> the job. She has a lot of experience.
4 I can't meet you this evening. A friend of mine <u>will come / is coming</u> t~~o~~
5 A: Have you decided where to go for your holidays?
   B: Yes, <u>we'll go / we're going</u> to Italy.
6 There's no need to be afraid of the dog. <u>It won't hurt / It isn't hurting</u> you.

22.2 Complete the sentences with will ('ll) + the following verbs:

be   come   get   like   live   look   meet   ~~pass~~

1 Don't worry about the exam. I'm sure you <u>'ll pass</u> .
2 Why don't you try on this jacket? It .... nice on you.
3 You must meet George sometime. I think you .... him.
4 It's raining. Don't go out. You .... wet.
5 Do you think people .... longer in the future?
6 Goodbye. I expect we .... again before long.
7 I've invited Sue to the party, but I don't think she ....
8 When the new road is finished, my journey to work .... much shorter.

22.3 Put in **will ('ll)** or **won't**.

1 Can you wait for me? I <u>won't</u> be very long.
2 There's no need to take an umbrella with you. It .... rain.
3 If you don't eat anything now, you .... be hungry later.
4 I'm sorry about what happened yesterday. It .... happen again.
5 I've got some incredible news! You .... never believe what happened.
6 Don't ask Amanda for advice. She .... know what to do.

22.4 Where do you think you will be at these times? Write true sentences about yourself. Use:
I'll be ...   *or*   **I'll probably be ...**   *or*   **I don't know where I'll be**

1 (next Monday evening at 7.45)   <u>I'll be at home.</u>
                          or <u>I'll probably be at home.</u>
                          or <u>I don't know where I'll be.</u>

2 (at 5 o'clock tomorrow morning)

....

3 (at 10.30 tomorrow morning)

....

4 (next Saturday afternoon at 4.15)

....

5 (this time next year)

....

22.5 Write questions using **do you think ... will ... ?** + the following:

be back   cost   end   get married   happen   ~~like~~   rain

1 I've bought Rosa this picture.   <u>Do you think she'll like it</u> .... ?
2 The weather doesn't look very good. Do you .... ?
3 The meeting is still going on. When do you .... ?
4 My car needs to be repaired. How much .... ?
5 Sally and David are in love. Do .... ?
6 'I'm going out now.' 'OK. What time .... ?'
7 The future situation is uncertain. What .... ?

→ Additional exercises 10–13 (pages 308–10)   45

will and I'm going to

Future actions

Study the difference between **will** and **(be) going to**:

Sue is talking to Helen:

SUE

HELEN

Let's have a party.

That's a great idea.
We'll **invite** lots of people.

will ('ll): We use **will** when we decide to do something at the time of speaking. The speaker has not decided before. The party is a new idea.

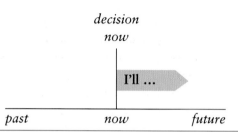

*decision
now*

I'll ...

past   now   future

Later that day, Helen meets Dave:

HELEN

DAVE

Sue and I have decided to have a party.
We're **going to invite** lots of people.

(be) going to: We use **(be) going to** when we have *already decided* to do something. Helen had already decided to invite lots of people *before* she spoke to Dave.

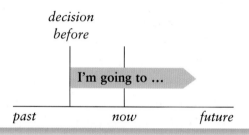

*decision
before*

I'm going to ...

past   now   future

Compare:
- □ 'Gary phoned while you were out.'   'OK. **I'll call** him back.'
  'Gary phoned while you were out.'   'Yes, I know. **I'm going to call** him back.'
- □ 'Ann is in hospital.'   'Oh really? I didn't know. **I'll go** and visit her.'
  'Ann is in hospital.'   'Yes, I know. **I'm going to visit** her this evening.'

B Future happenings and situations (predicting the future)

Sometimes there is not much difference between **will** and **going to**. For example, you can say:
- □ I think the weather **will** be nice this afternoon.
- □ I think the weather **is going to** be nice this afternoon.

When we say something **is going to** happen, we think this is because of the situation *now* (see Unit 20C). For example:
- □ Look at those black clouds. **It's going to rain.** (*not* It will rain)
  (We can see that it **is going to rain** from the clouds that are in the sky *now*.)
- □ I feel terrible. I think **I'm going to be** sick. (*not* I think I'll be sick)
  (I think **I'm going to be** sick because I feel terrible *now*.)

Do not use **will** in this type of situation.

In other situations, use **will**:
- □ Tom **will** probably **get** here at about 8 o'clock.
- □ I think Sarah **will like** the present we bought for her.
- □ These shoes are very well-made. They'll **last** a long time.

Exercises

23.1 Complete the sentences using **will ('ll)** or **going to**.

1 A: Why are you turning on the television?
  B: ....I'm going to watch.... the news. (I / watch)

2 A: Oh, I've just realised. I haven't got any money.
  B: Haven't you? Well, don't worry. .... you some. (I / lend)

3 A: I've got a headache.
  B: Have you? Wait a second and .... an aspirin for you. (I / get)

4 A: Why are you filling that bucket with water?
  B: .... the car. (I / wash)

5 A: I've decided to repaint this room.
  B: Oh, have you? What colour .... it? (you / paint)

6 A: Where are you going? Are you going shopping?
  B: Yes, ... something for dinner. (I / buy)

7 A: I don't know how to use this camera.
  B: It's easy. .... you. (I / show)

8 A: What would you like to eat?
  B: .... a sandwich, please. (I / have)

9 A: Did you post that letter for me?
  B: Oh, I'm sorry. I completely forgot. .... it now. (I / do)

10 A: The ceiling in this room doesn't look very safe, does it?
   B: No, it looks as if .... down. (it / fall)

11 A: Has George decided what to do when he leaves school?
   B: Yes. Everything is planned. .... a holiday for a few weeks.
      (he / have) Then .... a computer programming course. (he / do)

23.2 Read the situations and complete the sentences using **will ('ll)** or **going to**.

1 The phone rings and you answer. Somebody wants to speak to Jim.
  CALLER: Hello. Can I speak to Jim, please?
  YOU: Just a moment. ....I'll get.... him. (I / get)

2 It's a nice day, so you have decided to take a walk. Just before you go, you tell your friend.
  YOU: The weather's too nice to stay in. .... a walk. (I / take)
  FRIEND: Good idea. I think .... you. (I / join)

3 Your friend is worried because she has lost an important letter.
  YOU: Don't worry about the letter. I'm sure .... it. (you / find)
  FRIEND: I hope so.

4 There was a job advertised in the paper recently. At first you were interested, but then you
  decided not to apply.
  FRIEND: Have you decided what to do about that job you were interested in?
  YOU: Yes, ... for it. (I / not / apply)

5 You and a friend come home very late. Other people in the house are asleep. Your friend
  is noisy.
  YOU: Shh! Don't make so much noise. .... everybody up. (you / wake)

6 Paul has to go to the airport to catch a plane tomorrow morning.
  PAUL: Liz, I need somebody to take me to the airport tomorrow morning.
  LIZ: That's no problem. .... you. (I / take) What time is your flight?
  PAUL: 10.50.
  LIZ: OK, ... at about 9 o'clock then. (we / leave)
  Later that day, Joe offers to take Paul to the airport.
  JOE: Paul, do you want me to take you to the airport?
  PAUL: No thanks, Joe. .... me. (Liz / take)

→ Additional exercises 10–13 (pages 308–10)

A Study this example situation:

These people are standing in a queue to get into the cinema.

now

Half an hour from now, the cinema will be full. Everyone **will be watching** the film.

half an hour from now

Three hours from now, the cinema will be empty. The film **will have finished**. Everybody **will have gone** home.

three hours from now

B I **will be doing** something (*future continuous*) = I will be in the middle of doing it:
   □ This time next week I'll be on holiday. I'll **be lying** on the beach or **swimming** in the sea.
   □ You have no chance of getting the job. You'll **be wasting** your time if you apply for it.

Compare **will be** (do)**ing** and **will** (do):
   □ Don't phone between 7 and 8. We'll **be having** dinner.
   □ Let's wait for Liz to arrive and then we'll **have** dinner.

Compare **will be -ing** with other continuous forms:
   □ At 10 o'clock yesterday, Sally **was** in her office. She **was working**. *(past)*
   It's 10 o'clock now. She **is** in her office. She **is working**. *(present)*
   At 10 o'clock tomorrow, she **will be** in her office. She **will be working**.

C We also use **will be -ing** in a different way: to talk about complete actions in the future. For example:
   □ The government **will be making** a statement about the crisis later today.
   □ **Will** you **be going** away this summer?
   □ Later in the programme, I'll **be talking** to the Minister of Education …
   □ Our best player is injured and **won't be playing** in the game on Saturday.

Later in the programme I'll be talking to ...

In these examples **will be -ing** is similar to (**be**) **going to** … .

D We use **will have** (**done**) (*future perfect*) to say that something will already be complete before a time in the future. For example:
   □ Sally always leaves for work at 8.30 in the morning. She won't be at home at 9 o'clock – she**'ll have gone** to work.
   □ We're late. The film **will** already **have started** by the time we get to the cinema.

Compare **will have** (done) with other perfect forms:
   □ Ted and Amy **have been** married for 24 years. *(present perfect)*
   Next year they **will have been** married for 25 years.
   When their son was born, they **had been** married for three years. *(past perfect)*

Will → Units 21–22   **By then / by the time** → Unit 120   **The future** → Appendix 3

24.1 Read about Colin. Then tick (✓) the sentences which are true. In each group of sentences at least one is true.

Colin goes to work every day. He leaves home at 8 o'clock and arrives at work at about 8.45. He starts work immediately and continues until 12.30 when he has lunch (which takes about half an hour). He starts work again at 1.15 and goes home at exactly 4.30. Every day he follows the same routine and tomorrow will be no exception.

1 **At 7.45**
a he'll be leaving the house
b he'll have left the house
c he'll be at home ✓
d he'll be having breakfast ✓

4 **At 12.45**
a he'll have lunch
b he'll be having lunch
c he'll have finished his lunch
d he'll have started his lunch

2 **At 8.15**
a he'll be leaving the house
b he'll have left the house
c he'll have arrived at work
d he'll be arriving at work

5 **At 4 o'clock**
a he'll have finished work
b he'll finish work
c he'll be working
d he won't have finished work

3 **At 9.15**
a he'll be working
b he'll start work
c he'll have started work
d he'll be arriving at work

6 **At 4.45**
a he'll leave work
b he'll be leaving work
c he'll have left work
d he'll have arrived home

24.2 Put the verb into the correct form, **will be (do)ing** or **will have (done)**.

1 Don't phone between 7 and 8. _We'll be having_ (we / have) dinner then.
2 Phone me after 8 o'clock. .... (we / finish) dinner by then.
3 Tomorrow afternoon we're going to play tennis from 3 o'clock until 4.30. So at 4 o'clock, ... (we / play) tennis.
4 A: Can we meet tomorrow?
   B: Yes, but not in the afternoon. .... (I / work).
5 *B has to go to a meeting which begins at 10 o'clock. It will last about an hour.*
   A: Will you be free at 11.30?
   B: Yes, ... (the meeting / end) by then.
6 Ben is on holiday and he is spending his money very quickly. If he continues like this, ... (he / spend) all his money before the end of his holiday.
7 Do you think .... (you / still / do) the same job in ten years' time?
8 Lisa is from New Zealand. She is travelling around Europe at the moment. So far she has travelled about 1,000 miles. By the end of the trip, ... (she / travel) more than 3,000 miles.
9 If you need to contact me, ... (I / stay) at the Lion Hotel until Friday.
10 A: .... (you / see) Laura tomorrow?
    B: Yes, probably. Why?
    A: I borrowed this CD from her. Can you give it back to her?

→ Additional exercises 12–13 (pages 309–10)

When I do / When I've done   When and if

A

Study this example:

> Will you phone me tomorrow?

> Yes, I'll phone you **when I get** home from work.

'I'll phone you when I get home' is a sentence with two parts:

    the main part: 'I'll phone you'
and   *the when-part*:   '**when I get** home'

The time in the sentence is future ('tomorrow'), but we use a *present* tense (I **get**) in the **when**-part of the sentence.

We do *not* use **will** in the **when**-part of the sentence.

Some more examples:

- □ We'**ll** go out **when** it **stops** raining. (*not* when it will stop)
- □ **When** you **are** in London again, come and see us. (*not* When you will be)
- □ (*said to a child*) What do you want to be **when** you **grow** up? (*not* will grow)

The same thing happens after **while / before / after / as soon as / until** or **till**:

- □ I'm going to read a lot **while** I'**m** on holiday. (*not* while I will be)
- □ I'll probably go back home on Sunday. **Before I go**, I'd like to visit the museum.
- □ Wait here **until** (*or* **till**) I **come** back.

B

You can also use the present perfect (**have done**) after **when / after / until / as soon as**:

- □ Can I borrow that book **when** you'**ve finished** with it?
- □ Don't say anything while Ian is here. Wait **until** he **has gone**.

If you use the present perfect, one thing must be complete *before* the other (so the two things do *not* happen together):

- □ **When I've phoned** Kate, we can have dinner.
  (= First I'll phone Kate and *after that* we can have dinner.)

Do not use the present perfect if the two things happen together:

- □ **When I phone** Kate, I'll ask her about the party. (*not* When I've phoned)

It is often possible to use either the present simple or the present perfect:

- □ I'll come **as soon as I finish**.   *or*   I'll come **as soon as I've finished**.
- □ You'll feel better **after** you **have**   *or*   You'll feel better **after** you'**ve had** something to eat   something to eat.

C

After **if**, we normally use the present simple (**if I do / if I see** etc.) for the future:

- □ It's raining hard. We'll get wet **if** we **go** out. (*not* if we will go)
- □ I'll be angry **if** it **happens** again. (*not* if it will happen)
- □ Hurry up! **If** we **don't hurry**, we'll be late.

D

Compare **when** and **if**:

We use **when** for things which are *sure* to happen:

- □ I'm going shopping later. (for sure) **When** I go shopping, I'll buy some food.

We use **if** (*not* **when**) for things that will *possibly* happen:

- □ I might go shopping later. (it's possible) **If** I go shopping, I'll buy some food.
- □ **If** it is raining this evening, I won't go out. (*not* When it is raining)
- □ Don't worry **if** I'm late tonight. (*not* when I'm late)
- □ **If** they don't come soon, I'm not going to wait. (*not* When they don't come)

25.1 Complete the sentences using the verbs in brackets. All the sentences are about the future.
Use **will/won't** or the present simple (**I see** / he **plays** / it **is** etc.).

1 I .....'ll phone.... (phone) you when I .....get..... (get) home from work.
2 I want to see Julia before she .... (go) out.
3 We're going on holiday tomorrow. I .... (tell) you all about it when we
.... (come) back.
4 Brian looks very different now. When you .... (see) him again, you
.... (not / recognise) him.
5 .... (you / be) lonely without me while I .... (be) away?
6 We must do something soon before it .... (be) too late.
7 I don't want to go without you. I .... (wait) until you ....
(be) ready.
8 Sue has applied for the job, but she isn't very well-qualified for it. I ....
(be) surprised if she .... (get) it.
9 I hope to play tennis tomorrow if the weather .... (be) nice.
10 I'm going out now. If anybody .... (phone) while I .... (be)
out, can you take a message?

25.2 Make one sentence from two.

1 It will stop raining soon. Then we'll go out.
.....We'll go out..................................... when .....it stops raining.
2 I'll find somewhere to live. Then I'll give you my address.
I .... when ....
3 I'll do the shopping. Then I'll come straight back home.
.... after ....
4 It's going to get dark. Let's go home before that.
.... before ....
5 She must apologise to me first. I won't speak to her until then.
.... until ....

25.3 Read the situations and complete the sentences.

1 A friend of yours is going on holiday. You want to know what she is going to do.
You ask: What are you going to do when .....you are on holiday... ?
2 A friend of yours is visiting you. She has to go soon but maybe there's time for some more coffee.
You ask: Would you like some more coffee before .... ?
3 You want to sell your car. Jim is interested in buying it, but he hasn't decided yet.
You ask: Can you let me know as soon as .... ?
4 Your friends are going to New York soon. You want to know where they're going to stay.
You ask: Where are you going to stay when .... ?
5 The traffic is very bad in your town, but they are building a new road at the moment.
You say: I think things will be better when they ....

25.4 Put in **when** or **if**.

1 Don't worry .....if..... I'm late tonight.
2 Tom might phone while I'm out this evening. .... he does, can you take a message?
3 I'm going to Rome next week. .... I'm there, I hope to visit a friend of mine.
4 I think Jill will get the job. I'll be very surprised .... she doesn't get it.
5 I'm going shopping. .... you want anything, I can get it for you.
6 I'm going away for a few days. I'll phone you .... I get back.
7 I want you to come to the party, but .... you don't want to come, that's all right.
8 We can eat at home or, ... you prefer, we can go to a restaurant.

Unit 26

Can, could and (be) able to

A

We use **can** to say that something is possible or allowed, or that somebody has the ability to do something. We use **can** + *infinitive* (**can do** / **can see** etc.):

- □ We **can see** the lake from our bedroom window.
- □ 'I haven't got a pen.' 'You **can use** mine.'
- □ **Can** you **speak** any foreign languages?
- □ I **can come** and see you tomorrow if you like.
- □ The word 'play' **can be** a noun or a verb.

The negative is **can't** (= **cannot**):

- □ I'm afraid I **can't come** to the party on Friday.

B

You can say that somebody **is able to** do something, but **can** is more usual:

- □ We **are able to see** the lake from our bedroom window.

But **can** has only two forms: **can** (*present*) and **could** (*past*). So sometimes it is necessary to use **(be) able to**. Compare:

□ I **can't** sleep.	□ I **haven't been able to** sleep recently.
□ Tom **can** come tomorrow.	□ Tom **might be able to** come tomorrow.
□ Maria **can** speak French, Spanish and English.	□ Applicants for the job **must be able to** speak two foreign languages.

C

Could

Sometimes **could** is the past of **can**. We use **could** especially with:

see   hear   smell   taste   feel   remember   understand

- □ We had a lovely room in the hotel. We **could see** the lake.
- □ As soon as I walked into the room, I **could smell** gas.
- □ I was sitting at the back of the theatre and **couldn't hear** very well.

We also use **could** to say that somebody had the general ability or permission to do something:

- □ My grandfather **could speak** five languages.
- □ We were totally free. We **could do** what we wanted. (= we were allowed to do)

D

Could and was able to

We use **could** for *general* ability. But if you want to say that somebody did something in a specific situation, use **was/were able to** or **managed to** (*not* **could**):

- □ The fire spread through the building very quickly, but fortunately everybody **was able to escape** / **managed to escape**. (*not* could escape)
- □ We didn't know where David was, but we **managed to find** / **were able to find** him in the end. (*not* could find)

Compare:

- □ Mike was an excellent tennis player when he was younger. He **could beat** anybody.
  (= he had the general ability to beat anybody)
- *but*   Mike and Pete played tennis yesterday. Pete played very well, but Mike **managed to beat** him. (= he managed to beat him in this particular game)

The negative **couldn't** (**could not**) is possible in all situations:

- □ My grandfather **couldn't swim**.
- □ We looked for David everywhere, but we **couldn't find** him.
- □ Pete played well, but he **couldn't beat** Mike.

    Could (do) and could have (done) → Unit 27   Must and can't → Unit 28   Can/could you … ? → Unit 37

Exercises

26.1 Complete the sentences using **can** or **(be) able to**. Use **can** if possible; otherwise use **(be) able to.**

1 Gary has travelled a lot. He __can__ speak five languages.
2 I haven't _been able to_ sleep very well recently.
3 Nicole _____ drive, but she hasn't got a car.
4 I used to _____ stand on my head, but I can't do it now.
5 I can't understand Martin. I've never _____ understand him.
6 I can't see you on Friday, but I _____ meet you on Saturday morning.
7 Ask Catherine about your problem. She might _____ help you.

26.2 Write sentences about yourself using the ideas in brackets.

1 (something you used to be able to do)
   I used to be able to sing well.
2 (something you used to be able to do)
   I used _____
3 (something you would like to be able to do)
   I'd _____
4 (something you have never been able to do)
   I've _____

26.3 Complete the sentences with **can/can't/could/couldn't** + the following:

~~come~~   eat   hear   run   sleep   wait

1 I'm afraid I _can't come_ to your party next week.
2 When Tim was 16, he _____ 100 metres in 11 seconds.
3 'Are you in a hurry?' 'No, I've got plenty of time. I _____ .'
4 I was feeling sick yesterday. I _____ anything.
5 Can you speak a little louder? I _____ you very well.
6 'You look tired.' 'Yes, I _____ last night.'

26.4 Complete the answers to the questions with **was/were able to** ... .

1 A: Did everybody escape from the fire?
   B: Yes, although the fire spread quickly, everybody _was able to escape_ .
2 A: Did you finish your work this afternoon?
   B: Yes, there was nobody to disturb me, so I _____ .
3 A: Did you have difficulty finding our house?
   B: Not really. Your directions were good and we _____ .
4 A: Did the thief get away?
   B: Yes. No-one realised what was happening and the thief _____ .

26.5 Complete the sentences using **could, couldn't** or **managed to.**

1 My grandfather travelled a lot. He __could__ speak five languages.
2 I looked everywhere for the book, but I _couldn't_ find it.
3 They didn't want to come with us at first, but we _managed to_ persuade them.
4 Laura had hurt her leg and _____ walk very well.
5 Sue wasn't at home when I phoned, but I _____ contact her at her office.
6 I looked very carefully and I _____ see somebody in the distance.
7 I wanted to buy some tomatoes. The first shop I went to didn't have any, but I
   _____ get some in the next shop.
8 My grandmother loved music. She _____ play the piano very well.
9 A girl fell into the river, but fortunately we _____ rescue her.
10 I had forgotten to bring my camera, so I _____ take any photographs.

Could (do) and could have (done)

A We use **could** in a number of ways. Sometimes **could** is the past of **can** (see Unit 26):
- ☐ Listen. I **can hear** something. *(now)*
- ☐ I listened. I **could hear** something. *(past)*

But **could** is not only used in this way. We also use **could** to talk about possible actions *now* or *in the future* (especially to make suggestions).
For example:

- ☐ A: What shall we do this evening?
  - B: We **could go** to the cinema.
- ☐ A: When you go to Paris next month, you **could stay** with Julia.
  - B: Yes, I suppose I **could**.

What shall we do this evening?

*We **could go** to the cinema.*

Can is also possible in these sentences ('We **can** go to the cinema.' etc.). With **could**, the suggestion is less sure.

B We also use **could** (*not* **can**) for actions which are not realistic. For example:
- ☐ I'm so tired, I **could sleep** for a week. (*not* I can sleep for a week)

Compare **can** and **could**:
- ☐ I **can stay** with Julia when I go to Paris. (realistic)
- ☐ Maybe I **could stay** with Julia when I go to Paris. (possible, but less sure)
- ☐ This is a wonderful place. I **could stay** here for ever. (unrealistic)

C We also use **could** (*not* **can**) to say that something is possible now or in the future. The meaning is similar to **might** or **may** (see Unit 29):
- ☐ The story **could be** true, but I don't think it is. (*not* can be true)
- ☐ I don't know what time Liz is coming. She **could get** here at any time.

D We use **could have** (done) to talk about the past. Compare:
- ☐ I'm so tired, I **could sleep** for a week. *(now)*
  I was so tired, I **could have slept** for a week. *(past)*
- ☐ The situation is bad, but it **could be** worse. *(now)*
  The situation was bad, but it **could have been** worse. *(past)*

Something **could have** happened = it was possible but did *not* happen:
- ☐ Why did you stay at a hotel when you were in Paris? You **could have stayed** with Julia. (you didn't stay with her)
- ☐ I didn't know that you wanted to go to the concert. I **could have got** you a ticket. (I didn't get you a ticket)
- ☐ Dave was lucky. He **could have hurt** himself when he fell, but he's OK.

E We use **couldn't** to say that something would not be possible now:
- ☐ I **couldn't live** in a big city. I'd hate it. (= it wouldn't be possible for me)
- ☐ Everything is fine right now. Things **couldn't be** better.

For the past we use **couldn't have** (done):
- ☐ We had a really good holiday. It **couldn't have been** better.
- ☐ The trip was cancelled last week. Paul **couldn't have gone** anyway because he was ill. (= it would not have been possible for him to go)

Couldn't have (done) → Unit 28B **Could and might** → Unit 29C **Could I/you ... ?** → Unit 37
Could with if → Units 38C, 39E, 40D **Modal verbs (can/could/will/would etc.)** → Appendix 4

Exercises

27.1 Answer the questions with a suggestion. Use **could**.

1 Where shall we go for our holidays?
2 What shall we have for dinner tonight?
3 When shall I phone Angela?
4 What shall I give Ann for her birthday?
5 Where shall we hang this picture?

(to Scotland) _We could go to Scotland._
(fish) We ....
(now) You ....
(a book) ....
(in the kitchen) ....
....

27.2 In some of these sentences, you need **could** (not **can**). Change the sentences where necessary.

1 The story can be true, but I don't think it is.   _could be true_
2 It's a nice day. We can go for a walk.   _OK (could go is also possible)_
3 I'm so angry with him. I can kill him!   ....
4 If you're hungry, we can have dinner now.   ....
5 It's so nice here. I can stay here all day, but   ....
   unfortunately I have to go.
6 A: Where's my bag. Have you seen it?
   B: No, but it can be in the car.   ....
7 Peter is a keen musician. He plays the flute and
   he can also play the piano.   ....
8 A: I need to borrow a camera.
   B: You can borrow mine.   ....
9 The weather is nice now, but it can change later.   ....

27.3 Complete the sentences. Use **could** or **could have** + a suitable verb.

1 A: What shall we do this evening?
   B: I don't mind. We ...._could go_.... to the cinema.
2 A: I had a very boring evening at home yesterday.
   B: Why did you stay at home? You .... out with us.
3 A: There's an interesting job advertised in the paper. You .... for it.
   B: What sort of job? Show me the advertisement.
4 A: How was your exam? Was it difficult?
   B: It wasn't so bad. It .... worse.
5 A: I got very wet walking home in the rain last night.
   B: Why did you walk? You .... a taxi.
6 A: Where shall we meet tomorrow?
   B: Well, I .... to your house if you like.

27.4 Complete the sentences. Use **couldn't** or **couldn't have** + these verbs (in the correct form):

~~be~~   be   come   find   get   ~~live~~   wear

1 I ...._couldn't live_.... in a big city. I'd hate it.
2 We had a really good holiday. It ...._couldn't have been_.... better.
3 I .... that hat. I'd look silly and people would laugh at me.
4 We managed to find the restaurant you recommended, but we .... it
   without the map that you drew for us.
5 Paul has to get up at 4 o'clock every morning. I don't know how he does it. I
   .... up at that time every day.
6 The staff at the hotel were really nice when we stayed there last summer. They
   .... more helpful.
7 A: I tried to phone you last week. We had a party and I wanted to invite you.
   B: That was nice of you, but I .... anyway. I was away all last week.

Must and can't

Study this example:

My house is very near the motorway.

It **must be** very noisy.

You can use **must** to say that you believe something is certain:
- ☐ You've been travelling all day. You **must be** tired. (Travelling is tiring and you've been travelling all day, so you **must** be tired.)
- ☐ 'Jim is a hard worker.' 'Jim? You **must be joking**. He doesn't do anything.'
- ☐ Carol **must get** very bored in her job. She does the same thing every day.
- ☐ I'm sure Sally gave me her phone number. I **must have** it somewhere.

You can use **can't** to say that you believe something is not possible:
- ☐ You've just had lunch. You **can't be** hungry already. (People are not normally hungry just after eating a meal. You've just eaten, so you **can't** be hungry.)
- ☐ They haven't lived here for very long. They **can't know** many people.

Study the structure:

I/you/he (etc.)	must can't	be (tired / hungry / at work etc.) be (doing / going / joking etc.) do / get / know / have etc.

For the past we use **must have** (**done**) and **can't have** (**done**).

Study this example:

There's nobody at home. They **must have gone** out.

Martin and Lucy are standing at the door of their friends' house.
They have rung the doorbell twice, but nobody has answered. Lucy says:

They **must have gone** out.

- ☐ I didn't hear the phone. I **must have been** asleep.
- ☐ 'I've lost one of my gloves.' 'You **must have dropped** it somewhere.'
- ☐ Sue hasn't contacted me. She **can't have got** my message.
- ☐ Tom walked into a wall. He **can't have been looking** where he was going.

Study the structure:

I/you/he (etc.)	must can't	have	been (asleep / at work etc.) been (doing / looking etc.) gone / got / known etc.

You can use **couldn't have** instead of **can't have**:
- ☐ Sue **couldn't have got** my message.
- ☐ Tom **couldn't have been looking** where he was going.

Can't ('I can't swim' etc.) → Unit 26   Must ('I must go' etc.) → Units 31–32
Modal verbs (can/could/will/would etc.) → Appendix 4   American English → Appendix 7

Exercises

28.1 Put in **must** or **can't**.

1 You've been travelling all day. You ......*must*.... be tired.
2 That restaurant .... be very good. It's always full of people.
3 That restaurant .... be very good. It's always empty.
4 I'm sure I gave you the key. You .... have it. Have you looked in your bag?
5 You're going on holiday next week. You .... be looking forward to it.
6 It rained every day during their holiday, so they .... have had a very nice time.
7 Congratulations on passing your exam. You .... be very pleased.
8 You got here very quickly. You .... have walked very fast.
9 Bill and Sue always travel business class, so they .... be short of money.

28.2 Complete each sentence with a verb (one or two words) in the correct form.

1 I've lost one of my gloves. I must ......*have dropped*...... it somewhere.
2 They haven't lived here for very long. They can't .....*know*..... many people.
3 Ted isn't at work today. He must .... ill.
4 Ted wasn't at work last week. He must .... ill.
5 *(the doorbell rings)* I wonder who that is. It can't .... Mary. She's still at work at this time.
6 Sarah knows a lot about films. She must .... to the cinema a lot.
7 Look. James is putting on his hat and coat. He must .... out.
8 I left my bike outside the house last night and now it has gone. Somebody must .... it.
9 Amy was in a very difficult situation when she lost her job. It can't .... easy for her.
10 There is a man walking behind us. He has been walking behind us for the last twenty minutes. He must .... us.

28.3 Read the situations and use the words in brackets to write sentences with **must have** and **can't have**.

1 The phone rang, but I didn't hear it. (I / asleep)
   I must have been asleep.
2 Sue hasn't contacted me. (she / get / my message)
   She can't have got my message.
3 The jacket you bought is very good quality. (it / very expensive)
   ....
4 I haven't seen the people next door for ages. (they / go away)
   ....
5 I can't find my umbrella. (I / leave / it in the restaurant last night)
   ....
6 Dave, who is usually very friendly, walked past me without speaking. (he / see / me)
   ....
7 There was a man standing outside the café. (he / wait / for somebody)
   ....
8 Liz did the opposite of what I asked her to do. (she / understand / what I said)
   ....
9 When I got back to my car, the door was unlocked. (I / forget / to lock it)
   ....
10 I was woken up in the night by the noise next door. (the neighbours / have / a party)
   ....
11 The light was red, but the car didn't stop. (the driver / see / the red light)
   ....

May and might 1

A Study this example situation:

> You are looking for Bob. Nobody is sure where he is, but you get some suggestions.
>
> Where's Bob?
>
> He **may be** in his office. (= perhaps he is in his office)
>
> He **might be having** lunch. (= perhaps he is having lunch)
>
> Ask Ann. She **might know**. (= perhaps she knows)

We use **may** or **might** to say that something is a possibility. Usually you can use **may** or **might**, so you can say:

- □ It **may** be true. *or* It **might** be true. (= perhaps it is true)
- □ She **might** know. *or* She **may** know.

The negative forms are **may not** and **might not** (*or* **mightn't**):

- □ It **may not** be true. (= perhaps it isn't true)
- □ She **might not** work here any more. (= perhaps she doesn't work here)

Study the structure:

I/you/he (etc.)	may might	(not)	be (true / in his office etc.) be (doing / working / having etc.) know / work / want etc.

B For the past we use **may have** (**done**) or **might have** (**done**):

- □ A: I wonder why Kate didn't answer the phone.
  B: She **may have been** asleep. (= perhaps she was asleep)
- □ A: I can't find my bag anywhere.
  B: You **might have left** it in the shop. (= perhaps you left it in the shop)
- □ A: I was surprised that Kate wasn't at the meeting yesterday.
  B: She **might not have known** about it. (= perhaps she didn't know)
- □ A: I wonder why David was in such a bad mood yesterday.
  B: He **may not have been feeling** well. (= perhaps he wasn't feeling well)

Study the structure:

I/you/he (etc.)	may might	(not) have	been (asleep / at home etc.) been (doing / working / feeling etc.) known / had / wanted / left etc.

C **Could** is similar to **may** and **might**:

- □ It's a strange story, but it **could be** true. (= it may/might be true)
- □ You **could have left** your bag in the shop. (= you may/might have left it)

But **couldn't** (*negative*) is different from **may not** and **might not**. Compare:

- □ Sarah **couldn't have** got my message. Otherwise she would have replied.
  (= it is not possible that she got my message)
- □ I wonder why Sarah hasn't replied to my message. I suppose she **might not have** got it.
  (= perhaps she didn't get it, and perhaps she did)

Could → Unit 27   **May/might 2** → Unit 30   **May I … ?** → Unit 37C   **Might with if** → Units 30B, 38C, 40D
Modal verbs (**can/could/will/would** etc.) → Appendix 4

29.1 Write these sentences in a different way using **might**.

1 Perhaps Helen is in her office. *She might be in her office.*
2 Perhaps Helen is busy. ....
3 Perhaps she is working. ....
4 Perhaps she wants to be alone. ....
5 Perhaps she was ill yesterday. ....
6 Perhaps she went home early. ....
7 Perhaps she had to go home early. ....
8 Perhaps she was working yesterday. ....

In sentences 9–11 use **might not**.

9 Perhaps she doesn't want to see me. ....
10 Perhaps she isn't working today. ....
11 Perhaps she wasn't feeling well yesterday. ....

29.2 Complete each sentence with a verb in the correct form.

1 'Where's Sam?' 'I'm not sure. He might *be having* lunch.'
2 'Who is that man with Emily?' 'I'm not sure. It might .... her brother.'
3 A: Who was the man we saw with Anna yesterday?
   B: I'm not sure. It may .... her brother.
4 A: What are those people doing by the side of the road?
   B: I don't know. They might .... for a bus.
5 'Do you have a stamp?' 'No, but ask Simon. He may .... one.'

29.3 Read the situation and make sentences from the words in brackets. Use **might**.

1 I can't find Jeff anywhere. I wonder where he is.
   a (he / go / shopping) *He might have gone shopping.*
   b (he / play / tennis) *He might be playing tennis.*
2 I'm looking for Sarah. Do you know where she is?
   a (she / watch / TV / in her room) ....
   b (she / go / out) ....
3 I can't find my umbrella. Have you seen it?
   a (it / be / in the car) ....
   b (you / leave / in the restaurant last night) ....
4 Why didn't Dave answer the doorbell? I'm sure he was at home at the time.
   a (he / go / to bed early) ....
   b (he / not / hear / the doorbell) ....
   c (he / be / in the shower) ....

29.4 Complete the sentences using **might not have** ... or **couldn't have** ... .

1 A: Do you think Sarah got the message we sent her?
   B: No, she would have contacted us. *She couldn't have got it* .
2 A: I was surprised Kate wasn't at the meeting. Perhaps she didn't know about it.
   B: That's possible. *She might not have known about it* .
3 A: I wonder why they never replied to our letter. Do you think they received it?
   B: Maybe not. They ....
4 A: I wonder how the fire started. Was it an accident?
   B: No, the police say it ....
5 A: Mike says he needs to see you. He tried to find you yesterday.
   B: Well, he .... very hard. I was in my office all day.
6 A: The man you spoke to – are you sure he was American?
   B: No, I'm not sure. He ....

A

We use **may** and **might** to talk about possible actions or happenings in the future:

- ☐ I haven't decided yet where to go for my holidays. I **may go** to Ireland. (= perhaps I will go there)
- ☐ Take an umbrella with you. It **might rain** later. (= perhaps it will rain)
- ☐ The bus isn't always on time. We **might have** to wait a few minutes. (= perhaps we will have to wait)

The negative forms are **may not** and **might not** (**mightn't**):

- ☐ Liz **may not go** out tonight. She isn't feeling well. (= perhaps she will not go out)
- ☐ There **might not be** enough time to discuss everything at the meeting. (= perhaps there will not be enough time)

Compare **will** and **may/might**:

- ☐ I'll **be** late this evening. (for sure)
- ☐ I **may/might** be late this evening. (possible)

B

Usually you can use **may** or **might**. So you can say:

- ☐ I **may go** to Ireland. *or* I **might go** to Ireland.
- ☐ Jane **might be** able to help you. *or* Jane **may be** able to help you.

But we use only **might** (*not* may) when the situation is *not real*:

- ☐ If I were in Tom's position, I **might** look for another job.

The situation here is not real because I am *not* in Tom's position (so I'm not going to look for another job). **May** is not possible in this example.

C

There is also a continuous form: **may/might be -ing**. Compare this with **will be -ing**:

- ☐ Don't phone at 8.30. I'll **be watching** the film on television.
- ☐ Don't phone at 8.30. I **might be watching** (*or* I **may be watching**) the film on television. (= perhaps I'll be watching it)

We also use **may/might be -ing** for possible plans. Compare:

- ☐ I'm **going** to Ireland in July. (for sure)
- ☐ I **may be going** (*or* I **might be going**) to Ireland in July. (possible)

But you can also say 'I **may go** (*or* I **might go**) …' with little difference in meaning.

D **Might as well**

Rose and Clare have just missed the bus. The buses run every hour.

> What shall we do? Shall we walk?

> We **might as well**. It's a nice day and I don't want to wait here for an hour.

We **might as well** do something = We should do it because there is no better alternative. There is no reason not to do it.

May as well is also possible.

- ☐ A: What time are you going out?
  B: Well, I'm ready, so I **might as well go** now.
- ☐ Buses are so expensive these days, you **may as well get** a taxi. (= taxis are as good, no more expensive)

Exercises

30.1 Write sentences with **might**.

1 Where are you going for your holidays? (to Ireland???)
I haven't decided yet. _I might go to Ireland._

2 What sort of car are you going to buy? (a Mercedes???)
I'm not sure yet. I ....

3 What are you doing this weekend? (go to London???)
I haven't decided yet. ....

4 When is Tom coming to see us? (on Saturday???)
He hasn't said yet. ....

5 Where are you going to hang that picture? (in the dining room???)
I haven't made up my mind yet. ....

6 What is Julia going to do when she leaves school? (go to university???)
She's still thinking about it. ....

30.2 Complete the sentences using **might** + the following:

bite   break   need   ~~rain~~   slip   wake

1 Take an umbrella with you when you go out. It ...._might rain_....... later.
2 Don't make too much noise. You .... the baby.
3 Be careful of that dog. It .... you.
4 I don't think we should throw that letter away. We .... it later.
5 Be careful. The footpath is very icy. You ....
6 Don't let the children play in this room. They .... something.

30.3 Complete the sentences using **might be able to** or **might have to** + a suitable verb.

1 I can't help you, but why don't you ask Jane? She ....._might be able to help_..... you.
2 I can't meet you this evening, but I .... you tomorrow.
3 I'm not working on Saturday, but I .... on Sunday.
4 I can come to the meeting, but I .... before the end.

30.4 Write sentences with **might not**.

1 I'm not sure that Liz will come to the party.
Liz might not come to the party.

2 I'm not sure that I'll go out this evening.
I ....

3 I'm not sure that we'll get tickets for the concert.
We ....

4 I'm not sure that Sue will be able to come out with us this evening.
....

30.5 Read the situations and make sentences with **might as well**.

1 You and a friend have just missed the bus. The buses run every hour.
You say: We'll have to wait an hour for the next bus. _We might as well walk._

2 You have a free ticket for a concert. You're not very keen on the concert, but you decide to go.
You say: I .... to the concert. It's a pity to waste a free ticket.

3 You've just painted your kitchen. You still have a lot of paint, so why not paint the bathroom too?
You say: We .... There's plenty of paint left.

4 You and a friend are at home. You're bored. There's a film on TV starting in a few minutes.
You say: .... There's nothing else to do.

Have to and must

A

I **have to** do something = it is necessary to do it, I am obliged to do it:

- ☐ You can't turn right here. You **have to turn** left.
- ☐ I **have to wear** glasses for reading.
- ☐ George can't come out with us this evening. He **has to work** late.
- ☐ Last week Tina broke her arm and **had to go** to hospital.
- ☐ I haven't **had to go** to the doctor for ages.

> You **have to turn** left here.

We use **do/does/did** in questions and negative sentences (for the present and past simple):

- ☐ What **do I have to do** to get a new driving licence? (*not* What have I to do?)
- ☐ Karen **doesn't have to work** Saturdays. (*not* Karen hasn't to)
- ☐ Why **did** you **have to leave** early?

You can use **have to** with **will** and **might/may**:

- ☐ If the pain gets worse, you'**ll have to go** to the doctor.
- ☐ I **might have to work** late tomorrow evening. *or* I **may have to work** …
  (= it's possible that I will have to)

B

Must is similar to **have to**:

- ☐ It's later than I thought. I **must go**. *or* I **have to go**.

You can use **must** to give your own opinion (for example, to say what *you* think is necessary, or to recommend someone to do something). **Have to** is also possible:

- ☐ I haven't spoken to Sue for ages. I **must phone** her. (= I say this is necessary)
- ☐ Mark is a really nice person. You **must meet** him. (I recommend this)

We use **have to** (*not* **must**) to say what someone is *obliged* to do. The speaker is not giving his/her own opinion:

- ☐ I **have to work** from 8.30 to 5.30 every day. (a fact, not an opinion)
- ☐ Jane **has to travel** a lot for her work.

But **must** is often used in written rules and instructions:

- ☐ Applications for the job **must be received** by 18 May.
- ☐ *(exam instruction)* You **must write** your answers in ink.

You cannot use **must** to talk about the past:

- ☐ We **had** to leave early. (*not* we must)

C

Mustn't and **don't have to** are completely different:

You **mustn't** do something = it is necessary that you do *not* do it (so don't do it):	You **don't have to** do something = you don't need to do it (but you can if you want):
☐ You **must keep** it a secret. You **mustn't tell** anyone. (= don't tell anyone)	☐ You **don't have to tell** him, but you can if you want to.
☐ I promised I would be on time. I **mustn't be** late. (= I must be on time)	☐ I **don't have to be** at the meeting, but I think I'll go anyway.

D

You can use **have got to** instead of **have to**. So you can say:

- ☐ I'**ve got to** work tomorrow. *or* I **have to** work tomorrow.
- ☐ When **has** Liz **got to** go? *or* When **does** Liz **have to** go?

Must ('You must be tired') → Unit 28   Must/mustn't/needn't → Unit 32

Exercises

31.1 Complete the sentences with **have to / has to / had to**.

1 Bill starts work at 5 a.m. _He has to get up_ at four. (he / get up)
2 'I broke my arm last week.' ' _Did you have to go_ to hospital?' (you / go)
3 There was a lot of noise from the street. .... the window.
   (we / close)
4 Karen can't stay for the whole meeting. .... early. (she / leave)
5 How old .... to drive in your country? (you / be)
6 I don't have much time. .... (I / hurry)
7 How is Paul enjoying his new job? .... a lot? (he / travel)
8 'I'm afraid I can't stay long.' 'What time .... ?' (you / go)
9 'The bus was late again.' 'How long .... ?' (you / wait)
10 There was nobody to help me. I .... everything by myself. (I / do)

31.2 Complete the sentences using **have to** + the verbs in the list. Some sentences are positive (**I have to ...** etc.) and some are negative (**I don't have to ...** etc.):

ask   do   drive   ~~get up~~   go   make   make   pay   ~~show~~

1 I'm not working tomorrow, so I _don't have to get up_ early.
2 Steve didn't know how to use the computer, so I _had to show_ him.
3 Excuse me a moment – I .... a phone call. I won't be long.
4 I'm not so busy. I have a few things to do, but I .... them now.
5 I couldn't find the street I wanted. I .... somebody for directions.
6 The car park is free. You .... to park your car there.
7 A man was injured in the accident, but he .... to hospital because it
   wasn't serious.
8 Sue has a senior position in the company. She .... important decisions.
9 When Patrick starts his new job next month, he .... 50 miles to
   work every day.

31.3 In some of these sentences, **must** is wrong or unnatural. Correct the sentences where necessary.

1 It's later than I thought. I must go.   _OK (have to is also correct)_
2 I must work every day from 8.30 to 5.30.   _I have to work_
3 You must come and see us again soon.   ....
4 Tom can't meet us tomorrow. He must work.   ....
5 I must work late yesterday evening.   ....
6 I must get up early tomorrow. I have lots to do. ....
7 Julia wears glasses. She must wear glasses
   since she was very young.   ....

31.4 Complete the sentences with **mustn't** or **don't/doesn't have to**.

1 I don't want anyone to know about our plan. You _mustn't_ tell anyone.
2 Richard _doesn't have to_ wear a suit to work, but he usually does.
3 I can stay in bed tomorrow morning because I .... go to work.
4 Whatever you do, you .... touch that switch. It's very dangerous.
5 There's a lift in the building, so we .... climb the stairs.
6 You .... forget what I told you. It's very important.
7 Sue .... get up early, but she usually does.
8 Don't make so much noise. We .... wake the children.
9 I .... eat too much. I'm supposed to be on a diet.
10 You .... be a good player to enjoy a game of tennis.

→ Additional exercise 16 (page 311)

Unit 32

Must mustn't needn't

A **Must mustn't needn't**

You **must** do something = it is necessary that you do it:
- ☐ Don't tell anybody what I said. You **must** keep it a secret.
- ☐ We haven't got much time. We **must** hurry.

You **mustn't** do something = it is necessary that you do *not* do it (so don't do it):
- ☐ You **must** keep it a secret. You **mustn't** tell anybody else. (= don't tell anybody else)
- ☐ We **must** be very quiet. We **mustn't** make any noise.

You **needn't** do something = you don't need to do it (but you can if you like):
- ☐ You can come with me if you like, but you **needn't come** if you don't want to. (= it is not necessary for you to come)
- ☐ We've got plenty of time. We **needn't hurry**. (= it is not necessary to hurry)

B Instead of **needn't**, you can use **don't/doesn't need to**. So you can say:
- ☐ We **needn't** hurry. *or* We **don't need to** hurry.

Remember that we say **don't need to do**, but **needn't do** (*without* to).

C **Needn't have** (done)

Study this example situation:

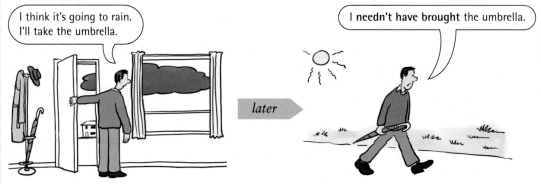

> I think it's going to rain. I'll take the umbrella.

> I **needn't have brought** the umbrella.

later

Paul had to go out. He thought it was going to rain, so he took the umbrella.

But it didn't rain, so the umbrella was not necessary. So he **needn't have taken** it.

He **needn't have taken** the umbrella = He took the umbrella, but this was not necessary.

Compare **needn't** (do) and **needn't have** (done):
- ☐ Everything will be OK. You **needn't worry**. (it's not necessary)
- ☐ Everything was OK. You **needn't have worried**. (you worried, but it was not necessary)

D **Didn't need to** (do) and **needn't have** (done)

I **didn't need to** … = it was not necessary for me to … (and I knew this at the time):
- ☐ I **didn't need to** get up early, so I didn't.
- ☐ I **didn't need to** get up early, but it was a lovely morning, so I did.

I **didn't have to** … is also possible in these examples.

I **needn't have done** something = I did it, but *now I know* that it was not necessary:
- ☐ I got up very early because I had to get ready to go away. But in fact it didn't take me long to get ready. So, I **needn't have got** up so early. I could have stayed in bed longer.

Must ('You must be tired') → Unit 28   Have to and must → Unit 31
Modal verbs (can/could/will/would etc.) → Appendix 4   American English → Appendix 7

32.1 Complete the sentences using **needn't** + the following verbs:

    ask   come   explain   ~~leave~~   tell   walk

1 We've got plenty of time. We ....*needn't leave*.... yet.
2 I can manage the shopping alone. You .... with me.
3 We .... all the way home. We can get a taxi.
4 Just help yourself if you'd like more to eat. You .... first.
5 We can keep this a secret between ourselves. We .... anybody else.
6 I understand the situation perfectly. You .... further.

32.2 Complete the sentences with **must**, **mustn't** or **needn't**.

1 We haven't got much time. We ....*must*.... hurry.
2 We've got plenty of time. We ....*needn't*.... hurry.
3 We have enough food at home, so we .... go shopping today.
4 Gary gave me a letter to post. I .... remember to post it.
5 Gary gave me a letter to post. I .... forget to post it.
6 There's plenty of time for you to make up your mind. You .... decide now.
7 You .... wash those tomatoes. They've already been washed.
8 This is a valuable book. You .... look after it carefully and you .... lose it.
9 A: What sort of house do you want to buy? Something big?
    B: Well, it .... be big – that's not so important. But it .... have a nice garden – that's essential.

32.3 Read the situations and make sentences with **needn't have**.

1 Paul went out. He took an umbrella because he thought it was going to rain. But it didn't rain.
    He needn't have taken an umbrella.
2 Linda bought some eggs when she went shopping. When she got home, she found that she already had plenty of eggs. She ....
3 A colleague got angry with you at work. He shouted at you, which you think was unnecessary. Later you say to him: You ....
4 Brian had money problems, so he sold his car. A few days later he won some money in a lottery. He ....
5 We took a camcorder with us on holiday, but we didn't use it in the end.
    We ....
6 I thought I was going to miss my train, so I rushed to the station. But the train was late and in the end I had to wait twenty minutes. ....

32.4 Write two sentences for each situation. Use **needn't have** in the first sentence and **could have** in the second (as in the example). For **could have**, see Unit 27.

1 Why did you rush? Why didn't you take your time?
    You needn't have rushed. You could have taken your time.
2 Why did you walk home? Why didn't you take a taxi?

    ....
3 Why did you stay at a hotel? Why didn't you stay with us?

    ....
4 Why did she phone me in the middle of the night? Why didn't she wait until the morning?

    ....

5 Why did you leave without saying anything? Why didn't you say goodbye?

    ....

Should 1

A You **should do** something = it is a good thing to do or the right thing to do. You can use **should** to give advice or to give an opinion:

- ☐ You look tired. You **should go** to bed.
- ☐ The government **should do** more to reduce crime.
- ☐ '**Should** we **invite** Susan to the party?' 'Yes, I think we **should**.'

We often use **should** with **I think / I don't think / Do you think** ... ?:

- ☐ **I think** the government **should do** more to reduce crime.
- ☐ **I don't think** you **should work** so hard.
- ☐ '**Do you think I should apply** for this job?' 'Yes, **I think you should**.'

You **shouldn't** do something = it isn't a good thing to do:

- ☐ You **shouldn't believe** everything you read in the newspapers.

Should is not as strong as **must** or **have to**:

- ☐ You **should** apologise. (= it would be a good thing to do)
- ☐ You **must** apologise. / You **have to** apologise. (= you have no alternative)

B You can use **should** when something is not right or what you expect:

- ☐ I wonder where Tina is. She **should be** here by now.
  (= she isn't here yet, and this is not normal)
- ☐ The price on this packet is wrong. It **should be** £2.50, not £3.50.
- ☐ That man on the motorbike **should be wearing** a helmet.

We also use **should** to say that we expect something to happen:

- ☐ She's been studying hard for the exam, so she **should pass**. (= I expect her to pass)
- ☐ There are plenty of hotels in the town. It **shouldn't be** difficult to find somewhere to stay.
  (= I don't expect it to be difficult)

C You **should have done** something = you didn't do it, but it would have been the right thing to do:

- ☐ You missed a great party last night. You **should have come**. Why didn't you?
  (= you didn't come, but it would have been good to come)
- ☐ I wonder why they're so late. They **should have arrived** long ago.

You **shouldn't have done** something = you did it, but it was the wrong thing to do:

- ☐ I'm feeling sick. I **shouldn't have eaten** so much. (= I ate too much)
- ☐ She **shouldn't have been listening** to our conversation. It was private.
  (= she was listening)

Compare **should** (do) and **should have** (done):

- ☐ You look tired. You **should go** to bed now.
- ☐ You went to bed very late last night. You **should have gone** to bed earlier.

D **Ought to ...**

You can use **ought to** instead of **should** in the sentences on this page. We say 'ought **to** do' (with **to**):

- ☐ Do you think I **ought to apply** for this job? (= Do you think I **should apply** ... ?)
- ☐ Jack **ought not to go** to bed so late. (= Jack **shouldn't go** ...)
- ☐ It was a great party last night. You **ought to have come**.
- ☐ She's been studying hard for the exam, so she **ought to pass**.

Exercises

33.1 For each situation, write a sentence with **should** or **shouldn't** + the following:

~~go away for a few days~~   go to bed so late   look for another job
put some pictures on the walls   take a photograph   use her car so much

1 Liz needs a change.   <u>She should go away for a few days.</u>
2 Your salary is very low.   You ....
3 Jack always has difficulty getting up.   He ....
4 What a beautiful view!   You ....
5 Sue drives everywhere. She never walks.   She ....
6 Bill's room isn't very interesting. ....

33.2 Read the situations and write sentences with **I think/I don't think ... should ...** .

1 Peter and Cathy are planning to get married. You think it's a bad idea.
   <u>I don't think they should get married.</u>
2 Jane has a bad cold but plans to go out this evening. You don't think this is a good idea. You
   say to her: ....
3 Peter needs a job. He's just seen an advertisement for a job which you think would be ideal for
   him, but he's not sure whether to apply or not. You say to him:
   I think ....
4 The government wants to increase taxes, but you don't think this is a good idea.
   ....

33.3 Complete the sentences with **should (have)** + the verb in brackets.

1 Diane <u>should pass</u> the exam. She's been studying very hard. (pass)
2 You missed a great party last night. <u>You should have come</u> . (come)
3 We don't see you enough. You .... and see us more often. (come)
4 I'm in a difficult position. What do you think I .... ? (do)
5 I'm sorry that I didn't take your advice. I .... what you said. (do)
6 I'm playing tennis with Jane tomorrow. She .... – she's much better
   than me. (win)
7 We lost the match, but we .... We were the better team. (win)
8 'Is Mike here yet?' 'Not yet, but he .... here soon.' (be)
9 I posted the letter three days ago, so it .... by now. (arrive)

33.4 Read the situations and write sentences with **should/shouldn't**. Some of the sentences are past
and some are present.

1 I'm feeling sick. I ate too much. <u>I shouldn't have eaten so much.</u>
2 That man on the motorbike isn't wearing a helmet. That's dangerous.
   He <u>should be wearing a helmet.</u>
3 When we got to the restaurant, there were no free tables. We hadn't reserved one.
   We ....
4 The notice says that the shop is open every day from 8.30. It is 9 o'clock now, but the shop
   isn't open yet. ....
5 The speed limit is 30 miles an hour, but Kate is doing 50.
   She ....
6 Laura gave me her address, but I didn't write it down. Now I can't remember it.
   I ....
7 I was driving behind another car. Suddenly, the driver in front stopped without warning and I
   drove into the back of his car. It wasn't my fault.
   The driver in front ....
8 I walked into a wall. I was looking behind me. I wasn't looking where I was going.
   ....

Unit 34

Should 2

A
You can use **should** after a number of verbs, especially:

>   demand   insist   propose   recommend   suggest

- [ ] They **insisted** that we **should have** dinner with them.
- [ ] I **demanded** that he **should apologise**.
- [ ] What do you **suggest I should do**?
- [ ] I **insist** that something **should be done** about the problem.

We also say 'It's important/vital/necessary/essential that ... should ...':

- [ ] It's **essential** that everyone **should be** here on time.

B
You can also leave out **should** in all the sentences in Section A:

- [ ] It's **essential** that everyone **be** here on time.   (= that everyone **should be** here)
- [ ] I **demanded** that he **apologise**. (= that he **should apologise**)
- [ ] What do you **suggest I do**?
- [ ] I **insist** that something **be done** about the problem.

This form (**be/do/have/apologise** etc.) is sometimes called the *subjunctive*. It is the same as the *infinitive* (without **to**).
You can also use normal present and past tenses:

- [ ] It's **essential** that everyone **is** here on time.
- [ ] I **demanded** that he **apologised**.

After **suggest**, you cannot use **to ...** ('to do / to buy' etc.). You can say:

- [ ] What do you **suggest we should do**?
or   What do you **suggest we do**? (*but not* What do you suggest us to do?)
- [ ] Jane **suggested** that I (**should**) **buy** a car.
or   Jane **suggested** that I **bought** a car. (*but not* Jane suggested me to buy)

You can also use **-ing** after **suggest**: What do you **suggest doing**? See Unit 53.

C
You can use **should** after a number of adjectives, especially:

>   strange   odd   funny   typical   natural   interesting   surprised   surprising

- [ ] It's **strange** that he **should be** late. He's usually on time.
- [ ] I was **surprised** that he **should say** such a thing.

D
If ... should ...

You can say 'If something **should** happen ...' . For example:

- [ ] If Tom **should phone** while I'm out, tell him I'll call him back later.
'If Tom **should phone**' is similar to 'If Tom **phones**'. With **should**, the speaker feels that the possibility is smaller. Another example:

- [ ] We have no jobs at present. But **if** the situation **should change**, we'll let you know.

You can also begin these sentences with **should** (**Should** something happen ...):

- [ ] **Should** Tom **phone**, tell him I'll call him back later.

E
You can use **I should ... / I shouldn't ...** to give somebody advice. For example:

- [ ] 'Shall I leave now?'   'No, **I should** wait a bit longer.'
Here, **I should wait** = I would wait if I were you, I advise you to wait.
Two more examples:

- [ ] 'I'm going out now. Is it cold?'   'Yes, **I should wear** a coat.
- [ ] **I shouldn't stay** up too late. You'll be tired tomorrow.

Should 1 → Unit 33   **American English** → Appendix 7

Exercises

34.1 Write a sentence (beginning in the way shown) that means the same as the first sentence.

1 'I think it would be a good idea to see a specialist,' the doctor said to me.
The doctor recommended that ....*I should see a specialist*.. .

2 'You really must stay a little longer,' she said to me.
She insisted that I ....

3 'Why don't you visit the museum after lunch?' I said to them.
I suggested that ....

4 'You must pay the rent by Friday,' the landlord said to us.
The landlord demanded that ....

5 'Why don't you go away for a few days?' Jack said to me.
Jack suggested that ....

34.2 Are these sentences right or wrong?

1 a Tom suggested that I should look for another job. ....*OK*..
  b Tom suggested that I look for another job. ....
  c Tom suggested that I looked for another job. ....
  d Tom suggested me to look for another job. ....

2 a Where do you suggest I go for my holiday? ....
  b Where do you suggest me to go for my holiday? ....
  c Where do you suggest I should go for my holiday? ....

34.3 Complete the sentences using **should** + the following:

    ask ~~**be**~~ **leave** **listen** **say** **worry**

1 It's strange that he ....*should be*.... late. He's usually on time.

2 It's funny that you .... that. I was going to say the same thing.

3 It's only natural that parents .... about their children.

4 Isn't it typical of Joe that he .... without saying goodbye to anybody?

5 I was surprised that they .... me for advice. What advice could I give them?

6 I'm going to give you all some essential information, so it's important that everybody
.... very carefully.

34.4 Use the words in brackets to complete these sentences. Use **If ... should ... .**

1 I'm going out now. ....*If Tom should phone*...., tell him I'll call him back this evening.
(Tom / phone)

2 I've hung the washing out to dry on the balcony. .... ,
can you bring the washing in, please? (it / rain)

3 I think everything will be OK. .... any problems,
I'm sure we'll be able to solve them. (there / be)

4 I don't want anyone to know where I'm going. .... ,
just say that you don't know. (anyone / ask)

Write sentences 3 and 4 again, this time beginning with **Should**.

5 (3) Should .... , I'm sure we'll be able to solve them.

6 (4) .... , just say that you don't know.

34.5 (Section E) Complete the sentences using **I should** + the following:

    buy **keep** **phone** ~~**wait**~~

1 'Shall I leave now?' 'No, ...*I should wait*.... a bit longer.'

2 'Shall I throw these things away?' 'No, ... them. You may need them.'

3 'Shall I go and see Paul?' 'Yes, but .... him first.'

4 'Is it worth repairing this TV set?' 'No, ... a new one.'

Had better   It's time ...

A

Had better (I'd better / you'd better etc.)

I'd better do something = it is advisable to do it. If I don't do it, there will be a problem or a danger:

- ☐ I have to meet Ann in ten minutes. **I'd better go** now or I'll be late.
- ☐ 'Shall I take an umbrella?' 'Yes, **you'd better**. It might rain.'
- ☐ **We'd better stop** for petrol soon. The tank is almost empty.

The negative is **I'd better not** (= I **had** better not):

- ☐ 'Are you going out tonight?' '**I'd better not**. I've got a lot to do.'
- ☐ You don't look very well. **You'd better not go** to work today.

Remember that:

> The form is '**had** better' (usually '**I'd** better / **you'd** better' etc. in spoken English).
> - ☐ **I'd better** phone Carol, **hadn't** I?
>
> **Had** is normally past, but the meaning of **had better** is present or future, *not* past.
> - ☐ **I'd better go** to the bank **now** / **tomorrow**.

We say 'I'd better **do**' (*not* to do).
- ☐ It might rain. We'd better **take** an umbrella. (*not* We'd better to take)

B

Had better and should

Had better is similar to **should** but not exactly the same. We use **had better** only for a specific situation (not for things in general). You can use **should** in all types of situations to give an opinion or give advice:

- ☐ It's late. You'd **better go**. / You **should go**. (a specific situation)
- ☐ You're always at home. You **should go** out more often. (in general – *not* 'had better go')

Also, with **had better**, there is always a danger or a problem if you don't follow the advice. **Should** only means 'it is a good thing to do'. Compare:

- ☐ It's a great film. You **should** go and see it. (but no problem if you don't)
- ☐ The film starts at 8.30. You'd **better** go now or you'll be late.

C

It's time ...

You can say **It's time** (for somebody) **to** ... :
- ☐ It's time **to go** home. / It's time for us **to go** home.

But you can also say:
- ☐ It's late. It's time **we went** home.

Here we use the past (**went**), but the meaning is present, *not* past:
- ☐ It's 10 o'clock and he's still in bed. **It's time** he **got** up. (*not* It's time he gets up)

It's time you did something = you should have already done it or started it. We often use this structure to criticise or to complain:

- ☐ **It's time** the children **were** in bed. It's long after their bedtime.
- ☐ You're very selfish. **It's time** you **realised** that you're not the most important person in the world.

You can also say **It's about time** ... . This makes the criticism stronger:
- ☐ Jack is a great talker. But **it's about time** he **did** something instead of just talking.

Should 1 → Unit 33

35.1 Read the situations and write sentences with **had better** or **had better not**. Use the words in brackets.

1 You're going out for a walk with Tom. It looks as if it might rain. You say to Tom:
  (an umbrella) _We'd better take an umbrella._

2 Michael has just cut himself. It's a bad cut. You say to him:
  (a plaster) ....

3 You and Kate plan to go to a restaurant this evening. It's a popular restaurant. You say to Kate:
  (reserve) We ....

4 Jill doesn't look very well – not well enough to go to work. You say to her:
  (work) ....

5 You received the phone bill four weeks ago, but you haven't paid it yet. If you don't pay soon, you could be in trouble. You say to yourself:
  (pay) ....

6 You want to go out, but you're expecting an important phone call. You say to your friend:
  (go out) I ....

7 You and Liz are going to the theatre. You've missed the bus and you don't want to be late. You say to Liz: (a taxi) ....

35.2 Put in **had better** where suitable. If **had better** is not suitable, use **should**.

1 I have an appointment in ten minutes. I __'d better__ go now or I'll be late.

2 It's a great film. You ...._should_.... go and see it. You'll really like it.

3 I .... get up early tomorrow. I've got a lot to do.

4 When people are driving, they .... keep their eyes on the road.

5 I'm glad you came to see us. You .... come more often.

6 She'll be upset if we don't invite her to the wedding, so we .... invite her.

7 These biscuits are delicious. You .... try one.

8 I think everybody .... learn a foreign language.

35.3 Complete the sentences. Sometimes you need only one word, sometimes two.

1 a I need some money. I'd better ...._go_.... to the bank.
  b John is expecting you to phone him. You .... better phone him now.
  c 'Shall I leave the window open?' 'No, you'd better .... it.'
  d We'd better leave as soon as possible, ... we?

2 a It's time the government .... something about the problem.
  b It's time something .... about the problem.
  c I think it's about time you .... about other people instead of only thinking about yourself.

35.4 Read the situations and write sentences with **It's time** (somebody **did** something).

1 You think the children should be in bed. It's already 11 o'clock.
  It's time the children were in bed.

2 You haven't had a holiday for a very long time. You need one now.
  It's time I ....

3 You're sitting on a train waiting for it to leave the station. It's already five minutes late.
  ....

4 You enjoy having parties. You haven't had one for a long time.
  ....

5 The company you work for has been badly managed for a long time. You think some changes should be made.
  ....

6 Andrew has been doing the same job for the last ten years. He should try something else.
  ....

Would

We use **would** (**'d**) / **wouldn't** when we *imagine* a situation or action (= we think of something that is not real):

- □ It **would be** nice to buy a new car, but we can't afford it.
- □ I**'d love** to live by the sea.
- □ A: Shall I tell Chris what happened?
  B: No, I **wouldn't say** anything.
  (= I wouldn't say anything in your situation)

We use **would have** (**done**) when we imagine situations or actions in the past (= things that didn't happen):

- □ They helped us a lot. I don't know what we**'d have done**
  (= we **would have done**) without their help.
- □ I didn't tell Sam what happened. He **wouldn't have been** pleased.

Compare **would** (**do**) and **would have** (**done**):

- □ I **would phone** Sue, but I haven't got her number. *(now)*
  I **would have phoned** Sue, but I didn't have her number. *(past)*
- □ I'm not going to invite them to the party. They **wouldn't come** anyway.
  I didn't invite them to the party. They **wouldn't have come** anyway.

We often use **would** in sentences with **if** (see Units 38–40):

- □ I **would phone** Sue **if** I had her number.
- □ I **would have phoned** Sue **if** I'd had her number.

Compare **will** (**'ll**) and **would** (**'d**):

- □ I**'ll stay** a bit longer. I've got plenty of time.
  I**'d stay** a bit longer, but I really have to go now. (so I can't stay longer)
- □ I**'ll phone** Sue. I've got her number.
  I**'d phone** Sue, but I haven't got her number. (so I can't phone her)

Sometimes **would/wouldn't** is the past of **will/won't**. Compare:

present		*past*
□ TOM: I**'ll phone** you on Sunday.	→	Tom said he**'d phone** me on Sunday.
□ ANN: I promise I **won't be** late.	→	Ann promised that she **wouldn't be** late.
□ LIZ: Damn! The car **won't start**.	→	Liz was annoyed because her car **wouldn't start**.

Somebody **wouldn't do** something = he/she refused to do it:

- □ I tried to warn him, but he **wouldn't listen** to me. (= he refused to listen)
- □ The car **wouldn't start**. (= it 'refused' to start)

You can also use **would** when you talk about things that happened regularly in the past:

- □ When we were children, we lived by the sea. In summer, if the weather was fine, we **would** all get up early and go for a swim. (= we did this regularly)
- □ Whenever Richard was angry, he **would** walk out of the room.

With this meaning, **would** is similar to **used to** (see Unit 18):

- □ Whenever Richard was angry, he **used to walk** out of the room.

 Will → Units 21–22   **Would you ... ?** → Unit 37A   **Would ... if** → Units 38–40   **Wish ... would** → Unit 41
Would like → Units 37E, 58   **Would prefer / would rather** → Unit 59   **Modal verbs** → Appendix 4

36.1 Write sentences about yourself. Imagine things you would like or wouldn't like.

1 (a place you'd love to live)   I'd love to live by the sea.
2 (a job you wouldn't like to do) ....
3 (something you would love to do) ....
4 (something that would be nice to have) ....
5 (a place you'd like to go to) ....

36.2 Complete the sentences using **would** + the following verbs (in the correct form):

be   be   ~~do~~   do   enjoy   enjoy   have   pass   stop

1 They helped us a lot. I don't know what we ....would have done.... without their help.
2 You should go and see the film. You .... it.
3 It's a pity you couldn't come to the concert yesterday. You .... it.
4 Shall I apply for the job or not? What .... you .... in my position?
5 I was in a hurry when I saw you. Otherwise I .... to talk.
6 We took a taxi home last night but got stuck in the traffic. It ....
   quicker to walk.
7 Why don't you go and see Clare? She .... very pleased to see you.
8 Why didn't you do the exam? I'm sure you .... it.
9 In an ideal world, everybody .... enough to eat.

36.3 Each sentence on the right follows a sentence on the left. Which follows which?

1 ~~I'd like to go to Australia one day.~~	a It wouldn't have been very nice.	....1c....
2 I wouldn't like to live on a busy road.	b It would have been fun.	....
3 I'm sorry the trip was cancelled.	c ~~It would be nice.~~	....
4 I'm looking forward to going out tonight.	d It won't be much fun.	....
5 I'm glad we didn't go out in the rain.	e It wouldn't be very nice.	....
6 I'm not looking forward to the trip.	f It will be fun.	....

36.4 Write sentences using **promised** + would/wouldn't.

1 I wonder why Laura is late.   She promised she wouldn't be late.
2 I wonder why Steve hasn't phoned. He promised ....
3 Why did you tell Jane what I said? You ....
4 I'm surprised they didn't wait for us. They ....

36.5 Complete the sentences. Use **wouldn't** + a suitable verb.

1 I tried to warn him, but he ....wouldn't listen.... to me.
2 I asked Amanda what had happened, but she .... me.
3 Paul was very angry about what I'd said and .... to me for two weeks.
4 Martina insisted on carrying all her luggage. She .... me help her.

36.6 These sentences are about things that often happened in the past. Complete the sentences
using **would** + the following: forget   help   shake   share   ~~walk~~

1 Whenever Richard was angry, he ....would walk.... out of the room.
2 We used to live next to a railway line. Every time a train went past, the house

   ....
3 George was a very kind man. He .... always .... you if you had a
   problem.
4 Brenda was always very generous. She didn't have much, but she ....
   what she had with everyone else.
5 You could never rely on Joe. It didn't matter how many times you reminded him to do
   something, he .... always ....

A Asking people to do things (requests)

We use **can** or **could** to ask people to do things:
- ☐ **Can you** wait a moment, please?
or **Could you** wait a moment, please?
- ☐ Liz, **can you** do me a favour?
- ☐ Excuse me, **could you** tell me how to get to the airport?

> **Could you** open the door, please?

Note that we say **Do you think** you **could ... ?** (*not* can):
- ☐ **Do you think you could** lend me some money until next week?

We also use **will** and **would** to ask people to do things (but **can/could** are more usual):
- ☐ Liz, **will you** do me a favour?
- ☐ **Would you** please be quiet? I'm trying to concentrate.

B Asking for things

To ask for something, we use **Can I have ... ?** or **Could I have ... ?**:
- ☐ *(in a shop)* **Can I have** these postcards, please?
- ☐ *(during a meal)* **Could I have** the salt, please?

May I have ... ? is also possible:
- ☐ **May I have** these postcards, please?

C Asking to do things

To ask to do something, we use **can, could** or **may**:
- ☐ *(on the phone)* Hello, **can I** speak to Steve, please?
- ☐ '**Could I** use your phone?' 'Yes, of course.'
- ☐ **Do you think I could** borrow your bike?
- ☐ '**May I** come in?' 'Yes, please do.'

May is more formal than **can** or **could**.

To ask to do something, you can also say **Do you mind if I ... ?** or **Is it all right / Is it OK if I ... ?**:
- ☐ '**Do you mind if I** use your phone?' 'Sure. Go ahead.'
- ☐ '**Is it all right if I** come in?' 'Yes, of course.'

D Offering to do things

To offer to do something, you can use **Can I ... ?**:
- ☐ '**Can I** get you a cup of coffee?' 'That would be nice.'
- ☐ '**Can I** help you?' 'No, it's all right. I can manage.'

E Offering and inviting

To offer or to invite, we use **Would you like ... ?** (*not* Do you like):
- ☐ '**Would you like** a cup of coffee?' 'Yes, please.'
- ☐ '**Would you like** to come to dinner tomorrow evening?' 'I'd love to.'

I'd like ... is a polite way of saying what you want:
- ☐ *(at a tourist information office)* **I'd like** some information about hotels, please.
- ☐ *(in a shop)* **I'd like** to try on this jacket, please.

Can and could → Units 26–27   **Mind -ing** → Unit 53   **Would like** → Units 55A, 58B
Modal verbs (can/could/will/would etc.) → Appendix 4

Exercises

37.1 Read the situations and write questions beginning **Can ...** or **Could ...** .

1 You're carrying a lot of things. You can't open the door yourself. There's a man standing near the door. You say to him: <u>Could you open the door, please?</u>

2 You phone Sue, but somebody else answers. Sue isn't there. You want to leave a message for her. You say: ....

3 You're a tourist. You want to go to the station, but you don't know how to get there. You ask at your hotel: ....

4 You are in a clothes shop. You see some trousers you like and you want to try them on. You say to the shop assistant: ....

5 You have a car. You have to go the same way as Steve, who is on foot. You offer him a lift. You say to him: ....

37.2 Read the situation and write a question using the word in brackets.

1 You want to borrow your friend's camera. What do you say to him?
(think) <u>Do you think I could borrow your camera?</u>

2 You are at a friend's house and you want to use her phone. What do you say?
(all right) <u>Is it all right if I use your phone?</u>

3 You've written a letter in English. Before you send it, you want a friend to check it for you. What do you ask?
(think) ....

4 You want to leave work early. What do you ask your boss?
(mind) ....

5 The woman in the next room is playing music. It's very loud. You want her to turn it down. What do you say to her?
(think) ....

6 You're on a train. The window is open and you're feeling cold. You'd like to close it, but first you ask the woman next to you.
(OK) ....

7 You're still on the train. The woman next to you has finished reading her newspaper, and you'd like to have a look at it. You ask her.
(think) ....

37.3 What would you say in these situations?

1 Paul has come to see you in your flat. You offer him something to eat.
YOU: <u>Would you like something to eat</u> .... ?
PAUL: No, thank you. I've just eaten.

2 You need help to change the film in your camera. You ask Kate.
YOU: I don't know how to change the film. .... ?
KATE: Sure. It's easy. All you have to do is this.

3 You're on a bus. You have a seat, but an elderly man is standing. You offer him your seat.
YOU: .... ?
MAN: Oh, that's very kind of you. Thank you very much.

4 You're the passenger in a car. Your friend is driving very fast. You ask her to slow down.
YOU: You're making me very nervous. .... ?
DRIVER: Oh, I'm sorry. I didn't realise I was going so fast.

5 You've finished your meal in a restaurant and now you want the bill. You ask the waiter:
YOU: .... ?
WAITER: Right. I'll get it for you now.

6 A friend of yours is interested in one of your books. You invite him to borrow it.
FRIEND: This looks very interesting.
YOU: Yes, it's a good book. .... ?

If I do ... and If I did ...

A Compare these examples:

(1) Lisa has lost her watch. She tells Sue:

> LISA: I've lost my watch. Have you seen it anywhere?
> SUE: No, but **if I find** it, I'll tell you.

In this example, Sue feels there is a real possibility that she will find the watch. So she says:
if I find ... , **I'll** ... .

---

(2) Joe says:

> If **I found** a wallet in the street, I'd take it to the police station.

This is a different type of situation. Here, Joe doesn't expect to find a wallet in the street; he is *imagining* a situation that will probably not happen. So he says:
if I found ... , **I'd** (= I **would**) ... . (*not* if I find ... , I'll ...)

When you imagine something like this, you use **if** + *past*
(**if** I **found** / **if** there **was** / **if** we **didn't** etc.).
But the meaning is *not* past:

If I won a million pounds ...

- □ What would you do **if** you **won** a million pounds?
  (we don't really expect this to happen)
- □ I don't really want to go to their party, but I probably will go. They'd be upset **if** I **didn't** go.
- □ If there **was** (*or* **were**) an election tomorrow, who would you vote for?

For **if** ... **was/were**, see Unit 39C.

B We do not normally use **would** in the **if**-part of the sentence:

- □ I'd be very frightened **if** somebody **pointed** a gun at me. (*not* if somebody would point)
- □ If I **didn't** go to their party, they'd be upset. (*not* If I wouldn't go)

But you can use **if** ... **would** when you ask somebody to do something:

- □ (*from a formal letter*) I would be grateful **if** you **would let** me know your decision as soon as possible.

C In the other part of the sentence (not the **if**-part) we use **would** ('**d**) / **wouldn't**:

- □ If you took more exercise, you'**d** (= you **would**) feel better.
- □ I'm not tired. If I went to bed now, I **wouldn't sleep**.
- □ **Would** you **mind** if I used your phone?

Could and **might** are also possible:

- □ If you took more exercise, you **might feel** better. (= it is possible that you would feel better)
- □ If it stopped raining, we **could go** out. (= we would be able to go out)

D Do not use **when** in sentences like those on this page:

- □ They'd be upset **if** I didn't go to their party. (*not* when I didn't go)
- □ What would you do **if** you were bitten by a snake? (*not* when you were bitten)

Will → Units 21–22   **If and when** → Unit 25D   **Would** → Unit 36   **If I knew** → Unit 39
If I had known → Unit 40

76

Exercises

38.1 Put the verb into the correct form.

1 They would be offended if I _didn't go_ to their party. (not / go)
2 If you took more exercise, you _would feel_ better. (feel)
3 If they offered me the job, I think I _would take_ it. (take)
4 A lot of people would be out of work if the car factory _closed down_ . (close down)
5 If I sold my car, I _wouldn't get_ much money for it. (not / get)
6 (in a lift) What would happen if somebody _pressed_ that red button? (press)
7 I don't think there's any chance that Gary and Emma will get married. I'd be absolutely astonished if they _did_ . (do)
8 Liz gave me this ring. She _would be_ very upset if I lost it. (be)
9 Dave and Kate are expecting us. They would be very disappointed if we _didn't come_ (not / come)
10 Would Steve mind if I _borrowed_ his bike without asking him? (borrow)
11 What would you do if somebody _walked_ in here with a gun? (walk)
12 I'm sure Sue _would understand_ if you explained the situation to her. (understand)

38.2 You ask a friend to imagine these situations. You ask **What would you do if ... ?**

1 (imagine – you win a lot of money)
  What would you do if you won a lot of money?
2 (imagine – you lose your passport)
  What _would you do if you lost your passport?_
3 (imagine – there's a fire in the building)
  What would you do if there were a fire in the bui
4 (imagine – you're in a lift and it stops between floors)
  What would you do if you were in a lift & it stops

38.3 Answer the questions in the way shown.

1 A: Shall we catch the 10.30 train?
  B: No. (arrive too early) _If we caught the 10.30 train, we'd arrive too early._
2 A: Is Kevin going to take his driving test?
  B: No. (fail) If he _took his driving test, he wouldn't fail_ (fail)
3 A: Why don't we stay at a hotel?
  B: No. (cost too much) If _we stayed at a hotel, it wouldn't cost too much_
4 A: Is Sally going to apply for the job?
  B: No. (not / get it) If _Sally applied for the job, she would not get it._
5 A: Let's tell them the truth.
  B: No. (not / believe us) If _we told them the truth, they wouldn't believe us_
6 A: Why don't we invite Bill to the party?
  B: No. (have to invite his friends too)
  If we invited Bill to party, we would have to invite his friends

38.4 Use your own ideas to complete these sentences.

1 If you took more exercise, _you'd feel better._
2 I'd be very angry if _____
3 If I didn't go to work tomorrow, _____
4 Would you go to the party if _____
5 If you bought some new clothes, _____
6 Would you mind if _____

If I knew ...   I wish I knew ...

A

Study this example situation:

Sarah wants to phone Paul, but she can't do this because she doesn't know his number.
She says:

If I knew his number, I **would phone** him.

Sarah says: **If I knew** his number ... . This tells us that she *doesn't* know his number. She is imagining the situation. The *real* situation is that she doesn't know his number.

If I **knew** his number ...

When you imagine a situation like this, you use **if** + *past* (if I **knew** / if you **were** / if we **didn't** etc.). But the meaning is present, *not* past:

- Tom would read more **if** he **had** more time. (but he doesn't have much time)
- If I **didn't** want to go to the party, I wouldn't go. (but I want to go)
- We wouldn't have any money **if** we **didn't** work. (but we work)
- If you **were** in my position, what would you do?
- It's a pity you can't drive. It would be useful **if** you **could**.

B

We use the past in the same way after **wish** (I wish I knew / I wish you were etc.). We use **wish** to say that we regret something, that something is not as we would like it to be:

- I **wish** I **knew** Paul's phone number.
  (= I don't know it and I regret this)
- Do you ever **wish** you **could** fly?
  (you can't fly)
- It rains a lot here. I **wish** it **didn't** rain so often.
- It's very crowded here. I **wish** there **weren't** so many people. (there are a lot of people)
- I **wish** I **didn't** have to work tomorrow, but unfortunately I do.

I wish I had an umbrella.

C

If I were / if I was

After **if** and **wish**, you can use **were** instead of **was** (if I **were** ... / I wish it **were** etc.). I **was** / it **was** are also possible. So you can say:

- If I **were** you, I wouldn't buy that coat.   *or*   If I **was** you, ...
- I'd go out **if** it **weren't** so cold.   *or*   ... if it **wasn't** so cold.
- I wish Carol **were** here.   *or*   I wish Carol **was** here.

D

We do not normally use **would** in the **if**-part of the sentence or after **wish**:

- If I **were** rich, I **would** have a yacht. (*not* If I would be rich)
- I **wish** I **had** something to read. (*not* I wish I would have)

Sometimes **wish ... would** is possible: I **wish** you **would listen**. See Unit 41.

E

Could sometimes means 'would be able to' and sometimes 'was/were able to':

- You **could** get a better job   (you **could** get = you would be able to get)
  if you **could** use a computer.   (you **could** use = you were able to use)

Could → Units 26–27   **If I do / if I did** → Unit 38   **If I had known / I wish I had known** → Unit 40
Wish → Unit 41

Exercises

39.1 Put the verb into the correct form.

1 If I __knew__ (know) his number, I would phone him.
2 I __wouldn't buy__ (not / buy) that coat if I were you.
3 I __would help__ (help) you if I could, but I'm afraid I can't.
4 We would need a car if we __lived__ (live) in the country.
5 If we had the choice, we __would live__ (live) in the country.
6 This soup isn't very good. It __would taste__ (taste) better if it wasn't so salty.
7 I wouldn't mind living in England if the weather __were/was__ (be) better.
8 If I were you, I __wouldn't wait__ (not / wait). I __went__ (go) now.
9 You're always tired. If you __didn't go__ (not / go) to bed so late every night, you wouldn't be tired all the time.
10 I think there are too many cars. If there __weren't__ (not / be) so many cars, there __wouldn't be__ (not / be) so much pollution.

39.2 Write a sentence with **if** ... for each situation.

1 We don't see you very often because you live so far away.
   __If you didn't live so far away, we'd see you more often.__
2 This book is too expensive, so I'm not going to buy it.
   I'd __not buy it__ if __this book wasn't expensive__
3 We don't go out very often – we can't afford it.
   We __wouldn't go out very often, if we couldn't afford it__
4 I can't meet you tomorrow – I have to work late.
   If __I had to work late I couldn't meet you tom.__
5 It's raining, so we can't have lunch outside.
   We __couldn't have lunch outside it if arern't raining__
6 I don't want his advice, and that's why I'm not going to ask for it.
   If __I wasn't ask for it, I wouldn't ask his adv.__

39.3 Write sentences beginning **I wish** ... .

1 I don't know many people (and I'm lonely). __I wish I knew more people.__
2 I don't have a mobile phone (and I need one). I wish __I had a mobile phone__
3 Helen isn't here (and I need to see her). __I wish helen was here__
4 It's cold (and I hate cold weather). __I wish it was cold__
5 I live in a big city (and I don't like it). __I wish I lived in a big city__
6 I can't go to the party (and I'd like to). __I wish I could go to the party__
7 I have to work tomorrow (but I'd like to stay in bed).
   __I wish I hadn't to work tom__
8 I don't know anything about cars (and my car has just broken down).
   __I wish I didn't know about car__
9 I'm not feeling well (and it's not nice).

39.4 Write your own sentences beginning **I wish** ... .

1 (somewhere you'd like to be now – on the beach, in New York, in bed etc.)
   I wish I
2 (something you'd like to have – a computer, a job, lots of money etc.)

3 (something you'd like to be able to do – sing, speak a language, fly etc.)

4 (something you'd like to be – beautiful, strong, rich etc.)

→ Additional exercises 19–21 (pages 313–14)

If I had known ...   I wish I had known ...

A

Study this example situation:

> Last month Gary was in hospital for a few days. Rachel didn't know this, so she didn't go to visit him. They met a few days ago. Rachel said:
>
> **If** I **had known** you were in hospital, I **would have gone** to see you.
>
> Rachel said: **If** I **had known** you were in hospital ... . This tells us that she *didn't* know he was in hospital.

We use **if** + **had** (**'d**) ... to talk about the past (**if** I **had known/been/done** etc.):
- I didn't see you when you passed me in the street. **If I'd seen** you, of course I would have said hello. (but I didn't see you)
- I decided to stay at home last night. I would have gone out **if I hadn't been** so tired. (but I was tired)
- **If** he **had been looking** where he was going, he wouldn't have walked into the wall. (but he wasn't looking)
- The view was wonderful. **If I'd had** a camera with me, I would have taken some photographs. (but I didn't have a camera)

Compare:
- I'm not hungry. **If I was** hungry, I would eat something. *(now)*
- I wasn't hungry. **If I had been** hungry, I would have eaten something. *(past)*

B

Do not use **would** in the **if**-part of the sentence. We use **would** in the other part of the sentence:
- **If I had seen** you, I **would have said** hello. (*not* If I would have seen you)

Note that **'d** can be **would** or **had**:
- If **I'd seen** you,   (I'd seen = I **had** seen)
  I'd have said hello.   (I'd have said = I **would** have said)

C

We use **had** (**done**) in the same way after **wish**. I **wish** something **had happened** = I am sorry that it didn't happen:
- I **wish I'd known** that Gary was ill. I would have gone to see him. (but I didn't know)
- I feel sick. I **wish I hadn't eaten** so much cake. (I ate too much cake)
- Do you **wish** you **had studied** science instead of languages? (you didn't study science)

Do not use **would have** ... after **wish**:
- The weather was cold while we were away. I wish it **had been** warmer. (*not* I wish it would have been)

D

Compare **would** (**do**) and **would have** (**done**):
- If I had gone to the party last night, I **would be** tired now. (I am not tired now – *present*)
- If I had gone to the party last night, I **would have met** lots of people. (I didn't meet lots of people – *past*)

Compare **would have**, **could have** and **might have**:
- If the weather hadn't been so bad, {
  - we **would have gone** out.
  - we **could have gone** out.
    - (= we would have been able to go out)
  - we **might have gone** out.
    - (= perhaps we would have gone out)

Had done → Unit 15   **If I do / if I did** → Unit 38   **If I knew / I wish I knew** → Unit 39   **Wish** → Unit 41

40.1 Put the verb into the correct form.

1 I didn't know you were in hospital. If __I'd known__ (I / know), __I would have gone__ (I / go) to see you.

2 Sam got to the station just in time to catch the train to the airport. If _he had missed_ (he / miss) the train, _he would have missed_ (he / miss) his flight.

3 I'm glad that you reminded me about Amanda's birthday. _I would have forgoten_ (I / forget) if _you didn't reminded_ (you / not / remind) me.

4 Unfortunately I forgot my address book when I went on holiday. If _I had had_ (I / have) your address, _I could have sent_ (I / send) you a postcard.

5 A: How was your holiday? Did you have a nice time?
   B: It was OK, but _we would have enjoyed_ (we / enjoy) it more if _the weather had been_ (the weather / be) nicer.

6 I took a taxi to the hotel, but the traffic was bad. _It would have been_ (it / be) quicker if _I had walked_ (I / walk).

7 I'm not tired. If _I werebeen_ (I / be) tired, I'd go home now.

8 I wasn't tired last night. If _I had weren_ (I / be) tired, I would have gone home earlier.

40.2 For each situation, write a sentence beginning with **If**.

1 I wasn't hungry, so I didn't eat anything.
   If I'd been hungry, I would have eaten something.

2 The accident happened because the road was icy.
   If the road _hadn't icy, There wouldn't have accident_

3 I didn't know that Joe had to get up early, so I didn't wake him up.
   If I _had known that Joe had_, _I wouldn't have woken him_

4 I was able to buy the car only because Jane lent me the money.
   If Jane had lend me the money, I would have able to bought th

5 Karen wasn't injured in the crash because she was wearing a seat belt.
   If karen hadn't been wearing a seat belt she would have injured

6 You didn't have any breakfast – that's why you're hungry now.
   If you had had brew, You wouldn't have been

7 I didn't get a taxi because I didn't have any money.
   _____

40.3 Imagine that you are in these situations. For each situation, write a sentence with **I wish**.

1 You've eaten too much and now you feel sick.
   You say: _I wish I hadn't eaten so much._

2 There was a job advertised in the newspaper. You decided not to apply for it. Now you think that your decision was wrong.
   You say: I wish I _had decided to apply for job_

3 When you were younger, you never learned to play a musical instrument. Now you regret this.
   You say: _____

4 You've painted the gate red. Now you think that red was the wrong colour.
   You say: _____

5 You are walking in the country. You'd like to take some photographs, but you didn't bring your camera.
   You say: _____

6 You have some unexpected guests. They didn't phone first to say they were coming. You are very busy and you are not prepared for them.
   You say (to yourself): _____

→ Additional exercises 19–21 (pages 313–14)

Unit 41 — Wish

A

You can say 'I wish you luck / every success / a happy birthday' etc. :
- ☐ I wish you every success in the future.
- ☐ I saw Tim before the exam and he wished me luck.

We say 'wish somebody *something*' (luck / a happy birthday etc.). But you cannot 'wish that something *happens*'. We use hope in this situation. For example:
- ☐ I hope you get this letter before you go away. (*not* I wish you get)

Compare I wish and I hope:
- ☐ I wish you a pleasant stay here.
- ☐ I hope you have a pleasant stay here. (*not* I wish you have)

B

We also use wish to say that we regret something, that something is not as we would like it. When we use wish in this way, we use the *past* (knew/lived etc.), but the meaning is *present*:
- ☐ I wish I knew what to do about the problem. (I don't know and I regret this)
- ☐ I wish you didn't have to go so soon. (you have to go)
- ☐ Do you wish you lived near the sea? (you don't live near the sea)
- ☐ Jack's going on a trip to Mexico soon. I wish I was going too. (I'm not going)

To say that we regret something in the past, we use wish + had ... (had known / had said) etc. :
- ☐ I wish I'd known about the party. I would have gone if I'd known. (I didn't know)
- ☐ It was a stupid thing to say. I wish I hadn't said it. (I said it)

For more examples, see Units 39 and 40.

C

I wish I could (do something) = I regret that I cannot do it:
- ☐ I'm sorry I have to go. I wish I could stay longer. (but I can't)
- ☐ I've met that man before. I wish I could remember his name. (but I can't)

I wish I could have (done something) = I regret that I could not do it:
- ☐ I hear the party was great. I wish I could have gone. (but I couldn't go)

D

You can say 'I wish (somebody) would (do something)'. For example:

I wish it would stop raining.

It's been raining all day. Jill doesn't like it. She says:
I wish it would stop raining.

Jill would like the rain to stop, but this will probably not happen.

We use I wish ... would when we would like something to happen or change. Usually, the speaker doesn't expect this to happen.

We often use I wish ... would to complain about a situation:
- ☐ The phone has been ringing for five minutes. I wish somebody would answer it.
- ☐ I wish you would do something instead of just sitting and doing nothing.

You can use I wish ... wouldn't ... to complain about things that people do repeatedly:
- ☐ I wish you wouldn't keep interrupting me.

We use I wish ... would ... for actions and changes, *not* situations. Compare:
- ☐ I wish Sarah would come. (= I want her to come)
- *but* I wish Sarah was (*or* were) here now. (*not* I wish Sarah would be)
- ☐ I wish somebody would buy me a car.
- *but* I wish I had a car. (*not* I wish I would have)

I wish I knew → Unit 39   I wish I was / I wish I were → Unit 39C   I wish I had known → Unit 40

41.1 Put in **wish(ed)** or **hope(d)**.

1 I _wish_ you a pleasant stay here.
2 Enjoy your holiday. I _hope_ you have a great time.
3 Goodbye. I _wish_ you all the best.
4 We said goodbye to each other and _wished_ each other luck.
5 We're going to have a picnic tomorrow, so I _hope_ the weather is nice.
6 I _wish_ you luck in your new job. I _hope_ it works out well for you.

41.2 What do you say in these situations? Write sentences with **I wish ... would ...** .

1 It's raining. You want to go out, but not in the rain.
   You say: _I wish it would stop raining._
2 You're waiting for Jane. She's late and you're getting impatient.
   You say to yourself: I wish _Jane would come soon_
3 You're looking for a job – so far without success. Nobody will give you a job.
   You say: I wish somebody _would give me job_
4 You can hear a baby crying. It's been crying for a long time and you're trying to study.
   You say: _I wish the baby would stop crying_
5 Brian has been wearing the same clothes for years. You think he needs some new clothes.
   You say to Brian: ....

For the following situations, write sentences with **I wish ... wouldn't ...** .

6 Your friend drives very fast. You don't like this.
   You say to your friend: I wish you _My friens wouldn't drive fast_
7 Joe leaves the door open all the time. This annoys you.
   You say to Joe: ....
8 A lot of people drop litter in the street. You don't like this.
   You say: I wish people ....

41.3 Are these sentences right or wrong? Correct them where necessary.

1 I wish Sarah would be here now.   _I wish Sarah were here now._
2 I wish you would listen to me.   ....
3 I wish I would have more free time.   ....
4 I wish our flat would be a bit bigger.   ....
5 I wish the weather would change.   ....
6 I wish you wouldn't complain all the time.   ....
7 I wish everything wouldn't be so expensive.   ....

41.4 Put the verb into the correct form.

1 It was a stupid thing to say. I wish I _hadn't said_ it. (I / not / say)
2 I'm fed up with this rain. I wish _it would stop_ . (it / stop)
3 It's a difficult question. I wish .... the answer. (I / know)
4 I should have listened to you. I wish .... your advice. (I / take)
5 You're lucky to be going away. I wish .... with you. (I / can / come)
6 I have no energy at the moment. I wish .... so tired. (I / not / be)
7 Aren't they ready yet? I wish .... up. (they / hurry)
8 It would be nice to stay here longer. I wish .... to leave now.
   (we / not / have)
9 When we were in London last year, we didn't have time to see all the things we wanted to see.
   I wish .... longer. (we / can / stay)
10 It's freezing today. I wish .... so cold. I hate cold weather. (it / not / be)
11 Joe still doesn't know what he wants to do. I wish .... (he / decide)
12 I really didn't enjoy the party. I wish .... (we / not / go)

Passive 1 (is done / was done)

A Study this example:

This house **was built** in 1935.

Was built is *passive*.

Compare active and passive:

Somebody **built** [this house] in 1935. *(active)*
subject   *object*

[This house] **was built** in 1935. *(passive)*
subject

When we use an active verb, we say *what the subject does*:
- ☐ My grandfather was a builder. **He built** this house in 1935.
- ☐ It's a big company. **It employs** two hundred people.

When we use a passive verb, we say *what happens to the subject*:
- ☐ This house is quite old. **It was built** in 1935.
- ☐ **Two hundred people are employed** by the company.

B When we use the passive, who or what causes the action is often unknown or unimportant:
- ☐ A lot of money **was stolen** in the robbery. (somebody stole it, but we don't know who)
- ☐ **Is** this room **cleaned** every day? (does somebody clean it? – it's not important who)

If we want to say who does or what causes the action, we use **by** ... :
- ☐ This house was built **by my grandfather**.
- ☐ Two hundred people are employed **by the company**.

C The passive is **be** (**is/was** etc.) + *past participle* (**done/cleaned/seen** etc.):
(**be**) **done**   (**be**) **cleaned**   (**be**) **damaged**   (**be**) **built**   (**be**) **seen** etc.
For irregular past participles (**done/seen/known** etc.), see Appendix 1.

Study the active and passive forms of the *present simple* and *past simple*:

Present simple
active: **clean(s) / see(s)** etc.

Somebody **cleans** [this room] every day.

passive: **am/is/are** + **cleaned/seen** etc.

[This room] **is cleaned** every day.

- ☐ Many accidents **are caused** by careless driving.
- ☐ **I'm not** often **invited** to parties.
- ☐ How **is** this word **pronounced**?

Past simple
active: **cleaned/saw** etc.

Somebody **cleaned** [this room] yesterday.

passive: **was/were** + **cleaned/seen** etc.

[This room] **was cleaned** yesterday.

- ☐ We **were woken** up by a loud noise during the night.
- ☐ 'Did you go to the party?'   'No, I **wasn't invited**.'
- ☐ How much money **was stolen** in the robbery?

Passive 2–3 → Units 42–43   By → Unit 128

Exercises

42.1 Complete the sentences using one of these verbs in the correct form, present or past:

~~cause~~   damage   hold   invite   make
overtake   show   surround   translate   write

1 Many accidents _are caused_ by dangerous driving.
2 Cheese _is made_ from milk.
3 The roof of the building _was damaged_ in a storm a few days ago.
4 You _weren't invited_ to the wedding. Why didn't you go?
5 A cinema is a place where films _are shown_ .
6 In the United States, elections for president _are held_ every four years.
7 Originally the book _was written_ in Spanish, and a few years ago it _was translated_ into English.
8 Although we were driving quite fast, we _were overtaken_ by a lot of other cars.
9 You can't see the house from the road. It _is surrounded_ by trees.

42.2 Write questions using the passive. Some are present and some are past.

1 Ask about glass. (how / make?) _How is glass made?_
2 Ask about television. (when / invent?) _When was television invented?_
3 Ask about mountains. (how / form?) _how are mountains formed?_
4 Ask about Pluto (*the planet*). (when / discover?) _when was Pluto discovered_
5 Ask about silver. (what / use for?) _what is used for silver?_

42.3 Put the verb into the correct form, present simple or past simple, active or passive.

1 It's a big factory. Five hundred people _are employed_ (employ) there.
2 _Did somebody clean_ (somebody / clean) this room yesterday?
3 Water _covers_ (cover) most of the earth's surface.
4 How much of the earth's surface _is covered_ (cover) by water?
5 The park gates _are locked_ (lock) at 6.30 p.m. every evening.
6 The letter _was posted_ (post) a week ago and it _arrived_ (arrive) yesterday.
7 The boat hit a rock and _sank_ (sink) quickly. Fortunately everybody _was rescued_ (rescue).
8 Richard's parents _died_ (die) when he was very young. He and his sister _were brought up_ (bring up) by their grandparents.
9 I was born in London, but I _grew up_ (grow up) in Canada.
10 While I was on holiday, my camera _was stolen_ (steal) from my hotel room.
11 While I was on holiday, my camera _disappeared_ (disappear) from my hotel room.
12 Why _did Sue resign_ (Sue / resign) from her job? Didn't she enjoy it?
13 Why _was Bill sacked_ (Bill / sack) from his job? What did he do wrong?
14 The company is not independent. It _is owned_ (own) by a much larger company.
15 I saw an accident last night. Somebody _called_ (call) an ambulance but nobody _was injured_ (injure), so the ambulance _wasn't need_ (not / need).
16 Where _were these Photos taken_ (these photographs / take)? In London? _Did you take_ (you / take) them, or somebody else?
17 Sometimes it's quite noisy living here, but it's not a problem for me – I _am not bothered_ (not / bother) by it.

42.4 Rewrite these sentences. Instead of using **somebody, they, people** etc., write a passive sentence.

1 Somebody cleans the room every day.   The room is cleaned every day.
2 They cancelled all flights because of fog.   All _flights were cancelled b-- of fog_
3 People don't use this road much.   _This road is not used_
4 Somebody accused me of stealing money.   I _was accused of stealing money_
5 How do people learn languages?   How _are languages learn by people_
6 Somebody warned us not to go out alone.   _we were warned not to go out alone_ .

85

Passive 2 (be done / been done / being done)

A

Study the following active and passive forms:

Infinitive

active: (to) **do/clean/see** etc.   Somebody **will clean** the room later.

passive: (to) **be + done/cleaned/seen** etc.   The room **will be cleaned** later.

- ☐ The situation is serious. Something must **be done** before it's too late.
- ☐ A mystery is something that can't **be explained**.
- ☐ The music was very loud and could **be heard** from a long way away.
- ☐ A new supermarket is going **to be built** next year.
- ☐ Please go away. I want **to be left** alone.

B

Perfect infinitive

active: (to) **have + done/cleaned/seen** etc.   Somebody **should have cleaned** the room .

passive: (to) **have been + done/cleaned/seen** etc.   The room **should have been cleaned**.

- ☐ I haven't received the letter yet. It might **have been sent** to the wrong address.
- ☐ If you hadn't left the car unlocked, it wouldn't **have been stolen**.
- ☐ There were some problems at first, but they seem **to have been solved**.

C

Present perfect

active: **have/has + done** etc.   The room looks nice. Somebody **has cleaned** it .

passive: **have/has been + done** etc.   The room looks nice. It **has been cleaned**.

- ☐ Have you heard? The concert **has been cancelled**.
- ☐ **Have** you ever **been bitten** by a dog?
- ☐ 'Are you going to the party?'   'No, I **haven't been invited**.'

Past perfect

active: **had + done** etc.   The room looked nice. Somebody **had cleaned** it .

passive: **had been + done** etc.   The room looked nice. It **had been cleaned**.

- ☐ The vegetables didn't taste very good. They **had been cooked** too long.
- ☐ The car was three years old but **hadn't been used** very much.

D

Present continuous

active: **am/is/are + (do)ing**   Somebody **is cleaning** the room at the moment.

passive: **am/is/are + being (done)**   The room **is being cleaned** at the moment.

- ☐ There's somebody walking behind us. I think we **are being followed**.
- ☐ *(in a shop)* 'Can I help you?'   'No, thank you. I'm **being served**.'

Past continuous

active: **was/were + (do)ing**   Somebody **was cleaning** the room when I arrived.

passive: **was/were + being (done)**   The room **was being cleaned** when I arrived.

- ☐ There was somebody walking behind us. We **were being followed**.

Passive 1, 3 → Units 42, 44

Exercises

43.1 What do these words mean? Use **it can ...** or **it can't ...** . Use a dictionary if necessary.

If something is
1 washable, *it can be washed* .
2 unbreakable, it *can't be broken* .
3 edible, *it can be eaten* .
4 unusable, *It can't be used* .
5 invisible, *It can't be seen* .
6 portable, *It can be arrested* .

43.2 Complete these sentences with the following verbs (in the correct form):

arrest   carry   cause   ~~do~~   make   repair   ~~send~~   spend   wake up

Sometimes you need **have** (**might have, should have** etc.).

1 The situation is serious. Something must __be done__ before it's too late.
2 I haven't received the letter. It might __have been sent__ to the wrong address.
3 A decision will not __be made__ until the next meeting.
4 Do you think that more money should __have been spent__ on education?
5 This road is in very bad condition. It should __have been repared__ a long time ago.
6 The injured man couldn't walk and had to __be carried__ .
7 It's not certain how the fire started, but it might __have been caused__ by an electrical fault.
8 I told the hotel receptionist I wanted to __be woken up__ at 6.30 the next morning.
9 If you hadn't pushed the policeman, you wouldn't __have been arrested__ .

43.3 Rewrite these sentences. Instead of using **somebody** or **they** etc., write a passive sentence.

1 Somebody has cleaned the room. __The room has been cleaned.__
2 They have postponed the meeting. The __meeting has been postponed__
3 Somebody is using the computer at the moment.
   The computer __is being used at the moment__
4 I didn't realise that somebody was recording our conversation.
   I didn't realise that __our conversation was being recorded.__
5 When we got to the stadium, we found that they had cancelled the game.
   When we got to the stadium, we found that __the game had been cancelled.__
6 They are building a new ring road round the city.
   __A new ring road is being built around the city.__
7 They have built a new hospital near the airport.
   __A new hospital has been built near the airport.__

43.4 Make sentences from the words in brackets. Sometimes the verb is active, sometimes passive.

1 There's somebody behind us. (I think / we / follow) __I think we're being followed.__
2 This room looks different. (you / paint / the walls?) __Have you painted the walls?__
3 My car has disappeared. (it / steal!) It __has been stolen.__
4 My umbrella has disappeared. (somebody / take) Somebody __has been taking__
5 Sam gets a higher salary now. (he / promote) He __has been promoted__
6 Ann can't use her office at the moment. (it / redecorate) It __can has been redecorate__
7 The photocopier broke down yesterday, but now it's OK. (it / work / again ; it / repair)
   It __was worked again__   It __has repaired__
8 When I went into the room, I saw that the table and chairs were not in the same place.
   (the furniture / move) The __furniture had been moved__
9 The man next door disappeared six months ago. (he / not / see / since then)
   He __hasn't been seen since then__
10 I wonder how Jane is these days. (I / not / see / for ages)
   I __am not being seen for ages__
11 A friend of mine was mugged on his way home a few nights ago. (you / ever / mug?)
   __you have ever mugged__

Passive 3

A

I was offered ... / we were given ... etc.

Some verbs can have two objects. For example, **give**:

- Somebody gave **the police** **the information**. (= Somebody gave the information to the police)

  object 1   *object 2*

So it is possible to make two passive sentences:

- **The police** were given the information.   *or*

  The information was given to the police.

Other verbs which can have two objects are:

ask   **offer**   **pay**   **show**   **teach**   **tell**

When we use these verbs in the passive, most often we begin with the *person*:

- **I was offered** the job, but I refused it. (= they offered me the job)
- **You will be given** plenty of time to decide. (= we will give you plenty of time)
- **Have you been shown** the new machine? (= has anybody shown you?)
- **The men were paid** £400 to do the work. (= somebody paid the men £400)

B

I don't like being ...

The passive of **doing/seeing** etc. is **being done / being seen** etc. Compare:

active: I don't like **people telling me** what to do.

passive: I don't like **being told** what to do.

- I remember **being taken** to the zoo when I was a child.

  (= I remember somebody taking me to the zoo)
- Steve hates **being kept** waiting. (= he hates people keeping him waiting)
- We managed to climb over the wall without **being seen**. (= without anybody seeing us)

C

I was born ...

We say 'I was born ...' (*not* I am born):

- I **was born** in Chicago.
- Where **were you born**? (*not* Where are you born?)   } *past*

but

- How many babies **are born** every day?   *present*

D

Get

You can use **get** instead of **be** in the passive:

- There was a fight at the party, but nobody **got hurt**. (= nobody **was** hurt)
- I don't often **get invited** to parties. (= I'm not often invited)
- I'm surprised Liz **didn't get offered** the job. (= Liz **wasn't offered** the job)

You can use **get** only when things *happen*. For example, you cannot use **get** in the following sentences:

- Jill **is liked** by everybody. (*not* gets liked – this is not a 'happening')
- He was a mystery man. Very little **was known** about him. (*not* got known)

We use **get** mainly in informal spoken English. You can use **be** in all situations.

We also use **get** in the following expressions (which are not passive in meaning):

get married, get divorced   **get lost** (= not know where you are)

get dressed (= put on your clothes)   **get changed** (= change your clothes)

Exercises

44.1 Write these sentences in another way, beginning in the way shown.

1 They didn't give me the information I needed.
I _wasn't given the information I needed._

2 They asked me some difficult questions at the interview.
I _was asked difficult que cu intre_

3 Linda's colleagues gave her a present when she retired.
Linda _was given present when she retired_

4 Nobody told me about the meeting.
I wasn't _being told about the meeting_

5 How much will they pay you for your work?
How much will you _be paid for your work_

6 I think they should have offered Tom the job.
I think Tom _should have been offered the job_

7 Has anybody shown you what to do?
Have you _been seen shown what to do._

44.2 Complete the sentences using **being** + the following (in the correct form):

give   invite   ~~keep~~   knock down   stick   treat

1 Steve hates _being kept_ waiting.
2 We went to the party without _being invited_ .
3 I like giving presents and I also like _being treated_ them.
4 It's a busy road and I don't like crossing it. I'm afraid of _being sticked_ .
5 I'm an adult. I don't like _being treated_ like a child.
6 You can't do anything about _tonecu decan_ in a traffic jam.

44.3 When were they born? Choose five of these people and write a sentence for each.
(Two of them were born in the same year.)

Beethoven	Galileo	Elvis Presley	1452	1869	1929
Agatha Christie	Mahatma Gandhi	Leonardo da Vinci	1564	1890	1935
~~Walt Disney~~	Martin Luther King	William Shakespeare	1770	~~1901~~	

1 _Walt Disney was born in 1901._
2
3
4
5
6
7 And you? I

44.4 Complete the sentences using **get/got** + the following verbs (in the correct form):

ask   damage   ~~hurt~~   pay   steal   sting   stop   use

1 There was a fight at the party, but nobody _got hurt_ .
2 Alex _got stung_ by a bee while he was sitting in the garden.
3 These tennis courts don't _get used_ very often. Not many people want to play.
4 I used to have a bicycle, but it _got stolen_ a few months ago.
5 Rachel works hard but doesn't _get paid_ very much.
6 Last night I _got stopped_ by the police as I was driving home. One of the lights on my car wasn't working.
7 Please pack these things very carefully. I don't want them to _get damaged_ .
8 People often want to know what my job is. I often _get asked_ that question.

A

Study this example situation:

Henry is very old. Nobody knows exactly how old he is, but:

It is said that | he | is 108 years old.

or | He | is said to be 108 years old.

Both these sentences mean: 'People say that he is 108 years old.'

You can use these structures with a number of other verbs, especially:

alleged   believed   considered   expected   known   reported   thought   understood

Compare the two structures:

☐ Cathy works very hard.
   It is said that she works 16 hours a day.   or   She **is said to work** 16 hours a day.
☐ The police are looking for a missing boy.
   It is believed that the boy is wearing   or   The boy **is believed to be wearing**
   a white pullover and blue jeans.   a white pullover and blue jeans.
☐ The strike started three weeks ago.
   It is expected that it will end soon.   or   The strike **is expected to end** soon.
☐ A friend of mine has been arrested.
   It is alleged that he hit a policeman.   or   He **is alleged to have hit** a policeman.
☐ The two houses belong to the same family.
   It is said that there is a secret tunnel   or   There **is said to be** a secret tunnel
   between them.   between them.

These structures are often used in news reports. For example, in a report about an accident:

☐ **It is reported that** two people were   or   Two people **are reported to have**
   injured in the explosion.   **been injured** in the explosion.

B

(Be) supposed to

Sometimes (**it is**) **supposed to ...** = (it is) **said to ...** :

☐ I want to see that film. It's **supposed to be** good. (= it is said to be good)
☐ Mark **is supposed to have hit** a policeman, but I don't believe it.

But sometimes **supposed to** has a different meaning. We use **supposed to** to say what is intended, arranged or expected. Often this is different from the real situation:

☐ The plan **is supposed to be** a secret, but everybody seems to know about it.
   (= the plan is intended to be a secret)
☐ What are you doing at work? You're **supposed to be** on holiday.
   (= you arranged to be on holiday)
☐ Our guests **were supposed to come** at 7.30, but they were late.
☐ Jane **was supposed to phone** me last night, but she didn't.
☐ I'd better hurry. I'm **supposed to be meeting** Chris in ten minutes.

You're **not supposed to** do something = it is not allowed or advisable:

☐ You're **not supposed to park** your car here. It's private parking only.
☐ Jeff is much better after his illness, but he's still **not supposed to do** any heavy work.

45.1 Write these sentences in another way, beginning as shown. Use the <u>underlined</u> word each time.

1 It is <u>expected</u> that the strike will end soon. The strike _is expected to end soon._

2 It is <u>expected</u> that the weather will be good tomorrow.
The weather is _expected to be good tomorrow_

3 It is <u>believed</u> that the thieves got in through a window in the roof.
The thieves _are believed to through a window in the roof._

4 It is <u>reported</u> that many people are homeless after the floods.
Many people _are reported to homeless after the floods._

5 It is <u>thought</u> that the prisoner escaped by climbing over a wall.
The prisoner _it is thought to climbing over a wall_

6 It is <u>alleged</u> that the man was driving at 110 miles an hour.
The man _is alleged to driving at 110 miles an hour._

7 It is <u>reported</u> that the building has been badly damaged by the fire.
The building _is reported badly damaged by the fire._

8 a It is <u>said</u> that the company is losing a lot of money.
The company _is said to losing lot of money._

b It is <u>believed</u> that the company lost a lot of money last year.
The company _is believed to lost a lot of money last year_

c It is <u>expected</u> that the company will make a loss this year.
The company _is expected to make a loss this year._

45.2 There are a lot of rumours about Alan. Here are some of the things people say about him:

1 (Alan speaks ten languages.)   2 (He knows a lot of famous people.)

3 (He is very rich.)   4 (He has twelve children.)   5 (He was an actor when he was younger.)

Alan

Nobody is sure whether these things are true. Write sentences about Alan using **supposed to.**

1 _Alan is supposed to speak ten languages._

2 He _is believed to knows a lot of famous people._

3 _He is thought to very rich._

4 _He is reported to has twelve children._

5 _He is known to an actor when he was younger._

45.3 Complete the sentences using **supposed to be** + the following:

on a diet   **a flower**   **my friend**   **a joke**   ~~a secret~~   **working**

1 Everybody seems to know about the plan, but it _is supposed to be a secret._

2 You shouldn't criticise me all the time. You _are supposed to be my friend_

3 I shouldn't be eating this cake really. I _am supposed to be on a diet_

4 I'm sorry for what I said. I was trying to be funny. It _is supposed to be a joke_

5 What's this drawing? Is it a tree? Or maybe it _is supposed to be a flower_

6 You shouldn't be reading the paper now. You _are supposed to be working._

45.4 Write sentences with **supposed to** + the following verbs:

arrive   **block**   ~~park~~   **phone**   **start**

Use the negative (**not supposed to**) where necessary.

1 You _'re not supposed to park_ here. It's private parking only.

2 We _are not supposed to arrive_ work at 8.15, but we rarely do anything before 8.30.

3 Oh, I _am not supposed to phone_ Helen, but I completely forgot.

4 This door is a fire exit. You _are supposed to block_ it.

5 My train _is supposed to start_ at 11.30, but it was an hour late.

→ Additional exercises 22–24 (pages 314–15)

Have something done

Study this example situation:

The roof of Lisa's house was damaged in a storm. Yesterday a workman came and repaired it.

Lisa **had** the roof **repaired** yesterday.

This means: Lisa arranged for somebody else to repair the roof. She didn't repair it herself.

LISA

We use **have something done** to say that we arrange for somebody else to do something for us. Compare:

- □ Lisa **repaired** the roof. (= she repaired it herself)
  Lisa **had** the roof **repaired**. (= she arranged for somebody else to repair it)

- □ 'Did you **make** those curtains yourself?' 'Yes, I enjoy making things.'
  'Did you **have** those curtains **made**?' 'No, I made them myself.'

B

Be careful with word order. The *past participle* (**repaired/cut** etc.) is after the *object*:

	have	object	past participle
Lisa	**had**	the roof	**repaired** yesterday.
Where did you	**have**	your hair	**cut**?
Your hair looks nice. Have you	**had**	it	**cut**?
Our neighbour has just	**had**	a garage	**built**.
We are	**having**	the house	**painted** at the moment.
How often do you	**have**	your car	**serviced**?
I think you should	**have**	that coat	**cleaned**.
I don't like	**having**	my photograph	**taken**.

C

Get something done

You can also say 'get something done' instead of 'have something done' (mainly in informal spoken English):

- □ When are you going to **get the roof repaired**? (= have the roof repaired)
- □ I think you should **get your hair cut** really short.

D

Sometimes **have something done** has a different meaning. For example:

- □ Paul and Karen **had all their money stolen** while they were on holiday.

This does not mean that they arranged for somebody to steal their money. 'They **had all their money stolen**' means only: 'All their money was stolen from them'.

With this meaning, we use **have something done** to say that something happens to somebody or their belongings. Usually what happens is not nice:

- □ Gary **had** his nose **broken** in a fight. (= his nose was broken)
- □ Have you ever **had** your passport **stolen**?

Exercises

46.1 Tick (✓) the correct sentence, (a) or (b), for each picture.

1 SARAH	2 BILL	3 JOHN	4 SUE
(a) Sarah is cutting her hair. (b) Sarah is having her hair cut.	(a) Bill is cutting his hair. (b) Bill is having his hair cut.	(a) John is cleaning his shoes. (b) John is having his shoes cleaned.	(a) Sue is taking a photograph. (b) Sue is having her photograph taken.

46.2 Answer the questions using **To have something done**. Choose from the boxes:

~~my car~~	my eyes	my jacket	my watch		clean	repair	~~service~~	test

1 Why did you go to the garage? _To have my car serviced._
2 Why did you go to the cleaner's? To _have my jacket cleaned_
3 Why did you go to the jeweller's? _To have my watch repaired_
4 Why did you go to the optician's? _To have my eyes tested._

46.3 Write sentences in the way shown.

1 Lisa didn't repair the roof herself. She _had it repaired._
2 I didn't cut my hair myself. I _had it cut here._
3 They didn't paint the house themselves. They _had Painted the house._
4 John didn't build that wall himself. _John had it built wall._
5 I didn't deliver the flowers myself. _I had it them delivered._

46.4 Use the words in brackets to complete the sentences. Use the structure **have something done**.

1 We _are having the house painted_ (the house / paint) at the moment.
2 I lost my key. I'll have to _have another key made_ (another key / make).
3 When was the last time you _had your hair cut_ (your hair / cut)?
✗ 4 _you are having delivered a news_ (you / a newspaper / deliver) to your house every day, or do you go out and buy one?
5 A: What are those workmen doing in your garden?
   B: Oh, we _are having a garage built_ (a garage / build).
6 A: Can I see the photographs you took when you were on holiday?
   B: I'm afraid I _am not having the film developed_ (not / the film / develop) yet.
7 This coat is dirty. I must _having it cleaned_ (it / clean).
8 If you want to wear earrings, why don't you _are having your ears pierced_ (your ears / pierce)?
9 A: I heard your computer wasn't working.
   B: That's right, but it's OK now. I _am having it repaired_ (it / repair).

In these items, use 'have something done' with its second meaning (see Section D).

10 Gary was in a fight last night. He _had his nose broken_ (his nose / break).
11 Did I tell you about Jane? She _had her handbag stolen_ (her handbag / steal) last week.
12 Did you hear about Pete? He _had his car vandalised_ (his car / vandalise) a few nights ago.

Reported speech 1 (He said that ...)

A Study this example situation:

I'm feeling ill.

PAUL

You want to tell somebody what Paul said. There are two ways of doing this:

You can repeat Paul's words (*direct* speech):
Paul said, '**I'm feeling ill.**'

Or you can use *reported* speech:
Paul said **that he was feeling ill.**

Compare:

direct	Paul said, ' I am feeling ill.'
reported	Paul said that he was feeling ill.

In writing we use these quotation marks to show direct speech.

B When we use reported speech, the main verb of the sentence is usually past (Paul **said** that ... / I **told** her that ... etc.). The rest of the sentence is usually past too:

□ Paul **said** that he **was feeling** ill.
□ I **told** Lisa that I **didn't have** any money.

You can leave out **that**. So you can say:

□ Paul **said that** he was feeling ill.   *or*   Paul **said** he was feeling ill.

In general, the *present* form in direct speech changes to the *past* form in reported speech:

am/is → was	do/does → did	will → would
are → were	have/has → had	can → could
want/like/know/go etc. → wanted/liked/knew/went etc.		

Compare direct speech and reported speech:

You met Jenny. Here are some of the things she said in *direct* speech:

Later you tell somebody what Jenny said. You use *reported* speech:

JENNY

'My parents **are** very well.'

'**I'm** going to learn to drive.'

'I **want** to buy a car.'
'John **has** a new job.'

'I **can't** come to the party on Friday.'

'I **don't** have much free time.'

'**I'm** going away for a few days. **I'll** phone you when I **get** back.'

□ Jenny said that her parents **were** very well.
□ She said that she **was** going to learn to drive.
□ She said that she **wanted** to buy a car.
□ She said that John **had** a new job.
□ She said that she **couldn't** come to the party on Friday.
□ She said she **didn't** have much free time.
□ She said that she **was** going away for a few days and **would** phone me when she **got** back.

C The *past simple* (**did/saw/knew** etc.) can usually stay the same in reported speech, or you can change it to the *past perfect* (**had done / had seen / had known** etc.):

□ *direct*   Paul said: '**I woke** up feeling ill, so I **didn't go** to work.'
   reported   Paul said (that) he **woke** up feeling ill, so he **didn't go** to work.   *or*
   Paul said (that) he **had woken** up feeling ill, so he **hadn't gone** to work.

Reported speech 2 → Unit 48   Reported questions → Unit 50B

Exercises

47.1 Yesterday you met a friend of yours, Steve. You hadn't seen him for a long time. Here are some of the things Steve said to you:

1 I'm living in London.

2 My father isn't very well.

3 Rachel and Mark are getting married next month.

4 My sister has had a baby.

5 I don't know what Frank is doing.

6 I saw Helen at a party in June and she seemed fine.

Steve

7 I haven't seen Diane recently.

8 I'm not enjoying my job very much.

9 You can come and stay at my place if you're ever in London.

10 My car was stolen a few days ago.

11 I want to go on holiday, but I can't afford it.

he said that he wanted to go on holiday, but he couldn't afford it.

12 I'll tell Chris I saw you.

he said that he would told Chris he had saw him.

Later that day you tell another friend what Steve said. Use reported speech.

1 Steve said that he was living in London.
2 He said that *his father wasn't very well.*
3 He *said that Rachel & Mark were getting married.*
4 *he said that his sister had had a baby.*
5 *he said the he didn't know what Frank was doing.*
6 *he said then he saw Helen at a party in June & she seemed*
7 *he said that he hadn't seen Diane recently.*
8 *he said that he was not enjoying his job very much.*
9 *he said that I could come & stayed at my you were*
10 *he said that his car was stolen*
11 ....
12 ....

47.2 Somebody says something to you which is the opposite of what they said earlier. Complete the answers.

1 A: That restaurant is expensive.
   B: Is it? I thought you said *it was cheap* .
2 A: Sue is coming to the party tonight.
   B: Is she? I thought you said she *was not coming tonight* .
3 A: Sarah likes Paul.
   B: Does she? Last week you said *Sarah did not likee Paul h* .
4 A: I know lots of people.
   B: Do you? I thought you said *You did not know people* .
5 A: Jane will be here next week.
   B: Will she? But didn't you say *Jane would be this week* ?
6 A: I'm going out this evening.
   B: Are you? But you said *you were staying at home* .
7 A: I can speak a little French.
   B: Can you? But earlier you said ....
8 A: I haven't been to the cinema for ages.
   B: Haven't you? I thought you said ....

→ Additional exercise 25 (page 316)

Reported speech 2

A

It is not always necessary to change the verb in reported speech. If you report something and the situation *hasn't changed*, you do not need to change the verb to the past:

- ☐ *direct*   Paul said, 'My new job **is** very interesting.'
  reported   Paul said that his new job **is** very interesting.
  (The situation hasn't changed. His job **is** still interesting.)

- ☐ *direct*   Helen said, '**I want** to go to New York next year.'
  reported   Helen told me that **she wants** to go to New York next year.
  (Helen still wants to go to New York next year.)

You can also change the verb to the past:

- ☐ Paul said that his new job **was** very interesting.
- ☐ Helen told me that she **wanted** to go to New York next year.

But if you are reporting a finished situation, you *must* use a past verb:

- ☐ Paul left the room suddenly. He said **he had** to go. (*not* has to go)

B

You need to use a past form when there is a difference between what was said and what is really true. For example:

You met Sonia a few days ago.
She said: '**Joe is in hospital.**' *(direct speech)*

Later that day you meet Joe in the street. You say:
'I didn't expect to see you, Joe. Sonia said you **were** in hospital.'
(*not* 'Sonia said you are in hospital', because clearly he is not)

C

Say and **tell**

If you say *who* somebody is talking to, use **tell**:

     TELL SOMEBODY

- ☐ Sonia **told me** that you were in hospital. (*not* Sonia said me)
- ☐ What did you **tell the police**? (*not* say the police)

Otherwise use **say**:

     SAY ~~SOMEBODY~~

- ☐ Sonia **said** that you were in hospital. (*not* Sonia told that …)
- ☐ What did you **say**?

But you can '**say** something **to** somebody':

- ☐ Ann **said** goodbye **to** me and left. (*not* Ann said me goodbye)
- ☐ What did you **say to** the police?

D

Tell/ask somebody **to** do something

We also use the infinitive (**to do / to stay** etc.) in reported speech, especially with **tell** and **ask** (for orders and requests):

- ☐ *direct*   '**Stay** in bed for a few days,' the doctor said to me.
  reported   The doctor **told me to** stay in bed for a few days.
- ☐ *direct*   '**Don't shout**,' I said to Jim.
  reported   I **told Jim not to** shout.
- ☐ *direct*   'Please **don't tell** anybody what happened,' Jackie said to me.
  reported   Jackie **asked me not to** tell anybody what (had) happened.

You can also say 'Somebody **said** (not) **to** do something':

- ☐ Jackie **said** not **to tell anyone**. (*but not* Jackie said me)

Reported speech → Unit 47   Reported questions → Unit 50B

Exercises

48.1 Here are some things that Sarah said to you:

> I've never been to the United States.

> I don't have any brothers or sisters.

> I can't drive.

> I don't like fish.

> Jane has a very well-paid job.

> I'm working tomorrow evening.

> Jane is a friend of mine.

> ~~Dave is lazy.~~

But later Sarah says something different to you. What do you say?

Sarah

1	Dave works very hard.
2	Let's have fish for dinner.
3	I'm going to buy a car.
4	Jane is always short of money.
5	My sister lives in Paris.
6	I think New York is a great place.
7	Let's go out tomorrow evening.
8	I've never spoken to Jane.

You

But you said he was lazy.

But *you said that you didn't like fish.*
but you said you could not drive.
but you said Jane had very over.
but You said you do not has and
but you said you had never
but you said you were won
but you said James is a foret

48.2 Complete the sentences with **say** or **tell** (in the correct form). Use only one word each time.

1 Ann __said__ goodbye to me and left.
2 .... us about your holiday. Did you have a nice time?
3 Don't just stand there! .... something!
4 I wonder where Sue is. She .... she would be here at 8 o'clock.
5 Dan .... me that he was bored with his job.
6 The doctor .... that I should rest for at least a week.
7 Don't .... anybody what I .... It's a secret just between us.
8 'Did she .... you what happened?' 'No, she didn't .... anything to me.'
9 Gary couldn't help me. He .... me to ask Caroline.
10 Gary couldn't help me. He .... to ask Caroline.

48.3 The following sentences are direct speech:

> Don't wait for me if I'm late.

> Mind your own business.

> Don't worry, Sue.

> Please slow down!

> Can you open your bag, please?

> Could you get a newspaper?

> ~~Hurry up!~~

> Will you marry me?

> Do you think you could give me a hand, Tom?

Now choose one of these to complete each of the sentences below. Use <u>reported</u> speech.

1 Bill was taking a long time to get ready, so I ....*told him to hurry up*............ .
2 Sarah was driving too fast, so I asked ....
3 Sue was nervous about the situation. I told ....
4 I couldn't move the piano alone, so I ....
5 The customs officer looked at me suspiciously and ....
6 Tom was going to the shop, so I ....
7 The man started asking me personal questions, so I ....
8 John was very much in love with Mary, so he ....
9 I didn't want to delay Helen, so I ....

→ Additional exercise 25 (page 316)

Questions 1

A

In questions we usually put the subject after the first verb:

subject	+ verb		verb	+ subject
Tom	will	→	will	Tom?
you	have	→	have	you?
the house	was	→	was	the house?

□ **Will Tom** be here tomorrow?
□ **Have you** been working hard?
□ When **was the house** built?

Remember that the subject comes after the *first* verb:
    □ **Is Catherine** working today? (*not* Is working Catherine)

B

In *present simple* questions, we use **do/does**:

you	live	→	**do**	you live?
the film	begins	→	**does**	the film begin?

□ **Do** you **live** near here?
□ What time **does** the film **begin**?

In *past simple* questions, we use **did**:

you	sold	→	**did**	you sell?
the train	stopped	→	**did**	the train stop?

□ **Did** you **sell** your car?
□ Why **did** the train **stop**?

But do not use **do/does/did** if **who/what** etc. is the subject of the sentence. Compare:

In these examples, **who/what** etc. is the *subject*:
    □ **Who wants** something to eat? (*not* Who does want)
    □ **What happened** to you last night? (*not* What did happen)
    □ **How many people came** to the meeting? (*not* did come)
    □ **Which bus goes** to the centre? (*not* does go)

C

Note the position of prepositions in questions beginning **Who/What/Which/Where** ... ?:
    □ **Who** do you want to speak **to**?   □ **What** was the weather **like** yesterday?
    □ **Which** job has Ann applied **for**?   □ **Where** are you **from**?

You can use *preposition* + **whom** in formal style:
    □ **To whom** do you wish to speak?

D

Isn't it ... ? / Didn't you ... ? etc. (negative questions)

We use negative questions especially to show surprise:
    □ **Didn't you** hear the doorbell? I rang it three times.
or when we expect the listener to agree with us:
    □ '**Haven't we** met somewhere before?' 'Yes, I think we have.'

Note the meaning of **yes** and **no** in answers to negative questions:
    □ **Don't you** want to go to the party? { **Yes.** (= Yes, I want to go)
                                        { **No.** (= No, I don't want to go)

Note the word order in negative questions beginning **Why** ... ?:
    □ **Why don't we** go out for a meal tonight? (*not* Why we don't go)
    □ **Why wasn't Mary** at work yesterday? (*not* Why Mary wasn't)

Questions 2 → Unit 50   Question tags (do you? isn't it? etc.) → Unit 52

Exercises

49.1 Ask Joe questions. (Look at his answers before you write the questions.)

1	(where / live?) _Where do you live?_ ~~e~~	In Manchester.
2	(born there?) _where did you born_	No, I was born in London.
3	(married?) _Are you married_	Yes.
4	(how long / married?) _How long have you married_	17 years.
5	(children?) _How many children do you_	Yes, two boys.
6	(how old / they?) _How old they are_	12 and 15.
7	(what / do?) _what do you do?_	I'm a journalist.
8	(what / wife / do?) _what does your wife do_	She's a doctor.

Joe

49.2 Make questions with **who** or **what**.

1	Somebody hit me.	_Who hit you?_
2	I hit somebody.	_Who did you hit?_
3	Somebody paid the bill.	Who _paid the bill?_
4	Something happened.	What _happened?_
5	Diane said something.	_what did Diane said_
6	This book belongs to somebody.	_To whom this book belongs to?_
7	Somebody lives in that house.	_who lives in that house?_
8	I fell over something.	_where you fell over?_
9	Something fell on the floor.	_what fell on the floor_
10	This word means something.	_what does this word mean_
11	I borrowed the money from somebody.	_To whom you borrowed the money_
12	I'm worried about something.	_what did you worried about?_

49.3 Put the words in brackets in the correct order. All the sentences are questions.

1 (when / was / built / this house) _When was this house built?_
2 (how / cheese / is / made) _How is cheese made?_
3 (when / invented / the computer / was) _when was the computer invented?_
4 (why / Sue / working / isn't / today) _why isn't Sue working today?_
5 (what time / coming / your friends / are) _what time your friends are coming_
6 (why / was / cancelled / the concert) _why was the concert cancelled_
7 (where / your mother / was / born) _where was your mother born_
8 (why / you / to the party / didn't / come) _why didn't you come to the p_
9 (how / the accident / did / happen) _how did the accident happen_
10 (why / this machine / doesn't / work) _why this machine doesn't work_

49.4 Write negative questions from the words in brackets. In each situation you are surprised.

1 A: We won't see Liz this evening.
   B: Why not? (she / not / come / to the party?) _Isn't she coming to the party?_
2 A: I hope we don't meet David tonight.
   B: Why? (you / not / like / him?) _Aren't you like him?_
3 A: Don't go and see that film.
   B: Why not? (it / not / good?) _isn't it good?_
4 A: I'll have to borrow some money.
   B: Why? (you / not / have / any?) _Haven't you any?_

Questions 2 (Do you know where ... ? / He asked me where ...)

A

Do you know where ... ? / I don't know why ... / Could you tell me what ... ? etc.

We say: Where **has Tom** gone?

but   **Do you know** where **Tom has** gone? (*not* Do you know where has Tom gone?)

When the question (**Where has Tom gone?**) is part of a longer sentence (**Do you know ... ? /
I don't know ... / Can you tell me ... ?** etc.), the word order changes. We say:

☐ What time **is** it?	*but*	**Do you know** what time **it is**?
☐ Who **are** those people?		**I don't know** who **those people are.**
☐ Where **can I** find Linda?		**Can you tell me** where **I can** find Linda?
☐ How much **will it** cost?		**Do you have any idea** how much **it will** cost?

Be careful with **do/does/did** questions. We say:

☐ What time **does the film begin**?	*but*	**Do you know** what time **the film begins?** (*not* does the film begin)
☐ What **do you mean**?		**Please explain** what **you mean.**
☐ Why **did she leave** early?		**I wonder** why **she left** early.

Use **if** or **whether** where there is no other question word (**what, why** etc.):

☐ Did anybody see you?	*but*	**Do you know** if anybody saw you? *or* ... **whether** anybody saw you?

B

He asked me where ... (reported questions)

The same changes in word order happen in reported questions. Compare:

    ☐ *direct*   The police officer said to us, 'Where are you going ?':

       reported   The police officer asked us where we were going .

    ☐ *direct*   Clare said, 'What time do the banks close ?'

       reported   Clare wanted to know what time the banks closed .

In reported speech the verb usually changes to the past (**were, closed** etc.). See Unit 47.

Study these examples. You had an interview for a job and these were some of the questions the
interviewer asked you:

> Are you willing to travel?

> Why did you apply for the job?

> What do you do in your spare time?

> Can you speak any foreign languages?

> How long have you been working in your present job?

> Do you have a driving licence?

Later you tell a friend what the interviewer asked you. You use *reported* speech:

    ☐ She asked if (*or* whether) **I was** willing to travel.
    ☐ She wanted to know what **I did** in my spare time.
    ☐ She asked how long **I had** been working in my present job.
    ☐ She asked why **I had** applied for the job. (*or* ... why **I applied**)
    ☐ She wanted to know if (*or* whether) **I could** speak any foreign languages.
    ☐ She asked if (*or* whether) **I had** a driving licence.

Reported speech → Units 47–48

Exercises

50.1 Make a new sentence from the question in brackets.

1 (Where has Tom gone?) Do you know _where Tom has gone?_
2 (Where is the post office?) Could you tell me where _the post office is._
3 (What's the time?) I wonder _what the time is?_
4 (What does this word mean?) I want to know _what this word means_
5 (What time did they leave?) Do you know _what time they leave / left_
6 (Is Sue going out tonight?) I don't know _Sue is going out to_
7 (Where does Caroline live?) Do you have any idea _where Caroline lives_
8 (Where did I park the car?) I can't remember _where I parked car_
9 (Is there a bank near here?) Can you tell me _there is a bank near here_
10 (What do you want?) Tell me _what you want_
11 (Why didn't Kate come to the party?) I don't know _why Kate come to the party_
12 (How much does it cost to park here?) Do you know _How much it cost to park here_
13 (Who is that woman?) I have no idea _who that woman is_
14 (Did Liz get my letter?) Do you know _Liz got my letter_
15 (How far is it to the airport?) Can you tell me _How far it is to the airport._

50.2 You are making a phone call. You want to speak to Sue, but she isn't there. Somebody else answers the phone. You want to know three things:
(1) Where has she gone? (2) When will she be back? and **(3) Did she go out alone?**
Complete the conversation:

A: Do you know where _she has gone_ ? (1)
B: Sorry, I've got no idea.
A: Never mind. I don't suppose you know _she will be came_ . (2)
B: No, I'm afraid not.
A: One more thing. Do you happen to know _when went out alone_ ? (3)
she
B: I'm afraid I didn't see her go out.
A: OK. Well, thank you anyway. Goodbye.

50.3 You have been away for a while and have just come back to your home town. You meet Tony, a friend of yours. He asks you a lot of questions:

1 (How are you?)
2 (Where have you been?)
3 (How long have you been back?)
4 (What are you doing now?)

5 (Why did you come back?)

Tony

6 (Where are you living?)
7 (Are you glad to be back?)
8 (Do you have any plans to go away again?)
9 (Can you lend me some money?)

Now you tell another friend what Tony asked you. Use reported speech.

1 _He asked me how I was._
2 He asked me _where I had been_
3 He _wanted to know how long I had been back_
4 _He asked me what I was doing now_
5 _He wanted to know when I came back_
6 _He asked me where I was living_
7 _He wanted to know I was glad to back_
8 _He wanted to know I had any plan to go away_
9 _He asked me I could lend him some money_

→ Additional exercise 25 (page 316)

Unit 51
Auxiliary verbs (have/do/can etc.)
I think so / I hope so etc.

A

In each of these sentences there is an auxiliary verb and a main verb:

I	have	lost	my keys.
She	can't	come	to the party.
The hotel	was	built	ten years ago.
Where	do you	live?	

In these examples **have/can't/was/do** are auxiliary (= helping) verbs.

You can use an auxiliary verb when you don't want to repeat something:
- ☐ 'Have you locked the door?' 'Yes, I **have**.' (= I have *locked the door*)
- ☐ George wasn't working, but Janet **was**. (= Janet was *working*)
- ☐ She could lend me the money, but she **won't**. (= she won't *lend me the money*)

Use **do/does/did** for the present and past simple:
- ☐ 'Do you like onions?' 'Yes, I **do**.' (= I *like onions*)
- ☐ 'Does Simon live in London?' 'He **did**, but he **doesn't** any more.'

You can use auxiliary verbs to deny what somebody says (= say it is not true):
- ☐ 'You're sitting in my place.' 'No, I'm **not**.' (= I'm not *sitting in your place*)
- ☐ 'You didn't lock the door before you left.' 'Yes, I **did**.' (= I *locked the door*)

B

We use **have you?** / **isn't she?** / **do they?** etc. to show interest in what somebody has said or to show surprise:
- ☐ 'I've just seen Simon.' 'Oh, **have you?** How is he?'
- ☐ 'Liz isn't very well today.' 'Oh, **isn't she?** What's wrong with her?'
- ☐ 'It rained every day during our holiday.' '**Did it?** What a pity!'
- ☐ 'Jim and Nora are getting married.' '**Are they?** Really?'

C

We use auxiliary verbs with **so** and **neither**:
- ☐ 'I'm feeling tired.' '**So am I**.' (= I'm feeling tired too)
- ☐ 'I never read newspapers.' '**Neither do I**.' (= I never read newspapers either)
- ☐ Sue hasn't got a car and **neither has Martin**.

Note the word order after **so** and **neither** (verb before subject):
- ☐ I passed the exam and **so did Paul**. (*not* so Paul did)

Instead of **neither**, you can use **nor**. You can also use **not ... either**:
- ☐ 'I don't know.' '**Neither do I**.' *or* '**Nor do I**.' *or* 'I **don't either**.'

D

I think so / I hope so etc.

After some verbs you can use **so** when you don't want to repeat something:
- ☐ 'Are those people English?' 'I **think so**.' (= I think *they are English*)
- ☐ 'Will you be at home this evening?' 'I **expect so**. (= I expect *I'll be at home ...*)
- ☐ 'Do you think Kate has been invited to the party?' 'I **suppose so**.'

In the same way we say: **I hope so**, **I guess so** and **I'm afraid so**.

The usual negative forms are:

I think so / I expect so	→	I **don't think so** / I **don't expect so**
I hope so / I'm afraid so / I guess so	→	I **hope not** / I'm **afraid not** / I **guess not**
I suppose so	→	I **don't suppose so** *or* I **suppose not**

- ☐ 'Is that woman American?' 'I **think so**. / I **don't think so**.'
- ☐ 'Do you think it will rain?' 'I **hope so**. / I **hope not**.' (*not* I don't hope so)

51.1 Complete each sentence with an auxiliary verb (**do/was/could** etc.). Sometimes the verb must be negative (**don't/wasn't** etc.).

1 I wasn't tired, but my friends ..... _were_ .
2 I like hot weather, but Ann ..... _doesn't_ .
3 'Is Colin here?' 'He ..... _was_ ..... five minutes ago, but I think he's gone home now.'
4 Liz said she might phone later this evening, but I don't think she ..... _was any u_
5 'Are you and Chris coming to the party?' 'I ..... _do_ ..... , but Chris ..... _wasn't_ .'
6 I don't know whether to apply for the job or not. Do you think I ..... _was_ ..... ?
7 'Please don't tell anybody what I said.' 'Don't worry. I ..... _don't_ .....'
8 'You never listen to me.' 'Yes, I ..... _do_ .....!'
9 'Can you play a musical instrument?' 'No, but I wish I ..... _was coul_ .'
10 'Please help me.' 'I'm sorry. I ..... _was_ ..... if I ..... _do_ ..... , but I ..... _don't_ .....'

51.2 You never agree with Sue. Answer in the way shown.

1 I'm hungry.   Are you? I'm not.
2 I'm not tired.   Aren't you? I am.
3 I like football.   ....
4 I didn't enjoy the film. .... You
5 I've never been to Australia. ....
Sue
6 I thought the exam was easy. ....

51.3 You are talking to Tina. If you're in the same position as Tina, reply with **So ...** or **Neither ...** as in the first example. Otherwise, ask questions as in the second example.

1 I'm feeling tired.   So am I.
2 I work hard.   Do you? What do you do?
3 I watched television last night. ....
4 I won't be at home tomorrow.   .... You
5 I like reading. I read a lot.   ....
Tina
6 I'd like to live somewhere else. ....
7 I can't go out tonight.   ....

51.4 In these conversations, you are B. Read the information in brackets and then answer with **I think so, I hope not** etc.

1 (You don't like rain.)
A: Do you think it will rain?   B: (hope) ..... _I hope not._
2 (You need more money quickly.)
A: Do you think you'll get a pay rise soon?   B: (hope) ....
3 (You think Diane will probably get the job that she applied for.)
A: Do you think Diane will get the job?   B: (expect) ....
4 (You're not sure whether Barbara is married – probably not.)
A: Is Barbara married?   B: (think) ....
5 (You are the receptionist at a hotel. The hotel is full.)
A: Have you got a room for tonight?   B: (afraid) ....
6 (You're at a party. You have to leave early.)
A: Do you have to leave already?   B: (afraid) ....
7 (Ann normally works every day, Monday to Friday. Tomorrow is Wednesday.)
A: Is Ann working tomorrow?   B: (suppose) ....
8 (You are going to a party. You can't stand John.)
A: Do you think John will be at the party?   B: (hope) ....
9 (You're not sure what time the concert is – probably 7.30.)
A: Is the concert at 7.30?   B: (think) ....

Question tags (do you? isn't it? etc.)

A Study these examples:

You haven't seen Kate today, **have you?**

No, I'm afraid not.

It was a good film, **wasn't it?**

Yes, it was great.

Have you? and **wasn't it?** are *question tags* (= mini-questions that we often put on the end of a sentence in spoken English). In question tags, we use an auxiliary verb (**have/was/will** etc.). We use **do/does/did** for the present and past simple (see Unit 51):

☐ 'Karen plays the piano, **doesn't** she?' 'Well, yes, but not very well.'
☐ 'You didn't lock the door, **did** you?' 'No, I forgot.'

B Normally we use a *negative* question tag after a *positive* sentence:

positive sentence +	*negative tag*
Kate **will** be here soon,	**won't she?**
There **was** a lot of traffic,	**wasn't there?**
Michael **should** pass the exam,	**shouldn't he?**

... and a *positive* question tag after a *negative* sentence:

negative sentence +	*positive tag*
Kate **won't** be late,	**will she?**
They **don't** like us,	**do they?**
You **haven't** got a car,	**have you?**

Notice the meaning of **yes** and **no** in answer to a negative sentence:

☐ You're **not** going out today, **are you?** { **Yes.** (= Yes, I am going out)
    No. (= No, I am not going out)

C The meaning of a question tag depends on how you say it. If your voice goes *down*, you are not really asking a question; you are only inviting the listener to agree with you:

☐ 'It's a nice day, **isn't it?**' 'Yes, beautiful.'
☐ 'Tim doesn't look well today, **does he?**' 'No, he looks very tired.'
☐ She's very funny. She's got a great sense of humour, **hasn't she?**

But if the voice goes *up*, it is a real question:

☐ 'You haven't seen Lisa today, **have you?**' 'No, I'm afraid I haven't.'
    (= Have you by chance seen Lisa today?)

You can use a *negative sentence + positive tag* to ask for things or information, or to ask somebody to do something. The voice goes *up* at the end of the tag in sentences like these:

☐ 'You haven't got a pen, **have you?**' 'Yes, here you are.'
☐ 'You couldn't do me a favour, **could you?**' 'It depends what it is.'
☐ 'You don't know where Karen is, **do you?**' 'Sorry, I have no idea.'

D After **Let's ...** the question tag is **shall we**:

☐ **Let's** go for a walk, **shall we?** (the voice goes *up*)

After **Don't ...** , the question tag is **will you**:

☐ **Don't** be late, **will you?** (the voice goes *down*)

After **I'm ...** , the negative question tag is **aren't I?** (= am I not?):

☐ I'm right, **aren't I?** 'Yes, you are.'

Auxiliary verbs (**have/do/can** etc.) → Unit 51

52.1 Put a question tag on the end of these sentences.

1	Kate won't be late, _will she_ ?	No, she's never late.
2	You're tired, _aren't you_ ?	Yes, a little.
3	You've got a camera, ... ?	Yes, I've got two actually.
4	You weren't listening, ... ?	Yes, I was!
5	Sue doesn't know Ann, ... ?	No, they've never met.
6	Jack's on holiday, ... ?	Yes, he's in Portugal.
7	Kate's applied for the job, ... ?	Yes, but she won't get it.
8	You can speak German, ... ?	Yes, but not very fluently.
9	He won't mind if I use his phone, ... ?	No, of course he won't.
10	There are a lot of people here, ... ?	Yes, more than I expected.
11	Let's go out tonight, ... ?	Yes, that would be great.
12	This isn't very interesting, ... ?	No, not very.
13	I'm too impatient, ... ?	Yes, you are sometimes.
14	You wouldn't tell anyone, ... ?	No, of course not.
15	Helen has lived here a long time, ... ?	Yes, 20 years.
16	I shouldn't have lost my temper, ... ?	No, but never mind.
17	He'd never met her before, ... ?	No, that was the first time.
18	Don't drop that vase, ... ?	No, don't worry.

52.2 Read the situation and write a sentence with a question tag. In each situation you are asking your friend to agree with you.

1 You look out of the window. The sky is blue and the sun is shining. What do you say to your friend? (nice day) __It's a nice day, isn't it?__

2 You're with a friend outside a restaurant. You're looking at the prices, which are very high. What do you say? (expensive) It ....

3 You and a colleague have just finished a training course. You really enjoyed it. What do you say to your colleague? (great) The course ....

4 Your friend's hair is much shorter than when you last met. What do you say to her/him? (have / your hair / cut) You ....

5 You and a friend are listening to a woman singing. You like her voice very much. What do you say to your friend? (a good voice) She ....

6 You are trying on a jacket in a shop. You look in the mirror and you don't like what you see. What do you say to your friend? (not / look / very good)
It ....

7 You and a friend are walking over a small wooden bridge. The bridge is very old and some parts are broken. What do you say? (not / very safe)
This bridge ....

52.3 In these situations you are asking for information, asking people to do things etc.

1 You need a pen. Perhaps Jane has got one. Ask her.
__Jane, you haven't got a pen, have you?__

2 Joe is just going out. You want him to get some stamps. Ask him.
Joe, you ....

3 You're looking for Diane. Perhaps Kate knows where she is. Ask her.
Kate, you ....

4 You need a bicycle pump. Perhaps Helen has got one. Ask her.
Helen, ...

5 Ann has a car and you need a lift to the station. Perhaps she'll take you. Ask her.
Ann, ...

6 You're looking for your keys. Perhaps Robert has seen them. Ask him.
Robert, ...

Verb + -ing (enjoy doing / stop doing etc.)

A

Look at these examples:

- □ I **enjoy** read**ing**. (*not* I enjoy to read)
- □ Would you **mind** clos**ing** the door?
  (*not* mind to close)
- □ Chris **suggested** go**ing** to the cinema.
  (*not* suggested to go)

> Would you mind closing the door?

After **enjoy**, **mind** and **suggest**, we use **-ing** (*not* **to** …).

Some more verbs that are followed by **-ing**:

stop	postpone	admit	avoid	imagine
finish	consider	deny	risk	fancy

- □ Suddenly everybody **stopped** talk**ing**. There was silence.
- □ I'll do the shopping when I've **finished** clean**ing** the flat.
- □ He tried to **avoid** answer**ing** my question.
- □ I don't **fancy** go**ing** out this evening. (= I'm not enthusiastic about it)
- □ Have you ever **considered** go**ing** to live in another country?

The negative form is **not -ing**:

- □ When I'm on holiday, I **enjoy not** hav**ing** to get up early.

B

We also use **-ing** after:

> **give up** (= stop)
> **put off** (= postpone)
> **go on / carry on** (= continue)
> **keep** *or* **keep on** (= do something continuously or repeatedly)

- □ I've **given up** read**ing** newspapers. I think it's a waste of time.
- □ Jenny doesn't want to retire. She wants to **go on** work**ing**. (*or* … to **carry on** working.)
- □ You **keep** interrupt**ing** when I'm talking! *or* You **keep on** interrupt**ing** …

C

With some verbs you can use the structure *verb* + somebody + **-ing**:

- □ I can't **imagine George** rid**ing** a motorbike.
- □ You can't **stop me** do**ing** what I want.
- □ 'Sorry to **keep you** wait**ing** so long.' 'That's all right.'

Note the passive form (**being done/seen/kept** etc.):

- □ I don't **mind being kept** waiting. (= I don't mind **people** keep**ing** me …)

D

When you are talking about finished actions, you can say **having done/stolen/said** etc. :

- □ They admitted **having stolen** the money.

But it is not necessary to use **having** (done). You can also say:

- □ They admitted **stealing** the money.
- □ I now regret **saying** (*or* **having said**) what I said.

For **regret**, see Unit 56B.

E

After some of the verbs on this page (especially **admit/deny/suggest**) you can also use **that** … :

- □ They **denied that** they had stolen the money. (*or* They **denied** stealing …)
- □ Sam **suggested that** we went to the cinema. (*or* Sam **suggested** going …)

Suggest → Unit 34   **Being done (passive)** → Unit 44B   **Verb + to …** → Unit 54   **Verb + to … and -ing** →
Units 55C, 56–58   **Regret / go on** → Unit 56B   **Go on / carry on / keep on** → Unit 141A

53.1 Complete each sentence with one of the following verbs (in the correct form):

~~answer~~ apply be forget listen live lose make read try use write

1 He tried to avoid ......*answering*...... my question.
2 Could you please stop .... so much noise?
3 I enjoy .... to music.
4 I considered .... for the job, but in the end I decided against it.
5 Have you finished .... the newspaper yet?
6 We need to change our routine. We can't go on .... like this.
7 I don't mind you .... the phone as long as you pay for all your calls.
8 My memory is getting worse. I keep .... things.
9 I've put off .... the letter so many times. I really must do it today.
10 What a stupid thing to do! Can you imagine anybody .... so stupid?
11 I've given up .... to lose weight – it's impossible.
12 If you invest your money on the stock market, you risk .... it.

53.2 Complete the sentences for each situation using **-ing**.

1 | What shall we do? | We could go to the zoo. | She suggested ......*going to*...... ......*the zoo*...... .

2 | Do you want to play tennis? | No, not really. | He didn't fancy ....

3 | You were driving too fast. | Yes, it's true. Sorry! | She admitted ....

4 | Why don't we go for a swim? | Good idea! | She suggested ....

5 | You broke the CD player. | No, I didn't! | He denied ....

6 | Can you wait a few minutes? | Sure, no problem. | They didn't mind ....

53.3 Complete the sentences so that they mean the same as the first sentence. Use **-ing**.

1 I can do what I want and you can't stop me.
   You ......*can't stop me doing what I want*...... .
2 It's not a good idea to travel during the rush hour.
   It's better to avoid ....
3 Shall we paint the kitchen next weekend instead of this weekend?
   Shall we postpone .... until .... ?
4 Could you turn the radio down, please?
   Would you mind .... ?
5 Please don't interrupt me all the time.
   Would you mind .... ?

53.4 Use your own ideas to complete these sentences. Use **-ing**.

1 She's a very interesting person. I always enjoy ......*talking to her*...... .
2 I'm not feeling very well. I don't fancy ....
3 I'm afraid there aren't any chairs. I hope you don't mind ....
4 It was a beautiful day, so I suggested ....
5 It was very funny. I couldn't stop ....
6 My car isn't very reliable. It keeps ....

Verb + to ... (decide to ... / forget to ... etc.)

A

offer	decide	hope	deserve	promise
agree	plan	manage	afford	threaten
refuse	arrange	fail	forget	learn

After these verbs you can use **to ...** (*infinitive*):
- ☐ It was late, so we **decided to take** a taxi home.
- ☐ Simon was in a difficult situation, so I **agreed to help** him.
- ☐ How old were you when you **learnt to drive**? (*or* learnt **how** to drive)
- ☐ I waved to Karen but **failed to attract** her attention.

The negative is **not to ...** :
- ☐ We **decided not to go** out because of the weather.
- ☐ I **promised not to be** late.

After some verbs **to ...** is not possible. For example, **enjoy/think/suggest**:
- ☐ I **enjoy** reading. (*not* enjoy to read)
- ☐ Tom **suggested** going to the cinema. (*not* suggested to go)
- ☐ Are you **thinking of** buying a car? (*not* thinking to buy)

For verb + **-ing**, see Unit 53. For verb + preposition + **-ing**, see Unit 62.

B

We also use **to ...** after:

seem	appear	tend	pretend	claim

For example:
- ☐ They **seem to have** plenty of money.
- ☐ I like Dan, but I think he **tends to talk** too much.
- ☐ Ann **pretended not to see** me when she passed me in the street.

There is also a *continuous* infinitive (**to be** doing) and a *perfect* infinitive (**to have** done):
- ☐ I **pretended to be** reading the newspaper. (= I pretended that I **was** reading)
- ☐ You **seem to have lost** weight. (= it seems that you **have lost** weight)
- ☐ Martin **seems to be** enjoying his new job. (= it seems that he **is** enjoying it)

C

After **dare** you can use the infinitive with or without **to**:
- ☐ I wouldn't **dare to tell** him. *or* I wouldn't **dare tell** him.

But after **dare not** (*or* **daren't**), you must use the infinitive without **to**:
- ☐ I **daren't tell** him what happened. (*not* I daren't to tell him)

D

After some verbs you can use a question word (**what/whether/how** etc.) + **to ...** . We use this structure especially after:

ask	decide	know	remember	forget	explain	learn	understand	wonder

We asked	how	to get	to the station.
Have you **decided**	where	to go	for your holidays?
I don't **know**	whether	to apply	for the job or not.
Do you **understand**	what	to do?	

Also **show/tell/ask/advise/teach** somebody **what/how/where** to do something:
- ☐ Can somebody **show me how to change** the film in this camera?
- ☐ Ask Jack. He'll **tell you what to do**.

Verb + **-ing** → Unit 53   Verb + object + **to ...** (want etc.) → Unit 55
Verb + **to ...** and **-ing** → Units 55C, 56–58

54.1 Complete the sentences for these situations.

1 [Shall we get married?] [Yes, let's.]   They decided _to get married_ .

2 [Please help me.] [OK.]   She agreed ....

3 [Can I carry your bag for you?] [No, thanks. I can manage.]   He offered ....

4 [Let's meet at 8 o'clock.] [OK, fine.]   They arranged ....

5 [What's your name?] [I'm not going to tell you.]   She refused ....

6 [Please don't tell anyone.] [I won't. I promise.]   She promised ....

54.2 Complete each sentence with a suitable verb.

1 Don't forget _to post_ the letter I gave you.
2 There was a lot of traffic, but we managed .... to the airport in time.
3 Jill has decided not .... a car.
4 We've got a new computer in our office. I haven't learnt .... it yet.
5 Karen failed .... a good impression at the job interview.
6 We were all afraid to speak. Nobody dared .... anything.

54.3 Put the verb into the correct form, to ... or –ing. (See Unit 53 for verbs + –ing.)

1 When I'm tired, I enjoy _watching_ television. It's relaxing. (watch)
2 It was a nice day, so we decided .... for a walk. (go)
3 It's a nice day. Does anyone fancy .... for a walk? (go)
4 I'm not in a hurry. I don't mind .... (wait)
5 They don't have much money. They can't afford .... out very often. (go)
6 I wish that dog would stop .... It's driving me mad. (bark)
7 Our neighbour threatened .... the police if we didn't stop the noise. (call)
8 We were hungry, so I suggested .... dinner early. (have)
9 Hurry up! I don't want to risk .... the train. (miss)
10 I'm still looking for a job, but I hope .... something soon. (find)

54.4 Make a new sentence using the verb in brackets.

1 You've lost weight.   (seem)   _You seem to have lost weight._
2 Tom is worried about something. (appear) Tom appears ....
3 You know a lot of people.   (seem)   You ....
4 My English is getting better.   (seem)   ....
5 That car has broken down.   (appear) ....
6 David forgets things.   (tend)   ....
7 They have solved the problem.   (claim) ....

54.5 Complete each sentence using what/how/whether + the following verbs:

do   ~~get~~   go   ride   say   use

1 Do you know _how to get_ to John's house?
2 Can you show me .... this washing machine?
3 Would you know .... if there was a fire in the building?
4 You'll never forget .... a bicycle once you've learnt.
5 I was really astonished. I didn't know ....
6 I've been invited to the party, but I haven't decided .... or not.

→ Additional exercises 26–28 (pages 317–19)

A

want	ask	help	would like
expect	beg	mean (= intend)	would prefer

These verbs are followed by **to** ... (*infinitive*). The structure can be:

verb + **to** ...   *or*   *verb* + *object* + **to** ...

☐ We **expected to be** late.   ☐ We **expected Dan to be** late.
☐ **Would** you **like to go** now?   ☐ Would you like **me to go** now?
☐ He doesn't **want to know**.   ☐ He doesn't want **anybody to know**.

Do not say 'want that':

☐ Do you **want me to come** with you? (*not* Do you want that I come)

After **help** you can use the infinitive with or without **to**. So you can say:

☐ Can you help me **to move** this table? *or* Can you help me **move** this table?

B

tell	remind	force	encourage	teach	enable
order	warn	invite	persuade	get (= persuade, arrange for)	

These verbs have the structure *verb* + *object* + **to** ... :

☐ Can you **remind me to phone** Sam tomorrow?
☐ Who **taught you to drive**?
☐ I didn't move the piano by myself. I **got somebody to help** me.
☐ Jim said the switch was dangerous and **warned me not to touch** it.

In the next example, the verb is *passive* (**I was warned / we were told** etc.):

☐ I **was warned not to touch** the switch.

You cannot use **suggest** with the structure *verb* + *object* + **to** ... :

☐ Jane **suggested that I should ask** your advice. (*not* Jane suggested me to ask)

C

After **advise**, **recommend** and **allow**, two structures are possible. Compare:

verb + **-ing** (without an object)   *verb* + *object* + **to** ...

☐ I wouldn't **advise/recommend** staying in that hotel.   ☐ I wouldn't **advise/recommend anybody to stay** in that hotel.
☐ They don't **allow** parking in front of the building.   ☐ They don't **allow people to park** in front of the building.

Study these examples with (**be**) **allowed** (*passive*):

☐ Parking **isn't allowed** in front of the building.   ☐ You **aren't allowed to park** in front of the building.

D

Make and **let**

These verbs have the structure *verb* + *object* + *infinitive* (without **to**):

☐ I **made him promise** that he wouldn't tell anybody what happened. (*not* to promise)
☐ Hot weather **makes me feel** tired. (= causes me to feel tired)
☐ Her parents wouldn't **let her go** out alone. (= wouldn't allow her to go out)
☐ **Let me carry** your bag for you.

We say '**make** somebody **do**' (*not* to do), but the *passive* is '(**be**) **made to do**' (with **to**):

☐ We **were made to wait** for two hours. (= They **made us wait** ...)

Suggest → Units 34, 53   **Tell/ask somebody to ...** → Unit 48D   **Verb + -ing** → Unit 53
Verb + to ... → Unit 54   **Verb + to ... and -ing** → Units 56–58   **Help** → Unit 57C

55.1 Complete the questions. Use **do you want me to ... ?** or **would you like me to ... ?** with these verbs (+ any other necessary words):

~~come~~   lend   repeat   show   shut   wait

1 Do you want to go alone, or   _do you want me to come with you_   ?
2 Do you have enough money, or do you want .... ?
3 Shall I leave the window open, or would you .... ?
4 Do you know how to use the machine, or would .... ?
5 Did you hear what I said, or do .... ?
6 Can I go now, or do .... ?

55.2 Complete the sentences for these situations.

1 Lock the door. / OK.   She told   _him to lock the door_   .

2 Why don't you come and stay with us? / That would be nice.   They invited him ....

3 Can I use your phone? / No!   She wouldn't let ....

4 Be careful. / Don't worry. I will.   She warned ....

5 Can you give me a hand? / Sure.   He asked ....

55.3 Complete each second sentence so that the meaning is similar to the first sentence.

1 My father said I could use his car.   My father allowed   _me to use his car._
2 I was surprised that it rained.   I didn't expect ....
3 Don't stop him doing what he wants.   Let ....
4 Tim looks older when he wears glasses.   Tim's glasses make ....
5 I think you should know the truth.   I want ....
6 Don't let me forget to phone my sister.   Remind ....
7 At first I didn't want to apply for the job, but Sarah persuaded me.   Sarah persuaded ....
8 My lawyer said I shouldn't say anything to the police.   My lawyer advised ....
9 I was told that I shouldn't believe everything he says.   I was warned ....
10 If you've got a car, you are able to get around more easily.   Having a car enables ....

55.4 Put the verb into the correct form: infinitive (**do/make/eat** etc.), to + infinitive, or **-ing**.

1 They don't allow people   _to park_   in front of the building. (park)
2 I've never been to Iceland, but I'd like .... there. (go)
3 I'm in a difficult position. What do you advise me .... ? (do)
4 The film was very sad. It made me .... (cry)
5 Diane's parents always encouraged her .... hard at school. (study)
6 I don't recommend .... in that restaurant. The food is terrible. (eat)
7 She said the letter was personal and wouldn't let me .... it. (read)
8 We are not allowed .... personal phone calls at work. (make)
9 'I don't think Alex likes me.' 'What makes you .... that?' (think)

Verb + -ing or to ... 1 (remember/regret etc.)

A Some verbs are followed by -ing and some are followed by to ... .

Verbs usually followed by -ing:		
admit	fancy	postpone
avoid	finish	risk
consider	imagine	stop
deny	keep (on)	suggest
enjoy	mind	

For examples, see Unit 53.

Verbs usually followed by to ... :		
afford	fail	offer
agree	forget	plan
arrange	hope	promise
decide	learn	refuse
deserve	manage	threaten

For examples, see Unit 54.

B Some verbs can be followed by -ing or to ... with a difference of meaning:

remember

I **remember doing** something = I did it and now I remember this.
You **remember doing** something *after* you have done it.
  □ I know I locked the door. I clearly **remember locking** it.
    (= I locked it, and now I remember this)
  □ He could **remember driving** along the road just before the accident, but he couldn't remember the accident itself.

I **remembered to do** something = I remembered that I had to do it, so I did it.
You **remember to do** something *before* you do it.
  □ I **remembered to lock** the door, but I forgot to shut the windows.
    (= I remembered that I had to lock it, and so I locked it)
  □ Please **remember to post** the letter.
    (= don't forget to post it)

regret

I **regret doing** something = I did it and now I'm sorry about it:
  □ I now **regret saying** what I said. I shouldn't have said it.
  □ It began to get cold and he **regretted not wearing** his coat.

I **regret to say** / **to tell** you / **to inform** you = I'm sorry that I have to say (etc.):
  □ *(from a formal letter)* We **regret to inform** you that we cannot offer you the job.

go on

Go on doing something = continue with the same thing:
  □ The president paused for a moment and then **went on talking**.
  □ We need to change. We can't **go on living** like this.

Go on to do something = do or say something new:
  □ After discussing the economy, the president then **went on to talk** about foreign policy.

C The following verbs can be followed by -ing or to ... :
  begin   start   continue   intend   bother

So you can say:
  □ It has **started raining**. *or* It has **started to rain**.
  □ John **intends buying** a house. *or* John **intends to buy** ...
  □ Don't **bother locking** the door. *or* Don't **bother to lock** ...

But normally we do not use -ing after -ing:
  □ It's starting **to rain**. (*not* It's starting raining)

Verb + -ing → Unit 53   Verb + to ... → Units 54–55   Other verbs + -ing or to ... → Units 57–58

56.1 Put the verb into the correct form, **-ing** or **to** ... . Sometimes either form is possible.

1 They denied ___stealing___ the money. (steal)
2 I don't enjoy .... very much. (drive)
3 I don't want .... out tonight. I'm too tired. (go)
4 I can't afford .... out tonight. I don't have enough money. (go)
5 Has it stopped .... yet? (rain)
6 Our team was unlucky to lose the game. We deserved .... (win)
7 Why do you keep .... me questions? Can't you leave me alone? (ask)
8 Please stop .... me questions! (ask)
9 I refuse .... any more questions. (answer)
10 One of the boys admitted .... the window. (break)
11 The boy's father promised .... for the window to be repaired. (pay)
12 If the company continues .... money, the factory may be closed. (lose)
13 'Does Sarah know about the meeting?' 'No, I forgot .... her.' (tell)
14 The baby began .... in the middle of the night. (cry)
15 Julia has been ill, but now she's beginning .... better. (get)
16 I've enjoyed .... you. I hope .... you again soon. (meet, see)

56.2 Here is some information about Tom when he was a child.

1 He was in hospital when he was four.
2 He went to Paris when he was eight.
3 He cried on his first day at school.
4 Once he fell into the river.
5 He said he wanted to be a doctor.
6 Once he was bitten by a dog.

He can still remember 1, 2 and 4. But he can't remember 3, 5 and 6. Write sentences beginning **He can remember** ... or **He can't remember** ... .

1 ___He can remember being in hospital when he was four.___
2 ....
3 ....
4 ....
5 ....
6 ....

56.3 Complete each sentence with a verb in the correct form, **-ing** or **to** ... .

1 a Please remember ___to lock___ the door when you go out.
  b A: You lent me some money a few months ago.
    B: Did I? Are you sure? I don't remember .... you any money.
  c A: Did you remember .... your sister?
    B: Oh no, I completely forgot. I'll phone her tomorrow.
  d When you see Steve, remember .... him my regards.
  e Someone must have taken my bag. I clearly remember .... it by the window and now it has gone.

2 a I believe that what I said was fair. I don't regret .... it.
  b I knew they were in trouble, but I regret .... I did nothing to help them.

3 a Ben joined the company nine years ago. He became assistant manager after two years, and a few years later he went on .... manager of the company.
  b I can't go on .... here any more. I want a different job.
  c When I came into the room, Liz was reading a newspaper. She looked up and said hello, and then went on .... her newspaper.

Verb + -ing or to ... 2 (try/need/help)

A | Try to ... and try -ing

Try to do = attempt to do, make an effort to do:
- ☐ I was very tired. I **tried to keep** my eyes open, but I couldn't.
- ☐ Please **try to be** quiet when you come home. Everyone will be asleep.

Try also means 'do something as an experiment or test'. For example:
- ☐ These cakes are delicious. You should **try** one. (= you should have one to see if you like it)
- ☐ We couldn't find anywhere to stay. We **tried** every hotel in the town, but they were all full. (= we went to every hotel to see if they had a room)

If **try** (with this meaning) is followed by a verb, we say **try -ing**:
- ☐ A: The photocopier doesn't seem to be working.
  B: **Try pressing** the green button.
    (= press the green button – perhaps this will help to solve the problem)

Compare:
- ☐ I **tried to move** the table, but it was too heavy. (so I couldn't move it)
- ☐ I didn't like the way the furniture was arranged, so I **tried moving** the table to the other side of the room. But it still didn't look right, so I moved it back again.

B | Need to ... and need -ing

I **need to do** something = it is necessary for me to do it:
- ☐ I **need to take** more exercise.
- ☐ He **needs to work** harder if he wants to make progress.
- ☐ I don't **need to come** to the meeting, do I?

Something **needs doing** = it needs to be done:
- ☐ The batteries in the radio **need changing**.
  (= they need to be changed)
- ☐ Do you think my jacket **needs cleaning**?
  (= ... needs to be cleaned)
- ☐ It's a difficult problem. It **needs thinking** about very carefully. (= it needs to be thought about)

> This room **needs tidying**.

C | Help and can't help

You can say **help to do** or **help do** (with or without **to**):
- ☐ Everybody **helped to clean** up after the party. *or*
  Everybody **helped clean** up ...
- ☐ Can you **help** me **to move** this table? *or*
  Can you **help** me **move** ...

I **can't help doing** something = I can't stop myself doing it:
- ☐ I don't like him, but he has a lot of problems. I **can't help feeling** sorry for him.
- ☐ She tried to be serious, but she **couldn't help laughing**.
  (= she couldn't stop herself laughing)
- ☐ I'm sorry I'm so nervous. I **can't help it**.
  (= I can't help **being** nervous)

Verb + -ing → Unit 53   Verb + to ... → Units 54–55   Other verbs + -ing or to ... → Units 56, 58

Exercises

57.1 Make suggestions. Each time use **try** + one of the following suggestions:

> phone his office   move the aerial   ~~change the batteries~~
> turn it the other way   take an aspirin

1   The radio isn't working. I wonder what's wrong with it.   Have you _tried changing the batteries?_

2   I can't open the door. The key won't turn.   Try ....

3   The TV picture isn't very good. What can I do about it?   Have you tried ....

4   I can't contact Fred. He's not at home. What shall I do?   Why don't you ....

5   I've got a terrible headache. I wish it would go.   Have you ....

57.2 For each picture, write a sentence with **need(s)** + one of the following verbs:

> ~~clean~~   cut   empty   paint   tighten

1	2	3	4	5

1 This jacket is dirty. _It needs cleaning._

2 The room isn't very nice. ....

3 The grass is very long. It ....

4 The screws are loose. ....

5 The bin is full. ....

57.3 Put the verb into the correct form.

1 a I was very tired. I tried _to keep_ (keep) my eyes open, but I couldn't.

    b I rang the doorbell, but there was no answer. Then I tried .... (knock) on the door, but there was still no answer.

    c We tried .... (put) the fire out but without success. We had to call the fire brigade.

    d Sue needed to borrow some money. She tried .... (ask) Gerry, but he was short of money too.

    e I tried .... (reach) the shelf, but I wasn't tall enough.

    f Please leave me alone. I'm trying .... (concentrate).

2 a I need a change. I need .... (go) away for a while.

    b My grandmother isn't able to look after herself any more. She needs .... (look) after.

    c The windows are dirty. They need .... (clean).

    d Your hair is getting very long. It needs .... (cut).

    e You don't need .... (iron) that shirt. It doesn't need .... (iron).

3 a They were talking very loudly. I couldn't help .... (overhear) what they said.

    b Can you help me .... (get) the dinner ready?

    c He looks so funny. Whenever I see him, I can't help .... (smile).

    d The fine weather helped .... (make) it a very enjoyable holiday.

Verb + –ing or to ... 3 (like / would like etc.)

A

Like / love / hate

When you talk about repeated actions, you can use **-ing** or **to** ... after these verbs.
So you can say:

- □ Do you **like getting** up early? *or* Do you **like to get** up early?
- □ Stephanie **hates flying**. *or* Stephanie **hates to fly**.
- □ I **love meeting** people. *or* I **love to meet** people.
- □ I don't **like being** kept waiting. *or* ... **like to be** kept waiting.
- □ I don't **like** friends **calling** me at work. *or* ... friends **to call** me at work.

but

(1) We use **-ing** (*not* **to** ...) when we talk about a situation that already exists (or existed).
For example:

- □ Paul lives in Berlin now. He **likes living** there. (He **likes living** in Berlin = He lives there and he likes it)
- □ Do you **like being** a student? (You are a student – do you like it?)
- □ The office I worked in was horrible. I **hated working** there. (I worked there and I hated it)

(2) There is sometimes a difference between **I like to do** and **I like doing**:

I like doing something = I do it and I enjoy it:
- □ I **like cleaning** the kitchen. (= I enjoy it.)

I like to do something = I think it is a good thing to do, but I don't necessarily enjoy it:
- □ It's not my favourite job, but I **like to clean** the kitchen as often as possible.

Note that **enjoy** and **mind** are always followed by **-ing** (*not* **to** ...):
- □ I **enjoy cleaning** the kitchen. (*not* I enjoy to clean)
- □ I don't **mind cleaning** the kitchen. (*not* I don't mind to clean)

B

Would like / would love / would hate / would prefer

Would like / would love etc. are usually followed by **to** ... :
- □ I'd **like** (= would like) **to go** away for a few days.
- □ **Would** you **like to come** to dinner on Friday?
- □ I **wouldn't like to go** on holiday alone.
- □ I'd **love to meet** your family.
- □ **Would** you **prefer to have** dinner now or later?

Compare **I like** and **I would like** (**I'd like**):
- □ I **like playing** tennis. / I **like to play** tennis. (= I like it in general)
- □ I'd **like to play** tennis today. (= I want to play today)

Would mind is always followed by **-ing** (*not* **to** ...):
- □ **Would** you **mind closing** the door, please?

C

I would like **to have done** something = I regret now that I didn't or couldn't do it:
- □ It's a pity we didn't see Val when we were in London. I **would like to have seen** her again.
- □ We'd **like to have gone** away, but we were too busy at home.

You can use the same structure after **would love / would hate / would prefer**:
- □ Poor old David! I **would hate to have been** in his position.
- □ I'd **love to have gone** to the party, but it was impossible.

Enjoy/mind → Unit 53   **Would like** → Units 37E, 55A   **Prefer** → Unit 59   **American English** → Appendix 7

Exercises

58.1 Write sentences about yourself. Say whether you like or don't like these activities. Choose one of these verbs for each sentence:

     like / don't like   love   hate   enjoy   don't mind

1 (fly) _I don't like flying._ or _I don't like to fly._
2 (play cards) ....
3 (be alone) ....
4 (go to museums) ....
5 (cook) ....

58.2 Make sentences from the words in brackets. Use **-ing** or **to ...** . Sometimes either form is possible.

1 Paul lives in Berlin now. It's nice. He likes it.
  (he / like / live / there) _He likes living there._
2 Jane is a biology teacher. She likes her job.
  (she / like / teach / biology) She ....
3 Joe always carries his camera with him and takes a lot of photographs.
  (he / like / take / photographs) ....
4 I used to work in a supermarket. I didn't like it much.
  (I / not / like / work / there) ....
5 Rachel is studying medicine. She likes it.
  (she / like / study / medicine) ....
6 Dan is famous, but he doesn't like it.
  (he / not / like / be / famous) ....
7 Jennifer is a very cautious person. She doesn't take many risks.
  (she / not / like / take / risks) ....
8 I don't like surprises.
  (I / like / know / things / in advance) ....

58.3 Complete each sentence with a verb in the correct form, **-ing** or **to ...** . In one sentence either form is possible.

1 It's good to visit other places – I enjoy _travelling_ .
2 'Would you like .... down?' 'No, thanks. I'll stand.'
3 I'm not quite ready yet. Would you mind .... a little longer?
4 When I was a child, I hated .... to bed early.
5 When I have to catch a train, I'm always worried that I'll miss it. So I like ....
  to the station in plenty of time.
6 I enjoy .... busy. I don't like it when there's nothing to do.
7 I would love .... to your wedding, but I'm afraid it isn't possible.
8 I don't like .... in this part of town. I want to move somewhere else.
9 Do you have a minute? I'd like .... to you about something.
10 If there's bad news and good news, I like .... the bad news first.

58.4 Write sentences using **would ... to have (done)**. Use the verbs in brackets.

1 It's a pity I couldn't go to the wedding. (like) _I would like to have gone to the wedding._
2 It's a pity I didn't see the programme. (like) ....
3 I'm glad I didn't lose my watch. (hate) ....
4 It's a pity I didn't meet your parents. (love) ....
5 I'm glad I wasn't alone. (not / like) ....
6 It's a pity I couldn't travel by train. (prefer) ....

→ Additional exercises 26–28 (pages 317–19)

A **Prefer to do** and **prefer doing**

You can use 'prefer to (do)' or 'prefer -ing' to say what you prefer in general:

☐ I don't like cities. I **prefer to live** in the country. *or* I **prefer living** in the country.

Study the differences in structure after **prefer**. We say:

	I prefer	something	**to** something else.
	I prefer	**doing** something	**to doing** something else.
but	I prefer	**to do** something	**rather than** (**do**) something else.

☐ I **prefer** this coat **to** the coat you were wearing yesterday.
☐ I **prefer** driv**ing to** travel**ling** by train.
but ☐ I **prefer to drive rather than travel** by train.
☐ Sarah **prefers** to live in the country **rather than** (**live**) in a city.

B **Would prefer** (**I'd prefer** ...)

We use **would prefer** to say what somebody wants in a specific situation (not in general):

☐ '**Would** you **prefer** tea or coffee?' 'Coffee, please.'

We say 'would prefer **to do** something' (*not* doing):

☐ 'Shall we go by train?' '**I'd prefer to drive.**' (*not* I'd prefer driving)
☐ **I'd prefer to stay** at home tonight **rather than go** to the cinema.

C **Would rather** (**I'd rather** ...)

Would rather (do) = **would prefer** (to do). We use **would rather** + *infinitive* (without **to**). Compare:

☐ 'Shall we go by train?' { 'I'd **prefer to** drive.'
    'I'd **rather** drive.' (*not* to drive)
☐ '**Would** you **rather have** tea or coffee?' 'Coffee, please.'

The negative is 'I'd **rather not** (do something)':

☐ I'm tired. I'd **rather not go** out this evening, if you don't mind.
☐ 'Do you want to go out this evening?' 'I'd **rather not.**'

We say '**would rather do** something **than do** something else':

☐ I'd **rather stay** at home tonight **than go** to the cinema.

D **I'd rather you did** something

We say 'I'd **rather** you **did** something' (*not* I'd rather you do). For example:

☐ 'Shall I stay here?' 'I'd **rather** you **came** with us.' (= I would prefer this)
☐ 'I'll repair your bike tomorrow, OK?' 'I'd **rather** you **did** it today.'
☐ 'Are you going to tell them what happened?' 'No. I'd **rather** they **didn't** know.'
☐ Shall I tell them, or **would** you **rather** they **didn't** know?

In this structure we use the *past* (**came**, **did** etc.), but the meaning is present *not* past. Compare:

☐ I'd rather **make** dinner now.
    I'd rather **you made** dinner now. (*not* I'd rather you make)

I'd rather you **didn't** (do something) = I'd prefer you not to do it:

☐ I'd **rather you didn't tell** anyone what I said.
☐ 'Shall I tell Linda what happened?' 'I'd **rather you didn't.**'

Would prefer → Unit 58B   **Prefer (one thing) to (another)** → Unit 136D

Exercises

59.1 Which do you prefer? Write sentences using **'I prefer (something) to (something else)'**. Put the verb into the correct form where necessary.

1 (drive / travel by train) _I prefer driving to travelling by train._
2 (basketball / football)
   I prefer ....
3 (phone people / send emails)
   I .... to ....
4 (go to the cinema / watch videos at home)
   ....

Now rewrite sentences 3 and 4 using the structure **'I prefer to (do something)'.**

5 (1) _I prefer to drive rather than travel by train._
6 (3) I prefer to ....
7 (4) ....

59.2 Write sentences using **I'd prefer ...** and **I'd rather ...** + the following:

| eat at home | ~~get a taxi~~ | go alone | wait a few minutes | listen to some music |
| stand | go for a swim | ~~wait till later~~ | think about it for a while | |

1	Shall we walk home?	(prefer)	_I'd prefer to get a taxi._
2	Do you want to eat now?	(rather)	_I'd rather wait till later._
3	Would you like to watch TV?	(rather)	....
4	Do you want to go to a restaurant?	(prefer)	....
5	Let's leave now.	(rather)	....
6	Shall we play tennis?	(rather)	....
7	I think we should decide now.	(prefer)	....
8	Would you like to sit down?	(rather)	....
9	Do you want me to come with you?	(prefer)	....

Now use the same ideas to complete these sentences using **than** and **rather than**.

10 I'd prefer to get a taxi _rather than walk home._
11 I'd prefer to go for a swim ....
12 I'd rather eat at home ....
13 I'd prefer to think about it for a while ....
14 I'd rather listen to some music ....

59.3 Complete the sentences using **would you rather I ...** .

1 Are you going to make dinner or _would you rather I made it_ ?
2 Are you going to tell Liz what happened or would you rather .... ?
3 Are you going to do the shopping or .... ?
4 Are you going to phone Diane or .... ?

59.4 Use your own ideas to complete these sentences.

1 'Shall I tell Ann the news?'   'No, I'd rather she _didn't_ know.'
2 Do you want me to go now or would you rather I .... here?
3 Do you want to go out this evening or would you rather .... at home?
4 This is a private letter addressed to me. I'd rather you .... read it.
5 I don't really like these shoes. I'd rather they .... a different colour.
6 A: Do you mind if I turn on the radio?
   B: I'd rather you .... I'm trying to study.

→ Additional exercises 27–28 (pages 318–19)

Preposition (in/for/about etc.) + -ing

A

If a preposition (**in/for/about** etc.) is followed by a verb, the verb ends in **-ing**:

	preposition	*verb* (**-ing**)	
Are you interested	**in**	work**ing**	for us?
I'm not very good	**at**	learn**ing**	languages.
Sue must be fed up	**with**	study**ing**.	
What are the advantages	**of**	hav**ing**	a car?
Thanks very much	**for**	invit**ing**	me to your party.
How	**about**	meet**ing**	for lunch tomorrow?
Why don't you go out	**instead of**	sitt**ing**	at home all the time?
Carol went to work	**in spite of**	feel**ing**	ill.

You can also say 'instead of **somebody** doing something', 'fed up with **people** doing something' etc. :

☐ I'm fed up with **people** telling me what to do.

B

Note the use of the following prepositions + **-ing**:

before -ing and **after -ing**:

☐ **Before** go**ing** out, I phoned Sarah. (*not* Before to go out)
☐ What did you do **after** leav**ing** school?

You can also say '**Before I went** out ...' and '... **after you left** school'.

by -ing (to say *how* something happens):

☐ The burglars got into the house **by** break**ing** a window and climb**ing** in.
☐ You can improve your English **by** read**ing** more.
☐ She made herself ill **by** not eat**ing** properly.
☐ Many accidents are caused **by** people driv**ing** too fast.

without -ing:

☐ We ran ten kilometres **without** stopp**ing**.
☐ It was a stupid thing to say. I said it **without** think**ing**.
☐ She needs to work **without** people disturb**ing** her. (*or* ... **without** be**ing** disturbed.)
☐ I have enough problems of my own **without** hav**ing** to worry about yours.

C

To -ing (look forward **to** do**ing** something etc.)

To is often part of the *infinitive* (**to do** / **to see** etc.):

☐ We decided **to go** out.
☐ Would you like **to meet** for lunch tomorrow?

But **to** is also a *preposition* (like **in/for/about/from** etc.). For example:

☐ We drove from London **to Edinburgh**.
☐ I prefer tea **to coffee**.
☐ Are you looking forward **to the weekend**?

If a preposition is followed by a verb, the verb ends in **-ing**:

in doing   **about** meeting   **without** stopping (etc.)

So, when **to** is a preposition and it is followed by a verb, you must say **to -ing**:

☐ I prefer driving **to** travel**ling** by train. (*not* to travel)
☐ Are you looking forward **to** go**ing** on holiday? (*not* looking forward to go)

Be/get used to -ing → Unit 61   **Verb + preposition + -ing** → Unit 62   **While/when -ing** → Unit 68B
In spite of → Unit 113   **Prepositions** → Units 121–136

60.1 Complete the second sentence so that it means the same as the first.

1 Why is it useful to have a car?
What are the advantages of ...<u>having a car</u>... ?

2 I don't intend to apply for the job.
I have no intention of ....

3 Helen has a good memory for names.
Helen is good at ....

4 Mark won't pass the exam. He has no chance.
Mark has no chance of ....

5 Did you get into trouble because you were late?
Did you get into trouble for .... ?

6 We didn't eat at home. We went to a restaurant instead.
Instead of ....

7 We got into the exhibition. We didn't have to queue.
We got into the exhibition without ....

8 Our team played well, but we lost the game.
Our team lost the game despite ....

60.2 Complete the sentences using **by -ing**. Use the following (with the verb in the correct form):

borrow too much money	~~break a window~~	drive too fast
put some pictures on the walls	stand on a chair	turn a key

1 The burglars got into the house ...<u>by breaking a window</u>.................... .
2 I was able to reach the top shelf ....
3 You start the engine of a car ....
4 Kevin got himself into financial trouble ....
5 You can put people's lives in danger ....
6 We made the room look nicer ....

60.3 Complete the sentences with a suitable word. Use only one word each time.

1 We ran ten kilometres without ...<u>stopping</u>.... .
2 He left the hotel without .... his bill.
3 It's a nice morning. How about .... for a walk?
4 We were able to translate the letter into English without .... a dictionary.
5 Before .... to bed, I like to have a hot drink.
6 It was a long journey. I was very tired after .... on a train for 36 hours.
7 I was annoyed because the decision was made without anybody .... me.
8 After .... the same job for ten years, I felt I needed a change.
9 We lost our way because we went straight on instead of .... left.
10 I like these photographs you took. You're good at .... photographs.

60.4 For each situation, write a sentence with **I'm (not) looking forward to**.

1 You are going on holiday next week. How do you feel?
<u>I'm looking forward to going on holiday.</u>..

2 Diane is a good friend of yours and she is coming to visit you soon. So you will see her again soon. How do you feel? I'm ....

3 You are going to the dentist tomorrow. You don't enjoy going to the dentist. How do you feel?
I'm not ....

4 Carol is a student at school. She hates it, but she is leaving school next summer.
How does she feel? ....

5 You've arranged to play tennis tomorrow. You like tennis a lot. How do you feel?
....

→ Additional exercises 26–28 (pages 317–19)   **121**

A   Study this example situation:

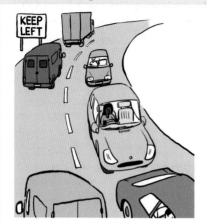

Lisa is American, but she lives in Britain. When she first drove a car in Britain, she found it very difficult because she had to drive on the left, not on the right. Driving on the left was strange and difficult for her because:

She **wasn't used to it**.
She **wasn't used to driving** on the left.

But after a lot of practice, driving on the left became less strange. So:
She **got used to driving** on the left.

Now it's no problem for Lisa:
She **is used to driving** on the left.

B   **I'm used to** something = it is not new or strange for me:
- Frank lives alone. He doesn't mind this because he has lived alone for 15 years. It is not strange for him. He **is used to it**. He **is used to living** alone.
- I bought some new shoes. They felt a bit strange at first because I **wasn't used to them**.
- Our new flat is on a very busy street. I expect we'll **get used to the noise**, but at the moment it's very disturbing.
- Diane has a new job. She has to get up much earlier now than before – at 6.30. She finds this difficult because she **isn't used to getting** up so early.
- Barbara's husband is often away from home. She doesn't mind this. She **is used to him** be**ing** away.

C   After **be/get used** you cannot use the infinitive (**to do / to drive** etc.). We say:
- She is used **to driving** on the left. (*not* She is used to drive)

When we say 'I am **used to** something', **to** is a *preposition*, not a part of the infinitive. So we say:
- Frank is used **to living** alone. (*not* Frank is used to live)
- Lisa had to get used **to driving** on the left. (*not* get used to drive)

D   Do not confuse **I am used to doing** and **I used to do**:

I **am** used to (**doing**) something = it isn't strange or new for me:
- I **am** used **to the weather** in this country.
- I **am** used **to driving** on the left because I've lived in Britain a long time.

I used **to do** something = I did it regularly in the past but no longer do it. You can use this only for the past, not for the present.
The structure is 'I **used to do**' (*not* 'I **am** used to do'):
- I **used to drive** to work every day, but these days I usually go by bike.
- We **used to live** in a small village, but now we live in London.

61.1 Look again at the situation in Section A on the opposite page ('Lisa is American ...').
The following situations are similar. Complete the sentences using **used to**.

1 Juan is Spanish and went to live in England. In Spain he usually had dinner late in the evening, but in England dinner was at 6 o'clock. This was very early for him and he found it very strange at first.

When Juan first went to England, he .... dinner so early, but after some time he .... it. Now he finds it normal. He .... at 6 o'clock.

2 Julia is a nurse. A year ago she started working nights. At first she found it hard and didn't like it.

She .... nights and it took her a few months to .... it. Now, after a year, she's quite happy. She .... nights.

61.2 What do you say in these situations? Use **I'm (not) used to ...** .

1 You live alone. You don't mind this. You have always lived alone.
FRIEND: Do you get a bit lonely sometimes?
YOU: No, _I'm used to living alone._

2 You sleep on the floor. You don't mind this. You have always slept on the floor.
FRIEND: Wouldn't you prefer to sleep in a bed?
YOU: No, I ....

3 You have to work long hours in your job. This is not a problem for you. You have always worked long hours.
FRIEND: You have to work very long hours in your job, don't you?
YOU: Yes, but I don't mind that. I ....

4 You usually go to bed early. Last night you went to bed very late (for you) and as a result you are very tired this morning.
FRIEND: You look tired this morning.
YOU: Yes, ...

61.3 Read the situations and complete the sentences using **used to**.

1 Some friends of yours have just moved into a flat on a busy street. It is very noisy.
They'll have to _get used to the noise._

2 The children at school had a new teacher. She was different from the teacher before her, but this wasn't a problem for the children. They soon ....

3 Sue moved from a big house to a much smaller one. She found it strange at first. She had to .... in a much smaller house.

4 Some people you know from Britain are going to live in your country. What will they have to get used to?
They'll have to ....

61.4 Complete the sentences using only one word each time (see Section C).

1 Lisa had to get used to _driving_ on the left.
2 We used to _live_ in a small village, but now we live in London.
3 Dan used to .... a lot of coffee. Now he prefers tea.
4 I feel very full after that meal. I'm not used to .... so much.
5 I wouldn't like to share an office. I'm used to .... my own office.
6 I used to .... a car, but I sold it a few months ago
7 When we were children, we used to .... swimming very often.
8 There used to .... a cinema here, but it was knocked down a few years ago.
9 I'm the boss here! I'm not used to .... told what to do.

→ Additional exercises 26–28 (pages 317–19)

Verb + preposition + -ing (succeed in -ing / accuse somebody of -ing etc.)

A

Many verbs have the structure *verb* + *preposition* (**in/for/about** etc.) + *object*.
For example:

verb +	preposition	+ object
We **talked**	**about**	the problem.
You must **apologise**	**for**	what you said.

If the *object* is another verb, it ends in **-ing**:

verb +	preposition	+ -ing (object)
We **talked**	**about**	**going** to America.
You must **apologise**	**for**	not **telling** the truth.

Some more verbs with this structure:

succeed (in)	Have you **succeeded**	**in**	**finding** a job yet?
insist (on)	They **insisted**	**on**	**paying** for the meal.
think (of)	I'm **thinking**	**of**	**buying** a house.
dream (of)	I wouldn't **dream**	**of**	**asking** them for money.
approve (of)	He doesn't **approve**	**of**	**swearing**.
decide (against)	We have **decided**	**against**	**moving** to London.
feel (like)	Do you **feel**	**like**	**going** out tonight?
look forward (to)	I'm **looking forward**	**to**	**meeting** her.

You can also say 'approve of **somebody** doing something', 'look forward to **somebody** doing something':

- ☐ I don't approve **of people** killing animals for fun.
- ☐ We are all looking forward **to Peter** coming home.

B

The following verbs can have the structure *verb* + *object* + *preposition* + **-ing**:

	verb +	object +	preposition	+ -ing (object)
congratulate (on)	I **congratulated**	Liz	**on**	**getting** a new job.
accuse (of)	They **accused**	us	**of**	**telling** lies.
suspect (of)	Nobody **suspected**	the general	**of**	**being** a spy.
prevent (from)	What **prevented**	you	**from**	**coming** to see us?
stop (from)	The rain didn't **stop**	us	**from**	**enjoying** our holiday.
thank (for)	I forgot to **thank**	them	**for**	**helping** me.
excuse (for)	Excuse	me	**for**	**being** so late.
forgive (for)	Please **forgive**	me	**for**	not **writing** to you.

You can say '**stop** somebody doing' or '**stop** somebody **from** doing':

- ☐ You can't **stop** me doing what I want. *or* You can't **stop** me **from** doing what I want.

Some of these verbs are often used in the *passive*. For example:

- ☐ We **were accused of** telling lies.
- ☐ The general **was suspected of** being a spy.

Note that we say 'apologise **to** somebody for ...':

- ☐ I apologised **to them** for keeping them waiting. (*not* I apologised them)

Decide to ... → Unit 54A   **Preposition + -ing** → Unit 60   **Verb + preposition** → Units 132–136

Exercises

62.1 Complete each sentence using only one word.

1 Our neighbours apologised for ....*making*.... so much noise.
2 I feel lazy. I don't feel like .... any work.
3 I wanted to go out alone, but Joe insisted on .... with me.
4 I'm fed up with my job. I'm thinking of .... something else.
5 We have decided against .... a new car because we can't really afford it.
6 I hope you get in touch with me soon. I'm looking forward to ....
   from you.
7 The weather was extremely bad and this prevented us from .... out.
8 The man who has been arrested is suspected of .... a false passport.
9 I think you should apologise to Sue for .... so rude to her.
10 Some parents don't approve of their children .... a lot of television.
11 I'm sorry I can't come to your party, but thank you very much for .... me.

62.2 Complete each sentence using a preposition + one of the following verbs (in the correct form):

carry   cause   escape   ~~go~~   interrupt   live   see   solve   spend   walk

1 Do you feel ....*like going*.... out this evening?
2 It took us a long time, but we finally succeeded .... the problem.
3 I've always dreamed .... in a small house by the sea.
4 The driver of the other car accused me .... the accident.
5 There's a fence around the lawn to stop people .... on the grass.
6 Excuse me .... you, but may I ask you something?
7 Where are you thinking .... your holiday this year?
8 The guards weren't able to prevent the prisoner ....
9 My bag wasn't very heavy, but Dan insisted .... it for me.
10 It's a pity Paul can't come to the party. I was really looking forward
   .... him.

62.3 Complete the sentences on the right.

1 YOU   KEVIN   It was nice of you to help me. Thanks very much.

   Kevin thanked ....*me for helping him*.... .

2 ANN   TOM   I'll drive you to the station. I insist.

   Tom insisted ....
   ....

3 YOU   DAN   I hear you got married. Congratulations!

   Dan congratulated me ....
   ....

4 SUE   JENNY   It was nice of you to come to see me. Thank you.

   Jenny thanked ....
   ....

5 YOU   KATE   I'm sorry I didn't phone earlier.

   Kate apologised ....
   ....

6 YOU   JANE   You're selfish.

   Jane accused ....
   ....

→ Additional exercises 27-28 (pages 318–19)

A When these expressions are followed by a verb, the verb ends in **-ing**:

> **It's no use / It's no good**
> □ There's nothing you can do about the situation, so **it's no use** worry**ing** about it.
> □ **It's no good** try**ing** to persuade me. You won't succeed.

> **There's no point in**
> □ **There's no point in** hav**ing** a car if you never use it.
> □ **There was no point in** wait**ing** any longer, so we went.
> But we usually say '**the point of** do**ing** something':
> □ **What's the point of** hav**ing** a car if you never use it?

> **It's (not) worth**
> □ I live only a short walk from here, so **it's not worth** tak**ing** a taxi.
> □ Our flight was very early in the morning, so **it wasn't worth** go**ing** to bed.

> You can say that a film is **worth seeing**, a book is **worth reading** etc. :
> □ What was the film like? Was it **worth seeing**?
> □ Thieves broke into the house but didn't take anything. There was nothing **worth stealing**.

B **Have difficulty -ing, have trouble -ing**

We say 'have difficulty do**ing** something' (*not* to do):
> □ I had no **difficulty** find**ing** a place to live. (*not* difficulty to find)
> □ Did you have any **difficulty** gett**ing** a visa?
> □ People often have **difficulty** read**ing** my writing.

You can also say 'have **trouble** doing something':
> □ I had no **trouble** finding a place to live.

C We use **-ing** after:

> **a waste of money / a waste of time**
> □ It was a **waste of time** read**ing** that book. It was rubbish.
> □ It's a **waste of money** buy**ing** things you don't need.

> **spend/waste** (time)
> □ He **spent** hours try**ing** to repair the clock.
> □ I **waste** a lot of time day-dream**ing**.

> **(be) busy**
> □ She said she couldn't see me. She was too **busy** do**ing** other things.

D **Go swimming / go fishing** etc.

We use **go -ing** for a number of activities (especially sports). For example, you can say:

go swimming   **go** sailing   **go** fishing   **go** climbing   **go** skiing   **go** jogging

Also **go** shopping, **go** sightseeing

> □ How often do you **go swimming**?
> □ I'd like to **go skiing**.
> □ When did you last **go shopping**?
> □ I've never **been** sailing. (For **gone** and **been**, see Unit 7D.)

63.1 Make sentences beginning **There's no point … .**

1 Why have a car if you never use it?
There's no point in having a car if you never use it.

2 Why work if you don't need money?
....

3 Don't try to study if you feel tired.
....

4 Why hurry if you've got plenty of time?
....

63.2 Complete the sentences on the right.

1	Shall we get a taxi home?	No, it isn't far. It's not worth _getting a taxi_ .
2	If you need help, why don't you ask Dave?	It's no use .... He won't be able to do anything.
3	I don't really want to go out tonight.	Well, stay at home! There's no point .... if you don't want to.
4	Shall I phone Liz now?	No, it's no good .... now. She won't be at home.
5	Are you going to complain about what happened?	No, it's not worth .... Nobody will do anything about it.
6	Do you ever read newspapers?	No, I think it's a waste ....
7	Do you want to keep these old clothes?	No, let's throw them away. They're not worth ....

63.3 Write sentences using **difficulty.**

1 I managed to get a visa, but it was difficult. I had difficulty _getting a visa_ .
2 I find it hard to remember people's names.
   I have difficulty ....
3 Lucy managed to get a job without difficulty.
   She had no ....
4 It won't be difficult to get a ticket for the game.
   You won't have any ....

63.4 Complete the sentences. Use only one word each time.

1 It's a waste of money ....buying.... things you don't need.
2 Every morning I spend about an hour .... the newspaper.
3 'What's Sue doing?' 'She's going away tomorrow, so she's busy ....'
4 I think you waste too much time .... television.
5 There's a beautiful view from that hill. It's worth .... to the top.
6 It's no use .... for the job. I know I wouldn't get it.
7 Just stay calm. There's no point in .... angry.

63.5 Complete these sentences with the following (with the verb in the correct form):

> **go riding**   ~~**go sailing**~~   **go shopping**   **go skiing**   **go swimming**

1 Barry lives by the sea and he's got a boat, so he often ....goes sailing.... .
2 It was a very hot day, so we .... in the lake.
3 There's plenty of snow in the mountains, so we'll be able to ....
4 Helen has got two horses. She .... regularly.
5 'Where's Dan?' 'He's .... There were a few things he needed to buy.'

→ Additional exercises 27–28 (pages 318–19)

To ... , for ... and so that ... (purpose)

A We use **to ...** to say why somebody does something (= the purpose of an action):

- □ 'Why are you going out?' 'To post a letter.'
- □ A friend of mine phoned **to invite** me to a party.
- □ We shouted **to warn** everybody of the danger.

We use **to ...** to say why something exists (= its purpose):

- □ This wall is **to keep** people out of the garden.
- □ The president has a team of bodyguards **to protect** him.

B We use **to ...** to say what can be done or must be done with something:

- □ It's difficult to find **a place to park** in the centre. (= a place where you can park)
- □ Would you like **something to eat**?
- □ Have you got **much work to do**? (= work that you must do)
- □ I get lonely if there's **nobody to talk to**.
- □ I need **something to open** this bottle **with**.

Also **money/time/chance/opportunity/energy/courage** etc. to (do something):

- □ They gave us **some money to buy** some food.
- □ Do you have **much opportunity to practise** your English?
- □ I need **a few days to think** about your proposal.

C **For ... and to ...**

Compare:

for + *noun*	**to** + *verb*
□ I'm going to Spain **for a holiday**.	□ I'm going to Spain **to learn** Spanish. (*not* for learn, *not* for learning)
□ What would you like **for dinner**?	□ What would you like **to eat**?
□ Let's go to the pool **for a swim**.	□ Let's go to the pool **to have** a swim.

You can say '**for** (somebody) **to** (do something)':

- □ There weren't any chairs **for us to sit on**, so we had to sit on the floor.

You can use **for -ing** or **to ...** to talk about the general purpose of something, or what it is generally used for:

- □ Do you use this brush **for washing** the dishes? (*or* ... **to wash** the dishes?)

You can use **What ... for?** to ask about purpose:

- □ **What** is this switch **for**?
- □ **What** did you do that **for**?

D **So that**

Sometimes you have to use **so that** for purpose.

We use **so that** (*not* **to ...**) especially

when the purpose is *negative* (**so that ... won't/wouldn't**):

- □ I hurried **so that** I **wouldn't** be late. (= because I didn't want to be late)
- □ Leave early **so that** you **won't** (*or* **don't**) miss the bus.

with **can** and **could** (**so that ... can/could**):

- □ She's learning English **so that** she **can** study in Canada.
- □ We moved to London **so that** we **could** see our friends more often.

Exercises

64.1 Choose from Box A and Box B to make a new sentence with **to** ... .

A
1 ~~I shouted~~
2 I had to go to the bank
3 I'm saving money
4 I went into hospital
5 I'm wearing two sweaters
6 I phoned the police

B
I want to keep warm
I wanted to report that my car had been stolen
I want to go to Canada
I had to have an operation
I needed to get some money
~~I wanted to warn people of the danger~~

1   *I shouted to warn people of the danger.*
2   I had to go to the bank ....
3   I ....
4   ....
5   ....
6   ....

64.2 Complete these sentences using a suitable verb.

1   The president has a team of bodyguards ..... *to protect* ..... him.
2   I didn't have enough time .... the newspaper today.
3   I came home by taxi. I didn't have the energy ....
4   'Would you like something .... ?'   'Yes, please. A cup of coffee.'
5   We need a bag .... these things in.
6   There will be a meeting next week .... the problem.
7   I wish we had enough money .... another car.
8   I saw Helen at the party, but we didn't have a chance .... to each other.
9   I need some new clothes. I don't have anything nice ....
10 They've just passed their exams. They're having a party ....
11 I can't do all this work alone. I need somebody .... me.

64.3 Put in **to** or **for**.

1   I'm going to Spain ..... *for* ..... a holiday.
2   You need a lot of experience .... this job.
3   You need a lot of experience .... do this job.
4   We'll need more time .... make a decision.
5   I went to the dentist .... a check-up.
6   I had to put on my glasses .... read the letter.
7   Do you have to wear glasses .... reading?
8   I wish we had a garden .... the children .... play in.

64.4 Write sentences with **so that**.

1   I hurried. I didn't want to be late.   *I hurried so that I wouldn't be late.*
2   I wore warm clothes. I didn't want to be cold.
    I wore ....
3   I left Dave my phone number. I wanted him to be able to contact me.
    I ....
4   We whispered. We didn't want anybody else to hear our conversation.
    .... nobody ....
5   Please arrive early. We want to be able to start the meeting on time.
    Please ....
6   Jennifer locked the door. She didn't want to be disturbed.
    ....
7   I slowed down. I wanted the car behind me to be able to overtake.
    ....

Adjective + to ...

A | Difficult to understand etc.

Compare sentences (a) and (b):

□ Jim doesn't speak very clearly. {
  (a) It is **difficult to understand** him .
  (b) He is **difficult to understand**.
}

Sentences (a) and (b) have the same meaning. Note that we say:
□ He is difficult **to understand**. (*not* He is difficult to understand him.)

You can use the same structures with:
**easy   hard   impossible   dangerous   safe   expensive   cheap   nice
good   interesting   exciting**

□ Do you think it is **safe** (for us) **to drink** this water?
Do you think this water is **safe** (for us) **to drink**? (*not* to drink it)
□ The questions in the exam were very difficult. It was **impossible to answer** them.
The questions in the exam were very difficult. They were **impossible to answer**.
(*not* to answer them)
□ Jill has lots of interesting ideas. It's **interesting to talk** to her.
Jill is **interesting to talk to**. (*not* to talk to her.)

You can also use this structure with *adjective + noun*:
□ This is a **difficult question** (for me) **to answer**. (*not* to answer it)

B | (It's) nice of (you) to ...

You can say 'It's **nice of** somebody **to** do something':
□ It was **nice of you to take** me to the airport. Thank you very much.

You can use many other adjectives in this way. For example:
kind   clever   sensible   mean   silly   stupid   careless   unfair   considerate:

□ It's **silly of Mary to give** up her job when she needs the money.
□ I think it was very **unfair of him to criticise** me.

C | I'm sorry to ... / I was surprised to ... etc.

You can use *adjective + to ...* to say how somebody reacts to something:
□ I was **sorry to hear** that your father is ill.

You can use many other adjectives in this way. For example:
happy   glad   pleased   sad   disappointed   surprised   amazed   astonished   relieved

□ Was Julia **surprised to see** you?
□ It was a long and tiring journey. We were **glad to get** home.

D | The first / the next (etc.) + to ...

You can use **to ...** after **the first/the last, the next, the only, the second** (etc.):
□ If I have any more news, you will be **the first** (person) **to know**.
□ **The next** train **to arrive** at platform 4 will be the 10.50 to Cardiff.
□ Everybody was late except me. I was **the only** one **to arrive** on time.

E | You can say that something is **sure/certain/likely/bound to** happen:
□ Carla is a very good student. She's **bound to pass** the exam. (= she is sure to pass)
□ I'm **likely to be** late home this evening. (= I will probably be late home)

Afraid/interested/sorry → Unit 66   **If ...** → Unit 84C   **Enough and too + adjective** → Unit 103

Exercises

65.1 (Section A) Write these sentences in another way, beginning as shown.

1 It's difficult to understand him.   He _is difficult to understand._
2 It's easy to use this machine.   This machine is ....
3 It was very difficult to open the window.   The window ....
4 It's impossible to translate some words.   Some words ....
5 It's expensive to maintain a car.   A ....
6 It's not safe to stand on that chair.   That ....

65.2 (Section A) Complete the second sentence. Use the adjective in brackets and **to ...** as in the example.

1 I couldn't answer the question.   (difficult)   It was a _difficult question to answer._
2 Everybody makes that mistake.   (easy)   It's an ....
3 I like living in this place.   (nice)   It's a ....
4 We enjoyed watching the game.   (good)   It was a ....

65.3 (Section B) Make a new sentence beginning **It ...** . Use one of these adjectives each time:

    careless   **inconsiderate**   ~~**kind**~~   **nice**

1 Sue has offered to help me.   _It's kind of Sue to offer to help me._
2 You make the same mistake again and again.
   It ....
3 Dan and Jenny invited me to stay with them.

   ....
4 The neighbours make so much noise at night.

   ....

65.4 (Section C) Use the following words to complete these sentences:

    sorry / hear   **glad / hear**   ~~**pleased / get**~~   **surprised / see**

1 We _were pleased to get_ your letter last week.
2 I got your message. I .... that you're keeping well.
3 We .... Paula at the party. We didn't expect her to come.
4 I .... that your mother isn't well. I hope she gets better soon.

65.5 (Section D) Complete the second sentence using the words in brackets + **to ...** .

1 Nobody left before me. (the first) I was _the first person to leave._
2 Everybody else arrived before Paul.
   (the last) Paul was the ....
3 Fiona passed the exam. All the other students failed.
   (the only) Fiona was ....
4 I complained to the restaurant manager about the service. Another customer had already complained.
   (the second) I was ....
5 Neil Armstrong walked on the moon in 1969. Nobody had done this before him.
   (the first) Neil Armstrong was ....

65.6 (Section E) Complete these sentences using the words in brackets and a suitable verb.

1 Diane is a very good student. She _is bound to pass_ the exam. (bound)
2 I'm not surprised you're tired. After such a long journey you .... tired. (bound)
3 Andy has a very bad memory. He .... what you tell him. (sure)
4 I don't think you need to take an umbrella. It .... (not likely)
5 The holidays begin this weekend. There .... a lot of traffic on the roads. (likely)

To ... (afraid to do) and preposition + -ing (afraid of -ing)

A Afraid to (do) and afraid of (do)ing

I am **afraid to do** something = I don't want to do it because it is dangerous or the result could be bad.
We use **afraid to do** for things we do intentionally; we can choose to do them or not:
- ☐ This part of town is dangerous. People are **afraid to walk** here at night.
  (= they don't want to walk here because it is dangerous – so they don't)
- ☐ James was **afraid to tell** his parents what had happened.
  (= he didn't want to tell them because he knew they would be angry, worried etc.)

I am **afraid of** something **happening** = it is possible that something bad will happen (for example, an accident).
We do not use **afraid of -ing** for things we do intentionally:
- ☐ The path was icy, so we walked very carefully. We were **afraid of falling**.
  (= it was possible that we would fall – *not* we were afraid to fall)
- ☐ I don't like dogs. I'm always **afraid of being** bitten. (*not* afraid to be bitten)

So, you are **afraid to do** something because you are **afraid of something happening** as a result:
- ☐ I was **afraid to go** near the dog because I **was afraid of being** bitten.

B Interested in (do)ing and interested to (do)

I'm **interested in doing** something = I'm thinking of doing it, I would like to do it:
- ☐ Let me know if you're **interested in joining** the club. (*not* to join)
- ☐ I tried to sell my car, but nobody was **interested in buying** it. (*not* to buy)

We use **interested to** ... to say how somebody reacts to what they **hear/see/read/learn/know/find**.
For example, 'I was **interested to hear** it' = I heard it and it was interesting for me:
- ☐ I was **interested to hear** that Tanya has left her job.
- ☐ Ask Mike for his opinion. I would be **interested to know** what he thinks. (= it would be interesting for me to know it)
This structure is the same as **surprised to** ... / **glad to** ... etc. (see Unit 65C):
- ☐ I was **surprised to hear** that Tanya has left her job.

C Sorry to (do) and sorry for/about (do)ing

We use **sorry to** ... to say we regret something that happens (see Unit 65C):
- ☐ I was **sorry to hear** that Nicky lost her job. (= I was sorry when I heard that ...)
- ☐ I've enjoyed my stay here. I'll be **sorry to leave**.
We also say **sorry to** ... to apologise at the time we do something:
- ☐ I'm **sorry to phone** you so late, but I need to ask you something.

You can use **sorry for** or **sorry about** (doing something) to apologise for something you did before:
- ☐ I'm **sorry for** (or **about**) **shouting** at you yesterday. (*not* sorry to shout)
You can also say:
- ☐ I'm **sorry I shouted** at you yesterday.

D We say:

I **want to** (do) / I'd **like to** (do)	*but*	I'm **thinking of** (do)ing / I **dream of** (do)ing
I **failed to** (do)	*but*	I **succeeded in** (do)ing
I **allowed** them **to** (do)	*but*	I **prevented** them **from** (do)ing
		I **stopped** them **from** (do)ing

For examples, see Units 54–55 and 62.

Verb + preposition + -ing → Unit 62   Adjective + preposition → Units 130–131   **Sorry about/for** → Unit 130

Exercises

66.1 Use the words in brackets to write sentences. Use **afraid to ...** or **afraid of –ing**.

1 The streets are unsafe at night.
   (a lot of people / afraid / go / out) _A lot of people are afraid to go out._

2 We walked very carefully along the icy path.
   (we / afraid / fall) _We were afraid of falling._

3 I don't usually carry my passport with me.
   (I / afraid / lose / it) ....

4 I thought she would be angry if I told her what had happened.
   (I / afraid / tell / her) ....

5 We rushed to the station.
   (we / afraid / miss / our train) ....

6 In the middle of the film there was an especially horrifying scene.
   (we / afraid / look) ....

7 The vase was very valuable, so I held it carefully.
   (I / afraid / drop / it) ....

8 I thought the food on my plate didn't look fresh.
   a (I / afraid / eat / it) ....
   b (I / afraid / get / sick) ....

66.2 Complete the sentences using **in ...** or **to ...** . Use these verbs:

~~buy~~   get   know   look   read   start

1 I'm trying to sell my car, but nobody is interested ....in buying.... it.

2 Julia is interested .... her own business.

3 I was interested .... your letter in the newspaper last week.

4 Ben wants to stay single. He's not interested .... married.

5 I met Mark a few days ago. You'll be interested .... that he's just got a job in Paris.

6 I don't enjoy sightseeing. I'm not interested .... at old buildings.

66.3 Complete each sentence using **sorry for/about ...** or **sorry to ...** . Use the verb in brackets.

1 I'm ....sorry to phone.... you so late, but I need to ask you something. (phone)

2 I was .... that you didn't get the job you applied for. (hear)

3 I'm .... all those bad things about you. I didn't mean them. (say)

4 I'm .... you, but do you have a pen I could borrow? (disturb)

5 I'm .... the book you lent me. I'll buy you another one. (lose)

66.4 Complete each sentence using the verb in brackets.

1 a We wanted ...to leave.... the building. (leave)
   b We weren't allowed .... the building. (leave)
   c We were prevented .... the building. (leave)

2 a Peter failed .... the problem. (solve)
   b Chris succeeded .... the problem. (solve)

3 a I'm thinking .... away next week. (go)
   b I'm hoping .... away next week. (go)
   c I'd like .... away next week. (go)
   d I'm looking forward .... away next week. (go)

4 a Helen wanted .... me lunch. (buy)
   b Helen promised .... me lunch. (buy)
   c Helen insisted .... me lunch. (buy)
   d Helen wouldn't dream .... me lunch. (buy)

→ Additional exercise 27 (page 318)

See somebody do and see somebody doing

Study this example situation:

Tom got into his car and drove away. You saw this.
You can say:

☐ I saw Tom **get** into his car and **drive** away.

In this structure we use **get/drive/do** etc.
(*not* to get / to drive / to do).

| Somebody **did** something | + | I saw this |

    I saw somebody **do** something

TOM

But after a *passive* ('he **was seen**' etc.), we use **to**:

☐ He was seen **to** get in the car.

Study this example situation:

Yesterday you saw Kate. She was waiting for a bus.
You can say:

☐ I saw Kate **waiting** for a bus.

In this structure we use **-ing** (wait**ing**/do**ing** etc.):

| Somebody **was doing** something | + | I saw this |

    I saw somebody **doing** something

KATE

Study the difference in meaning between the two structures:

I saw him **do** something = he **did** something (*past simple*) and I saw this. I saw the complete action from beginning to end:

☐ He **fell** off the wall. I saw this. → I saw him **fall** off the wall.
☐ The accident **happened**. Did you see it? → Did you see the accident **happen**?

I saw him **doing** something = he **was doing** something (*past continuous*) and I saw this. I saw him when he was in the middle of doing it. This does not mean that I saw the complete action:

☐ He **was walking** along the street.
I saw this when I drove past in my car. } I saw him **walking** along the street.

Sometimes the difference is not important and you can use either form:

☐ I've never seen her **dance**. *or* I've never seen her **dancing**.

We use these structures with **see** and **hear**, and a number of other verbs:

☐ I didn't **hear** you **come** in. (you came in – I didn't hear this)
☐ Liz suddenly **felt** somebody **touch** her on the shoulder.
☐ Did you **notice** anyone **go** out?

☐ I could **hear** it **raining**. (it was raining – I could hear it)
☐ The missing children were last **seen playing** near the river.
☐ **Listen to** the birds **singing**!
☐ Can you **smell** something **burning**?
☐ I **found** Sue in my room **reading** my letters.

67.1 Complete the answers to the questions.

1	Did anybody go out?	I don't think so. I didn't see __anybody go out__ .
2	Has Sarah arrived yet?	Yes, I think I heard her _____ .
3	How do you know I took the money?	I know because I saw you _____ .
4	Did the doorbell ring?	I don't think so. I didn't hear _____ .
5	Can Tom play the piano?	I've never heard _____ .
6	Did I lock the door when I went out?	Yes, I saw _____ .
7	How did the woman fall?	I don't know. I didn't see _____ .

67.2 In each of these situations you and a friend saw, heard or smelt something. Look at the pictures and complete the sentences.

1 _Look! There's Kate._
2 _Look! There's Dave and Helen._
3
4 _Listen! That's Bill._
5 _Can you smell burning?_ / _Yes! It's the dinner._
Look! There's Clare.
Look! There's Linda.

1 __We saw Kate waiting for a bus__ .
2 We saw Dave and Helen _____ .
3 We saw _____ in a restaurant.
4 We heard _____ .
5 We could _____ .
6 _____ .

67.3 Complete these sentences. Use the following verbs (in the correct form):

climb ~~come~~ crawl cry explode ride run say ~~sing~~ slam sleep tell

1 Listen to the birds __singing__ !
2 I didn't hear you __come__ in.
3 We listened to the old man _____ his story from beginning to end.
4 Listen! Can you hear a baby _____ ?
5 I looked out of the window and saw Dan _____ his bike along the road.
6 I thought I heard somebody _____ 'Hi', so I looked round.
7 We watched two men _____ across the garden and _____ through an open window into the house.
8 Everybody heard the bomb _____ . It was a tremendous noise.
9 Oh! I can feel something _____ up my leg! It must be an insect.
10 I heard somebody _____ the door in the middle of the night. It woke me up.
11 When we got home, we found a cat _____ on the kitchen table.

-ing clauses
(Feeling tired, I went to bed early.)

A Study these situations:

> Joe was playing football. He hurt his knee.
> You can say:
> > ☐ Joe hurt his knee **playing football**.
>
> You were feeling tired. So you went to bed early.
> You can say:
> > ☐ **Feeling tired**, I went to bed early.
>
> 'Playing football' and 'feeling tired' are **-ing** clauses.
> If the **-ing** clause is at the beginning of the sentence (as in the second example), we write a comma (,) after it.

B When two things happen at the same time, you can use an **-ing** clause.
> ☐ Kate is in the kitchen **making coffee**.
> > (= she is in the kitchen *and* she is making coffee)
> ☐ A man ran out of the house **shouting**.
> > (= he ran out of the house *and* he was shouting)
> ☐ Do something! Don't just stand there **doing nothing!**

We also use **-ing** when one action happens during another action. We use **-ing** for the longer action:
> ☐ Joe hurt his knee **playing football**. (= while he was playing)
> ☐ Did you cut yourself **shaving**? (= while you were shaving)

You can also use **-ing** after **while** or **when**:
> ☐ Jim hurt his knee **while playing** football.
> ☐ Be careful **when crossing** the road. (= when you are crossing)

C When one action happens before another action, we use **having** (**done**) for the first action:
> ☐ **Having found** a hotel, we looked for somewhere to have dinner.
> ☐ **Having finished** her work, she went home.

You can also say **after -ing**:
> ☐ **After finishing** her work, she went home.

If one short action follows another short action, you can use the simple **-ing** form (**doing** instead of **having done**) for the first action:
> ☐ **Taking** a key out of his pocket, he opened the door.

These structures are used more in written English than in spoken English.

D You can use an **-ing** clause to explain something, or to say why somebody does something. The **-ing** clause usually comes at the beginning of the sentence:
> ☐ **Feeling tired**, I went to bed early. (= because I felt tired)
> ☐ **Being** unemployed, he hasn't got much money. (= because he is unemployed)
> ☐ **Not having** a car, she finds it difficult to get around.
> > (= because she doesn't have a car)
> ☐ **Having** already **seen** the film twice, I didn't want to go to the cinema.
> > (= because I had already seen it twice)

These structures are used more in written English than in spoken English.

-ing and -ed clauses → Unit 97

68.1 Choose from Box A and Box B to make sentences. Use an **–ing** clause.

A	
	1 ~~Kate was in the kitchen.~~
	2 Diane was sitting in an armchair.
	3 Sue opened the door carefully.
	4 Sarah went out.
	5 Linda was in London for two years.
	6 Mary walked around the town.

B	
	She was trying not to make a noise.
	She looked at the sights and took photographs.
	She said she would be back in an hour.
	She was reading a book.
	~~She was making coffee.~~
	She worked as a tourist guide.

1   *Kate was in the kitchen making coffee.*
2 Diane was sitting ....
3 Sue ....
4 ....
5 ....
6 ....

68.2 Make one sentence from two using an **–ing** clause.

1 Joe was playing football. He hurt his knee.   *Joe hurt his knee playing football.*
2 I was watching television. I fell asleep.
   I ....
3 A friend of mine slipped and fell. He was getting off a bus.
   A friend of mine ....
4 I was walking home in the rain. I got very wet.
   I ....
5 Laura was driving to work yesterday. She had an accident.
....
6 Two firefighters were overcome by smoke. They were trying to put out the fire.
....

68.3 Make sentences beginning **Having** ... .

1 She finished her work. Then she went home.   *Having finished her work, she went home.*
2 We bought our tickets. Then we went into the theatre.
....
3 They had dinner and then they continued their journey.
....
4 After I'd done the shopping, I went for a cup of coffee.
....

68.4 Make sentences beginning **–ing** or **Not –ing** (like those in Section D). Sometimes you need to begin with **Having** (done something).

1 I felt tired. So I went to bed early.
   Feeling tired, I went to bed early.
2 I thought they might be hungry. So I offered them something to eat.
....
3 She is a foreigner. So she needs a visa to work in this country.
....
4 I didn't know his phone number. So I wasn't able to contact him.
....
5 Sarah has travelled a lot. So she knows a lot about other countries.
....
6 I wasn't able to speak the local language. So I had trouble communicating.
....
7 We had spent nearly all our money. So we couldn't afford to stay at a hotel.

A

A noun can be *countable* or *uncountable*:

Countable
- □ I eat **a banana** every day.
- □ I like **bananas**.

Banana is a *countable* noun.

A countable noun can be singular (**banana**) or plural (**bananas**).

We can use numbers with countable nouns. So we can say 'one banana', 'two bananas' etc.

Examples of nouns usually countable:
- □ Kate was singing **a song**.
- □ There's **a nice beach** near here.
- □ Do you have **a ten-pound note**?
- □ It wasn't your fault. It was **an accident**.
- □ There are no **batteries** in the radio.
- □ We haven't got enough **cups**.

Uncountable
- □ I eat **rice** every day.
- □ I like **rice**.

Rice is an *uncountable* noun.

An uncountable noun has only one form (**rice**).

We cannot use numbers with uncountable nouns. We cannot say 'one rice', 'two rices' etc.

Examples of nouns usually uncountable:
- □ Kate was listening to (some) **music**.
- □ There's **sand** in my shoes.
- □ Do you have any **money**?
- □ It wasn't your fault. It was bad **luck**.
- □ There is no **electricity** in this house.
- □ We haven't got enough **water**.

B

You can use **a/an** with singular countable nouns:

a beach   a student   an umbrella

You cannot use singular countable nouns alone (without **a/the/my** etc.):
- □ I want **a banana**. (*not* I want banana)
- □ There's been **an accident**. (*not* There's been accident)

You can use *plural* countable nouns alone:
- □ I like **bananas**. (= bananas in general)
- □ **Accidents** can be prevented.

You cannot normally use **a/an** with uncountable nouns. We do not say 'a sand', 'a music', 'a rice'.
But you can often use **a … of**. For example:
a bowl / a packet / a grain of rice

You can use uncountable nouns alone (without **the/my/some** etc.):
- □ I eat **rice** every day.
- □ There's **blood** on your shirt.
- □ Can you hear **music**?

C

You can use **some** and **any** with plural countable nouns:
- □ We sang **some songs**.
- □ Did you buy **any apples**?

We use **many** and **few** with plural countable nouns:
- □ We didn't take **many photographs**.
- □ I have a **few things** to do.

You can use **some** and **any** with uncountable nouns:
- □ We listened to **some music**.
- □ Did you buy **any apple juice**?

We use **much** and **little** with uncountable nouns:
- □ We didn't do **much shopping**.
- □ I have a **little work** to do.

Countable and uncountable 2 → Unit 70   **Some and any** → Unit 85   **Many/much/few/little** → Unit 87
Children / the children → Unit 75

138

Exercises

69.1 Some of these sentences need **a/an**. Correct the sentences where necessary.

1 Joe goes everywhere by bike. He hasn't got car.   *He hasn't got a car.*
2 Helen was listening to music when I arrived.   OK
3 We went to very nice restaurant last weekend.   ✓
4 I clean my teeth with toothpaste.   ✓
5 I use toothbrush to clean my teeth.   *a tooth*
6 Can you tell me if there's bank near here?   *a*
7 My brother works for insurance company in London.
8 I don't like violence.
9 Can you smell paint?
10 When we were in Rome, we stayed in big hotel.   *a big*
11 We need petrol. I hope we come to petrol station soon.   *a*
12 I wonder if you can help me. I have problem.   *a*
13 I like your suggestion. It's very interesting idea.
14 John has got interview for job tomorrow.   *an*
15 I like volleyball. It's good game.
16 Liz doesn't usually wear jewellery.   *a*
17 Jane was wearing beautiful necklace.   *a*

69.2 Complete the sentences using the following words. Use **a/an** where necessary.

accident   biscuit   blood   coat   decision   electricity
interview   key   moment   music   question   sugar

1 It wasn't your fault. It was *an accident* .
2 Listen! Can you hear *music* ?
3 I couldn't get into the house because I didn't have *a key* .
4 It's very warm today. Why are you wearing *a coat* ?
5 Do you take *sugar* in your coffee?
6 Are you hungry? Would you like *a biscuit* with your coffee?
7 Our lives would be very difficult without *electricity* .
8 'I had *an interview* for a job yesterday.'   'Did you? How did it go?'
9 The heart pumps *blood* through the body.
10 Excuse me, but can I ask you *a question* ?
11 I'm not ready yet. Can you wait *a moment* , please?
12 We can't delay much longer. We have to make *a decision* soon.

69.3 Complete the sentences using the following words. Sometimes the word needs to be plural (**-s**), and sometimes you need to use **a/an**.

air   day   friend   language   letter   meat
patience   people   photograph   queue   space   umbrella

1 I had my camera, but I didn't take any *photographs* .
2 There are seven *days* in a week.
3 A vegetarian is a person who doesn't eat *meat* .
4 Outside the cinema there was *a queue* of people waiting to see the film.
5 I'm not very good at writing *letters* .
6 Last night I went out with some *friends* of mine.
7 There were very few *people* in town today. The streets were almost empty.
8 I'm going out for a walk. I need some fresh *air* .
9 Gary always wants things quickly. He hasn't got much *patience* .
10 I think it's going to rain. Do you have *an umbrella* I could borrow?
11 Do you speak any foreign *languages* ?
12 Our flat is very small. We haven't got much *space* .

Countable and uncountable 2

A Many nouns can be used as countable or uncountable nouns, usually with a difference in meaning. Compare:

Countable	*Uncountable*
□ Did you hear **a noise** just now? (= a specific noise)	□ I can't work here. There's too much **noise**. (*not* too many noises)
□ I bought **a paper** to read. (= a newspaper)	□ I need **some paper** to write on. (= material for writing on)
□ There's **a hair** in my soup! (= one single hair)	□ You've got very long **hair**. (*not* hairs) (= all the hair on your head)
□ You can stay with us. There is **a spare room**. (= a room in a house)	□ You can't sit here. There isn't **room**. (= space)
□ I had some interesting **experiences** while I was travelling. (= things that happened to me)	□ They offered me the job because I had a lot of **experience**. (*not* experiences)
□ Enjoy your trip. Have **a good time!**	□ I can't wait. I haven't got **time**.

Coffee/tea/juice/beer etc. (drinks) are normally uncountable:
  □ I don't like **coffee** very much.
But you can say **a coffee** (= a cup of coffee), **two coffees** (= two cups) etc. :
  □ **Two** coffees and **an orange juice**, please.

B The following nouns are usually uncountable:

accommodation	behaviour	damage	luck	permission	traffic
advice	bread	furniture	luggage	progress	weather
baggage	chaos	information	news	scenery	work

You cannot use **a/an** with these nouns:
  □ I'm going to buy **some bread**. *or* ... **a loaf of bread**. (*not* a bread)
  □ Enjoy your holiday! I hope you have good **weather**. (*not* a good weather)

These nouns are not usually plural (so we do not say 'breads', 'furnitures' etc.):
  □ Where are you going to put all your **furniture**? (*not* furnitures)
  □ Let me know if you need more **information**. (*not* informations)

News is uncountable, not plural:
  □ The **news was** very depressing. (*not* The news were)

Travel (*noun*) means 'travelling in general' (uncountable). We do not say 'a travel' to mean **a trip** or **a journey**:
  □ They spend a lot of money on **travel**.
  □ We had **a very good trip/journey**. (*not* a good travel)

Compare these countable and uncountable nouns:

Countable	*Uncountable*
□ I'm looking for **a job**.	□ I'm looking for **work**. (*not* a work)
□ What **a beautiful view!**	□ What beautiful **scenery!**
□ It's **a nice day** today.	□ It's nice **weather** today.
□ We had a lot of **bags** and **cases**.	□ We had a lot of **baggage/luggage**.
□ **These chairs** are mine.	□ **This furniture** is mine.
□ That's **a good suggestion**.	□ That's good **advice**.

Exercises

70.1 Which of the <u>underlined</u> parts of these sentences is correct?

1 'Did you hear ~~noise~~ / a noise just now?' 'No, I didn't hear anything.' (<u>a noise</u> *is correct*).
2 a If you want to know the news, you can read paper / (a paper.)
   b I want to print some documents, but the printer is out of paper / papers.
3 a I thought there was somebody in the house because there was light / (a light) on inside.
   b (Light / A light) comes from the sun.
4 a I was in a hurry this morning. I didn't have (time) / a time for breakfast.
   b 'Did you enjoy your holiday?' 'Yes, we had wonderful time / (a wonderful time.')
5 This is nice room / (a nice room.) Did you decorate it yourself?
6 Sue was very helpful. She gave us some very useful (advice) / advices.
7 Did you have (nice weather) / a nice weather when you were away?
8 We were very unfortunate. We had (bad luck) / a bad luck.
9 Is it difficult to find a work / (job) at the moment?
10 Our travel / (journey) from Paris to Moscow by train was very tiring.
11 When the fire alarm rang, there was (total chaos) / a total chaos.
12 I had to buy a / (some) bread because I wanted to make some sandwiches.
13 Bad news don't / (doesn't) make people happy.
14 (Your hair is) / Your hairs are too long. You should have (it) / them cut.
15 (The damage) / the damages caused by the storm will cost a lot to repair.

70.2 Complete the sentences using the following words. Use the plural (-s) where necessary.

advice	chair	experience	experience	furniture	hair
information	job	~~luggage~~	permission	progress	work

1 I didn't have much *luggage* – just two small bags.
2 They'll tell you all you want to know. They'll give you plenty of *information* .
3 There is room for everybody to sit down. There are plenty of *chairs* .
4 We have no *furniture* , not even a bed or a table.
5 'What does Alan look like?' 'He's got a long beard and very short *hair* .'
6 Carla's English is better than it was. She's made *progress* .
7 Mike is unemployed. He can't get a *job* .
8 Mike is unemployed. He can't get *work* .
9 If you want to leave early, you have to ask for *permission* .
10 I didn't know what to do. So I asked Chris for *advice* .
11 I don't think Dan will get the job. He doesn't have enough *experience* .
12 Paul has done many interesting things. He could write a book about his *experiences*

70.3 What do you say in these situations? Complete each sentence using one of the words from Section B.

1 Your friends have just arrived at the station. You can't see any cases or bags. You ask them:
   Have *you got any luggage* ?
2 You go into the tourist office. You want to know about places to see in the town. You say:
   I'd like *to see places* .
3 You are a student. You want your teacher to advise you about which courses to do. You say:
   Can you give me *advice which course I have to do* ?
4 You want to watch the news on TV, but you don't know when it is on. You ask your friend:
   What time ?
5 You are at the top of a mountain. You can see a very long way. It's beautiful. You say:
   It , isn't it?
6 You look out of the window. The weather is horrible: cold, wet and windy. You say:
   What !

Countable nouns with **a/an** and **some**

A Countable nouns can be *singular* or *plural*:

a **dog**	a **child**	the **evening**	this **party**	an **umbrella**
dogs	some **children**	the **evenings**	these **parties**	two **umbrellas**

Before singular countable nouns you can use **a/an**:
- ☐ Goodbye! Have **a** nice **evening**.
- ☐ Do you need **an umbrella**?

You cannot use singular countable nouns alone (without **a/the/my** etc.):
- ☐ She never wears **a** hat. (*not* She never wears hat)
- ☐ Be careful of **the** dog. (*not* Be careful of dog)
- ☐ What **a** beautiful day!
- ☐ I've got **a** headache.

B We use **a/an** ... to say what kind of thing or person something/somebody is:
- ☐ That's **a nice table**.

In the plural we use the noun alone (*not* some ...):
- ☐ Those are **nice chairs**. (*not* some nice chairs)

Compare singular and plural:

☐ A dog is **an animal**.	☐ Dogs are **animals**.
☐ I'm **an optimist**.	☐ We're **optimists**.
☐ Tim's father is **a doctor**.	☐ Most of my friends are **students**.
☐ Are you **a good driver**?	☐ Are they **good students**?
☐ Jill is **a really nice person**.	☐ Jill's parents are **really nice people**.
☐ What **a lovely dress**!	☐ What **awful shoes**!

We say that somebody has **a long nose** / **a nice face** / **blue eyes** / **small hands** etc. :

☐ Jack has got **a** long **nose**. (*not* the long nose)	☐ Jack has got **blue eyes**. (*not* the blue eyes)

Remember to use **a/an** when you say what somebody's job is:
- ☐ Sandra is **a nurse**. (*not* Sandra is nurse)
- ☐ Would you like to be **an English teacher**?

C You can use **some** with plural countable nouns. We use **some** in two ways.

(1) **Some** = a number of / a few of / a pair of:
- ☐ I've seen **some** good **films** recently. (*not* I've seen good films)
- ☐ **Some friends** of mine are coming to stay at the weekend.
- ☐ I need **some** new **sunglasses**. (= a new pair of sunglasses)

Do *not* use **some** when you are talking about things in general (see Unit 75):
- ☐ I love **bananas**. (*not* some bananas)
- ☐ My aunt is a writer. She writes **books**. (*not* some books)

Sometimes you can make sentences with or without **some** (with no difference in meaning):
- ☐ There are (**some**) eggs in the fridge if you're hungry.

(2) **Some** = some but not all:
- ☐ **Some children** learn very quickly. (but not all children)
- ☐ Tomorrow there will be rain in **some places**, but most of the country will be dry.

Countable and uncountable → Units 69–70   A/an and the → Unit 72   Some and any → Unit 85

Exercises

71.1 What are these things? Use a dictionary if necessary.

1 an ant? _It's an insect._
2 ants and bees? _They're insects._
3 a cauliflower? _This is cauliflower_
4 chess? _It is chess_
5 a violin, a trumpet and a flute?
 They are musical instrument
6 a skyscraper? ....

7 Earth, Mars, Venus and Jupiter?
8 a tulip? ....
9 the Nile, the Rhine and the Mississippi?

10 a pigeon, an eagle and a crow?

Who were these people?

11 Beethoven? _He was a composer._
12 Shakespeare? ....
13 Albert Einstein?
....
14 Washington, Lincoln and Kennedy?

15 Marilyn Monroe?

16 Elvis Presley and John Lennon?

17 Van Gogh, Renoir and Picasso?

71.2 Read about what these people do, and say what their jobs are. Choose from:

chef   interpreter   journalist   ~~nurse~~   plumber   surgeon   travel agent   waiter

1 Sarah looks after patients in hospital. _She's a nurse._
2 Gary works in a restaurant. He brings the food to the tables. He _is a waiter_
3 Martina arranges people's holidays for them. She _is a travel agent_
4 Kevin works in a hospital. He operates on people. _he is a surgeon_
5 Jonathan cooks in a restaurant. _he is a chef_
6 Jane writes articles for a newspaper. _he is a journalist_
7 Dave installs and repairs water pipes. _he is plumber_
8 Linda translates what people are saying from one language into another, so that they can understand each other. _her is an interpreter_

71.3 Put in a/an or some where necessary. If no word is necessary, leave the space empty.

1 I've seen _some_ good films recently.
2 What's wrong with you? Have you got _a_ headache?
3 I know a lot of people. Most of them are _—_ students.
4 When I was _a_ child, I used to be very shy.
5 Would you like to be _an_ actor? ✓
6 Do you collect _some_ stamps?
7 What _a_ beautiful garden!
8 _Some_ birds, for example the penguin, cannot fly.
9 Do you enjoy going to _—_ concerts?
10 I've been walking for three hours. I've got _some_ sore feet.
11 I don't feel very well this morning. I've got _a_ sore throat.
12 Maria speaks _some_ English, but not very much.
13 It's a pity we don't have _a_ camera. I'd like to take _a_ photograph of that house.
14 Those are _—_ nice shoes. Where did you get them?
15 I'm going shopping. I want to buy _some_ new shoes.
16 You need _a_ visa to visit _some_ countries, but not all of them.
17 Jane is _a_ teacher. Her parents were _—_ teachers too.
18 I don't believe him. He's _a_ liar. He's always telling _some_ lies.

A/an and the

Study this example:

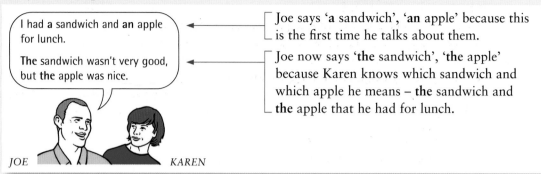

I had **a** sandwich and **an** apple for lunch.

The sandwich wasn't very good, but **the** apple was nice.

⎡ Joe says 'a sandwich', 'an apple' because this
⎣ is the first time he talks about them.

⎡ Joe now says 'the sandwich', 'the apple'
│ because Karen knows which sandwich and
│ which apple he means – **the** sandwich and
⎣ **the** apple that he had for lunch.

JOE   KAREN

Compare **a** and **the** in these examples:

- ☐ **A** man and **a** woman were sitting opposite me. **The** man was American, but I think **the** woman was British.
- ☐ When we were on holiday, we stayed at **a** hotel. Sometimes we ate at **the** hotel and sometimes we went to **a** restaurant.

We use **the** when we are thinking of a specific thing. Compare **a/an** and **the**:

- ☐ Tim sat down on **a** chair. (perhaps one of many chairs in the room)
  Tim sat down on **the** chair **nearest the door**. (a specific chair)
- ☐ Paula is looking for **a** job. (not a specific job)
  Did Paula get **the** job **she applied for**? (a specific job)
- ☐ Have you got **a** car? (not a specific car)
  I cleaned **the** car yesterday. (= my car)

We use **the** when it is clear in the situation which thing or person we mean. For example, in a room we talk about **the** light / **the** floor / **the** ceiling / **the** door / **the** carpet etc. :

- ☐ Can you turn off **the** light, please? (= the light in this room)
- ☐ I took a taxi to **the** station. (= the station in that town)
- ☐ *(in a shop)* I'd like to speak to **the** manager, please. (= the manager of this shop)

In the same way, we say (go to) **the** bank, **the** post office:

- ☐ I have to go to **the** bank and then I'm going to **the** post office. (The speaker is usually thinking of a specific bank or post office.)

We also say (go to) **the** doctor / **the** dentist:

- ☐ Caroline isn't very well. She's gone to **the** doctor. (= her usual doctor)
- ☐ I don't like going to **the** dentist.

Compare **the** and **a**:

- ☐ I have to go to **the** bank today.
  Is there **a** bank near here?
- ☐ I don't like going to **the** dentist.
  My sister is **a** dentist.

We say 'once **a** week / three times **a** day / £1.50 **a** kilo' etc. :

- ☐ 'How often do you go to the cinema?' 'About once **a** month.'
- ☐ 'How much are those potatoes?' '£1.50 **a** kilo.'
- ☐ Helen works eight hours **a** day, six days **a** week.

A/an → Unit 71   **The** → Units 73–78

72.1 Put in a/an or the.

1 This morning I bought ___*a*___ newspaper and ___*a*___ magazine. ___the___ newspaper is in my bag, but I can't remember where I put ___the___ magazine.

2 I saw ___an___ accident this morning. ___The___ car crashed into ___the/a___ tree. ___The___ driver of ___a/the___ car wasn't hurt, but ___the___ car was badly damaged.

3 There are two cars parked outside: ___the___ blue one and ___the___ grey one. ___The___ blue one belongs to my neighbours; I don't know who ___the___ owner of ___the___ grey one is.

4 My friends live in ___an___ old house in ___a___ small village. There is ___a___ beautiful garden behind ___the___ house. I would like to have ___a___ garden like that.

72.2 Put in a/an or the.

1 a This house is very nice. Has it got ___a___ garden?

  b It's a beautiful day. Let's sit in ___the___ garden.

  c I like living in this house, but it's a pity that ___the___ garden is so small.

2 a Can you recommend ___a___ good restaurant?

  b We had dinner in ___a___ very nice restaurant.

  c We had dinner in ___the___ best restaurant in town.

3 a She has ___a___ French name, but in fact she's English, not French.

  b What's ___the___ name of that man we met yesterday?

  c We stayed at a very nice hotel – I can't remember ___the___ name now.

4 a There isn't ___an___ airport near where I live. ___The___ nearest airport is 70 miles away.

  b Our flight was delayed. We had to wait at ___the___ airport for three hours.

  c Excuse me, please. Can you tell me how to get to ___the___ airport?

5 a 'Are you going away next week?' 'No, ___the___ week after next.'

  b I'm going away for ___a___ week in September.

  c Gary has a part-time job. He works three mornings ___a___ week.

72.3 Put in a/an or the where necessary.

1 Would you like apple? ___Would you like an apple?___

2 How often do you go to dentist? ___the___

3 Could you close door, please? ___the___

4 I'm sorry. I didn't mean to do that. It was mistake. ___a___

5 Excuse me, where is bus station, please? ___the___

6 I have problem. Can you help me? ___a___

7 I'm just going to post office. I won't be long. ___the___

8 There were no chairs, so we sat on floor. ___the___

9 Have you finished with book I lent you? ___the___

10 My sister has just got job in bank in Manchester. ___a / the___

11 We live in small flat in city centre. ___a / the___

12 There's supermarket at end of street I live in. ___a / the___

72.4 Answer these questions about yourself. Where possible, use the structure in Section D (**once a week / three times a day** etc.).

1 How often do you go to the cinema? ___Three or four times a year.___

2 How much does it cost to hire a car in your country? ___About £20 a day.___

3 How often do you go to the cinema? ___once a week___

4 How often do you go away on holiday? ___about once a year___

5 What's the usual speed limit in towns in your country? ___about 30 miles a day___

6 How much sleep do you need? ___about 8 hours a day___

7 How often do you go out in the evening? ___twice a week___

8 How much television do you watch (on average)?

→ Additional exercise 29 (page 319)

The 1

A

We use **the** when there is only one of something:

□ What is **the** longest river in **the** world? (there is only one longest river)

□ **The** earth goes round **the** sun and **the** moon goes round **the** earth.

□ Have you ever crossed **the** equator?

□ I'm going away at **the** end of this month.

Don't forget **the**:

□ Paris is **the** capital of France. (*not* Paris is capital of …)

But we use **a/an** to say what kind of thing something is (see Unit 71B). Compare **the** and **a**:

□ **The** sun is **a** star. (= one of many stars)

□ **The** hotel we stayed at was **a** very nice hotel.

B

We say: **the sky, the sea, the ground, the country, the environment.**

□ We looked up at all the stars in **the sky**. (*not* in sky)

□ Would you like to live in **the country**? (= not in a town)

□ We must do more to protect **the environment**. (= the natural world around us)

But we say **space** (without **the**) when we mean 'space in the universe'. Compare:

□ There are millions of stars **in space**. (*not* in the space)

□ I tried to park my car, but **the space** was too small.

C

We use **the** before **same** (**the same**):

□ Your pullover is **the same** colour as mine. (*not* is same colour)

□ 'Are these keys **the same**?' 'No, they're different.'

D

We say: (go to) **the cinema, the theatre.**

□ I go to **the cinema** a lot, but I haven't been to **the theatre** for ages.

When we say **the cinema / the theatre**, we do not necessarily mean a specific cinema or theatre.

We usually say **the radio**, but **television** (without **the**). Compare:

□ I listen to **the radio** a lot.   *but*   I watch **television** a lot.

□ We heard the news on **the radio**. *but*   We watched the news on **television**.

The television = the television set:

□ Can you turn off **the television**, please?

E

Breakfast   lunch   dinner

We do *not* normally use **the** with the names of meals (**breakfast, lunch** etc.):

□ What did you have for **breakfast**?

□ We had **lunch** in a very nice restaurant.

□ What time is **dinner**?

But we use **a** if there is an adjective before **breakfast, lunch** etc. :

□ We had **a** very **nice lunch**. (*not* We had very nice lunch)

F

Platform 5   Room 126 etc.

We do *not* use **the** before *noun + number*. For example, we say:

□ Our train leaves from **Platform 5**. (*not* the Platform 5)

□ *(in a shop)* Have you got these shoes in **size 43**? (*not* the size 43)

In the same way, we say: **Room 126** (in a hotel), **page 29** (of a book), **question 3** (in an exam), **Gate 10** (at an airport) etc.

73.1 Put in **the** or **a/an** where necessary. If no word is necessary, leave the space empty.

1 A: Where did you have ___—___ lunch?
  B: We went to ___a___ restaurant.
2 A: Did you have ___a___ nice holiday?
  B: Yes, it was ___the___ best holiday I've ever had.
3 A: Where's ___the___ nearest shop?
  B: There's one at ___the___ end of this street.
4 A: Do you often listen to ___the___ radio?
  B: No. In fact I haven't got ___the___ radio.
5 A: Would you like to travel in ___the___ space?
  B: Yes, I'd love to go to ___the___ moon.
6 A: Do you go to ___the___ cinema very often?
  B: No, not very often. But I watch a lot of films on ___a___ television.
7 A: It was ___the___ nice day yesterday, wasn't it?
  B: Yes, it was beautiful. We went for a walk by ___the___ sea.
8 A: What did you have for ___—___ breakfast this morning?
  B: Nothing. I never eat ___—___ breakfast.
9 A: Excuse me, where is ___a___ Room 25, please?
  B: It's on ___the___ second floor.
10 A: We spent all our money because we stayed at ___the___ most expensive hotel in town.
  B: Why didn't you stay at ___a___ cheaper hotel?

73.2 Put in **the** where necessary. If you don't need **the**, leave the space empty.

1 I haven't been to ___the___ cinema for ages.
2 I lay down on ___the___ ground and looked up at ___the___ sky.
3 Sarah spends most of her free time watching ___the___ television.
4 ___the___ television was on, but nobody was watching it.
5 Lisa and I arrived at ___the___ same time.
6 Have you had ___—___ dinner yet?
7 You'll find ___the___ information you need at ___the___ top of ___—___ page 15.
8 What's ___the___ capital city of Canada?

73.3 Put in **the** or **a/an** where necessary. (See Unit 72 for **a/an** and **the** if necessary.)

1 Sun is star. ___The sun is a star.___
2 Paul lives in small village in country. _____
3 Moon goes round earth every 27 days. ___The Moon___
4 I'm fed up with doing same thing every day. _____
5 It was very hot day. It was hottest day of year. _____
6 I don't usually have lunch, but I always eat good breakfast. _____
7 If you live in foreign country, you should try and learn language. _____
8 We missed our train because we were waiting on wrong platform. _____
9 Next train to London leaves from Platform 3. _____

73.4 Complete the sentences using the following. Use **the** where necessary.

breakfast   cinema   ~~dinner~~   gate   Gate 21   question 8   sea

1 'Are you going out this evening?' 'Yes, after ___dinner___ .'
2 There was no wind, so ___the sea___ was very calm.
3 The test wasn't too difficult, but I couldn't answer ___question 8___ .
4 'I'm going to ___the cinema___ tonight.' 'Are you? What are you going to see?'
5 I didn't have time for ___breakfast___ this morning because I was in a hurry.
6 Oh, ___the gate___ is open. I must have forgotten to shut it.
7 (airport announcement) Flight AB123 to Rome is now boarding at ___Gate 21___ .

→ Additional exercise 29 (page 319)

The 2 (school / the school etc.)

A

Compare **school** and **the school**:

ALISON

Alison is ten years old. Every day she goes to **school**. She's at **school** now. **School** begins at 9 and finishes at 3.

We say a child goes to **school** or is at **school** (as a pupil). We are not necessarily thinking of a specific school. We are thinking of **school** as a general idea.

Today Alison's mother wants to speak to her daughter's teacher. So she has gone to **the school** to see her. She's at **the school** now.

Alison's mother is not a pupil. She is not 'at school', she doesn't 'go to school'. If she wants to see Alison's teacher, she goes to **the school** (= Alison's school, a specific building).

B

We use **prison, hospital, university, college** and **church** in a similar way. We do not use **the** when we are thinking of the general idea of these places and what they are used for. Compare:

☐ Ken's brother is in **prison** for robbery. (He is a prisoner. We are not thinking of a specific prison.)

☐ Joe had an accident last week. He was taken to **hospital**. He's still in **hospital** now. (as a patient)

☐ When I leave **school**, I want to go to **university/college**.

☐ Sally's father goes to **church** every Sunday. (to a religious service)

☐ Ken went to **the prison** to visit his brother.
(He went as a visitor, not as a prisoner.)

☐ Jane has gone to **the hospital** to visit Joe. She's at **the hospital** now. (as a visitor)

☐ Excuse me, where is **the university**, please? (= the university buildings)

☐ Some workmen went to **the church** to repair the roof. (not for a religious service)

With most other places, you need **the**. For example, **the cinema**, **the bank** (see Units 72C and 73D).

C

Bed   work   home

We say **go to bed / be in bed** etc. (*not* the bed):

☐ It's time to go to **bed** now.

☐ Do you ever have breakfast in **bed**?

but ☐ I sat down on **the bed**. (a specific piece of furniture)

go to work / be at work / start work / finish work etc. (*not* the work):

☐ Chris didn't go to **work** yesterday.

☐ What time do you usually finish **work**?

go home / come home / arrive home / get home / be at home etc. :

☐ It's late. Let's go **home**.

☐ Will you be at **home** tomorrow afternoon?

D

We say **go to sea / be at sea** (without **the**) when the meaning is 'go/be on a voyage':

☐ Keith works on ships. He is at **sea** most of the time.

but ☐ I'd like to live near **the sea**.

☐ It can be dangerous to swim in **the sea**.

The → Units 72–73, 75–78   **Prepositions** (at school / in hospital etc.) → Units 123–125   **Home** → Unit 126D
American English → Appendix 7

148

74.1 Complete each sentence using a preposition (to/at/in etc.) + one of these words:

bed   home   ~~hospital~~   hospital   prison   school   university   work

1 Two people were injured in the accident and were taken _to hospital_ .
2 In Britain, children from the age of five have to go _to school_ .
3 Mark didn't go out last night. He stayed _at the home_ .
4 There is a lot of traffic in the morning when everybody is going _to work_ .
5 Cathy's mother has just had an operation. She is still _in the hospital_ .
6 When Julia leaves school, she wants to study economics _at the university_ .
7 Bill never gets up before 9 o'clock. It's 8.30 now, so he is still _in the bed_ .
8 If you commit a serious crime, you could be sent _to prison_ .

74.2 Complete the sentences with the word given (**school** etc.). Use **the** where necessary.

1 (**school**)
  a Every term parents are invited to _the school_ to meet the teachers.
  b Why aren't your children at _school_ today? Are they ill?
  c When he was younger, Ted hated _to school_ .
  d What time does _school_ usually start in the mornings in your country?
  e A: How do your children get home from _the school_ ? By bus?
    B: No, they walk. _The school_ isn't very far.
  f What sort of job does Jenny want to do when she leaves _school_ ?
  g There were some people waiting outside _the school_ to meet their children.

2 (**university**)
  a In your country do many people go to _the university_ ?
  b If you want to get a degree, you normally have to study at _university_ .
  c This is only a small town, but _the university_ is one of the biggest in the country.

3 (**hospital**)
  a My brother has always been very healthy. He's never been in _hospital_ .
  b When Ann was ill, I went to _the hospital_ to visit her. When I was there,
    I met Lisa who is a nurse at _the hospital_ .
  c Peter was injured in an accident and was kept in _the hospital_ for a few days.

4 (**church**)
  a John's mother is a regular churchgoer. She goes to _the church_ every Sunday.
  b John himself doesn't go to _church_ .
  c John went to _the church_ to take some photographs of the building.

5 (**prison**)
  a In some places people are in _prison_ because of their political beliefs.
  b A few days ago the fire brigade were called to _the prison_ to put out a fire.
  c The judge decided to fine the man £500 instead of sending him to _the prison_ .

6 (**home/work/bed**)
  a I like to read in _bed_ before I go to sleep.
  b It's nice to travel around, but there's no place like _the home_ !
  c Shall we meet after _the work_ tomorrow evening?
  d If I'm feeling tired, I go to _the bed_ early.
  e What time do you usually start _work_ in the morning?
  f The economic situation was very bad. Many people were out of _the work_ .

7 (**sea**)
  a There's a nice view from the window. You can see _the sea_ .
  b It was a long voyage. We were at _sea_ for four weeks.
  c I love swimming in _the sea_ .

→ Additional exercise 29 (page 319)

The 3 (children / the children)

A

When we are talking about things or people in general, we do *not* use **the**:

- □ I'm afraid of **dogs**. (*not* the dogs)
  (**dogs** = dogs in general, not a specific group of dogs)
- □ **Doctors** are paid more than **teachers**.
- □ Do you collect **stamps**?
- □ **Crime** is a problem in most big cities. (*not* The crime)
- □ **Life** has changed a lot in the last thirty years. (*not* The life)
- □ Do you like **classical music / Chinese food / fast cars**?
- □ My favourite sport is **football/skiing/athletics**.
- □ My favourite subject at school was **history/physics/English**.

We say '**most** people / **most** books / **most** cars' etc. (*not* the most …):

- □ **Most hotels** accept credit cards. (*not* The most hotels)

B

We use **the** when we mean specific things or people.
Compare:

In general (without **the**)	*Specific people or things* (with **the**)
□ **Children** learn from playing. (= children in general)	□ We took **the children** to the zoo. (= a specific group, perhaps the speaker's children)
□ I couldn't live without **music**.	□ The film wasn't very good, but I liked **the music**. (= the music in the film)
□ All **cars** have wheels.	□ All **the cars** in this car park belong to people who work here.
□ **Sugar** isn't very good for you.	□ Can you pass **the sugar**, please? (= the sugar on the table)
□ **English people** drink a lot of tea. (= English people in general)	□ **The English people I know** drink a lot of tea. (= only the English people I know, not English people in general)

C

The difference between 'something in general' and 'something specific' is not always very clear.
Compare:

In general (without **the**)	*Specific people or things* (with **the**)
□ I like working with **people**. (= people in general)	
□ I like working with **people who are lively**. (not all people, but 'people who are lively' is still a general idea)	□ I like **the people I work with**. (= a specific group of people)
□ Do you like **coffee**? (= coffee in general)	
□ Do you like **strong black coffee**? (not all coffee, but 'strong black coffee' is still a general idea)	□ Did you like **the coffee we had after dinner last night**? (= specific coffee)

The 1–2 → Units 73–74   The + adjective (the young / the English etc.) → Unit 76

Exercises

75.1 Choose four of these things and write whether you like them or not:

boxing	cats	fast food restaurants	football	~~hot weather~~
maths	opera	small children	rock music	zoos

Begin each sentence with one of these:

I like … / I don't like …   I don't mind …
I love … / I hate …   I'm interested in … / I'm not interested in …

1 _I don't like hot weather very much._ ....

2 ....

3 ....

4 ....

5 ....

75.2 Complete the sentences using the following. Use **the** where necessary.

~~(the) basketball~~	(the) **grass**	(the) **patience**	(the) **people**
(the) **questions**	(the) **meat**	~~(the) information~~	(the) **shops**
(the) **history**	(the) **water**	(the) **spiders**	(the) **lies**

1 My favourite sport is _basketball_ .

2 _The information_ we were given wasn't correct.

3 Some people are afraid of ....

4 A vegetarian is somebody who doesn't eat ....

5 The test wasn't very difficult. I answered .... without difficulty.

6 Do you know .... who live next door?

7 .... is the study of the past.

8 George always tells the truth. He never tells ....

9 It was late when we arrived in the town, and .... were shut.

10 .... in the pool didn't look very clean, so we didn't go for a swim.

11 Don't sit on .... It's wet after the rain.

12 You need .... to teach young children.

75.3 Choose the correct form, with or without **the**.

1 I'm afraid of <u>dogs</u> / ~~the dogs~~. (<u>dogs</u> *is correct*)

2 Can you pass ~~salt~~ / <u>the salt</u>, please? (<u>the salt</u> *is correct*)

3 <u>Apples / The apples</u> are good for you.

4 Look at <u>apples / the apples</u> on that tree! They're very big.

5 <u>Women / The women</u> live longer than <u>men / the men</u>.

6 I don't drink <u>tea / the tea</u>. I don't like it.

7 We had a very good meal. <u>Vegetables / The vegetables</u> were especially good.

8 <u>Life / The life</u> is strange sometimes. Some very strange things happen.

9 I like <u>skiing / the skiing</u>, but I'm not very good at it.

10 Who are <u>people / the people</u> in this photograph?

11 What makes <u>people / the people</u> violent? What causes <u>aggression / the aggression</u>?

12 <u>All books / All the books</u> on the top shelf belong to me.

13 Don't stay in that hotel. It's very noisy and <u>beds / the beds</u> are very uncomfortable.

14 A pacifist is somebody who is against <u>war / the war</u>.

15 <u>First World War / The First World War</u> lasted from 1914 until 1918.

16 I'd like to go to Egypt and see <u>Pyramids / the Pyramids</u>.

17 Someone gave me a book about <u>history / the history</u> of <u>modern art / the modern art</u>.

18 Ron and Brenda got married, but <u>marriage / the marriage</u> didn't last very long.

19 <u>Most people / The most people</u> believe that <u>marriage / the marriage</u> and
<u>family life / the family life</u> are the basis of <u>society / the society</u>.

→ Additional exercise 29 (page 319)

The 4 (the giraffe / the telephone / the piano etc. ; the + adjective)

A

Study these sentences:
- □ **The giraffe** is the tallest of all animals.
- □ **The bicycle** is an excellent means of transport.
- □ When was **the telephone** invented?
- □ **The dollar** is the currency (= the money) of the United States.

In these examples, **the** ... does not mean one specific thing. **The giraffe** = a specific type of animal, not a specific giraffe. We use **the** (+ singular countable noun) in this way to talk about a type of animal, machine etc.

In the same way we use **the** for musical instruments:
- □ Can you play **the** guitar?
- □ **The piano** is my favourite instrument.

Compare **a** and **the**:
- □ I'd like to have **a piano**.   *but*   I can't play **the piano**.
- □ We saw **a giraffe** at the zoo.   *but*   **The giraffe** is my favourite animal.

Note that we use **man** (= human beings in general / the human race) without **the**:
- □ What do you know about the origins of **man**? (*not* the man)

B

The + adjective

We use **the** + adjective (without a noun) to talk about groups of people, especially:

the young	the rich	the sick	the blind	the injured
the old	the poor	the disabled	the deaf	the dead
the elderly	the homeless	the unemployed		

The young = young people, **the rich** = rich people etc. :
- □ Do you think **the rich** should pay higher taxes?
- □ The government has promised to provide more money to help **the homeless**.

These expressions are always *plural* in meaning. For example, you cannot say 'a young' or 'the injured' for one person. You must say 'a young **person**', 'the injured **woman**' etc.

Note that we say 'the **poor**' (*not* the poors), 'the **young**' (*not* the youngs) etc.

C

The + nationality

You can use **the** + nationality adjectives that end in -ch or -sh (**the French / the English / the Spanish** etc.) The meaning is 'the people of that country':
- □ **The French** are famous for their food. (= the people of France)

The French / the English etc. are plural in meaning. We do not say 'a French / an English'. You have to say **a Frenchman / an Englishwoman** etc.

You can also use **the** + nationality words ending in -ese (**the Chinese / the Sudanese / the Japanese** etc.):
- □ **The Chinese** invented printing.

But these words can also be singular (**a Japanese, a Sudanese** etc.).
Also **a Swiss** (singular) and **the Swiss** (= the people of Switzerland)

With other nationalities, the plural noun ends in -s. For example:
    an Italian → Italians   **a Mexican → Mexicans**   **a Turk → Turks**

With these words (**Italians** etc.), we do not normally use **the** to talk about the people in general (see Unit 75).

A/an and the → Unit 72   **The 1–3** → Units 73–75   **Names with and without the** → Units 77–78

Exercises

Unit 76

76.1 Answer the questions. Choose the right answer from the box. Don't forget **the**. Use a dictionary if necessary.

1

animals	
tiger	elephant
rabbit	cheetah
giraffe	kangaroo

2

birds	
eagle	penguin
swan	owl
parrot	robin

3

inventions	
telephone	wheel
telescope	laser
helicopter	typewriter

4

currencies	
dollar	peso
euro	rupee
rouble	yen

1 a Which of the animals is tallest? ..... the giraffe .....
  b Which animal can run fastest? .....
  c Which of these animals is found in Australia? .....
2 a Which of these birds has a long neck? .....
  b Which of these birds cannot fly? .....
  c Which bird flies at night? .....
3 a Which of these inventions is oldest? .....
  b Which one is most recent? .....
  c Which one was especially important for astronomy? .....
4 a What is the currency of India? .....
  b What is the currency of Canada? .....
  c And the currency of your country? .....

76.2 Put in **the** or **a**.
1 When was ..... the ..... telephone invented?
2 Can you play ..... musical instrument?
3 Jill plays ..... violin in an orchestra.
4 There was ..... piano in the corner of the room.
5 Can you play ..... piano?
6 Our society is based on ..... family.
7 Martin comes from ..... large family.
8 ..... computer has changed the way we live.

76.3 Complete these sentences using **the** + the following:

injured   poor   rich   sick   unemployed   ~~young~~

1 ..... The young ..... have the future in their hands.
2 Ambulances arrived at the scene of the accident and took ..... to hospital.
3 Life is all right if you have a job, but things are not so easy for ..... .
4 Julia has been a nurse all her life. She has spent her life caring for ..... .
5 In England there is an old story about a man called Robin Hood. It is said that he robbed ..... and gave the money to ..... .

76.4 What do you call the people of these countries?

	one person (a/an ...)	the people in general
1 Canada	a Canadian	Canadians
2 Germany		
3 France		
4 Russia		
5 China		
6 Brazil		
7 England		
8 and your country		

Names with and without **the** 1

A

We do *not* use **the** with names of people ('Helen', 'Helen Taylor' etc.). In the same way, we do *not* normally use **the** with names of places. For example:

continents	Africa (*not* the Africa), Europe, South America
countries, states etc.	France (*not* the France), Japan, Switzerland, Texas
islands	Sicily, Bermuda, Tasmania
cities, towns etc.	Cairo, New York, Bangkok
mountains	Everest, Etna, Kilimanjaro

But we use **the** in names with **Republic, Kingdom, States** etc. :

    the Czech **Republic**   the United **Kingdom** (**the UK**)

    the Dominican **Republic**   the United **States** of America (**the USA**)

Compare:

    ☐ Have you been to **Canada** or **the United States?**

B

When we use **Mr/Mrs/Captain/Doctor** etc. + a name, we do not use **the**. So we say:

    Mr Johnson / **Doctor** Johnson / **Captain** Johnson / **President** Johnson etc. (*not* the …)

    Uncle Robert / **Saint** Catherine / **Princess** Maria etc. (*not* the …)

Compare:

    ☐ We called **the doctor.**

    We called **Doctor** Johnson. (*not* the Doctor Johnson)

We use **mount** (= mountain) and **lake** in the same way (without **the**):

    Mount Everest (*not* the …)   **Mount** Etna   **Lake** Superior   **Lake** Constance

    ☐ They live near **the lake.**

    They live near **Lake** Constance. (*not* the Lake Constance)

C

We use **the** with the names of oceans, seas, rivers and canals:

    the Atlantic (Ocean)   **the** Red Sea   **the** Amazon

    the Indian Ocean   **the** Channel (between   **the** Nile

    the Mediterranean (Sea)   France and Britain)   **the** Suez Canal

We use **the** with the names of deserts:

    the Sahara (Desert)   **the** Gobi Desert

D

We use **the** with *plural* names of people and places:

people	**the** Taylors (= the Taylor family), **the** Johnsons
countries	**the** Netherlands, **the** Philippines, **the** United States
groups of islands	**the** Canaries / **the** Canary Islands, **the** Bahamas
mountain ranges	**the** Rocky Mountains / **the** Rockies, **the** Andes, **the** Alps

    ☐ The highest mountain in **the Alps** is **Mont Blanc.**

E

We say:

    the north (of Brazil)   *but*   **northern** Brazil (*without* the)

    the south-east (of Spain)   *but*   **south-eastern** Spain

Compare:

    ☐ Sweden is in **northern Europe**; Spain is in **the south.**

Also **the** Middle East, **the** Far East

We also use **north/south** etc. (without **the**) in the names of some regions and countries:

    North America   **South Africa**

Note that on maps, **the** is not usually included in the name.

77.1 Put in **the** where necessary. Leave the space empty if the sentence is already complete.

1 Who is _____--_____ Doctor Johnson? (*the sentence is complete without* the)
2 I was ill, so I went to see _____ doctor.
3 The most powerful person in _____ United States is _____ president.
4 _____ President Kennedy was assassinated in 1963.
5 Do you know _____ Wilsons? They're a very nice couple.
6 Do you know _____ Professor Brown's phone number?

77.2 Some of these sentences are correct, but some need **the** (sometimes more than once). Correct the sentences where necessary.

1 Everest was first climbed in 1953.	*OK*
2 Milan is <u>in north</u> of Italy.	*in the north of Italy*
3 Africa is much larger than Europe.	....
4 Last year I visited Mexico and United States.	....
5 South of England is warmer than north.	....
6 Portugal is in western Europe.	....
7 France and Britain are separated by Channel.	....
8 Jim has travelled a lot in Middle East.	....
9 Chicago is on Lake Michigan.	....
10 Next year we're going skiing in Swiss Alps.	....
11 UK consists of Great Britain and Northern Ireland.	....
12 Seychelles are a group of islands in Indian Ocean.	....
13 Africa's highest mountain is Kilimanjaro (5895 metres).	....
14 River Volga flows into Caspian Sea.	....

77.3 Here are some geography questions. Choose the right answer from one of the boxes and write **the** if necessary. You do not need all the names in the boxes. Use an atlas if necessary.

continents	countries	oceans and seas	mountains	rivers and canals	
Africa	Canada	~~Atlantic~~	Alps	Amazon	Rhine
Asia	Denmark	Indian Ocean	Andes	Danube	Thames
Australia	Indonesia	Pacific	Himalayas	Nile	Volga
Europe	Sweden	Black Sea	Rockies	Suez Canal	
North America	Thailand	Mediterranean	Urals	Panama Canal	
South America	United States	Red Sea			

1 What do you have to cross to travel from Europe to America? _____the Atlantic_____
2 Where is Argentina? ....
3 Which is the longest river in Africa? ....
4 Of which country is Stockholm the capital? ....
5 Of which country is Washington the capital? ....
6 What is the name of the mountain range in the west of North America? ....
7 What is the name of the sea between Africa and Europe? ....
8 Which is the smallest continent in the world? ....
9 What is the name of the ocean between North America and Asia? ....
10 What is the name of the ocean between Africa and Australia? ....
11 Which river flows through London? ....
12 Which river flows through Vienna, Budapest and Belgrade? ....
13 Of which country is Bangkok the capital? ....
14 What joins the Atlantic and Pacific Oceans? ....
15 Which is the longest river in South America? ....

Names with and without **the** 2

A

Names without **the**

We do not use **the** with names of most city streets/roads/squares/parks etc. :

Wall **Street** (*not* the …)   Fifth **Avenue**   Hyde **Park**
Queens **Road**   **Broadway**   Times **Square**

Names of important public buildings and institutions (for example, airports, stations, universities) are often two words:

Manchester Airport   **Harvard University**

The first word is the name of a place ('Manchester') or a person ('Harvard'). These names are usually without **the**. In the same way, we say:

Victoria **Station** (*not* the …)   Canterbury **Cathedral**   Edinburgh **Castle**
Buckingham Palace   Cambridge **University**   Sydney **Harbour**

Compare:

Buckingham Palace (*not* the …)   *but*   **the Royal Palace**
('Royal' is an adjective – it is not a name like 'Buckingham'.)

B

Most other buildings have names with **the**. For example:

hotels/restaurants	**the** Sheraton Hotel, **the** Bombay Restaurant, **the** Holiday Inn
theatres/cinemas	**the** Palace Theatre, **the** Odeon (cinema)
museums/galleries	**the** Guggenheim Museum, **the** Hayward Gallery
other buildings	**the** Empire State (Building), **the** White House, **the** Eiffel Tower

We often leave out the noun:

the Sheraton (Hotel)   **the Palace** (Theatre)   **the Guggenheim** (Museum)

Some names are only **the** + *noun*, for example:

the Acropolis   **the Kremlin**   **the Pentagon**

C

Names with **of** usually have **the**. For example:

the Bank **of** England   **the** Museum **of** Modern Art
the Great Wall **of** China **the** Tower **of** London

Note that we say:

the University **of** Cambridge   *but*   **Cambridge University** (*without* **the**)

D

Many shops, restaurants, hotels, banks etc. are named after the people who started them. These names end in -'s or -s. We do not use **the** with these names:

Lloyds Bank (*not* the …)   **Brown's Restaurant**   **Macy's** (department store)

Churches are often named after saints:

St John's Church (*not* the St Johns Church)   **St Patrick's Cathedral**

E

Most newspapers and many organisations have names with **the**:

newspapers	**the** Washington Post, **the** Financial Times, **the** Sun
organisations	**the** European Union, **the** BBC (= British Broadcasting Corporation), **the** Red Cross

Names of companies, airlines etc. are usually without **the**:

Fiat (*not* the Fiat)   **Sony**   **British Airways**
Kodak   **IBM**   **Yale University Press**

78.1 Use the map to answer the questions. Write the name of the place and the street it is in.
Use **the** if necessary. (Remember that on maps we do not normally use **the**.)

1	Is there a cinema near here?	Yes, <u>the Odeon in Market Street</u> .
2	Is there a supermarket near here?	Yes, ... in ....
3	Is there a hotel near here?	Yes, ... in ....
4	Is there a church near here?	Yes, ...
5	Is there a museum near here?	Yes, ...
6	Is there a bookshop near here?	Yes, ...
7	Is there a park near here?	Yes, ... at the end of
		....
8	Is there a restaurant near here?	There are two. ....
		or ....

78.2 Where are the following? Use **the** where necessary.

Acropolis	Broadway	Buckingham Palace	Eiffel Tower
Kremlin	White House	Gatwick Airport	~~Times Square~~

1 <u>Times Square</u> is in New York.   5 .... is in Moscow.
2 .... is in Paris.   6 .... is in New York.
3 .... is in London.   7 .... is in Athens.
4 .... is in Washington.   8 .... is near London.

78.3 Choose the correct form, with or without **the**.

1 Have you ever been to ~~British Museum~~ / the British Museum? (<u>the British Museum</u> *is correct*)
2 <u>Hyde Park</u> / The Hyde Park is a very large park in central London.
3 Another park in central London is <u>St James's Park</u> / the St James's Park.
4 <u>Grand Hotel</u> / The Grand Hotel is in <u>Baker Street</u> / the Baker Street.
5 <u>Dublin Airport</u> / The Dublin Airport is situated about 12 kilometres from the city centre.
6 Frank is a student at <u>Liverpool University</u> / the Liverpool University.
7 If you're looking for a department store, I would recommend <u>Harrison's</u> / the Harrison's.
8 If you're looking for a place to have lunch, I would recommend <u>Ship Inn</u> / the Ship Inn.
9 <u>Statue of Liberty</u> / The Statue of Liberty is at the entrance to <u>New York Harbour</u> / the New York Harbour.
10 You should go to <u>Science Museum</u> / the Science Museum. It's very interesting.
11 John works for <u>IBM</u> / the IBM now. He used to work for <u>British Telecom</u> / the British Telecom.
12 'Which cinema are you going to this evening?' '<u>Classic</u> / The Classic.'
13 I'd like to go to China and see <u>Great Wall</u> / the Great Wall.
14 'Which newspaper do you want?' '<u>Herald</u> / The Herald.'
15 This book is published by <u>Cambridge University Press</u> / the Cambridge University Press.

→ Additional exercise 29 (page 319)

Unit 79

Singular and plural

A

Sometimes we use a *plural* noun for one thing that has two parts. For example:

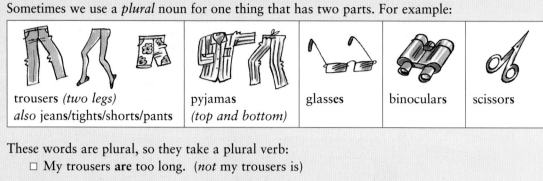

| trousers *(two legs)* also jeans/tights/shorts/pants | pyjamas *(top and bottom)* | glasses | binoculars | scissors |

These words are plural, so they take a plural verb:
- My trousers **are** too long. (*not* my trousers is)

You can also use **a pair of** + these words:
- **Those are** nice **jeans**. *or* That's a nice **pair of** jeans. (*not* a nice jeans)
- I need **some** new **glasses**. *or* I need a new **pair of** glasses.

B

Some nouns end in **-ics**, but are not usually plural. For example:
athletics economics electronics gymnastics maths (= mathematics) **physics politics**
- **Gymnastics is** my favourite sport. (*not* Gymnastics are)

News is not plural (see Unit 70B):
- What time **is the news** on television? (*not* are the news)

Some words ending in **-s** can be singular or plural. For example:

means	**a means** of transport	**many means** of transport
series	**a** television **series**	**two** television **series**
species	**a species** of bird	**200 species** of bird

C

Some singular nouns are often used with a plural verb. For example:
audience committee company family firm government staff team

These nouns are all groups of people. We often think of them as a number of people (= they), not as one thing (= it). So we often use a plural verb:
- **The government** (= they) **want** to increase taxes.
- **The staff** at the school (= they) **are** not happy with **their** new working conditions.

In the same way, we often use a plural verb after the name of a sports team or a company:
- **Italy are** playing Brazil next week (in a football match).
- **Shell have** increased the price of petrol.

A singular verb (The government **wants** … / Shell **has** … etc.) is also possible.

We use a plural verb with **police**:
- **The police are** investigating the murder, but **haven't** arrested anyone yet.
  (*not* The police is … hasn't)

Note that we say **a police officer / a policeman / a policewoman** (*not* a police).

D

We do not often use the plural of **person** ('persons'). We normally use **people** (a *plural* word):
- He's **a** nice **person**. *but* They are nice **people**. (*not* nice persons)
- **Many people don't** have enough to eat. (*not* Many people doesn't)

E

We think of a sum of money, a period of time, a distance etc. as *one* thing. So we use a singular verb:
- **Twenty thousand pounds** (= it) **was** stolen in the robbery. (*not* were stolen)
- **Three years** (= it) **is** a long time to be without a job. (*not* Three years are)
- **Six miles is** a long way to walk every day.

American English → Appendix 7

79.1 Complete each sentence using a word from Sections A or B. Sometimes you need **a** or **some**.

1 My eyesight isn't very good. I need ......*glasses*...... .
2 ...*A species*... is a group of animals or plants that have the same characteristics.
3 Footballers don't wear trousers when they play. They wear ....
4 The bicycle is .... of transport.
5 The bicycle and the car are .... of transport.
6 I want to cut this piece of material. I need ....
7 A friend of mine is writing .... of articles for the local newspaper.
8 There are a lot of American TV .... shown on British television.
9 While we were out walking, we saw many different .... of bird.

79.2 In each example the words on the left are connected with an activity (for example, a sport or an academic subject). Write the name of the activity. The beginning of the word is given.

1 calculate   algebra   equation   ...*mathematics*.........................
2 government   election   minister   p...
3 finance   trade   employment   e...
4 running   jumping   throwing   a...
5 light   heat   gravity   ph..
6 exercises   somersault   parallel bars   gy..
7 computer   silicon chip   video games   el..

79.3 Choose the correct form of the verb, singular or plural. In one sentence either the singular or plural verb is possible.

1 Gymnastics <u>is</u> / <s>are</s> my favourite sport. (<u>is</u> *is correct*)
2 The trousers you bought for me <u>doesn't / don't</u> fit me.
3 The police <u>want / wants</u> to interview two men about the robbery last week.
4 Physics <u>was / were</u> my best subject at school.
5 Can I borrow your scissors? Mine <u>isn't / aren't</u> sharp enough.
6 Fortunately the news <u>wasn't / weren't</u> as bad as we expected.
7 Where <u>does / do</u> your family live?
8 Three days <u>isn't / aren't</u> long enough for a good holiday.
9 I can't find my binoculars. Do you know where <u>it is / they are</u>?
10 It's a nice place to visit. The people <u>is / are</u> very friendly.
11 <u>Does / Do</u> the police know how the accident happened?
12 I don't like very hot weather. Thirty degrees <u>is / are</u> too hot for me.

79.4 Most of these sentences are wrong. Correct them where necessary.

1 Three years are a long time to be without a job.   *Three years is a long time*
2 The government want to increase taxes.   *OK* (wants *is also correct*)
3 Susan was wearing a black jeans.   ....
4 Brazil are playing Italy in a football match next week. ....
5 I like Martin and Jane. They're very nice persons.   ....
6 I need more than ten pounds. Ten pounds aren't enough.   ....
7 I'm going to buy a new pyjama.   ....
8 The committee haven't made a decision yet.   ....
9 There was a police directing traffic in the street.   ....
10 What is the police going to do?   ....
11 This scissors isn't very sharp.   ....

Noun + noun (a tennis ball / a headache)

A

You can use two nouns together (*noun + noun*) to mean *one* thing/person/idea etc. For example:

    a **tennis** ball   a **bank** manager   a **road** accident   **income** tax   the **city** centre

The first noun is like an adjective. It tells us what kind of thing/person/idea etc. For example:

> a **tennis** ball = a **ball** used to play **tennis**
> a **road** accident = an **accident** that happens on the **road**
> **income** tax = **tax** that you pay on your **income**
> the **water** temperature = the **temperature** of the **water**
> a **London** doctor = a **doctor** from **London**
> my **life** story = the **story** of my **life**

So you can say:

    a **television** camera   a **television** programme   a **television** studio   a **television** producer
    (these are all different things or people to do with television)
    language **problems**   marriage **problems**   health **problems**   work **problems**
    (these are all different kinds of problems)

Compare:

    garden vegetables (= **vegetables** that are grown in a garden)
    a **vegetable** garden (= a **garden** where vegetables are grown)

Sometimes the first word ends in **-ing**. Usually these are things used for doing something:

    a **frying** pan (= a pan for frying)   a **washing** machine   a **swimming** pool   a **dining** room

Sometimes there are more than two nouns together:

- ☐ I waited at the **hotel reception desk**.
- ☐ We watched the **World Swimming Championships** on television.
- ☐ If you want to play **table tennis** (= a game), you need a **table tennis table** (= a table).

B

When two nouns are together like this, sometimes we write them as one word and sometimes as two separate words. For example:

    a **headache**   **toothpaste**   a **weekend**   a **car park**   a **road sign**

There are no clear rules for this. If you are not sure, write two words.

C

Note the difference between:

    a **sugar bowl** (perhaps empty) and a **bowl of sugar** (= a bowl with sugar in it)
    a **shopping bag** (perhaps empty) and a **bag of shopping** (= a bag full of shopping)

D

When we use *noun + noun*, the first noun is like an *adjective*. It is normally singular, but the meaning is often plural. For example: a **book**shop is a shop where you can buy **books**, an **apple** tree is a tree that has **apples**.

In the same way we say:

    a **three-hour** journey (= a journey that takes three **hours**)
    a **ten-pound** note (*not* pounds)
    a **four-week** course (*not* weeks)
    two **14-year**-old girls (*not* years)
    a **six-page** letter (*not* pages)

Compare:

- ☐ It was a **four-week** course. *but* The course lasted four **weeks**.

–'s and of ... → Unit 81   **A week's holiday / three weeks' holiday etc.** → Unit 81E

Exercises

80.1 What do we call these things and people?

1 A ticket for a concert is ..... *a concert ticket* ..... .
2 Problems concerning health are ..... *health problems* ..... .
3 A magazine about computers is ..... .
4 Photographs taken on your holiday are your ..... .
5 Chocolate made with milk is ..... .
6 Somebody whose job is to inspect factories is ..... .
7 A horse that runs in races is ..... .
8 A race for horses is ..... .
9 A hotel in central London is ..... .
10 The results of your exams are your ..... .
11 The carpet in the dining room is ..... .
12 A scandal involving an oil company is ..... .
13 Workers at a car factory are ..... .
14 A scheme to improve a road is ..... .
15 A course that lasts five days is ..... .
16 A question that has two parts is ..... .
17 A girl who is seven years old is ..... .

80.2 Answer the questions using two of the following words each time:

~~accident~~	belt	card	credit	editor	forecast	newspaper
number	~~road~~	room	seat	shop	weather	window

1 This can be caused by bad driving. ..... *a road accident* .....
2 If you're staying at a hotel, you need to remember this. your .....
3 You should wear this when you're in a car. a .....
4 You can often use this to pay for things instead of cash. a .....
5 If you want to know if it's going to rain, you can read or listen to this. the .....
6 This person is a top journalist. a .....
7 You might stop to look in this when you're walking along a street. a .....

80.3 Complete the sentences using the following:

15 minute(s)	**60 minute(s)**	**two hour(s)**	**five day(s)**	**two year(s)**	**500 year(s)**
six mile(s)	**six mile(s)**	**20 pound(s)**	**five course(s)**	~~**ten page(s)**~~	~~**450 page(s)**~~

Sometimes you need the singular (**day/page** etc.) and sometimes the plural (**days/pages** etc.).

1 It's quite a long book. There are ..... *450 pages* ..... .
2 A few days ago I received a ..... *ten-page* ..... letter from Julia.
3 I didn't have any change. I only had a ..... note.
4 At work in the morning I usually have a ..... break for coffee.
5 There are ..... in an hour.
6 It's only a ..... flight from London to Madrid.
7 It was a very big meal. There were ..... .
8 Mary has just started a new job. She's got a ..... contract.
9 The oldest building in the city is the ..... castle.
10 I work ..... a week. Saturday and Sunday are free.
11 We went for a long walk in the country. We must have walked ..... .
12 We went for a ..... walk in the country.

A

We use -'s (*apostrophe* + s) mostly for people or animals:

- □ **Tom's** computer isn't working. (*not* the computer of Tom)
- □ How old are **Chris's** children? (*not* the children of Chris)
- □ What's (= What is) **your sister's** name?
- □ What's **Tom's sister's** name?
- □ Be careful. Don't step on **the cat's** tail.

Note that you can use -'s without a following noun:

- □ This isn't my book. It's **my sister's**. (= my sister's book)

We do not always use -'s for people. For example, we would use **of** ... in this sentence:

- □ What was the name **of the man who phoned you?** ('the man who phoned you' is too long to be followed by -'s)

Note that we say **a woman's hat** (= a hat for a woman), **a boy's name** (= a name for a boy), **a bird's egg** (= an egg laid by a bird) etc.

B

With a *singular* noun we use -'s:

    my **sister's** room (= **her** room – one sister)   **Mr Carter's** house (= **his** house)

With a *plural* noun (sisters, friends etc.) we put an apostrophe at the end of the word (-s'):

    my **sisters'** room (= **their** room – *two or more* sisters)

    the **Carters'** house (= **their** house – Mr and Mrs Carter)

If a plural noun does not end in -s (for example **men/women/children/people**) we use -'s:

    the **men's** changing room   a **children's** book (= a book for children)

Note that you can use -'s after more than one noun:

    Jack and Karen's wedding   **Mr and Mrs Carter's** house

C

For things, ideas etc., we normally use **of** (... **of the book** / ... **of the restaurant** etc.):

    the door **of the garage** (*not* the garage's door)

    the name **of the book**   the owner **of the restaurant**

Sometimes the structure *noun + noun* is possible (see Unit 80):

    the **garage door**   the **restaurant owner**

We say **the beginning/end/middle of** ... , **the top/bottom of** ... , **the front/back/side of** ... :

    the beginning of the month (*not* the month's beginning)

    the top of the hill   **the back of** the car

D

You can usually use -'s or **of** ... for an organisation (= a group of people). So you can say:

    the **government's** decision   *or*   the decision **of the government**

    the **company's** success   *or*   the success **of the company**

It is also possible to use -'s for places. So you can say:

    the **city's** streets   the **world's** population   **Italy's** prime minister

E

You can also use -'s with time expressions (**yesterday** / **next week** etc.):

- □ Do you still have **yesterday's** newspaper?
- □ **Next week's** meeting has been cancelled.

In the same way, you can say **today's** / **tomorrow's** / **this evening's** / **Monday's** etc.

We also use -'s (or -s' with plural words) with periods of time:

- □ I've got **a week's** holiday starting on Monday.
- □ Julia has got **three weeks'** holiday.
- □ I live near the station – it's only about **ten minutes'** walk.

Exercises

81.1 In some of these sentences, it would be more natural to use **-'s** or **-'**. Change the underlined parts where necessary.

1 Who is <u>the owner of this restaurant</u>?   *OK*
2 Where are <u>the children of Chris</u>?   *Chris's children*
3 Is this <u>the umbrella of your friend</u>?
4 Write your name at <u>the top of the page</u>.
5 I've never met <u>the daughter of Charles</u>.
6 Have you met <u>the son of Mary and Dan</u>?
7 We don't know <u>the cause of the problem</u>.
8 Do we still have <u>the newspaper of yesterday</u>?
9 What's <u>the name of this street</u>?
10 What is <u>the cost of a new computer</u>?
11 <u>The friends of your children</u> are here.
12 <u>The garden of our neighbours</u> is very nice.
13 I work on <u>the ground floor of the building</u>.
14 <u>The hair of Bill</u> is very long.
15 I couldn't go to <u>the party of Catherine</u>.
16 What's <u>the name of the woman who lives next door</u>?
17 Have you seen <u>the car of the parents of Mike</u>?
18 What's <u>the meaning of this expression</u>?
19 Do you agree <u>with the economic policy of the government</u>?

81.2 What is another way of saying these things? Use **-'s**.

1 a hat for a woman   *a woman's hat*
2 a name for a boy
3 clothes for children
4 a school for girls
5 a nest for a bird
6 a magazine for women

81.3 Read each sentence and write a new sentence beginning with the <u>underlined</u> words.

1 The meeting <u>tomorrow</u> has been cancelled.
     Tomorrow's meeting has been cancelled.
2 The storm <u>last week</u> caused a lot of damage.
Last
3 The only cinema in <u>the town</u> has closed down.
The
4 The weather in <u>Britain</u> is very changeable.

5 Tourism is the main industry in <u>the region</u>.

81.4 Use the information given to complete the sentences.

1 If I leave my house at 9 o'clock and drive to the airport, I arrive at about 11.
So it's about ___*two hours' drive*___ from my house to the airport. (drive)
2 If I leave my house at 8.40 and walk to the centre, I get there at 9 o'clock.
So it's _____ from my house to the centre. (walk)
3 I'm going on holiday on the 12th. I have to be back at work on the 26th.
So I've got _____ . (holiday)
4 I went to sleep at 3 o'clock this morning and woke up an hour later. After that I couldn't sleep. So last night I only had _____ . (sleep)

A Study this example:

Hi, I'm Steve.

STEVE

Steve **introduced himself** to the other guests.

We use **myself/yourself/himself** etc. (*reflexive pronouns*) when the *subject* and *object* are the same:

Steve	introduced	himself
subject		*object*

The reflexive pronouns are:

singular: my**self**   your**self** *(one person)*   him**self**/her**self**/it**self**
plural: our**selves**   your**selves** *(more than one person)*   them**selves**

- □ I don't want you to pay for me. I'll pay for **myself**. (*not* I'll pay for me)
- □ Julia had a great holiday. **She** really enjoyed **herself**.
- □ Do **you** talk to **yourself** sometimes? (*said to one person*)
- □ If you want more to eat, help **yourselves**. (*said to more than one person*)

Compare:
- □ It's not our fault. **You** can't blame **us**.
- □ It's our own fault. **We** should blame **ourselves**.

B We do not use **myself** etc. after feel/relax/concentrate/meet:
- □ I feel nervous. I can't **relax**.
- □ You must try and **concentrate**. (*not* concentrate yourself)
- □ What time shall we **meet**? (*not* meet ourselves, *not* meet us)

We normally use **wash/shave/dress** *without* **myself** etc. :
- □ He got up, **washed**, **shaved** and **dressed**. (*not* washed himself etc.)
You can also say **get dressed** (He **got dressed**).

C Compare -**selves** and **each other**:
- □ Kate and Joe stood in front of the mirror and looked   **themselves**
  at **themselves**. (= *Kate and Joe* looked at *Kate and Joe*)
- □ Kate looked at Joe; Joe looked at Kate. They looked
  at **each other**.   **each other**

You can use **one another** instead of **each other**:
- □ How long have you and Bill known **each other**?   *or*   ... known **one another**?
- □ Sue and Ann don't like **each other**.   *or*   ... don't like **one another**.
- □ Do you and Sarah live near **each other**?   *or*   ... near **one another**?

D We also use **myself/yourself** etc. in another way. For example:
- □ 'Who repaired your bike for you?' 'I repaired it **myself**.'

I repaired it myself = I repaired it, not anybody else. Here, **myself** is used to emphasise 'I' (= it makes it stronger). Some more examples:
- □ I'm not going to do your work for you. **You** can do it **yourself**. (= you, not me)
- □ Let's paint the house **ourselves**. It will be much cheaper.
- □ **The film itself** wasn't very good, but I loved the music.
- □ I don't think Liz will get the job. **Liz herself** doesn't think she'll get it. (*or* Liz doesn't think she'll get it **herself**.)

82.1 Complete the sentences using **myself/yourself** etc. + the following verbs (in the correct form):

blame   burn   enjoy   express   hurt   ~~introduce~~   put

1 Steve ....*introduced himself*.... to the other guests at the party.
2 Bill fell down some steps, but fortunately he didn't ....
3 It isn't Sue's fault. She really shouldn't ....
4 Please try and understand how I feel. .... in my position.
5 The children had a great time at the beach. They really ....
6 Be careful! That pan is very hot. Don't ....
7 Sometimes I can't say exactly what I mean. I wish I could .... better.

82.2 Put in **myself/yourself/ourselves** etc. or **me/you/us** etc.

1 Julia had a great holiday. She enjoyed ....*herself*.... .
2 It's not my fault. You can't blame ....
3 What I did was really bad. I'm ashamed of ....
4 We've got a problem. I hope you can help ....
5 'Can I take another biscuit?'   'Of course. Help .... !'
6 You must meet Sarah. I'll introduce .... to her.
7 Don't worry about us. We can look after ....
8 I gave them a key to our house so that they could let .... in.
9 I didn't want anybody to see the letters, so I burned ....

82.3 Complete these sentences. Use **myself/yourself** etc. only where necessary. Use the following verbs (in the correct form):

concentrate   defend   dry   feel   meet   relax   ~~shave~~   wash

1 Martin decided to grow a beard because he was fed up with ....*shaving*.... .
2 I wasn't very well yesterday, but I .... much better today.
3 I climbed out of the swimming pool and .... with a towel.
4 I tried to study, but I couldn't ....
5 If somebody attacks you, you need to be able to ....
6 I'm going out with Chris this evening. We're .... at 7.30.
7 You're always rushing around. Why don't you sit down and .... ?
8 There was no water, so we couldn't ....

82.4 Complete the sentences with **–selves** or **each other**.

1 How long have you and Bill known ....*each other*.... ?
2 If people work too hard, they can make .... ill.
3 I need you and you need me. We need ....
4 In Britain friends often give .... presents at Christmas.
5 Some people are very selfish. They only think of ....
6 Tracy and I don't see .... very often these days.
7 We couldn't get back into the house. We had locked .... out.
8 They've had an argument. They're not speaking to .... at the moment.
9 We'd never met before, so we introduced .... to ....

82.5 Complete the answers to the questions using **myself/yourself/itself** etc.

1	Who repaired the bike for you?	Nobody. I ....*repaired it myself*....
2	Who cuts Brian's hair for him?	Nobody. He cuts ....
3	Do you want me to post that letter for you?	No, I'll ....
4	Who told you that Linda was going away?	Linda ....
5	Can you phone John for me?	Why can't you .... ?

→ Additional exercise 30 **(page 320)**

A friend of mine   my own house
on my own / by myself

A   **A friend of mine / a friend of Tom's etc.**

We say '(a friend) **of mine/yours/his/hers/ours/theirs**':
- ☐ I'm going to a wedding on Saturday. **A friend of mine** is getting married. (*not* a friend of me)
- ☐ We went on holiday with **some friends of ours**. (*not* some friends of us)
- ☐ Michael had an argument with **a neighbour of his**.
- ☐ It was **a good idea of yours** to go to the cinema.

In the same way we say '(a friend) **of my sister's** / (a friend) **of Tom's**' etc. :
- ☐ That woman over there is **a friend of my sister's**.
- ☐ It was **a good idea of Tom's** to go to the cinema.

B   **My own … / your own … etc.**

We use **my/your/his/her/its/our/their** before **own**:
   my own house   **your own** car   **her own** room
(*not* an own house, an own car etc.)

My own … / your own … etc. = something that is only mine/yours, not shared or borrowed:
- ☐ I don't want to share a room with anybody. I want **my own room**.
- ☐ Vicky and George would like to have **their own house**.
- ☐ It's a pity that the flat hasn't got **its own parking space**.
- ☐ It's **my own fault** that I've got no money. I buy too many things I don't need.
- ☐ Why do you want to borrow my car? Why don't you use **your own**? (= your own car)

You can also use **own** to say that you do something yourself instead of somebody else doing it for you. For example:
- ☐ Brian usually cuts **his own hair**.
  (= he cuts it himself; he doesn't
  go to the hairdresser's)
- ☐ I'd like to have a garden so that
  I could grow **my own vegetables**.
  (= grow them myself instead of
  buying them from shops)

BRIAN

C   **On my own / by myself**

On my own and **by myself** both mean 'alone'. We say:

on { my/your his/her/its our/their } own	=	by { myself / yourself (*singular*) himself / herself / itself ourselves / yourselves (*plural*) / themselves }

- ☐ I like living **on my own / by myself**.
- ☐ 'Did you go on holiday **on your own / by yourself**?' 'No, with a friend.'
- ☐ David was sitting **on his own / by himself** in a corner of the café.
- ☐ Learner drivers are not allowed to drive **on their own / by themselves**.

Myself/yourself/themselves etc. → Unit 82

83.1 Write new sentences with the same meaning. Change the <u>underlined</u> words and use the structure in Section A (**a friend of mine** etc.).

1 I am meeting <u>one of my friends</u> tonight.   *I'm meeting a friend of mine tonight.*
2 We met <u>one of your relatives</u>.   We met a ....
3 Henry borrowed <u>one of my books</u>.   Henry ....
4 Liz invited <u>some of her friends</u> to her flat.   Liz ....
5 We had dinner with <u>one of our neighbours</u>.   ....
6 I went on holiday with <u>two of my friends</u>.   ....
7 Is that man <u>one of your friends</u>?   ....
8 I met <u>one of Jane's friends</u> at the party.   ....

83.2 Complete the sentences using **my own / your own** etc. + the following:

~~bedroom~~   business   opinions   private beach   words

1 I share a kitchen and bathroom, but I have ...*my own bedroom*............... .
2 Gary doesn't think the same as me. He's got ....
3 Julia is fed up with working for other people. She wants to start ....
4 We stayed at a luxury hotel by the sea. The hotel had ....
5 In the test we had to read a story, and then write it in ....

83.3 Complete the sentences using **my own / your own** etc.

1 Why do you want to borrow my car? ...*Why don't you use your own car*............... ?
2 How can you blame me? It's not my fault. It's ....
3 She's always using my ideas. Why can't she use .... ?
4 Please don't worry about my problems. You've got ....
5 I can't make his decisions for him. He must make ....

83.4 Complete the sentences using **my own / your own** etc. Use the following verbs:

bake   ~~cut~~   make   write

1 Brian never goes to the hairdresser.
He ...*cuts his own hair*............... .
2 Mary doesn't often buy clothes.
She usually ....
3 We don't often buy bread.
We usually ....
4 Paul is a singer. He sings songs written by other people, but he also
....

83.5 Complete the sentences using **on my own / by myself** etc.

1 Did you go on holiday on ...*your own*............... ?
2 I'm glad I live with other people. I wouldn't like to live on ....
3 The box was too heavy for me to lift by ....
4 'Who was Tom with when you saw him?' 'Nobody. He was by ....'
5 Very young children should not go swimming by ....
6 I don't think she knows many people. When I see her, she is always by ....
7 I don't like strawberries with cream. I like them on ....
8 Do you like working with other people or do you prefer working by .... ?
9 We had no help decorating the flat. We did it completely on ....
10 I went out with Sally because she didn't want to go out on ....

A
There and it

There's a new restaurant in King Street.

Yes, I know. I went there last night. It's very good.

We use **there** ... when we talk about something for the first time, to say that it exists:
- □ **There's** a new restaurant in King Street. (*not* A new restaurant is in King Street)
- □ I'm sorry I'm late. **There was** a lot of traffic. (*not* It was a lot of traffic)
- □ Things are more expensive now. **There has been** a big rise in the cost of living.

It = a specific thing, place, fact, situation etc. (but see also section C):
- □ We went to the new restaurant. **It's** very good. (It = the restaurant)
- □ I wasn't expecting them to come. **It** was a complete surprise. (It = that they came)

Compare **there** and **it**:
- □ I don't like this town. **There's** nothing to do here. **It's** a boring place.

There also means 'to/at/in that place':
- □ The new restaurant is very good. I went **there** (= to the restaurant) last night.
- □ When we got to the party, there were already a lot of people **there** (= at the party).

B

You can say **there will be / there must be / there might be / there used to be** etc. :
- □ **Will there be** many people at the party?
- □ 'Is there a flight to Paris this evening?' '**There might be.** I'll phone the airport.'
- □ If people drove more carefully, **there wouldn't be** so many accidents.

Also **there must have been, there should have been** etc. :
- □ There was a light on. **There must have been** somebody at home.

Compare **there** and **it**:
- □ They live on a busy road. **There must be** a lot of noise from the traffic.
  They live on a busy main road. **It must be** very noisy.
- □ **There used to be** a cinema in King Street, but it closed a few years ago.
  That building is now a supermarket. **It used to be** a cinema.

You can also say **there is sure/certain/likely/bound** to be ... :
- □ **There is bound** (= sure) **to be** a flight to Paris this evening.

C

We also use **it** in sentences like this:
- □ **It's** dangerous **to walk in the road.**

We do not usually say 'To walk in the road is dangerous'. Normally we begin with **It** ... .
Some more examples:
- □ **It** didn't take us long **to get here.**
- □ **It's** a pity **(that) Sandra can't come to the party.**
- □ Let's go. **It's** not worth **waiting any longer.**

We also use **it** to talk about distance, time and weather:
- □ How far is **it** from here to the airport.
- □ What day is **it** today?
- □ **It's** a long time since we saw you last.
- □ **It** was windy yesterday. (*but* **There** was **a cold wind.**)

It's worth / it's no use / there's no point → Unit 63A   Sure to / bound to ... etc. → Unit 65E
There is + -ing/-ed → Unit 97

Exercises

84.1 Put in **there is/was** or **it is/was**. Some sentences are questions (**is there ... ? / is it ... ?** etc.) and some are negative (**isn't/wasn't**).

1 The journey took a long time. _There was_ a lot of traffic.
2 What's the new restaurant like? _Is it_ good?
3 '............................. a bookshop near here?' 'Yes, ... one in Hill Street.'
4 When we got to the cinema, ... a queue outside. .... a very long queue, so we decided not to wait.
5 I couldn't see anything. .... completely dark.
6 .... trouble at the club last night. They had to call the police.
7 How far .... from Milan to Rome?
8 .... Keith's birthday yesterday. We had a party.
9 .... three years since I last went to the theatre.
10 I wanted to visit the museum, but .... enough time.
11 '............................. time to leave?' 'Yes, ... nearly midnight.'
12 A few days ago .... a storm. .... a lot of damage.
13 .... a beautiful day yesterday. We had a picnic.
14 .... anything on television, so I turned it off.
15 .... an accident in King Street, but .... very serious.

84.2 Read the first sentence and then write a sentence beginning **There ...** .

1 The roads were busy today.   _There was a lot of traffic._
2 This soup is very salty.   There .... in the soup.
3 The box was empty.   .... in the box.
4 The film was very violent.   ....
5 The shops were very crowded.   ....
6 I like this town – it's lively.   ....

84.3 Complete the sentences. Use **there will be**, **there would be** etc. Choose from:

will   may   ~~would~~   wouldn't   should   used to   (be) going to

1 If people drove more carefully, _there would be_ fewer accidents.
2 'Do we have any eggs?' 'I'm not sure. .... some in the fridge.'
3 I think everything will be OK. I don't think .... any problems.
4 Look at the sky. .... a storm.
5 'Is there a school in the village?' 'Not now. .... one, but it closed.'
6 People drive too fast on this road. I think .... a speed limit.
7 If people weren't aggressive, ... any wars.

84.4 Are these sentences right or wrong? Change **it** to **there** where necessary.

1 They live on a busy road. It must be a lot of noise.   _There must be a lot of noise._
2 Last winter it was very cold and it was a lot of snow.   ....
3 It used to be a church here, but it was knocked down.   ....
4 Why was she so unfriendly? It must have been a reason.   ....
5 It's a long way from my house to the nearest shop.   ....
6 A: Where can we park the car?
  B: Don't worry. It's sure to be a car park somewhere.   ....
7 After the lecture it will be an opportunity to ask questions.   ....
8 I like the place where I live, but it would be nicer to live by the sea.   ....
9 I was told that it would be somebody to meet me at the station, but it wasn't anybody.   ....
10 The situation is still the same. It has been no change.   ....
11 I don't know who'll win, but it's sure to be a good game.   ....

A In general we use **some** (*also* **somebody/someone/something**) in positive sentences and **any** (*also* **anybody** etc.) in negative sentences:

some	any
□ We bought **some** flowers.	□ We didn't buy **any** flowers.
□ He's busy. He's got **some** work to do.	□ He's lazy. He **never** does **any** work.
□ There's **somebody** at the door.	□ There isn't **anybody** at the door.
□ I'm hungry. I want **something** to eat.	□ I'm not hungry. I don't want **anything** to eat.

We use **any** in the following sentences because the meaning is negative:
   □ She went out **without any** money. (she didn't take **any** money with her)
   □ He **refused** to eat **anything**. (he didn't eat **anything**)
   □ **Hardly anybody** passed the examination. (= almost **nobody** passed)

B We use both **some** and **any** in questions. We use **some** to talk about a person or thing that we know exists, or we think exists:
   □ Are you waiting for **somebody**? (I think you are waiting for somebody)
We use **some** in questions when we offer or ask for things:
   □ Would you like **something** to eat? (there is something to eat)
   □ Can I have **some** sugar, please? (there is probably some sugar I can have)

But in most questions, we use **any**. We do not know if the thing or person exists:
   □ 'Have you got **any** luggage?' 'No, I haven't.'
   □ I can't find my bag. Has **anybody** seen it?

C We often use **any** after **if**:
   □ If there are **any** letters for me, can you send them on to this address?
   □ **If anyone** has any questions, I'll be pleased to answer them.
   □ Let me know **if** you need **anything**.

The following sentences have the idea of **if**:
   □ I'm sorry for **any** trouble I've caused. (= if I have caused any trouble)
   □ **Anyone** who wants to do the exam must tell me by Friday. (= if there is anyone)

D We also use **any** with the meaning 'it doesn't matter which':
   □ You can take **any** bus. They all go to the centre. (= it doesn't matter which bus you take)
   □ 'Sing a song.' 'Which song shall I sing?' '**Any** song. I don't mind.' (= it doesn't matter which song)
   □ Come and see me **any** time you want.
   □ 'Let's go out somewhere.' 'Where shall we go?' '**Anywhere**. I just want to go out.'
   □ We left the door unlocked. **Anybody** could have come in.

Compare **something** and **anything**:
   □ A: I'm hungry. I want **something** to eat.
      B: What would you like?
      A: I don't mind. **Anything**. (= it doesn't matter what)

E **Somebody/someone/anybody/anyone** are singular words:
   □ **Someone** is here to see you.
But we often use **they/them/their** after these words:
   □ **Someone** has forgotten **their** umbrella. (= his or her umbrella)
   □ If **anybody** wants to leave early, **they** can. (= he or she can)

Exercises

85.1 Put in **some** or **any**.

1 We didn't buy .....*any*..... flowers.
2 This evening I'm going out with .... friends of mine.
3 A: Have you seen .... good films recently?
   B: No, I haven't been to the cinema for ages.
4 I didn't have .... money, so I had to borrow ....
5 Can I have .... milk in my coffee, please?
6 I was too tired to do .... work.
7 You can cash these traveller's cheques at .... bank.
8 Can you give me .... information about places of interest in the town?
9 With the special tourist train ticket, you can travel on .... train you like.
10 If there are .... words you don't understand, use a dictionary.

85.2 Complete the sentences with **some-** or **any-** + **-body/-thing/-where**.

1 I was too surprised to say .....*anything*..... .
2 There's .... at the door. Can you go and see who it is?
3 Does .... mind if I open the window?
4 I wasn't feeling hungry, so I didn't eat ....
5 You must be hungry. Would you like .... to eat?
6 Quick, let's go! There's .... coming and I don't want .... to see us.
7 Sarah was upset about .... and refused to talk to ....
8 This machine is very easy to use. .... can learn to use it very quickly.
9 There was hardly .... on the beach. It was almost deserted.
10 'Do you live .... near Joe?' 'No, he lives in another part of town.'
11 'Where shall we go on holiday?' 'Let's go .... warm and sunny.'
12 They stay at home all the time. They never seem to go ....
13 I'm going out now. If .... phones while I'm out, can you tell them I'll be back at 11.30?
14 Why are you looking under the bed? Have you lost .... ?
15 The police have asked that .... who saw the accident should contact them.
16 'Can I ask you .... ?' 'Sure. What do you want to ask?'
17 Sue is very secretive. She never tells .... (*2 words*)

85.3 Complete the sentences. Use **any** (+ noun) or **anybody/anything/anywhere**.

1	Which bus do I have to catch?	.....*Any bus*..... . They all go to the centre.
2	Which day shall I come?	I don't mind. ....
3	What do you want to eat?	.... I don't mind. Whatever you have.
4	Where shall I sit?	It's up to you. You can sit .... you like.
5	What sort of job are you looking for?	.... It doesn't matter.
6	What time shall I phone tomorrow?	.... I'll be in all day.
7	Who shall I invite to the party?	I don't mind. .... you like.
8	Which newspaper shall I buy?	.... Whatever they have in the shop.

A No and none

We use **no** + *noun*. **No** = **not a** or **not any**:
- □ We had to walk home because there was **no bus**. (= there wasn't **a** bus)
- □ Sue will have **no difficulty** finding a job. (= Sue won't have **any** difficulty …)
- □ There were **no shops** open. (= There weren't **any** shops open.)

You can use **no** + *noun* at the beginning of a sentence:
- □ **No reason** was given for the change of plan.

We use **none** *without* a noun:
- □ 'How much money do you have?' '**None**.' (= no money)
- □ All the tickets have been sold. There are **none** left. (= no tickets left)

Or we use **none of** … :
- □ This money is all yours. **None of it** is mine.

After **none of** + *plural* (none of **the students**, none of **them** etc.) the verb can be singular or plural. A plural verb is more usual:
- □ None of the shops **were** (*or* **was**) open.

B Nothing   nobody/no-one   nowhere

You can use these negative words at the beginning of a sentence or alone (as answers to questions):
- □ **Nobody** (*or* **No-one**) came to visit me while I was in hospital.
- □ 'What happened?' '**Nothing**.'
- □ 'Where are you going?' '**Nowhere**. I'm staying here.'

You can also use these words after a verb, especially after **be** and **have**:
- □ The house is empty. There's **nobody** living there.
- □ We **had nothing** to eat.

Nothing/nobody etc. = **not** + **anything/anybody** etc. :
- □ I didn't say **anything**. (= I said **nothing**.)
- □ Jane didn't tell **anybody** about her plans. (= Jane told **nobody** …)
- □ They haven't got **anywhere** to live. (= They've got **nowhere** to live.)

With **nothing/nobody** etc., do *not* use a negative verb (**isn't, didn't** etc.):
- □ I **said** nothing. (*not* I didn't say nothing)
- □ Nobody **tells** me anything. (*not* Nobody doesn't tell me)

C We also use **any/anything/anybody** etc. (*without* not) to mean 'it doesn't matter which/what/who' (see Unit 85D). Compare **no-** and **any-**:
- □ There was **no** bus, so we walked home.
  You can take **any** bus. They all go to the centre. (= it doesn't matter which)
- □ 'What do you want to eat?' '**Nothing**. I'm not hungry.'
  I'm so hungry. I could eat **anything**. (= it doesn't matter what)
- □ The exam was extremely difficult. **Nobody** passed. (= everybody failed)
  The exam was very easy. **Anybody** could have passed. (= it doesn't matter who)

D After **nobody/no-one** you can use **they/them/their** (see also Unit 85E):
- □ **Nobody** phoned, did **they**? (= did he or she)
- □ **No-one** did what I asked **them** to do. (= him or her)
- □ **Nobody** in the class did **their** homework. (= his or her homework)

Some and any → Unit 85   **None of …** → Unit 88   **Any bigger / no better etc.** → Unit 106B

86.1 Complete these sentences with **no, none** or **any**.

1 It was a public holiday, so there were ......*no*...... shops open.
2 I haven't got ......*any*...... money. Can you lend me some?
3 We had to walk home because there were .... taxis.
4 We had to walk home because there weren't .... taxis.
5 'How many eggs have we got?' '......................... . Do you want me to get some?'
6 We took a few photographs, but .... of them were very good.
7 What a stupid thing to do! .... intelligent person would do such a thing.
8 I'll try and answer .... questions you ask me.
9 I couldn't answer .... of the questions they asked me.
10 We cancelled the party because .... of the people we invited were able to come.
11 I tried to phone Chris, but there was .... answer.

86.2 Answer these questions using **none/nobody/nothing/nowhere**.

1	What did you do?	*Nothing.*
2	Who were you talking to?	....
3	How much luggage have you got?	....
4	Where are you going?	....
5	How many mistakes did you make?	....
6	How much did you pay?	....

Now answer the same questions using complete sentences with **any/anybody/anything/anywhere**.

7 (1) ...*I didn't do anything.*.........................
8 (2) I ....
9 (3) ....
10 (4) ....
11 (5) ....
12 (6) ....

86.3 Complete these sentences with **no-** or **any-** + **-body/-thing/-where**.

1 I don't want ...*anything*...... to drink. I'm not thirsty.
2 The bus was completely empty. There was .... on it.
3 'Where did you go for your holidays?' '......................... . I stayed at home.'
4 I went to the shops, but I didn't buy ....
5 'What did you buy?' '......................... . I couldn't find .... I wanted.'
6 The town is still the same as it was years ago. .... has changed.
7 Have you seen my watch? I can't find it ....
8 There was complete silence in the room. .... said ....

86.4 Choose the right word.

1 She didn't tell ~~nobody~~ / anybody about her plans. (anybody *is correct*)
2 The accident looked serious, but fortunately nobody / anybody was badly injured.
3 I looked out of the window, but I couldn't see no-one / anyone.
4 My job is very easy. Nobody / Anybody could do it.
5 'What's in that box?' 'Nothing / Anything. It's empty.'
6 The situation is uncertain. Nothing / Anything could happen.
7 I don't know nothing / anything about economics.

→ Additional exercise 30 (page 320)

Unit 87

Much, many, little, few, a lot, plenty

A

We use **much** and **little** with *uncountable* nouns:

much time   much luck   little energy   little money

We use **many** and **few** with *plural* nouns:

many friends   many people   few cars   few countries

B

We use **a lot of / lots of / plenty of** with both *uncountable* and *plural* nouns:

a lot of luck   lots of time   plenty of money
a lot of friends   lots of people   plenty of ideas

Plenty = more than enough:

☐ There's no need to hurry. We've got **plenty of time.**

C

Much is unusual in positive sentences (especially in spoken English). Compare:

☐ We didn't spend **much** money.

but   We spent **a lot of** money. (*not* We spent much money)

☐ Do you see David **much?**

but   I see David **a lot.** (*not* I see David much)

We use **many** and **a lot** of in all kinds of sentences:

☐ **Many** people drive too fast.   *or*   **A lot of** people drive too fast.
☐ Do you know **many** people?   *or*   Do you know **a lot of** people?
☐ There aren't **many** tourists here.   *or*   There aren't **a lot of** tourists here.

Note that we say **many years / many weeks / many days** (*not* a lot of ...):

☐ We've lived here for **many years.** (*not* a lot of years)

D

Little and **few** (*without* a) are negative ideas (= not much / not many):

☐ Gary is very busy with his job. He has **little time** for other things. (= not much time, less time than he would like)
☐ Vicky doesn't like living in London. She has **few friends** there. (= not many, not as many as she would like)

You can say **very little** and **very few:**

☐ Gary has **very little** time for other things.
☐ Vicky has **very few** friends in London.

E

A little and **a few** have a more positive meaning.

A little = some, a small amount:

☐ Let's go and have a coffee. We have **a little** time before the train leaves.
(a little time = some time, enough time to have a coffee)
☐ 'Do you speak English?'   '**A little.**'   (so we can talk a bit)

A few = some, a small number:

☐ I enjoy my life here. I have **a few** friends and we meet quite often.
(a few friends = not many but enough to have a good time)
☐ 'When was the last time you saw Clare?'   '**A few** days ago.'   (= some days ago)

Compare:

☐ He spoke **little** English, so it was difficult to communicate with him.
He spoke **a little** English, so we were able to communicate with him.
☐ She's lucky. She has **few** problems. (= not many problems)
Things are not going so well for her. She has **a few** problems. (= some problems)

You can say **only a little** and **only a few:**

☐ Hurry! We **only** have **a little** time. (*not* only little time)
☐ The village was very small. There were **only a few** houses. (*not* only few houses)

174   Countable and uncountable → Units 69–70

Exercises

87.1 In some of these sentences **much** is incorrect or unnatural. Change **much** to **many** or **a lot (of)** where necessary. Write 'OK' if the sentence is correct.

1 We didn't spend much money.   _OK_
2 Sue drinks <u>much tea</u>.   _a lot of tea_
3 Joe always puts much salt on his food.
4 We'll have to hurry. We haven't got much time.
5 It cost much to repair the car.
6 Did it cost much to repair the car?
7 I don't know much people in this town.
8 I use the phone much at work.
9 There wasn't much traffic this morning.
10 You need much money to travel round the world.

87.2 Complete the sentences using **plenty (of)** + the following:

> hotels   money   room   things to see   ~~time~~   to learn

1 There's no need to hurry. There's ___ plenty of time. ___
2 He's got no financial problems. He's got
3 Come and sit with us. There's
4 She knows a lot, but she still has
5 It's an interesting town to visit. There
6 I'm sure we'll find somewhere to stay.

87.3 Put in **much/many/few/little** (one word only).

1 She isn't very popular. She has ___ few ___ friends.
2 Ann is very busy these days. She has ___ free time.
3 Did you take ___ photographs when you were on holiday?
4 I'm not very busy today. I haven't got ___ to do.
5 This is a very modern city. There are ___ old buildings.
6 The weather has been very dry recently. We've had ___ rain.
7 'Do you know Rome?' 'No, I haven't been there for ___ years.'

87.4 Put in **a** where necessary. Write 'OK' if the sentence is already complete.

1 She's lucky. She has <u>few problems</u>.   _OK_
2 Things are not going so well for her. She has <u>few problems</u>.   _a few problems_
3 Can you lend me <u>few dollars</u>?
4 There was <u>little traffic</u>, so the journey didn't take very long.
5 I can't give you a decision yet. I need <u>little time</u> to think.
6 It was a surprise that he won the match. <u>Few people</u> expected him to win.
7 I don't know much Spanish – <u>only few words</u>.
8 I wonder how Sam is. I haven't seen him for <u>few months</u>.

87.5 Put in **little / a little / few / a few**.

1 Gary is very busy with his job. He has ___ little ___ time for other things.
2 Listen carefully. I'm going to give you ___ advice.
3 Do you mind if I ask you ___ questions?
4 It's not a very interesting place to visit, so ___ tourists come here.
5 I don't think Jill would be a good teacher. She's got ___ patience.
6 'Would you like milk in your coffee?' 'Yes, ___ .'
7 This is a very boring place to live. There's ___ to do.
8 'Have you ever been to Paris?' 'Yes, I've been there ___ times.'

175

A

all	some	any	most	much/many	little/few	no

You can use the words in the box with a noun (**some food / few books** etc.):

- **All cars** have wheels.
- **Some cars** can go faster than others.
- *(on a notice)* **NO CARS.** (= no cars allowed)
- **Many people** drive too fast.
- I don't go out very often. I'm at home **most days**.

NO CARS

You cannot say 'all of cars', 'some of people' etc. (see also Section B):

- **Some people** learn languages more easily than others. (*not* Some of people)

Note that we say **most** (*not* the most):

- **Most tourists** don't visit this part of the town. (*not* The most tourists)

B

all	some	any	most	much/many	little/few	half	none

You can use the words in the box with **of** (**some of / most of** etc.).
We use **some of / most of / none of** etc. + **the/this/that/these/those/my** ... etc. So you can say
'some **of the people**', 'some **of those people**' (*but not* 'some of people'):

- **Some of the people** I work with are not very friendly.
- **None of this money** is mine.
- Have you read **any of these books**?
- I was sick yesterday. I spent **most of the day** in bed.

You don't need **of** after **all** or **half**. So you can say:

- **All my friends** live in Los Angeles. *or* All **of** my friends ...
- **Half this money** is mine. *or* Half **of** this money ...

Compare:

- **All flowers** are beautiful. (= all flowers in general)
  All (of) the flowers in this garden are beautiful. (= a specific group of flowers)
- **Most problems** have a solution. (= most problems in general)
  We were able to solve **most of the problems** we had. (= a specific group of problems)

C

You can use **all of / some of / none of** etc. + **it/us/you/them**:

- 'How many of these people do you know?' '**None of them. / A few of them.**'
- Do **any of you** want to come to a party tonight?
- 'Do you like this music?' '**Some of it. Not all of it.**'

We say: **all of us / all of you / half of it / half of them** etc. You cannot leave out **of** before
it/us/you/them:

- **All of us** were late. (*not* all us)
- I haven't finished the book yet. I've only read **half of it**. (*not* half it)

D

You can also use **some/most** etc. alone, *without* a noun:

- Some cars have four doors and **some** have two.
- A few of the shops were open, but **most** (of them) were closed.
- Half this money is mine, and **half** (of it) is yours. (*not* the half)

Some and any → Unit 85   **No and none** → Unit 86   **Much/many/little/few** → Unit 87
All → Units 90, 110C   **All of whom / most of which** etc. → Unit 96B

Exercises

88.1 Put in **of** where necessary. Leave the space empty if the sentence is already complete.

1 All ....–........ cars have wheels. (*the sentence is already complete*)
2 None .....of..... this money is mine.
3 Some .... films are very violent.
4 Some .... the films I've seen recently have been very violent.
5 Joe never goes to museums. He says that all .... museums are boring.
6 I think some .... people watch too much television.
7 'Are any .... those letters for me?' 'No, they're all for me.'
8 Kate has lived in London most .... her life.
9 Jim has lived in Chicago all .... his life.
10 Most .... days I get up before 7 o'clock.

88.2 Choose from the list and complete the sentences. Use **of** (some of / most of etc.) where necessary.

accidents	European countries	my dinner	the players
birds	her friends	my spare time	the population
~~cars~~	her opinions	the buildings	~~these books~~

1 I haven't read many .....of these books..... .
2 All .....cars..... have wheels.
3 I spend much .... gardening.
4 Many .... are caused by bad driving.
5 It's a historic town. Many .... are over 400 years old.
6 When she got married, she kept it a secret. She didn't tell any ....
7 Not many people live in the north of the country. Most .... live in the south.
8 Not all .... can fly. For example, the penguin can't fly.
9 Our team played badly and lost the game. None .... played well.
10 Julia and I have very different ideas. I don't agree with many ....
11 Sarah travels a lot in Europe. She has been to most ....
12 I had no appetite. I could only eat half ....

88.3 Use your own ideas to complete these sentences.

1 The building was damaged in the explosion. All .....the windows..... were broken.
2 We had a very lazy holiday. We spent most of .... on the beach.
3 I went to the cinema by myself. None of .... wanted to come.
4 The test was difficult. I could only answer half ....
5 Some of .... you took at the wedding were very good.
6 'Have you spent all .... I gave you?' 'No, there's still some left.'

88.4 Complete the sentences. Use:
   all of / some of / none of + it/them/us (all of it / some of them etc.)

1 These books are all Jane's. .....None of them..... belong to me.
2 'How many of these books have you read?' '........................ . Every one.'
3 We all got wet in the rain because .... had an umbrella.
4 Some of this money is yours and .... is mine.
5 I asked some people for directions, but .... was able to help me.
6 She invented the whole story from beginning to end. .... was true.
7 Not all the tourists in the group were Spanish. .... were French.
8 I watched most of the film, but not ....

Both / both of   neither / neither of
either / either of

A

We use **both/neither/either** for *two* things. You can use these words with a *noun* (**both books**, **neither book** etc.).

For example, you are going out to eat. There are two possible restaurants. You say:

□ **Both restaurants** are very good. (*not* The both restaurants)
□ **Neither restaurant** is expensive.
□ We can go to **either restaurant**. I don't mind.
   (**either** = one or the other, it doesn't matter which one)

B

Both of … / neither of … / either of …

We use **both of / neither of / either of** + **the/these/my/Tom's** … etc. So we say 'both of **the** restaurants', 'both of **those** restaurants' etc. (*but not* both of restaurants):

□ **Both of these** restaurants are very good.
□ **Neither of the** restaurants we went to was (*or* were) expensive.
□ I haven't been to **either of those** restaurants. (= I haven't been to one or the other)

You don't need **of** after **both**. So you can say:

□ **Both my parents** are from London. *or* Both **of** my parents …

You can use **both of / neither of / either of** + **us/you/them**:

□ *(talking to two people)* Can **either of you** speak Spanish?
□ I asked two people the way to the station, but **neither of them** could help me.

You must say 'both **of**' before **us/you/them**:

□ **Both of us** were very tired. (*not* Both us were …)

After **neither of …** a *singular* or a *plural* verb is possible:

□ Neither of the children **wants** (*or* **want**) to go to bed.

C

You can also use **both/neither/either** alone, *without* a noun:

□ I couldn't decide which of the two shirts to buy. I liked **both**. (*or* I liked **both** of them.)
□ 'Is your friend British or American?' '**Neither**. She's Australian.'
□ 'Do you want tea or coffee?' '**Either**. I don't mind.'

D

You can say:

both … and …	□ **Both** Chris **and** Pat were late.
	□ I was **both** tired **and** hungry when I arrived home.
neither … nor …	□ **Neither** Chris **nor** Pat came to the party.
	□ Tom said he would contact me, but he **neither** wrote **nor** phoned.
either … or …	□ I'm not sure where Maria's from. She's **either** Spanish **or** Italian.
	□ **Either** you apologise **or** I'll never speak to you again.

E

Compare **either/neither/both** (two things) and **any/none/all** (more than two):

□ There are **two** good hotels here. You could stay at **either** of them.	□ There are **many** good hotels here. You could stay at **any** of them.
□ We tried **two** hotels. { **Neither** of them had any rooms. { **Both** of them were full.	□ We tried **a lot of** hotels. { **None** of them had any rooms. { **All** of them were full.

89.1 Complete the sentences with **both/neither/either**.

1 'Do you want tea or coffee?' '__Either__ . I really don't mind.'
2 'What day is it today – the 18th or the 19th?' '_____ . It's the 20th.'
3 A: Where did you go for your holidays – Scotland or Ireland?
   B: We went to _____ . A week in Scotland and a week in Ireland.
4 'When shall I phone, in the morning or afternoon?' '_____ . I'll be in all day.'
5 'Where's Liz? Is she at work or at home?' '_____ . She's away on holiday.'

89.2 Complete the sentences with **both/neither/either**. Use **of** where necessary.

1 __Both__ my parents are from London.
2 To get to the town centre, you can go along the footpath by the river or you can go along the road. You can go _____ way.
3 I tried twice to phone George, but _____ times he was out.
4 _____ Tom's parents is English. His father is Polish and his mother is Italian.
5 I saw an accident this morning. One car drove into the back of another. Fortunately _____ driver was injured, but _____ cars were badly damaged.
6 I've got two sisters and a brother. My brother is working, but _____ my sisters are still at school.

89.3 Complete the sentences with **both/neither/either + of us/them**.

1 I asked two people the way to the station, but __neither of them__ could help me.
2 I was invited to two parties last week, but I couldn't go to _____ .
3 There were two windows in the room. It was very warm, so I opened _____ .
4 Sarah and I play tennis together regularly, but _____ can play very well.
5 I tried two bookshops for the book I wanted, but _____ had it.

89.4 Write sentences with **both ... and ... / neither ... nor ... / either ... or ...** .

1 Chris was late. So was Pat. __Both Chris and Pat were late.__
2 He didn't write and he didn't phone. __He neither wrote nor phoned.__
3 Joe is on holiday and so is Sam. _____
4 Joe hasn't got a car. Sam hasn't got one either. _____
5 Brian doesn't watch TV and he doesn't read newspapers.
   _____
6 It was a boring film. It was long too.
   The film _____
7 Is that man's name Richard? Or is it Robert? It's one of the two.
   That man's name _____
8 I haven't got time to go on holiday. And I haven't got the money.
   I've got _____
9 We can leave today or we can leave tomorrow – whichever you prefer.
   We _____

89.5 Complete the sentences with **neither/either/none/any**.

1 We tried a lot of hotels, but __none__ of them had any rooms.
2 I took two books with me on holiday, but I didn't read _____ of them.
3 I took five books with me on holiday, but I didn't read _____ of them.
4 There are a few shops at the end of the street, but _____ of them sells newspapers.
5 You can phone me at _____ time during the evening. I'm always at home.
6 I can meet you next Monday or Friday. Would _____ of those days be convenient for you?
7 John and I couldn't get into the house because _____ of us had a key.

A   All and everybody/everyone

We do not normally use **all** to mean **everybody/everyone**:
- ☐ **Everybody** enjoyed the party. (*not* All enjoyed)

But we say **all of us/you/them** (*not* everybody of ...):
- ☐ **All of us** enjoyed the party. (*not* Everybody of us)

B   All and everything

Sometimes you can use **all** or **everything**:
- ☐ I'll do **all I can** to help.   *or*   I'll do **everything I can** to help.

You can say 'all **I can**' / 'all **you need**' etc., but we do not normally use **all** *alone*:
- ☐ He thinks he knows **everything**. (*not* he knows all)
- ☐ Our holiday was a disaster. **Everything** went wrong. (*not* All went wrong)

But you can say **all about**:
- ☐ He knows **all about** computers.

We also use **all** (*not* everything) to mean 'the only thing(s)':
- ☐ **All** I've eaten today is a sandwich. (= the only thing I've eaten today)

C   **Every / everybody / everyone / everything** are *singular* words, so we use a *singular* verb:
- ☐ **Every seat** in the theatre **was** taken.
- ☐ **Everybody has** arrived. (*not* have arrived)

But you can use **they/them/their** after **everybody/everyone**:
- ☐ **Everybody** said **they** enjoyed **themselves**. (= he or she enjoyed himself or herself)

D   Whole and all

Whole = complete, entire. Most often we use **whole** with *singular* nouns:
- ☐ Did you read **the whole book**? (= all the book, not just a part of it)
- ☐ Emily has lived **her whole life** in Scotland.
- ☐ I was so hungry, I ate **a whole packet** of biscuits. (= a complete packet)

We use **the/my/her** etc. before **whole**. Compare **whole** and **all**:
   the whole book / **all the** book   **her whole** life / **all her** life

We do not normally use **whole** with *uncountable* nouns. We say:
- ☐ I've spent **all the money** you gave me. (*not* the whole money)

E   Every/all/whole with time words

We use **every** to say how often something happens (**every day** / **every Monday** / **every ten minutes** / **every three weeks** etc.):
- ☐ When we were on holiday, we went to the beach **every day**. (*not* all days)
- ☐ The bus service is excellent. There's a bus **every ten minutes**.
- ☐ We don't see each other very often – about **every six months**.

All day / the whole day = the complete day from beginning to end:
- ☐ We spent **all day / the whole day** on the beach.
- ☐ Dan was very quiet. He didn't say a word **all evening / the whole evening**.

Note that we say **all day** (*not* all the day), **all week** (*not* all the week) etc.

Compare **all the time** and **every time**:
- ☐ They never go out. They are at home **all the time**. (= always, continuously)
- ☐ **Every time** I see you, you look different. (= each time, on every occasion)

Countable and uncountable → Units 69–70   **All / all of** → Unit 88   **Each and every** → Unit 91
Every one → Unit 91D   **All (word order)** → Unit 110C

90.1 Complete these sentences with **all**, **everything** or **everybody/everyone**.

1 It was a good party. .....*Everybody*..... enjoyed it.
2 .....*All*..... I've eaten today is a sandwich.
3 .... has their faults. Nobody is perfect.
4 Nothing has changed. .... is the same as it was.
5 Kate told me .... about her new job. It sounds quite interesting.
6 Can .... write their names on a piece of paper, please?
7 Why are you always thinking about money? Money isn't ....
8 I didn't have much money with me. .... I had was ten pounds.
9 When the fire alarm rang, ... left the building immediately.
10 Sue didn't say where she was going. .... she said was that she was going away.
11 We have completely different opinions. I disagree with .... she says.
12 We all did well in the examination. .... in our class passed.
13 We all did well in the examination. .... of us passed.
14 Why are you so lazy? Why do you expect me to do .... for you?

90.2 Write sentences with **whole**.

1 I read the book from beginning to end. .....*I read the whole book.*.....
2 Everyone in the team played well.
The ....
3 Paul opened a box of chocolates. When he finished eating, there were no chocolates left in the box. He ate ....
4 The police came to the house. They were looking for something. They searched everywhere, every room. They ....
5 Everyone in Dave and Jane's family plays tennis. Dave and Jane play, and so do all their children. The ....
6 Ann worked from early in the morning until late in the evening.

....
7 Jack and Jill went on holiday to the seaside for a week. It rained from the beginning of the week to the end. It ....

Now write sentences 6 and 7 again using **all** instead of **whole**.

8 (6) Ann ....
9 (7) ....

90.3 Complete these sentences using **every** with the following:

| five minutes | ~~ten minutes~~ | four hours | six months | four years |

1 The bus service is very good. There's a bus .....*every ten minutes*..... .
2 Tom is ill. He has some medicine. He has to take it ....
3 The Olympic Games take place ....
4 We live near a busy airport. A plane flies over our house ....
5 Martin has a check-up with his dentist ....

90.4 Which is the correct alternative?

1 I've spent ~~the whole money~~ / all the money you gave me. (all the money *is correct*)
2 Sue works every day / all days except Sunday.
3 I'm tired. I've been working hard all the day / all day.
4 It was a terrible fire. Whole building / The whole building was destroyed.
5 I've been trying to phone her, but every time / all the time I phone the line is busy.
6 I don't like the weather here. It rains every time / all the time.
7 When I was on holiday, all my luggage / my whole luggage was stolen.

→ Additional exercise 30 (page 320)

Each and every

A Each and every are similar in meaning. Often it is possible to use **each** or **every**:
- □ **Each** time (*or* **Every** time) I see you, you look different.
- □ There's a telephone in **each** room (*or* **every** room) of the house.

But **each** and **every** are not exactly the same. Study the difference:

We use **each** when we think of things separately, one by one. □ Study **each sentence** carefully. (= study the sentences one by one) each = **X + X + X + X** **Each** is more usual for a small number: □ There were four books on the table. **Each book** was a different colour. □ *(in a card game)* At the beginning of the game, **each player** has three cards.	We use **every** when we think of things as a group. The meaning is similar to **all**. □ **Every sentence** must have a verb. (= all sentences in general) every = (X X X X X X X X X X X X X X X X X X X X X X X X X X X X X X X) **Every** is more usual for a large number: □ Kate loves reading. She has read **every book** in the library. (= all the books) □ I would like to visit **every country** in the world. (= all the countries)

Each (but not **every**) can be used for two things:
- □ In a football match, **each team** has eleven players. (*not* every team)

We use **every** (not **each**) to say how often something happens:
- □ 'How often do you use your computer?' 'Every day.' (*not* Each day)
- □ There's a bus **every ten minutes**. (*not* each ten minutes)

B Compare the structures we use with **each** and **every**:

You can use **each** with a noun:
   each book   **each student**
You can use **each** alone (without a noun):
□ None of the rooms was the same. **Each** (= each room) was different.
Or you can use **each one**:
□ **Each one** was different.
You can say **each of** (the … / these … / them etc.):
□ Read **each of these** sentences carefully.
□ **Each of the** books is a different colour.
□ **Each of them** is a different colour.
	You can use **every** with a noun:
	   every book **every student**
	You can't use **every** alone, but you can say **every one**:
	□ A: Have you read all these books?
	   B: Yes, **every one**.
	
	You can say **every one of** … (*but not* every of):
	□ I've read **every one of those** books. (*not* every of those books)
	□ I've read **every one of them**.

C You can also use **each** in the middle or at the end of a sentence. For example:
- □ The students were **each** given a book. (= Each student was given a book.)
- □ These oranges cost 15 pence **each**.

D **Everyone and every one**

Everyone (one word) is only for people (= everybody).
Every one (two words) is for things or people, and is similar to **each one** (see Section B).
- □ **Everyone** enjoyed the party. (= Everybody …)
- □ Sarah is invited to lots of parties and she goes to **every one**. (= to every party)

Each other → Unit 82C **All and every** → Unit 90

Exercises

91.1 Look at the pictures and complete the sentences with **each** or **every**.

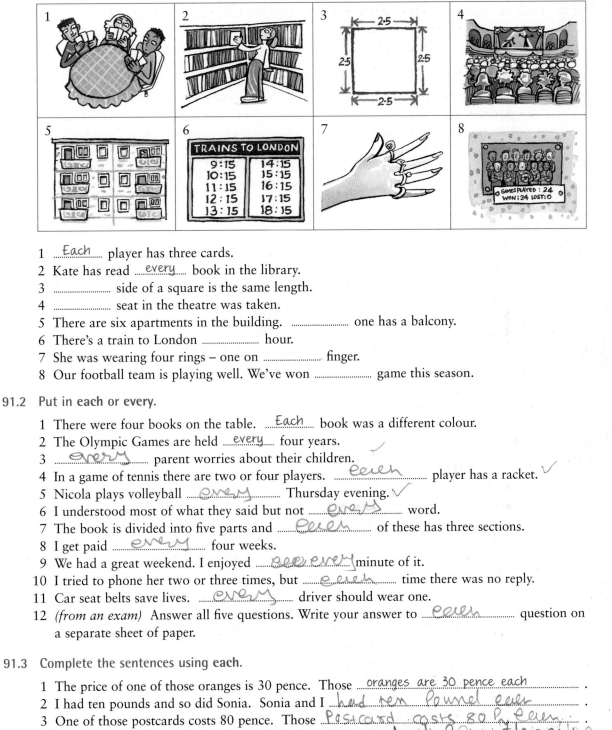

1 __Each__ player has three cards.
2 Kate has read __every__ book in the library.
3 .... side of a square is the same length.
4 .... seat in the theatre was taken.
5 There are six apartments in the building. .... one has a balcony.
6 There's a train to London .... hour.
7 She was wearing four rings – one on .... finger.
8 Our football team is playing well. We've won .... game this season.

91.2 Put in **each** or **every**.

1 There were four books on the table. __Each__ book was a different colour.
2 The Olympic Games are held __every__ four years.
3 __every__ parent worries about their children.
4 In a game of tennis there are two or four players. __each__ player has a racket. ✓
5 Nicola plays volleyball __every__ Thursday evening. ✓
6 I understood most of what they said but not __every__ word.
7 The book is divided into five parts and __each__ of these has three sections.
8 I get paid __every__ four weeks.
9 We had a great weekend. I enjoyed __every__ minute of it.
10 I tried to phone her two or three times, but __each__ time there was no reply.
11 Car seat belts save lives. __every__ driver should wear one.
12 *(from an exam)* Answer all five questions. Write your answer to __each__ question on a separate sheet of paper.

91.3 Complete the sentences using **each**.

1 The price of one of those oranges is 30 pence. Those __oranges are 30 pence each__ .
2 I had ten pounds and so did Sonia. Sonia and I __had ten Pound each__ .
3 One of those postcards costs 80 pence. Those __Postcard costs 80 P. each__ .
4 The hotel was expensive. I paid £120 and so did you. We __had Paid £120 each__

91.4 Put in **everyone** (1 word) or **every one** (2 words).

1 Sarah is invited to a lot of parties and she goes to __every one__ .
2 As soon as __every one__ had arrived, we began the meeting.
3 I asked her lots of questions and she answered __every one__ correctly.
4 She's very popular. __everyone__ likes her.
5 I dropped a tray of glasses. Unfortunately .... broke.

Relative clauses 1:
clauses with **who/that/which**

A Look at this example sentence:

The woman | who lives next door | is a doctor.
— relative clause —

A *clause* is a part of a sentence. A *relative clause* tells us which person or thing (or what kind of person or thing) the speaker means:

☐ The woman **who lives next door** … ('who lives next door' tells us which woman)
☐ People **who live in the country** … ('who live in the country' tells us what kind of people)

We use **who** in a relative clause when we are talking about people (not things):

the woman – she lives next door – is a doctor

⟶ The woman **who lives next door** is a doctor.

we know a lot of people – they live in the country

⟶ We know a lot of people **who live in the country**.

☐ An architect is someone **who designs buildings**.
☐ What was the name of the person **who phoned you?**
☐ Anyone **who wants to apply for the job** must do so by Friday.

You can also use **that** (instead of **who**), but you can't use **which** for people:
☐ The woman **that lives next door** is a doctor. (*not* the woman which)

Sometimes you must use **who** (*not* that) for people – see Unit 95.

B When we are talking about things, we use **that** or **which** (*not* who) in a relative clause:

where is the cheese? – it was in the fridge

⟶ Where is the cheese { that / which } was in the fridge?

☐ I don't like stories **that have unhappy endings.** (*or* stories **which** have …)
☐ Barbara works for a company **that makes furniture.** (*or* a company **which** makes furniture)
☐ The machine **that broke down** is working again now. (*or* The machine **which** broke down)

That is more usual than **which**, but sometimes you must use **which** – see Unit 95.

C **What** = 'the thing(s) that'. Compare **what** and **that**:
☐ **What** happened was my fault. (= the thing that happened)
☐ Everything **that happened** was my fault. (*not* Everything what happened)
☐ The machine **that broke down** is now working again. (*not* The machine what broke down)

D Remember that in relative clauses we use **who/that/which**, not **he/she/they/it**:
☐ I've never spoken to the woman **who lives** next door. (*not* the woman she lives)

92.1 In this exercise you have to explain what some words mean. Choose the right meaning from the box and then write a sentence with **who**. Use a dictionary if necessary.

he/she	{	steals from a shop ~~designs buildings~~ doesn't believe in God is not brave	he/she {	buys something from a shop pays rent to live in a house or flat breaks into a house to steal things expects the worst to happen

1 (an architect) *An architect is someone who designs buildings.*
2 (a burglar) A burglar is someone *who steals from the shop.*
3 (a customer) *is someone who buys something from shop.*
4 (a shoplifter) *is someone who*
5 (a coward) ....
6 (an atheist) ....
7 (a pessimist) ....
8 (a tenant) ....

92.2 Make one sentence from two. Use **who/that/which**.

1 A girl was injured in the accident. She is now in hospital.
   The girl who was injured in the accident is now in hospital.
2 A waitress served us. She was impolite and impatient.
   The *waitress who served us was impolite & impatient.*
3 A building was destroyed in the fire. It has now been rebuilt.
   The *building which was destroyed in the fire has now been rebuilt*
4 Some people were arrested. They have now been released.
   The *People that were arrested now have been released.*
5 A bus goes to the airport. It runs every half hour.
   The *bus that goes to the airport runs every half anhur.*

92.3 Complete the sentences. Choose the best ending from the box and change it into a relative clause.

he invented the telephone	~~it makes furniture~~
she runs away from home	it gives you the meaning of words
they stole my car	it can support life
they were on the wall	it cannot be explained

1 Barbara works for a company *that makes furniture* .
2 The book is about a girl ....
3 What happened to the pictures *the ones that* ?
4 A mystery is something ....
5 The police have caught the men ....
6 A dictionary is a book ....
7 Alexander Bell was the man ....
8 It seems that the earth is the only planet ....

92.4 Are these sentences right or wrong? Correct them where necessary.

1 I don't like stories who have unhappy endings. *stories that have*
2 What was the name of the person who phoned you? *OK*
3 Where's the nearest shop who sells newspapers? ....
4 The driver which caused the accident was fined £500. ....
5 Do you know the person that took these photographs? ....
6 We live in a world what is changing all the time. ....
7 Dan said some things about me that were not true. ....
8 What was the name of the horse it won the race? ....

A Look at these example sentences from Unit 92:

☐ The woman │ who │ **lives next door** is a doctor. (*or* The woman **that** lives …)

The woman │ │ lives next door. **who** (= the woman) is the *subject*

☐ Where is the cheese │ that │ **was in the fridge?** (*or* the cheese **which** was …)

The cheese │ │ was in the fridge. **that** (= the cheese) is the *subject*

You must use **who/that/which** when it is the subject of the relative clause. So you cannot say 'The woman lives next door is a doctor' or 'Where is the cheese was in the fridge?'.

B Sometimes **who/that/which** is the *object* of the verb. For example:

☐ The woman │ who │ **I wanted to see** was away on holiday.

I wanted to see │ the woman │ **who** (= the woman) is the *object*
I is the *subject*

☐ Have you found the keys │ that │ **you lost?**

You lost │ the keys. │ **that** (= the keys) is the *object*
you is the *subject*

When **who/that/which** is the object, you can leave it out. So you can say:

☐ **The woman I wanted to see** was away. *or* The woman **who** I wanted to see …
☐ Have you found **the keys you lost?** *or* … the keys **that** you lost?
☐ **The dress Liz bought** doesn't fit her very well. *or* The dress **that** Liz bought …
☐ Is there **anything I can do?** *or* … anything **that** I can do?

Note that we say:

the keys you lost (*not* the keys you lost them)
the dress Liz bought (*not* the dress Liz bought it)

C Note the position of prepositions (**in/to/for** etc.) in relative clauses:

Tom is talking │ to │ a woman – do you know her?

⟶ Do you know the woman (who/that) **Tom is talking** │ to │ ?

I slept │ in │ a bed last night – it wasn't very comfortable

⟶ The bed (that/which) **I slept** │ in │ **last night** wasn't very comfortable.

☐ Are these the books **you were looking for?** *or* … the books **that/which** you were …
☐ The woman **he fell in love with** left him after a month. *or* The woman **who/that** he …
☐ The man **I was sitting next to on the plane** talked all the time. *or*
The man **who/that** I was sitting next to …

Note that we say:
the books you were looking for (*not* the books you were looking for them)

D You cannot use **what** in sentences like these (see also Unit 92C):

☐ **Everything (that) they said** was true. (*not* Everything what they said)
☐ I gave her **all the money (that) I had.** (*not* all the money what I had)

What = 'the thing(s) that':

☐ Did you hear **what they said?** (= the things that they said)

Relative clauses 1 → Unit 92   Relative clauses 3–5 → Units 94–96   Whom → Unit 94B

93.1 In some of these sentences you need **who** or **that**. Correct the sentences where necessary.

1 <u>The woman lives next door</u> is a doctor.   *The woman who lives next door*
2 Have you found the keys you lost?   OK
3 The people we met last night were very nice.   *The People who we met*
4 The people work in the office are very nice.
5 The people I work with are very nice.   *O.k*
6 What have you done with the money I gave you?
7 What happened to the money was on the table?   *there was on*
8 What's the worst film you've ever seen?   *O.k*
9 What's the best thing it has ever happened to you?

93.2 What do you say in these situations? Complete each sentence with a relative clause.

1 Your friend lost some keys. You want to know if he has found them. You say:
   Have you found ___*the keys you lost*___ ?
2 A friend is wearing a dress. You like it. You tell her:
   I like the dress ___*you are wearing.*___ .
3 A friend is going to see a film. You want to know the name of the film. You say:
   What's the name of the film _____ ?
4 You wanted to visit a museum. It was shut when you got there. You tell a friend:
   The museum _____ was shut when we got there.
5 You invited some people to your party. Some of them couldn't come. You tell someone:
   Some of the people _____ couldn't come.
6 Your friend had to do some work. You want to know if she has finished. You say:
   Have you finished the work _____ ?
7 You hired a car. It broke down after a few miles. You tell a friend:
   The car _____ broke down after a few miles.
8 You stayed at a hotel. Tom had recommended it to you. You tell a friend:
   We stayed at a hotel _____ .

93.3 Complete each sentence using a relative clause with a preposition. Choose from the box.

we went to a party last night	you can rely on Gary	we were invited to a wedding
I work with some people	I applied for a job	you told me about a hotel
~~you were looking for some books~~	I saw you with a man	

1 Are these the books ___*you were looking for*___ ?
2 Unfortunately we couldn't go to the wedding _____ .
3 I enjoy my job. I like the people _____ .
4 What's the name of that hotel _____ ?
5 The party _____ wasn't very enjoyable.
6 I didn't get the job _____ .
7 Gary is a good person to know. He's somebody _____ .
8 Who was that man _____ in the restaurant?

93.4 Put in **that** or **what** where necessary. If the sentence is already complete, leave the space empty.

1 I gave her all the money ___–___ I had. (all the money **that** I had *is also correct*)
2 Did you hear ___*what*___ they said?
3 They give their children everything _____ they want.
4 Tell me _____ you want and I'll try to get it for you.
5 Why do you blame me for everything _____ goes wrong?
6 I won't be able to do much, but I'll do _____ I can.
7 I won't be able to do much, but I'll do the best _____ I can.
8 I don't agree with _____ you've just said.
9 I don't trust him. I don't believe anything _____ he says.

Relative clauses 3: whose/whom/where

A Whose

We use **whose** in relative clauses instead of **his/her/their**:

we saw some people – their car had broken down

—→ We saw some people whose car had broken down.

We use **whose** mostly for people:

- □ A widow is a woman **whose husband is dead**. (**her** husband is dead)
- □ What's the name of the man **whose car you borrowed**? (you borrowed **his** car)
- □ I met someone **whose brother I went to school with**. (I went to school with **his/her** brother)

Compare **who** and **whose**:

- □ I met a man **who** knows you. (**he** knows you)
- □ I met a man **whose sister** knows you. (**his sister** knows you)

B Whom

Whom is possible instead of **who** when it is the *object* of the verb in the relative clause (like the sentences in Unit 93B):

- □ The woman **whom I wanted to see** was away. (I wanted to see **her**)

You can also use **whom** with a preposition (**to whom / from whom / with whom** etc.):

- □ The people **with whom I work** are very nice. (I work **with them**)

But we do not often use **whom** in spoken English. We usually prefer **who** or **that**, or nothing (see Unit 93). So we usually say:

- □ The woman **I wanted to see** … *or* The woman **who/that** I wanted to see …
- □ The people **I work with** … *or* The people **who/that** I work with …

C Where

You can use **where** in a relative clause to talk about a place:

the restaurant – we had dinner there – it was near the airport

—→ The restaurant where we had dinner was near the airport.

- □ I recently went back to **the town where I grew up**.
  (*or* … the town I grew up in *or* … the town **that** I grew up in)
- □ I would like to live in **a place where there is plenty of sunshine**.

D We say:

the day / the year / the time etc. { something happens *or*
{ **that** something happens

- □ Do you remember **the day (that) we went to the zoo**?
- □ **The last time (that) I saw her**, she looked fine.
- □ I haven't seen them since **the year (that) they got married**.

E We say:

the reason { something happens *or*
{ **that/why** something happens

- □ **The reason I'm phoning you** is to ask your advice.
  (*or* The reason **that** I'm phoning / The reason **why** I'm phoning)

Relative clauses 1–2 → Units 92–93   Relative clauses 4–5 → Units 95–96   Whom → Unit 96

Exercises

94.1 You met these people at a party:

The next day you tell a friend about these people. Complete the sentences using **who** or **whose**.

1 I met somebody *whose mother writes detective stories* .
2 I met a man ....
3 I met a woman ....
4 I met somebody ....
5 I met a couple ....
6 I met somebody ....

94.2 Read the situations and complete the sentences using **where**.

1 You grew up in a small town. You went back there recently. You tell someone this.
I recently went back to the small town *where I grew up* .
2 You want to buy some postcards. You ask a friend where you can do this.
Is there a shop near here .... ?
3 You work in a factory. The factory is going to close down next month. You tell a friend:
The factory .... is going to close down next month.
4 Sue is staying at a hotel. You want to know the name of the hotel. You ask a friend:
Do you know the name of the hotel .... ?
5 You play football in a park on Sundays. You show a friend the park. You say:
This is the park .... on Sundays.

94.3 Complete each sentence using **who/whom/whose/where**.

1 What's the name of the man ......*whose*...... car you borrowed?
2 A cemetery is a place .... people are buried.
3 A pacifist is a person .... believes that all wars are wrong.
4 An orphan is a child .... parents are dead.
5 What was the name of the person to .... you spoke on the phone?
6 The place .... we spent our holidays was really beautiful.
7 This school is only for children .... first language is not English.
8 The woman with .... he fell in love left him after a month.

94.4 Use your own ideas to complete these sentences. They are like the examples in Sections D and E.

1 I'll always remember the day *I first met you* .
2 I'll never forget the time ....
3 The reason .... was that I didn't know your address.
4 Unfortunately I wasn't at home the evening ....
5 The reason .... is that they don't need one.
6 .... was the year ....

189

A There are two types of relative clause. In these examples, the relative clauses are <u>underlined</u>. Compare:

Type 1	Type 2
□ The woman <u>who lives next door</u> is a doctor. □ Barbara works for a company <u>that makes furniture</u>. □ We stayed at the hotel <u>(that) you recommended</u>.	□ My brother Rob, <u>who lives in Australia</u>, is a doctor. □ Colin told me about his new job, <u>which he's enjoying very much</u>. □ We stayed at the Park Hotel, <u>which a friend of ours recommended</u>.
In these examples, the relative clause tells you which person or thing (or what kind of person or thing) the speaker means: 'The woman **who lives next door**' tells us *which* woman. 'A company **that makes furniture**' tells us *what kind* of company. 'The hotel (**that**) **Ann recommended**' tells us *which* hotel.	In these examples, the relative clauses do not tell you which person or thing the speaker means. We already know which thing or person is meant: 'My brother Rob', 'Colin's new job' and 'the Park Hotel'. The relative clauses in these sentences give us *extra information* about the person or thing.
We do not use commas (,) with these clauses: □ We know a lot of people <u>who live in London</u>.	We use commas (,) with these clauses: □ My brother Rob, <u>who lives in London</u>, is a doctor.

B In both types of relative clause we use **who** for people and **which** for things. But:

Type 1	Type 2
You can use **that**: □ Do you know anyone **who/that** speaks French and Italian? □ Barbara works for a company **which/that** makes furniture.	You cannot use **that**: □ John, **who** (*not* that) speaks French and Italian, works as a tourist guide. □ Colin told me about his new job, **which** (*not* that) he's enjoying very much.
You can leave out **who/which/that** when it is the object (see Unit 93): □ We stayed at the hotel (that/which) you recommended. □ This morning I met somebody (who/that) I hadn't seen for ages.	You cannot leave out **who** or **which**: □ We stayed at the Park Hotel, **which** a friend of ours recommended. □ This morning I met Chris, **who** I hadn't seen for ages.
We do not often use **whom** in this type of clause (see Unit 94B).	You can use **whom** for people (when it is the object): □ This morning I met Chris, **whom** I hadn't seen for ages.

In both types of relative clause you can use **whose** and **where**:

□ We met some people **whose** car had broken down. □ What's the name of the place **where** you went on holiday?	□ Liz, **whose** car had broken down, was in a very bad mood. □ Jill has just been to Sweden, **where** her daughter lives.

Relative clauses (Type 1) → Units 92–94   Relative clauses (Type 2) → Unit 96

95.1 Make one sentence from two. Use the sentence in brackets to make a relative clause (Type 2). You will need to use **who(m)/whose/which/where**.

1 Catherine is very friendly. (She lives next door.)
Catherine, who lives next door, is very friendly.

2 We stayed at the Park Hotel. (A friend of ours had recommended it.)
We stayed at the Park Hotel, which a friend of ours had recommended.

3 We often go to visit our friends in Bristol. (It is not very far away.)
....

4 I went to see the doctor. (He told me to rest for a few days.)
....

5 John is one of my closest friends. (I have known him for a very long time.)
John ....

6 Sheila is away from home a lot. (Her job involves a lot of travelling.)
....

7 The new stadium will be opened next month. (It can hold 90,000 people.)
....

8 Glasgow is the largest city in Scotland. (My brother lives there.)
....

9 A friend of mine helped me to get a job. (His father is the manager of a company.)
....

95.2 Read the information and complete each sentence. Use a relative clause of Type 1 or Type 2. Use commas where necessary.

1 There's a woman living next door to me. She's a doctor.
The woman _who lives next door to me is a doctor._

2 I've got a brother called Rob. He lives in Australia. He's a doctor.
My brother Rob _, who lives in Australia, is a doctor._

3 There was a strike at the car factory. It began ten days ago. It is now over.
The strike at the car factory ....

4 I was looking for a book this morning. I've found it now.
I've found ....

5 London was once the largest city in the world, but the population is now falling.
The population of London ....

6 A job was advertised. A lot of people applied for it. Few of them had the necessary qualifications.
Few of ....

7 Amy has a son. She showed me a photograph of him. He's a policeman.
Amy showed me ....

95.3 Correct the sentences that are wrong and put in commas where necessary. If the sentence is correct, write 'OK'.

1 Colin told me about his <u>new job that</u> he's enjoying very much.
Colin told me about his new job, which he's enjoying very much.

2 My office that is on the second floor is very small.
....

3 The office I'm using at the moment is very small.
....

4 Ben's father that used to be a teacher now works for a TV company.
....

5 The doctor that examined me couldn't find anything wrong.
....

6 The sun that is one of millions of stars in the universe provides us with heat and light.
....

Relative clauses 5: extra information clauses (2)

A

Prepositions + whom/which

You can use a *preposition* before **whom** (for people) and **which** (for things). So you can say:
to whom / with whom / about which / without which etc. :

- ☐ Mr Lee, **to whom** I spoke at the meeting, is very interested in our proposal.
- ☐ Fortunately we had a map, **without which** we would have got lost.

In informal English we often keep the preposition after the verb in the relative clause. When we do this, we normally use **who** (*not* whom) for people:

- ☐ This is my friend from Canada, **who** I was telling you **about**.
- ☐ Yesterday we visited the City Museum, **which** I'd never been **to** before.

B

All of / most of etc. **+ whom/which**

Study these examples:

Mary has three brothers. All of them are married. *(2 sentences)*

→ Mary has three brothers, **all of** whom are married. *(1 sentence)*

They asked me a lot of questions. I couldn't answer most of them . *(2 sentences)*

→ They asked me a lot of questions, **most of** which I couldn't answer. *(1 sentence)*

In the same way you can say:

none of / neither of / any of / either of
some of / many of / much of / (a) few of } **+ whom** (people)
both of / half of / each of / one of / two of etc. } **+ which** (things)

- ☐ Martin tried on three jackets, **none of which** fitted him.
- ☐ Two men, **neither of whom** I had seen before, came into the office.
- ☐ They've got three cars, **two of which** they rarely use.
- ☐ Sue has a lot of friends, **many of whom** she was at school with.

You can also say **the cause of which / the name of which** etc. :

- ☐ The building was destroyed in a fire, **the cause of which** was never established.
- ☐ We stayed at a beautiful hotel, **the name of which** I can't remember now.

C

Which (*not* what)

Study this example:

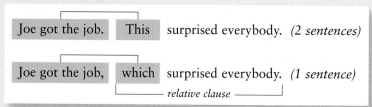

Joe got the job. This surprised everybody. *(2 sentences)*

Joe got the job, which surprised everybody. *(1 sentence)*
———— relative clause ————

In this example, **which** = 'the fact that he got the job'. You must use **which** (*not* what) in sentences like these:

- ☐ Sarah couldn't meet us, **which** was a pity. (*not* what was a pity)
- ☐ The weather was good, **which** we hadn't expected. (*not* what we hadn't expected)

For **what**, see Units 92C and 93D.

All of / most of etc. → Unit 88   **Both of** etc. → Unit 89   Relative clauses 1–4 → Units 92–95

Exercises

96.1 Write the relative clauses in a more formal way using a preposition + **whom/which**.

1 Yesterday we visited the City Museum, which I'd never been to before.
Yesterday we visited the City Museum, _to which I'd never been before_ .

2 My brother showed us his new car, which he's very proud of.
My brother showed us his new car, ...

3 This is a photograph of our friends Chris and Sam, who we went on holiday with.
This is a photograph of our friends Chris and Sam, ...

4 The wedding, which only members of the family were invited to, took place on Friday.
The wedding, ... ,
took place on Friday.

96.2 Use the information in the first sentence to complete the second sentence. Use **all of / most of** etc. or **the ... of** + **whom/which**.

1 All of Mary's brothers are married.
Mary has three brothers, _all of whom are married_ .

2 Most of the information we were given was useless.
We were given a lot of information, ...

3 Jane has received neither of the letters I sent her.
I sent Jane two letters, ...

4 None of the ten people who applied for the job was suitable.
Ten people applied for the job, ...

5 Kate hardly ever uses one of her computers.
Kate has got two computers, ...

6 Mike gave half of the £50,000 he won to his parents.
Mike won £50,000, ...

7 Both of Julia's sisters are teachers.
Julia has two sisters, ...

8 I went to a party – I knew only a few of the people there.
There were a lot of people at the party, ...

9 The sides of the road we drove along were lined with trees.
We drove along the road, the ....

10 The aim of the company's new business plan is to save money.
The company has a new business plan, ...

96.3 Join sentences from the boxes to make new sentences. Use **which**.

1 ~~Laura couldn't come to the party.~~
2 Jane doesn't have a phone.
3 Neil has passed his exams.
4 Our flight was delayed.
5 Kate offered to let me stay at her house.
6 The street I live in is very noisy at night.
7 Our car has broken down.

This was very kind of her.
This means we can't go away tomorrow.
This makes it difficult to contact her.
This makes it difficult to sleep sometimes.
~~This was a pity~~.
This is good news.
This meant we had to wait three hours at the airport.

1 Laura couldn't come to the party, _which was a pity._ ....

2 Jane ....

3 ....

4 ....

5 ....

6 ....

7 ....

A A *clause* is a part of a sentence. Some clauses begin with -ing or -ed. For example:

Do you know the woman **talking to Tom** ?
└── -ing *clause* ──┘

TOM

the woman talking to Tom

The boy **injured in the accident** was taken to hospital.
└────── -ed *clause* ──────┘

the boy injured in the accident

B We use **-ing** clauses to say what somebody (or something) is (or was) doing at a particular time:

- □ Do you know the woman **talking to Sam?** (the woman **is talking** to Sam)
- □ Police **investigating the crime** are looking for three men. (police **are investigating** the crime)
- □ Who were those people **waiting outside?** (they **were waiting**)
- □ I was woken up by a bell **ringing.** (a bell **was ringing**)

You can also use an **-ing** clause to say what happens all the time, not just at a particular time. For example:

- □ The road **connecting the two villages** is very narrow. (the road **connects** the two villages)
- □ I have a large room **overlooking the garden.** (the room **overlooks** the garden)
- □ Can you think of the name of a flower **beginning with T?** (the name **begins** with T)

C **-ed** clauses have a *passive* meaning:

- □ The boy **injured in the accident** was taken to hospital. (he **was injured** in the accident)
- □ George showed me some pictures **painted by his father.** (they **had been painted** by his father)

Injured and **invited** are *past participles*. Note that many past participles are irregular and do not end in **-ed** (**stolen/made/written** etc.):

- □ The police never found the money **stolen in the robbery.**
- □ Most of the goods **made in this factory** are exported.

You can use **left** in this way, with the meaning 'not used, still there':

- □ We've eaten nearly all the chocolates. There are only a few **left.**

D We often use **-ing** and **-ed** clauses after **there is / there was** etc. :

- □ **There were** some children **swimming** in the river.
- □ **Is there** anybody **waiting?**
- □ **There was** a big red car **parked** outside the house.

See/hear somebody doing something → Unit 67   **-ing clauses** → Unit 68   **There (is)** → Unit 84
Irregular past participles (made/stolen etc.) → Appendix 1

Exercises

97.1 Make one sentence from two. Complete the sentences with an **-ing** clause.

1 A bell was ringing. I was woken up by it.
I was woken up by ___a bell ringing___ .

2 A man was sitting next to me on the plane. I didn't talk much to him.
I didn't talk much to the _____ .

3 A taxi was taking us to the airport. It broke down.
The _____ broke down.

4 There's a path at the end of this street. The path leads to the river.
At the end of the street there's a _____ .

5 A factory has just opened in the town. It employs 500 people.
A _____ has just opened in the town.

6 The company sent me a brochure. It contained the information I needed.
The company sent me _____ .

97.2 Make one sentence from two, beginning as shown. Each time make an **-ed** clause.

1 A boy was injured in the accident. He was taken to hospital.
The boy ___injured in the accident___ was taken to hospital.

2 A gate was damaged in the storm. It has now been repaired.
The gate _____ has now been repaired.

3 A number of suggestions were made at the meeting. Most of them were not very practical.
Most of the _____ were not very practical.

4 Some paintings were stolen from the museum. They haven't been found yet.
The _____ haven't been found yet.

5 A man was arrested by the police. What was his name?
What was the name of _____ ?

97.3 Complete the sentences using the following verbs in the correct form:

blow   call   ~~invite~~   live   offer   read   ~~ring~~   sit   study   work

1 I was woken up by a bell ___ringing___ .

2 Some of the people ___invited___ to the party can't come.

3 Life must be very unpleasant for people _____ near busy airports.

4 A few days after the interview, I received a letter _____ me the job.

5 Somebody _____ Jack phoned while you were out.

6 There was a tree _____ down in the storm last night.

7 The waiting room was empty except for a young man _____ by the window
_____ a magazine.

8 Ian has a brother _____ in a bank in London and a sister _____
economics at university in Manchester.

97.4 Use the words in brackets to make sentences using **There is / There was** etc.

1 That house is empty. (nobody / live / in it) ___There's nobody living in it.___

2 The accident wasn't serious. (nobody / injure) ___There was nobody injured.___

3 I can hear footsteps. (somebody / come)
There _____

4 The train was full. (a lot of people / travel)
_____

5 We were the only guests at the hotel. (nobody else / stay there)
_____

6 The piece of paper was blank. (nothing / write / on it)
_____

7 The college offers English courses in the evening. (a course / begin / next Monday)
_____

Adjectives ending in **-ing** and **-ed** (boring/bored etc.)

A There are many adjectives ending in **-ing** and **-ed**, for example: **boring** and **bored**. Study this example situation:

bored

boring

Jane has been doing the same job for a very long time. Every day she does exactly the same thing again and again. She doesn't enjoy her job any more and would like to do something different.

Jane's job is **boring**.

Jane is **bored** (with her job).

Somebody is **bored** if something (or somebody else) is **boring**. Or, if something is **boring**, it makes you **bored**. So:

- ☐ Jane is **bored** because her job is **boring**.
- ☐ Jane's job is **boring**, so Jane is **bored**. (*not* Jane is boring)

If a person is **boring**, this means that they make other people **bored**:

- ☐ George always talks about the same things. He's really **boring**.

B Compare adjectives ending in **-ing** and **-ed**:

☐ My job is { boring. interesting. tiring. satisfying. depressing. etc.	☐ I'm **bored** with my job. ☐ I'm not **interested** in my job any more. ☐ I get very **tired** doing my job. ☐ I'm not **satisfied** with my job. ☐ My job makes me **depressed**. etc.
In these examples, the **-ing** adjective tells you about the job.	In these examples, the **-ed** adjective tells you how somebody feels (about the job).

Compare these examples:

interesting
- ☐ Julia thinks politics is **interesting**.

- ☐ Did you meet anyone **interesting** at the party?

surprising
- ☐ It was **surprising** that he passed the exam.

disappointing
- ☐ The film was **disappointing**. We expected it to be much better.

shocking
- ☐ The news was **shocking**.

interested
- ☐ Julia is **interested** in politics. (*not* interesting in politics)
- ☐ Are you **interested** in buying a car? I'm trying to sell mine.

surprised
- ☐ Everybody was **surprised** that he passed the exam.

disappointed
- ☐ We were **disappointed** with the film. We expected it to be much better.

shocked
- ☐ I was **shocked** when I heard the news.

Exercises

98.1 Complete the sentences for each situation. Use the word in brackets + -ing or -ed.

1 The film wasn't as good as we had expected. (**disappoint…**)
   a The film was ___disappointing___ .
   b We were ___disappointed___ with the film.

2 Donna teaches young children. It's a very hard job, but she enjoys it. (**exhaust…**)
   a She enjoys her job, but it's often _____ .
   b At the end of a day's work, she is often _____ .

3 It's been raining all day. I hate this weather. (**depress…**)
   a This weather is _____ .
   b This weather makes me _____ .
   c It's silly to get _____ because of the weather.

4 Clare is going to Mexico next month. She has never been there before. (**excit…**)
   a It will be an _____ experience for her.
   b Going to new places is always _____ .
   c She is really _____ about going to Mexico.

98.2 Choose the correct word.

1 I was ~~disappointing~~ / disappointed with the film. I had expected it to be better.
   (disappointed *is correct*)

2 Are you interesting / interested in football?

3 The football match was very exciting / excited. I enjoyed it.

4 It's sometimes embarrassing / embarrassed when you have to ask people for money.

5 Do you easily get embarrassing / embarrassed?

6 I had never expected to get the job. I was really amazing / amazed when I was offered it.

7 She has really learnt very fast. She has made astonishing / astonished progress.

8 I didn't find the situation funny. I was not amusing / amused.

9 It was a really terrifying / terrified experience. Afterwards everybody was very shocking / shocked.

10 Why do you always look so boring / bored? Is your life really so boring / bored?

11 He's one of the most boring / bored people I've ever met. He never stops talking and he never says anything interesting / interested.

98.3 Complete each sentence using a word from the box.

amusing/amused	annoying/annoyed	boring/bored
confusing/confused	disgusting/disgusted	exciting/excited
exhausting/exhausted	interesting/interested	~~surprising~~/surprised

1 He works very hard. It's not ___surprising___ that he's always tired.

2 I've got nothing to do. I'm _____ .

3 The teacher's explanation was _____ . Most of the students didn't understand it.

4 The kitchen hadn't been cleaned for ages. It was really _____ .

5 I seldom visit art galleries. I'm not particularly _____ in art.

6 There's no need to get _____ just because I'm a few minutes late.

7 The lecture was _____ . I fell asleep.

8 I've been working very hard all day and now I'm _____ .

9 I'm starting a new job next week. I'm very _____ about it.

10 Steve is very good at telling funny stories. He can be very _____ .

11 Liz is a very _____ person. She knows a lot, she's travelled a lot and she's done lots of different things.

Unit 99

Adjectives: a **nice new** house, you look **tired**

A

Sometimes we use two or more adjectives together:
- ☐ My brother lives in a **nice new** house.
- ☐ In the kitchen there was a **beautiful large round wooden** table.

Adjectives like **new/large/round/wooden** are *fact* adjectives. They give us factual information about age, size, colour etc.
Adjectives like **nice/beautiful** are *opinion* adjectives. They tell us what somebody thinks of something or somebody.
Opinion adjectives usually go before fact adjectives.

	opinion	*fact*	
a	**nice**	**long**	summer holiday
an	**interesting**	**young**	man
	delicious	**hot**	vegetable soup
a	**beautiful**	**large round wooden**	table

B

Sometimes we use two or more fact adjectives together. Usually (but not always) we put fact adjectives in this order:

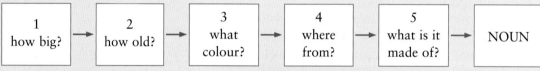

| 1 how big? | 2 how old? | 3 what colour? | 4 where from? | 5 what is it made of? | NOUN |

    a **tall young** man (1 → 2)   a **large wooden** table (1 → 5)
    big blue eyes (1 → 3)   an **old Russian** song (2 → 4)
    a **small black plastic** bag (1 → 3 → 5)   an **old white cotton** shirt (2 → 3 → 5)

Adjectives of size and length (**big/small/tall/short/long** etc.) usually go before adjectives of shape and width (**round/fat/thin/slim/wide** etc.):
    a **large round** table   a **tall thin** girl   a **long narrow** street
When there are two or more colour adjectives, we use **and**:
    a **black and white** dress   a **red, white and green** flag
This does not usually happen with other adjectives before a noun:
    a **long black** dress (*not* a long and black dress)

C

We use adjectives after **be/get/become/seem**:
- ☐ Be **careful**!
- ☐ I'm **tired** and I'm getting **hungry**.
- ☐ As the film went on, it **became** more and more **boring**.
- ☐ Your friend **seems** very **nice**.

We also use adjectives to say how somebody/something looks, feels, sounds, tastes or smells:
- ☐ You **look tired**. / I **feel tired**. / She **sounds tired**.
- ☐ The dinner **smells good**.
- ☐ This tea **tastes** a bit **strange**.

But to say *how* somebody does something you must use an *adverb* (see Units 100–101):
- ☐ Drive **carefully**! (*not* Drive careful)
- ☐ Susan plays the piano very **well**. (*not* plays … very good)

D

We say 'the **first two** days / the **next few** weeks / the **last ten** minutes' etc. :
- ☐ I didn't enjoy the **first two** days of the course. (*not* the two first days)
- ☐ They'll be away for the **next few** weeks. (*not* the few next weeks)

Adverbs → Units 100–101   Comparison (**cheaper** etc.) → Units 105–107
Superlatives (**cheapest** etc.) → Unit 108

99.1 Put the adjectives in brackets in the correct position.

1 a beautiful table (wooden / round)   *a beautiful round wooden table*
2 an unusual ring (gold)
3 an old house (beautiful)
4 black gloves (leather)
5 an American film (old)
6 a long face (thin)
7 big clouds (black)
8 a sunny day (lovely)
9 an ugly dress (yellow)
10 a wide avenue (long)
11 a red car (old / little)
12 a new sweater (green / nice)
13 a metal box (black / small)
14 a big cat (fat / black)
15 a little village (old / lovely)
16 long hair (black / beautiful)
17 an old painting (interesting / French)
18 an enormous umbrella (red / yellow)

99.2 Complete each sentence with a verb (in the correct form) and an adjective from the boxes.

feel	look	~~seem~~		awful	fine	interesting
smell	sound	taste		nice	~~upset~~	wet

1 Helen ___seemed upset___ this morning. Do you know what was wrong?
2 I can't eat this. I've just tried it and it _____ .
3 I wasn't very well yesterday, but I _____ today.
4 What beautiful flowers! They _____ too.
5 You _____ . Have you been out in the rain?
6 Jim was telling me about his new job. It _____ – much better than his old job.

99.3 Put in the correct word.

1 This tea tastes a bit ___strange___ . (strange / strangely)
2 I always feel _____ when the sun is shining. (happy / happily)
3 The children were playing _____ in the garden. (happy / happily)
4 The man became _____ when the manager of the restaurant asked him to leave.
(violent / violently)
5 You look _____ ! Are you all right? (terrible / terribly)
6 There's no point in doing a job if you don't do it _____ . (proper / properly)
7 The soup tastes _____ . (good / well)
8 Hurry up! You're always so _____ . (slow / slowly)

99.4 Write the following in another way using **the first ... / the next ... / the last ...** .

1 the first day and the second day of the course   *the first two days of the course*
2 next week and the week after   *the next two weeks*
3 yesterday and the day before yesterday
4 the first week and the second week of May
5 tomorrow and a few days after that
6 questions 1, 2 and 3 in the exam
7 next year and the year after
8 the last day of our holiday and the two days
before that

→ Additional exercise 31 (page 320)

Adjectives and adverbs 1 (quick/quickly)

A Look at these examples:
- □ Our holiday was too short – the time passed very **quickly**.
- □ Two people were **seriously** injured in the accident.

Quickly and **seriously** are *adverbs*. Many adverbs are formed from an adjective + **-ly**:

adjective:	quick	serious	careful	quiet	heavy	bad
adverb:	quickly	seriously	carefully	quietly	heavily	badly

For spelling, see Appendix 6.

Not all words ending in **-ly** are adverbs. Some *adjectives* end in **-ly** too, for example:
friendly   lively   elderly   lonely   silly   lovely

B Adjective or adverb?

Adjectives (**quick/careful** etc.) tell us about a *noun* (somebody or something). We use adjectives before nouns:	Adverbs (**quickly/carefully** etc.) tell us about a *verb* (*how* somebody does something or *how* something happens):
□ Sam is a **careful driver**. (*not* a carefully driver)	□ Sam **drove carefully** along the narrow road. (*not* drove careful)
□ We didn't go out because of the **heavy rain**.	□ We didn't go out because it was **raining heavily**. (*not* raining heavy)

Compare:

□ She speaks **perfect English**. *adjective + noun*	□ She **speaks** English **perfectly**. *verb + noun + adverb*

We also use adjectives after some verbs, especially **be**, and also **look/feel/sound** etc.
Compare:

□ Please **be quiet**.	□ Please **speak quietly**.
□ I was disappointed that my exam results **were** so **bad**.	□ I was unhappy that I **did** so **badly** in the exam. (*not* did so bad)
□ Why do you always **look** so **serious**?	□ Why do you never **take** me **seriously**?
□ I **feel happy**.	□ The children were **playing happily**.

C We also use adverbs before *adjectives* and *other adverbs*. For example:

reasonably cheap	*(adverb + adjective)*
terribly sorry	*(adverb + adjective)*
incredibly quickly	*(adverb + adverb)*

- □ It's a **reasonably cheap** restaurant and the food is **extremely good**.
- □ I'm **terribly sorry**. I didn't mean to push you. (*not* terrible sorry)
- □ Maria learns languages **incredibly quickly**.
- □ The examination was **surprisingly easy**.

You can also use an adverb before a *past participle* (**injured/organised/written** etc.):
- □ Two people were **seriously injured** in the accident. (*not* serious injured)
- □ The meeting was very **badly organised**.

Adjectives after be/look/feel etc. → Unit 99C   Adjectives and adverbs 2 → Unit 101

100.1 Complete each sentence with an adverb. The first letters of the adverb are given.

1 We didn't go out because it was raining he_avily____ .
2 Our team lost the game because we played very ba_____ .
3 I had little difficulty finding a place to live. I found a flat quite ea_____ .
4 We had to wait for a long time, but we didn't complain. We waited pat_____ .
5 Nobody knew Steve was coming to see us. He arrived unex_____ .
6 Mike keeps fit by playing tennis reg_____ .
7 I don't speak French very well, but I can understand per_____ if people speak
    sl_____ and cl_____ .

100.2 Put in the correct word.

1 Two people were ____seriously____ injured in the accident. (serious / seriously)
2 The driver of the car had ____serious____ injuries. (serious / seriously)
3 I think you behaved very _____ . (selfish / selfishly)
4 Rose is _____ upset about losing her job. (terrible / terribly)
5 There was a _____ change in the weather. (sudden / suddenly)
6 Everybody at the party was _____ dressed. (colourful / colourfully)
7 Linda likes wearing _____ clothes. (colourful / colourfully)
8 Liz fell and hurt herself quite _____ . (bad / badly)
9 Joe says he didn't do well at school because he was _____ taught. (bad / badly)
10 Don't go up that ladder. It doesn't look _____ . (safe / safely)

100.3 Complete each sentence using a word from the box. Sometimes you need the adjective (careful etc.) and sometimes the adverb (carefully etc.).

careful(ly)	complete(ly)	continuous(ly)	financial(ly)	fluent(ly)
happy/happily	nervous(ly)	perfect(ly)	~~quick(ly)~~	special(ly)

1 Our holiday was too short. The time passed very ____quickly____ .
2 Steve doesn't take risks when he's driving. He's always _____ .
3 Sue works _____ . She never seems to stop.
4 Rachel and Patrick are very _____ married.
5 Maria's English is very _____ although she makes quite a lot of mistakes.
6 I cooked this meal _____ for you, so I hope you like it.
7 Everything was very quiet. There was _____ silence.
8 I tried on the shoes and they fitted me _____ .
9 Do you usually feel _____ before examinations?
10 I'd like to buy a car, but it's _____ impossible for me at the moment.

100.4 Choose two words (one from each box) to complete each sentence.

absolutely	badly	completely	changed	~~cheap~~	damaged
~~reasonably~~	seriously	slightly	enormous	ill	long
unnecessarily	unusually		planned	quiet	

1 I thought the restaurant would be expensive, but it was ____reasonably cheap____ .
2 Steve's mother is _____ in hospital.
3 What a big house! It's _____ .
4 It wasn't a serious accident. The car was only _____ .
5 The children are normally very lively, but they're _____ today.
6 When I returned home after 20 years, everything had _____ .
7 The film was _____ . It could have been much shorter.
8 A lot went wrong during our holiday because it was _____ .

→ Additional exercise 31 (page 320)

A Good/well

Good is an *adjective*. The *adverb* is **well**:

- ☐ Your English is **good**.   *but*   You **speak** English **well**.
- ☐ Susan is a **good** pianist.   *but*   Susan **plays** the piano **well**.

We use **well** (*not* good) with *past participles* (**dressed/known** etc.):

well-dressed   well-known   well-educated   well-paid

- ☐ Gary's father is a **well-known** writer.

But **well** is also an adjective with the meaning 'in good health':

- ☐ 'How are you today?   'I'm very **well**, thanks.'

B Fast/hard/late

These words are both adjectives and adverbs:

adjective	*adverb*
☐ Darren is a very **fast** runner.	Darren can **run** very **fast**.
☐ Kate is a **hard** worker.	Kate **works hard**. (*not* works hardly)
☐ I was **late**.	I **got up late** this morning.

Lately = recently:

- ☐ Have you seen Tom **lately**?

C Hardly

Hardly = very little, almost not. Study these examples:

- ☐ Sarah wasn't very friendly at the party. She **hardly** spoke to me.
  (= she spoke to me very little, almost not at all)
- ☐ We've only met once or twice. We **hardly** know each other.

Hard and **hardly** are different. Compare:

- ☐ He tried **hard** to find a job, but he had no luck. (= he tried a lot, with a lot of effort)
- ☐ I'm not surprised he didn't find a job. He **hardly** tried to find one. (= he tried very little)

You can use **hardly + any/anybody/anyone/anything/anywhere**:

- ☐ A: How much money have we got?
  B: **Hardly any**. (= very little, almost none)
- ☐ These two cameras are very similar. There's **hardly any** difference between them.
- ☐ The exam results were very bad. **Hardly anybody** in our class passed. (= very few students passed)

> There's **hardly anything** in the fridge.

Note that you can say:

- ☐ She said **hardly anything**.   *or*   She **hardly** said **anything**.
- ☐ We've got **hardly any** money.   *or*   We've **hardly** got **any** money.

I can hardly do something = it's very difficult for me, almost impossible:

- ☐ Your writing is terrible. **I can hardly** read it. (= it is almost impossible to read it)
- ☐ My leg was hurting me. **I could hardly** walk.

Hardly ever = almost never:

- ☐ I'm nearly always at home in the evenings. I **hardly ever** go out.

Hardly also means 'certainly not'. For example:

- ☐ It's **hardly surprising** that you're tired. You haven't slept for three days.
  (= it's certainly not surprising)
- ☐ The situation is serious, but it's **hardly a crisis**. (= it's certainly not a crisis)

Exercises

101.1 Put in **good** or **well**.

1 I play tennis but I'm not very ___good___ .
2 Your exam results were very ....
3 You did .... in your exams.
4 The weather was .... while we were on holiday.
5 I didn't sleep .... last night.
6 How are you? Are you .... ?
7 Lucy speaks German very ....
8 Lucy's German is very ....
9 Our new business isn't doing very .... at the moment.
10 I like your hat. It looks .... on you.
11 I've met her a few times, but I don't know her ....

101.2 Complete these sentences using **well** + the following words:

~~behaved~~   dressed   informed   kept   known   paid   written

1 The children were very good. They were ___well-behaved___ .
2 I'm surprised you haven't heard of her. She is quite ....
3 Our neighbours' garden is neat and tidy. It is very ....
4 I enjoyed the book you lent me. It's a great story and it's very ....
5 Tania knows a lot about many things. She is very ....
6 Mark's clothes are always smart. He is always ....
7 Jane has a lot of responsibility in her job, but she isn't very ....

101.3 Are the <u>underlined</u> words right or wrong? Correct them where necessary.

1 I'm tired because I've been working <u>hard</u>.   ___OK___
2 I tried <u>hard</u> to remember her name, but I couldn't.   ....
3 This coat is practically unused. I've <u>hardly</u> worn it. ....
4 Judy is a good tennis player. She hits the ball <u>hardly</u>. ....
5 Don't walk so <u>fast</u>! I can't keep up with you.   ....
6 I had plenty of time, so I was walking <u>slow</u>.   ....

101.4 Complete the sentences. Use **hardly** + the following verbs (in the correct form):

change   hear   ~~know~~   recognise   say   sleep   speak

1 Scott and Tracy have only met once before. They ___hardly know___ each other.
2 You're speaking very quietly. I can .... you.
3 I'm very tired this morning. I .... last night.
4 We were so shocked when we heard the news, we could ....
5 Kate was very quiet this evening. She .... a word.
6 You look the same now as you looked 15 years ago. You've ....
7 I met Dave a few days ago. I hadn't seen him for a long time and he looks very different now. I .... him.

101.5 Complete these sentences with **hardly** + any/anybody/anything/anywhere/ever.

1 I'll have to go shopping. There's ___hardly anything___ to eat.
2 It was a very warm day and there was .... wind.
3 'Do you know much about computers?'   'No, ...'
4 The hotel was almost empty. There was .... staying there.
5 I listen to the radio quite often, but I .... watch television.
6 Our new boss is not very popular. .... likes her.
7 It was very crowded in the room. There was .... to sit.
8 We used to be good friends, but we .... see each other now.
9 It was nice driving this morning. There was .... traffic.
10 I hate this town. There's .... to do and .... to go.

→ Additional exercise 31 (page 320)

A   Compare **so** and **such**:

We use **so** + *adjective/adverb*:
     so stupid   so quick
     so nice   so quickly

- ☐ I didn't like the book. The story was **so stupid.**
- ☐ I like Liz and Joe. They are **so nice.**

We use **such** + *noun*:
     such a story   such people
We also use **such** + *adjective* + *noun*:
     such a stupid **story**   such nice **people**

- ☐ I didn't like the book. It was **such** a stupid **story.** (*not* a so stupid story)
- ☐ I like Liz and Joe. They are **such nice people.** (*not* so nice people)

We say **such a** … (*not* a such):
     such a big **dog** (*not* a such big dog)

B   **So** and **such** make the meaning of an adjective (or adverb) stronger:

- ☐ It's a beautiful day, isn't it? It's **so warm.** (= really warm)
- ☐ It's difficult to understand him because he talks **so quietly.**

You can use **so** … **that**:
- ☐ The book was **so good that** I couldn't put it down.
- ☐ I was **so tired that** I fell asleep in the armchair.

We usually leave out **that**:
- ☐ I was **so tired** I fell asleep.

- ☐ It was a great holiday. We had **such a good time.** (= a really good time)

You can use **such** … **that**:
- ☐ It was **such a good book that** I couldn't put it down.
- ☐ It was **such nice weather that** we spent the whole day on the beach.

We usually leave out **that**:
- ☐ It was **such nice weather** we spent …

C   We also use **so** and **such** with the meaning 'like this':

- ☐ Somebody told me the house was built 100 years ago. I didn't realize it was **so old.** (= as old as it is)
- ☐ I'm tired because I got up at six. I don't usually get up **so early.**
- ☐ I expected the weather to be cooler. I'm surprised it is **so warm.**

- ☐ I didn't realise it was **such an old house.**
- ☐ You know it's not true. How can you say **such a thing?**

Note the expression **no such** … :
- ☐ You won't find the word 'blid' in the dictionary. There's **no such word.** (= this word does not exist)

D   Compare:

so long
- ☐ I haven't seen her for **so long** I've forgotten what she looks like.

so far
- ☐ I didn't know it was **so far.**

so much, so many
- ☐ I'm sorry I'm late – there was **so much** traffic.

such a long time
- ☐ I haven't seen her for **such a long time.** (*not* so long time)

such a long way
- ☐ I didn't know it was **such a long way.**

such a lot (of)
- ☐ I'm sorry I'm late – there was **such a lot** of traffic.

Not so … as → Unit 107A   **Such as** → Unit 117B

102.1 Put in **so**, **such** or **such a**.

1 It's difficult to understand him because he speaks .....<u>so</u>.... quietly.

2 I like Liz and Joe. They're ....<u>such</u>.... nice people.

3 It was a great holiday. We had ....<u>such a</u>.... good time.

4 I was surprised that he looked .... well after his recent illness.

5 Everything is .... expensive these days, isn't it?

6 The weather is beautiful, isn't it? I didn't expect it to be .... nice day.

7 I have to go. I didn't realise it was .... late.

8 He always looks good. He wears .... nice clothes.

9 It was .... boring film that I fell asleep while I was watching it.

10 I couldn't believe the news. It was .... shock.

11 I think she works too hard. She looks .... tired all the time.

12 The food at the hotel was .... awful. I've never eaten .... awful food.

13 They've got .... much money they don't know what to do with it.

14 I didn't realise you lived .... long way from the city centre.

15 The party was really great. It was .... pity you couldn't come.

102.2 Make one sentence from two. Use **so** or **such**.

1 ~~She worked hard.~~	You could hear it from miles away.
2 ~~It was a beautiful day.~~	You would think it was her native language.
3 I was tired.	We spent the whole day indoors.
4 We had a good time on holiday.	~~She made herself ill.~~
5 She speaks English well.	I couldn't keep my eyes open.
6 I've got a lot to do.	I didn't eat anything else for the rest of the day.
7 The music was loud.	~~We decided to go to the beach.~~
8 I had a big breakfast.	I didn't know what to say.
9 It was horrible weather.	I don't know where to begin.
10 I was surprised.	We didn't want to come home.

1 <u>She worked so hard she made herself ill.</u>

2 <u>It was such a beautiful day we decided to go to the beach.</u>

3 I was ....

4 ....

5 ....

6 ....

7 ....

8 ....

9 ....

10 ....

102.3 Use your own ideas to complete these pairs of sentences.

1 a We enjoyed our holiday. It was so ....<u>relaxing</u>.. .

  b We enjoyed our holiday. We had such ....<u>a good time</u>............................... .

2 a I like Catherine. She's so ....

  b I like Catherine. She's such ....

3 a I like New York. It's so ....

  b I like New York. It's such ....

4 a I wouldn't like to be a teacher. It's so ....

  b I wouldn't like to be a teacher. It's such ....

5 a It's great to see you again! I haven't seen you for so ....

  b It's great to see you again! I haven't seen you for such ....

A Enough goes *after* adjectives and adverbs:

- [ ] I can't run very far. I'm not **fit enough**. (*not* enough fit)
- [ ] Let's go. We've waited **long enough**.
- [ ] Is Joe going to apply for the job? Is he **experienced enough**?

> I'm not fit enough.

Compare **too** ... and **not** ... enough:

- [ ] You never stop working. You work **too hard**.
  (= more than is necessary)
- [ ] You're lazy. You don't work **hard enough**.
  (= less than is necessary)

B Enough normally goes *before* nouns:

- [ ] I can't run very far. I haven't got **enough energy**. (*not* energy enough)
- [ ] Is Joe going to apply for the job? Does he have **enough experience**?
- [ ] We've got **enough money**. We don't need any more.
- [ ] Some of us had to sit on the floor because there weren't **enough chairs**.

Note that we say:

- [ ] We didn't have **enough time**. (*not* the time wasn't enough)
- [ ] There is **enough money**. (*not* the money is enough)

You can use **enough** alone (without a noun):

- [ ] We don't need any more money. We've got **enough**.

Compare **too much/many** and **enough**:

- [ ] There's **too much furniture** in this room. There's not **enough space**.
- [ ] There were **too many people** and not **enough chairs**.

C We say **enough/too ... for** somebody/something:

- [ ] We haven't got **enough** money **for a holiday**.
- [ ] Is Joe experienced **enough for the job**?
- [ ] This shirt is **too** big **for me**. I need a smaller size.

But we say **enough/too ... to** do something (*not* for doing). For example:

- [ ] We haven't got **enough money to go** on holiday. (*not* for going)
- [ ] Is Joe **experienced enough to do** the job?
- [ ] They're **too young to get** married. / They're not **old enough to get** married.
- [ ] Let's get a taxi. It's **too far to walk** home from here.
- [ ] The bridge is just **wide enough** for two cars **to pass** each other.

D We say:

	The food was very hot. We couldn't eat **it**.
and	The food was so hot that we couldn't eat **it**.
but	The food was **too** hot **to eat**. (*without* it)

Some more examples like this:

- [ ] These boxes are **too heavy to carry**.
  (*not* too heavy to carry them)
- [ ] The wallet was **too big to put** in my pocket.
  (*not* too big to put it)
- [ ] This chair isn't **strong enough to stand on**.
  (*not* strong enough to stand on it)

To ... and for ... (purpose) → Unit 64   **Adjective + to ... (difficult to understand etc.)** → Unit 65

103.1 Complete the sentences using **enough** + the following words:

big   ~~chairs~~   cups   ~~fit~~   milk   money   qualifications   room   time   warm   well

1 I can't run very far. I'm not ......*fit enough*...... .
2 Some of us had to sit on the floor because there weren't ......*enough chairs*...... .
3 I'd like to buy a car, but I haven't got .... at the moment.
4 Have you got .... in your coffee or would you like some more?
5 Are you .... ? Or shall I switch on the heating?
6 It's only a small car. There isn't .... for all of us.
7 Steve didn't feel .... to go to work this morning.
8 I enjoyed my trip to Paris, but there wasn't .... to do everything
   I wanted.
9 Do you think I've got .... to apply for the job?
10 Try this jacket on and see if it's .... for you.
11 There weren't .... for everybody to have coffee at the same time.

103.2 Complete the answers to the questions. Use **too** or **enough** + the word(s) in brackets.

#	Question	(word)	Answer
1	Are they going to get married?	(old)	No, they're not *old enough to get married* .
2	I need to talk to you about something.	(busy)	Well, I'm afraid I'm .... to you now.
3	Let's go to the cinema.	(late)	No, it's .... to the cinema.
4	Why don't we sit outside?	(warm)	It's not .... outside.
5	Would you like to be a politician?	(shy)	No, I'm .... a politician.
6	Would you like to be a teacher?	(patience)	No, I haven't got .... a teacher.
7	Did you hear what he was saying?	(far away)	No, we were .... what he was saying.
8	Can he read a newspaper in English?	(English)	No, he doesn't know .... a newspaper.

103.3 Make one sentence from two. Complete the new sentence using **too** or **enough**.

1 We couldn't carry the boxes. They were too heavy.
   The boxes were too heavy to carry.
2 I can't drink this coffee. It's too hot.
   This coffee is ....
3 Nobody could move the piano. It was too heavy.
   The piano ....
4 Don't eat these apples. They're not ripe enough.
   These apples ....
5 I can't explain the situation. It is too complicated.
   The situation ....
6 We couldn't climb over the wall. It was too high.
   The wall ....
7 Three people can't sit on this sofa. It isn't big enough.
   This sofa ....
8 You can't see some things without a microscope. They are too small.
   Some ....

A You can use **quite/pretty/rather/fairly** + adjectives or adverbs. So you can say:

☐ It's **quite** cold.   It's **pretty** cold.   It's **rather** cold.   It's **fairly** cold.

Quite/pretty/rather/fairly = less than 'very' but more than 'a little'.

B Quite and **pretty** are very similar in meaning:

☐ You'll need a coat when you go out. It's **quite cold / pretty cold**. (= less than 'very cold', but more than 'a little cold')
☐ I'm surprised you haven't heard of her. She's **quite famous / pretty famous**.
☐ Amanda lives **quite near** me, so we see each other **pretty often**.

Pretty is an informal word and is used mainly in spoken English.

Quite goes before **a/an**:

☐ We live in **quite an old house**. (*not* a quite old house)

Compare:

☐ Sally has **quite a** good job.
  Sally has **a pretty** good job.

You can also use **quite** (but not **pretty**) in the following ways:

quite a/an + noun (without an adjective):

☐ I didn't expect to see them. It was **quite a surprise**. (= quite a big surprise)

quite a lot (of …):

☐ There were **quite a lot of** people at the meeting.

quite + verb, especially **like** and **enjoy**:

☐ I **quite like** tennis, but it's not my favourite sport.

C Rather is similar to **quite** and **pretty**. We often use **rather** for negative ideas:

☐ The weather isn't so good. It's **rather cloudy**.
☐ Paul is **rather shy**. He doesn't talk very much.

Quite and **pretty** are also possible in these examples.

When we use **rather** for positive ideas (**good/nice** etc.), it means 'unusually' or 'surprisingly':

☐ These oranges are **rather good**. Where did you get them?

D Fairly is weaker than **quite/rather/pretty**. For example, if something is **fairly good**, it is not very good and it could be better:

☐ My room is **fairly big**, but I'd prefer a bigger one.
☐ We see each other **fairly often**, but not as often as we used to.

E Quite also means 'completely'. For example:

☐ 'Are you sure?' 'Yes, **quite sure**.' (= completely sure)

Quite means 'completely' with a number of adjectives, especially:

sure	right	true	clear	different	incredible	amazing
certain	wrong	safe	obvious	unnecessary	extraordinary	impossible

☐ She was **quite different** from what I expected. (= completely different)
☐ Everything they said was **quite true**. (= completely true)

We also use **quite** (= completely) with some verbs. For example:

☐ I **quite agree** with you. (= I completely agree)

Not quite = not completely:

☐ They **haven't quite finished** their dinner yet.
☐ I **don't quite understand** what you mean.
☐ 'Are you ready yet?' '**Not quite**.' (= not completely)

104.1 Complete the sentences using **quite** + the following:

~~famous~~   good   hungry   late   noisy   often   old   surprised

1 I'm surprised you haven't heard of her. She's _quite famous_ .
2 I'm .... Is there anything to eat?
3 'How were the photographs you took?' '................................ . Better than usual.'
4 I go to the cinema .... – maybe once a month.
5 We live near a very busy road, so it's often ....
6 I didn't expect Laura to contact me. I was .... when she phoned.
7 I went to bed .... last night, so I'm a bit tired this morning.
8 I don't know exactly when these houses were built, but they're ....

104.2 Complete the sentences using **quite** + the following:

| a busy day | a good voice | a nice time | a lot of traffic |
| ~~a nice day~~ | a long way | a strong wind | |

1 The weather was better than we had expected. It was _quite a nice day_ .
2 Tom often sings. He's got ....
3 The bus stop wasn't very near the hotel. We had to walk ....
4 It's warm today, but there's ....
5 The journey took longer than I expected. There was ....
6 I'm tired. I've had ....
7 Our holiday was OK. We had ....

104.3 Use your own ideas to complete these sentences. Use **rather** + adjective.

1 The weather isn't so good. It's _rather cloudy_ .
2 I enjoyed the film, but it was ....
3 The hotel we stayed at wasn't very good. I was ....
4 I think it's .... that Chris went away without telling anybody.
5 Lucy doesn't like having to wait. Sometimes she's ....

104.4 What does **quite** mean in these sentences? Tick (✓) the right meaning.

	more than a little, less than very (Section B)	completely (Section E)
1 It's <u>quite cold</u>. You'd better wear your coat.	✓	
2 'Are you sure?' 'Yes, <u>quite sure</u>.'		✓
3 Maria's English is <u>quite good</u>.		
4 I couldn't believe it. It was <u>quite incredible</u>.		
5 My bedroom is <u>quite big</u>.		
6 I'm <u>quite tired</u>. I think I'll go to bed.		
7 I <u>quite agree</u> with you.		

104.5 Complete these sentences using **quite** + the following:

different   impossible   right   safe   sure   ~~true~~   unnecessary

1 I didn't believe her at first, but in fact what she said was _quite true_ .
2 You won't fall. The ladder is ....
3 I'm afraid I can't do what you ask. It's ....
4 I couldn't agree with you more. You are ....
5 You can't compare the two things. They are ....
6 You needn't have done that. It was ....
7 I think I saw them go out, but I'm not ....

Comparison 1
(cheaper, more expensive etc.)

A

Study these examples:

How shall we travel? By car or by train?

Let's go by car. It's **cheaper**.
Don't go by train. It's **more expensive**.

Cheaper and **more expensive** are *comparative* forms.

After comparatives you can use **than** (see Unit 107):

☐ It's **cheaper** to go by car **than** by train.
☐ Going by train is **more expensive than** going by car.

B

The comparative form is **-er** or **more** ... .

We use **-er** for short words (one syllable):	We use **more** ... for longer words (two syllables or more):
cheap → cheaper fast → faster	more serious more often
large → larger thin → thinner	more expensive more comfortable
We also use **-er** for two-syllable words that end in **-y** (**-y** → **ier**):	We also use **more** ... for adverbs that end in **-ly**:
lucky → luckier early → earlier	more slowly more seriously
easy → easier pretty → prettier	more quietly more carefully
For spelling, see Appendix 6.	

Compare these examples:

☐ You're **older** than me.	☐ You're **more patient** than me.
☐ The exam was fairly easy – **easier** than I expected.	☐ The exam was quite difficult – **more difficult** than I expected.
☐ Can you walk a bit **faster**?	☐ Can you walk a bit **more slowly**?
☐ I'd like to have a **bigger** car.	☐ I'd like to have a **more reliable** car.
☐ Last night I went to bed **earlier** than usual.	☐ I don't play tennis much these days. I used to play **more often**.

You can use **-er** *or* **more** ... with some two-syllable adjectives, especially:

clever   narrow   quiet   shallow   simple

☐ It's too noisy here. Can we go somewhere **quieter / more quiet**?

C

A few adjectives and adverbs have irregular comparative forms:

good/well → **better**

☐ The garden looks **better** since you tidied it up.
☐ I know him **well** – probably **better** than anybody else knows him.

bad/badly → **worse**:

☐ 'How is your headache? Better?' 'No, it's **worse**.'
☐ He did very badly in the exam – **worse** than expected.

far → **further** (*or* **farther**):

☐ It's a long walk from here to the park – **further** than I thought. (*or* **farther** than)

Further (*but not* farther) can also mean 'more' or 'additional':

☐ Let me know if you hear any **further** news. (= any more news)

105.1 Complete the sentences using a comparative form (older / more important etc.).

1 It's too noisy here. Can we go somewhere ....*quieter*.... ?
2 This coffee is very weak. I like it a bit ....
3 The hotel was surprisingly big. I expected it to be ....
4 The hotel was surprisingly cheap. I expected it to be ....
5 The weather is too cold here. I'd like to live somewhere ....
6 My job is a bit boring sometimes. I'd like to do something ....
7 It's a pity you live so far away. I wish you lived ....
8 I was surprised how easy it was to use the computer. I thought it would be

    ....
9 Your work isn't very good. I'm sure you can do ....
10 Don't worry. The situation isn't so bad. It could be ....
11 I was surprised we got here so quickly. I expected the journey to take ....
12 You're talking very loudly. Can you speak a bit .... ?
13 You hardly ever phone me. Why don't you phone me .... ?
14 You're standing too near the camera. Can you move a bit .... away?
15 You were a bit depressed yesterday, but you look .... today.

105.2 Complete the sentences. Each time use the comparative form of one of the words in the box. Use **than** where necessary.

big	crowded	~~early~~	easily	high	important
interested	peaceful	~~reliable~~	serious	simple	thin

1 I was feeling tired last night, so I went to bed ....*earlier than*.... usual.
2 I'd like to have a ....*more reliable*.... car. The one I've got keeps breaking down.
3 Unfortunately her illness was .... we thought at first.
4 You look .... Have you lost weight?
5 I want a .... flat. We don't have enough space here.
6 He doesn't study very hard. He's .... in having a good time.
7 Health and happiness are .... money.
8 The instructions were very complicated. They could have been ....
9 There were a lot of people on the bus. It was .... usual.
10 I like living in the countryside. It's .... living in a town.
11 You'll find your way around the town .... if you have a good map.
12 In some parts of the country, prices are .... in others.

105.3 Read the situations and complete the sentences. Use a comparative form (**-er** or **more ...**).

1 Yesterday the temperature was six degrees. Today it's only three degrees.
    It's ....*colder today than it was yesterday.*...
2 The journey takes four hours by car and five hours by train.
    It takes ....
3 Dave and I went for a run. I ran ten kilometres. Dave stopped after eight kilometres.
    I ran ....
4 Chris and Joe both did badly in the test. Chris got 30%, but Joe only got 25%.
    Joe did ....
5 I expected my friends to arrive at about 4 o'clock. In fact they arrived at 2.30.
    My friends ....
6 You can go by bus or by train. The buses run every 30 minutes. The trains run every hour.
    The buses ....
7 We were very busy at work today. We're not usually as busy as that.
    We ....

Comparison 2 (much better / any better / better and better / the sooner the better)

A Before comparatives you can use:

much **a lot** **far** (= a lot) **a bit** **a little** **slightly** (= a little)

- □ Let's go by car. It's **much cheaper**. (*or* **a lot cheaper**)
- □ 'How do you feel?' '**Much better**, thanks.'
- □ Don't go by train. It's **a lot more expensive**. (*or* **much more expensive**)
- □ Could you speak **a bit more slowly**? (*or* **a little more slowly**)
- □ This bag is **slightly heavier** than the other one.
- □ Her illness was **far more serious** than we thought at first. (*or* **much more serious / a lot more serious**)

B You can use **any** and **no** + comparative (**any longer / no bigger** etc.):

- □ I've waited long enough. I'm not waiting **any longer**. (= not even a little longer)
- □ We expected their house to be very big, but it's **no bigger** than ours. *or*
  … it isn't **any bigger** than ours. (= not even a little bigger)
- □ How do you feel now? Do you feel **any better**?
- □ This hotel is better than the other one, and it's **no more expensive**.

C **Better and better / more and more** etc.

We repeat comparatives (**better and better** etc.) to say that something changes continuously:

- □ Your English is improving. It's getting **better and better**.
- □ The city is growing fast. It's getting **bigger and bigger**.
- □ Cathy got **more and more bored** in her job. In the end she left.
- □ These days **more and more** people are learning English.

D **The … the …**

You can say **the** (sooner/bigger/more etc.) **the better**:

- □ 'What time shall we leave?' '**The sooner the better**.' (= as soon as possible)
- □ A: What sort of box do you want? A big one?
  B: Yes, **the bigger the better**. (= as big as possible)
- □ When you're travelling, **the less luggage** you have **the better**.

We also use **the … the …** to say that one thing depends on another thing:

- □ **The warmer** the weather, **the better** I feel. (= if the weather is warmer, I feel better)
- □ **The sooner** we leave, **the earlier** we will arrive.
- □ **The younger** you are, **the easier** it is to learn.
- □ **The more expensive** the hotel, **the better** the service.
- □ **The more electricity** you use, **the higher** your bill will be.
- □ **The more** I thought about the plan, **the less** I liked it.

E **Older** and **elder**

The comparative of **old** is **older**:

- □ David looks **older** than he really is.

You can use **elder** (*or* **older**) when you talk about people in a family. You can say (**my/your** etc.) **elder sister/brother/daughter/son**:

- □ **My elder sister** is a TV producer. (*or* My **older** sister …)

We say 'my **elder sister**', but we do not say that 'somebody is elder':

- □ My sister is **older** than me. (*not* elder than me)

Any/no → Unit 86 **Comparison 1, 3** → Units 105, 107 **Eldest** → Unit 108D
Even + comparative → Unit 112C

106.1 Use the words in brackets to complete the sentences. Use **much / a bit** etc. + a comparative form. Use **than** where necessary.

1 Her illness was ...*much more serious than*... we thought at first. (much / serious)
2 This bag is too small. I need something .... (much / big)
3 I'm afraid the problem is .... it seems. (much / complicated)
4 It was very hot yesterday. Today it's .... (a bit / cool)
5 I enjoyed our visit to the museum. It was .... I expected.
   (far / interesting)
6 You're driving too fast. Can you drive .... ? (a bit / slowly)
7 It's .... to learn a foreign language in a country where it is
   spoken. (a lot / easy)
8 I thought she was younger than me, but in fact she's ....
   (slightly / old)

106.2 Complete the sentences using **any/no** + comparative. Use **than** where necessary.

1 I've waited long enough. I'm not waiting ...*any longer*... .
2 I'm sorry I'm a bit late, but I couldn't get here ....
3 This shop isn't expensive. The prices are .... anywhere else.
4 I need to stop for a rest. I can't walk ....
5 The traffic isn't particularly bad today. It's .... usual.

106.3 Complete the sentences using the structure in Section C (... **and** ...).

1 Cathy got ...*more and more bored*... in her job. In the end she left. (bored)
2 That hole in your sweater is getting .... (big)
3 My bags seemed to get .... as I carried them. (heavy)
4 As I waited for my interview, I became .... (nervous)
5 As the day went on, the weather got .... (bad)
6 Health care is becoming .... (expensive)
7 Since Anna went to Canada, her English has got .... (good)
8 As the conversation went on, Paul became .... (talkative)

106.4 These sentences are like those in Section D. Use the words in brackets (in the correct form) to complete the sentences.

1 I like warm weather.
   The warmer the weather, ...*the better I feel*... . (feel)
2 I didn't really like him when we first met.
   But the more I got to know him, ... (like)
3 If you're in business, you want to make a profit.
   The more goods you sell, ... (profit)
4 It's hard to concentrate when you're tired.
   The more tired you are, ... (hard)
5 Kate had to wait a very long time.
   The longer she waited, ... (impatient / become)

106.5 Which is correct, **older** or **elder**? Or both of them?

        ✓   ✓
1 My <u>older</u> / <u>elder</u> sister is a TV producer. (<u>older</u> and <u>elder</u> are both correct)
2 I'm surprised Diane is only 25. I thought she was <u>older</u> / <u>elder</u>.
3 Jane's younger sister is still at school. Her <u>older</u> / <u>elder</u> sister is a nurse.
4 Martin is <u>older</u> / <u>elder</u> than his brother.

Comparison 3 (as ... as / than)

A Study this example situation:

Sarah, Joe and David are all very rich. Sarah has £20 million, Joe has £15 million and David has £10 million. So:

Joe is rich.
He is **richer than** David.
But he **isn't as rich as** Sarah.
(= Sarah is **richer than** he is)

SARAH   JOE   DAVID

Some more examples of **not as ... (as)**:

- ☐ Richard **isn't as old as** he looks. (= he looks **older than** he is)
- ☐ The town centre **wasn't as crowded as** usual. (= it is usually **more crowded**)
- ☐ Jenny **didn't** do **as well** in the exam **as** she had hoped. (= she had hoped to do **better**)
- ☐ The weather is better today. It's **not as cold**. (= yesterday was **colder**)
- ☐ I **don't** know **as many** people **as** you do. (= you know **more** people)
- ☐ 'How much did it cost? Fifty pounds?' 'No, **not as much** as that.' (= less than fifty pounds)

You can also say **not so ... (as)**:

- ☐ It's not warm, but it isn't **so cold as** yesterday. (= it isn't **as cold as** ...)

Less ... than is similar to **not as ... as**:

- ☐ I spent **less money than** you. (= I **didn't** spend **as much money as** you)
- ☐ The city centre was **less crowded than** usual. (= it **wasn't as** crowded **as** usual)

B We also use **as ... as** (*but not* so ... as) in positive sentences and in questions:

- ☐ I'm sorry I'm late. I got here **as fast as** I could.
- ☐ There's plenty of food. You can have **as much as** you want.
- ☐ Let's walk. It's **just as quick as** taking the bus.
- ☐ Can you send me the money **as soon as possible**, please?

Also **twice as ... as, three times as ... as** etc. :

- ☐ Petrol is **twice as expensive as** it was a few years ago.
- ☐ Their house is about **three times as big as** ours.

C We say **the same as** (*not* the same like):

- ☐ Laura's salary is **the same as** mine. *or* Laura gets **the same** salary **as** me.
- ☐ David is **the same** age **as** James.
- ☐ 'What would you like to drink?' 'I'll have **the same as** you.'

D **Than me / than I am** etc.

You can say:

- ☐ You're taller **than I am**. *or* You're taller **than me**.
  (*not usually* You're taller than I)
- ☐ He's not as clever **as she is**. *or* He's not as clever **as her**.
- ☐ They have more money **than we have**. *or* They have more money **than us**.
- ☐ I can't run as fast as **he can**. *or* I can't run as fast as **him**.

Comparison 1–2 → Units 105–106   **As long as** → Unit 115B   **As and like** → Unit 117

107.1 Complete the sentences using **as ... as**.

1 I'm quite tall, but you are taller. I'm not _as tall as you_ .
2 My salary is high, but yours is higher. My salary isn't ....
3 You know a bit about cars, but I know more.
   You don't ....
4 It's still cold, but it was colder yesterday.
   It isn't ....
5 I still feel quite tired, but I felt a lot more tired yesterday.
   I don't ....
6 Our neighbours have lived here for quite a long time, but we've lived here longer.
   Our neighbours haven't ....
7 I was a bit nervous before the interview, but usually I'm a lot more nervous.
   I wasn't ....

107.2 Write a new sentence with the same meaning.

1 Richard is younger than he looks. Richard isn't _as old as he looks_ .
2 I didn't spend as much money as you. You _spent more money than me_ .
3 The station was nearer than I thought. The station wasn't ....
4 The meal didn't cost as much as I expected. The meal cost ....
5 I go out less than I used to. I don't ....
6 Karen's hair isn't as long as it used to be. Karen used to ....
7 I know them better than you do. You don't ....
8 There are fewer people at this meeting than at the last one.
   There aren't ....

107.3 Complete the sentences using **as ... as** + the following:

   bad   comfortable   ~~fast~~   long   often   quietly   soon   well   well-qualified

1 I'm sorry I'm late. I got here _as fast as_ I could.
2 It was a difficult question. I answered it .... I could.
3 'How long can I stay with you?' 'You can stay .... you like.'
4 I need the information quickly, so let me know .... possible.
5 I like to keep fit, so I go swimming .... I can.
6 I didn't want to wake anybody, so I came in .... I could.

   In the following sentences use **just as ... as**.

7 I'm going to sleep on the floor. It's .... the bed.
8 Why did he get the job rather than me? I'm .... him.
9 At first I thought he was nice, but really he's .... everybody else.

107.4 Write sentences using **the same as**.

1 David and James are both 22 years old. David _is the same age as James_ .
2 You and I both have dark brown hair. Your hair ....
3 I arrived at 10.25 and so did you. I ....
4 My birthday is 5 April. Tom's birthday is 5 April too. My ....

107.5 Complete the sentences with **than ...** or **as ...** .

1 I can't reach as high as you. You are taller _than me_ .
2 He doesn't know much. I know more ....
3 I don't work particularly hard. Most people work as hard ....
4 We were very surprised. Nobody was more surprised ....
5 She's not a very good player. I'm a better player ....
6 They've been very lucky. I wish we were as lucky ....

Superlatives
(the longest / the most enjoyable etc.)

A   Study these examples:

> What is **the longest** river in the world?
> What was **the most enjoyable** holiday you've ever had?
>
> **Longest** and **most enjoyable** are *superlative* forms.

B   The superlative form is **-est** or **most** ... . In general, we use **-est** for short words and **most** ...
for longer words. The rules are the same as those for the comparative – see Unit 105.

long → longest	**hot** → hottest	**easy** → easiest	**hard** → hardest
but **most** famous	**most** boring	**most** difficult	**most** expensive

A few adjectives are irregular:

   good → **best**   bad → **worst**   far → **furthest/farthest**

For spelling, see Appendix 6.

C   We normally use **the** before a superlative (**the** longest / **the** most famous etc.):

- ☐ Yesterday was **the hottest** day of the year.
- ☐ The film was really boring. It was **the most boring** film I've ever seen.
- ☐ She is a really nice person – one of **the nicest** people I know.
- ☐ Why does he always come to see me at **the worst** possible moment?

Compare superlative and comparative:

- ☐ This hotel is **the cheapest** in town. *(superlative)*
  This hotel is **cheaper** than all the others in town. *(comparative)*
- ☐ He's **the most patient** person I've ever met.
  He's much **more patient** than I am.

D   **Oldest** and **eldest**

The superlative of **old** is **oldest**:

- ☐ That church is **the oldest** building in the town. *(not* the eldest)

We use **eldest** (*or* **oldest**) when we are talking about people in a family:

- ☐ **My eldest son** is 13 years old. *(or* My **oldest** son)
- ☐ Are you **the eldest** in your family? *(or* the **oldest**)

E   After superlatives we normally use **in** with places:

- ☐ What's the longest river **in the world**? *(not* of the world)
- ☐ We had a nice room. It was one of the best **in the hotel**. *(not* of the hotel)

We also use **in** for organisations and groups of people (a class / a company etc.):

- ☐ Who is the youngest student **in the class**? *(not* of the class)

For a period of time, we normally use **of**:

- ☐ What was the happiest day **of your life**?
- ☐ Yesterday was the hottest day **of the year**.

F   We often use the *present perfect* (I **have done**) after a superlative (see also Unit 8A):

- ☐ What's **the most important** decision **you've ever had** to make?
- ☐ That was **the best** holiday **I've had** for a long time.

Comparison (cheaper / more expensive etc.) → Units 105–107   **Elder** → Unit 106E

108.1 Complete the sentences. Use a superlative (**-est** or **most ...**) + a preposition (**of** or **in**).

1 It's a very good room. It _is the best room in_ the hotel.
2 It's a very cheap restaurant. It's .... the town.
3 It was a very happy day. It was .... my life.
4 She's a very intelligent student. She .... the class.
5 It's a very valuable painting. It .... the gallery.
6 Spring is a very busy time for me. It .... the year.

In the following sentences use **one of** + a superlative + a preposition.

7 It's a very good room. It _is one of the best rooms in_ the hotel.
8 He's a very rich man. He's one .... the world.
9 It's a very big castle. It .... Britain.
10 She's a very good player. She .... the team.
11 It was a very bad experience. It .... my life.
12 He's a very dangerous criminal. He .... the country.

108.2 Complete the sentences. Use a superlative (**-est** or **most ...**) or a comparative (**-er** or **more ...**).

1 We stayed at _the cheapest_ hotel in the town. (cheap)
2 Our hotel was _cheaper_ than all the others in the town. (cheap)
3 The United States is very large, but Canada is .... (large)
4 What's .... country in the world? (small)
5 I wasn't feeling well yesterday, but I feel a bit .... today. (good)
6 It was an awful day. It was .... day of my life. (bad)
7 What is .... sport in your country? (popular)
8 Everest is .... mountain in the world. It is ....
   than any other mountain. (high)
9 We had a great holiday. It was one of .... holidays we've ever
   had. (enjoyable)
10 I prefer this chair to the other one. It's .... (comfortable)
11 What's .... way of getting from here to the station? (quick)
12 Sue and Kevin have got three daughters. .... is 14 years old. (old)

108.3 What do you say in these situations? Use a superlative + **ever**. Use the words in brackets (in the correct form).

1 You've just been to the cinema. The film was extremely boring. You tell your friend:
   (boring / film / see) That's _the most boring film I've ever seen_ .
2 Your friend has just told you a joke, which you think is very funny. You say:
   (funny / joke / hear) That's ....
3 You're drinking coffee with a friend. It's really good coffee. You say:
   (good / coffee / taste) This ....
4 You are talking to a friend about Mary. Mary is very generous. You tell your friend about her:
   (generous / person / meet) She ....
5 You have just run ten kilometres. You've never run further than this. You say to your friend:
   (far / run) That ....
6 You decided to give up your job. Now you think this was a bad mistake. You say to your
   friend:
   (bad / mistake / make) It ....
7 Your friend meets a lot of people, some of them famous. You ask your friend:
   (famous / person / meet?) Who .... ?

A Verb + object

The *verb* and the *object* normally go together. We do not usually put other words between them:

	verb +	*object*	
I	like	my job	very much. (*not* I like very much my job)
Did you	see	your friends	yesterday?
Liz often	plays	tennis.	

Study these examples. The verb and the object go together each time:

- □ Do you **eat** **meat** every day?
  (*not* Do you eat every day meat?)

- □ Everybody **enjoyed** **the party** very much.
  (*not* enjoyed very much the party)

- □ Our guide **spoke** **English** fluently.
  (*not* spoke fluently English)

- □ I lost all my money and I also **lost** **my passport** .
  (*not* I lost also my passport)

- □ At the end of the street you'll **see** **a supermarket** on your left.
  (*not* see on your left a supermarket)

B Place and time

Usually the *verb* and the *place* (where?) go together:
  go home   **live in a city**   **walk to work** etc.

If the verb has an *object*, the place comes after the *verb + object*:
  take somebody home   **meet a friend in the street**

Time (when? / how often? / how long?) usually goes after *place*:

	place	+	*time*	
Ben walks	to work		every morning.	(*not* every morning to work)
Sam has been	in Canada		since April.	
We arrived	at the airport		early.	

Study these examples. *Time* goes after *place*:

- □ I'm going **to Paris** **on Monday** . (*not* I'm going on Monday to Paris)

- □ They have lived **in the same house** **for a long time** .

- □ Don't be late. Make sure you're **here** **by 8 o'clock** .

- □ Sarah gave me a lift **home** **after the party** .

- □ You really shouldn't go **to bed** **so late** .

It is often possible to put *time* at the beginning of the sentence:
- □ **On Monday** I'm going to Paris.
- □ **Every morning** Ben walks to work.

Some time words (for example, **always/never/often**) usually go with the verb in the middle of the sentence. See Unit 110.

Word order in questions → Units 49–50   Adjective order → Unit 99   Word order 2 → Unit 110

Exercises

109.1 Is the word order right or wrong? Correct the sentences where necessary.

1 Everybody enjoyed the party very much.   *OK*
2 Ben walks every morning to work.   *Ben walks to work every morning.*
3 Joe doesn't like very much football.
4 I drink three or four cups of coffee every morning.
5 I ate quickly my breakfast and went out.
6 Are you going to invite to the party a lot of people?
7 I phoned Tom immediately after hearing the news.
8 Did you go late to bed last night?
9 Did you learn a lot of things at school today?
10 I met on my way home a friend of mine.

109.2 Put the parts of the sentence in the correct order.

1 (the party / very much / everybody enjoyed)   *Everybody enjoyed the party very much.*
2 (we won / easily / the game)
3 (quietly / the door / I closed)
4 (Diane / quite well / speaks / German)
5 (Sam / all the time / TV / watches)
6 (again / please don't ask / that question)

7 (football / every weekend / does Kevin play?)

8 (some money / I borrowed / from a friend of mine)

109.3 Complete the sentences. Put the parts in the correct order.

1 (for a long time / have lived / in the same house)
They   *have lived in the same house for a long time*   .
2 (to the supermarket / every Friday / go)
I   .
3 (home / did you come / so late)
Why   ?
4 (her children / takes / every day / to school)
Sarah   .
5 (been / recently / to the cinema)
I haven't   .
6 (at the top of the page / your name / write)
Please   .
7 (her name / after a few minutes / remembered)
I   .
8 (around the town / all morning / walked)
We   .
9 (on Saturday night / didn't see you / at the party)
I   .
10 (some interesting books / found / in the library)
We   .
11 (her umbrella / last night / in a restaurant / left)
Jackie   .
12 (opposite the park / a new hotel / are building)
They   .

Word order 2: adverbs with the verb

A Some adverbs (for example, **always, also, probably**) go with the verb in the middle of a sentence:
- Helen **always drives** to work.
- We were feeling very tired and we **were also** hungry.
- The concert **will probably be cancelled**.

B Study these rules for the position of adverbs in the middle of a sentence. (They are only general rules, so there are exceptions.)

(1) If the verb is one word (**drives/fell/cooked** etc.), the adverb usually goes *before* the verb:

	adverb	*verb*	
Helen	**always**	**drives**	to work.
I	**almost**	**fell**	as I was going down the stairs.

- I cleaned the house and **also cooked** the dinner. (*not* cooked also)
- Lucy **hardly ever watches** television and **rarely reads** newspapers.
- 'Shall I give you my address?' 'No, I **already have** it.'

Note that these adverbs (**always/often/also** etc.) go before **have to ... :**
- Joe never phones me. I **always have** to phone him. (*not* I have always to phone)

(2) But adverbs go *after* **am/is/are/was/were**:
- We were feeling very tired and we **were also** hungry.
- Why are you **always** late? You're **never** on time.
- The traffic **isn't usually** as bad as it was this morning.

(3) If the verb is two or more words (for example, **can remember / doesn't eat / will be cancelled**), the adverb usually goes *after the first verb* (**can/doesn't/will** etc.):

	verb 1	*adverb*	*verb 2*	
I	**can**	**never**	**remember**	her name.
Clare	**doesn't**	**often**	**eat**	meat.
	Are you	**definitely**	**going**	away next week?
The concert	**will**	**probably**	**be**	cancelled.

- You **have always been** very kind to me.
- Jack can't cook. He **can't even boil** an egg.
- **Do** you **still work** for the same company?
- The house **was only built** a year ago and it's **already falling** down.

Note that **probably** goes before a negative (**isn't/won't** etc.). So we say:
- I **probably won't see** you. *or* I will **probably not** see you. (*not* I won't probably)

C We also use **all** and **both** in these positions:
- We **all felt** ill after the meal. (*not* we felt all ill)
- My parents **are both** teachers. (*not* my parents both are teachers)
- Sarah and Jane **have both applied** for the job.
- We **are all going** out this evening.

D Sometimes we use **is/will/did** etc. instead of repeating part of a sentence (see Unit 51). Note the position of **always/never** etc. in these sentences:
- He always says he won't be late, but he **always is**. (= he is always late)
- I've never done it and I **never will**. (= I will never do it)

We normally put **always/never** etc. *before* the verb in sentences like these.

Word order 1 → Unit 109

Exercises

110.1 Are the <u>underlined</u> words in the right position or not? Correct the sentences where necessary.

1 Helen drives <u>always</u> to work.   <u>Helen always drives to work.</u>
2 I cleaned the house and <u>also</u> cooked the dinner.   <u>OK</u>
3 I have <u>usually</u> a shower in the morning. ....
4 We <u>soon</u> found the solution to the problem. ....
5 Steve gets <u>hardly ever</u> angry. ....
6 I did some shopping and I went <u>also</u> to the bank. ....
7 Jane has <u>always</u> to hurry in the morning. ....
8 We <u>all</u> were tired, so we <u>all</u> fell asleep. ....
9 She <u>always</u> says she'll phone me, but she <u>never</u> does. ....

110.2 Rewrite the sentences to include the word in brackets.

1 Clare doesn't eat meat. (often)   <u>Clare doesn't often eat meat.</u>
2 a We were on holiday in Spain. (all) ....
   b We were staying at the same hotel. (all) ....
   c We enjoyed ourselves. (all) ....
3 Catherine is very generous. (always) ....
4 I don't have to work on Saturdays. (usually) ....
5 Do you watch TV in the evenings? (always) ....
6 Martin is learning French, and he is learning Italian. (also)
   Martin is learning French and he ....
7 a The new hotel is very expensive. (probably) ....
   b It costs a lot to stay there. (probably) ....
8 a I can help you. (probably) ....
   b I can't help you. (probably) ....

110.3 Complete the sentences. Use the words in brackets in the correct order.

1 I <u>can never remember</u> her name. (remember / never / can)
2 I .... sugar in coffee. (take / usually)
3 I .... hungry when I get home from work. (am / usually)
4 A: Where's Joe?
   B: He .... home early. (gone / has / probably)
5 Mark and Diane .... in Manchester. (both / were / born)
6 Liz is a good pianist. She .... very well. (sing / also / can)
7 Our cat .... under the bed. (often / sleeps)
8 They live in the same street as me, but I .... to them.
   (never / have / spoken)
9 We .... a long time for the bus. (have / always / to wait)
10 My eyesight isn't very good. I .... with glasses.
   (read / can / only)
11 I .... early tomorrow. (probably / leaving / will / be)
12 I'm afraid I .... able to come to the party.
   (probably / be / won't)
13 It's difficult to contact Sue. She .... at home when I phone
   her. (is / hardly ever)
14 We .... in the same place. We haven't moved.
   (still / are / living)
15 If we hadn't taken the same train, we .... each other.
   (never / met / would / have)
16 A: Are you tired?
   B: Yes, I .... at this time of day. (am / always)

Still, yet and already
Any more / any longer / no longer

A   Still

We use **still** to say that a situation or action is continuing. It hasn't changed or stopped:
- ☐ It's ten o'clock and Joe is **still** in bed.
- ☐ When I went to bed, Chris was **still** working.
- ☐ Do you **still** want to go away or have you changed your mind?

Still usually goes in the middle of the sentence with the verb (see Unit 110).

B   Any more / any longer / no longer

We use **not … any more** or **not … any longer** to say that a situation has changed. **Any more** and **any longer** go at the end of a sentence:
- ☐ Lucy doesn't work here **any more** (*or* any longer). She left last month.
  (*not* Lucy doesn't still work here.)
- ☐ We used to be good friends, but we aren't **any more** (*or* any longer).

You can also use **no longer**. **No longer** goes in the middle of the sentence:
- ☐ Lucy **no longer** works here.

Note that we do not normally use **no more** in this way:
- ☐ We are **no longer** friends. (*not* We are no more friends.)

Compare **still** and **not … any more**:
- ☐ Sally **still** works here, but Lucy doesn't work here **any more**.

C   Yet

Yet = until now. We use **yet** mainly in negative sentences (**He isn't** here **yet**) and questions (**Is he** here **yet?**). **Yet** shows that the speaker is expecting something to happen.
Yet usually goes at the end of a sentence:
- ☐ It's 10 o'clock and Joe **isn't** here **yet**.
- ☐ **Have you met** your new neighbours **yet?**
- ☐ 'Where are you going for your holidays?' 'We **don't** know **yet**.'

We often use **yet** with the *present perfect* (**Have** you met … **yet?**'). See Unit 7C.

Compare **yet** and **still**:
- ☐ Mike lost his job six months ago and **is still** unemployed.
  Mike lost his job six months ago and **hasn't found** another job **yet**.
- ☐ **Is** it **still** raining?
  Has it **stopped** raining **yet?**

Still is also possible in *negative* sentences (before the negative):
- ☐ She said she would be here an hour ago and she **still hasn't** come.

This is similar to 'she hasn't come **yet**'. But **still … not** shows a stronger feeling of surprise or impatience. Compare:
- ☐ I wrote to him last week. He **hasn't** replied **yet**. (but I expect he will reply soon)
- ☐ I wrote to him months ago and he **still** hasn't replied. (he should have replied before now)

D   Already

We use **already** to say that something happened sooner than expected. **Already** usually goes in the middle of a sentence (see Unit 110):
- ☐ 'What time is Sue leaving?' 'She has **already** left.' (= sooner than you expected)
- ☐ Shall I tell Joe what happened or does he **already** know?
- ☐ I've only just had lunch and I'm **already** hungry.

Present perfect + already/yet → Unit 7C   Word order → Unit 110

111.1 Compare what Paul said a few years ago with what he says now. Some things are the same as before and some things have changed. Write sentences with **still** and **any more**.

I travel a lot.
I work in a shop.
I write poems.
I want to be a teacher.
I'm interested in politics.
I'm single.
I go fishing a lot.

Paul a few
years ago

I travel a lot.
I work in a hospital.
I gave up writing poems.
I want to be a teacher.
I'm not interested in politics.
I'm single.
I haven't been fishing for years.

Paul now

1 (travel)   _He still travels a lot._
2 (shop)   _He doesn't work in a shop_
      any more.
3 (poems)   He ....
4 (teacher) ....

5 (politics) ....
      ....
6 (single) ....
7 (fishing) ....
8 (beard) ....

Now write three sentences about Paul using **no longer**.
9   _He no longer works in a shop._   11 ....
10 ....   12 ....

111.2 For each sentence (with **still**) write a sentence with a similar meaning using **not ... yet** + one of the following verbs:

    decide   **find**   **finish**   **go**   ~~**stop**~~   **take off**   **wake up**

1 It's still raining.   _It hasn't stopped raining yet._
2 Gary is still here.   He ....
3 They're still repairing the road.   They ....
4 The children are still asleep.   ....
5 Is Ann still looking for a place to live?   ....?
6 I'm still wondering what to do.   ....
7 The plane is still waiting on the runway.   ....

111.3 Put in **still**, **yet**, **already** or **any more** in the underlined sentence (or part of the sentence). Study the examples carefully.

1 Mike lost his job a year ago and he is unemployed.   _he is still unemployed_
2 Shall I tell Joe what happened or does he know?   _does he already know_
3 I'm hungry. Is dinner ready?   _Is dinner ready yet?_
4 I was hungry earlier, but I'm not hungry.   _I'm not hungry any more_
5 Can we wait a few minutes? I don't want to go out. ....
6 Jenny used to work at the airport, but she doesn't work there. ....
7 I used to live in Amsterdam. I have a lot of friends there. ....
8 'Shall I introduce you to Joe?'   'There's no need. We've met.' ....
9 Do you live in the same place or have you moved? ....
10 Would you like to eat with us or have you eaten? ....
11 'Where's John?'   'He's not here. He'll be here soon.' ....
12 Tim said he'd be here at 8.30. It's 9 o'clock now and he isn't here. ....
13 Do you want to join the club or are you a member? ....
14 It happened a long time ago, but I can remember it very clearly. ....
15 I've put on weight. These trousers don't fit me. ....
16 'Have you finished with the paper?'   'No, I'm reading it.'
....

A Study this example situation:

> Tina loves watching television.
>
> She has a TV set in every room of the house – **even** the bathroom.
>
> We use **even** to say that something is unusual or surprising. It is not usual to have a TV set in the bathroom.

Some more examples:
- ☐ These photographs are really awful. **Even I** take better photographs than these. (and I'm certainly not a good photographer)
- ☐ He always wears a coat – **even in hot weather**.
- ☐ Nobody would help her – **not even her best friend**.
- *or* **Not even** her best friend would help her.

B Very often we use **even** with the verb in the middle of a sentence (see Unit 110):
- ☐ Sue has travelled all over the world. She has **even** been to the Antarctic. (It's especially unusual to go to the Antarctic, so she must have travelled a lot.)
- ☐ They are very rich. They **even** have their own private jet.

Study these examples with **not even**:
- ☐ I can't cook. I **can't even** boil an egg. (and boiling an egg is very easy)
- ☐ They weren't very friendly to us. They **didn't even** say hello.
- ☐ Jenny is very fit. She's just run five miles and she's **not even** out of breath.

C You can use **even** + *comparative* (**cheaper** / **more expensive** etc.):
- ☐ I got up very early, but Jack got up **even earlier**.
- ☐ I knew I didn't have much money, but I've got **even less** than I thought.
- ☐ We were surprised to get a letter from her. We were **even more surprised** when she came to see us a few days later.

D **Even though / even when / even if**

You can use **even though / even when / even if** + *subject* + *verb*:
- ☐ **Even though she can't** drive, she has bought a car.
        subject + verb
- ☐ He never shouts, **even when he's** angry.
- ☐ I'll probably see you tomorrow. But **even if I don't see** you tomorrow, we're sure to see each other before the weekend.

You cannot use **even** in this way (+ *subject* + *verb*). We say:
- ☐ **Even though she can't** drive, she has bought a car. (*not* Even she can't drive)
- ☐ I can't reach the shelf **even if I stand** on a chair. (*not* even I stand)

Compare **even if** and **if**:
- ☐ We're going to the beach tomorrow. It doesn't matter what the weather is like. We're going **even if** it's raining.
- ☐ We want to go to the beach tomorrow, but we won't go **if** it's raining.

If and when → Unit 25D   **Though / even though** → Unit 113E

112.1 Julie, Sarah and Amanda are three friends who went on holiday together. Use the information given about them to complete the sentences using **even** or **not even**.

Julie 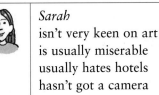 is usually happy is usually on time likes getting up early is very interested in art	*Sarah* is almost always late isn't very keen on art is usually miserable usually hates hotels hasn't got a camera	*Amanda* is almost always late is a keen photographer loves staying in hotels isn't very good at getting up

1 They stayed at a hotel. Everybody liked it, __even Sarah__ .
2 They arranged to meet. They all arrived on time, ...
3 They went to an art gallery. Nobody enjoyed it, ...
4 Yesterday they had to get up early. They all managed to do this, ...
5 They were together yesterday. They were all in a good mood, ...
6 None of them took any photographs, ...

112.2 Make sentences with **even**. Use the words in brackets.

1 Sue has been all over the world. (the Antarctic) __She has even been to the Antarctic.__
2 We painted the whole room. (the floor) We ....
3 Rachel has met lots of famous people. (the prime minister)
  She ....
4 You could hear the noise from a long way away. (from the next street)
  You ....

In the following sentences you have to use **not ... even**.

5 They didn't say anything to us. (hello) __They didn't even say hello.__
6 I can't remember anything about her. (her name) I ....
7 There isn't anything to do in this town. (a cinema) ....
8 He didn't tell anybody where he was going. (his wife)
  ....
9 I don't know anyone in our street. (the people next door)
  ....

112.3 Complete the sentences using **even + comparative**.

1 It was very hot yesterday, but today it's __even hotter__ .
2 The church is 500 years old, but the house next to it is ....
3 That's a very good idea, but I've got an .... one.
4 The first question was very difficult to answer. The second one was ....
5 I did very badly in the exam, but most of my friends did ....
6 Neither of us was hungry. I ate very little and my friend ate ....

112.4 Put in **if**, **even**, **even if** or **even though**.

1 __Even though__ she can't drive, she has bought a car.
2 The bus leaves in five minutes, but we can still catch it .... we run.
3 The bus leaves in two minutes. We won't catch it now .... we run.
4 His Spanish isn't very good – .... after three years in Spain.
5 His Spanish isn't very good .... he's lived in Spain for three years.
6 .... with the heating on, it was very cold in the house.
7 I couldn't sleep .... I was very tired.
8 I won't forgive them for what they did, ... they apologise.
9 .... I hadn't eaten anything for 24 hours, I wasn't hungry.

→ Additional exercise 32 (page 321)

A Study this example situation:

Last year Paul and Joanne had a holiday by the sea. It rained a lot, but they enjoyed themselves.

You can say:
Although it rained a lot, they enjoyed themselves.
(= It rained a lot, *but* they …)
or
In spite of
Despite } the rain, they enjoyed themselves.

B After **although** we use a *subject + verb*:
- **Although it rained** a lot, we enjoyed our holiday.
- I didn't get the job **although I had** the necessary qualifications.

Compare the meaning of **although** and **because**:
- We went out **although** it was raining.
- We didn't go out **because** it was raining.

C After **in spite of** or **despite**, we use a *noun*, a *pronoun* (**this/that/what** etc.) or **-ing**:
- **In spite of the rain**, we enjoyed our holiday.
- I didn't get the job **in spite of having** the necessary qualifications.
- She wasn't well, but **in spite of this** she went to work.
- **In spite of what** I said yesterday, I still love you.

Despite is the same as **in spite of**. We say **in spite of**, but **despite** (*without* of):
- She wasn't well, but **despite this** she went to work. (*not* despite of this)

You can say **in spite of the fact (that)** … and **despite the fact (that)** … :
- I didn't get the job { **in spite of the fact (that)**
despite the fact (that) } I had the necessary qualifications.

Compare **in spite of** and **because of**:
- We went out **in spite of the rain**. (*or* … despite the rain.)
- We didn't go out **because of the rain**.

D Compare **although** and **in spite of / despite**:
- **Although the traffic was bad,**
In spite of the traffic, } we arrived on time. (*not* In spite of the traffic was bad)

- I couldn't sleep { **although I was** very tired.
despite being very tired. (*not* despite I was tired)

E Sometimes we use **though** instead of **although**:
- I didn't get the job **though** I had the necessary qualifications.

In spoken English we often use **though** at the end of a sentence:
- The house isn't very nice. I like the garden **though**. (= but I like the garden)
- I see them every day. I've never spoken to them **though**. (= but I've never spoken to them)

Even though (*but not* 'even' alone) is a stronger form of **although**:
- **Even though** I was really tired, I couldn't sleep. (*not* Even I was really tired …)

Exercises

113.1 Complete the sentences. Use **although** + a sentence from the box.

I didn't speak the language	~~he has a very important job~~
I had never seen her before	we don't like them very much
it was quite cold	the heating was on
I'd met her twice before	we've known each other a long time

1 __Although he has a very important job__ , he isn't particularly well-paid.
2 .... , I recognised her from a photograph.
3 She wasn't wearing a coat ....
4 We thought we'd better invite them to the party ....
5 .... , I managed to make myself understood.
6 .... , the room wasn't warm.
7 I didn't recognise her ....
8 We're not very good friends ....

113.2 Complete the sentences with **although / in spite of / because / because of**.

1 __Although__ it rained a lot, we enjoyed our holiday.
2 a .... all our careful plans, a lot of things went wrong.
  b .... we'd planned everything carefully, a lot of things went wrong.
3 a I went home early .... I was feeling unwell.
  b I went to work the next day .... I was still feeling unwell.
4 a She only accepted the job .... the salary, which was very high.
  b She accepted the job .... the salary, which was rather low.
5 a I managed to get to sleep .... there was a lot of noise.
  b I couldn't get to sleep .... the noise.

Use your own ideas to complete the following sentences:

6 a He passed the exam although ....
  b He passed the exam because ....
7 a I didn't eat anything although ....
  b I didn't eat anything in spite of ....

113.3 Make one sentence from two. Use the word(s) in brackets in your sentences.

1 I couldn't sleep. I was very tired. (despite)
  __I couldn't sleep despite being very tired.__
2 They have very little money. They are happy. (in spite of)
  In spite ....
3 My foot was injured. I managed to walk to the nearest village. (although)
  ....
4 I enjoyed the film. The story was silly. (in spite of)
  ....
5 We live in the same street. We hardly ever see each other. (despite)
  ....
6 I got very wet in the rain. I was only out for five minutes. (even though)
  ....

113.4 Use the words in brackets to make a sentence with **though** at the end.

1 The house isn't very nice. (like / garden) __I like the garden though.__
2 It's warm today. (very windy) ....
3 We didn't like the food. (ate) ....
4 Liz is very nice. (don't like / husband) I ....

→ Additional exercise 32 (page 321)

A Study this example situation:

Your car should have a spare wheel because it is possible you will have a puncture.

Your car should have a spare wheel **in case** you have a puncture.

In case you have a puncture = because it is possible you will have a puncture.

Some more examples of **in case**:

- ☐ I'll leave my mobile phone switched on **in case Jane calls**. (= because it is possible she will call)
- ☐ I'll draw a map for you **in case you have difficulty finding our house**. (= because it is possible you will have difficulty)
- ☐ I'll remind them about the meeting **in case they've forgotten**. (= because it is possible they have forgotten)

We use **just in case** for a smaller possibility:

- ☐ I don't think it will rain, but I'll take an umbrella **just in case**. (= **just in case** it rains)

Do not use **will** after **in case**. Use a present tense for the future (see Unit 25):

- ☐ I'll leave my phone switched on **in case** Jane **calls**. (*not* in case Jane will call)

B **In case** is not the same as **if**. We use **in case** to say *why* somebody does (or doesn't do) something. You do something *now* **in case** something happens *later*.

Compare:

in case	if
☐ We'll buy some more food **in case** Tom comes. (= Perhaps Tom will come; we'll buy some more food now, whether he comes or not; then we'll *already* have the food *if* he comes.)	☐ We'll buy some more food **if** Tom comes. (= Perhaps Tom will come; if he comes, we'll buy some more food; if he doesn't come, we won't buy any more food.)
☐ I'll give you my phone number **in case** you need to contact me.	☐ You can phone me at the hotel **if** you need to contact me.
☐ You should insure your bike **in case** it is stolen.	☐ You should inform the police **if** your bike is stolen.

C You can use **in case** + *past* to say why somebody did something:

- ☐ I left my phone switched on **in case Jane called**. (= because it was possible that Jane would call)
- ☐ I drew a map for Sarah **in case she had difficulty finding the house**.
- ☐ We rang the doorbell again **in case they hadn't heard it the first time**.

D **In case of** is not the same as **in case**. **In case of** ... = if there is ... (especially on notices etc.):

- ☐ **In case of fire**, please leave the building as quickly as possible. (= if there is a fire)
- ☐ **In case of emergency**, telephone this number. (= if there is an emergency)

114.1 Barbara is going for a long walk in the country. You think she should take:

~~some chocolate~~   **a map**   **an anorak**   **a camera**   **some water**

You think she should take these things because:

it's possible she'll get lost	~~she might get hungry~~
perhaps she'll be thirsty	maybe it will rain
she might want to take some photographs	

What do you say to Barbara? Write sentences with **in case**.

1 _Take some chocolate with you in case you get hungry._
2 Take ....
3 ....
4 ....
5 ....

114.2 What do you say in these situations? Use **in case**.

1 It's possible that Mary will need to contact you, so you give her your phone number.
   You say: Here's my phone number _in case you need to contact me_ .
2 A friend of yours is going away for a long time. Maybe you won't see her again before she
   goes, so you decide to say goodbye now.
   You say: I'll say goodbye now ....
3 You are shopping in a supermarket with a friend. You think you have everything you need,
   but perhaps you've forgotten something. Your friend has the list. You ask her to check it.
   You say: Can you .... ?
4 You are giving a friend some advice about using a computer. You think he should back up
   (= *copy*) his files because the computer might crash (and he would lose all his data).
   You say: You should back up ....

114.3 Write sentences with **in case**.

1 There was a possibility that Jane would call. So I left my phone switched on.
   I left _my phone switched on in case Jane called_ .
2 Mike thought that he might forget the name of the book. So he wrote it down.
   He wrote down ....
3 I thought my parents might be worried about me. So I phoned them.
   I phoned ....
4 I sent an email to Liz, but she didn't reply. So I sent another email because perhaps she hadn't
   received the first one.
   I sent ....
5 I met some people when I was on holiday in France. They said they might come to London
   one day. I live in London, so I gave them my address.
   I gave ....

114.4 Put in **in case** or **if**.

1 I'll draw a map for you _in case_ you have difficulty finding our house.
2 You should tell the police _if_ you have any information about the crime.
3 I hope you'll come to London sometime. .... you come, you can stay with us.
4 This letter is for Susan. Can you give it to her .... you see her?
5 Write your name and address on your bag .... you lose it.
6 Go to the lost property office .... you lose your bag.
7 The burglar alarm will ring .... somebody tries to break into the house.
8 You should lock your bike to something .... somebody tries to steal it.
9 I was advised to get insurance .... I needed medical treatment while I was abroad.

→ Additional exercise 32 (page 321)

Unless   As long as   Provided/providing

A

Unless

Study this example situation:

> The club is for members only.
>
> You can't go in **unless you are a member**.
>
> This means:
> You can't go in *except if* you are a member.   *or*
> You can go in *only if* you are a member.
>
> **Unless** = except if.

Some more examples of **unless**:

- ☐ I'll see you tomorrow **unless I have to work late**. (= except if I have to work late)
- ☐ There are no buses to the beach. **Unless you have a car**, it's difficult to get there.
  (= except if you have a car)
- ☐ 'Shall I tell Liz what happened?' '**Not unless** she asks you.' (= only if she asks you)
- ☐ Sally hates complaining. She wouldn't complain about something **unless it was really bad**.
  (= except if it was really bad)
- ☐ We can take a taxi to the restaurant – **unless you'd prefer to walk**. (= except if you'd prefer to walk)

Instead of **unless** it is often possible to say **if … not**:

- ☐ **Unless we leave now**, we'll be late.   *or*   **If we don't leave now**, we'll …

B

As long as etc.

> as long as *or* so long as
> provided **(that)** *or* providing **(that)** } All these expressions mean 'if' or 'on condition that'.

For example:

- ☐ You can borrow my car { **as long as** / **so long as** } you promise not to drive too fast.

  (= you can borrow my car, but you must promise not to drive too fast – this is a condition)

- ☐ Travelling by car is convenient { **provided (that)** / **providing (that)** } you have somewhere to park.

  (= but only if you have somewhere to park)

- ☐ **Providing (that)** / **Provided (that)** } the room is clean, I don't mind which hotel we stay at.

  (= the room must be clean – otherwise I don't mind)

C

When you are talking about the future, do *not* use **will** after **unless / as long as / so long as / provided / providing**. Use a *present* tense (see Unit 25):

- ☐ I'm not going out **unless** it **stops** raining. (*not* unless it will stop)
- ☐ **Providing** the weather **is** good, we're going to have a picnic. (*not* providing it will be good)

115.1 Write a new sentence with the same meaning. Use **unless** in your sentence.

1 You must try a bit harder or you won't pass the exam.
   <u>You won't pass the exam unless you try a bit harder.</u>

2 Listen carefully or you won't know what to do.
   You won't know what to do ....

3 She must apologise to me or I'll never speak to her again.
   ....

4 You have to speak very slowly or he won't be able to understand you.
   ....

5 Business must improve soon, or the company will have to close.
   ....

115.2 Write sentences with **unless**.

1 The club isn't open to everyone. You are allowed in only if you're a member.
   <u>You aren't allowed in the club unless you're a member.</u>

2 I don't want to go to the party alone. I'm going only if you go too.
   I'm not going ....

3 Don't worry about the dog. It will attack you only if you move suddenly.
   The dog ....

4 Ben isn't very talkative. He'll speak to you only if you ask him something.
   Ben ....

5 Today is a public holiday. The doctor will see you only if it's an emergency.
   The doctor ....

115.3 Choose the correct word or expression for each sentence.

1 You can borrow my car <u>unless / as long as</u> you promise not to drive too fast. (<u>as long as</u> *is correct*)

2 I'm playing tennis tomorrow <u>unless / providing</u> it rains.

3 I'm playing tennis tomorrow <u>unless / providing</u> it doesn't rain.

4 I don't mind if you come home late <u>unless / as long as</u> you come in quietly.

5 I'm going now <u>unless / provided</u> you want me to stay.

6 I don't watch TV <u>unless / as long as</u> I've got nothing else to do.

7 Children are allowed to use the swimming pool <u>unless / provided</u> they are with an adult.

8 <u>Unless / provided</u> they are with an adult, children are not allowed to use the swimming pool.

9 We can sit here in the corner <u>unless / as long as</u> you'd rather sit over there by the window.

10 A: Our holiday cost a lot of money.
   B: Did it? Well, that doesn't matter <u>unless / as long as</u> you enjoyed yourselves.

115.4 Use your own ideas to complete these sentences.

1 We'll be late unless <u>we get a taxi</u> .

2 I like hot weather as long as ....

3 It takes Kate about 20 minutes to drive to work provided ....

4 I don't mind walking home as long as ....

5 I like to walk to work in the morning unless ....

6 We can meet tomorrow unless ....

7 You can borrow the money providing ....

8 You won't achieve anything unless ....

→ Additional exercise 32 (page 321)

A

As = at the same time as

You can use **as** when two things happen at the same time:

- We all waved goodbye to Liz **as** she drove away.
  (We **waved** and she **drove** away at the same time)
- I watched her **as** she opened the letter.
- **As** I walked along the street, I looked in the shop windows.
- Can you turn off the light **as** you go out, please?

Or you can say that something happened **as you were doing** something else (in the middle of doing something else):

- Kate slipped **as she was getting off** the bus.
- We met Paul **as we were leaving** the hotel.

For the *past continuous* (**was getting / were going** etc.), see Unit 6.

You can also use **just as** (= exactly at that moment):

- **Just as** I sat down, the phone rang.
- I had to leave **just as** the conversation was getting interesting.

We also use **as** when two things happen together in a longer period of time:

- **As** the day went on, the weather got worse.
- I began to enjoy the job more **as** I got used to it.

the day went on

the weather got worse

Compare **as** and **when**:

We use **as** only if two things happen at the same time.	Use **when** (*not* as) if one thing happens after another.
□ **As we walked home**, we talked about what we would have for dinner. (= at the same time)	□ **When we got home**, we started cooking the dinner. (*not* As we got home)

B

As = because

As also means 'because':

- **As I was hungry**, I decided to find somewhere to eat. (= because I was hungry)
- **As it was a public holiday** last Thursday, most of the shops were shut.
  (= because it was a public holiday)
- **As we have plenty of time** before our flight, let's go and have a coffee.
- Yesterday we watched television all evening **as we didn't have anything better to do**.
- **As I don't often watch television any more**, I've decided to give my TV set to a friend of mine.

You can also use **since** in this way:

- **Since** we have plenty of time, let's go and have a coffee.

Compare **as** and **when**:

□ I couldn't contact David **as he was away on holiday** and he doesn't have a mobile phone. (= because he was away)	□ David's passport was stolen **when he was away on holiday**. (= during the time he was away)
□ **As they lived near us**, we used to see them quite often. (= because they lived near us)	□ **When they lived near us**, we used to see them quite often. (= at the time they lived near us)

As ... as → Unit 107   Like and as → Unit 117   As if → Unit 118

Exercises

116.1 (Section A) Use **as** to join sentences from the boxes.

1 ~~we all waved goodbye to Liz~~	we were driving along the road
2 we all smiled	I was taking a hot dish out of the oven
3 I burnt myself	~~she drove away~~
4 the crowd cheered	we posed for the photograph
5 a dog ran out in front of the car	the two teams ran onto the field

1   We all waved goodbye to Liz as she drove away. ....

2   ....

3   ....

4   ....

5   ....

116.2 (Section B) Join sentences from the boxes. Begin each sentence with **as**.

1 ~~it was a public holiday~~	I went in
2 it was a nice day	we came in very quietly
3 we didn't want to wake anybody up	~~most of the shops were shut~~
4 the door was open	we didn't know what time it was
5 none of us had a watch	we went for a walk by the sea

1   As it was a public holiday, most of the shops were shut. ....

2   ....

3   ....

4   ....

5   ....

116.3 What does **as** mean in these sentences?

	because	*at the same time as*
1 **As** they live near me, I see them quite often.	✓	
2 Kate slipped **as** she was getting off the bus.		✓
3 **As** I was tired, I went to bed early.		
4 Unfortunately, **as** I was parking the car, I hit the car behind.		
5 **As** we climbed the hill, we got more and more tired.		
6 We decided to go out to eat **as** we had no food at home.		
7 **As** we don't use the car very often, we've decided to sell it.		

116.4 In some of these sentences, you need **when** (not **as**). Correct the sentences where necessary.

1   Julia got married <u>as she was 22</u>.   *when she was 22*

2   As the day went on, the weather got worse.   *OK*

3   He dropped the glass as he was taking it out of the cupboard.   ....

4   My camera was stolen as I was asleep on the beach.   ....

5   As I left school, I went to work in a shop.   ....

6   The train slowed down as it approached the station.   ....

7   I used to live near the sea as I was a child.   ....

116.5 Use your own ideas to complete these sentences.

1   I saw you as ....

2   It started to rain just as ....

3   As I didn't have enough money for a taxi, ...

4   Just as I took the photograph, ...

→ Additional exercise 32 (page 321)

A Like = 'similar to', 'the same as'. You cannot use **as** in this way:

- What a beautiful house! It's **like a palace**. (*not* as a palace)
- 'What does Sandra do?' 'She's a teacher, **like me**.' (*not* as me)
- Be careful! The floor has been polished. It's **like walking on ice**. (*not* as walking)
- It's raining again. I hate weather **like this**. (*not* as this)

In these sentences, **like** is a *preposition*. So it is followed by a *noun* (like **a palace**), a *pronoun* (like **me** / like **this**) or *-ing* (like walk**ing**).
You can also say '... **like** (somebody/something) do**ing** something':

- 'What's that noise?' 'It sounds **like a baby** cry**ing**.'

B Sometimes **like** = for example:

- Some sports, **like motor-racing**, can be dangerous.

You can also use **such as** (= for example):

- Some sports, **such as** motor-racing, can be dangerous.

C As = in the same way as, or in the same condition as. We use **as** before *subject + verb*:

- I didn't move anything. I left everything **as it was**.
- You should have done it **as I showed you**.

Like is also possible in informal spoken English:

- I left everything **like it was**.

Compare **as** and **like**:

- You should have done it **as I showed you**. (*or* like **I showed you**)
- You should have done it **like this**. (*not* as this)

Note that we say **as usual** / **as always**:

- You're late **as usual**.
- **As always**, Nick was the first to complain.

D Sometimes **as** (+ *subject + verb*) has other meanings. For example, after **do**:

- You can do **as you like**. (= do what you like)
- They did **as they promised**. (= They did what they promised.)

We also say **as you know** / **as I said** / **as she expected** / **as I thought** etc. :

- **As you know**, it's Emma's birthday next week. (= you know this already)
- Andy failed his driving test, **as he expected**. (= he expected this before)

Like is not usual in these expressions, except with **say** (**like I said**):

- **As I said** yesterday, I'm sure we can solve the problem.   *or*   **Like I said** yesterday ...

E As can also be a *preposition*, but the meaning is different from **like**. Compare:

□ Sue Casey is the manager of a company. **As the manager**, she has to make many important decisions. (**As the manager** = in her position as the manager.)	□ Mary Stone is the assistant manager. **Like the manager** (Sue Casey), she also has to make important decisions. (**Like the manager** = similar to the manager)

As (*preposition*) = in the position of, in the form of etc. :

- A few years ago I worked **as a taxi driver**. (*not* like a taxi driver)
- We haven't got a car, so we use the garage **as a workshop**.
- Many words, for example 'work' and 'rain', can be used **as verbs or nouns**.
- London is fine **as a place to visit**, but I wouldn't like to live there.
- The news of the tragedy came **as a great shock**.

As ... as → Unit 107   As (= at the same time as / because)→ Unit 116   As if → Unit 118

Exercises

117.1 In some of these sentences, you need **like** (not **as**). Correct the sentences where necessary.

1 It's raining again. I hate weather as this.   <u>weather like this</u>
2 Andy failed his driving test, as he expected.   <u>OK</u>
3 Do you think Caroline looks as her mother?   ....
4 Tim gets on my nerves. I can't stand people as him.   ....
5 Why didn't you do it as I told you to do it?   ....
6 Brian is a student, as most of his friends.   ....
7 You never listen. Talking to you is as talking to the ....
   wall.
8 As I said yesterday, I'm thinking of changing my job. ....
9 Tom's idea seems a good one. Let's do as he suggests. ....
10 I'll phone you tomorrow as usual, OK?   ....
11 Suddenly there was a terrible noise. It was as a bomb ....
   exploding.
12 She's a very good swimmer. She swims as a fish.   ....

117.2 Complete the sentences using **like** or **as** + the following:

a beginner	blocks of ice	~~a palace~~	a birthday present
a child	a church	winter	a tourist guide

1 This house is beautiful. It's __like a palace__ .
2 My feet are really cold. They're ....
3 I've been playing tennis for years, but I still play ....
4 Marion once had a part-time job ....
5 I wonder what that building with the tower is. It looks ....
6 My brother gave me this watch .... a long time ago.
7 It's very cold for the middle of summer. It's ....
8 He's 22 years old, but he sometimes behaves ....

117.3 Put in **like** or **as**. Sometimes either word is possible.

1 We heard a noise __like__ a baby crying.
2 Your English is very fluent. I wish I could speak .... you.
3 Don't take my advice if you don't want to. You can do .... you like.
4 You waste too much time doing things .... sitting in cafés all day.
5 I wish I had a car .... yours.
6 You don't need to change your clothes. You can go out .... you are.
7 My neighbour's house is full of lots of interesting things. It's .... a museum.
8 We saw Kevin last night. He was very cheerful, ... always.
9 Sally has been working .... a waitress for the last two months.
10 While we were on holiday, we spent most of our time doing energetic things .... sailing,
   water skiing and swimming.
11 You're different from the other people I know. I don't know anyone .... you.
12 We don't need all the bedrooms in the house, so we use one of them .... a study.
13 The news that Sue and Gary were getting married came .... a complete surprise to me.
14 .... her father, Catherine has a very good voice.
15 At the moment I've got a temporary job in a bookshop. It's OK .... a temporary job,
   but I wouldn't like to do it permanently.
16 .... you can imagine, we were very tired after such a long journey.
17 This tea is awful. It tastes .... water.
18 I think I prefer this room .... it was, before we decorated it.

A You can use **as if** or **as though** to say how somebody or something **looks/sounds/feels**:

- That house **looks as if** it's going to fall down.
- Helen **sounded as if** she had a cold, didn't she?
- I've just come back from holiday, but I feel very tired. I don't **feel as if** I've just had a holiday.

You can use **as though** in all these examples:

- I don't feel **as though** I've just had a holiday.

In informal spoken English you can also use **like**:

- That house **looks like** it's going to fall down.

Compare:

- You look **tired**. (**look** + *adjective*)
  You look **as if you haven't slept**. (**look as if** + *subject* + *verb*)

B You can say **It looks as if ... / It sounds as if ...** :

- Sandra is very late, isn't she? **It looks as if** she isn't coming.
- We took an umbrella because **it looked as if** it was going to rain.
- Do you hear that music next door? **It sounds as if** they are having a party.

> It sounds as if they're having a party next door.

You can also use **as though** or **like**:

- **It looks as though** she isn't coming. *or*
  It looks like she isn't coming.

C You can use **as if** or **as though** with other verbs to say how somebody does something:

- He ran **as if he was running** for his life.
- After the interruption, the speaker went on talking **as if nothing had happened**.
- When I told them my plan, they looked at me **as though I was mad**.

In informal spoken English, you can also use **like** in these examples.

D After **as if** (or **as though**), we sometimes use the *past* when we are talking about the *present*. For example:

- I don't like Tim. He talks as if he **knew** everything.

The meaning is not past in this sentence. We use the past (as if he **knew**) because the idea is not real: Tim does *not* know everything. We use the past in the same way in **if** sentences and after **wish** (see Unit 39).
Some more examples:

- She's always asking me to do things for her – **as if I didn't** have enough to do already. (I *do* have enough to do)
- Gary's only 40. Why do you talk about him **as if he was** an old man? (he isn't an old man)

When you use the past in this way, you can use **were** instead of **was**:

- Why do you talk about him **as if he were** (*or* **was**) an old man?
- They treat me **as if I were** (*or* **was**) their own son. (I'm not their son)

If I was/were → Unit 39C **Look/sound etc. + adjective →** Unit 99C **Like and as →** Unit 117

Exercises

118.1 What do you say in these situations? Use **look/sound/feel** + **as if** ... . Use the words in brackets to make your sentence.

1 You meet Bill. He has a black eye and some plasters on his face. (be / a fight)
   You say to him: _You look as if you've been in a fight._

2 Christine comes into the room. She looks absolutely terrified. (see / a ghost)
   You say to her: What's the matter? You ....

3 Joe is on holiday. He's talking to you on the phone and sounds very happy. (enjoy / yourself)
   You say to him: You ....

4 You have just run one kilometre. You are absolutely exhausted. (run / a marathon)
   You say to a friend: I ....

118.2 Make sentences beginning **It looks as if ... / It sounds as if ...** .

you should see a doctor	there's been an accident	they are having an argument
it's going to rain	~~she isn't coming~~	we'll have to walk

1 Sandra said she would be here an hour ago.
   You say: _It looks as if she isn't coming._

2 The sky is full of black clouds.
   You say: It ....

3 You hear two people shouting at each other next door.
   You say: ....

4 You see an ambulance, some policemen and two damaged cars at the side of the road.
   You say: ....

5 You and a friend have just missed the last bus home.
   You say: ....

6 Dave isn't feeling well. He tells you all about it.
   You say: ....

118.3 Complete the sentences with **as if**. Choose from the box, putting the verbs in the correct form.

she / enjoy / it	I / go / be sick	he / not / eat / for a week
~~he / need / a good rest~~	she / hurt / her leg	he / mean / what he / say
I / not / exist	she / not / want / come	

1 Mark looks very tired. He looks _as if he needs a good rest_ .

2 I don't think Paul was joking. He looked ....

3 What's the matter with Liz? She's walking ....

4 Peter was extremely hungry and ate his dinner very quickly.
   He ate ....

5 Caroline had a bored expression on her face during the concert.
   She didn't look ....

6 I've just eaten too many chocolates. Now I don't feel well.
   I feel ....

7 I phoned Liz and invited her to the party, but she wasn't very enthusiastic about it.
   She sounded ....

8 I went into the office, but nobody spoke to me or looked at me.
   Everybody ignored me ....

118.4 These sentences are like the ones in Section D. Complete each sentence using **as if**.

1 Brian is a terrible driver. He drives _as if he were_ the only driver on the road.

2 I'm 20 years old, so please don't talk to me .... I .... a child.

3 Steve has never met Nicola, but he talks about her .... his best friend.

4 It was a long time ago that we first met, but I remember it .... yesterday.

237

For, during and while

A   For and during

We use **for** + a period of time to say how long something goes on:

| for **two hours** | for a **week** | for **ages** |

- ☐ We watched television **for two hours** last night.
- ☐ Diane is going away **for a week** in September.
- ☐ Where have you been? I've been waiting **for ages**.
- ☐ Are you going away **for the weekend**?

We use **during** + *noun* to say when something happens (*not* how long):

| during **the film** | during **our holiday** | during **the night** |

- ☐ I fell asleep **during the film**.
- ☐ We met some really nice people **during our holiday**.
- ☐ The ground is wet. It must have rained **during the night**.

With 'time words' (for example: **the morning / the afternoon / the summer**), you can usually say **in** or **during**:

- ☐ It must have rained **in the night**. (*or* during the night)
- ☐ I'll phone you sometime **during the afternoon**. (*or* in the afternoon)

You cannot use **during** to say how long something goes on:

- ☐ It rained **for** three days without stopping. (*not* during three days)

Compare **during** and **for**:

- ☐ I fell asleep **during the film**. I was asleep **for half an hour**.

B   During and while

Compare:

We use **during** + *noun*:	We use **while** + *subject* + *verb*:
☐ I fell asleep **during the film**. 　　　　　　 └─*noun*─┘	☐ I fell asleep **while I was watching TV**. 　　　　　　 └─*subject + verb*─┘
☐ We met a lot of interesting people **during our holiday**.	☐ We met a lot of interesting people **while we were on holiday**.
☐ Robert suddenly began to feel ill **during the exam**.	☐ Robert suddenly began to feel ill **while he was doing the exam**.

Some more examples of **while**:

- ☐ We saw Clare **while we were waiting** for the bus.
- ☐ **While you were** out, there was a phone call for you.
- ☐ Chris read a book **while I watched** television.

When you are talking about the future, use the *present* (*not* will) after **while**:

- ☐ I'll be in London next week. I hope to see Tom **while I'm there**. (*not* while I will be there)
- ☐ What are you going to do **while you are** waiting? (*not* while you will be waiting)

See also Unit 25.

For and since → Unit 12A　　**While** + –ing → Unit 68B

119.1 Put in **for** or **during**.

1 It rained ....for.... three days without stopping.
2 I fell asleep ....during.... the film.
3 I went to the theatre last night. I met Sue .... the interval.
4 Martin hasn't lived in Britain all his life. He lived in Brazil .... four years.
5 Production at the factory was seriously affected .... the strike.
6 I felt really ill last week. I could hardly eat anything .... three days.
7 I waited for you .... half an hour and decided that you weren't coming.
8 Sarah was very angry with me. She didn't speak to me .... a week.
9 We usually go out at weekends, but we don't often go out .... the week.
10 Jack started a new job a few weeks ago. Before that he was out of work .... six months.
11 I need a change. I think I'll go away .... a few days.
12 The president gave a long speech. She spoke .... two hours.
13 We were hungry when we arrived. We hadn't had anything to eat .... the journey.
14 We were hungry when we arrived. We hadn't had anything to eat .... eight hours.

119.2 Put in **during** or **while**.

1 We met a lot of interesting people ....while.... we were on holiday.
2 We met a lot of interesting people ....during.... our holiday.
3 I met Mike .... I was shopping.
4 .... I was on holiday, I didn't read any newspapers or watch TV.
5 .... our stay in Paris, we visited a lot of museums and galleries.
6 The phone rang three times .... we were having dinner.
7 The phone rang three times .... the night.
8 I had been away for many years. .... that time, many things had changed.
9 What did they say about me .... I was out of the room?
10 I went out for dinner last night. Unfortunately I began to feel ill .... the meal and had to go home.
11 Please don't interrupt me .... I'm speaking.
12 There were many interruptions .... the president's speech.
13 Can you lay the table .... I get the dinner ready?
14 We were hungry when we arrived. We hadn't had anything to eat .... we were travelling.

119.3 Use your own ideas to complete these sentences.

1 I fell asleep while ...I was watching television.................................
2 I fell asleep during ...the film..............
3 I hurt my arm while ....
4 Can you wait here while ....
5 Most of the students looked bored during ....
6 I was asked a lot of questions during ....
7 Don't open the car door while ....
8 The lights suddenly went out while ....
9 It started to rain during ....
10 It started to rain while ....

→ Additional exercise 33 (page 321)

By and until   By the time ...

A

By (+ a time) = not later than:

- ☐ I sent the letter to them today, so they should receive it **by Monday**. (= on or before Monday, not later than Monday)
- ☐ We'd better hurry. We have to be home **by 5 o'clock**. (= at or before 5 o'clock, not later than 5 o'clock)
- ☐ Where's Sarah? She should be here **by now**. (= now or before now – so she should have already arrived)

This milk has to be used **by 14 August**.

B

We use **until** (*or* **till**) to say *how long* a situation continues:

- ☐ 'Shall we go now?' 'No, let's **wait until** (*or* **till**) it stops raining.
- ☐ I couldn't get up this morning. { I **stayed in bed until** half past ten. / I **didn't get up until** half past ten. }

Compare **until** and **by**:

Something *continues* **until** a time in the future:	Something *happens* **by** a time in the future:
☐ David **will be away until** Monday. (so he'll be back *on* Monday)	☐ David **will be back by** Monday. (= he'll be back not later than Monday)
☐ I'll **be working until** 11.30. (so I'll stop working *at* 11.30)	☐ I'll **have finished my work by** 11.30. (= I'll finish my work not later than 11.30.)

C

You can say '**by the time** something happens'. Study these examples:

- ☐ It's too late to go to the bank now. **By the time we get there**, it will be closed. (= the bank will close between now and the time we get there)
- ☐ *(from a postcard)* Our holiday ends tomorrow. So **by the time you receive this postcard**, I'll be back home. (= I will arrive home between tomorrow and the time you receive this postcard)
- ☐ Hurry up! **By the time we get to the cinema**, the film will already have started.

You can say '**by the time** something happened' (for the past):

- ☐ Karen's car broke down on the way to the party last night. **By the time she arrived**, most of the other guests had left. (= it took her a long time to get to the party and most of the guests left during this time)
- ☐ I had a lot of work to do yesterday evening. I was very tired **by the time I finished**. (= it took me a long time to do the work, and I became more and more tired during this time)
- ☐ We went to the cinema last night. It took us a long time to find somewhere to park the car. **By the time we got to the cinema**, the film had already started.

Also **by then** *or* **by that time**:

- ☐ Karen finally arrived at the party at midnight, but **by then** (*or* **by that time**), most of the guests had left.

Will be doing and will have done → Unit 24   **By (other uses)** → Units 42B, 60B, 128

Exercises

120.1 Make sentences with **by**.

1 We have to be home not later than 5 o'clock.
   We have to be home by 5 o'clock.

2 I have to be at the airport not later than 8.30.
   I have to be at the airport ....

3 Let me know not later than Saturday whether you can come to the party.
   Let me know ....

4 Please make sure that you're here not later than 2 o'clock.
   Please make sure that ....

5 If we leave now, we should arrive not later than lunchtime.
   If we leave now, ...

120.2 Put in **by** or **until**.

1 Steve has gone away. He'll be away ....._until_.... Monday.

2 Sorry, but I must go. I have to be home .... 5 o'clock.

3 I've been offered a job. I haven't decided yet whether to accept it or not. I have to decide
   .... Friday.

4 I think I'll wait .... Thursday before making a decision.

5 It's too late to go shopping. The shops are open only .... 5.30. They'll be closed
   .... now.

6 I'd better pay the phone bill. It has to be paid .... tomorrow.

7 Don't pay the bill today. Wait .... tomorrow.

8 A: Have you finished redecorating your house?
   B: Not yet. We hope to finish .... the end of the week.

9 A: I'm going out now. I'll be back at about 10.30. Will you still be here?
   B: I don't think so. I'll probably have gone out .... then.

10 I'm moving into my new flat next week. I'm staying with a friend .... then.

11 I've got a lot of work to do. .... the time I finish, it will be time to go to bed.

12 If you want to take part in the competition, you have to apply .... 3 April.

120.3 Use your own ideas to complete these sentences. Use **by** or **until**.

1 David is away at the moment. He'll be away _until Monday_ .

2 David is away at the moment. He'll be back _by Monday_ .

3 I'm just going out. I won't be very long. Wait here ....

4 I'm going out to buy a few things. It's 4.30 now. I won't be long. I'll be back ....

5 If you want to apply for the job, your application must be received ....

6 Last night I watched TV ....

120.4 Read the situations and complete the sentences using **By the time** ... .

1 I was invited to a party, but I got there much later than I intended.
   By the time I got to the party , most of the other guests had left.

2 I intended to catch a train, but it took me longer than expected to get to the station.
   .... , my train had already left.

3 I wanted to go shopping after finishing my work. But I finished much later than expected.
   .... , it was too late to go shopping.

4 I saw two men who looked as if they were trying to steal a car. I called the police, but it was
   some time before they arrived.
   .... , the two men had disappeared.

5 We climbed a mountain and it took us a very long time to get to the top. There wasn't
   much time to enjoy the view.
   .... , we had to come down again.

→ Additional exercise 33 (page 321)

A Compare **at**, **on** and **in**:

    ☐ They arrived **at** 5 o'clock.
    ☐ They arrived **on** Friday.
    ☐ They arrived **in** October. / They arrived **in** 1968.

We use:

at for the time of day   **at** five o'clock   **at** 11.45   **at** midnight   **at** lunchtime   **at** sunset etc.
on for days and dates   **on** Friday / **on** Fridays   **on** 16 May 1999   **on** Christmas Day   **on** my birthday

in for longer periods (for example: months/years/seasons)
    in October   **in** 1988   **in** the 18th century   **in** the past
    in (the) winter   **in** the 1990s   **in** the Middle Ages   **in** (the) future

B We use **at** in these expressions:

at night	☐ I don't like going out **at night**.
at the weekend / at weekends	☐ Will you be here **at the weekend**?
at Christmas	☐ Do you give each other presents **at Christmas**?
at the moment / at present	☐ Mr Benn is busy **at the moment / at present**.
at the same time	☐ Emily and I arrived **at the same time**.

C We say:

in the morning(s)	*but*	**on Friday morning(s)**
in the afternoon(s)		**on Sunday afternoon(s)**
in the evening(s)		**on Monday evening(s)** etc.

    ☐ I'll see you **in the morning**.   ☐ I'll see you **on Friday morning**.
    ☐ Do you work **in the evenings**?   ☐ Do you work **on Saturday evenings**?

D We do not use **at/on/in** before **last/next/this/every**:

    ☐ I'll see you **next Friday**. (*not* on next Friday)
    ☐ They got married **last March**.

In spoken English we often leave out **on** before days (**Sunday/Monday** etc.). So you can say:

    ☐ I'll see you **on Friday**. *or* I'll see you **Friday**.
    ☐ I don't go out **on Monday mornings**. *or* I don't go out **Monday mornings**.

E **In a few minutes / in six months** etc.

    ☐ The train will be leaving **in a few minutes**. (= a few minutes from now)
    ☐ Andy has gone away. He'll be back **in a week**. (= a week from now)
    ☐ She'll be here **in a moment**. (= a moment from now)

You can also say 'in six months' time', 'in a week's time' etc. :

    ☐ They're getting married **in six months' time**. *or* … **in six months**.

We also use **in** … to say how long it takes to do something:

    ☐ I learnt to drive **in four weeks**. (= it took me four weeks to learn)

On/in time, at/in the end → Unit 122   In/at/on (position) → Units 123–125
In/at/on (other uses) → Unit 127   American English → Appendix 7

Exercises

121.1 Complete the sentences. Use **at**, **on** or **in** + the following:

the evening	about 20 minutes	~~1492~~	the same time
the moment	21 July 1969	the 1920s	night
Saturdays	the Middle Ages	11 seconds	

1 Columbus made his first voyage from Europe to America ...._in 1492_........ .
2 If the sky is clear, you can see the stars ....
3 After working hard during the day, I like to relax ....
4 Neil Armstrong was the first man to walk on the moon ....
5 It's difficult to listen if everyone is speaking ....
6 Jazz became popular in the United States ....
7 I'm just going out to the shop. I'll be back ....
8 *(on the phone)* 'Can I speak to Dan?' 'I'm afraid he's not here .... ,'
9 Many of Europe's great cathedrals were built ....
10 Ben is a very fast runner. He can run 100 metres ....
11 Liz works from Monday to Friday. Sometimes she also works ....

121.2 Put in **at**, **on** or **in**.

1 Mozart was born in Salzburg ...._in_.... 1756.
2 I haven't seen Kate for a few days. I last saw her .... Tuesday.
3 The price of electricity is going up .... October.
4 .... weekends, we often go for long walks in the country.
5 I've been invited to a wedding .... 14 February.
6 Jonathan is 63. He'll be retiring from his job .... two years' time.
7 I'm busy just now, but I'll be with you .... a moment.
8 Jenny's brother is an engineer, but he doesn't have a job .... the moment.
9 There are usually a lot of parties .... New Year's Eve.
10 I don't like driving .... night.
11 My car is being repaired at the garage. It will be ready .... two hours.
12 The telephone and the doorbell rang .... the same time.
13 Mary and David always go out for dinner .... their wedding anniversary.
14 It was a short book and easy to read. I read it .... a day.
15 .... Saturday night I went to bed .... midnight.
16 We travelled overnight to Paris and arrived .... 5 o'clock .... the morning.
17 The course begins .... 7 January and ends sometime .... April.
18 I might not be at home .... Tuesday morning, but I'll be there .... the afternoon.

121.3 Which is correct: a, b, or both of them?

1 a I'll see you on Friday.	b I'll see you Friday.	_both_
2 a I'll see you on next Friday.	b I'll see you next Friday.	_b_
3 a Paul got married in April.	b Paul got married April.	....
4 a They never go out on Sunday evenings.	b They never go out Sunday evenings.	....
5 a We often have a short holiday on Christmas.	b We often have a short holiday at Christmas.	....
6 a What are you doing the weekend?	b What are you doing at the weekend?	....
7 a Will you be here on Tuesday?	b Will you be here Tuesday?	....
8 a We were ill at the same time.	b We were ill in the same time.	....
9 a Sue got married at 18 May 1996.	b Sue got married on 18 May 1996.	....
10 a He left school last June.	b He left school in last June.	....

→ Additional exercise 33 **(page 321)**

On time and in time
At the end and in the end

On time and in time

On time = punctual, not late. If something happens **on time**, it happens at the time which was planned:
- The 11.45 train left **on time**. (= it left at 11.45)
- 'I'll meet you at 7.30.' 'OK, but please be **on time**.' (= don't be late, be there at 7.30)
- The conference was well-organised. Everything began and finished **on time**.

The opposite of **on time** is **late**:
- Be **on time**. Don't be **late**.

In time (for something / to do something) = soon enough:
- Will you be home **in time for dinner**? (= soon enough for dinner)
- I've sent Emma a birthday present. I hope it arrives **in time** (for her birthday).
  (= on or before her birthday)
- I'm in a hurry. I want to be home **in time to see** the game on television.
  (= soon enough to see the game)

The opposite of **in time** is **too late**:
- I got home **too late** to see the game on television.

You can say **just in time** (= almost too late):
- We got to the station **just in time** for our train.
- A child ran into the road in front of the car – I managed to stop **just in time**.

At the end and in the end

At the end (of something) = at the time when something ends. For example:

| at the end of the month | at the end of January | at the end of the game |
| at the end of the film | at the end of the course | at the end of the concert |

- I'm going away **at the end of January** / **at the end of the month**.
- **At the end of the concert**, there was great applause.
- The players shook hands **at the end of the game**.

You cannot say 'in the end of ...'. So you cannot say 'in the end of January' or 'in the end of the concert'.

The opposite of **at the end** (of ...) is **at the beginning** (of ...):
- I'm going away **at the beginning of January**. (*not* in the beginning)

In the end = finally.

We use **in the end** when we say what the final result of a situation was:
- We had a lot of problems with our car. We sold it **in the end**. (= finally we sold it)
- He got more and more angry. **In the end** he just walked out of the room.
- Alan couldn't decide where to go for his holidays. He didn't go anywhere **in the end**.
  (*not* at the end)

The opposite of **in the end** is usually **at first**:
- **At first** we didn't get on very well, but **in the end** we became good friends.

Exercises

122.1 Complete the sentences with on time or in time.

1 The bus was late this morning, but it's usually _on time_ .
2 The film was supposed to start at 8.30, but it didn't begin ....
3 I like to get up .... to have a big breakfast before going to work.
4 We want to start the meeting .... , so please don't be late.
5 I've just washed this shirt. I want to wear it this evening, so I hope it will be dry

   ....
6 The train service isn't very good. The trains are rarely ....
7 I nearly missed my flight this morning. I got to the airport just ....
8 I nearly forgot that it was Joe's birthday. Fortunately I remembered ....
9 Why are you never .... ? You always keep everybody waiting.

122.2 Read the situations and make sentences using just in time.

1 A child ran into the road in front of your car. You saw the child at the last moment.
   (manage / stop) _I managed to stop just in time._
2 You were walking home. Just after you got home, it started to rain very heavily.
   (get / home) I ....
3 Tim was going to sit on the chair you had just painted. You said, 'Don't sit on that chair!',
   so he didn't. (stop / him) I ....
4 You and a friend went to the cinema. You were late and you thought you would miss the
   beginning of the film. But the film began just as you sat down in the cinema.
   (get / cinema / beginning of the film)
   We ....

122.3 Complete the sentences using at the end + the following:

the course	~~the game~~	the interview	the month	the race

1 The players shook hands _at the end of the game_ .
2 I usually get paid ....
3 The students had a party ....
4 Two of the runners collapsed ....
5 To my surprise, I was offered the job ....

122.4 Write sentences with In the end. Use the verb in brackets.

1 We had a lot of problems with our car. (sell) _In the end we sold it._
2 Judy got more and more fed up with her job.
   (resign) ....
3 I tried to learn German, but I found it too difficult.
   (give up) ....
4 We couldn't decide whether to go to the party or not.
   (not / go) ....

122.5 Put in at or in.

1 I'm going away _at_ the end of the month.
2 It took me a long time to find a job. .... the end I got a job in a hotel.
3 Are you going away .... the beginning of August or .... the end?
4 I couldn't decide what to buy Laura for her birthday. I didn't buy her anything ....
   the end.
5 We waited ages for a taxi. We gave up .... the end and walked home.
6 I'll be moving to a new address .... the end of September.
7 We had a few problems at first, but .... the end everything was OK.
8 I'm going away .... the end of this week.
9 A: I didn't know what to do.
   B: Yes, you were in a difficult position. What did you do .... the end?

A **In**

in a room
in a building
in a box

in a garden
in a town/country
in the city centre

in a pool
in the sea
in a river

- ☐ There's no-one **in the room** / **in the building** / **in the garden**.
- ☐ What have you got **in your hand** / **in your mouth**?
- ☐ When we were **in Italy**, we spent a few days **in Venice**.
- ☐ I have a friend who lives **in a small village in the mountains**.
- ☐ There were some people swimming **in the pool** / **in the sea** / **in the river**.

B **At**

at the bus stop
at the door
at the window

at the roundabout

at reception

- ☐ Do you know that man standing **at the door** / **at the window**?
- ☐ Turn left **at the traffic lights** / **at the church** / **at the roundabout**.
- ☐ We have to get off the bus **at the next stop**.
- ☐ When you leave the hotel, please leave your key **at reception**. (= at the reception desk)

C **On**

on the ceiling
on the door
on the table
on the wall
on the floor

on her nose

on a page

on an island

- ☐ I sat **on the floor** / **on the ground** / **on the grass** / **on the beach** / **on a chair**.
- ☐ There's a dirty mark **on the wall** / **on the ceiling** / **on your nose** / **on your shirt**.
- ☐ Have you seen the notice **on the notice board** / **on the door**?
- ☐ You'll find details of TV programmes **on page seven** (of the newspaper).
- ☐ The hotel is **on a small island** in the middle of the lake.

D Compare **in** and **at**:

- ☐ There were a lot of people **in the shop**. It was very crowded.
  Go along this road, then turn left **at the shop**.
- ☐ I'll meet you **in the hotel lobby**.
  I'll meet you **at the entrance to the hotel**.

Compare **in** and **on**:

- ☐ There is some water **in the bottle**.
  There is a label **on the bottle**.

Compare **at** and **on**:

- ☐ There is somebody **at the door**. Shall I go and see who it is?
  There is a notice **on the door**. It says 'Do not disturb'.

in the bottle

on the bottle

123.1 Answer the questions about the pictures. Use **in**, **at** or **on** with the words below the pictures.

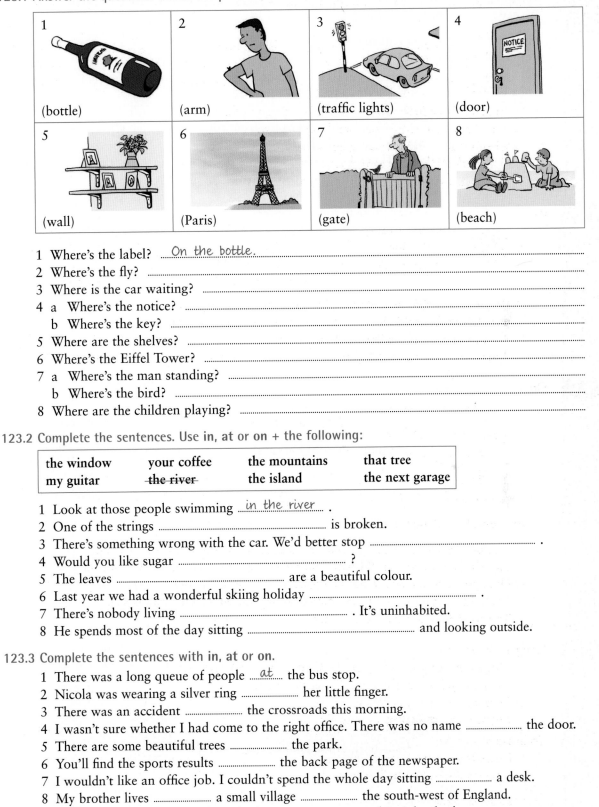

1 (bottle)	2 (arm)	3 (traffic lights)	4 (door)
5 (wall)	6 (Paris)	7 (gate)	8 (beach)

1 Where's the label? *On the bottle.* ....
2 Where's the fly? ....
3 Where is the car waiting? ....
4 a Where's the notice? ....
   b Where's the key? ....
5 Where are the shelves? ....
6 Where's the Eiffel Tower? ....
7 a Where's the man standing? ....
   b Where's the bird? ....
8 Where are the children playing? ....

123.2 Complete the sentences. Use **in**, **at** or **on** + the following:

the window	your coffee	the mountains	that tree
my guitar	~~the river~~	the island	the next garage

1 Look at those people swimming ...*in the river*... .
2 One of the strings .... is broken.
3 There's something wrong with the car. We'd better stop ....
4 Would you like sugar .... ?
5 The leaves .... are a beautiful colour.
6 Last year we had a wonderful skiing holiday ....
7 There's nobody living .... It's uninhabited.
8 He spends most of the day sitting .... and looking outside.

123.3 Complete the sentences with **in**, **at** or **on**.

1 There was a long queue of people ...*at*... the bus stop.
2 Nicola was wearing a silver ring .... her little finger.
3 There was an accident .... the crossroads this morning.
4 I wasn't sure whether I had come to the right office. There was no name .... the door.
5 There are some beautiful trees .... the park.
6 You'll find the sports results .... the back page of the newspaper.
7 I wouldn't like an office job. I couldn't spend the whole day sitting .... a desk.
8 My brother lives .... a small village .... the south-west of England.
9 The man the police are looking for has a scar .... his right cheek.
10 The headquarters of the company are .... Milan.
11 I like that picture hanging .... the wall .... the kitchen.
12 If you come here by bus, get off .... the stop after the traffic lights.

→ Additional exercise 34 (page 322)

In/at/on (position) 2

A

We say that somebody/something is:

in a line / in a row / in a queue	in bed
in the sky / in the world	in the country / in the countryside
in an office / in a department	in a photograph / in a picture
in a book / in a (news)paper / in a magazine / in a letter	

□ When I go to the cinema, I like to sit **in the front row**.
□ James isn't up yet. He's still **in bed**.
□ It was a lovely day. There wasn't a cloud **in the sky**.
□ I've just started working **in the sales department**.
□ Who is the woman **in that photograph**?
□ Have you seen this picture **in today's paper**?

in a row

B

on the left / on the right   on the left-hand side / right-hand side
on the ground floor / on the first floor / on the second floor etc.
on a map / on a menu / on a list
on a farm

□ In Britain we drive **on the left**. (*or* ... **on the left-hand side**.)
□ Our flat is **on the second floor** of the building.
□ Here's a shopping list. Don't buy anything that's not **on the list**.
□ Have you ever worked **on a farm**?

We say that a place is **on a river** / **on a road** / **on the coast**:
□ Budapest is **on the (river) Danube**.
□ Portsmouth is **on the south coast** of England.

Also **on the way**:
□ We stopped at a small village **on the way** to London.

BUDAPEST

DANUBE

C

at the top (of) / **at the bottom** (of) / **at the end** (of)
□ Write your name **at the top of the page**.
□ Jane's house is **at the other end of the street**.

at the top (of the page)

at the bottom (of the page)

D

in the front / **in the back** of a car
□ I was sitting **in the back** (of the car) when we crashed.

at the front / **at the back** of a building / theatre / group of people etc.
□ The garden is **at the back of the house**.
□ Let's sit **at the front** (of the cinema).
□ We were **at the back**, so we couldn't see very well.

on the front / **on the back** of a letter / piece of paper etc.
□ I wrote the date **on the back of the photograph**.

at the back

at the front

E

in the corner of a room
□ The television is **in the corner** of the room.

at the corner *or* **on the corner** of a street
□ There is a post box **at/on the corner** of the street.

in the corner

at/on the corner

In the world → Unit 108E   **In/at/on (position)** → Units 123, 125   **American English** → Appendix 7

124.1 Answer the questions about the pictures. Use **in**, **at** or **on** with the words below the pictures.

1 SUE (sales department)	2 (second floor)	3 (corner)	4 (corner)	5 (top / stairs)
6 (back / car)	7 (front) LIZ	8 (left)	9 GARY (back row)	10 (farm)

1 Where does Sue work? ___In the sales department.___
2 Sue lives in this building. Where's her flat exactly? ....
3 Where is the woman standing? ....
4 Where is the man standing? ....
5 Where's the cat? ....
6 Where's the dog? ....
7 Liz is in this group of people. Where is she? ....
8 Where's the post office? ....
9 Gary is at the cinema. Where is he sitting? ....
10 Where does Kate work? ....

124.2 Complete the sentences. Use **in**, **at** or **on** + the following:

the west coast	the world	the back of the class	~~the sky~~
the front row	the right	the back of this card	the way to work

1 It was a lovely day. There wasn't a cloud ___in the sky___ .
2 In most countries people drive ....
3 What is the tallest building .... ?
4 I usually buy a newspaper .... in the morning.
5 San Francisco is .... of the United States.
6 We went to the theatre last night. We had seats ....
7 I couldn't hear the teacher. She spoke quietly and I was sitting ....
8 I don't have your address. Could you write it .... ?

124.3 Complete the sentences with **in**, **at** or **on**.

1 Write your name ___at___ the top of the page.
2 Is your sister .... this photograph? I don't recognise her.
3 I didn't feel very well when I woke up, so I stayed .... bed.
4 We normally use the front entrance to the building, but there's another one .... the back.
5 Is there anything interesting .... the paper today?
6 There was a list of names, but my name wasn't .... the list.
7 .... the end of the street, there is a path leading to the river.
8 I love to look up at the stars .... the sky at night.
9 When I'm a passenger in a car, I prefer to sit .... the front.
10 It's a very small village. You probably won't find it .... your map.
11 Joe works .... the furniture department of a large store.
12 Paris is .... the river Seine.
13 I don't like cities. I'd much prefer to live .... the country.
14 My office in .... the top floor. It's .... the left as you come out of the lift.

→ Additional exercise 34 (page 322)

In/at/on (position) 3

A   In hospital / at home etc.

We say that somebody is **in hospital / in prison / in jail**:
- [ ] Ann's mother is **in hospital**.

We say that somebody is **at home / at work / at school / at university / at college**:
- [ ] I'll be **at work** until 5.30, but I'll be **at home** all evening.
- [ ] Julia is studying chemistry **at university**.

Also **at sea** (= on a voyage). Compare **at sea** and **in the sea**:
- [ ] It was a long voyage. We were **at sea** for 30 days.
- [ ] I love swimming **in the sea**.

B   At a party / at a concert etc.

We say that somebody is **at an event** (**at a party / at a conference** etc.):
- [ ] Were there many people **at the party / at the meeting / at the wedding**?
- [ ] I saw Steve **at a football match / at a concert** on Saturday.

C   In and at for buildings

You can often use **in** or **at** with buildings. For example, you can eat **in a restaurant** or **at a restaurant**; you can buy something **in a supermarket** or **at a supermarket**. We usually say **at** when we say where an event takes place (for example: a concert, a film, a party, a meeting):
- [ ] We went to a concert **at the Royal Festival Hall**.
- [ ] The meeting took place **at the company's head office** in Frankfurt.

We say **at the station / at the airport**:
- [ ] Don't meet me **at the station**. I can get a taxi.

We say **at somebody's house**:
- [ ] I was **at Sue's house** last night.   *or*   I was **at Sue's** last night.
Also **at the doctor's, at the hairdresser's** etc.

We use **in** when we are thinking about the building itself. Compare:
- [ ] We had dinner **at the hotel**.
  All the rooms **in the hotel** have air conditioning. (*not* at the hotel)
- [ ] I was **at Sue's (house)** last night.
  It's always cold **in Sue's house**. The heating doesn't work very well. (*not* at Sue's house)

D   In and at for towns etc.

We normally use **in** with cities, towns and villages:
- [ ] Sam's parents live **in Nottingham**. (*not* at Nottingham)
- [ ] The Louvre is a famous art museum **in Paris**. (*not* at Paris)

But you can use **at** *or* **in** when you think of the place as *a point or station on a journey*:
- [ ] Does this train stop **at** (*or* **in**) **Nottingham**? (= at Nottingham station)
- [ ] We stopped **at** (*or* **in**) a small **village** on the way to London.

E   On a bus / in a car etc.

We usually say **on a bus / on a train / on a plane / on a ship**   *but*   **in a car / in a taxi**:
- [ ] **The bus** was very full. There were too many people **on it**.
- [ ] Mary arrived **in a taxi**.

We say **on a bike** (= bicycle) / **on a motorbike / on a horse**:
- [ ] Jane passed me **on her bike**.

At school / in hospital etc. → Unit 74   **In/at/on (position)** → Units 123–24   **To/at/in/into** → Unit 126
By car / by bike etc. → Unit 128B

125.1 Complete the sentences about the pictures. Use **in**, **at** or **on** with the words below the pictures.

1 AIRPORT CAR HIRE (the airport)	**2** DAVE (a train)	**3** CONFERENCE (a conference) KAREN	**4** MARTIN (hospital)
5 JUDY (the hairdresser's)	**6** GARY (his bike)	**7** (New York)	**8** THE SAVOY THEATRE (the Savoy Theatre)

1 You can hire a car _at the airport_ .   5 Judy is ....
2 Dave is ....   6 I saw Gary ....
3 Karen is ....   7 We spent a few days ....
4 Martin is ....   8 We went to a show ....

125.2 Complete the sentences. Use **in**, **at** or **on** + the following:

sea	hospital	a taxi	~~the station~~	the cinema
the plane	school	prison	the airport	the sports centre

1 My train arrives at 11.30. Can you meet me ___at the station___ ?
2 We walked to the restaurant, but we went home ....
3 I'd like to see a film. What's on .... this week?
4 Some people are .... for crimes that they did not commit.
5 'What does your sister do? Has she got a job?' 'No, she's still ....'
6 I play basketball .... on Friday evenings.
7 A friend of mine was injured in an accident a few days ago. She's still ....
8 Our flight was delayed. We had to wait .... for four hours.
9 I enjoyed the flight, but the food .... wasn't very nice.
10 Bill works on ships. He is .... most of the time.

125.3 Complete these sentences with **in**, **at** or **on**.

1 We went to a concert ___at___ the Royal Festival Hall.
2 It was a very slow train. It stopped .... every station.
3 My parents live .... a small village about 50 miles from London.
4 I haven't seen Kate for some time. I last saw her .... David's wedding.
5 We stayed .... a very nice hotel when we were .... Amsterdam.
6 There were fifty rooms .... the hotel.
7 I don't know where my umbrella is. Perhaps I left it .... the bus.
8 I wasn't in when you phoned. I was .... my sister's house.
9 There must be somebody .... the house. The lights are on.
10 The exhibition .... the Museum of Modern Art finished on Saturday.
11 Shall we travel .... your car or mine?
12 What are you doing .... home? I expected you to be .... work.
13 'Did you like the film?' 'Yes, but it was too hot .... the cinema.'
14 Paul lives .... Birmingham. He's a student .... Birmingham University.

→ Additional exercise 34 **(page 322)**   **251**

To/at/in/into

A

We say **go/come/travel** (etc.) **to** a place or event. For example:

go to China	**go to** bed	**come to** my house
go back to Italy	**go to** the bank	**be taken to** hospital
return to London	**go to** a concert	**be sent to** prison
welcome (somebody) **to** (a place)		**drive to** the airport

TO → □

- □ When are your friends **going back to** Italy? (*not* going back in Italy)
- □ Three people were injured in the accident and **taken to** hospital.
- □ **Welcome to** our country! (*not* Welcome in)

In the same way we say 'a **journey to** / a **trip to** / a **visit to** / on **my way to** ...' etc. :
- □ Did you enjoy **your trip to** Paris / **your visit to** the zoo?

Compare **to** (for *movement*) and **in/at** (for *position*):
- □ They are **going to** France.   *but*   They **live in** France.
- □ Can you **come to** the party?   *but*   I'll **see you at** the party.

B

Been to

We say '**been to** (a place)':
- □ I've **been to** Italy four times, but I've never **been to** Rome.
- □ Amanda has never **been to a football match** in her life.

C

Get and arrive

We say **get to** (a place):
- □ What time did they **get to London** / **to work** / **to the party**?

But we say **arrive in** ... or **arrive at** ... (*not* arrive to).
We say **arrive in** a town or country:
- □ They **arrived in London** / **in Spain** a week ago.

For other places (buildings etc.) or events, we say **arrive at**:
- □ When did they **arrive at the hotel** / **at the airport** / **at the party**?

D

Home

We say: **go home** / **come home** / **get home** / **arrive home** / **on the way home** etc. (no preposition).
We do not say 'to home':
- □ I'm tired. Let's **go home** now. (*not* go to home)
- □ I met Linda **on my way home**. (*not* my way to home)

E

Into

Go into, **get into** ... etc. = enter (a room / a building / a car etc.):
- □ I opened the door, **went into** the room and sat down.
- □ A bird **flew into** the kitchen through the window.

INTO → □

With some verbs (especially **go/get/put**) we often use **in** (instead of **into**):
- □ She **got in** the car and drove away. (*or* She **got into** the car ...)
- □ I read the letter and **put it** back **in** the envelope.

The opposite of **into** is **out of**:
- □ She **got out of** the car and **went into** a shop.

We usually say '**get on/off** a bus / a train / a plane' (*not usually* get into/out of):
- □ She **got on the bus** and I never saw her again.

126.1 Put in **to/at/in/into** where necessary. If no preposition is necessary, leave the space empty.

1 Three people were taken __to__ hospital after the accident.
2 I met Kate on my way __—__ home. *(no preposition)*
3 We left our luggage .... the station and went to find something to eat.
4 Shall we take a taxi .... the station or shall we walk?
5 I have to go .... the bank today to change some money.
6 The river Rhine flows .... the North Sea.
7 'Have you got your camera?' 'No, I left it .... home.'
8 Have you ever been .... China?
9 I had lost my key, but I managed to climb .... the house through a window.
10 We got stuck in a traffic jam on our way .... the airport.
11 We had lunch .... the airport while we were waiting for our plane.
12 Welcome .... the hotel. We hope you enjoy your stay here.
13 We drove along the main road for about a kilometre and then turned .... a narrow side street.
14 Did you enjoy your visit .... the zoo?
15 I'm tired. As soon as I get .... home, I'm going .... bed.
16 Marcel is French. He has just returned .... France after two years .... Brazil.
17 Carl was born .... Chicago, but his family moved .... New York when he was three. He still lives .... New York.

126.2 Have you been to these places? If so, how many times? Choose three of the places and write a sentence using **been to**.

Athens   **Australia**   **Ireland**   **Paris**   **Rome**   **Sweden**   **Tokyo**   **the United States**

1 *(example answers)* I've never been to Australia. / I've been to Ireland once.
2 ....
3 ....
4 ....

126.3 Put in **to/at/in** where necessary. If no preposition is necessary, leave the space empty.

1 What time does this train get __to__ London?
2 What time does this train arrive .... London?
3 What time did you get .... home last night?
4 What time do you usually arrive .... work in the morning?
5 When we got .... the cinema, there was a long queue outside.
6 I arrived .... home feeling very tired.

126.4 Write sentences using **got + into / out of / on / off**.

1 You were walking home. A friend passed you in her car. She saw you, stopped and offered you a lift. She opened the door. What did you do? I got into the car.
2 You were waiting for the bus. At last your bus came. The doors opened. What did you do then? I ....
3 You drove home in your car. You stopped outside your house and parked the car. What did you do then? ....
4 You were travelling by train to Manchester. When the train got to Manchester, what did you do? ....
5 You needed a taxi. After a few minutes a taxi stopped for you. You opened the door. What did you do then? ....
6 You were travelling by air. At the end of your flight, your plane landed at the airport and stopped. The doors were opened, you took your bag and stood up. What did you do then?
....

→ Additional exercise 34 (**page 322**)

A   Expressions with **in**

in the rain / in the sun (= sunshine) / **in the shade / in the dark / in bad weather** etc.
- ☐ We sat **in the shade**. It was too hot to sit **in the sun**.
- ☐ Don't go out **in the rain**. Wait until it stops.

(write) **in ink / in biro / in pencil**
- ☐ When you do the exam, you're not allowed to write **in pencil**.

Also   (write) **in words / in figures / in BLOCK CAPITALS** etc.
- ☐ Please write your name **in block capitals**.
- ☐ Write the story **in your own words**.   (= don't copy somebody else)

(be/fall) **in love** (with somebody)
- ☐ Have you ever been **in love with** anybody?

in (my) **opinion**
- ☐ **In my opinion**, the film wasn't very good.

B   **At the age of ...** etc.

We say 'at the age of 16 / at 120 miles an hour / at 100 degrees etc.':
- ☐ Tracy left school **at 16**. *or* ... **at the age of** 16.
- ☐ The train was travelling **at 120 miles an hour**.
- ☐ Water boils **at 100 degrees Celsius**.

> We are now flying **at a speed of** 800 kilometres an hour and **at an altitude** of 9,000 metres.

C   **On holiday / on a tour** etc.

We say: (be/go) **on holiday / on business / on a trip / on a tour / on a cruise** etc.
- ☐ I'm going **on holiday** next week.
- ☐ Emma's away **on business** at the moment.
- ☐ One day I'd like to go **on a world tour**.

You can also say 'go to a place **for a holiday / for my holiday(s)**':
- ☐ Steve has gone to France **for a holiday**.

D   Other expressions with **on**

on television / on the radio
- ☐ I didn't watch the news **on television**, but I heard it **on the radio**.

on the phone/telephone
- ☐ I've never met her, but I've spoken to her **on the phone** a few times.

(be/go) **on strike**
- ☐ There are no trains today. The drivers are **on strike**.

(be/go) **on a diet**
- ☐ I've put on a lot of weight. I'll have to go **on a diet**.

(be) **on fire**
- ☐ Look! That car is **on fire**.

on the whole (= in general)
- ☐ Sometimes I have problems at work, but **on the whole** I enjoy my job.

on purpose (= intentionally)
- ☐ I'm sorry. I didn't mean to annoy you. I didn't do it **on purpose**.

127.1 Complete the sentences using **in** + the following:

block capitals	cold weather	love	my opinion
pencil	~~the rain~~	the shade	

1 Don't go out ____in the rain____ . Wait until it stops.
2 Matt likes to keep warm, so he doesn't go out much ....
3 If you write .... and make a mistake, you can rub it out and correct it.
4 They fell .... almost immediately and were married in a few weeks.
5 Please write your address clearly, preferably ....
6 It's too hot in the sun. I'm going to sit ....
7 Amanda thought the restaurant was OK, but .... it wasn't very good.

127.2 Complete the sentences using **on** + the following:

business	a diet	~~fire~~	holiday	the phone
purpose	strike	television	a tour	the whole

1 Look! That car is ____on fire____ ! Somebody call the fire brigade.
2 Workers at the factory have gone .... for better pay and conditions.
3 Soon after we arrived, we were taken .... of the city.
4 I feel lazy this evening. Is there anything worth watching .... ?
5 I'm sorry. It was an accident. I didn't do it ....
6 Richard has put on a lot of weight recently. I think he should go ....
7 Jane's job involves a lot of travelling. She often has to go away ....
8 A: I'm going .... next week.
   B: Where are you going? Somewhere nice?
9 A: Is Sarah here?
   B: Yes, but she's .... at the moment. She won't be long.
10 A: How was your exam?
    B: Well, there were some difficult questions, but .... it was OK.

127.3 Complete the sentences with **on, in, at** or **for.**

1 Water boils ____at____ 100 degrees Celsius.
2 When I was 14, I went .... a trip to France organised by my school.
3 There was panic when people realised that the building was .... fire.
4 Julia's grandmother died recently .... the age of 79.
5 Can you turn the light on, please? I don't want to sit .... the dark.
6 We didn't go .... holiday last year. We stayed at home.
7 I'm going to Switzerland .... a short holiday next month.
8 I won't be here next week. I'll be .... holiday.
9 Technology has developed .... great speed.
10 Alan got married .... 17, which is rather young to get married.
11 I heard an interesting programme .... the radio this morning.
12 .... my opinion, violent films should not be shown .... television.
13 I wouldn't like to go .... a cruise. I think I'd get bored.
14 I mustn't eat too much. I'm supposed to be .... a diet.
15 I wouldn't like his job. He spends most of his time talking .... the phone.
16 The earth travels round the sun .... 107,000 kilometres an hour.
17 'Did you enjoy your holiday?' 'Not every minute, but .... the whole, yes.'
18 When you write a cheque, you have to write the amount .... words and figures.

→ Additional exercise 34 (page 322)

A

We use **by** in many expressions to say how we do something. For example, you can:

send something **by post**   contact somebody **by phone / by email / by fax**

do something **by hand**   pay **by cheque / by credit card**

□ Can I pay **by credit card**?

□ You can contact me **by phone, by fax** or **by email**.

But we say **pay cash** or **pay in cash** (*not* by cash).

We also say **by mistake / by accident / by chance**:

□ We hadn't arranged to meet. We met **by chance**.

But we say 'do something **on purpose**' (= you mean to do it):

□ I didn't do it **on purpose**. It was an accident.

Note that we say **by chance, by cheque** etc. (*not* by the chance / by a cheque). In these expressions we use **by** + *noun* without **the** or **a**.

B

In the same way we use **by** ... to say how somebody travels:

by car / by train / by plane / by boat / by ship / by bus / by bike etc.

by road / by rail / by air / by sea / by underground

□ Joanne usually goes to work **by bus**.

□ Do you prefer to travel **by air** or **by train**?

But we say **on foot**:

□ Did you come here **by car** or **on foot**?

You cannot use **by** if you say **my car / the train / a taxi** etc. We use **by** + *noun* without 'a/the/my' etc. We say:

by car   *but*   **in my** car (*not* by my car)

by train *but*   **on the** train (*not* by the train)

We use **in** for cars and taxis:

□ They didn't come **in their car**. They came **in a taxi**.

We use **on** for bicycles and public transport (buses, trains etc.):

□ We travelled **on the 6.45 train**.

C

We say that 'something is done **by** somebody/something' (*passive*):

□ Have you ever been bitten **by a dog**?

□ The programme was watched **by millions of people**.

Compare **by** and **with**:

□ The door must have been opened **with a key**. (*not* by a key)

   (= somebody used a key to open it)

□ The door must have been opened **by somebody** with a key.

We say 'a play **by Shakespeare**' / 'a painting **by Rembrandt**' / 'a novel **by Tolstoy**' etc. :

□ Have you read anything **by Ernest Hemingway**?

D

By also means 'beside':

□ Come and sit **by me**. (= beside me)

□ 'Where's the light switch?' '**By the door**.'

switch

E

Note the following use of **by**:

□ Clare's salary has just gone up **from £2,000** a month **to £2,200**. So it has increased **by £200 / by ten per cent**.

□ Carl and Mike had a race over 200 metres. Carl won **by about three metres**.

new salary ——— £2,200

increased **by £200**

old salary ——— £2,000

Passive + by → Unit 42B   **By + -ing** → Unit 60B   **By myself** → Unit 83C   **By (time)** → Unit 120

128.1 Complete the sentences using by + the following:

~~chance~~   credit card   hand   mistake   satellite

1 We hadn't arranged to meet. We met __by chance__ .
2 I didn't intend to take your umbrella. I took it _____ .
3 Don't put the sweater in the washing machine. It has to be washed _____ .
4 I don't need cash. I can pay the bill _____ .
5 The two cities were connected _____ for a television programme.

128.2 Put in by, in or on.

1 Joanne usually goes to work __by__ bus.
2 I saw Jane this morning. She was _____ the bus.
3 How did you get here? Did you come _____ train?
4 I decided not to go _____ car. I went _____ my bike instead.
5 I didn't feel like walking home, so I came home _____ a taxi.
6 Sorry we're late. We missed the bus, so we had to come _____ foot.
7 How long does it take to cross the Atlantic _____ ship?

128.3 Write three sentences like the examples. Write about a song, a painting, a film, a book etc.

1 _War and Peace is a book by Tolstoy._
2 _Romeo and Juliet is a play by Shakespeare._
3 _____
4 _____
5 _____

128.4 Put in by, in, on or with.

1 Have you ever been bitten __by__ a dog?
2 The plane was badly damaged _____ lightning.
3 We managed to put the fire out _____ a fire extinguisher.
4 Who is that man standing _____ the window?
5 These photographs were taken _____ a friend of mine.
6 I don't mind going _____ car, but I don't want to go _____ your car.
7 There was a small table _____ the bed _____ a lamp and a clock _____ it.

128.5 All these sentences have a mistake. Correct them.

1 Did you come here by Kate's car or yours?   _in Kate's car_
2 I don't like travelling on bus.   _____
3 These photographs were taken by a very good camera. _____
4 I know this music is from Beethoven, but I can't
   remember what it's called.   _____
5 I couldn't pay by cash – I didn't have any money on me. _____
6 We lost the game only because of a mistake of one of
   our players.

128.6 Complete the sentences using by.

1 Clare's salary was £2,000 a month. Now it is £2,200.
   Her salary _has increased by £200 a month._
2 My daily newspaper used to cost 60 pence. From today it costs 70 pence.
   The price has gone up _____
3 There was an election. Helen won. She got 25 votes and Norman got 23.
   Helen won _____
4 I went to Kate's house to see her, but she had gone out five minutes before I arrived.
   I missed _____

→ Additional exercise 34 (page 322)

Noun + preposition
(reason for, cause of etc.)

A   Noun + **for** ...

a **cheque FOR** (a sum of money)
- [ ] They sent me a **cheque for** £150.

a **demand** / a **need FOR** ...
- [ ] The company closed down because there wasn't enough **demand for** its product.
- [ ] There's no excuse for behaviour like that. There's no **need for** it.

a **reason FOR** ...
- [ ] The train was late, but nobody knew the **reason for** the delay. (*not* reason of)

B   Noun + **of** ...

an **advantage** / a **disadvantage OF** ...
- [ ] The **advantage of living alone** is that you can do what you like.

but there is an advantage in (*or* to) doing something
- [ ] **There are** many advantages **in** living alone. (*or* ... **to** living alone)

a **cause OF** ...
- [ ] The **cause of** the explosion is unknown.

a **photograph** / a **picture** / a **map** / a **plan** / a **drawing** (etc.) **OF** ...
- [ ] Rachel showed me some **photographs of** her family.
- [ ] I had a **map of** the town, so I was able to find my way around.

C   Noun + **in** ...

an **increase** / a **decrease** / a **rise** / a **fall IN** (prices etc.)
- [ ] There has been an **increase in** the number of road accidents recently.
- [ ] Last year was a bad one for the company. There was a big **fall in** sales.

D   Noun + **to** ...

damage **TO** ...
- [ ] The accident was my fault, so I had to pay for the **damage to** the other car.

an **invitation TO** ... (a party / a wedding etc.)
- [ ] Did you get an **invitation to** the party?

a **solution TO** (a problem) / a **key TO** (a door) / an **answer TO** (a question) / a **reply TO** (a letter) / a **reaction TO** ...
- [ ] I hope we'll find a **solution to** the problem. (*not* a solution of the problem)
- [ ] I was surprised at her **reaction to** my suggestion.

an **attitude TO** ... (*or* **TOWARDS** ...)
- [ ] His **attitude to** his job is very negative. *or* His **attitude towards** his job ...

E   Noun + **with** ... / **between** ...

a **relationship** / a **connection** / contact **WITH** ...
- [ ] Do you have a good **relationship with** your parents?
- [ ] The police want to question a man in **connection with** the robbery.

but a **relationship** / a **connection** / contact / a **difference BETWEEN** two things or people
- [ ] The police believe that there is no **connection between** the two crimes.
- [ ] There are some **differences between** British and American English.

Exercises

129.1 Complete the second sentence so that it has the same meaning as the first.

1 What caused the explosion? What was the cause _of the explosion_ ?
2 We're trying to solve the problem. We're trying to find a solution ....
3 Sue gets on well with her brother. Sue has a good relationship ....
4 The cost of living has gone up a lot.
   There has been a big increase ....
5 I don't know how to answer your question.
   I can't think of an answer ....
6 I don't think that a new road is necessary.
   I don't think there is any need ....
7 I think that working at home has many advantages.
   I think that there are many advantages ....
8 The number of people without jobs fell last month.
   Last month there was a fall ....
9 Nobody wants to buy shoes like these any more.
   There is no demand ....
10 In what way is your job different from mine?
   What is the difference .... ?

129.2 Complete the sentences using the following nouns + the correct preposition:

cause	connection	contact	damage	invitation
key	~~map~~	pictures	reason	reply

1 On the wall there were some pictures and a ....._map of_.... the world.
2 Thank you for the .... your party next week.
3 Since she left home two years ago, Sophie has had little .... her family.
4 I can't open this door. Have you got a .... the other door?
5 The .... the fire at the hotel last night is still unknown.
6 I emailed Jim last week, but I still haven't received a .... my message.
7 The two companies are completely independent. There is no .... them.
8 Jane showed me some old .... the city as it looked 100 years ago.
9 Carol has decided to give up her job. I don't know her .... doing this.
10 It wasn't a bad accident. The .... the car wasn't serious.

129.3 Complete the sentences with the correct preposition.

1 There are some differences ....._between_.... British and American English.
2 Money isn't the solution .... every problem.
3 There has been an increase .... the amount of traffic using this road.
4 When I opened the envelope, I was delighted to find a cheque .... £500.
5 The advantage .... having a car is that you don't have to rely on public transport.
6 There are many advantages .... being able to speak a foreign language.
7 Everything can be explained. There's a reason .... everything.
8 When Paul left home, his attitude .... his parents seemed to change.
9 Ben and I used to be good friends, but I don't have much contact .... him now.
10 There has been a sharp rise .... property prices in the past few years.
11 What was Emma's reaction .... the news?
12 If I give you the camera, can you take a photograph .... me?
13 The company has rejected the workers' demands .... a rise .... pay.
14 What was the answer .... question 3 in the test?
15 The fact that Jane was offered a job has no connection .... the fact that she is a friend of the managing director.

→ Additional exercise 35 (page 322)

A It was **nice of** you to …

> **nice / kind / good / generous / polite / stupid / silly** etc. **OF** somebody (to do something)
> - ☐ Thank you. It was very **kind of you** to help me.
> - ☐ It is **stupid of me** to go out without a coat in such cold weather.
>
> *but* (be) **nice / kind / good / generous / polite / rude / friendly / cruel** etc. **TO** somebody
> - ☐ They have always been very **nice to** me. (*not* with me)
> - ☐ Why were you so **unfriendly to** Lucy?

B *Adjective* + **about** / **with**

> **angry / annoyed / furious** $\begin{cases} \textbf{ABOUT} \text{ something} \\ \textbf{WITH} \text{ somebody } \textbf{FOR} \text{ doing something} \end{cases}$
>
> - ☐ It's stupid to get **angry about** things that don't matter.
> - ☐ Are you **annoyed with** me **for** being late?
>
> **excited / worried / upset / nervous / happy** etc. **ABOUT** a situation
> - ☐ Are you **excited about** going away next week?
> - ☐ Lisa is **upset about** not being invited to the party.
>
> **delighted / pleased / satisfied / happy / disappointed WITH** something you receive, or the result of something
> - ☐ I was **delighted with** the present you gave me.
> - ☐ Were you **happy with** your exam results?

C *Adjective* + **at** / **by** / **with**

> **surprised / shocked / amazed / astonished AT / BY** something
> - ☐ Everybody was **surprised AT** (*or* **BY**) the news.
> - ☐ I hope you weren't **shocked BY** (*or* **AT**) what I said.
>
> **impressed WITH / BY** somebody/something
> - ☐ I'm very **impressed with** (*or* by) her English. It's very good.
>
> **fed up / bored WITH** something
> - ☐ I don't enjoy my job any more. I'm **fed up with** it. / I'm **bored with** it.

D Sorry **about** / **for**

> **sorry ABOUT** a situation or something that happened
> - ☐ I'm **sorry about** the mess. I'll clear it up later.
> - ☐ We're all **sorry about** Julie losing her job.
>
> **sorry FOR / ABOUT** something you did
> - ☐ Alex is very **sorry for** what he said. (*or* **sorry about** what he said)
> - ☐ I'm **sorry for** shouting at you yesterday. (*or* **sorry about** shouting)
> You can also say 'I'm sorry I (did something)':
> - ☐ I'm **sorry I shouted** at you yesterday.
>
> **feel / be sorry FOR** somebody who is in a bad situation
> - ☐ I **feel sorry for** Matt. He's had a lot of bad luck. (*not* I feel sorry about Matt)

Preposition + -ing → Unit 60   Adjective + to … → Unit 65   Sorry to … / sorry for … → Unit 66C
Adjective + preposition 2 → Unit 131

130.1 Write sentences using **nice of ...** , **kind of ...** etc.

1	I went out in the cold without a coat.	(silly) *That was silly of you.*
2	Sue offered to drive me to the airport.	(nice) That was .... her.
3	I needed money and Tom gave me some.	(generous) That ....
		....
4	They didn't invite us to their party.	(not very nice) That ....
		....
5	Can I help you with your luggage?	(very kind) .... you.
6	Kevin didn't thank me for the present.	(not very polite) ....
		....
7	They've had an argument and now they refuse to speak to each other.	(a bit childish) ....

130.2 Complete the sentences using the following adjectives + the correct preposition:

annoyed   annoyed   astonished   bored   ~~excited~~   impressed   kind   sorry

1 Are you ......*excited about*...... going away next week?
2 Thank you for all your help. You've been very .... me.
3 I wouldn't like to be in her position. I feel .... her.
4 What have I done wrong? Why are you .... me?
5 Why do you always get so .... things that don't matter?
6 I wasn't very .... the service in the restaurant. We had to wait ages before our food arrived.
7 Ben isn't very happy at college. He says he's .... the course he's doing.
8 I had never seen so many people before. I was .... the crowds.

130.3 Put in the correct preposition.

1 I was delighted ...*with*... the present you gave me.
2 It was very nice .... you to do my shopping for me. Thank you very much.
3 Why are you always so rude .... your parents? Can't you be nice .... them?
4 It was careless .... you to leave the door unlocked when you went out.
5 They didn't reply to our letter, which wasn't very polite .... them.
6 We always have the same food every day. I'm fed up .... it.
7 I can't understand people who are cruel .... animals.
8 We enjoyed our holiday, but we were a bit disappointed .... the hotel.
9 I was surprised .... the way he behaved. It was completely out of character.
10 I've been trying to learn Spanish, but I'm not very satisfied .... my progress.
11 Linda doesn't look very well. I'm worried .... her.
12 Are you angry .... what happened?
13 I'm sorry .... what I did. I hope you're not angry .... me.
14 The people next door are furious .... us .... making so much noise last night.
15 Jill starts her new job next week. She's quite excited .... it.
16 I'm sorry .... the smell of paint in this room. I've just decorated it.
17 I was shocked .... what I saw. I'd never seen anything like it before.
18 The man we interviewed for the job was intelligent, but we weren't very impressed .... his appearance.
19 Are you still upset .... what I said to you yesterday?
20 He said he was sorry .... the situation, but there was nothing he could do.
21 I felt sorry .... the children when we went on holiday. It rained every day and they had to spend most of the time indoors.

→ Additional exercise 35 **(page 322)**

Adjective + preposition 2

Adjective + of (1)

afraid / frightened / terrified / scared OF ...
- □ 'Are you **afraid of** spiders?' 'Yes, I'm **terrified of** them.'

fond / proud / ashamed / jealous / envious OF ...
- □ Why are you always so **jealous of** other people?

suspicious / critical / tolerant OF ...
- □ He didn't trust me. He was **suspicious of** my intentions.

Adjective + of (2)

aware / conscious OF ...
- □ 'Did you know he was married?' 'No, I wasn't **aware of** that.'

capable / incapable OF ...
- □ I'm sure you are **capable of** passing the examination.

full / short OF ...
- □ The letter I wrote was **full of** mistakes. (*not* full with)
- □ I'm a bit **short of** money. Can you lend me some?

typical OF ...
- □ He's late again. It's **typical of** him to keep everybody waiting.

tired / sick OF ...
- □ Come on, let's go! I'm **tired of** waiting. (= I've had enough of waiting.)

certain / sure OF *or* **ABOUT ...**
- □ I think she's arriving this evening, but I'm not **sure of** that. *or* ... **sure about** that.

Adjective + at / to / from / in / on / with / for

good / bad / brilliant / better / hopeless etc. **AT ...**
- □ I'm not very **good at** repairing things. (*not* good in repairing things)

married / engaged TO ...
- □ Linda is **married to** an American. (*not* married with)
- *but* Linda is married **with three children**. (= she is married and has three children)

similar TO ...
- □ Your writing is **similar to** mine.

different FROM *or* **different TO ...**
- □ The film was **different from** what I'd expected. (*or* **different to** what I'd expected.)

interested IN ...
- □ Are you **interested in** art?

keen ON ...
- □ We stayed at home because Chris wasn't very **keen on** going out.

dependent ON ... (*but* **independent OF ...**)
- □ I don't want to be **dependent on** anybody.

crowded WITH (people etc.)
- □ The streets were **crowded with** tourists. (*but* **full of** tourists)

famous FOR ...
- □ The Italian city of Florence is **famous for** its art treasures.

responsible FOR ...
- □ Who was **responsible for** all that noise last night?

Preposition + -ing → Unit 60   Afraid of/to ... → Unit 66A   Adjective + preposition 1 → Unit 130
American English → Appendix 7

131.1 Complete the second sentence so that it has the same meaning as the first.

1 There were lots of tourists in the streets.   The streets were crowded __with tourists__ .
2 There was a lot of furniture in the room.   The room was full ....
3 I don't like sport very much.   I'm not very keen ....
4 We don't have enough time.   We're a bit short ....
5 I'm not a very good tennis player.   I'm not very good ....
6 Catherine's husband is Russian.   Catherine is married ....
7 I don't trust Robert.   I'm suspicious ....
8 My problem is not the same as yours.   My problem is different ....

131.2 Complete the sentences using the following adjectives + the correct preposition:

afraid   **different**   **interested**   **proud**   **responsible**   **similar**   ~~sure~~

1 I think she's arriving this evening, but I'm not __sure of__ that.
2 Your camera is .... mine, but it isn't exactly the same.
3 Don't worry. I'll look after you. There's nothing to be ....
4 I never watch the news on television. I'm not .... the news.
5 The editor is the person who is .... what appears in a newspaper.
6 Sarah is a keen gardener. She's very .... her garden and loves showing it to visitors.
7 I was surprised when I met Lisa for the first time. She was .... what I expected.

131.3 Put in the correct preposition.

1 The letter I wrote was full __of__ mistakes.
2 My home town is not an especially interesting place. It's not famous .... anything.
3 Kate is very fond .... her younger brother.
4 I don't like going up ladders. I'm scared .... heights.
5 You look bored. You don't seem interested .... what I'm saying.
6 Did you know that Liz is engaged .... a friend of mine?
7 I'm not ashamed .... what I did. In fact I'm quite proud .... it.
8 I suggested that we should all go out for a meal, but nobody else was keen .... the idea.
9 These days everybody is aware .... the dangers of smoking.
10 The station platform was crowded .... people waiting for the train.
11 Sue is much more successful than I am. Sometimes I feel a bit jealous .... her.
12 I'm tired .... doing the same thing every day. I need a change.
13 Do you know anyone who might be interested .... buying an old car?
14 We've got plenty to eat. The fridge is full .... food.
15 She is a very honest person. I don't think she is capable .... telling a lie.
16 Helen works hard and she's extremely good .... her job.
17 I'm not surprised he changed his mind at the last moment. That's typical .... him.
18 Mark has no money of his own. He's totally dependent .... his parents.
19 We're short .... staff in our office at the moment. We need more people to do the work.

131.4 Write sentences about yourself. Are you good at these things or not? Use the following:

good   **quite good**   **not very good**   **hopeless**

1 (repairing things)   __I'm not very good at repairing things.__
2 (telling jokes)   ....
3 (mathematics)   ....
4 (remembering names)   ....

→ Additional exercise 35 **(page 322)**

A   *Verb +* **to**

talk / speak TO somebody   (**with** is also possible but less usual)
- ☐ Who was that man you were **talking to?**

listen TO …
- ☐ We spent the evening **listening to** music.   (*not* listening music)

write (a letter) **TO** …
- ☐ I **wrote to** the hotel complaining about the poor service we had received.

apologise TO somebody (**for** …)
- ☐ They **apologised to me** for what happened.   (*not* They apologised me)

explain something **TO** somebody
- ☐ Can you **explain** this word **to me?**   (*not* explain me this word)

explain / describe (**to** somebody) what/how/why …
- ☐ I **explained to them** why I was worried.   (*not* I explained them)
- ☐ Let me **describe to you** what I saw.   (*not* Let me describe you)

B   We do not use **to** with these verbs:

phone / telephone / call somebody
- ☐ Did you **phone your father** yesterday?   (*not* phone to your father)

answer somebody/something
- ☐ He refused to **answer my question.**   (*not* answer to my question)

ask somebody
- ☐ Can I **ask you** a question?   (*not* ask to you)

thank somebody (**for** something)
- ☐ He **thanked me** for helping him.   (*not* He thanked to me)

C   *Verb +* **at**

look / stare / glance AT … , **have a look / take a look AT** …
- ☐ Why are you **looking at** me like that?

laugh AT …
- ☐ I look stupid with this haircut. Everybody will **laugh at** me.

aim / point (something) **AT** … , **shoot / fire** (a gun) **AT** …
- ☐ Don't **point** that knife **at** me. It's dangerous.
- ☐ We saw someone with a gun **shooting at** birds, but he didn't hit any.

D   Some verbs can be followed by **at** or **to,** with a difference of meaning. For example:

shout AT somebody   (when you are angry)
- ☐ He got very angry and started **shouting at** me.

shout TO somebody   (so that they can hear you)
- ☐ He **shouted to** me from the other side of the street.

throw something **AT** somebody/something   (in order to hit them)
- ☐ Somebody **threw** an egg **at** the minister.

throw something **TO** somebody   (for somebody to catch)
- ☐ Lisa shouted 'Catch!' and **threw** the keys **to** me from the window.

Verb + preposition 2–4 → Units 133–136   **Ask for** → Unit 133C   **Apologise for / thank somebody for**
→ Unit 135B   **Other verbs + to** → Unit 136D   **American English** → Appendix 7

132.1 You ask somebody to explain things that you don't understand. Write questions beginning **Can you explain ... ?**

1 (I don't understand this word.)
   Can you explain this word to me?
2 (I don't understand what you mean.)
   Can you explain to me what you mean?
3 (I don't understand this question.)
   Can you explain ....
4 (I don't understand the problem.)
   Can ....
5 (I don't understand how this machine works.)
   ....
6 (I don't understand what I have to do.)
   ....

132.2 Put in **to** where necessary. If the sentence is already complete, leave the space empty.

1 I know who she is, but I've never spoken ....*to*.... her.
2 Why didn't you answer ....*–*.... my letter?
3 I like to listen .... the radio while I'm having breakfast.
4 We'd better phone .... the restaurant to reserve a table.
5 'Did Mike apologise .... you?' 'Yes, he said he was very sorry.'
6 I explained .... everybody the reasons for my decision.
7 I thanked .... everybody for all the help they had given me.
8 Ask me what you like, and I'll try and answer .... your questions.
9 Mike described .... me exactly what happened.
10 Karen won't be able to help you, so there's no point in asking .... her.

132.3 Complete the sentences. Use the following verbs (in the correct form) + the correct preposition:

~~explain~~   glance   ~~laugh~~   listen   point   speak   throw   throw

1 I look stupid with this haircut. Everybody will ....*laugh at*.... me.
2 I don't understand this. Can you ....*explain*.... it ....*to*.... me?
3 Sue and Kevin had an argument and now they're not .... one another.
4 Be careful with those scissors! Don't .... them .... me!
5 I .... my watch to see what the time was.
6 Please .... me! I've got something important to tell you.
7 Don't .... stones .... the birds! It's cruel.
8 If you don't want that sandwich, ... it .... the birds. They'll eat it.

132.4 Put in **to** or **at**.

1 I wrote ....*to*.... the hotel complaining about the poor service we had received.
2 Look .... these flowers. Aren't they pretty?
3 Please don't shout .... me! Try to calm down.
4 I saw Sue as I was cycling along the road. I shouted .... her, but she didn't hear me.
5 Don't listen .... what he says. He doesn't know what he's talking about.
6 What's so funny? What are you laughing .... ?
7 Do you think I could have a look .... your magazine, please?
8 I'm a bit lonely. I need somebody to talk ....
9 She was so angry she threw a book .... the wall.
10 The woman sitting opposite me on the train kept staring .... me.
11 Can I speak .... you a moment? There's something I want to ask you.

→ Additional exercise 36 (page 323)   **265**

A   Verb + about

talk / read / know ABOUT … , tell somebody ABOUT …
- □ We **talked about** a lot of things at the meeting.

have a discussion ABOUT something, *but* **discuss** something (no preposition)
- □ We had **a discussion about** what we should do.
- □ We **discussed** a lot of things at the meeting. (*not* discussed about)

do something ABOUT something = *do something to improve a bad situation*
- □ If you're worried about the problem, you should **do** something **about** it.

B   Care about, care for and take care of

care ABOUT somebody/something = *think that somebody/something is important*
- □ He's very selfish. He doesn't **care about** other people.

We say '**care what/where/how** …' etc. (*without* about)
- □ You can do what you like. I don't **care what** you do.

care FOR somebody/something
(1) = *like something* (usually in questions and negative sentences)
- □ Would you **care for** a cup of coffee? (= Would you like … ?)
- □ I don't **care for** very hot weather. (= I don't like …)
(2) = *look after somebody*
- □ Alan is 85 and lives alone. He needs somebody to **care for** him.

take care OF … = *look after*
- □ Have a nice holiday. **Take care of** yourself! (= look after yourself)

C   Verb + for

ask (somebody) FOR …
- □ I wrote to the company **asking** them **for** more information about the job.

but 'I **asked** him **the way** to …', 'She **asked** me **my name**' (no preposition)

apply (TO a person, a company etc.) FOR a job etc.
- □ I think you'd be good at this job. Why don't you **apply for** it?

wait FOR …
- □ Don't **wait for** me. I'll join you later.
- □ I'm not going out yet. I'm **waiting for** the rain to stop.

search (a person / a place / a bag etc.) FOR …
- □ I've **searched** the house **for** my keys, but I still can't find them.

leave (a place) FOR another place
- □ I haven't seen her since she **left** (home) **for** the office this morning.
   (*not* left to the office)

D   Look for and look after

look FOR … = *search for, try to find*
- □ I've lost my keys. Can you help me to **look for** them?

look AFTER … = *take care of*
- □ Alan is 85 and lives alone. He needs somebody to **look after** him. (*not* look for)
- □ You can borrow this book, but you must promise to **look after** it.

133.1 Put in the correct preposition. If no preposition is necessary, leave the space empty.

1 I'm not going out yet. I'm waiting ...for... the rain to stop.
2 I couldn't find the street I was looking for, so I stopped someone to ask .... directions.
3 I've applied .... a job at the factory. I don't know if I'll get it.
4 I've applied .... three colleges. I hope one of them accepts me.
5 I've searched everywhere .... John, but I haven't been able to find him.
6 I don't want to talk .... what happened last night. Let's forget it.
7 I don't want to discuss .... what happened last night. Let's forget it.
8 We had an interesting discussion .... the problem, but we didn't reach a decision.
9 We discussed .... the problem, but we didn't reach a decision.
10 I don't want to go out yet. I'm waiting .... the post to arrive.
11 Ken and Sonia are touring Italy. They're in Rome at the moment, but tomorrow they leave .... Venice.
12 The roof of the house is in very bad condition. I think we ought to do something .... it.
13 We waited .... Steve for half an hour, but he never came.
14 Tomorrow morning I have to catch a plane. I'm leaving my house .... the airport at 7.30.

133.2 Complete the sentences with the following verbs (in the correct form) + preposition:

    apply   ask   do   leave   look   ~~search~~   talk   wait

1 Police are ...searching for... the man who escaped from prison.
2 We're still .... a reply to our letter. We haven't heard anything yet.
3 I think Ben likes his job, but he doesn't .... it much.
4 When I'd finished my meal, I .... the waiter .... the bill.
5 Cathy is unemployed. She has .... several jobs, but she hasn't had any luck.
6 If something is wrong, why don't you .... something .... it?
7 Linda's car is very old, but it's in excellent condition. She .... it very well.
8 Diane is from Boston, but now she lives in Paris. She .... Boston .... Paris when she was 19.

133.3 Put in the correct preposition after **care**. If no preposition is necessary, leave the space empty.

1 He's very selfish. He doesn't care ...about... other people.
2 Are you hungry? Would you care .... something to eat?
3 She doesn't care .... the exam. She doesn't care whether she passes or fails.
4 Please let me borrow your camera. I promise I'll take good care .... it.
5 'Do you like this coat?' 'Not really. I don't care .... the colour.'
6 Don't worry about the shopping. I'll take care .... that.
7 I want to have a good holiday. I don't care .... the cost.
8 I want to have a good holiday. I don't care .... how much it costs.

133.4 Complete the sentences with **look for** or **look after**. Use the correct form of **look** (looks/looked/looking).

1 I ...looked for... my keys, but I couldn't find them anywhere.
2 Kate is .... a job. I hope she finds one soon.
3 Who .... you when you were ill?
4 I'm .... Elizabeth. Have you seen her?
5 The car park was full, so we had to .... somewhere else to park.
6 A babysitter is somebody who .... other people's children.

→ Additional exercise 36 (page 323)

A

dream ABOUT ... (when you are asleep)
- ☐ I **dreamt about** you last night.

dream OF/ABOUT being something / doing something = *imagine*
- ☐ Do you **dream of/about** being rich and famous?

(I) **wouldn't dream OF** doing something = *I would never do it*
- ☐ 'Don't tell anyone what I said.'   'No, I **wouldn't dream of** it.' (= I would never do it)

B

hear ABOUT ... = *be told about something*
- ☐ Did you **hear about** what happened at the club on Saturday night?

hear OF ... = *know that somebody/something exists*
- ☐ 'Who is Tom Hart?'   'I have no idea. I've never **heard of** him'. (*not* heard from him)

hear FROM ... = *receive a letter, phone call or message from somebody*
- ☐ 'Have you **heard from** Jane recently?'   'Yes, she phoned a few days ago.'

C

think ABOUT ... and **think OF** ...

When you **think ABOUT** something, you consider it, you concentrate your mind on it:
- ☐ I've **thought about** what you said and I've decided to take your advice.
- ☐ 'Will you lend me the money?'   'I'll **think about** it.'

When you **think OF** something, the idea comes to your mind:
- ☐ He told me his name, but I can't **think of** it now. (*not* think about it)
- ☐ That's a good idea. Why didn't I **think of** that? (*not* think about that)

We also use **think of** when we ask or give an opinion:
- ☐ 'What did you **think of** the film?'   'I didn't **think** much **of** it.' (= I didn't like it much)

The difference is sometimes very small and you can use **of** or **about**:
- ☐ When I'm alone, I often **think of** (*or* **about**) you.

You can say **think of** *or* **think about** doing something (for possible future actions):
- ☐ My sister is **thinking of** (*or* **about**) going to Canada. (= she is considering it)

D

remind somebody **ABOUT** ... = *tell somebody not to forget*
- ☐ I'm glad you **reminded** me **about** the meeting. I'd completely forgotten about it.

remind somebody **OF** ... = *cause somebody to remember*
- ☐ This house **reminds** me **of** the one I lived in when I was a child.
- ☐ Look at this photograph of Richard. Who does he **remind** you **of**?

E

complain (**TO** somebody) **ABOUT** ... = *say that you are not satisfied*
- ☐ We **complained to** the manager of the restaurant **about** the food.

complain OF a pain, an illness etc. = *say that you have a pain etc.*
- ☐ We called the doctor because George was **complaining of** a pain in his stomach.

F

warn somebody **ABOUT** a person or thing which is bad, dangerous, unusual etc.
- ☐ I knew he was a strange person. I had been **warned about** him. (*not* warned of him)
- ☐ Vicky **warned me about** the traffic. She said it would be bad.

warn somebody **ABOUT/OF** a danger, something bad which might happen later
- ☐ Scientists have **warned** us **about/of** the effects of global warming.

Remind/warn somebody to ... → Unit 55B

134.1 Put in the correct preposition.

1 Did you hear __about__ what happened at the party on Saturday?
2 'I had a strange dream last night.' 'Did you? What did you dream .... ?'
3 Our neighbours complained .... us .... the noise we made last night.
4 Kevin was complaining .... pains in his chest, so he went to the doctor.
5 I love this music. It reminds me .... a warm day in spring.
6 He loves his job. He thinks .... his job all the time, he dreams .... it, he talks
   .... it and I'm fed up with hearing .... it.
7 I tried to remember the name of the book, but I couldn't think .... it.
8 Jackie warned me .... the water. She said it wasn't safe to drink.
9 We warned our children .... the dangers of playing in the street.

134.2 Complete the sentences using the following verbs (in the correct form) + the correct preposition:

complain   dream   hear   remind   remind   think   think   warn

1 That's a good idea. Why didn't I __think of__ that?
2 Bill is never satisfied. He is always .... something.
3 I can't make a decision yet. I need time to .... your proposal.
4 Before you go into the house, I must .... you .... the dog. He is very
   aggressive sometimes, so be careful.
5 She's not a well-known singer. Not many people have .... her.
6 A: You wouldn't go away without telling me, would you?
   B: Of course not. I wouldn't .... it.
7 I would have forgotten my appointment if Jane hadn't .... me .... it.
8 Do you see that man over there? Does he .... you .... anybody you know?

134.3 Complete the sentences using hear or heard + the correct preposition (about/of/from).

1 I've never __heard of__ Tom Hart. Who is he?
2 'Did you .... the accident last night?' 'Yes, Vicky told me.'
3 Jill used to phone quite often, but I haven't .... her for a long time now.
4 A: Have you .... a writer called William Hudson?
   B: No, I don't think so. What sort of writer is he?
5 Thank you for your letter. It was good to .... you again.
6 'Do you want to .... our holiday?' 'Not now. Tell me later.'
7 I live in a small town in the north of England. You've probably never .... it.

134.4 Complete the sentences using think about or think of. Sometimes both about and of are possible. Use the correct form of think (think/thinking/thought).

1 You look serious. What are you __thinking about__ ?
2 I like to have time to make decisions. I like to .... things carefully.
3 I don't know what to get Sarah for her birthday. Can you .... anything?
4 A: I've finished reading the book you lent me.
   B: Have you? What did you .... it? Did you like it?
5 We're .... going out for a meal this evening. Would you like to come?
6 I don't really want to go out with Tom tonight. I'll have to .... an
   excuse.
7 When I was offered the job, I didn't accept immediately. I went away and
   .... it for a while. In the end I decided to take the job.
8 I don't .... much .... this coffee. It's like water.
9 Carol is very homesick. She's always .... her family back home.

A Verb + **of**

accuse / suspect somebody **OF** …
- ☐ Sue **accused** me **of** being selfish.
- ☐ Some students were **suspected of** cheating in the exam.

approve / disapprove OF …
- ☐ His parents don't **approve of** what he does, but they can't stop him.

die OF (*or* **FROM**) an illness etc.
- ☐ 'What did he **die of**?' 'A heart attack.'

consist OF …
- ☐ We had an enormous meal. It **consisted of** seven courses.

B Verb + **for**

pay (somebody) **FOR** …
- ☐ I didn't have enough money to **pay for** the meal. (*not* pay the meal)
but **pay** a bill / a fine / tax / rent / a sum of money etc. (no preposition)
- ☐ I didn't have enough money to **pay the rent**.

thank / forgive somebody **FOR** …
- ☐ I'll never **forgive** them **for** what they did.

apologise (to somebody) **FOR** …
- ☐ When I realised I was wrong, I **apologised** (to them) **for** my mistake.

blame somebody/something **FOR** … , somebody is **to blame FOR** …
- ☐ Everybody **blamed** me **for** the accident.
- ☐ Everybody said that I was **to blame for** the accident.

blame (a problem etc.) **ON** …
- ☐ Everybody **blamed** the accident **on** me.

C Verb + **from**

suffer FROM an illness etc.
- ☐ The number of people **suffering from** heart disease has increased.

protect somebody/something **FROM** (*or* **AGAINST**) …
- ☐ Sun block **protects** the skin **from** the sun. (*or* … **against** the sun.)

D Verb + **on**

depend / rely ON …
- ☐ 'What time will you be home?' 'I don't know. It **depends on** the traffic.'
- ☐ You can **rely on** Jill. She always keeps her promises.

You can use **depend** + **when/where/how** etc. with or without **on**:
- ☐ 'Are you going to buy it?' 'It **depends how much** it is.' (*or* It **depends on** how much)

live ON money/food
- ☐ Michael's salary is very low. It isn't enough to **live on**.

congratulate / compliment somebody **ON** …
- ☐ I **congratulated** her **ON** her success in the exam.

Verb + preposition + -ing → Unit 62   Other verbs + for → Unit 133   Other verbs + on → Unit 136E

135.1 Complete the second sentence so that it means the same as the first.

1 Sue said I was selfish. Sue accused me __of being selfish__ .
2 The misunderstanding was my fault, so I apologised.
   I apologised ....
3 Jane won the tournament, so I congratulated her.
   I congratulated Jane ....
4 He has enemies, but he has a bodyguard to protect him.
   He has a bodyguard to protect him ....
5 There are eleven players in a football team.
   A football team consists ....
6 Sandra eats only bread and eggs. She lives ....

135.2 Complete the second sentence using **for** or **on**. These sentences all have **blame**.

1 Liz said that what happened was Joe's fault. Liz blamed Joe __for what happened__ .
2 You always say everything is my fault.
   You always blame me ....
3 Do you think the economic crisis is the fault of the government?
   Do you blame the government .... ?
4 I think the increase in violent crime is the fault of television.
   I blame the increase in violent crime ....

Now rewrite sentences 3 and 4 using **to blame for**.
5 (3) Do you think the government .... ?
6 (4) I think that ....

135.3 Complete the sentences using the following verbs (in the correct form) + the correct
preposition:

   accuse   apologise   ~~approve~~   congratulate   depend   live   pay

1 His parents don't ....__approve of__.... what he does, but they can't stop him.
2 When you went to the theatre with Paul, who .... the tickets?
3 It's not very pleasant when you are .... something you didn't do.
4 A: Are you going to the beach tomorrow?
   B: I hope so. It .... the weather.
5 Things are very cheap there. You can .... very little money.
6 When I saw David, I .... him .... passing his driving test.
7 You were very rude to Liz. Don't you think you should .... her?

135.4 Put in the correct preposition. If no preposition is necessary, leave the space empty.

1 Some students were suspected ....__of__.... cheating in the exam.
2 Sally is often not well. She suffers .... very bad headaches.
3 You know that you can rely .... me if you ever need any help.
4 It is terrible that some people are dying .... hunger while others eat too much.
5 Are you going to apologise .... what you did?
6 The accident was my fault, so I had to pay .... the repairs.
7 I didn't have enough money to pay .... the bill.
8 I complimented her .... her English. She spoke very fluently and her pronunciation was
   excellent.
9 She hasn't got a job. She depends .... her parents for money.
10 I don't know whether I'll go out tonight. It depends .... how I feel.
11 They wore warm clothes to protect themselves .... the cold.
12 The apartment consists .... three rooms, a kitchen and bathroom.

→ Additional exercise 36 **(page 323)**

A   Verb + in

believe IN ...
- ☐ Do you **believe in** God? (= Do you believe that God exists?)
- ☐ I **believe in** saying what I think. (= I believe it is right to say what I think)

but   'believe something' (= believe it is true), 'believe somebody' (= believe they are telling the truth)
- ☐ The story can't be true. I don't **believe it.** (*not* believe in it)

specialise IN ...
- ☐ Helen is a lawyer. She **specialises in** company law.

succeed IN ...
- ☐ I hope you **succeed in** finding the job you want.

B   Verb + into

break INTO ...
- ☐ Our house was **broken into** a few days ago, but nothing was stolen.

crash / drive / bump / run INTO ...
- ☐ He lost control of the car and **crashed into** a wall.

divide / cut / split something INTO two or more parts
- ☐ The book is **divided into** three parts.

translate a book etc. FROM one language INTO another
- ☐ Ernest Hemingway's books have been **translated into** many languages.

C   Verb + with

collide WITH ...
- ☐ There was an accident this morning. A bus **collided with** a car.

fill something WITH ... (*but* **full of ...** – see Unit 131B)
- ☐ Take this saucepan and **fill** it **with** water.

provide / supply somebody WITH ...
- ☐ The school **provides** all its students **with** books.

D   Verb + to

happen TO ...
- ☐ What **happened to** that gold watch you used to have? (= where is it now?)

invite somebody TO a party / a wedding etc.
- ☐ They only **invited** a few people **to** their wedding.

prefer one thing/person TO another
- ☐ I **prefer** tea **to** coffee

E   Verb + on

concentrate ON ...
- ☐ Don't look out of the window. **Concentrate on** your work.

insist ON ...
- ☐ I wanted to go alone, but some friends of mine **insisted on** coming with me.

spend (money) ON ...
- ☐ How much do you **spend on** food each week?

136.1 Complete the second sentence so that it means the same as the first.

1 There was a collision between a bus and a car.
A bus collided __with a car__ .

2 I don't mind big cities, but I prefer small towns.
I prefer _____ .

3 I got all the information I needed from Jane.
Jane provided me _____ .

4 This morning I bought a pair of shoes, which cost £70.
This morning I spent _____ .

136.2 Complete the sentences using the following verbs (in the correct form) + the correct preposition:

believe   concentrate   divide   drive   fill   happen   ~~insist~~   invite   succeed

1 I wanted to go alone, but Sue __insisted on__ coming with me.

2 I haven't seen Mike for ages. I wonder what has _____ him.

3 We've been _____ the party, but unfortunately we can't go.

4 It's a very large house. It's _____ four flats.

5 I don't _____ ghosts. I think people only imagine that they see them.

6 Steve gave me an empty bucket and told me to _____ it _____ water.

7 I was driving along when the car in front of me stopped suddenly. Unfortunately I couldn't stop in time and _____ the back of it.

8 Don't try and do two things together. _____ one thing at a time.

9 It wasn't easy, but in the end we _____ finding a solution to the problem.

136.3 Put in the correct preposition. If the sentence is already complete, leave the space empty.

1 The school provides all its students __with__ books.

2 A strange thing happened _____ me a few days ago.

3 Mark decided to give up sport so that he could concentrate _____ his studies.

4 I don't believe _____ working very hard. It's not worth it.

5 My present job isn't wonderful, but I prefer it _____ what I did before.

6 I hope you succeed _____ getting what you want.

7 As I was coming out of the room, I collided _____ somebody who was coming in.

8 There was an awful noise as the car crashed _____ a tree.

9 Patrick is a photographer. He specialises _____ sports photography.

10 Do you spend much money _____ clothes?

11 The country is divided _____ six regions.

12 I prefer travelling by train _____ driving. It's much more pleasant.

13 I was amazed when Joe walked into the room. I couldn't believe _____ it.

14 Somebody broke _____ my car and stole the radio.

15 I was quite cold, but Tom insisted _____ having the window open.

16 Some words are difficult to translate _____ one language _____ another.

17 What happened _____ the money I lent you? What did you spend it _____ ?

18 The teacher decided to split the class _____ four groups.

19 I filled the tank, but unfortunately I filled it _____ the wrong kind of petrol.

136.4 Use your own ideas to complete these sentences. Use a preposition.

1 I wanted to go out alone, but my friend insisted __on coming with me__ .

2 I spend a lot of money _____ .

3 I saw the accident. The car crashed _____ .

4 Chris prefers basketball _____ .

5 Shakespeare's plays have been translated _____ .

→ Additional exercise 36 (page 323)

A We often use verbs with the following words:

in	on	up	away	round	about	over	by
out	off	down	back	through	along	forward	

So you can say **look out / get on / take off / run away** etc. These are *phrasal verbs*.

We often use **on/off/out** etc. with verbs of movement. For example:

get on	□	The bus was full. We couldn't **get on**.
drive off	□	A woman got into the car and **drove off**.
come back	□	Sally is leaving tomorrow and **coming back** on Saturday.
turn round	□	When I touched him on the shoulder, he **turned round**.

But often the second word (**on/off/out** etc.) gives a special meaning to the verb. For example:

break down	□	Sorry I'm late. The car **broke down**. (= the engine stopped working)
look out	□	**Look out!** There's a car coming. (= be careful)
take off	□	It was my first flight. I was nervous as the plane **took off**. (= went into the air)
get on	□	How was the exam? How did you **get on**? (= How did you do?)
get by	□	My French isn't very good, but it's enough to **get by**. (= manage)

For more phrasal verbs, see Units 138–145.

B Sometimes a phrasal verb is followed by a *preposition*. For example:

phrasal verb	*preposition*	
run away	**from**	□ Why did you **run away from** me?
keep up	**with**	□ You're walking too fast. I can't **keep up with** you.
look up	**at**	□ We **looked up at** the plane as it flew above us.
look forward	**to**	□ Are you **looking forward to** your holiday?

C Sometimes a phrasal verb has an *object*. Usually there are two possible positions for the object.
So you can say:

> I **turned on** the light.   *or*   I **turned** the light **on**.
> object   object

If the object is a *pronoun* (**it/them/me/him** etc.), only one position is possible:

> I **turned** it **on**. (*not* I turned on it)

Some more examples:

□ Could you { **fill in** this form? / **fill** this form **in**? }

but They gave me a form and told me to **fill it in**. (*not* fill in it)

□ Don't { **throw away** this postcard. / **throw** this postcard **away**. }

but I want to keep this postcard, so don't **throw it away**. (*not* throw away it)

□ I'm going to { **take off** my shoes. / **take** my shoes **off**. }

but These shoes are uncomfortable. I'm going to **take them off**. (*not* take off them)

□ Don't { **wake up** the baby. / **wake** the baby **up**. }

but The baby is asleep. Don't **wake her up**. (*not* wake up her)

Exercises

137.1 Complete each sentence using a verb from A (in the correct form) + a word from B. You can use a word more than once.

A | fly   get   go   look   sit   speak |

B | away   by   down   on   out   round   up |

1 The bus was full. We couldn't _____get on_____ .
2 I've been standing for the last two hours. I'm going to _____ for a bit.
3 A cat tried to catch the bird, but it _____ just in time.
4 We were trapped in the building. We couldn't _____ .
5 I can't hear you very well. Can you _____ a little?
6 'Do you speak German?'   'Not very well, but I can _____ .'
7 House prices are very high. They've _____ a lot in the last few years.
8 I thought there was somebody behind me, but when I _____ , there was nobody there.

137.2 Complete the sentences using a word from A and a word from B. You can use a word more than once.

A | away   back   forward   in   up |

B | at   through   to   with |

1 You're walking too fast. I can't keep _____up with_____ you.
2 My holidays are nearly over. Next week I'll be _____ work.
3 We went _____ the top floor of the building to admire the view.
4 Are you looking _____ the party next week?
5 There was a bank robbery last week. The robbers got _____ £50,000.
6 I love to look _____ the stars in the sky at night.
7 I was sitting in the kitchen when suddenly a bird flew _____ the open window.

137.3 Complete the sentences using the following verbs + it/them/me:

~~fill in~~   get out   give back   switch on   take off   wake up

1 They gave me a form and told me to _____fill it in_____ .
2 I'm going to bed now. Can you _____ at 6.30?
3 I've got something in my eye and I can't _____ .
4 I don't like it when people borrow things and don't _____ .
5 I want to use the kettle. How do I _____ ?
6 My shoes are dirty. I'd better _____ before going into the house.

137.4 Use your own ideas to complete the sentences. Use a noun (**this newspaper** etc.) or a pronoun (**it/them** etc.) + the word in brackets (**away/up** etc.).

1 Don't throw _____away this newspaper_____ . I want to keep it. (away)
2 'Do you want this postcard?'   'No, you can throw _____it away_____ .' (away)
3 I borrowed these books from the library. I have to take _____ tomorrow. (back)
4 We can turn _____ . Nobody is watching it. (off)
5 A: How did the vase get broken?
  B: I'm afraid I knocked _____ while I was cleaning. (over)
6 Shh! My mother is asleep. I don't want to wake _____ . (up)
7 It's quite cold. You should put _____ if you're going out. (on)
8 It was only a small fire. I was able to put _____ quite easily. (out)
9 A: Is this hotel more expensive than when we stayed here last year?
  B: Yes, they've put _____ . (up)
10 It's a bit dark in this room. Shall I turn _____ ? (on)

→ Additional exercises 37–41 (pages 323–25)

A Compare **in** and **out**:

in = into a room, a building, a car etc.	**out** = out of a room, building, a car etc.
☐ How did the thieves **get in**?	☐ He just stood up and **walked out**.
☐ Here's a key, so you can **let yourself in**.	☐ I had no key, so I was **locked out**.
☐ Sally walked up to the edge of the pool and **dived in**. (= into the water)	☐ She swam up and down the pool, and then **climbed out**.
☐ I've got a new flat. I'm **moving in** on Friday.	☐ Tim opened the window and **looked out**.
☐ As soon as I got to the airport, I **checked in**.	☐ *(at a hotel)* What time do we have to **check out**?
In the same way you can say **go in**, **come in**, **walk in**, **break in** etc.	In the same way you can say **go out**, **get out**, **move out**, **let** somebody **out** etc.
Compare **in** and **into**:	Compare **out** and **out of**:
☐ I'm moving **in** next week.	☐ He walked **out**.
☐ I'm moving **into my new flat** on Friday.	☐ He walked **out of the room**.

B Other verbs + **in**

drop in / **call in** = *visit somebody for a short time without arranging to do this*
 ☐ I **dropped in** to see Chris on my way home.

join in = *take part in an activity that is already going on*
 ☐ We're playing a game. Why don't you **join in**?

plug in an electrical machine = *connect it to the electricity supply*
 ☐ The fridge isn't working because you haven't **plugged** it **in**.

plug in

fill in a form, a questionnaire etc. = *write the necessary information on a form*
 ☐ Please **fill in** the application form and send it to us by 28 February.
You can also say **fill out** a form.

take somebody **in** = *deceive somebody*
 ☐ The man said he was a policeman and I believed him. I was completely **taken in**.

C Other verbs + **out**

eat out = *eat at a restaurant, not at home*
 ☐ There wasn't anything to eat at home, so we decided to **eat out**.

drop out of college / university / a course / a race = *stop before you have completely finished a course/race etc.*
 ☐ Gary went to university but **dropped out** after a year.

get out of something that you arranged to do = *avoid doing it*
 ☐ I promised I'd go to the wedding. I don't want to go, but I can't **get out** of it now.

cut something **out** (of a newspaper etc.)
 ☐ There was a beautiful picture in the magazine, so I **cut** it **out** and kept it.

leave something **out** = *omit it, not include it*
 ☐ In the sentence 'She said that she was ill', you can **leave out** the word 'that'.

cross something **out** / **rub** something **out**
 ☐ Some of the names on the list had been **crossed out**.   ~~Sarah~~   *cross out*

138.1 Complete each sentence using a verb in the correct form.

1 Here's a key so that you can ....*let*.... yourself in.
2 Liz doesn't like cooking, so she .... out a lot.
3 Eve isn't living in this flat any more. She .... out a few weeks ago.
4 If you're in our part of town, you must .... in and see us.
5 When I .... in at the airport, I was told my flight would be delayed.
6 There were some advertisements in the paper that I wanted to keep, so I ....
them out.
7 I wanted to iron some clothes, but there was nowhere to .... the iron in.
8 I hate .... in questionnaires.
9 Steve was upset because he'd been .... out of the team.
10 Be careful! The water's not very deep here, so don't .... in.
11 If you write in pencil and you make a mistake, you can .... it out.
12 Paul started doing a Spanish course, but he .... out after a few weeks.

138.2 Complete the sentences with in, into, out or out of.

1 I've got a new flat. I'm moving ....*in*.... on Friday.
2 We checked .... the hotel as soon as we arrived.
3 As soon as we arrived at the hotel, we checked ....
4 The car stopped and the driver got ....
5 Thieves broke .... the house while we were away.
6 Why did Sarah drop .... college? Did she fail her exams?

138.3 Complete each sentence using a verb + in or out (of).

1 Sally walked to the edge of the pool, ...*dived in*.... and swam to the other end.
2 Not all the runners finished the race. Three of them ....
3 I went to see Joe and Sue in their new house. They .... last week.
4 I've told you everything you need to know. I don't think I've ....
anything.
5 Some people in the crowd started singing. Then a few more people ....
and soon everybody was singing.
6 We go to restaurants a lot. We like ....
7 Don't be .... by him. If I were you, I wouldn't believe anything he says.
8 I .... to see Laura a few days ago. She was fine.
9 A: Can we meet tomorrow morning at ten?
    B: Probably. I'm supposed to go to another meeting, but I think I can
    .... it.

138.4 Complete the sentences. Use the word in brackets in the correct form.

1 A: The fridge isn't working.
    B: That's because you haven't ....*plugged it in*.... . (plug)
2 A: What do I have to do with these forms?
    B: .... and send them to this address. (fill)
3 A: I've made a mistake on this form.
    B: That's all right. Just .... and correct it. (cross)
4 A: Did you believe the story they told you?
    B: Yes, I'm afraid they completely .... (take)
5 A: Have you been to that new club in Bridge Street?
    B: We wanted to go there a few nights ago, but the doorman wouldn't ....
    because we weren't members. (let)

→ Additional exercises 37–41 (pages 323–25)

A

out = not burning, not shining

go out	□ Suddenly all the lights in the building **went out**.
put out a fire / a cigarette / a light	□ We managed to **put** the fire **out**.
turn out a light	□ I **turned** the lights **out** before leaving.
blow out a candle	□ We don't need the candle. You can **blow** it **out**.

B

work out

work out = *do physical exercises*
  □ Rachel **works out** at the gym three times a week.

work out = *develop, progress*
  □ Good luck for the future. I hope everything **works out** well for you.
  □ A: Why did James leave the company?
    B: Things didn't **work out**. (= things didn't work out well)

work out (for mathematical calculations)
  □ The total bill for three people is £84.60. That **works out** at £28.20 each.

work something **out** = *calculate, think about a problem and find the answer*
  □ 345 × 76? I need to do this on paper. I can't **work** it **out** in my head.

C

Other verbs + **out**

carry out an order / an experiment / a survey / an investigation / a plan etc.
  □ Soldiers are expected to **carry out** orders.
  □ An investigation into the accident will be **carried out** as soon as possible.

fall out (**with** somebody) = *stop being friends*
  □ They used to be very good friends. I'm surprised to hear that they have **fallen out**.
  □ David **fell out with** his father and left home.

find out that/what/when … etc., **find out about** something = *get information*
  □ The police never **found out** who committed the murder.
  □ I've just **found out** that it's Helen's birthday today.
  □ I called the tourist office to **find out** about hotels in the town.

give/hand things **out** = *give to each person*
  □ At the end of the lecture, the speaker **gave out** information sheets to the audience.

point something **out** (**to** somebody) = *draw attention to something*
  □ As we drove through the city, our guide **pointed out** all the sights.
  □ I didn't realise I'd made a mistake until somebody **pointed** it **out to** me.

run out (**of** something)
  □ We **ran out of** petrol on the motorway. (= we used all our petrol)

sort something **out** = *find a solution to, put in order*
  □ There are a few problems we need to **sort out**.
  □ All these papers are mixed up. I'll have to **sort** them **out**.

turn out to be … / **turn out** good/nice etc. / **turn out** that …
  □ Nobody believed Paul at first, but he **turned out** to be right. (= it became clear in the end that he was right)
  □ The weather wasn't so good in the morning, but it **turned out** nice later.
  □ I thought they knew each other, but it **turned out** that they'd never met.

try out a machine, a system, a new idea etc. = *test it to see if it is OK*
  □ The company is **trying out** a new computer system at the moment.

Phrasal verbs 1 (Introduction) → Unit 137   More verbs + **out** → Unit 138

Exercises

139.1 Which words can go together? Choose from the box.

a candle	a cigarette	~~a light~~	a mess	a mistake	a new product	an order

1 turn out ..... *a light* .....
2 point out .....
3 blow out .....
4 carry out .....
5 put out .....
6 try out .....
7 sort out .....

139.2 Complete each sentence using a verb + **out**.

1 The company is ..... *trying out* ..... a new computer system at the moment.
2 Steve is very fit. He does a lot of sport and ..... regularly.
3 The road will be closed for two days next week while building work is ..... .
4 We didn't manage to discuss everything at the meeting. We ..... of time.
5 You have to ..... the problem yourself. I can't do it for you.
6 I phoned the station to ..... what time the train arrived.
7 The new drug will be ..... on a small group of patients.
8 I thought the two books were the same until a friend of mine ..... the difference.
9 They got married a few years ago but it didn't ..... , and they separated.
10 There was a power cut and all the lights ..... .
11 We thought she was American at first, but she ..... to be Swedish.
12 Sometimes it ..... cheaper to eat in a restaurant than to cook at home.
13 I haven't applied for the job yet. I want to ..... more about the company first.
14 It took the fire brigade two hours to ..... the fire.

139.3 For each picture, complete the sentence using a verb + **out**.

1	2	3 *earlier* *now*
They've *run out of petrol* .	The man with the beard is ..... leaflets.	The weather has ....
4 *I don't like her any more* *I don't like him any more*	5 POST *JOE*	6 *LISA* CAMERA INSTRUCTIONS
They've	One of Joe's jobs in the office is	Lisa is trying to ..... how ..... .

139.4 Complete the sentences. Each time use a verb + **out**.

1 A: Shall I leave the light on?
  B: No, you can ..... *turn it out* ..... .
2 A: This recipe looks interesting.
  B: Yes, let's ..... .
3 A: How much money do I owe you exactly?
  B: Just a moment. I'll have to ..... .
4 A: What happened about your problem with your bank?
  B: It's OK now. I went to see them and we ..... .

→ Additional exercises 37–41 (pages 323–25)

A   On and off for lights, machines etc.

We say: the light **is on** / **put** the light **on** / **leave** the light **on** etc.
         turn the light **on/off**   or   **switch** the light **on/off**

- ☐ Shall **I leave** the lights **on** or **turn** them **off**?
- ☐ '**Is** the heating **on**?'   'No, I **switched** it **off**.'
- ☐ We need some boiling water, so I'll **put** the kettle **on**.

Also **put on** some music / a CD / a video etc.

- ☐ I haven't listened to this CD yet. Shall I **put** it **on**?

B   On and off for events etc.

go on = *happen*
- ☐ What's all that noise? What's **going on**? (= what's happening)

call something **off** = *cancel it*
- ☐ The open air concert had to be **called off** because of the weather.

put something **off**, **put off** doing something = *delay it*
- ☐ The wedding has been **put off** until January.
- ☐ We can't **put off** making a decision. We have to decide now.

C   On and off for clothes etc.

put on clothes, glasses, make-up, a seat belt etc.
- ☐ My hands were cold, so I **put** my gloves **on**.
Also **put on** weight = *get heavier*
- ☐ I've **put on** two kilograms in the last month.

try on clothes (to see if they fit)
- ☐ I **tried on** a jacket in the shop, but it didn't fit me very well.

take off clothes, glasses etc.
- ☐ It was warm, so I **took off** my jacket.

D   Off = away from a person or place

be off (to a place)
- ☐ Tomorrow **I'm off** to Paris / **I'm off** on holiday.
   (= I'm going to Paris / I'm going on holiday)

walk off / **run off** / **drive off** / **ride off** / **go off** (similar to **walk away** / **run away** etc.)
- ☐ Diane got on her bike and **rode off**.
- ☐ Mark left home at the age of eighteen and **went off** to Canada.

set off = *start a journey*
- ☐ We **set off** very early to avoid the traffic. (= We left early)

take off = *leave the ground (for planes)*
- ☐ After a long delay the plane finally **took off**.

see somebody **off** = *go with them to the airport/station to say goodbye*
- ☐ Helen was going away. We went to the station with her to **see her off**.

Phrasal verbs 1 (Introduction) → Unit 137   More verbs + on/off → Unit 141

Exercises

Unit **140**

140.1 Complete the sentences using **put on** + the following:

a CD   **the heating**   **the kettle**   ~~the light~~   **the oven**

1 It was getting dark, so I ....._put the light on_..... .
2 It was getting cold, so I ....
3 I wanted to bake a cake, so I ....
4 I wanted to make some tea, so I ....
5 I wanted to listen to some music, so I ....

140.2 Complete the sentences. Each time use a verb + **on** or **off**.

1 It was warm, so I ....._took off_..... my jacket.
2 What are all these people doing? What's .... ?
3 The weather was too bad for the plane to .... , so the flight was delayed.
4 I didn't want to be disturbed, so I .... my mobile phone.
5 Rachel got into her car and .... at high speed.
6 Tim has .... weight since I last saw him. He used to be quite thin.
7 A: What time are you leaving tomorrow?
   B: I'm not sure yet, but I'd like to .... as early as possible.
8 Don't .... until tomorrow what you can do today.
9 There was going to be a strike by bus drivers, but now they have been offered more money and the strike has been ....
10 Are you cold? Shall I get you a sweater to .... ?
11 When I go away, I prefer to be alone at the station or airport. I don't like it when people come to .... me ....

140.3 Look at the pictures and complete the sentences.

1	2
Her hands were cold, so she ....._put her gloves on_..... .	The plane .... at 10.55.
3	**4**
Maria .... , but it was too big for her.	The match .... because of the weather.
5	**6**
Mark's parents went to the airport to	He took his sunglasses out of his pocket and ....

→ Additional exercises 37–41 (pages 323–25)

281

A

Verb + **on** = continue doing something

drive on / walk on / play on = *continue walking/driving/playing etc.*
- ☐ Shall we stop at this petrol station or shall we **drive on** to the next one?

go on = *continue*
- ☐ The party **went on** until 4 o'clock in the morning.

go on / carry on (doing something) = *continue (doing something)*
- ☐ We can't **go on** spending money like this. We'll have nothing left soon.
- ☐ I don't want to **carry on** working here. I'm going to look for another job.

Also **go on with / carry on with** something
- ☐ Don't let me disturb you. Please **carry on with** what you're doing.

keep on doing something = *do it continuously or repeatedly*
- ☐ He **keeps on** criticising me. I'm fed up with it!

B

Get on

get on = *progress*
- ☐ How are you **getting on** in your new job? (= How is it going?)

get on (**with** somebody) = *have a good relationship*
- ☐ Joanne and Karen don't **get on**. They're always arguing.
- ☐ Richard **gets on** well **with** his neighbours. They're all very friendly.

get on with something = *continue doing something you have to do, usually after an interruption*
- ☐ I must **get on with** my work. I have a lot to do.

C

Verb + **off**

doze off / drop off / nod off = *fall asleep*
- ☐ The lecture wasn't very interesting. In fact I **dropped off** in the middle of it.

finish something **off** = *do the last part of something*
- ☐ A: Have you finished painting the kitchen?
   B: Nearly. I'll **finish** it **off** tomorrow.

go off = *explode*
- ☐ A bomb **went off** in the city centre, but fortunately nobody was hurt.

Also an alarm can **go off** = *ring*
- ☐ Did you hear the alarm **go off**?

put somebody **off** (doing something) = *cause somebody not to want something or to do something*
- ☐ We wanted to go to the exhibition, but we were **put off** by the long queue.
- ☐ What **put** you **off** applying for the job? Was the salary too low?

rip somebody **off** = *cheat somebody (informal)*
- ☐ Did you really pay £1,000 for that painting? I think you were **ripped off**.
   (= you paid too much)

show off = *try to impress people with your ability, your knowledge etc.*
- ☐ Look at that boy on the bike riding with no hands. He's just **showing off**.

tell somebody **off** = *speak angrily to somebody because they did something wrong*
- ☐ Clare's mother **told** her **off** for wearing dirty shoes in the house.

Exercises

141.1 Change the underlined words. Keep the same meaning, but use a verb + **on** or **off**.

1 Did you hear the bomb <u>explode</u>?
Did you hear the bomb ....*go off*.... ?

2 The meeting <u>continued</u> longer than I expected.
The meeting .... longer than I expected.

3 We didn't stop to rest. We <u>continued walking</u>.
We didn't stop to rest. We ....

4 I <u>fell asleep</u> while I was watching TV.
I .... while I was watching TV.

5 Gary doesn't want to retire. He wants to <u>continue</u> working.
Gary doesn't want to retire. He wants to .... working.

6 The fire alarm <u>rang</u> in the middle of the night.
The fire alarm .... in the middle of the night.

7 Martin <u>phones me continuously</u>. It's very annoying.
Martin .... It's very annoying.

141.2 Complete each sentence using a verb + **on** or **off**.

1 We can't ....*go on*.... spending money like this. We'll have nothing left soon.
2 I was standing by the car when suddenly the alarm ....
3 I'm not ready to go home yet. I have a few things to ....
4 'Shall I stop the car here?' 'No, ...'
5 Bill paid too much for the car he bought. I think he was ....
6 'Is Emma enjoying her course at university?' 'Yes, she's .... very well.'
7 I was very tired at work today. I nearly .... at my desk a couple of times.
8 Ben was .... by his boss for being late for work repeatedly.
9 I really like working with my colleagues. We all .... really well together.
10 There was a very loud noise. It sounded like a bomb ....
11 I .... making the same mistake. It's very frustrating.
12 I've just had a coffee break, and now I must .... with my work.
13 Peter is always trying to impress people. He's always ....
14 We decided not to go into the museum. We were .... by the cost of tickets.

141.3 Complete the sentences. Use the following verbs (in the correct form) + **on** or **off**. Sometimes you will need other words as well:

> carry   finish   ~~get~~   get   get   go   rip   tell

1 A: How ....*are you getting on*.... in your new job?
B: Fine, thanks. It's going very well.

2 A: Have you written the letter you had to write?
B: I've started it. I'll .... in the morning.

3 A: We took a taxi to the airport. It cost £40.
B: £40! Normally it costs about £20. You ....

4 A: Why were you late for work this morning?
B: I overslept. My alarm clock didn't ....

5 A: How .... in your interview? Do you think you'll get the job?
B: I hope so. The interview was OK.

6 A: Did you stop playing tennis when it started to rain?
B: No, we .... The rain wasn't very heavy.

7 A: Some children at the next table in the restaurant were behaving very badly.
B: Why didn't their parents .... ?

8 A: Why does Paul want to leave his job?
B: He .... his boss.

→ Additional exercises 37–41 (pages 323–25)

Phrasal verbs 6   up/down

A   Compare **up** and **down**:

put something **up** (on a wall etc.)
- □ I **put** some pictures **up** on the wall.

pick something **up**
- □ There was a letter on the floor. I **picked** it **up** and looked at it.

stand up
- □ Alan **stood up** and walked out.

turn something **up**
- □ I can't hear the TV. Can you **turn** it **up** a bit?

take something **down** (from a wall etc.)
- □ I didn't like the picture, so I **took** it **down**.

put something **down**
- □ I stopped writing and **put down** my pen.

sit down / **bend down** / **lie down**
- □ I **bent down** to tie my shoelace.

turn something **down**
- □ The oven is too hot. **Turn** it **down** to 150 degrees.

B   **Knock down** etc.

knock down a building / **blow** something **down** / **cut** something **down** etc.
- □ Some old houses were **knocked down** to make way for the new shopping centre.
- □ Why did you **cut down** the tree in your garden?

Also be **knocked down** (by a car etc.)
- □ A man was **knocked down** by a car and taken to hospital.

C   **Down** = getting less

slow down = *go more slowly*
- □ You're driving too fast. **Slow down.**

calm (somebody) **down** = *become calmer, make somebody calmer*
- □ **Calm down.** There's no point in getting angry.

cut down (on something) = *eat, drink or do something less often*
- □ I'm trying to **cut down** on coffee. I drink far too much of it.

D   Other verbs + **down**

break down = *stop working (for machines, cars, relationships etc.)*
- □ The car **broke down** and I had to phone for help.
- □ Their marriage **broke down** after only a few months.

close down / **shut down** = *stop doing business*
- □ There used to be a shop at the end of the street; it **closed down** a few years ago.

let somebody **down** = *disappoint somebody because you didn't do what they hoped*
- □ You can always rely on Pete. He'll never **let** you **down**.

turn somebody/something **down** = *refuse an application, an offer etc.*
- □ I applied for several jobs, but I was **turned down** for each one.
- □ Rachel was offered the job, but she decided to **turn** it **down**.

write something **down** = *write something on paper because you may need the information later*
- □ I can't remember Tim's address. I **wrote** it **down**, but I can't find it.

142.1 Complete the sentences. Use the following verbs (in the correct form) + **up** or **down**:

calm   let   put   ~~take~~   turn   turn

1 I don't like this picture on the wall. I'm going to __take it down__ .
2 The music is too loud. Can you _____ ?
3 David was very angry. I tried to _____ .
4 I've bought some new curtains. Can you help me _____ ?
5 I promised I would help Anna. I don't want to _____ .
6 I was offered the job, but I decided I didn't want it. So I _____ .

142.2 For each picture, complete the sentences using a verb + **up** or **down**. In most sentences you will need other words as well.

1 There used to be a tree next to the house, but we __cut it down__ .
2 There used to be some shelves on the wall, but I _____ .
3 The ceiling was so low, he couldn't _____ straight.
4 She couldn't hear the radio very well, so she _____ .
5 While they were waiting for the bus, they _____ on the ground.
6 A few trees _____ in the storm last week.
7 Sarah gave me her phone number. I _____ on a piece of paper.
8 Liz dropped her keys, so she _____ and _____ .

142.3 Complete each sentence using a verb (in the correct form) + **down**.

1 I stopped writing and __put down__ my pen.
2 I was really angry. It took me a long time to _____ .
3 The train _____ as it approached the station.
4 Sarah applied to study medicine at university, but she _____ .
5 Our car is very reliable. It has never _____ .
6 I need to spend less money. I'm going to _____ on things I don't really need.
7 I didn't play very well. I felt that I had _____ the other players in the team.
8 The shop _____ because it was losing money.
9 This is a very ugly building. Many people would like it to _____ .
10 I can't understand why you _____ the chance of working abroad for a year. It would have been a great experience for you.
11 A: Did you see the accident? What happened exactly?
   B: A man _____ by a car as he was crossing the road.
12 Peter got married when he was 20, but unfortunately the marriage _____ a few years later.

→ Additional exercises 37–41 (pages 323–25)

A

go up / come up / walk up (to …) = *approach*
  □ A man **came up to** me in the street and asked me for money.

catch up (with somebody), **catch** somebody **up** = *move faster than somebody in front of you so that you reach them*
  □ I'm not ready to go yet. You go on and I'll **catch up with** you / I'll **catch** you **up**.

keep up (with somebody) = *continue at the same speed or level*
  □ You're walking too fast. I can't **keep up** (**with** you).
  □ You're doing well. **Keep** it **up!**

B

set up an organisation, a company, a business, a system, a website etc. = *start it*
  □ The government has **set up** a committee to investigate the problem.

take up a hobby, a sport, an activity etc. = *start doing it*
  □ Laura **took up** photography a few years ago. She takes really good pictures.

fix up a meeting etc. = *arrange it*
  □ We've **fixed up** a meeting for next Monday.

C

grow up = *become an adult*
  □ Sarah was born in Ireland but **grew up** in England.

bring up a child = *raise, look after a child*
  □ Her parents died when she was a child and she was **brought up** by her grandparents.

D

clean up / clear up / tidy up something = *make it clean, tidy etc.*
  □ Look at this mess! Who's going to **tidy up**? (*or* **tidy** it **up**)

wash up = *wash the plates, dishes etc. after a meal*
  □ I hate **washing up**. (*or* I hate **doing the washing-up**.)

E

end up somewhere, **end up** doing something etc.
  □ There was a fight in the street and three men **ended up** in hospital. (= that's what happened to these men in the end)
  □ I couldn't find a hotel and **ended up** sleeping on a bench at the station. (= that's what happened to me in the end)

give up = *stop trying*, **give** something **up** = *stop doing it*
  □ Don't **give up**. Keep trying!
  □ Sue got bored with her job and decided to **give** it **up**. (= stop doing it)

make up something / be **made up of** something
  □ Children under 16 **make up** half the population of the city. (= half the population are children under 16)
  □ Air is **made up** mainly **of** nitrogen and oxygen. (= Air consists of …)

take up space or time = *use space or time*
  □ Most of the space in the room was **taken up** by a large table.

turn up / show up = *arrive, appear*
  □ We arranged to meet Dave last night, but he didn't **turn up**.

use something **up** = *use all of it so that nothing is left*
  □ I'm going to take a few more photographs. I want to **use up** the rest of the film.

143.1 Look at the pictures and complete the sentences. Use <u>three</u> words each time, including a verb from Section A.

1 A man ....*came up to*.... me in the street and asked me the way to the station.

2 Sue .... the front door of the house and rang the doorbell.

3 Tom was a long way behind the other runners, but he managed to .... them.

4 Tanya was running too fast for Paul. He couldn't .... her.

143.2 Complete the sentences. Use the following verbs (in the correct form) + **up**:

~~end~~   end   give   give   grow   make   take   take   turn   use   wash

1 I couldn't find a hotel and ....*ended up*.... sleeping on a bench at the station.
2 I'm feeling very tired now. I've .... all my energy.
3 After dinner I .... and put the dishes away.
4 People often ask children what they want to be when they ....
5 We invited Tim to the party, but he didn't ....
6 Two years ago Mark .... his studies to be a professional footballer.
7 A: Do you do any sports?
   B: Not at the moment, but I'm thinking of .... tennis.
8 You don't have enough determination. You .... too easily.
9 Karen travelled a lot for a few years and .... in Canada, where she still lives.
10 I do a lot of gardening. It .... most of my free time.
11 There are two universities in the city, and students .... 20 per cent of the population.

143.3 Complete the sentences. Use the following verbs + **up** (with any other necessary words):

bring   ~~catch~~   fix   ~~give~~   go   keep   keep   make   set   tidy

1 Sue got bored with her job and decided to ....*give it up*.... .
2 I'm not ready yet. You go on and I'll ....*catch up with*.... you.
3 The room is in a mess. I'd better ....
4 We expect to go away on holiday sometime in July, but we haven't .... yet.
5 Stephen is having problems at school. He can't .... the rest of the class.
6 Although I .... in the country, I have always preferred cities.
7 Our team started the game well, but we couldn't .... , and in the end we lost.
8 I saw Mike at the party, so I .... him and said hello.
9 When I was on holiday, I joined a tour group. The group .... two Americans, three Germans, five Italians and myself.
10 Helen has her own internet website. A friend of hers helped her to ....

→ Additional exercises 37–41 (pages 323–25)

Phrasal verbs 8 up (2)

A

bring up a topic etc. = *introduce it in a conversation*
- ☐ I don't want to hear any more about this matter. Please don't **bring** it **up** again.

come up = *be introduced in a conversation*
- ☐ Some interesting matters **came up** in our discussion yesterday.

come up with an idea, a suggestion etc. = *produce an idea*
- ☐ Sarah is very creative. She's always **coming up with** new ideas.

make something **up** = *invent something that is not true*
- ☐ What Kevin told you about himself wasn't true. He **made** it all **up**.

B

cheer up = *be happier*, **cheer** somebody **up** = *make somebody feel happier*
- ☐ You look so sad! **Cheer up!**
- ☐ Helen is depressed at the moment. What can we do to **cheer her up?**

save up for something / to do something = *save money to buy something*
- ☐ Dan is **saving up** for a trip round the world.

clear up = *become bright (for weather)*
- ☐ It was raining when I got up, but it **cleared up** during the morning.

C

blow up = *explode*, **blow** something **up** = *destroy it with a bomb etc.*
- ☐ The engine caught fire and **blew up**.
- ☐ The bridge was **blown up** during the war.

tear something **up** = *tear it into pieces*
- ☐ I didn't read the letter. I just **tore** it **up** and threw it away.

beat somebody **up** = *hit someone repeatedly so that they are badly hurt*
- ☐ A friend of mine was attacked and **beaten up** a few days ago. He was badly hurt and had to go to hospital.

D

break up / split up (with somebody) = *separate*
- ☐ I'm surprised to hear that Sue and Paul have **split up**. They seemed very happy together when I last saw them.

do up a coat, a shoelace, buttons etc. = *fasten, tie etc.*
- ☐ It's quite cold. **Do up** your coat before you go out.

do up a building, a room etc. = *repair and improve it*
- ☐ The kitchen looks great now that it has been **done up**.

look something **up** in a dictionary/encyclopaedia etc.
- ☐ If you don't know the meaning of a word, you can **look** it **up** in a dictionary.

put up with something = *tolerate it*
- ☐ We live on a busy road, so we have to **put up with** a lot of noise from the traffic.

hold up a person, a plan etc. = *delay*
- ☐ Don't wait for me. I don't want to **hold** you **up**.
- ☐ Plans to build a new factory have been **held up** because of the company's financial problems.

mix up people/things, **get** people/things **mixed up** = *you think one is the other*
- ☐ The two brothers look very similar. Many people **mix** them **up**. (*or* ... **get** them **mixed up**)

Phrasal verbs 1 (Introduction) → Unit 137   More verbs + up → Units 142–143

144.1 Which goes with which?

1 I'm going to tear up	A a new camera	1 __F__
2 Jane came up with	B a lot of bad weather	2 ....
3 Paul is always making up	C your jacket	3 ....
4 I think you should do up	D an interesting suggestion	4 ....
5 I don't think you should bring up	E excuses	5 ....
6 I'm saving up for	F ~~the letter~~	6 ....
7 We had to put up with	G that subject	7 ....

144.2 Look at the pictures and complete the sentences. You will need two or three words each time.

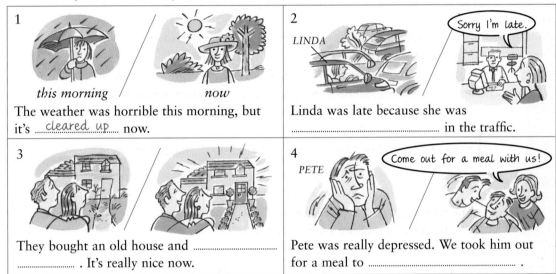

1 *this morning* / *now*

The weather was horrible this morning, but it's ....*cleared up*.... now.

2 LINDA — Sorry I'm late.

Linda was late because she was .... in the traffic.

3 They bought an old house and .... It's really nice now.

4 PETE — Come out for a meal with us!

Pete was really depressed. We took him out for a meal to ....

144.3 Complete the sentences. Each time use a verb (in the correct form) + up. Sometimes you will need other words as well.

1 Some interesting matters ....*came up*.... in our discussion yesterday.

2 The ship .... and sank. The cause of the explosion was never discovered.

3 Two men have been arrested after a man was .... outside a restaurant last night. The injured man was taken to hospital.

4 'Is Robert still going out with Tina?'   'No, they've ....'

5 I put my shoes on and .... the shoelaces.

6 The weather is horrible this morning, isn't it? I hope it .... later.

7 I wanted to phone Chris, but I dialled Laura's number by mistake. I got their phone numbers ....

144.4 Complete the sentences. Each time use a verb + up. Sometimes you will need other words as well.

1 Don't wait for me. I don't want to ....*hold you up*.... .

2 I don't know what this word means. I'll have to ....

3 There's nothing we can do about the problem. We'll just have to .... it.

4 'Was that story true?'   'No, I ....'

5 I think we should follow Tom's suggestion. Nobody has .... a better plan.

6 I hate this photograph. I'm going to ....

7 I'm trying to spend less money at the moment. I'm .... a trip to Australia.

→ Additional exercises 37–41 (pages 323–25)

Phrasal verbs 9   away/back

A
Compare **away** and **back**:

away = away from home
- □ We're **going away** on holiday today.

away = away from a place, a person etc.
- □ The woman got into her car and **drove away**.
- □ I tried to take a picture of the bird, but it **flew away**.
- □ I dropped the ticket and it **blew away** in the wind.
- □ The police searched the house and **took away** a computer.

In the same way you can say:
walk away, run away, look away etc.

back = back home
- □ We'll **be back** in three weeks.

back = back to a place, a person etc.
- □ A: I'm going out now.
   B: What time will you **be back**?
- □ After eating at a restaurant, we **walked back** to our hotel.
- □ I've still got Jane's keys. I forgot to **give** them **back** to her.
- □ When you've finished with that book, can you **put** it **back** on the shelf?

In the same way you can say:
go back, come back, get back, take something **back** etc.

B
Other verbs + **away**

get away = escape, leave with difficulty
- □ We tried to catch the thief, but he managed to **get away**.

get away with something = do something wrong without being caught
- □ I parked in a no-parking zone, but I **got away with** it.

keep away (from …) = don't go near
- □ **Keep away from** the edge of the pool. You might fall in.

give something **away** = give it to somebody else because you don't want it any more
- □ 'Did you sell your old computer?' 'No, I **gave** it **away**.'

put something **away** = put it in the place where it is kept, usually out of sight
- □ When the children had finished playing with their toys, they **put** them **away**.

throw something **away** = put it in the rubbish
- □ I kept the letter, but I **threw away** the envelope.

C
Other verbs + **back**

wave back / smile back / shout back / write back / hit somebody **back**
- □ I waved to her and she **waved back**.

call/phone/ring (somebody) **back** = return a phone call
- □ I can't talk to you now. I'll **call** you **back** in ten minutes.

get back to somebody = reply to them by phone etc.
- □ I sent him an email, but he never **got back to** me.

look back (on something) = think about what happened in the past
- □ My first job was in a travel agency. I didn't like it very much at the time but, **looking back on** it, I learnt a lot and it was a very useful experience.

pay back money, **pay** somebody **back**
- □ If you borrow money, you have to **pay** it **back**.
- □ Thanks for lending me the money. I'll **pay** you **back** next week.

Phrasal verbs 1 (Introduction) → Unit 137

145.1 Complete each sentence using a verb in the correct form.

1 The woman got into her car and ___drove___ away.
2 Here's the money you need. .... me back when you can.
3 Don't .... that box away. It could be useful.
4 Jane doesn't do anything at work. I don't know how she .... away with it.
5 I'm going out now. I'll .... back at about 10.30.
6 You should think more about the future; don't .... back all the time.
7 Gary is very generous. He won some money in the lottery and .... it all away.
8 I'll .... back to you as soon as I have the information you need.

145.2 Complete the sentences. Each time use a verb + away or back.

1 I was away all day yesterday. I ___got back___ very late.
2 I haven't seen our neighbours for a while. I think they must ....
3 'I'm going out now.'   'OK. What time will you .... ?'
4 A man was trying to break into a car. When he saw me, he ....
5 I smiled at him, but he didn't ....
6 If you cheat in the exam, you might .... with it. But you might get caught.
7 Be careful! That's an electric fence. .... from it.

145.3 Look at the pictures and complete the sentences.

1	2	3
She waved to him and he ___waved back___ .	It was windy. I dropped a twenty-pound note and it	SUE Sue opened the letter, read it and .... in the envelope.
4	5 ELLIE BEN	6
He tried to talk to her, but she just	Ellie threw the ball to Ben and he	His shoes were worn out, so he ....

145.4 Complete the sentences. Use the verb in brackets + away or back.

1 A: Do you still have my keys?
   B: No. Don't you remember? I ___gave them back___ to you yesterday? (give)
2 A: Do you want this magazine?
   B: No, I've finished with it. You can .... (throw)
3 A: How are your new jeans? Do they fit you OK?
   B: No, I'm going to .... to the shop. (take)
4 A: Here's the money you asked me to lend you.
   B: Thanks. I'll .... as soon as I can. (pay)
5 A: What happened to all the books you used to have?
   B: I didn't want them any more, so I .... (give)
6 A: Did you phone Sarah?
   B: She wasn't there. I left a message asking her to .... (call)

→ Additional exercises 37–41 (pages 323–25)

Appendix 1
Regular and irregular verbs

1.1   *Regular verbs*

If a verb is regular, the past simple and past participle end in **-ed**. For example:

infinitive	clean	finish	use	paint	stop	carry
past simple *past participle* }	cleaned	finished	used	painted	stopped	carried

For spelling rules, see Appendix 6.

For the *past simple* (I **cleaned** / they **finished** / she **carried** etc.), see Unit 5.

We use the *past participle* to make the perfect tenses and all the passive forms.
Perfect tenses (**have/has/had** cleaned):

- ☐ I **have cleaned** the windows. *(present perfect – see Units 7–8)*
- ☐ They were still working. They **had**n't **finished**. *(past perfect – see Unit 15)*

Passive (**is** cleaned / **was** cleaned etc.):

- ☐ He **was carried** out of the room. *(past simple passive)*
- ☐ This gate has just **been painted**. *(present perfect passive)* } see Units 42–44

1.2   *Irregular verbs*

When the past simple and past participle do *not* end in **-ed** (for example, **I saw / I have seen**), the verb is *irregular*.

With some irregular verbs, all three forms (*infinitive, past simple* and *past participle*) are the same. For example, **hit**:

- ☐ Don't **hit** me. *(infinitive)*
- ☐ Somebody **hit** me as I came into the room. *(past simple)*
- ☐ I've never **hit** anybody in my life. *(past participle – present perfect)*
- ☐ George was **hit** on the head by a stone. *(past participle – passive)*

With other irregular verbs, the past simple is the same as the past participle (but different from the infinitive). For example, **tell → told**:

- ☐ Can you **tell** me what to do? *(infinitive)*
- ☐ She **told** me to come back the next day. *(past simple)*
- ☐ Have you **told** anybody about your new job? *(past participle – present perfect)*
- ☐ I was **told** to come back the next day. *(past participle – passive)*

With other irregular verbs, all three forms are different. For example, **wake → woke/woken**:

- ☐ I'll **wake** you up. *(infinitive)*
- ☐ I **woke** up in the middle of the night. *(past simple)*
- ☐ The baby has **woken** up. *(past participle – present perfect)*
- ☐ I was **woken** up by a loud noise. *(past participle – passive)*

1.3   The following verbs can be regular or irregular:

burn	→	burned	*or*	burnt	**smell**	→	smelled	*or*	smelt
dream	→	dreamed	*or*	dreamt [dremt]*	**spell**	→	spelled	*or*	spelt
lean	→	leaned	*or*	leant [lent]*	**spill**	→	spilled	*or*	spilt
learn	→	learned	*or*	learnt	**spoil**	→	spoiled	*or*	spoilt

* *pronunciation*

So you can say:

- ☐ I **leant** out of the window. *or* I **leaned** out of the window.
- ☐ The dinner has been **spoiled**. *or* The dinner has been **spoilt**.

In British English the irregular form (**burnt/learnt** etc.) is more usual. For American English, see Appendix 7.

1.4   List of irregular verbs

infinitive	past simple	past participle
be	was/were	been
beat	beat	beaten
become	became	become
begin	began	begun
bend	bent	bent
bet	bet	bet
bite	bit	bitten
blow	blew	blown
break	broke	broken
bring	brought	brought
broadcast	broadcast	broadcast
build	built	built
burst	burst	burst
buy	bought	bought
catch	caught	caught
choose	chose	chosen
come	came	come
cost	cost	cost
creep	crept	crept
cut	cut	cut
deal	dealt	dealt
dig	dug	dug
do	did	done
draw	drew	drawn
drink	drank	drunk
drive	drove	driven
eat	ate	eaten
fall	fell	fallen
feed	fed	fed
feel	felt	felt
fight	fought	fought
find	found	found
flee	fled	fled
fly	flew	flown
forbid	forbade	forbidden
forget	forgot	forgotten
forgive	forgave	forgiven
freeze	froze	frozen
get	got	got
give	gave	given
go	went	gone
grow	grew	grown
hang	hung	hung
have	had	had
hear	heard	heard
hide	hid	hidden
hit	hit	hit
hold	held	held
hurt	hurt	hurt
keep	kept	kept
kneel	knelt	knelt
know	knew	known
lay	laid	laid
lead	led	led
leave	left	left
lend	lent	lent
let	let	let
lie	lay	lain

infinitive	past simple	past participle
light	lit	lit
lose	lost	lost
make	made	made
mean	meant	meant
meet	met	met
pay	paid	paid
put	put	put
read	read [red]*	read [red]*
ride	rode	ridden
ring	rang	rung
rise	rose	risen
run	ran	run
say	said	said
see	saw	seen
seek	sought	sought
sell	sold	sold
send	sent	sent
set	set	set
sew	sewed	sewn/sewed
shake	shook	shaken
shine	shone	shone
shoot	shot	shot
show	showed	shown/showed
shrink	shrank	shrunk
shut	shut	shut
sing	sang	sung
sink	sank	sunk
sit	sat	sat
sleep	slept	slept
slide	slid	slid
speak	spoke	spoken
spend	spent	spent
spit	spat	spat
split	split	split
spread	spread	spread
spring	sprang	sprung
stand	stood	stood
steal	stole	stolen
stick	stuck	stuck
sting	stung	stung
stink	stank	stunk
strike	struck	struck
swear	swore	sworn
sweep	swept	swept
swim	swam	swum
swing	swung	swung
take	took	taken
teach	taught	taught
tear	tore	torn
tell	told	told
think	thought	thought
throw	threw	thrown
understand	understood	understood
wake	woke	woken
wear	wore	worn
weep	wept	wept
win	won	won
write	wrote	written

* *pronunciation*

Appendix 2
Present and past tenses

	simple	*continuous*
present	**I do** *present simple* (→ Units 2–4) ☐ Ann often **plays** tennis. ☐ I **work** in a bank, but I **don't enjoy** it much. ☐ **Do** you **like** parties? ☐ It **doesn't rain** so much in summer.	**I am doing** *present continuous* (→ Units 1, 3–4) ☐ 'Where's Ann?' 'She's **playing** tennis.' ☐ Please don't disturb me now. I'm **working**. ☐ Hello. **Are** you **enjoying** the party? ☐ It **isn't raining** at the moment.
present perfect	**I have done** *present perfect simple* (→ Units 7–8, 10–14) ☐ Ann **has played** tennis many times. ☐ I've **lost** my key. **Have** you **seen** it anywhere? ☐ How long **have** you and Chris **known** each other? ☐ A: Is it still raining? B: No, it **has stopped**. ☐ The house is dirty. I **haven't cleaned** it for weeks.	**I have been doing** *present perfect continuous* (→ Units 9–11) ☐ Ann is tired. She **has been playing** tennis. ☐ You're out of breath. **Have** you **been running**? ☐ How long **have** you **been learning** English? ☐ It's still raining. It **has been raining** all day. ☐ I **haven't been feeling** well recently. Perhaps I should go to the doctor.
past	**I did** *past simple* (→ Units 5–6, 13–14) ☐ Ann **played** tennis yesterday afternoon. ☐ I **lost** my key a few days ago. ☐ There was a film on TV last night, but we **didn't watch** it. ☐ What **did** you **do** when you finished work yesterday?	**I was doing** *past continuous* (→ Unit 6) ☐ I saw Ann at the sports centre yesterday. She **was playing** tennis. ☐ I dropped my key when I **was trying** to open the door. ☐ The television was on, but we **weren't watching** it. ☐ What **were** you **doing** at this time yesterday?
past perfect	**I had done** *past perfect* (→ Unit 15) ☐ It wasn't her first game of tennis. She **had played** many times before. ☐ They couldn't get into the house because they **had lost** the key. ☐ The house was dirty because I **hadn't cleaned** it for weeks.	**I had been doing** *past perfect continuous* (→ Unit 16) ☐ Ann was tired yesterday evening because she **had been playing** tennis in the afternoon. ☐ George decided to go to the doctor because he **hadn't been feeling** well.

For the passive, see Units 42–44.

Appendix 3
The future

3.1 *List of future forms:*

☐ I'm **leaving** tomorrow.	*present continuous*	(→ Unit 19A)
☐ My train **leaves** at 9.30.	*present simple*	(→ Unit 19B)
☐ I'm **going to leave** tomorrow.	**(be) going to**	(→ Units 20, 23)
☐ I'll **leave** tomorrow.	**will**	(→ Units 21–23)
☐ I'll **be leaving** tomorrow.	*future continuous*	(→ Unit 24)
☐ I'll **have left** by this time tomorrow.	*future perfect*	(→ Unit 24)
☐ I hope to see you before I **leave** tomorrow.	*present simple*	(→ Unit 25)

3.2 *Future actions*

We use the present continuous (**I'm doing**) for arrangements:
- ☐ **I'm leaving** tomorrow. I've got my plane ticket. (already planned and arranged)
- ☐ 'When **are** they **getting** married?' 'On 24 July.'

We use the present simple (I **leave** / it **leaves** etc.) for timetables, programmes etc. :
- ☐ My train **leaves** at 11.30. (according to the timetable)
- ☐ What time **does** the film **begin**?

We use (**be**) **going to** … to say what somebody has already decided to do:
- ☐ I've decided not to stay here any longer. **I'm going to leave** tomorrow. (*or* I'm **leaving** tomorrow.)
- ☐ 'Your shoes are dirty.' 'Yes, I know. **I'm going to clean** them.'

We use **will** ('**ll**) when we decide or agree to do something at the time of speaking:
- ☐ A: I don't want you to stay here any longer.
  B: OK. **I'll leave** tomorrow. (B decides this at the time of speaking)
- ☐ That bag looks heavy. **I'll help** you with it.
- ☐ I **won't tell** anybody what happened. I promise. (**won't = will not**)

3.3 *Future happenings and situations*

Most often we use **will** to talk about future happenings ('something **will happen**') or situations ('something **will be**'):
- ☐ I don't think John is happy at work. I think he**'ll leave** soon.
- ☐ This time next year I**'ll be** in Japan. Where **will** you **be**?

We use (**be**) **going to** when the situation *now* shows what **is going to happen** *in the future*:
- ☐ Look at those black clouds. It**'s going to rain**. (you can see the clouds *now*)

3.4 *Future continuous and future perfect*

Will be (do)**ing** = will be in the middle of (doing something):
- ☐ This time next week I'll be on holiday. **I'll be lying** on a beach or **swimming** in the sea.

We also use **will be -ing** for future actions (see Unit 24C):
- ☐ What time **will** you **be leaving** tomorrow?

We use **will have** (**done**) to say that something will already be complete before a time in the future:
- ☐ I won't be here this time tomorrow. **I'll have** already **left**.

3.5 We use the *present* (*not* will) after **when/if/while/before** etc. (see Unit 25):
- ☐ I hope to see you **before** I **leave** tomorrow. (*not* before I will leave)
- ☐ **When** you **are** in London again, come and see us. (*not* When you will be)
- ☐ **If** we **don't hurry**, we'll be late.

Appendix 4
Modal verbs (can/could/will/would etc.)

This appendix is a summary of modal verbs. For more information, see Units 21–41.

4.1   Compare **can/could** etc. for actions:

can **could**	☐ I **can go** out tonight. (= there is nothing to stop me) ☐ I **can't go** out tonight. ☐ I **could go** out tonight, but I'm not very keen. ☐ I **couldn't go** out last night. (= I wasn't able)
can *or* **may**	☐ **Can** / **May** I **go** out tonight? (= do you allow me)
will/won't **would**	☐ I think I**'ll go** out tonight. ☐ I promise I **won't go** out. ☐ I **would go** out tonight, but I have too much to do. ☐ I promised I **wouldn't go** out.
shall	☐ **Shall** I **go** out tonight? (do you think it is a good idea?)
should *or* **ought to**	☐ I { **should** / **ought to** } **go** out tonight. (= it would be a good thing to do)
must **needn't**	☐ I **must go** out tonight. (= it is necessary) ☐ I **mustn't go** out tonight. (= it is necessary that I do *not* go out) ☐ I **needn't go** out tonight. (= it is not necessary)

Compare **could have …** / **would have …** etc. :

could	☐ I **could have gone** out last night, but I decided to stay at home.
would	☐ I **would have gone** out last night, but I had too much to do.
should *or* **ought to**	☐ I { **should** / **ought to** } **have gone** out last night. I'm sorry I didn't.
needn't	☐ I **needn't have gone** out last night. (= I went out, but it was not necessary)

4.2   We use **will/would/may** etc. to say whether something is possible, impossible, probable, certain etc. Compare:

will **would**	☐ 'What time **will** she **be** here?' 'She**'ll be** here soon.' ☐ She **would be** here now, but she's been delayed.
should *or* **ought to**	☐ She { **should** / **ought to** } **be** here soon. (= I expect she will be here soon)
may *or* **might** *or* **could**	☐ She { **may** / **might** / **could** } **be** here now. I'm not sure. (= it's possible that she is here)
must **can't**	☐ She **must be** here. I saw her come in. ☐ She **can't** possibly **be** here. I know for certain that she's away on holiday.

Compare **would have …** / **should have …** etc. :

will **would**	☐ She **will have arrived** by now. (= before now) ☐ She **would have arrived** earlier, but she was delayed.
should *or* **ought to**	☐ I wonder where she is. She { **should** / **ought to** } **have arrived** by now.
may *or* **might** *or* **could**	☐ She { **may** / **might** / **could** } **have arrived**. I'm not sure. (= it's possible that she has arrived)
must **can't**	☐ She **must have arrived** by now. (= I'm sure – there is no other possibility) ☐ She **can't** possibly **have arrived** yet. It's much too early. (= it's impossible)

Appendix 5
Short forms (I'm / you've / didn't etc.)

5.1 In spoken English we usually say **I'm / you've / didn't** etc. (*short forms* or *contractions*) rather than **I am / you have / did not** etc. We also use these short forms in informal writing (for example, a letter or message to a friend).

When we write short forms, we use an *apostrophe* (') for the missing letter(s):

I'm = I <u>a</u>m   you've = you <u>ha</u>ve   didn't = did n<u>o</u>t

5.2 List of short forms:

'm = am 's = is *or* has 're = are 've = have 'll = will 'd = would *or* had	I'm I've I'll I'd	he's he'll he'd	she's she'll she'd	it's	you're you've you'll you'd	we're we've we'll we'd	they're they've they'll they'd

's can be **is** or **has**:
- She's ill. (= She **is** ill.)
- She's gone away. (= She **has** gone.)

but **let's** = let **us**:
- Let's go now. (= Let **us** go)

'd can be **would** or **had**:
- I'd see a doctor if I were you. (= I **would** see)
- I'd never seen her before. (= I **had** never seen)

We use some of these short forms (especially **'s**) after question words (**who/what** etc.) and after **that/there/here**:

who's   what's   where's   how's   that's   there's   here's   who'll   there'll   who'd
- **Who's** that woman over there? (= who **is**)
- **What's** happened? (= what **has**)
- Do you think **there'll** be many people at the party? (= there **will**)

We also use short forms (especially **'s**) after a noun:
- **Catherine's** going out tonight. (= Catherine **is**)
- **My best friend's** just got married. (= My best friend **has**)

You cannot use **'m / 's / 're / 've / 'll / 'd** at the end of a sentence (because the verb is stressed in this position):
- 'Are you tired?' 'Yes, I **am**.' (*not* Yes, I'm.)
- Do you know where she **is**? (*not* Do you know where she's?)

5.3 Negative short forms

isn't	(= is not)	don't	(= do not)	haven't	(= have not)
aren't	(= are not)	doesn't	(= does not)	hasn't	(= has not)
wasn't	(= was not)	didn't	(= did not)	hadn't	(= had not)
weren't	(= were not)				
can't	(= cannot)	couldn't	(= could not)	mustn't	(= must not)
won't	(= will not)	wouldn't	(= would not)	needn't	(= need not)
shan't	(= shall not)	shouldn't	(= should not)	daren't	(= dare not)

Negative short forms for **is** and **are** can be:

he **isn't** / she **isn't** / it **isn't**   *or*   he's **not** / she's **not** / it's **not**
you **aren't** / we **aren't** / they **aren't**   *or*   you're **not** / we're **not** / they're **not**

Appendix 6
Spelling

6.1 Nouns, verbs and adjectives can have the following endings:

noun + -s/-es *(plural)*	books	ideas	matches
verb + -s/-es (after **he/she/it**)	works	enjoys	washes
verb + -ing	working	enjoying	washing
verb + -ed	worked	enjoyed	washed
adjective + -er *(comparative)*	cheaper	quicker	brighter
adjective + -est *(superlative)*	cheapest	quickest	brightest
adjective + -ly *(adverb)*	cheaply	quickly	brightly

When we use these endings, there are sometimes changes in spelling. These changes are listed below.

6.2 Nouns and verbs + -s/-es

The ending is -es when the word ends in -s/-ss/-sh/-ch/-x:

bus/buses	miss/misses	wash/washes
match/matches	search/searches	box/boxes

Note also:

potato/potatoes	tomato/tomatoes
do/does	go/goes

6.3 Words ending in -y (baby, carry, easy etc.)

> If a word ends in a *consonant** + y (-by/-ry/-sy/-vy etc.)
>
> y changes to **ie** before the ending -s:
>
> | | | | |
> |---|---|---|---|
> | baby/babies | story/stories | country/countries | secretary/secretaries |
> | hurry/hurries | study/studies | apply/applies | try/tries |
>
> y changes to **i** before the ending -ed:
>
> | | | | |
> |---|---|---|---|
> | hurry/hurried | study/studied | apply/applied | try/tried |
>
> y changes to **i** before the endings -er and -est:
>
> | | | |
> |---|---|---|
> | easy/easier/easiest | heavy/heavier/heaviest | lucky/luckier/luckiest |
>
> y changes to **i** before the ending -ly:
>
> | | | |
> |---|---|---|
> | easy/easily | heavy/heavily | temporary/temporarily |

y does *not* change before -ing:

hurrying	studying	applying	trying

y does *not* change if the word ends in a *vowel** + y (-ay/-ey/-oy/-uy):

play/plays/played	monkey/monkeys	enjoy/enjoys/enjoyed	buy/buys

An exception is: **day/daily**
Note also: **pay/paid**   **lay/laid**   **say/said**

6.4 Verbs ending in -ie (die, lie, tie)

If a verb ends in -ie, ie changes to **y** before the ending -ing:

die/dying	lie/lying	tie/tying

---

* **a e i o u** are *vowel* letters.
The other letters (**b c d f g** etc.) are *consonant* letters.

6.5 Words ending in -e (hope, dance, wide etc.)

> *Verbs*
>
> If a verb ends in -e, we leave out e before the ending -ing:
>
> hope/hop**ing**   smile/smil**ing**   dance/danc**ing**   confuse/confus**ing**
>
> Exceptions are be/**being**
> *and* verbs ending in -ee: see/see**ing**   agree/agree**ing**
>
> If a verb ends in -e, we add -d for the past (of regular verbs):
>
> hope/hope**d**   smile/smile**d**   dance/dance**d**   confuse/confuse**d**

> *Adjectives and adverbs*
>
> If an adjective ends in -e, we add -r and -st for the comparative and superlative:
>
> wide/wide**r**/wide**st**   late/late**r**/late**st**   large/large**r**/large**st**
>
> If an adjective ends in -e, we *keep* e before -ly in the adverb:
>
> polite/polite**ly**   extreme/extreme**ly**   absolute/absolute**ly**
>
> If an adjective ends in -le (simple, terrible etc.), the adverb ending is -**ply**, -**bly** etc. :
>
> sim**ple**/sim**ply**   terri**ble**/terri**bly**   reasona**ble**/reasona**bly**

6.6 Doubling consonants (**stop/stopping/stopped, wet/wetter/wettest** etc.)

Sometimes a word ends in *vowel + consonant*. For example:

stop   plan   rub   big   wet   thin   prefer   regret

Before the endings -ing/-ed/-er/-est, we double the consonant at the end. So **p → pp**,
n → nn etc. For example:

stop	p → pp	stopping	stopped
plan	n → nn	planning	planned
rub	b → bb	rubbing	rubbed
big	g → gg	bigger	biggest
wet	t → tt	wetter	wettest
thin	n → nn	thinner	thinnest

If the word has more than one syllable (**prefer, begin** etc.), we double the consonant at the end
only if the final syllable is stressed:

preFER / preferring / preferred   perMIT / permitting / permitted
reGRET / regretting / regretted   beGIN / beginning

If the final syllable is not stressed, we do *not* double the final consonant:

VISit / visiting / visited   deVELop / developing / developed
HAPpen / happening / happened   reMEMber / remembering / remembered

In British English, verbs ending in -l have -ll- before -ing and -ed whether the final syllable is
stressed or not:

travel / travelling / travelled   cancel / cancelling / cancelled

For American spelling, see Appendix 7.

> Note that
>
> we do *not* double the final consonant if the word ends in *two* consonants (-rt, -lp, -ng etc.):
>
> star**t** / starting / started   hel**p** / helping / helped   lon**g** / longer / longest
>
> we do *not* double the final consonant if there are *two* vowel letters before it (-oil, -eed etc.):
>
> b**oi**l / boiling / boiled   n**ee**d / needing / needed   expl**ai**n / explaining / explained
> ch**ea**p / cheaper / cheapest   l**ou**d / louder / loudest   q**ui**et / quieter / quietest
>
> we do *not* double y or w at the end of words. (At the end of words y and w are not
> consonants.)
>
> sta**y** / staying / stayed   gro**w** / growing   ne**w** / newer / newest

There are a few grammatical differences between British English and American English:

Unit	BRITISH	AMERICAN
7A–B and 13A	The *present perfect* is used for an action in the past with a result now: □ **I've lost** my key. **Have** you **seen** it? □ Sally isn't here. She**'s gone** out. The *present perfect* is used with **just, already** and **yet**: □ I'm not hungry. **I've just had** lunch. □ A: What time is Mark leaving? B: He **has already left**. □ **Have** you **finished** your work **yet**?	The *present perfect* OR *past simple* can be used: □ **I've lost** my key. **Have** you **seen** it? or I **lost** my key. **Did** you **see** it? □ Sally isn't here. { She**'s gone** out. / She **went** out. The *present perfect* OR *past simple* can be used: □ I'm not hungry. { **I've just had** lunch. / I **just had** lunch. □ A: What time is Mark leaving? B: { He **has already left**. / He **already left**. □ **Have** you **finished** your work **yet**? or **Did** you **finish** your work **yet**?
17C	British speakers usually say: **have** a bath **have** a shower **have** a break **have** a holiday	American speakers say: **take** a bath **take** a shower **take** a break **take** a vacation
21D and 22D	**Will** or **shall** can be used with **I/we**: □ I **will/shall** be late this evening. **Shall I** … ? and **shall we** … ? are used to ask for advice etc. : □ Which way **shall we** go?	**Shall** is unusual: □ I **will** be late this evening. **Should I** … ? and **should we** … ? are more usual to ask for advice etc. : □ Which way **should we** go?
28	British speakers use **can't** to say they believe something is not probable: □ Sue hasn't contacted me. She **can't** have got my message.	American speakers use **must not** in this situation: □ Sue hasn't contacted me. She **must not** have gotten my message.
32	You can use **needn't** or **don't need to**: □ We **needn't** hurry. or We **don't need to** hurry.	**Needn't** is unusual. The usual form is **don't need to**: □ We **don't need to** hurry.
34A–B	After **demand, insist** etc. you can use **should**: □ I demanded that he **should apologise**. □ We insisted that something **should be** done about the problem.	The *subjunctive* is normally used. **Should** is unusual after **demand, insist** etc. : □ I demanded that he **apologize**.* □ We insisted that something **be** done about the problem.
51B	British speakers generally use **Have you?** / **Isn't she?** etc. □ A: Liz isn't feeling well. B: **Isn't she?** What's wrong with her?	American speakers generally use **You have?** / **She isn't?** etc. : □ A: Liz isn't feeling well. B: **She isn't?** What's wrong with her?
70B	**Accommodation** is usually uncountable: □ There isn't enough **accommodation**.	**Accommodation** can be countable: □ There aren't enough **accommodations**.

* Many verbs ending in **-ise** in British English (apolog**ise**/organ**ise**/special**ise** etc.) are spelt with **-ize** (apolog**ize**/organ**ize**/special**ize** etc.) in American English.

Unit	BRITISH	AMERICAN
74B	to/in **hospital** (without **the**): □ Three people were injured and taken to **hospital**.	to/in **the hospital**: □ Three people were injured and taken to **the hospital**.
79C	Nouns like **government/team/family** etc. can have a singular or plural verb: □ The team **is/are** playing well.	These nouns normally take a singular verb in American English: □ The team **is** playing well.
121B	**at the weekend / at weekends**: □ Will you be here **at the weekend**?	**on the weekend / on weekends**: □ Will you be here **on the weekend**?
124D	**at the front / at the back** (of a group etc.): □ Let's sit **at the front** (of the cinema).	**in the front / in the back** (of a group etc.): □ Let's sit **in the front** (of the movie theater).
131C	**different from** or **different to**: □ It was **different from/to** what I'd expected.	**different from** or **different than**: □ It was **different from/than** what I'd expected.
132A	**write to** somebody: □ Please **write to** me soon.	**write (to)** somebody (with or without **to**): □ Please **write (to)** me soon.
137A	British speakers use both **round** and **around**: □ He turned **round**. *or* He turned **around**.	American speakers use **around** (not usually 'round') □ He turned **around**.
137C	British speakers use both **fill in** and **fill out**: □ Can you **fill in** this form? *or* Can you **fill out** this form?	American speakers use **fill out**: □ Can you **fill out** this form?
141B	**get on** = *progress* □ How are you **getting on** in your new job? **get on** (with somebody): □ Richard **gets on** well with his new neighbours.	American speakers do not use **get on** in this way. **get along** (with somebody): □ Richard **gets along** well with his new neighbors.
144D	**do up** a room etc. : □ The kitchen looks great now that it has been **done up**.	**do over** a room etc. : □ The kitchen looks great now that it has been **done over**.

Appendix	BRITISH	AMERICAN
1.3	The verbs in this section (**burn, spell** etc.) can be regular or irregular (**burned** *or* **burnt, spelled** *or* **spelt** etc.). The past participle of **get** is **got**: □ Your English has **got** much better. (= has become much better) **Have got** is also an alternative to **have**: □ I've **got** two brothers. (= I have two brothers.)	The verbs in this section are normally regular (**burned, spelled** etc.). The past participle of **get** is **gotten**: □ Your English has **gotten** much better. **Have got** = have (as in British English): □ I've **got** two brothers.
6.6	British spelling: travel → travelling / travelled cancel → cancelling / cancelled	American spelling: travel → traveling / traveled cancel → canceling / canceled

Additional exercises

These exercises are divided into the following sections:

Present and past   Units 1–6, Appendix 2

1   Put the verb into the correct form: present simple (**I do**), present continuous (**I am doing**), past simple (**I did**) or past continuous (**I was doing**).

1   We can go out now. It __isn't raining__ (not / rain) any more.
2   Catherine __was waiting__ (wait) for me when I __arrived__ (arrive).
3   I __am getting__ (get) hungry. Let's go and have something to eat.
4   What __do you doing__ (you / do) in your spare time? Do you have any hobbies?
5   The weather was horrible when we __arrived__ (arrive). It was cold and it __was raining__ (rain) hard.
6   Louise usually __phones__ (phone) me on Fridays, but she __didn't phone__ (not / phone) last Friday.
7   A: When I last saw you, you __were thinking__ (think) of moving to a new flat.
    B: That's right, but in the end I __decided__ (decide) to stay where I was.
8   Why __are you looking__ (you / look) at me like that? What's the matter?
9   It's usually dry here at this time of the year. It __doesn't rain__ (not / rain) much.
10 The phone __rang / was ringing__ (ring) three times while we __were having__ (have) dinner last night.
11 Linda was busy when we __went__ (go) to see her yesterday. She had an exam today and she __was preparing__ (prepare) for it. We __didn't want__ (not / want) to disturb her, so we __didn't stay__ (not / stay) very long.
12 When I first __told__ (tell) Tom the news, he __didn't believe__ (not / believe) me. He __thinks / thought__ (think) that I __was joking__ (joke).

302

Present and past

2 Which is correct?

1 Everything is going well. We ~~didn't have~~ / haven't had any problems so far.
(haven't had *is correct*)
2 Lisa ~~didn't go~~ / hasn't gone to work yesterday. She wasn't feeling well.
3 Look! That man over there ~~wears~~ / is wearing the same sweater as you.
4 Your son is much taller than when I last saw him. He ~~grew~~ / has grown a lot.
5 I still don't know what to do. I ~~didn't decide~~ / haven't decided yet. ✓
6 I wonder why Jim ~~is~~ / is being so nice to me today. He isn't usually like that.
7 Jane had a book open in front of her, but she ~~didn't read~~ / wasn't reading it.
8 I wasn't very busy. I ~~didn't have~~ / wasn't having much to do. ✓
9 ~~It begins~~ / It's beginning to get dark. Shall I turn on the light?
10 After leaving school, Tim ~~got~~ / has got a job in a factory. ✓
11 When Sue heard the news, she ~~wasn't~~ / hasn't been very pleased. ✓
12 This is a nice restaurant, isn't it? Is this the first time ~~you are~~ / you've been here? ✓
13 I need a new job. ~~I'm doing~~ / I've been doing the same job for too long. ✓
14 'Anna has gone out.' 'Oh, has she? What time ~~did she go~~ / has she gone?' ✓
15 'You look tired.' 'Yes, ~~I've played~~ / I've been playing basketball.' ✓
16 Where ~~are you coming~~ / do you come from? Are you American? ✓
17 I'd like to see Tina again. It's a long time since I saw her / ~~that I didn't see her~~.
18 Robert and Maria have been married ~~since 20 years~~ / for 20 years. ✓

3 Complete each question using a suitable verb.

1 A: I'm looking for Paul. _Have you seen_ him?
B: Yes, he was here a moment ago.
2 A: Why _did you go_ to bed so early last night?
B: I was feeling very tired.
3 A: Where _are you going_ ?
B: Just to the post box. I want to post these letters. I'll be back in a few minutes.
4 A: _Do you watch_ television every evening?
B: No, only if there's something special on.
5 A: Your house is very beautiful. How long _have you been living_ here?
B: Nearly ten years.
6 A: How was your holiday? _Did you have_ a nice time?
B: Yes, thanks. It was great.
7 A: _Have you seen_ Julie recently?
B: Yes, I met her a few days ago.
8 A: Can you describe the woman you saw? What _was she wearing_ ?
B: A red sweater and black jeans.
9 A: I'm sorry to keep you waiting. _Have you been waiting_ long?
B: No, only about ten minutes.
10 A: How long _does it take_ you to get to work in the morning?
B: Usually about 45 minutes. It depends on the traffic.
11 A: _Have you finished_ with that magazine yet?
B: No, I'm still reading it. I won't be long.
12 A: _Have you been_ to the United States?
B: No, never, but I went to Canada a few years ago.

4   Use your own ideas to complete B's sentences.

1   A: What's the new restaurant like? Is it good?
    B: I've no idea. _I've never been_ .... there.

2   A: How well do you know Bill?
    B: Very well. We _have been together_ .... since we were children.

3   A: Did you enjoy your holiday?
    B: Yes, it was really good. It's the best holiday _I ever enjoy had_ .

4   A: Is David still here?
    B: No, I'm afraid he isn't. _He just gone_ .... about ten minutes ago.

5   A: I like your suit. I haven't seen it before.
    B: It's new. It's the first time _are you wearing I have worn_ .

6   A: How did you cut your knee?
    B: I slipped and fell when _I was playing_ .... tennis.

7   A: Do you ever go swimming?
    B: Not these days. I haven't _been for_ .... a long time.

8   A: How often do you go to the cinema?
    B: Very rarely. It's nearly a year _I been_ .... to the cinema.

9   A: I've bought some new shoes. Do you like them?
    B: Yes, they're very nice. Where _did you get_ .... them?

Present and past   Units 1–17, 110, Appendix 2

5   Put the verb into the correct form: past simple (**I did**), past continuous (**I was doing**), past perfect (**I had done**) or past perfect continuous (**I had been doing**).

Yesterday afternoon Sarah ...._went_.... (go) to the station to meet Paul. When she
.....*got*..... (get) there, Paul _had already waiting_ ...... (already / wait)
for her. His train ....._arrived_..... (arrive) early.

When I got home, Bill _was lying_ .... (lie) on the sofa. The television was on,
but he _was not watching_ .... (not / watch) it. He _had fallen_ ...... (fall)
asleep and ..._was snoring_.... (snore) loudly. I ...._turned_.... (turn) the
television off and just then he _had woken / woke_ .... (wake) up.

3

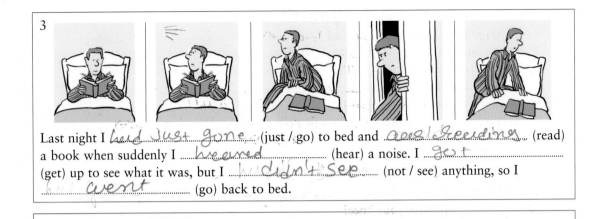

Last night I _had just gone_ (just / go) to bed and _was reading_ (read)
a book when suddenly I _heared_ (hear) a noise. I _got_
(get) up to see what it was, but I _didn't see_ (not / see) anything, so I
went (go) back to bed.

4

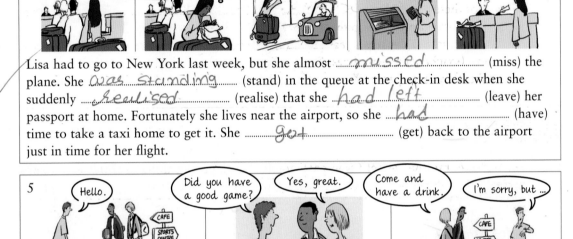

Lisa had to go to New York last week, but she almost _missed_ (miss) the
plane. She _was standing_ (stand) in the queue at the check-in desk when she
suddenly _realised_ (realise) that she _had left_ (leave) her
passport at home. Fortunately she lives near the airport, so she _had_ (have)
time to take a taxi home to get it. She _got_ (get) back to the airport
just in time for her flight.

5

I _met_ (meet) Peter and Lucy yesterday as I _was walking_
(walk) through the park. They _had been_ (be) to the Sports Centre where
they _had been playing_ (play) tennis. They _were going_ (go) to a café
and _invited_ (invite) me to join them, but I _had arranged_
(arrange) to meet another friend and _didn't have_ (not / have) time.

6   Make sentences from the words in brackets. Put the verb into the correct form: present perfect
(**I have done**), present perfect continuous (**I have been doing**), past perfect (**I had done**) or
past perfect continuous (**I had been doing**).

1 Amanda is sitting on the ground. She's out of breath.
   (she / run) _She has been running._

2 Where's my bag? I left it under this chair.
   (somebody / take / it) _Somebody has taken it_

3 We were all surprised when Jenny and Andy got married last year.
   (they / only / know / each other / a few weeks)
   They had only been known each other for a few weeks

4 It's still raining. I wish it would stop.
   (it / rain / all day) _It had been raining all day_

5 Suddenly I woke up. I was confused and didn't know where I was.
   (I / dream) _I had been dreaming_

6 I wasn't hungry at lunchtime, so I didn't have anything to eat.
(I / have / a big breakfast) *I had had a big breakfast.*

7 Every year Robert and Tina spend a few days at the same hotel by the sea.
(they / go / there for years) *They have been going there for you*

8 I've got a headache.
(I / have / it / since I got up) *I have had it it since I got up*

9 Next week Gary is going to run in a marathon.
(he / train / very hard for it) *He has been training very hard for*

7 Put the verb into the correct form.

Julia and Kevin are old friends. They meet by chance at a rail station.

JULIA: Hello, Kevin. (1) *I have not seen* (I / not / see)
you for ages. How are you?

KEVIN: I'm fine. How about you?
(2) *You are looking* (you / look) well.

JULIA: Yes, I'm very well thanks.
So, (3) *are you going* (you / go) somewhere or
(4) *are you meeting* (you / meet) somebody off a train?

KEVIN: (5) *I am going* (I / go) to London for a business meeting.

JULIA: Oh. (6) *Do you often go* (you / often / go) away on business?

KEVIN: Quite often, yes. And you? Where (7) *are you going* (you / go)?

JULIA: Nowhere. (8) *am meeting* (I / meet) a friend. Unfortunately
her train (9) *has been* (be) delayed –
(10) *I have been waiting* (I / wait) here for nearly an hour.

KEVIN: How are your children?

JULIA: They're all fine, thanks. The youngest (11) *has just started* (just / start)
school.

KEVIN: How (12) *is she getting* (she / get) on?
(13) *Does she like* (she / like) it?

JULIA: Yes, (14) *she thinks* (she / think) it's great.

KEVIN: (15) *are you working* (you / work) at the moment? When I last
(16) *spspoke* (speak) to you, (17) *you had been going* (you / work) in a travel agency.
were

JULIA: That's right. Unfortunately the company (18) *has gone went* (go) out
of business a couple of months after (19) *I had started* (I / start)
work there, so (20) *I had lost* (I / lose) my job.

KEVIN: And (21) *you have not had* (you / not / have) a job since then?

JULIA: Not a permanent job. (22) *I have had* (I / have) a few temporary
jobs. By the way, (23) *have you seen* (you / see) Joe recently?

KEVIN: Joe? He's in Canada.

JULIA: Really? How long (24) *has he been* (he / be) in Canada?
he

KEVIN: About a year now. (25) *I had seen saw* (I / see) him a few days before
(26) *he went* (he / go). (27) *he had been* (he / be)
unemployed for months, so (28) *he decided* (he / decide) to try his
luck somewhere else. (29) *he was really looking* (he / really / look forward)
to going. *forward*

JULIA: So, what (30) *is he doing* (he / do) there?

KEVIN: I've no idea. (31) *I have not heard* (I / not / hear) from him since
(32) *he left* (he / leave). Anyway, I must go and catch my
train. It was really nice to see you again.

JULIA: You too. Bye. Have a good trip.

KEVIN: Thanks. Bye.

8   Put the verb into the most suitable form.

1   Who _____invented_____ (invent) the bicycle?
2   'Do you still have a headache?' 'No, _____it has gone_____ (it / go). I'm all right now.'
3   I was the last to leave the office yesterday evening. Everybody else _____had gone_____ (go) home when I _____locked the evening_____ (leave).
4   What _____did you do_____ (you / do) last weekend? _____Did you go_____ (you / go) away?
5   I like your car. How long _____have you had_____ (you / have) it?
6   It's a pity the trip was cancelled. I _____was looking_____ (look) forward to it.
7   Jane is an experienced teacher. _____she has been teaching_____ (she / teach) for 15 years.
8   _____I had bought_____ (I / buy) a new jacket last week, but _____I haven't worn_____ (I / not / wear) it yet.
9   A few days ago _____I saw_____ (I / see) a man at a party whose face _____was_____ (be) very familiar. At first I couldn't think where _____I had seen_____ (I / see) him before. Then suddenly _____I remembered_____ (I / remember) who _____it was_____ (it / be).
10 _____Have you heard_____ (you / hear) of Agatha Christie? _____she was_____ (she / be) a writer who _____had died_____ (die) in 1976. _____She wrote_____ (she / write) more than 70 detective novels. _____Have you read_____ (you / read) any of them?
11 A: What _____does this word mean_____ (this word / mean)?
    B: I've no idea. _____I have never seen_____ (I / never / see) it before. Look it up in the dictionary.
12 A: _____Did you get_____ (you / get) to the theatre in time for the play last night?
    B: No, we were late. By the time we got there, _____it had already begun_____ (it / already / begin).
13 I went to Sarah's room and _____knocked_____ (knock) on the door, but there _____was_____ (be) no answer. Either _____she had gone_____ (she / go) out or _____she didn't want_____ (she / not / want) to see anyone.
14 Patrick asked me how to use the photocopier. _____he had never used_____ (he / never / use) it before, so _____he didn't know_____ (he / not / know) what to do.
15 Liz _____went_____ (go) for a swim after work yesterday. _____She needed_____ (she / need) some exercise because _____she had been sitting_____ (she / sit) in an office all day in front of a computer.

Past continuous and used to   Units 6, 18

9   Complete the sentences using the past continuous (was/were –ing) or used to ... . Use the verb in brackets.

1   I haven't been to the cinema for ages now. We _____used to go_____ a lot. (go)
2   Ann didn't see me wave to her. She _____was looking_____ in the other direction. (look)
3   I _____used to drive_____ a lot but, I don't use my car very much these days. (drive)
4   I asked the taxi driver to slow down. She _____was driving_____ too fast. (drive)
5   Rosemary and Jonathan met for the first time when they _____were working_____ in the same bank. (work)
6   When I was a child, I _____used to have_____ a lot of bad dreams. (have)
7   I wonder what Joe is doing these days. He _____was living_____ in Spain when I last heard from him. (live)
8   'Where were you yesterday afternoon?' 'I _____was playing_____ volleyball.' (play)
9   'Do you do any sports?' 'Not these days, but I _____used to play_____ volleyball.' (play)
10 George looked very nice at the party. He _____was wearing_____ a very smart suit. (wear)

The future

10   What do you say to your friend in these situations? Use the words given in brackets. Use the present continuous (**I am doing**), **going to** or **will (I'll)**.

1   You have made all your holiday arrangements. Your destination is Jamaica.
FRIEND: Have you decided where to go for your holiday yet?
YOU: *I'm going to Jamaica.*   (I / go)

2   You have made an appointment with the dentist for Friday morning.
FRIEND: Shall we meet on Friday morning?
YOU: I can't on Friday. *I am going* (I / go)

3   You and some friends are planning a holiday in Britain. You have decided to hire a car, but you haven't arranged this yet.
FRIEND: How do you plan to travel round Britain? By train?
YOU: No, *we are going to hire a car* (we / hire)

4   Your friend has two young children. She wants to go out tomorrow evening. You offer to look after the children.
FRIEND: I want to go out tomorrow evening, but I haven't got a babysitter.
YOU: That's no problem. *I will look after your children* (I / look after)

5   You have already arranged to have lunch with Sue tomorrow.
FRIEND: Are you free at lunchtime tomorrow?
YOU: No, *I am having my lunch with Sue* (have lunch)

6   You are in a restaurant. You and your friend are looking at the menu. Maybe your friend has decided what to have. You ask her/him.
YOU: What *are you going to have* ? (you / have)
FRIEND: I don't know. I can't make up my mind.

7   You and a friend are reading. It's getting a bit dark and your friend is having trouble reading. You decide to turn on the light.
FRIEND: It's getting a bit dark, isn't it? It's difficult to read.
YOU: Yes. *I will turn on light on light* (I / turn on)

8   You and a friend are reading. It's getting a bit dark and you decide to turn on the light. You stand up and walk towards the light switch.
FRIEND: What are you doing?
YOU: *I am going to turn on light* (I / turn on)

11   Put the verb into the most suitable form. Use a present tense (simple or continuous), **will (I'll)** or **shall**.

Conversation 1 (*in the morning*)

JENNY: (1) *Are you doing* (you / do) anything tomorrow evening, Helen?
HELEN: No, why?
JENNY: Well, do you fancy going to the cinema? *Strangers on a Plane* is on. I want to see it, but I don't want to go alone.
HELEN: OK, (2) *I will come* (I / come) with you. What time (3) *shall we meet* (we / meet)?
JENNY: Well, the film (4) *will begins* (begin) at 8.45, so (5) *shall I meet* (I / meet) you at about 8.30 outside the cinema, OK?
HELEN: Fine. (6) *I am seeing* (I / see) Tina later this evening. (7) *Shall I ask* (I / ask) her if she wants to come too?
JENNY: Yes, do that. (8) *I'll see* (I / see) you tomorrow then. Bye.

Conversation 2 (*later the same day*)

HELEN: Jenny and I (9) *are going* (go) to the cinema tomorrow
night to see *Strangers on a Plane*. Why don't you come too?

TINA: I'd love to come. What time (10) *the film begins* (the film / begin)?

HELEN: 8.45.

TINA: (11) *will you meet* (you / meet) outside the cinema?

HELEN: Yes, at 8.30. Is that OK for you?

TINA: Yes, (12) *I will be* (I / be) there at 8.30.

12　Put the verb into the most suitable form. Sometimes there is more than one possibility.

1　*A has decided to learn a language.*

A: I've decided to try and learn a foreign language.

B: Have you? Which language (1) *are you going to learn* (you / learn)?

A: Spanish.

B: (2) *are you going to do* (you / do) a course?

A: Yes, (3) *it's starting* (it / start) next week.

B: That's great. I'm sure (4) *you will enjoy* (you / enjoy) it.

A: I hope so. But I think (5) *it will be* (it / be) quite difficult.

2　*A wants to know about B's holiday plans.*

A: I hear (1) *you are going* (you / go) on holiday soon.

B: That's right. (2) *we are going* (we / go) to Finland.

A: I hope (3) *you will have* (you / have) a nice time.

B: Thanks. (4) *I'll send* (I / send) you a postcard and (5) *I'll get*
(I / get) in touch with you when (6) *I get* (I / get) back.

3　*A invites B to a party.*

A: (1) *I am having* (I / have) a party next Saturday. Can you come?

B: On Saturday? I'm not sure. Some friends of mine (2) *are coming* (come) to
stay with me next week, but I think (3) *they will be gone* (they / go) by
Saturday. But if (4) *they are* (they / be) still here,
(5) *I won't be* (I / not / be) able to come to the party.

A: OK. Well, tell me as soon as (6) *you know* (you / know).

B: Right. (7) *I'll phone* (I / phone) you during the week.

4　*A and B are two secret agents arranging a meeting. They are talking on the phone.*

A: Well, what time (1) *shall we meet*
(we / meet)?

B: Come to the café by the station at 4 o'clock.
(2) *I'll be waiting* (I / wait) for you
when (3) *you arrive* (you / arrive).
(4) *I'll be sitting* (I / sit) by the window
and (5) *I will be wearing* (I / wear) a bright green sweater.

A: OK? (6) *will Agent 307 come* (Agent 307 / come) too?

B: No, she can't be there.

A: Oh. (7) *shall I bring* (I / bring) the documents?

B: Yes. (8) *I will explain* (I / explain) everything when
(9) *I see you* (I / see) you. And don't be late.

A: OK. (10) *I will try* (I / try) to be on time.

13 Put the verb into the correct form. Choose from the following:

present continuous (**I am doing**)	**will** (**'ll**) / **won't**
present simple (**I do**)	**will be doing**
going to (**I'm going to do**)	**shall**

1 I feel a bit hungry. I think _I' shall have_ (I / have) something to eat.

2 Why are you putting on your coat? _are you going_ (you / go) somewhere?

3 What time _shall I phone_ (I / phone) you this evening? About 7.30?

4 Look! That plane is flying towards the airport. _It going landing_ (it / land).

5 We must do something soon, before _it is_ (it / be) too late.

6 I'm sorry you've decided to leave the company. _I will miss_ (I / miss) you when _you will be going_ (you / go).

7 _Shall I give_ (I / give) you my address? If _I give_ (I / give) you my address, _you send_ (you / send) me a postcard?

8 Are you still watching that programme? What time _it will end_ (it / end)?

9 _I am going_ (I / go) to London next weekend for a wedding. My sister _is getting_ (get) married.

10 I'm not ready yet. _shall I tell_ (I / tell) you when _I am_ (I / be) ready. I promise _I won't be_ (I / not / be) very long.

11 A: Where are you going?
   B: To the hairdresser's. _I am having_ (I / have) my hair cut.

12 She was very rude to me. I refuse to speak to her again until _she apologises_ (she / apologise).

13 I wonder where _we are will be living_ (we / live) ten years from now?

14 What do you plan to do when _you are finishing finish_ (you / finish) your course at college?

Past, present and future | Units 1–25

14 Use your own ideas to complete B's sentences.

1 A: How did the accident happen?
   B: I _was going_ too fast and couldn't stop in time.

2 A: Is that a new camera?
   B: No, I _have had bought_ it a long time.

3 A: Is that a new computer?
   B: Yes, I _have bought_ it a few weeks ago.

4 A: I can't talk to you right now. You can see I'm very busy.
   B: OK. I _will be come_ back in about half an hour.

5 A: This is a nice restaurant. Do you come here often?
   B: No, it's the first time I _have ever been_ here.

6 A: Do you do any sport?
   B: No, I _used to playing_ football, but I gave it up.

7 A: I'm sorry I'm late.
   B: That's OK. I _am not waiting_ long.

8 A: When you went to the US last year, was it your first visit?
   B: No, I _had been_ there twice before.

9 A: Do you have any plans for the weekend?
   B: Yes, I _am going_ to a party on Saturday night.

10 A: Do you know what Steve's doing these days?
   B: No, I _have not met_ him for ages.

11 A: Will you still be here by the time I get back?
   B: No, I _will be out_ by then. _have left_

15   Robert is travelling in North America. He sends
an email to a friend in Winnipeg (Canada). Put
the verb into the most suitable form.

CANADA

Winnipeg — USA — Minneapolis
— Kansas City

Hi

(1) __I've just arrived__ (I / just / arrive) in Minneapolis. (2) _have been travelling_
(I / travel) for more than a month now, and (3) _I am beginning_ (I / begin) to think about
coming home. Everything (4) _I have seen_ (I / see) so far (5) _has been_ (be)
really interesting, and (6) _I met_ (I / meet) some really kind people.

(7) _I had left_ (I / leave) Kansas City a week ago. (8) _I had stayed_
(I / stay) there with Emily, the aunt of a friend from college. She was really helpful and hospitable
and although (9) _I was planning_ (I / plan) to stay only a couple of days,
(10) _I ended up_ (I / end up) staying more than a week.

(11) _I enjoyed_ (I / enjoy) the journey from Kansas City to here. (12) _I took/given_
(I / take) the Greyhound bus and (13) _met_ (meet) some really
interesting people – everybody was really friendly.

So now I'm here, and (14) _I am staying_ (I / stay) here for a few days before (15) _I continue_
(I / continue) up to Canada. I'm not sure exactly when (16) _I am getting ... own get_
(I / get) to Winnipeg – it depends what happens while (17) _I am_ (I / be) here. But
(18) _I'll let_ (I / let) you know as soon as (19) _I know_ (I / know) myself.

(20) _I am staying_ (I / stay) with a family here – they're friends of some people
I know at home. Tomorrow (21) _we are visiting_ (we / visit) some people they
know who (22) _are building_ (build) a house in the mountains. It isn't finished
yet, but (23) _it will be_ (it / be) interesting to see what it's like.

Anyway, that's all for now. (24) _I will be_ (I / be) in touch again soon.

Robert

Modal verbs (can/must/would etc.)   **Units 26–36, Appendix 4**

16   Which alternatives are correct? Sometimes only one alternative is correct, and sometimes two
of the alternatives are possible.

1   'What time will you be home tonight?'   'I'm not sure. I __A or B__ late.'
    A may be   B might be   C can be   (both A and B are correct)

2   I can't find the theatre tickets. They .... out of my pocket.
    A must have fallen   B should have fallen   C had to fall

3   Somebody ran in front of the car as I was driving. Fortunately I .... just in time.
    A could stop   B could have stopped   C managed to stop

4   We've got plenty of time. We .... yet.
    A mustn't leave   B needn't leave   C don't need to leave

5   I .... out but I didn't feel like it, so I stayed at home.
    A could go   B could have gone   C must have gone

6 I'm sorry I .... come to your party last week.
   A couldn't come   B couldn't have come   C wasn't able to come

7 'What do you think of my theory?' 'I'm not sure. You .... right.'
   A could be   B must be   C might be

8 I couldn't wait for you any longer. I .... , and so I went.
   A must go   B must have gone   C had to go

9 'Do you know where Liz is?' 'No. I suppose she .... shopping.'
   A should have gone   B may have gone   C could have gone

10 At first they didn't believe me when I told them what had happened, but in the end
   I .... them that I was telling the truth.
   A was able to convince   B managed to convince   C could convince

11 I promised I'd phone Gary this evening. I ....
   A mustn't forget   B needn't forget   C don't have to forget

12 Why did you leave without me? You .... for me.
   A must have waited   B had to wait   C should have waited

13 Lisa phoned me and suggested .... lunch together.
   A we have   B we should have   C to have

14 You look nice in that jacket, but you hardly ever wear it. .... it more often.
   A You'd better wear   B You should wear   C You ought to wear

15 Shall I buy a car? What's your advice? What .... ?
   A will you do   B would you do   C shall you do

17   Make sentences from the words in brackets.

1 Don't phone them now. (they might / have / lunch)
   They might be having lunch.

2 I ate too much. Now I feel sick. (I shouldn't / eat / so much)
   I shouldn't have eaten so much.

3 I wonder why Tom didn't phone me. (he must / forget)
   ....

4 Why did you go home so early? (you needn't / go / home so early)
   ....

5 You've signed the contract. (it / can't / change / now)
   ....

6 'What's Linda doing?' 'I'm not sure.' (she may / watch / television)
   ....

7 Laura was standing outside the cinema. (she must / wait / for somebody)
   ....

8 He was in prison at the time that the crime was committed. (he couldn't / do / it)
   ....

9 Why weren't you here earlier? (you ought / be / here earlier)
   ....

10 Why didn't you ask me to help you? (I would / help / you)
   ....

11 I'm surprised you weren't told that the road was dangerous. (you should / warn / about it)
   ....

12 Gary was in a strange mood yesterday. (he might not / feel / very well)
   ....

18 Complete B's sentences using **can/could/might/must/should/would** + the verb in brackets. In some sentences you need to use **have: must have ... / should have ...** etc. In some sentences you need the negative (**can't/couldn't** etc.).

1 A: I'm hungry.
  B: But you've just had lunch. You ....*can't be*.... hungry already. (be)
2 A: I haven't seen our neighbours for ages.
  B: No. They ...*must have gone*... away. (go)
3 A: What's the weather like? Is it raining?
  B: Not at the moment, but it .... later. (rain)
4 A: Where has Julia gone?
  B: I'm not sure. She .... to the bank. (go)
5 A: I didn't see you at Michael's party last week.
  B: No, I had to work that night, so I .... (go)
6 A: I saw you at Michael's party last week.
  B: No, you .... me. I didn't go to Michael's party. (see)
7 A: What time will we get to Sue's house?
  B: Well, it takes about one and a half hours, so if we leave at 3 o'clock, we .... there by 4.30. (get)
8 A: When was the last time you saw Bill?
  B: Years ago. I .... him if I saw him now. (recognise)
9 A: Did you hear the explosion?
  B: What explosion?
  A: There was a loud explosion about an hour ago. You .... it. (hear)
10 A: We weren't sure which way to go. In the end we turned right.
  B: You went the wrong way. You .... left. (turn)

---

if (conditional)   Units 25, 38–40

19 Put the verb into the correct form.

1 If you ....*found*.... a wallet in the street, what would you do with it? (find)
2 I must hurry. My friend will be annoyed if I ...*'m not*... on time. (not / be)
3 I didn't realise that Gary was in hospital. If I ...*had known*... he was in hospital, I would have gone to visit him. (know)
4 If the phone .... , can you answer it? (ring)
5 I can't decide what to do. What would you do if you .... in my position? (be)
6 A: What shall we do tomorrow?
  B: Well, if it .... a nice day, we can go to the beach. (be)
7 A: Let's go to the beach.
  B: No, it's too cold. If it .... warmer, I wouldn't mind going. (be)
8 A: Did you go to the beach yesterday?
  B: No, it was too cold. If it .... warmer, we might have gone. (be)
9 If you .... enough money to go anywhere in the world, where would you go? (have)
10 I'm glad we had a map. I'm sure we would have got lost if we .... one. (not / have)
11 The accident was your fault. If you .... more carefully, it wouldn't have happened. (drive)
12 A: Why do you read newspapers?
  B: Well, if I .... newspapers, I wouldn't know what was happening in the world. (not / read)

20 Complete the sentences.

1 Liz is tired all the time. She shouldn't go to bed so late.
If *Liz didn't go to bed so late, she wouldn't be tired all the time.*

2 It's rather late. I don't think Sarah will come to see us now.
I'd be surprised if Sarah ....

3 I'm sorry I disturbed you. I didn't know you were busy.
If I'd known you were busy, I ....

4 I don't want them to be upset, so I've decided not to tell them what happened.
They'd .... if ....

5 The dog attacked you, but only because you frightened it.
If ....

6 Unfortunately I didn't have an umbrella and so I got very wet in the rain.
I ....

7 Martin failed his driving test last week. He was very nervous and that's why he failed.
If he ....

21 Use your own ideas to complete the sentences.

1 I'd go out this evening if ....
2 I'd have gone out last night if ....
3 If you hadn't reminded me, ...
4 We wouldn't have been late if ....
5 If I'd been able to get tickets, ...
6 Who would you phone if .... ?
7 Cities would be nicer places if ....
8 If there was no television, ...

Passive	Units 42–45

22 Put the verb into the most suitable passive form.

1 There's somebody behind us. I think we *are being followed* (follow).

2 A mystery is something that *can't be explained* (can't / explain).

3 We didn't play football yesterday. The match .... (cancel).

4 The television .... (repair). It's working again now.

5 In the middle of the village there is a church which .... (restore)
at the moment. The work is almost finished.

6 The tower is the oldest part of the church. It .... (believe) to be
over 600 years old.

7 If I didn't do my job properly, I .... (would / sack).

8 A: I left a newspaper on the desk last night and it isn't there now.
B: It .... (might / throw) away.

9 I learnt to swim when I was very young. I .... (teach) by my
mother.

10 After .... (arrest), I was taken to the police station.

11 '.. (you / ever / arrest)?' 'No, never.'

12 Two people .... (report) to .... (injure)
in an explosion at a factory in Birmingham early this morning.

23 Put the verb into the correct form, active or passive.

1 This house is quite old. It _was built_ (build) over 100 years ago.
2 My grandfather was a builder. He _built_ (build) this house many years ago.
3 'Is your car still for sale?' 'No, I .... (sell) it.'
4 A: Is the house at the end of the street still for sale?
   B: No, it .... (sell).
5 Sometimes mistakes .... (make). It's inevitable.
6 I wouldn't leave your car unlocked. It .... (might / steal).
7 My bag has disappeared. It .... (must / steal).
8 I can't find my hat. Somebody .... (must / take) it by mistake.
9 It's a serious problem. I don't know how it .... (can / solve).
10 We didn't leave early enough. We .... (should / leave) earlier.
11 Nearly every time I travel by plane, my flight .... (delay).
12 A new bridge .... (build) across the river. Work started last year
   and the bridge .... (expect) to open next year.

24 Read these newspaper reports and put the verbs into the most suitable form.

1 **Castle Fire**

Winton Castle (1) _was damaged_ (damage) in a fire last night. The fire, which (2) .... (discover) at about 9 o'clock, spread very quickly. Nobody (3) .... (injure), but two people had to (4) .... (rescue) from an upstairs room. A number of paintings (5) .... (believe / destroy). It (6) .... (not / know) how the fire started.

2 **SHOP ROBBERY**

In Paxham yesterday a shop assistant (1) .... (force) to hand over £500 after (2) .... (threaten) by a man with a knife. The man escaped in a car which (3) .... (steal) earlier in the day. The car (4) .... (later / find) in a car park where it (5) .... (abandon) by the thief. A man (6) .... (arrest) in connection with the robbery and (7) .... (still / question) by the police.

3 **ROAD DELAYS**

Repair work started yesterday on the Paxham–Longworth road. The road (1) .... (resurface) and there will be long delays. Drivers (2) .... (ask) to use an alternative route if possible. The work (3) .... (expect) to last two weeks. Next Sunday the road (4) .... (close), and traffic (5) .... (divert).

4 **Accident**

A woman (1) .... (take) to hospital after her car collided with a lorry near Norstock yesterday. She (2) .... (allow) home later after treatment. The road (3) .... (block) for an hour after the accident, and traffic had to (4) .... (divert). A police inspector said afterwards: 'The woman was lucky. She could (5) .... (kill).'

Reported speech

25 Complete the sentences using reported speech.

1

Can I speak to Paul, please?

I'll try again later.

Paul has gone out. I don't know when he'll be back. Do you want to leave a message?

YOU

A woman phoned at lunchtime yesterday and asked _if she could speak to Paul_ . I told
Paul had gone out and _she didn't know when
he would be back_ . I asked _Did she know when Paul could be
back_ , but she said _it I wanted to try
call_ later. But she never did.

2

We have no record of any reservation in your name.

We're sorry, but the hotel is full.

RECEPTION

I went to London recently, but my visit didn't begin well. I had reserved a hotel room, but
when I got to the hotel they told _me they had no record of any reservation
in my name_ . When I asked _them that Did they had any rooms then
they said they say my_ , but _the hotel was full_ .
There was nothing I could do. I just had to look for somewhere else to stay.

3

Why are you visiting the country?

How long do you intend to stay?

Where will you be staying during your visit?

We're on holiday.

After getting off the plane, we had to queue for an hour to get through immigration. Finally
it was our turn. The immigration official asked us _why any are we were visiting the
country_ , and we told _him that we were on holiday_ .
Then he wanted to know _how long did we intend to stay_ and
where we would be staying during our visit .
He seemed satisfied with our answers, checked our passports and wished us a pleasant stay.

4

I'll phone you from the airport when I arrive.

SUE

Don't come to the airport. I'll take the bus.

A: What time is Sue arriving this afternoon?
B: About three. She said _would phoned us from the airport
when she arrived_ .
A: Aren't you going to meet her?
B: No, she said _not to come to the airport_ . She said
that she would take the bus .

5

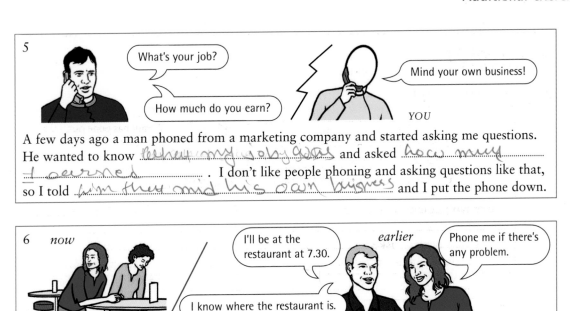

A few days ago a man phoned from a marketing company and started asking me questions. He wanted to know _whether my job was_ and asked _how much I earned_ . I don't like people phoning and asking questions like that, so I told _him they mind his own business_ and I put the phone down.

6

Louise and Sarah are in a restaurant waiting for Paul.

LOUISE: I wonder where Paul is. He said _he will be at the res. at 7:30_
SARAH: Maybe he's got lost.
LOUISE: I don't think so. He said _that he knew where the res was_
        And I told _him that phone me it there was any me_

7

JOE: Is there anything to eat?
JANE: You just said _you were not hungry_.
JOE: Well, I am now. I'd love a banana.
JANE: A banana? But you said _you didn't like bananas_
      You told _me that didn't buy some not_

-ing and infinitive   **Units 53–66**

26   Put the verb into the correct form.

1 How old were you when you learnt _to drive_ ? (drive)
2 I don't mind _walking_ home, but I'd rather _get_ a taxi. (walk, get)
3 I can't make a decision. I keep _changing_ my mind. (change)
4 He had made his decision and refused _to change_ his mind. (change)
5 Why did you change your decision? What made you _change_ your mind? (change)
6 It was a really good holiday. I really enjoyed _being_ by the sea again. (be)
7 Did I really tell you I was unhappy? I don't remember _saying_ that. (say)
8 'Remember _to phone_ Tom tomorrow.' 'OK. I won't forget.' (phone)
9 The water here is not very good. I'd avoid _drinking_ it if I were you. (drink)

10 I pretended .... interested in the conversation, but really it was very boring. (be)

11 I got up and looked out of the window .... what the weather was like. (see)

12 I have a friend who claims .... able to speak five languages. (be)

13 I like .... carefully about things before .... a decision. (think, make)

14 I had a flat in the centre of town but I didn't like .... there, so I decided .... (live, move)

15 Steve used .... a footballer. He had to stop .... because of an injury. (be, play)

16 After .... by the police, the man admitted .... the car but denied .... at 100 miles an hour. (stop, steal, drive)

17 A: How do you make this machine .... ? (work)
    A: I'm not sure. Try .... that button and see what happens. (press)

27 Make sentences from the words in brackets.

1 I can't find the tickets. (I / seem / lose / them)
   I seem to have lost them.

2 I haven't got far to go. (it / not / worth / take / a taxi)
   It's not worth taking a taxi.

3 I'm feeling a bit tired. (I / not / fancy / go / out)
   I haven't fancy to go out

4 Tim isn't very reliable. (he / tend / forget / things)

5 I've got a lot of luggage. (you / mind / help / me?)

6 There's nobody at home. (everybody / seem / go out)

7 We don't like our flat. (we / think / move)

8 The vase was very valuable. (I / afraid / touch / it)

9 Bill never carries money with him. (he / afraid / robbed)

10 I wouldn't go to see the film. (it / not / worth / see)

11 I'm very tired after that long walk. (I / not / used / walk / so far)

12 Sue is on holiday. I received a postcard from her yesterday. (she / seem / enjoy / herself)

13 Dave had lots of photographs he'd taken while on holiday. (he / insist / show / them to me)

14 I don't want to do the shopping. (I'd rather / somebody else / do / it)

28 Complete the second sentence so that the meaning is similar to the first.

1 I was surprised I passed the exam.
   I didn't expect __to pass the exam__ .
2 Did you manage to solve the problem?
   Did you succeed __in solving the problem__ ?
3 I don't read newspapers any more.
   I've given up ....
4 I'd prefer not to go out tonight.
   I'd rather ....
5 He can't walk very well.
   He has difficulty ....
6 Shall I phone you this evening?
   Do you want .... ?
7 Nobody saw me come in.
   I came in without ....
8 They said I was a cheat.
   I was accused ....
9 It will be good to see them again.
   I'm looking forward ....
10 What do you think I should do?
   What do you advise me .... ?
11 It's a pity I couldn't go out with you.
   I'd like ....
12 I'm sorry that I didn't take your advice.
   I regret ....

---

a/an and the   Units 69–78

29 Put in a/an or the where necessary. Leave the space empty if the sentence is already complete.

1 I don't usually like staying at __−__ hotels, but last summer we spent a few days at __a__ very
   nice hotel by __the__ sea.
2 __−__ tennis is my favourite sport. I play once or twice __a__ week if I can, but I'm not
   .... very good player.
3 I won't be home for __the__ dinner this evening. I'm meeting some friends after __−__ work
   and we're going to __the__ cinema.
4 __−__ unemployment is increasing at the moment and it's getting difficult for __the__ people
   to find .... work.
5 There was __an__ accident as I was going __to the__ home last night. Two people were taken to
   __the__ hospital. I think __the__ most accidents are caused by .... people driving too fast.
6 Carol is __an__ economist. She used to work in __an__ investment department of __the__
   Lloyds Bank. Now she works for __an__ American bank in __the__ United States.
7 A: What's __the__ name of __a__ hotel where you're staying?
   B: __The__ Imperial. It's in __−__ Queen Street in __the__ city centre. It's near __the__ station.
8 I have two brothers. __−__ older one is training to be __a__ pilot with __the__ British
   Airways. __The__ younger one is still at __−__ school. When he leaves __the__ school, he
   wants to go to __an__ university to study __−__ law.

---

30   Which alternatives are correct? Sometimes only one alternative is correct, and sometimes two
     alternatives are possible.

     1 I don't remember ......A..... about the accident.   (A *is correct*)
        A anything   B something   C nothing
     2 Chris and I have known .... for quite a long time.
        A us   B each other   C ourselves
     3 'How often do the buses run?'   '... twenty minutes.'
        A All   B Each   C Every
     4 I shouted for help, but .... came.
        A nobody   B no-one   C anybody
     5 Last night we went out with some friends of ....
        A us   B our   C ours
     6 It didn't take us a long time to get here. .... traffic.
        A It wasn't much   B There wasn't much   C It wasn't a lot
     7 Can I have .... milk in my coffee, please?
        A a little   B any   C some
     8 Sometimes I find it difficult to ....
        A concentrate   B concentrate me   C concentrate myself
     9 There's .... on at the cinema that I want to see, so there's no point in going.
        A something   B anything   C nothing
     10 I drink .... water every day.
        A much   B a lot of   C lots of
     11 .... in the city centre are open on Sunday.
        A Most of shops   B Most of the shops   C The most of the shops
     12 There were about twenty people in the photo. I didn't recognise .... of them.
        A any   B none   C either
     13 I've been waiting .... for Sarah to phone.
        A all morning   B the whole morning   C all the morning
     14 I can't afford to buy anything in this shop. .... so expensive.
        A All is   B Everything is   C All are

---

31   There are mistakes in some of these sentences. Correct the sentences where necessary. Write
     'OK' if the sentence is already correct.

     1 The building was total destroyed in the fire.   *totally destroyed*
     2 I didn't like the book. It was such a stupid story.   *OK*
     3 The city is very polluted. It's the more polluted place
        I've ever been to.
     4 I was disappointing that I didn't get the job. I was well-
        qualified and the interview went well.
     5 It's warm today, but there's quite a strong wind.
     6 Joe works hardly, but he doesn't get paid very much.
     7 The company's offices are in a modern large building.
     8 Dan is a very fast runner. I wish I could run as fast as him.
     9 I missed the three last days of the course because I was ill.
     10 You don't look happy. What's the matter?

11 The weather has been unusual cold for the time of the year. ....

12 The water in the pool was too dirty to swim in it. ....

13 I got impatient because we had to wait so long time. ....

14 Is this box big enough or do you need a bigger one? ....

15 This morning I got up more early than usual. ....

Conjunctions   Units 25, 38, 112–118

32   Which is correct?

1 I'll try to be on time, but don't worry if / ~~when~~ I'm late. (if is *correct*)

2 Don't throw that bag away. If / When you don't want it, I'll have it.

3 Please report to reception if / when you arrive at the hotel.

4 We've arranged to play tennis tomorrow, but we won't play if / when it's raining.

5 Jennifer is in her final year at school. She still doesn't know what she's going to do if / when she leaves.

6 What would you do if / when you lost your keys?

7 I hope I'll be able to come to the party, but I'll let you know if / unless I can't.

8 I don't want to be disturbed, so don't phone me if / unless it's something important.

9 Please sign the contract if / unless you're happy with the conditions.

10 I like travelling by ship as long as / unless the sea is not rough.

11 You might not remember the name of the hotel, so write it down if / in case you forget it.

12 It's not cold now, but take your coat with you if / in case it gets cold later.

13 Take your coat with you and then you can put it on if / in case it gets cold later.

14 They always have the television on, even if / if nobody is watching it.

15 Even / Although we played very well, we lost the match.

16 Despite / Although we've known each other a long time, we're not particularly close friends.

17 'When did you leave school?' 'As / When I was 17.'

18 I think Ann will be very pleased as / when she hears the news.

Prepositions (time)   Units 12, 119–122

33   Put in one of the following: **at   on   in   during   for   since   by   until**

1 Jack has gone away. He'll be back ...*in*... a week.

2 We're having a party .... Saturday. Can you come?

3 I've got an interview next week. It's .... 9.30 .... Tuesday morning.

4 Sue isn't usually here .... weekends. She goes away.

5 The train service is very good. The trains are nearly always .... time.

6 It was a confusing situation. Many things were happening .... the same time.

7 I couldn't decide whether or not to buy the sweater. .... the end I decided to leave it.

8 The road is busy all the time, even .... night.

9 I met a lot of nice people .... my stay in New York.

10 I saw Helen .... Friday, but I haven't seen her .... then.

11 Brian has been doing the same job .... five years.

12 Lisa's birthday is .... the end of March. I'm not sure exactly which day it is.

13 We have some friends staying with us .... the moment. They're staying .... Friday.

14 If you're interested in applying for the job, your application must be received .... Friday.

15 I'm just going out. I won't be long – I'll be back .... ten minutes.

Prepositions (position and other uses)

Units 123–128

34   Put in the missing preposition.

1 I'd love to be able to visit every country .... the world.
2 Jessica White is my favourite author. Have you read anything .... her?
3 'Is there a bank near here?' 'Yes, there's one .... the end of this road.'
4 Tim is away at the moment. He's .... holiday.
5 We live .... the country, a long way from the nearest town.
6 I've got a stain .... my jacket. I'll have to have it cleaned.
7 We went .... a party .... Linda's house on Saturday.
8 Boston is .... the east coast of the United States.
9 Look at the leaves .... that tree. They're a beautiful colour.
10 'Have you ever been .... Tokyo?' 'No, I've never been .... Japan.'
11 Mozart died .... Vienna in 1791 .... the age of 35.
12 'Are you .... this photograph?' 'Yes, that's me, ... the left.'
13 We went .... the theatre last night. We had seats .... the front row.
14 'Where's the light switch?' 'It's .... the wall .... the door.'
15 It was late when we arrived .... the hotel.
16 I couldn't decide what to eat. There was nothing .... the menu that I liked.
17 We live .... a tower block. Our flat is .... the fifteenth floor.
18 A: What did you think of the film?
   B: Some parts were a bit stupid, but .... the whole I enjoyed it.
19 'When you paid the hotel bill, did you pay cash?' 'No, I paid .... credit card.'
20 'How did you get here? .... the bus?' 'No, ... car.'
21 A: I wonder what's .... television this evening. Have you got a newspaper?
   B: Yes, the TV programmes are .... the back page.
22 Helen works for a telecommunications company. She works .... the customer services department.
23 Anna spent two years working .... London before returning .... Italy.
24 'Did you enjoy your trip .... the beach?' 'Yes, it was great.'
25 Next summer we're going .... a trip to Canada.

Noun/adjective + preposition

Units 129–131

35   Put in the missing preposition.

1 The plan has been changed, but nobody seems to know the reason .... this.
2 Don't ask me to decide. I'm not very good .... making decisions.
3 Some people say that Sue is unfriendly, but she's always very nice .... me.
4 What do you think is the best solution .... the problem?
5 There has been a big increase .... the price of land recently.
6 He lives a rather lonely life. He doesn't have much contact .... other people.
7 Paul is a keen photographer. He likes taking pictures .... people.
8 Michael got married .... a woman he met when he was studying at college.
9 He's very brave. He's not afraid .... anything.
10 I'm surprised .... the amount of traffic today. I didn't think it would be so busy.
11 Thank you for lending me the guidebook. It was full .... useful information.
12 Please come in and sit down. I'm sorry .... the mess.

Verb + preposition   Units 132–136

36 Complete each sentence with a preposition where necessary. If no preposition is necessary, leave the space empty.

1   She works quite hard. You can't accuse her _____ being lazy.
2   Who's going to look _____ your children while you're at work?
3   The problem is becoming serious. We have to discuss _____ it.
4   The problem is becoming serious. We have to do something _____ it.
5   I prefer this chair _____ the other one. It's more comfortable.
6   I must phone _____ the office to tell them I won't be at work today.
7   The river divides the city _____ two parts.
8   'What do you think _____ your new boss?' 'She's all right, I suppose.'
9   Can somebody please explain _____ me what I have to do?
10 I said hello to her, but she didn't answer _____ me.
11 'Do you like staying at hotels?' 'It depends _____ the hotel.'
12 'Have you ever been to Borla?' 'No, I've never heard _____ it. Where is it?'
13 You remind me _____ somebody I knew a long time ago. You look just like her.
14 This is wonderful news! I can't believe _____ it.
15 George is not an idealist – he believes _____ being practical.
16 What's funny? What are you laughing _____ ?
17 What have you done with all the money you had? What did you spend it _____ ?
18 If Kevin asks _____ you _____ money, don't give him any.
19 I apologised _____ Sarah _____ keeping her waiting so long.
20 Lisa was very helpful. I thanked _____ her _____ everything she'd done.

Phrasal verbs   Units 137–145

37 A says something and B replies. Which goes with which?

A		B		
1	~~I've made a mistake on this form.~~	a	Don't worry. I'll tidy it up.	1 ___d___
2	I'm too warm with my coat on.	b	No problem. I can fix it up.	2 _____
3	This jacket looks nice.	c	Kate pointed it out.	3 _____
4	My phone number is 576920.	d	~~That's OK. Just cross it out and correct it.~~	4 _____
5	This room is in a mess.			5 _____
6	What's 45 euros in dollars?	e	Yes, why don't you try it on?	6 _____
7	How did you find the mistake?	f	OK, I won't bring it up.	7 _____
8	I'm not sure whether to accept their offer or not.	g	Just a moment. I'll write it down.	8 _____
9	I need a place to stay when I'm in London.	h	Why don't you take it off then?	9 _____
10	It's a subject he doesn't like to talk about.	i	You can look it up.	10 _____
11	I don't know what this word means.	j	I think you should turn it down.	11 _____
		k	Give me a moment to work it out.	

38   Only one alternative is correct. Which is it?

1   Nobody believed Paul at first but he ......B...... to be right.   (B *is correct*)
    A came out   B turned out   C worked out   D carried out

2   Here's some good news. It will ....
    A turn you up   B put you up   C blow you up   D cheer you up

3   I was annoyed with the way the children were behaving, so I ....
    A told them up   B told them off   C told them out   D told them over

4   The club committee is .... of the president, the secretary and seven other members.
    A set up   B made up   C set out   D made out

5   You were going to apply for the job, and then you decided not to. So what .... ?
    A put you off   B put you out   C turned you off   D turned you away

6   I had no idea that he was lying to me. I was completely ....
    A taken in   B taken down   C taken off   D taken over

7   Barbara started a course at college, but she .... after six months.
    A went out   B fell out   C turned out   D dropped out

8   You can't predict everything. Often things don't .... as you expect.
    A make out   B break out   C work out   D get out

9   Why are all these people here? What's .... ?
    A going off   B getting off   C going on   D getting on

10 It's a very busy airport. There are planes .... or landing every few minutes.
    A going up   B taking off   C getting up   D driving off

11 The traffic was moving slowly because a bus had .... and was blocking the road.
    A broken down   B fallen down   C fallen over   D broken up

12 How are you .... in your new job? Are you enjoying it?
    A keeping on   B going on   C carrying on   D getting on

39   Complete the sentences. Use two words each time.

1   Keep ....*away from*.... the edge of the pool. You might fall in.
2   I didn't notice that the two pictures were different until Liz pointed it .... me.
3   I asked Dan if he had any suggestions about what we should do, but he didn't come .... anything.
4   I'm glad Sarah is coming to the party. I'm really looking .... seeing her again.
5   Things are changing all the time. It's difficult to keep .... all these changes.
6   Unfortunately I ran .... film, so I couldn't take any more photographs.
7   Don't let me interrupt you. Carry .... your work.
8   Steve was very happy in his job until he fell .... his boss. After that, it was impossible for them to work together, and Steve decided to leave.
9   I've had enough of being treated like this. I'm not going to put .... it any more.
10 I didn't enjoy the trip very much at the time, but when I look .... it now, I realise it was a good experience and I'm glad I went on it.
11 The wedding was supposed to be a secret, so how did you find .... it? Did Jenny tell you?
12 There is a very nice atmosphere in the office where I work. Everybody gets .... everybody else.

40   Complete each sentence using a phrasal verb that means the same as the words in brackets.

1 The football match had to be ....*called off*.... because of the weather. (cancelled)

2 The story Kate told wasn't true. She ....*made it up*.... . (invented it)

3 A bomb .... near the station, but no-one was injured. (exploded)

4 George finally .... nearly an hour late. (arrived)

5 Here's an application form. Can you .... and sign it, please? (complete it)

6 A number of buildings are going to be .... to make way for the new road. (demolished)

7 I'm having a few problems with my computer which need to be .... as soon as possible. (put right)

8 Be positive! You must never ....! (stop trying)

9 I was very tired and .... in front of the television. (fell asleep)

10 After eight years together, they've decided to .... (separate)

11 The noise is terrible. I can't .... any longer. (tolerate it)

12 We don't have a lot of money, but we have enough to .... (manage)

13 I'm sorry I'm late. The meeting .... later than I expected. (continued)

14 We need to make a decision today at the latest. We can't .... any longer. (delay it)

41   Complete the sentences. Use one word each time.

1 You're driving too fast. Please ....*slow*.... down.

2 It was only a small fire and I managed to .... it out with a bucket of water.

3 The house is empty at the moment, but I think the new tenants are .... in next week.

4 I've .... on weight. My clothes don't fit any more.

5 Their house is really nice now. They've .... it up really well.

6 I was talking to the woman sitting next to me on the plane, and it .... out that she works for the same company as my brother.

7 'Do you know what happened?' 'Not yet, but I'm going to .... out.'

8 There's no need to get angry. .... down!

9 If you're going on a long walk, plan your route carefully before you .... off.

10 Sarah has just phoned to say that she'll be late. She's been .... up.

11 You've written my name wrong. It's Martin, not Marin – you .... out the T.

12 Three days at £45 a day – that .... out at £135.

13 We had a really interesting discussion, but Jane didn't .... in. She just listened.

14 Jonathan is pretty fit. He .... out in the gym every day.

15 Come and see us more often. You must .... in any time you like.

16 We are still discussing the contract. There are still a couple of things to .... out.

17 My alarm clock .... off in the middle of the night and .... me up.

Study guide

This guide is to help you decide which units you need to study. The sentences in the guide are grouped together (*Present and past*, *Articles and nouns* etc.) in the same way as the units in the *Contents* (pages iii–vi).

Each sentence can be completed using one or more of the alternatives (A, B, C etc.). There are between two and five alternatives each time. IN SOME SENTENCES MORE THAN ONE ALTERNATIVE IS POSSIBLE.

If you don't know or if you are not sure which alternatives are correct, then you probably need to study the unit(s) in the list on the right. You will also find the correct sentence in this unit. (If two or three units are listed, you will find the correct sentence in the first one.)

There is a key to this study guide on page 372.

IF YOU ARE NOT SURE WHICH IS RIGHT	STUDY UNIT

Present and past

1.1   At first I didn't like my job, but _____*A*_____ to enjoy it now.   **1, 3**
  A I'm beginning   B I begin

1.2   I don't understand this sentence. What _____*B*_____ ?   **2, 49**
  A does mean this word   B does this word mean   C means this word

1.3   Robert _____*C*_____ away two or three times a year.   **2, 3, 110**
  A is going usually   B is usually going   C usually goes   D goes usually

1.4   How _____*B*_____ now? Better than before?   **4**
  A you are feeling   B do you feel   C are you feeling

1.5   It was a boring weekend. _____*C*_____ anything.   **5**
  A I didn't   B I don't do   C I didn't do

1.6   Matt _____*A*_____ while we were having dinner.   **6, 14**
  A phoned   B was phoning   C has phoned

Present perfect and past

2.1   Jim is on holiday. He _____*B*_____ to Italy.   **7**
  A is gone   B has gone   C has been

2.2   Everything is going well. We _____*C*_____ any problems so far.   **8**
  A didn't have   B don't have   C haven't had

2.3   Sarah has lost her passport again. It's the second time this _____*A*_____ .   **8**
  A has happened   B happens   C happened   D is happening

2.4   You're out of breath. _____*C*_____ ?   **9**
  A Are you running   B Have you run   C Have you been running

2.5   Where's the book I gave you? What _____*A*_____ with it?   **10**
  A have you done   B have you been doing   C are you doing

2.6   '_____*B*_____ each other for a long time?' 'Yes, since we were at school.'   **11, 10**
  A Do you know   B Have you known   C Have you been knowing

2.7   Sally has been working here _____*A*_____ .   **12**
  A for six months   B since six months   C six months ago

326

IF YOU ARE NOT SURE WHICH IS RIGHT

STUDY UNIT

2.8   It's two years .... Joe.   **12**
       A that I don't see   B that I haven't seen   C since I didn't see
       D since I last saw

2.9   It .... raining for a while, but now it's raining again.   **13**
       A stopped   B has stopped   C was stopped

2.10   My mother .... in Scotland.   **13, 15**
       A grew up   B has grown up   C had grown up

2.11   .... a lot of sweets when you were a child?   **14**
       A Have you eaten   B Had you eaten   C Did you eat

2.12   Ian .... in Scotland for ten years. Now he lives in London.   **14, 11**
       A lived   B has lived   C has been living

2.13   The man sitting next to me on the plane was very nervous. He **15**
       before.
       A hasn't flown   B didn't fly   C hadn't flown   D wasn't flying

2.14   Cathy was sitting in an armchair resting. She was tired because
       .... very hard.   **16**
       A she was working   B she's been working   C she'd been working

2.15   .... a car when you were living in London?   **17, 14**
       A Had you   B Were you having   C Have you had   D Did you have

2.16   I .... tennis a lot, but I don't play very often now.   **18**
       A was playing   B was used to play   C used to play

Future

3.1   I'm tired. .... to bed now. Goodnight.   **19**
       A I go   B I'm going

3.2   .... tomorrow, so we can go out somewhere.   **19, 21**
       A I'm not working   B I don't work   C I won't work

3.3   That bag looks heavy. .... you with it.   **21**
       A I'm helping   B I help   C I'll help

3.4   I think the weather .... be nice this afternoon.   **23, 22**
       A will   B shall   C is going to

3.5   'Ann is in hospital.' 'Yes, I know. .... her this evening.'   **23, 20**
       A I visit   B I'm going to visit   C I'll visit

3.6   We're late. The film .... by the time we get to the cinema.   **24**
       A will already start   B will be already started   C will already have started

3.7   Don't worry .... late tonight.   **25**
       A if I'm   B when I'm   C when I'll be   D if I'll be

IF YOU ARE NOT SURE WHICH IS RIGHT

Modals

4.1 The fire spread through the building very quickly, but fortunately everybody ....

A was able to escape   B managed to escape   C could escape

26

4.2 I'm so tired I .... for a week.
A can sleep   B could sleep   B could have slept

27

4.3 The story .... be true, but I don't think it is.
A might   B can   C could   D may

27, 29

4.4 Why did you stay at a hotel when you were in Paris? You .... with Julia.
A can stay   B could stay   C could have stayed

27

4.5 'I've lost one of my gloves.' 'You .... it somewhere.'
A must drop   B must have dropped   C must be dropping
D must have been dropping

28

4.6 'I was surprised that Kate wasn't at the meeting yesterday.' 'She .... about it.'
A might not know   B may not know   C might not have known
D may not have known

29

4.7 What was the problem? Why .... leave early?
A had you to   B did you have to   C must you   D you had to

31

4.8 We've got plenty of time. We .... hurry.
A don't need to   B mustn't   C needn't

32

4.9 You missed a great party last night. You .... Why didn't you?
A must have come   B should have come   C ought to have come
D had to come

33

4.10 Jane .... a car with the money I'd won in the lottery.
A suggested that I buy   B suggested that I should buy
C suggested me to buy   D suggested that I bought

34

4.11 You're always at home. You .... out more often.
A should go   B had better go   C had better to go

35

4.12 It's late. It's time .... home.
A we go   B we must go   C we should go   D we went   E to go

35

4.13 .... a bit longer, but I really have to go now.
A I'd stay   B I'll stay   C I can stay   D I'd have stayed

36

If and wish

5.1 I'm not tired enough to go to bed. If I .... to bed now, I wouldn't sleep.
A go   B went   C had gone   D would go

38

5.2 If I were rich, ... a yacht.
A I'll have   B I can have   C I'd have   D I had

39

5.3 I wish I .... have to work tomorrow, but unfortunately I do.
A don't   B didn't   C wouldn't   D won't

39, 41

IF YOU ARE NOT SURE WHICH IS RIGHT

5.4　The view was wonderful. If .... a camera with me,
I would have taken some photographs.
A I had　　B I would have　　C I would have had　　D I'd had

40

5.5　The weather is horrible. I wish it .... raining.
A would stop　　B stopped　　C stops　　D will stop

41

Passive

6.1　We ....C............... by a loud noise during the night.
A woke up　　B are woken up　　C were woken up　　D were waking up

42

6.2　A new supermarket is going to ....B........... next year.
A build　　B be built　　C be building　　D building

43

6.3　There's somebody walking behind us. I think ......B.....D..... .
A we are following　　B we are being following　　C we are followed
D we are being followed

43

6.4　'Where ....A............ ?' 'In London.'
A were you born　　B are you born　　C have you been born
D did you born

44

6.5　There was a fight at the party, but nobody .....A..B......... .
A was hurt　　B got hurt　　C hurt

44

6.6　Jane .......A....C..... to phone me last night, but she didn't.
A supposed　　B is supposed　　C was supposed

45

6.7　Where ....D........... ? Which hairdresser did you go to?
A did you cut your hair　　　　B have you cut your hair
C did you have cut your hair　　D did you have your hair cut

46

Reported speech

7.1　Paul left the room suddenly. He said he ....A........ to go.
A had　　B has　　C have

48, 47

7.2　Hello, Joe. I didn't expect to see you today. Sonia said you
.........B......... in hospital.
A are　　B were　　C was　　D should be

48, 47

7.3　Ann ....A.......... and left.
A said goodbye to me　　B said me goodbye　　C told me goodbye

48

Questions and auxiliary verbs

8.1　'What time .... ?' 'At 8.30.'
A begins the film　　B does begin the film　　C does the film begin

49

8.2　'Do you know where .... ?' 'No, he didn't say.'
A Tom has gone　　B has Tom gone　　C has gone Tom

50

8.3　The police officer stopped us and asked us where ....
A were we going　　B are we going　　C we are going　　D we were going

50

IF YOU ARE NOT SURE WHICH IS RIGHT

8.4	'Do you think it will rain?' '_____ '	51
	A I hope not. B I don't hope. C I don't hope so.	
8.5	'You don't know where Karen is, _____ ?' 'Sorry, I have no idea.'	52
	A don't you B do you C is she D are you	

-ing and the infinitive

9.1	You can't stop me _____ what I want.	53
	A doing B do B to do C that I do	
9.2	I must go now. I promised _____ late.	54, 36
	A not being B not to be C to not be D I wouldn't be	
9.3	Do you want _____ with you or do you want to go alone?	55
	A me coming B me to come C that I come D that I will come	
9.4	I know I locked the door. I clearly remember _____ it.	56
	A locking B to lock C to have locked	
9.5	She tried to be serious, but she couldn't help _____ .	57
	A laughing B to laugh C that she laughed D laugh	
9.6	Paul lives in Berlin now. He likes _____ there.	58
	A living B to live	
9.7	It's not my favourite job, but I like _____ the kitchen as often as possible.	58
	A cleaning B clean C to clean D that I clean	
9.8	I'm tired. I'd rather _____ out this evening, if you don't mind.	59
	A not going B not to go C don't go D not go	
9.9	'Shall I stay here?' 'I'd rather _____ with us.'	59
	A you come B you to come C you came D you would come	
9.10	Are you looking forward _____ on holiday?	60, 62
	A going B to go C to going D that you go	
9.11	When Lisa came to Britain, she had to get used _____ on the left.	61
	A driving B to driving C to drive	
9.12	I'm thinking _____ a house. Do you think that's a good idea?	62, 66
	A to buy B of to buy C of buying	
9.13	I had no _____ a place to live. In fact it was surprisingly easy.	63
	A difficulty to find B difficulty finding C trouble to find	
	D trouble finding	
9.14	A friend of mine phoned _____ me to a party.	64
	A for invite B to invite C for inviting D for to invite	
9.15	Jim doesn't speak very clearly. _____	65
	A It is difficult to understand him. B He is difficult to understand.	
	C He is difficult to understand him.	

IF YOU ARE NOT SURE WHICH IS RIGHT

9.16   The path was icy, so we walked very carefully. We were afraid   66
     A of falling   **B** from falling   **C** to fall   **D** to falling

9.17   I didn't hear you .... in. You must have been very quiet.   67
     A come   **B** to come   **C** came

9.18   .... a hotel, we looked for somewhere to have dinner.   68
     A Finding   **B** After finding   **C** Having found   **D** We found

Articles and nouns

10.1   It wasn't your fault. It was   69
     A accident   **B** an accident   **C** some accident

10.2   Where are you going to put all your .... ?   70
     A furniture   **B** furnitures

10.3   'Where are you going?' 'I'm going to buy ....'   70
     A a bread   **B** some bread   **C** a loaf of bread

10.4   Sandra is .... She works at a large hospital.   71, 72
     A nurse   **B** a nurse   **C** the nurse

10.5   Helen works six days .... week.   72
     A in   **B** for   **C** a   **D** the

10.6   There are millions of stars in   73
     A space   **B** a space   **C** the space

10.7   Every day .... begins at 9 and finishes at 3.   74
     A school   **B** a school   **C** the school

10.8   .... a problem in most big cities.   75
     A Crime is   **B** The crime is   **C** The crimes are

10.9   When .... invented?   76
     A was telephone   **B** were telephones   **C** were the telephones
     D was the telephone

10.10   Have you been to .... ?   77
     A Canada or United States   **B** the Canada or the United States
     C Canada or the United States   **D** the Canada or United States

10.11   On our first day in Moscow, we visited   78
     A Kremlin   **B** a Kremlin   **C** the Kremlin

10.12   What time .... on television?   79, 70
     A is the news   **B** are the news   **C** is news   **D** is the new

10.13   It took us quite a long time to get here. It was .... journey.   80
     A three hour   **B** a three-hours   **C** a three-hour

10.14   This isn't my book. It's   81
     A my sister   **B** my sister's   **C** from my sister   **D** of my sister
     E of my sister's

IF YOU ARE NOT SURE WHICH IS RIGHT

Pronouns and determiners

11.1   What time shall we .... tomorrow?
       A meet   **B** meet us   **C** meet ourselves   82

11.2   I'm going to a wedding on Saturday. .... is getting married.
       A A friend of me   **B** A friend of mine   **C** One my friends   83

11.3   They live on a busy road. .... a lot of noise from the traffic.
       A It must be   **B** It must have   **C** There must have   **D** There must be   84

11.4   He's lazy. He never does .... work.
       A some   **B** any   **C** no   85

11.5   'What would you like to eat?' 'I don't mind. ....
       – whatever you have.'   85
       A Something   **B** Anything   **C** Nothing

11.6   We couldn't buy anything because .... of the shops were open.
       A all   **B** no-one   **C** none   **D** nothing   86

11.7   We went shopping and spent .... money.
       A a lot of   **B** much   **C** lots of   **D** many   87

11.8   .... don't visit this part of the town.
       A The most tourists   **B** Most of tourists   **C** Most tourists   88

11.9   I asked two people the way to the station, but .... of them   89
       could help me.
       A none   **B** either   **C** both   **D** neither

11.10 .... enjoyed the party. It was great.
       A Everybody   **B** All   **C** All of us   **D** Everybody of us   90

11.11 The bus service is excellent. There's a bus .... ten minutes.   90, 91
       A each   **B** every   **C** all

Relative clauses

12.1   I don't like stories .... have unhappy endings.
       A that   **B** they   **C** which   **D** who   92

12.2   I didn't believe them at first, but in fact everything .... was true.   93
       A they said   **B** that they said   **C** what they said

12.3   What's the name of the man .... ?   94
       A you borrowed his car   **B** which car you borrowed
       C whose car you borrowed   **D** his car you borrowed

12.4   Colin told me about his new job, ... very much.   95
       A that he's enjoying   **B** which he's enjoying   **C** he's enjoying
       D he's enjoying it

12.5   Sarah couldn't meet us, ... was a pity.   96
       A that   **B** it   **C** what   **D** which

12.6   George showed me some pictures .... by his father.   97, 92
       A painting   **B** painted   **C** that were painted   **D** they were painted

IF YOU ARE NOT SURE WHICH IS RIGHT

Adjectives and adverbs

13.1   Jane doesn't enjoy her job any more. She's .... because every day she does exactly the same thing.
A boring   B bored

98

13.2   Lisa was carrying a .... bag.
A black small plastic   B small and black plastic   C small black plastic
D plastic small black

99

13.3   Maria's English is excellent. She speaks ....
A perfectly English   B English perfectly   C perfect English
D English perfect

100

13.4   He .... to find a job, but he had no luck.
A tried hard   B tried hardly   C hardly tried

101

13.5   I haven't seen her for .... , I've forgotten what she looks like.
A so long   B so long time   C a such long time   D such a long time

102

13.6   We haven't got .... on holiday at the moment.
A money enough to go   B enough money to go
C money enough for going   D enough money for going

103

13.7   Sally is doing OK at the moment. She has ....
A a quite good job   B quite a good job   C a pretty good job

104

13.8   The exam was fairly easy – .... I expected.
A more easy that   B more easy than   C easier than   D easier as

105

13.9   The more electricity you use, ...
A your bill will be higher   B will be higher your bill
C the higher your bill will be   D higher your bill will be

106

13.10   Patrick is a fast runner. I can't run as fast as ....
A he   B him   C he can

107

13.11   The film was really boring. It was .... I've ever seen.
A most boring film   B the more boring film   C the film more boring
D the most boring film

108

13.12   Ben likes walking. ....
A Every morning he walks to work.   B He walks to work every morning.
C He walks every morning to work.   D He every morning walks to work.

109

13.13   Joe never phones me. ....
A Always I have to phone him.   B I always have to phone him.
C I have always to phone him.   D I have to phone always him.

110

13.14   Lucy .... She left last month.
A still doesn't work here   B doesn't still work here
C no more works here   D doesn't work here any more.

111

13.15   .... she can't drive, she has bought a car.
A Even   B Even when   C Even if   D Even though

112, 113

IF YOU ARE NOT SURE WHICH IS RIGHT

Conjunctions and prepositions

14.1 I couldn't sleep .... very tired.
A although I was   B despite I was   C despite of being   D in spite of being
113

14.2 You should insure your bike .... stolen.
A in case it will be   B if it will be   C in case it is   D if it is
114

14.3 The club is for members only. You .... you're a member.
A can't go in if   B can go in only if   C can't go in unless
D can go in unless
115

14.4 Yesterday we watched television all evening .... we didn't have anything better to do.
A when   B as   C while   D since
116

14.5 'What's that noise?' 'It sounds .... a baby crying.'
A as   B like   C as if   D as though
117, 118

14.6 They are very kind to me. They treat me .... their own son.
A like I'm   B as if I'm   C as if I was   D as if I were
118

14.7 I'll be in London next week. I hope to see Tom .... there.
A while I'll be   B while I'm   C during my visit   D during I'm
119

14.8 David is away at the moment. I don't know exactly when he's coming back, but I'm sure he'll be back .... Monday.
A by   B until
120

Prepositions

15.1 Goodbye! I'll see you ....
A at Friday morning   B on Friday morning   C in Friday morning
D Friday morning
121

15.2 I'm going away .... the end of January.
A at   B on   C in
122

15.3 When we were in Italy, we spent a few days .... Venice.
A at   B to   C in
123, 125

15.4 Our flat is .... the second floor of the building.
A at   B on   C in   D to
124

15.5 I saw Steve .... a concert on Saturday.
A at   B on   C in   D to
125

15.6 When did they .... the hotel?
A arrive to   B arrive at   C arrive in   D get to   E get in
126

15.7 I'm going .... holiday next week. I'll be away for two weeks.
A at   B on   C in   D for
127

15.8 We travelled .... 6.45 train, which arrived at 8.30.
A in the   B on the   C by the   D by
128

15.9 'Have you read anything .... Ernest Hemingway?' 'No, what sort of books did he write?'
A of   B from   C by
128

IF YOU ARE NOT SURE WHICH IS RIGHT

15.10   The accident was my fault, so I had to pay for the damage .... the other car.
     A of   **B** for   **C** to   **D** on   **E** at   129

15.11   I like them very much. They have always been very nice .... me.
     A of   **B** for   **C** to   **D** with   130

15.12   I'm not very good .... repairing things.
     A at   **B** for   **C** in   **D** about   131

15.13   I don't understand this sentence. Can you .... ?
     A explain to me this word   **B** explain me this word
     C explain this word to me   132

15.14   If you're worried about the problem, you should do something .... it.
     A for   **B** about   **C** against   **D** with   133

15.15   'Who is Tom Hart?' 'I have no idea. I've never heard .... him.'
     A about   **B** from   **C** after   **D** of   134

15.16   'What time will you be home?' 'I don't know. It depends .... the traffic.'
     A of   **B** for   **C** from   **D** on   135

15.17   I prefer tea .... coffee.
     A to   **B** than   **C** against   **D** over   136, 59

Phrasal verbs

16.1   These shoes are uncomfortable. I'm going to ....
     A take off   **B** take them off   **C** take off them   137

16.2   We're playing a game. Why don't you .... ?
     A join in   **B** come in   **C** get in   **D** break in   138

16.3   Nobody believed Paul at first, but he .... to be right.
     A worked out   **B** came out   **C** found out   **D** turned out   139

16.4   We can't .... making a decision. We have to decide now.
     A put away   **B** put over   **C** put off   **D** put out   140

16.5   'Have you finished painting the kitchen?' 'Nearly. I'll .... tomorrow.'
     A finish it up   **B** finish it over   **C** finish it off   141

16.6   You can always rely on Pete. He'll never ....
     A put you up   **B** let you down   **C** take you over   **D** see you off   142

16.7   Children under 16 .... half the population of the city.
     A make up   **B** put up   **C** take up   **D** bring up   143

16.8   I'm surprised to hear that Sue and Paul have .... They seemed very happy together when I last saw them.
     A broken up   **B** ended up   **C** finished up   **D** split up   144

16.9   I parked in a no-parking zone, but I .... it.
     A came up with   **B** got away with   **C** made off with   **D** got on with   145

Key to Exercises

In some of the exercises you have to use your own ideas to write sentences. Example answers are given in the Key. If possible, check your answers with somebody who speaks English well.

UNIT 1

1.1
2 'm looking / am looking
3 's getting / is getting
4 're staying / are staying
5 is losing
6 's starting / is starting
7 're making / are making ... 'm trying / am trying
8 's happening / is happening

1.2
3 'm not listening / am not listening
4 's having / is having
5 'm not eating / am not eating
6 's learning / is learning
7 aren't speaking / 're not speaking / are not speaking
8 'm getting / am getting
9 isn't working / 's not working / is not working

1.3
1 What's / What is he studying Is he enjoying
2 are you getting on things are getting he isn't enjoying / he's not enjoying he's beginning / he is beginning

1.4
2 is changing
3 's getting / is getting
4 is rising
5 is beginning

UNIT 2

2.1
2 drink
3 opens
4 causes
5 live
6 take
7 connects

2.2
2 do the banks close
3 don't use
4 does Martin come
5 do you do
6 takes ... does it take
7 does this word mean
8 doesn't do

2.3
3 rises
4 make
5 don't eat

6 doesn't believe
7 translates
8 don't tell
9 flows

2.4
2 Does your sister play tennis?
3 Which newspaper do you read?
4 What does your brother do?
5 How often do you go to the cinema?
6 Where do your grandparents live?

2.5
2 I promise
3 I insist
4 I apologise
5 I recommend

UNIT 3

3.1
3 is trying
4 are they talking
5 OK
6 It's getting / It is getting
7 OK
8 I'm coming / I am coming
9 are you getting
10 He always gets
11 OK

3.2
3 's waiting / is waiting
4 Are you listening
5 Do you listen
6 flows
7 's flowing / is flowing
8 grow ... aren't growing / 're not growing / are not growing
9 's improving / is improving
10 's staying / is staying ... stays
11 'm starting / am starting
12 'm learning / am learning ... 's teaching / is teaching
13 finish ... 'm working / am working
14 live ... do your parents live
15 's looking / is looking ... 's staying / is staying
16 does your brother do ... isn't working / 's not working / is not working
17 enjoy ... 'm not enjoying / am not enjoying

3.3
2 It's always breaking down.
3 I'm always making the same mistake. / ... that mistake.

4 You're always forgetting your glasses.

UNIT 4

4.1
2 Do you believe
3 OK
4 It tastes
5 I think

4.2
2 What are you doing? I'm thinking.
3 Who does this umbrella belong to?
4 The dinner smells good.
5 Is anybody sitting there?
6 These gloves don't fit me.

4.3
2 'm using / am using
3 need
4 does he want
5 is he looking
6 believes
7 don't remember / do not remember or can't remember
8 'm thinking / am thinking
9 think ... don't use
10 consists

4.4
2 's being / is being
3 's / is
4 are you being
5 Is he

UNIT 5

5.1
2 had
3 She walked to work
4 It took her (about) half an hour
5 She started work
6 She didn't have (any) lunch. / ... eat (any) lunch.
7 She finished work
8 She was tired when she got home.
9 She cooked
10 She didn't go
11 She went to bed
12 She slept

5.2
2 taught
3 sold
4 fell ... hurt
5 threw ... caught
6 spent ... bought ... cost

5.3

2 did you travel / did you go
3 did it take (you) / were you there
4 did you stay
5 Was the weather good/nice? *or* Did you have good/nice weather?
6 Did you go to / Did you see / Did you visit

5.4

3 didn't disturb
4 left
5 didn't sleep
6 flew
7 didn't cost
8 didn't have
9 were

UNIT 6

6.1

Example answers:
3 I was working.
4 I was in bed asleep.
5 I was getting ready to go out.
6 I was watching TV at home.

6.2

Example answers:
2 was having a shower
3 were waiting for the bus
4 was reading the paper
5 was watching it

6.3

1 didn't see ... was looking
2 met ... were going ... was going ... had ... were waiting / waited
3 was cycling ... stepped ... was going ... managed ... didn't hit

6.4

2 were you doing
3 Did you go
4 were you driving ... happened
5 took ... wasn't looking
6 didn't know
7 saw ... was trying
8 was walking ... heard ... was following ... started
9 wanted
10 dropped ... was doing ... didn't break

UNIT 7

7.1

2 She's broken her leg. / She has broken ...
3 The bus fare has gone up.
4 Her English has improved.
5 He's grown a beard. / He has grown ...
6 The letter has arrived.
7 The temperature has fallen.

7.2

2 Yes, I've just seen her. / Yes, I have just seen her.
3 He's already left. / He has already left.
4 I haven't read it yet.
5 No, she's already seen the film. / No, she has already seen ...
6 Yes, they've just arrived. / Yes, they have just arrived.
7 We haven't told him yet.

7.3

2 he's just gone out / he has just gone out
3 I haven't finished yet.
4 I've already done it. / I have already done it.
5 Have you found a place to live yet?
6 I haven't decided yet.
7 she's just come back / she has just come back

7.4

2 been
3 gone
4 gone
5 been

UNIT 8

8.1

2 Have you ever been to California?
3 Have you ever run (in) a marathon?
4 Have you ever spoken to a famous person?
5 What's the most beautiful place you've ever visited?

8.2

2 haven't seen
3 haven't eaten
4 I haven't played (it)
5 I've had / I have had
6 I haven't read
7 I've never been / I haven't been
8 's been / has been
9 I've never tried / I haven't tried *or* I've never eaten / I haven't eaten
10 it's happened / it has happened *or* that's happened / that has happened
11 I've never seen / I haven't seen

8.3

2 haven't read one / haven't read a newspaper
3 it's made a loss / it has made a loss / it hasn't made a profit
4 she hasn't worked hard this term
5 it hasn't snowed (much) this winter

6 haven't won many/any games this season

8.4

2 Have you played tennis before?
No, this is the first time I've played tennis.
3 Have you ridden a horse before? / Have you been on a horse before?
No, this is the first time I've ridden a horse. / ... I've been on a horse.
4 Have you been to London before?
No, this is the first time I've been to London.

UNIT 9

9.1

2 's been watching television / has been watching television
3 've been playing tennis / have been playing tennis
4 's been running / has been running

9.2

2 Have you been waiting long?
3 What have you been doing?
4 How long have you been working there?
5 How long have you been selling computers?

9.3

2 've been waiting / have been waiting
3 've been learning Spanish / have been learning Spanish
4 She's been working there / She has been working there
5 They've been going there / They have been going there

9.4

2 I've been looking / I have been looking
3 are you looking
4 She's been teaching / She has been teaching
5 I've been thinking / I have been thinking
6 he's working / he is working
7 she's been working / she has been working

UNIT 10

10.1

2 She's been travelling for three months. / She has been travelling ...
She's visited six countries so far. / She has visited ...

3 He's won the national championships four times. / He has won …
  He's been playing tennis since he was ten. / He has been playing …
4 They've made five films since they left college. / They have made …
  They've been making films since they left college. / They have been making …

10.2

2 Have you been waiting long?
3 Have you caught any fish?
4 How many people have you invited?
5 How long have you been teaching?
6 How many books have you written?
  How long have you been writing books?
7 How long have you been saving?
  How much money have you saved?

10.3

2 Somebody's broken / Somebody has broken
3 Have you been working
4 Have you ever worked
5 has she gone
6 He's appeared / He has appeared
7 I haven't been waiting
8 it's stopped / it has stopped
9 I've lost / I have lost … Have you seen
10 I've been reading / I have been reading … I haven't finished
11 I've read / I have read

UNIT 11

11.1

3 have been married
4 *OK*
5 It's been raining / It has been raining
6 have you been living
7 has been working
8 *OK*
9 I haven't drunk
10 have you had

11.2

2 How long have you been teaching English? / How long have you taught …
3 How long have you known Caroline?
4 How long has your brother been in Australia?

5 How long have you had that jacket?
6 How long has Joe been working at the airport? / How long has Joe worked …
7 How long have you been learning to drive?
8 Have you always lived in Chicago?

11.3

3 's been / has been
4 've been waiting / have been waiting
5 've known / have known
6 haven't played
7 's been watching / has been watching
8 haven't watched
9 've had / have had
10 hasn't been
11 've been feeling / have been feeling *or* 've felt / have felt
12 's lived / has lived *or* 's been living / has been living
13 haven't been
14 've always wanted / have always wanted

UNIT 12

12.1

2 since
3 for
4 for
5 since
6 for
7 since
8 since
9 for

12.2

2 How long has Kate been learning Japanese?
  When did Kate start learning Japanese?
3 How long have you known Simon?
  When did you first meet Simon? / When did you and Simon first meet?
4 How long have Rebecca and David been married?
  When did Rebecca and David get married? / When did Rebecca and David marry?

12.3

3 He has been ill since Sunday.
4 He has been ill for a few days.
5 She got married a year ago.
6 I've had a headache since I woke up.
7 She went to Italy three weeks ago.
8 I've been working in a hotel for six months. / I've worked in a hotel for six months.

12.4

2 No, I haven't seen Sarah/her for about a month.
3 No, I haven't been to the cinema for a long time.
4 No, I haven't eaten in a restaurant for ages. / No, I haven't been to a restaurant for ages.
6 No, it's about a month since I (last) saw Sarah/her. / No, it's been about a month since …
7 No, it's a long time since I (last) went to the cinema. / No, it's been a long time since …
8 No, it's ages since I (last) ate in a restaurant. / No, it's been ages since … *or* … since I went to a restaurant.

UNIT 13

13.1

2 has gone
3 forgot
4 went
5 had
6 has broken

13.2

3 've forgotten / have forgotten
4 arrested
5 's improved / has improved
6 've finished / have finished
7 applied
8 was
9 's been / has been
10 broke *or* 's broken / has broken … did (that) happen … fell

13.3

3 did Shakespeare write
4 *OK*
5 *OK*
6 The Chinese invented
7 were you born
8 *OK*
9 Albert Einstein was … who developed

UNIT 14

14.1

3 *OK*
4 I bought
5 Where were you
6 Lucy left school
7 *OK*
8 *OK*
9 *OK*
10 When was this book published?

14.2

2 The weather has been cold recently.
3 It was cold last week.

4 I didn't read a newspaper yesterday.
5 I haven't read a newspaper today.
6 Emily has earned a lot of money this year.
7 She didn't earn so much last year.
8 Have you had a holiday recently?

14.3
2 got ... was ... went
3 Have you finished or Did you finish
4 wasn't / was not
5 worked
6 's lived / has lived
7 Did you go ... was ... was
8 died ... never met
9 've never met / have never met
10 's gone / has gone or went ... did he go
11 have you lived / have you been living ... did you live ... did you live

14.4
Example answers:
2 I haven't bought anything today.
3 I didn't watch TV yesterday.
4 I went out with some friends yesterday evening.
5 I haven't been to the cinema recently.
6 I've read a lot of books recently.

UNIT 15

15.1
2 It had changed a lot.
3 She'd arranged to do something else. / She had arranged ...
4 The film had already begun.
5 I hadn't seen him for five years.
6 She'd just had breakfast. / She had just had ...

15.2
2 I'd never seen her before. / I had never seen ...
3 He'd never played (tennis) before. / He had never played ...
4 We'd never been there before. / We had never been ...

15.3
1 called the police
2 there was ... had gone
3 He'd just come back from / He had just come back from
He looked

4 got a phone call
was
'd sent her / had sent her
'd never replied to them / had never replied to them

15.4
2 went
3 had gone
4 broke
5 saw ... had broken ... stopped

UNIT 16

16.1
2 They'd been playing football. / They had been playing ...
3 I'd been looking forward to it. / I had been looking forward ...
4 She'd been dreaming. / She had been dreaming.
5 He'd been watching a film. / He had been watching ...

16.2
2 I'd been waiting for 20 minutes when I (suddenly) realised that I was in the wrong restaurant. or ... that I had come to the wrong restaurant.
3 At the time the factory closed down, Sarah had been working there for five years.
4 The orchestra had been playing for about ten minutes when a man in the audience started shouting.
5 *Example answer:*
I'd been walking along the road for about ten minutes when a car suddenly stopped just behind me.

16.3
3 was walking
4 'd been running / had been running
5 were eating
6 'd been eating / had been eating
7 was looking
8 was waiting ... 'd been waiting / had been waiting
9 'd had / had had
10 'd been travelling / had been travelling

UNIT 17

17.1
3 I haven't got a ladder. / I don't have a ladder.
4 We didn't have enough time.
5 He didn't have a map.
6 She hasn't got any money. /

She doesn't have any money.
7 I haven't got enough energy. / I don't have enough energy.
8 They didn't have a camera.

17.2
2 Have you got / Do you have
3 Did you have
4 Have you got / Do you have
5 Have you got / Do you have
6 did you have
7 Did you have

17.3
Example answers:
2 I haven't got a bike (now).
I had a bike (ten years ago).
3 I've got a mobile phone (now).
I didn't have a mobile phone (ten years ago).
4 I haven't got a dog (now).
I didn't have a dog (ten years ago).
5 I've got a guitar (now).
I had a guitar (ten years ago).
6 I haven't got long hair (now).
I didn't have long hair (ten years ago).
7 I've got a driving licence (now).
I didn't have a driving licence (ten years ago).

17.4
2 has a break
3 had a party
4 have a look
5 's having / is having a nice time
6 had a chat
7 Did you have difficulty
8 had a baby
9 was having a shower
10 Did you have a good flight?

UNIT 18

18.1
2 used to have/ride
3 used to live
4 used to eat/like/love
5 used to be
6 used to take
7 used to be
8 did you use to go

18.2
3–6
He used to go to bed early.
He didn't use to go out in the evening.
He used to run three miles every morning.
He didn't use to spend much money. / ... a lot of money.

18.3

2–10

She used to have lots of friends, but she doesn't know many people these days.

She used to be very lazy, but she works very hard these days.

She didn't use to like cheese, but she eats lots of cheese now.

She used to be a hotel receptionist, but she works in a bookshop now.

She used to play the piano, but she hasn't played the piano for years.

She never used to read newspapers, but she reads a newspaper every day now.

She didn't use to drink tea, but she likes it now.

She used to have a dog, but it died two years ago.

She used to go to a lot of parties, but she hasn't been to a party for ages.

UNIT 19

19.1

2 How long are you going for?
3 When are you leaving?
4 Are you going alone?
5 Are you travelling by car?
6 Where are you staying?

19.2

2 I'm working late. / I'm working till 9 o'clock.
3 I'm going to the theatre.
4 I'm meeting Julia.

19.3

Example answers:

2 I'm working tomorrow morning.
3 I'm not doing anything tomorrow evening.
4 I'm playing football next Sunday.
5 I'm going to a party this evening.

19.4

3 're having / are having
4 finishes
5 'm not going / am not going … 'm staying / am staying
6 Are you doing
7 're going / are going … starts
8 'm leaving / am leaving
9 're meeting / are meeting
10 does this train get
11 'm going / am going … Are you coming
12 does it end
13 'm not using / am not using

14 's coming / is coming … 's travelling / is travelling … arrives

UNIT 20

20.1

2 What are you going to wear?
3 Where are you going to put it?
4 Who are you going to invite?

20.2

2 I'm going to take it back.
3 I'm not going to accept it.
4 I'm going to phone her tonight.
5 I'm going to complain.

20.3

2 He's going to be late.
3 The boat is going to sink.
4 They're going to run out of petrol.

20.4

2 was going to buy
3 were going to play
4 was going to phone
5 was going to give up
6 were going to have

UNIT 21

21.1

2 I'll turn / I'll switch / I'll put
3 I'll go
4 I'll do
5 I'll show / I'll teach
6 I'll have
7 I'll send
8 I'll give / I'll bring
9 I'll stay / I'll wait

21.2

2 I'll go to bed.
3 I think I'll walk.
4 I'll play tennis (today).
5 I don't think I'll go swimming.

21.3

3 I'll meet
4 I'll lend
5 I'm having
6 I won't forget
7 does your train leave
8 won't tell
9 Are you doing
10 Will you come

21.4

2 Shall I buy it?
3 What shall I give/buy/get Helen (for her birthday)?
4 Where shall we go (on holiday)?
5 Shall we go by car or (shall we) walk? / … or (shall we go) on foot?
6 What time shall I phone (you)?

UNIT 22

22.1

2 I'm going
3 will get
4 is coming
5 we're going
6 It won't hurt

22.2

2 will look
3 'll like / will like
4 'll get / will get
5 will live
6 'll meet / will meet
7 'll come / will come
8 will be

22.3

2 won't
3 'll / will
4 won't
5 'll / will
6 won't

22.4

Example answers:

2 I'll be in bed.
3 I'll be at work.
4 I'll probably be at home.
5 I don't know where I'll be this time next year.

22.5

2 Do you think it will rain?
3 When do you think it will end?
4 How much do you think it will cost?
5 Do you think they'll get married? / … they will get married?
6 What time do you think you'll be back? / … you will be back?
7 What do you think will happen?

UNIT 23

23.1

2 I'll lend
3 I'll get
4 I'm going to wash
5 are you going to paint
6 I'm going to buy
7 I'll show
8 I'll have
9 I'll do
10 it's going to fall
11 He's going to have … he's going to do

23.2

2 I'm going to take … I'll join
3 you'll find
4 I'm not going to apply
5 You'll wake
6 I'll take … we'll leave … Liz is going to take

UNIT 24

24.1
2 b *is true*
3 a *and* c *are true*
4 b *and* d *are true*
5 c *and* d *are true*
6 c *is true*

24.2
2 We'll have finished
3 we'll be playing
4 I'll be working
5 the meeting will have ended
6 he'll have spent
7 you'll still be doing
8 she'll have travelled
9 I'll be staying
10 Will you be seeing

UNIT 25

25.1
2 goes
3 'll tell / will tell ... come
4 see ... won't recognise / will not recognise
5 Will you be ... 'm/am
6 's/is
7 'll wait / will wait ... 're/are
8 'll be / will be ... gets
9 is
10 phones ... 'm/am

25.2
2 I'll give you my address when I find somewhere to live. *or* ... when I've found somewhere to live.
3 I'll come straight back home after I do the shopping. *or* ... after I've done the shopping.
4 Let's go home before it gets dark.
5 I won't speak to her until she apologises. *or* ... until she has apologised.

25.3
2 you go / you leave
3 you decide *or* you've decided / you have decided
4 you're in New York / you go to New York
5 finish the new road / 've finished the new road / have finished the new road *or* build the new road / 've built the new road / have built the new road

25.4
2 If
3 When
4 if
5 If
6 when
7 if
8 if

UNIT 26

26.1
3 can
4 be able to
5 been able to
6 can
7 be able to

26.2
Example answers:
2 I used to be able to run fast.
3 I'd like to be able to play the piano.
4 I've never been able to get up early.

26.3
2 could run
3 can wait
4 couldn't eat
5 can't hear
6 couldn't sleep

26.4
2 was able to finish it
3 were able to find it
4 was able to get away

26.5
4 couldn't
5 managed to
6 could
7 managed to
8 could
9 managed to
10 couldn't

UNIT 27

27.1
2 We could have fish.
3 You could phone (her) now.
4 You could give her a book.
5 We could hang it in the kitchen.

27.2
3 I could kill him!
4 *OK* – could have *is also possible*
5 I could stay here all day
6 it could be in the car (may/might *are also possible*)
7 *OK*
8 *OK* – could borrow *is also possible*
9 it could change later (may/might *are also possible*)

27.3
2 could have come/gone
3 could apply
4 could have been
5 could have got/taken
6 could come

27.4
3 couldn't wear
4 couldn't have found
5 couldn't get
6 couldn't have been
7 couldn't have come/gone

UNIT 28

28.1
2 must
3 can't
4 must
5 must
6 can't
7 must
8 must
9 can't

28.2
3 be
4 have been
5 be
6 go *or* have been
7 be going
8 have taken / have stolen / have moved
9 have been
10 be following

28.3
3 It must have been very expensive.
4 They must have gone away.
5 I must have left it in the restaurant last night.
6 He can't have seen me. *or* He couldn't have seen me.
7 He must have been waiting for somebody
8 She can't have understood what I said. *or* She couldn't have understood what I said.
9 I must have forgotten to lock it.
10 The neighbours must have been having a party.
11 The driver can't have seen the red light. *or* The driver couldn't have seen ...

UNIT 29

29.1
2 She might be busy.
3 She might be working.
4 She might want to be alone.
5 She might have been ill yesterday.
6 She might have gone home early.
7 She might have had to go home early.
8 She might have been working yesterday.
9 She might not want to see me.

10 She might not be working today.
11 She might not have been feeling well yesterday.
You can use **may** *instead of* **might** *in all these sentences.*

29.2
2 be
3 have been
4 be waiting
5 have

29.3
2 a She might be watching TV in her room.
  b She might have gone out.
3 a It might be in the car.
  b You might have left it in the restaurant last night.
4 a He might have gone to bed early.
  b He might not have heard the doorbell.
  c He might have been in the shower.
You can use **may** *instead of* **might** *in all these sentences.*

29.4
3 might not have received it
4 couldn't have been an accident
5 couldn't have tried
6 might not have been American

UNIT 30

30.1
2 I might buy a Mercedes.
3 I might go to London.
4 He might come on Saturday.
5 I might hang it in the dining room.
6 She might go to university.
You can use **may** *instead of* **might** *in all these sentences.*

30.2
2 might wake
3 might bite
4 might need
5 might slip
6 might break
You can use **may** *instead of* **might** *in all these sentences.*

30.3
2 might be able to meet/see
3 might have to work
4 might have to go/leave
You can use **may** *instead of* **might** *in all these sentences.*

30.4
2 I might not go out this evening.
3 We might not get tickets for the concert.
4 Sue might not be able to come out with us this evening.

You can use **may** *instead of* **might** *in all these sentences.*

30.5
2 I might as well go to the concert.
3 We might as well paint the bathroom.
4 We might as well watch the film.
You can use **may** *instead of* **might** *in all these sentences.*

UNIT 31

31.1
3 We had to close
4 She has to leave
5 do you have to be
6 I have to hurry
7 Does he have to travel
8 do you have to go
9 did you have to wait
10 had to do

31.2
3 have to make
4 don't have to do
5 had to ask
6 don't have to pay
7 didn't have to go
8 has to make
9 will have to drive

31.3
3 OK (have to *is also correct*)
4 He **has** to work.
5 I **had to** work late yesterday evening.
6 OK (have to *is also correct*)
7 She **has had to** wear glasses since she was very young. (*For the present perfect* (**has had**) *with* **for** *and* **since,** *see Units 11–12.*)

31.4
3 don't have to
4 mustn't
5 don't have to
6 mustn't
7 doesn't have to
8 mustn't
9 mustn't
10 don't have to

UNIT 32

32.1
2 needn't come
3 needn't walk
4 needn't ask
5 needn't tell
6 needn't explain

32.2
3 needn't
4 must
5 mustn't

6 needn't
7 needn't
8 must … mustn't
9 needn't … must

32.3
2 She needn't have bought (any) eggs.
3 You needn't have shouted at me.
4 He needn't have sold his car.
5 We needn't have taken the camcorder (with us).
6 I needn't have rushed (to the station).

32.4
2 You needn't have walked home. You could have taken a taxi.
3 You needn't have stayed at a hotel. You could have stayed with us.
4 She needn't have phoned me in the middle of the night. She could have waited until the morning.
5 You needn't have left without saying anything. You could have said goodbye.

UNIT 33

33.1
2 You should look for another job.
3 He shouldn't go to bed so late.
4 You should take a photograph.
5 She shouldn't use her car so much.
6 He should put some pictures on the walls.

33.2
2 I don't think you should go out. / I think you should stay at home.
3 I think you should apply for it. / … for the job.
4 I don't think the government should increase taxes.

33.3
3 should come
4 should do
5 should have done
6 should win
7 should have won
8 should be
9 should have arrived

33.4
3 We should have reserved a table.
4 The shop should be open (now). / The shop should have opened by now. *or* It should …

5 She shouldn't be doing 50. / She shouldn't be driving so fast. / She should be driving more slowly.

6 I should have written down her address. / I should have written her address down. *or* I should have written it down.

7 The driver in front shouldn't have stopped without warning. / ... shouldn't have stopped so suddenly.

8 I should have been looking where I was going. / I shouldn't have been looking behind me.

UNIT 34

34.1

2 I should stay / I stay / I stayed a little longer

3 they should visit / they visit / they visited the museum after lunch

4 we should pay / we pay / we paid the rent by Friday

5 I should go / I go / I went away for a few days

34.2

1 b *OK*
  c *OK*
  d *wrong*
2 a *OK*
  b *wrong*
  c *OK*

34.3

2 should say
3 should worry
4 should leave
5 should ask
6 should listen

34.4

2 If it should rain
3 If there should be
4 If anyone should ask
5 Should there be any problems
6 Should anyone ask (where I'm going)

34.5

2 I should keep
3 I should phone
4 I should buy

UNIT 35

35.1

2 You'd better put a plaster on it.
3 We'd better reserve a table.
4 You'd better not go to work.
5 I'd better pay the phone bill (soon).
6 I'd better not go out (yet).
7 We'd better take/get a taxi.

35.2

3 'd better
4 should
5 should
6 'd better
7 should
8 should

35.3

1 b 'd/had
  c close/shut
  d hadn't
2 a did
  b was done
  c thought

35.4

2 It's time I had a holiday.
3 It's time the train left.
4 It's time I/we had a party.
5 It's time some changes were made.
6 It's time he tried something else.

UNIT 36

36.1

Example answers:
2 I wouldn't like to be a teacher.
3 I'd love to learn to fly a plane.
4 It would be nice to have a big garden.
5 I'd like to go to Mexico.

36.2

2 'd enjoy / would enjoy
3 'd have enjoyed / would have enjoyed
4 would you do
5 'd have stopped / would have stopped
6 would have been
7 'd be / would be
8 'd have passed / would have passed
9 would have

36.3

2 e
3 b
4 f
5 a
6 d

36.4

2 He promised he'd phone. / ... he would phone.
3 You promised you wouldn't tell her.
4 They promised they'd wait (for us). / ... they would wait.

36.5

2 wouldn't tell
3 wouldn't speak
4 wouldn't let

36.6

2 would shake

3 would always help
4 would share
5 would always forget

UNIT 37

37.1

2 Can/Could I leave a message (for her)? *or* Can/Could you give her a message?
3 Can/Could you tell me how to get to the station? *or* ... the way to the station? *or* ... where the station is?
4 Can/Could I try on these trousers? *or* Can/Could I try these (trousers) on?
5 Can I give/offer you a lift?

37.2

3 Do you think you could check this letter (for me)? / ... check my letter?
4 Do you mind if I leave work early?
5 Do you think you could turn the music down? / ... turn it down?
6 Is it OK if I close the window?
7 Do you think I could have a look at your newspaper?

37.3

2 Can/Could/Would you show me? *or* Do you think you could show me? *or* ... do it for me?
3 Would you like to sit down? *or* Would you like a seat? *or* Can I offer you a seat?
4 Can/Could/Would you slow down? *or* Do you think you could ...?
5 Can/Could/May I/we have the bill, please? *or* Do you think I/we could have ... ?
6 Would you like to borrow it?

UNIT 38

38.1

3 'd take / would take
4 closed down
5 wouldn't get
6 pressed
7 did
8 'd be / would be
9 didn't come
10 borrowed
11 walked
12 would understand

38.2

2 What would you do if you lost your passport?
3 What would you do if there was/were a fire in the building?

343

4 What would you do if you were in a lift and it stopped between floors?

38.3

2 If he took his driving test, he'd fail (it). / ... he would fail (it).
3 If we stayed at a hotel, it would cost too much.
4 If she applied for the job, she wouldn't get it.
5 If we told them the truth, they wouldn't believe us.
6 If we invited Bill, we'd have to invite his friends too. / ... we would have to ...

38.4
Example answers:
2 I'd be very angry if somebody broke into my house.
3 If I didn't go to work tomorrow, I'd have a much nicer day than usual.
4 Would you go to the party if you were invited?
5 If you bought some new clothes, you'd feel much better.
6 Would you mind if I didn't go out with you this evening?

UNIT 39

39.1

3 'd help / would help
4 lived
5 'd live / would live
6 would taste
7 were/was
8 wouldn't wait ... 'd go / would go
9 didn't go
10 weren't ... wouldn't be

39.2

2 I'd buy it / I would buy it if it weren't/wasn't so expensive.
or ... if it were/was cheaper.
3 We'd go out / We would go out more often if we could afford it.
4 If I didn't have to work late, I could meet you tomorrow. *or* ... I'd meet / I would meet ...
or ... I'd be able to meet ...
5 We could have lunch outside if it weren't raining / wasn't raining.
6 If I wanted his advice, I'd ask for it / I would ask for it.

39.3

2 I wish I had a mobile phone.
3 I wish Helen were/was here.
4 I wish it weren't/wasn't (so) cold.
5 I wish I didn't live in a big city.
6 I wish I could go to the party.

7 I wish I didn't have to work tomorrow.
8 I wish I knew something about cars.
9 I wish I were feeling / was feeling better.

39.4
Example answers:
1 I wish I was at home.
2 I wish I had a big garden.
3 I wish I could tell jokes.
4 I wish I was taller.

UNIT 40

40.1

2 If he'd missed / he had missed the train, he'd have missed / he would have missed his flight.
3 I'd have forgotten / I would have forgotten ... you hadn't reminded
4 I'd had / I had had ... I'd have sent / I would have sent
5 we'd have enjoyed / we would have enjoyed ... the weather had been
6 It would have been ... I'd walked / I had walked
7 I were / I was
8 I'd been / I had been

40.2

2 If the road hadn't been icy, the accident wouldn't have happened.
3 If I'd known / If I had known (that Joe had to get up early), I'd have woken / I would have woken him up.
4 If Jane hadn't lent me the money, I wouldn't have been able to buy the car. *or* ... I couldn't have bought the car.
5 If Karen hadn't been wearing a seat belt, she'd have been injured / she would have been injured (in the crash).
6 If you'd had / If you had had (some) breakfast, you wouldn't be hungry now.
7 If I'd had / If I had had (some) money, I'd have got / I would have got a taxi.

40.3

2 I wish I'd applied / I wish I had applied for it. *or* ... for the job.
3 I wish I'd learned / I wish I had learned to play a musical instrument (when I was younger).
4 I wish I hadn't painted it red.
or ... the gate red.
5 I wish I'd brought / I wish I had brought my camera.

6 I wish they'd phoned / I wish they had phoned first (to say they were coming). *or* I wish I'd known / I wish I had known they were coming.

UNIT 41

41.1

2 hope
3 wish
4 wished
5 hope
6 wish ... hope

41.2

2 I wish Jane/she would come. *or* ... would hurry up.
3 I wish somebody would give me a job.
4 I wish the/that baby would stop crying.
5 I wish you would buy some new clothes. *or* I wish you would get some new clothes.
6 I wish you wouldn't drive so fast.
7 I wish you wouldn't leave the door open (all the time).
8 I wish people wouldn't drop litter in the street.

41.3

2 *OK*
3 I wish I had more free time.
4 I wish our flat was/were a bit bigger.
5 *OK*
6 *OK*
7 I wish everything wasn't/weren't so expensive.

41.4

3 I knew
4 I'd taken / I had taken
5 I could come
6 I wasn't / I weren't
7 they'd hurry / they would hurry
8 we didn't have
9 we could have stayed
10 it wasn't / weren't
11 he'd decide / he would decide
12 we hadn't gone

UNIT 42

42.1

2 is made
3 was damaged
4 were invited
5 are shown
6 are held
7 was written ... was translated
8 were overtaken
9 is surrounded

42.2

2 When was television invented?
3 How are mountains formed?
4 When was Pluto discovered?
5 What is silver used for?

42.3

3 covers
4 is covered
5 are locked
6 was posted ... arrived
7 sank ... was rescued
8 died ... were brought up
9 grew up
10 was stolen
11 disappeared
12 did Sue resign
13 was Bill sacked
14 is owned
15 called ... was injured ...
wasn't needed
16 were these photographs taken
... Did you take
17 'm not bothered / am not
bothered

42.4

2 All flights were cancelled
because of fog.
3 This road isn't used much.
4 I was accused of stealing
money.
5 How are languages
learned/learnt?
6 We were warned not to go out
alone.

UNIT 43

43.1

2 it can't be broken
3 it can be eaten
4 it can't be used
5 it can't be seen
6 it can be carried

43.2

3 be made
4 be spent
5 have been repaired
6 be carried
7 have been caused
8 be woken up
9 have been arrested

43.3

2 The meeting has been
postponed.
3 The computer is being used at
the moment.
4 I didn't realise that our
conversation was being
recorded.
5 ... we found that the game
had been cancelled.
6 A new ring road is being built
round the city.
7 A new hospital has been built
near the airport.

43.4

3 It's been stolen! / It has been
stolen!
4 Somebody has taken it. *or*
... taken my umbrella.
5 He's been promoted. / He has
been promoted.
6 It's being redecorated. / It is
being redecorated.
7 It's working again. / It is
working again. ... It's been
repaired. / It has been repaired.
8 The furniture had been
moved.
9 He hasn't been seen since
then.
10 I haven't seen her for ages.
11 Have you ever been mugged?

UNIT 44

44.1

2 I was asked some difficult
questions at the interview.
3 Linda was given a present by
her colleagues when she
retired.
4 I wasn't told about the
meeting.
5 How much will you be paid
for your work?
6 I think Tom should have been
offered the job.
7 Have you been shown what to
do?

44.2

2 being invited
3 being given
4 being knocked down
5 being treated
6 being stuck

44.3

2–6 Beethoven was born in 1770.
Agatha Christie was born in
1890.
Galileo was born in 1564.
Mahatma Gandhi was born in
1869.
Martin Luther King was born
in 1929.
Elvis Presley was born in
1935.
Leonardo da Vinci was born
in 1452.
William Shakespeare was
born in 1564.
7 I was born in ...

44.4

2 got stung
3 get used
4 got stolen
5 get paid
6 got stopped
7 get damaged
8 get asked

UNIT 45

45.1

2 The weather is expected to be
good tomorrow.
3 The thieves are believed to
have got in through a window
in the roof.
4 Many people are reported to
be homeless after the floods.
5 The prisoner is thought to
have escaped by climbing over
a wall.
6 The man is alleged to have
been driving at 110 miles an
hour.
7 The building is reported to
have been badly damaged by
the fire.
8 a The company is said to be
losing a lot of money.
b The company is believed to
have lost a lot of money
last year.
c The company is expected
to make a loss this year.

45.2

2 He is supposed to know a lot
of famous people.
3 He is supposed to be very rich.
4 He is supposed to have twelve
children.
5 He is supposed to have been
an actor when he was
younger.

45.3

2 You're / You are supposed to
be my friend.
3 I'm / I am supposed to be on
a diet.
4 It was supposed to be a joke.
5 Or maybe it's / it is supposed
to be a flower.
6 You're / You are supposed to
be working.

45.4

2 're / are supposed to start
3 was supposed to phone
4 aren't / 're not / are not
supposed to block
5 was supposed to arrive

UNIT 46

46.1

1 b
2 a
3 a
4 b

46.2

2 To have my jacket cleaned.
3 To have my watch repaired.
4 To have my eyes tested.

46.3
2 I had it cut.
3 They had it painted.
4 He had it built.
5 I had them delivered.

46.4
2 have another key made
3 had your hair cut
4 Do you have a newspaper delivered
5 're having / are having a garage built
6 haven't had the film developed
7 have it cleaned
8 have your ears pierced
9 've had it repaired / have had it repaired *or* had it repaired
11 had her handbag stolen
12 had his car vandalised

UNIT 47

47.1
2 He said (that) his father wasn't very well.
3 He said (that) Rachel and Mark were getting married next month.
4 He said (that) his sister had had a baby.
5 He said (that) he didn't know what Frank was doing.
6 He said (that) he'd seen / he had seen Helen at a party in June and she'd seemed / she had seemed fine. *or* He said (that) he saw Helen … and she seemed …
7 He said (that) he hadn't seen Diane recently.
8 He said (that) he wasn't enjoying his job very much.
9 He said (that) I could come and stay at his place if I was ever in London.
10 He said (that) his car had been stolen a few days ago. *or* … his car was stolen a few days ago.
11 He said (that) he wanted to go on holiday, but (he) couldn't afford it.
12 He said (that) he'd tell / he would tell Chris he'd seen / he had seen me. *or* … he saw me.

47.2
Example answers:
2 she wasn't coming / … she was going somewhere else / … she was staying at home
3 she didn't like him
4 you didn't know anybody

5 she wouldn't be here / … she would be away / … she was going away
6 you were staying at home / … you weren't going out
7 you couldn't speak (any) French
8 you went to the cinema last week / … you had been/gone to the cinema last week

UNIT 48

48.1
2 But you said you didn't like fish.
3 But you said you couldn't drive.
4 But you said she had a very well-paid job.
5 But you said you didn't have any brothers or sisters.
6 But you said you'd / you had never been to the United States.
7 But you said you were working tomorrow evening.
8 But you said she was a friend of yours.

48.2
2 Tell
3 Say
4 said
5 told
6 said
7 tell … said
8 tell … say
9 told
10 said

48.3
2 her to slow down
3 her not to worry
4 asked Tom to give me a hand *or* … to help me
5 asked me to open my bag
6 asked him to get a newspaper
7 told him to mind his own business
8 asked her to marry him
9 told her not to wait (for me) if I was late

UNIT 49

49.1
2 Were you born there?
3 Are you married?
4 How long have you been married?
5 Have you got (any) children? *or* Do you have (any) children?
6 How old are they?
7 What do you do?
8 What does your wife do?

49.2
3 Who paid the bill?
4 What happened?
5 What did she/Diane say?
6 Who does it / this book belong to?
7 Who lives in that house? / Who lives there?
8 What did you fall over?
9 What fell on the floor?
10 What does it / this word mean?
11 Who did you borrow it / the money from?
12 What are you worried about?

49.3
2 How is cheese made?
3 When was the computer invented?
4 Why isn't Sue working today?
5 What time are your friends coming?
6 Why was the concert cancelled?
7 Where was your mother born?
8 Why didn't you come to the party?
9 How did the accident happen?
10 Why doesn't this machine work?

49.4
2 Don't you like him?
3 Isn't it good?
4 Haven't you got any? *or* Don't you have any?

UNIT 50

50.1
2 Could you tell me where the post office is?
3 I wonder what the time is.
4 I want to know what this word means.
5 Do you know what time they left?
6 I don't know if/whether Sue is going out tonight.
7 Do you have any idea where Caroline lives?
8 I can't remember where I parked the car.
9 Can you tell me if/whether there is a bank near here?
10 Tell me what you want.
11 I don't know why Kate didn't come to the party.
12 Do you know how much it costs to park here?
13 I have no idea who that woman is.
14 Do you know if/whether Liz got my letter?
15 Can you tell me how far it is to the airport?

50.2

1 Do you know where she has gone?
2 I don't suppose you know when she'll be back / she will be back.
3 Do you happen to know if/whether she went out alone?

50.3

2 He asked me where I'd been. / ... where I had been.
3 He asked me how long I'd been back. / ... how long I had been back.
4 He asked me what I was doing now.
5 He asked me why I'd come back. / ... why I had come back. *or* ... why I came back.
6 He asked me where I was living.
7 He asked me if/whether I was glad to be back.
8 He asked me if/whether I had any plans to go away again.
9 He asked me if/whether I could lend him some money.

UNIT 51

51.1

2 doesn't
3 was
4 will
5 am ... isn't *or* 'm not ... is
6 should
7 won't
8 do
9 could
10 would ... could ... can't

51.2

3 Do you? I don't.
4 Didn't you? I did.
5 Haven't you? I have.
6 Did you? I didn't.

51.3

Example answers:
3 So did I. *or* Did you? What did you watch?
4 Neither will I. *or* Won't you? Where will you be?
5 So do I. *or* Do you? What sort of books do you like?
6 So would I. *or* Would you? Where would you like to live?
7 Neither can I. *or* Can't you? Why not?

51.4

2 I hope so.
3 I expect so.
4 I don't think so.
5 I'm afraid not.
6 I'm afraid so.
7 I suppose so.

8 I hope not.
9 I think so.

UNIT 52

52.1

3 haven't you
4 were you
5 does she
6 isn't he
7 hasn't she
8 can't you
9 will he
10 aren't there
11 shall we
12 is it
13 aren't I
14 would you
15 hasn't she
16 should I
17 had he
18 will you

52.2

2 It's (very) expensive, isn't it?
3 The course was great, wasn't it?
4 You've had your hair cut, haven't you?
5 She has a good voice, hasn't she? *or* She's got / She has got ...
6 It doesn't look very good, does it?
7 This bridge isn't very safe, is it?

52.3

2 Joe, you couldn't get (me) some stamps, could you?
3 Kate, you don't know where Diane is, do you? *or* ... you haven't seen Diane, have you?
4 Helen, you haven't got a bicycle pump, have you? *or* ... you don't have a bicycle pump, do you?
5 Ann, you couldn't take me to the station, could you? *or* ... you couldn't give me a lift to the station, could you?
6 Robert, you haven't seen my keys, have you?

UNIT 53

53.1

2 making
3 listening
4 applying
5 reading
6 living
7 using
8 forgetting
9 writing
10 being
11 trying
12 losing

53.2

2 playing tennis
3 driving too fast
4 going for a swim
5 breaking the CD player
6 waiting a few minutes

53.3

2 travelling during the rush hour
3 painting the kitchen until next weekend
4 turning the radio down
5 not interrupting me all the time

53.4

Example answers:
2 going out
3 sitting on the floor
4 having a picnic
5 laughing
6 breaking down

UNIT 54

54.1

2 to help him
3 to carry her bag (for her)
4 to meet at 8 o'clock
5 to tell him her name / to give him her name
6 not to tell anyone

54.2

2 to get
3 to buy / to have / to rent / to hire
4 (how) to use / (how) to operate
5 to make
6 say *or* to say

54.3

2 to go
3 going
4 waiting
5 to go
6 barking
7 to call
8 having
9 missing
10 to find

54.4

2 Tom appears to be worried about something.
3 You seem to know a lot of people.
4 My English seems to be getting better.
5 That car appears to have broken down.
6 David tends to forget things.
7 They claim to have solved the problem.

54.5

2 how to use
3 what to do
4 how to ride

5 what to say / what to do

6 whether to go

UNIT 55

55.1

2 or do you want me to lend you some

3 or would you like me to shut it

4 or would you like me to show you

5 or do you want me to repeat it

6 or do you want me to wait

55.2

2 to stay with them

3 him use her phone

4 him to be careful

5 her to give him a hand

55.3

2 I didn't expect it to rain.

3 Let him do what he wants.

4 Tim's glasses make him look older.

5 I want you to know the truth.

6 Remind me to phone my sister.

7 Sarah persuaded me to apply for the job.

8 My lawyer advised me not to say anything to the police.

9 I was warned not to believe everything he says.

10 Having a car enables you to get around more easily.

55.4

2 to go

3 to do

4 cry

5 to study

6 eating

7 read

8 to make

9 think

UNIT 56

56.1

2 driving

3 to go

4 to go

5 raining

6 to win

7 asking

8 asking

9 to answer

10 breaking

11 to pay

12 losing *or* to lose

13 to tell

14 crying *or* to cry

15 to get

16 meeting ... to see

56.2

2 He can remember going to Paris when he was eight.

3 He can't remember crying on his first day at school.

4 He can remember falling into the river.

5 He can't remember saying he wanted to be a doctor. *or* He can't remember wanting to be a doctor.

6 He can't remember being bitten by a dog.

56.3

1 b lending

  c to phone / to call

  d to give

  e leaving/putting

2 a saying

  b to say

3 a to become

  b working

  c reading

UNIT 57

57.1

2 Try turning it the other way.

3 Have you tried moving the aerial?

4 Why don't you try phoning his office?

5 Have you tried taking an aspirin?

57.2

2 It needs painting.

3 It needs cutting.

4 They need tightening.

5 It needs emptying.

57.3

1 b knocking

  c to put

  d asking

  e to reach

  f to concentrate

2 a to go

  b looking

  c cleaning

  d cutting

  e You don't need to iron ... It doesn't need ironing

3 a overhearing

  b get *or* to get

  c smiling

  d make *or* to make

UNIT 58

58.1

Example answers:

2 I don't mind playing cards.

3 I don't like being alone. *or* ... to be alone.

4 I enjoy going to museums.

5 I love cooking. *or* I love to cook.

58.2

2 She likes teaching biology.

3 He likes taking photographs. *or* He likes to take photographs.

4 I didn't like working there.

5 She likes studying medicine.

6 He doesn't like being famous.

7 She doesn't like taking risks. *or* She doesn't like to take risks.

8 I like to know things in advance.

58.3

2 to sit

3 waiting

4 going *or* to go

5 to get

6 being

7 to come / to go

8 living

9 to talk

10 to have / to know / to get / to hear / to be told

58.4

2 I would like / I'd like to have seen the programme.

3 I would hate / I'd hate to have lost my watch.

4 I would love / I'd love to have met your parents.

5 I wouldn't like to have been alone.

6 I would prefer / I'd prefer to have travelled by train. *or* I would have preferred to travel ...

UNIT 59

59.1

Example answers:

2 I prefer basketball to football.

3 I prefer sending emails to phoning people.

4 I prefer going to the cinema to watching videos at home.

6 I prefer to send emails rather than phone people.

7 I prefer to go to the cinema rather than watch videos at home.

59.2

3 I'd rather listen to some music.

4 I'd prefer to eat at home.

5 I'd rather wait a few minutes.

6 I'd rather go for a swim.

7 I'd prefer to think about it for a while.

8 I'd rather stand.

9 I'd prefer to go alone.

11 I'd prefer to go for a swim rather than play tennis.

12 I'd rather eat at home than go to a restaurant.

13 I'd prefer to think about it for a while rather than decide now.

14 I'd rather listen to some music than watch TV.

59.3
2 (would you rather) I told her
3 would you rather I did it
4 would you rather I phoned her

59.4
2 stayed/remained/waited
3 stay
4 didn't
5 were
6 didn't

UNIT 60

60.1
2 applying for the job
3 remembering names
4 passing the exam
5 being late
6 eating at home, we went to a restaurant
7 having to queue *or* queuing
8 playing well

60.2
2 by standing on a chair
3 by turning a key
4 by borrowing too much money
5 by driving too fast
6 by putting some pictures on the walls

60.3
2 paying/settling
3 going
4 using
5 going
6 being/travelling/sitting
7 asking/telling/consulting
8 doing/having
9 turning/going
10 taking

60.4
2 I'm looking forward to seeing her/Diane.
3 I'm not looking forward to going to the dentist (tomorrow).
4 She's looking forward to leaving school (next summer).
5 I'm looking forward to playing tennis (tomorrow).

UNIT 61

61.1
1 When Juan first went to England, he **wasn't used to having** dinner so early, but after some time he **got used to** it. Now he finds it normal. He **is used to eating / is used to having dinner** at 6 o'clock.

2 She **wasn't used to working** nights and it took her a few months to **get used to** it. Now, after a year, she's quite happy. She **is used to working** nights.

61.2
2 No, I'm used to sleeping on the floor.
3 I'm used to working long hours.
4 Yes, I'm not used to going to bed so late.

61.3
2 They soon got used to her. / … to the/their new teacher.
3 She had to get used to living in a much smaller house.
4 (*example answers*) They'll have to get used to the weather. / … to the food. / … to speaking a foreign language.

61.4
3 drink
4 eating
5 having
6 have
7 go
8 be
9 being

UNIT 62

62.1
2 doing
3 coming/going
4 doing/trying
5 buying/having
6 hearing
7 going
8 having/using
9 being
10 watching
11 inviting/asking

62.2
2 in solving
3 of living
4 of causing
5 (from) walking
6 for interrupting
7 of spending
8 from escaping
9 on carrying
10 to seeing

62.3
2 on driving Ann to the station
3 on getting married
4 Sue for coming to see her
5 (to me) for not phoning earlier
6 me of being selfish

UNIT 63

63.1
2 There's no point in working if you don't need money.
3 There's no point in trying to study if you feel tired.
4 There's no point in hurrying if you've got plenty of time.

63.2
2 asking Dave
3 in going out
4 phoning her/Liz
5 complaining (about what happened)
6 of time reading newspapers
7 keeping

63.3
2 remembering people's names
3 difficulty getting a job
4 difficulty getting a ticket for the game

63.4
2 reading
3 packing / getting ready
4 watching
5 going/climbing/walking
6 applying
7 getting / being

63.5
2 went swimming
3 go skiing
4 goes riding
5 gone shopping

UNIT 64

64.1
2 I had to go to the bank to get some money.
3 I'm saving money to go to Canada.
4 I went into hospital to have an operation.
5 I'm wearing two sweaters to keep warm.
6 I phoned the police to report that my car had been stolen.

64.2
2 to read
3 to walk / to go on foot
4 to drink
5 to put / to carry
6 to discuss / to consider / to talk about
7 to buy / to get
8 to talk / to speak
9 to wear / to put on
10 to celebrate
11 to help / to assist

64.3
2 for
3 to

4 to
5 for
6 to
7 for
8 for … to

64.4

2 I wore warm clothes so that I wouldn't be cold.
3 I left Dave my phone number so that he could contact me. / … would be able to contact me.
4 We whispered so that nobody else would hear our conversation. / … so that nobody else could hear … / would be able to hear …
5 Please arrive early so that we can start the meeting on time. / … so that we'll be able to start …
6 Jennifer locked the door so that she wouldn't be disturbed.
7 I slowed down so that the car behind me could overtake. / … would be able to overtake.

UNIT 65

65.1

2 This machine is easy to use.
3 The window was very difficult to open.
4 Some words are impossible to translate.
5 A car is expensive to maintain.
6 That chair isn't safe to stand on.

65.2

2 It's an easy mistake to make.
3 It's a nice place to live. *or* … a nice place to live in.
4 It was a good game to watch.

65.3

2 It's careless of you to make the same mistake again and again.
3 It was nice of them to invite me (to stay with them). / It was nice of Dan and Jenny to …
4 It's inconsiderate of them to make so much noise (at night). / It's inconsiderate of the neighbours to …

65.4

2 'm/am glad to hear *or* was glad to hear
3 were surprised to see
4 'm/am sorry to hear *or* was sorry to hear

65.5

2 Paul was the last (person) to arrive.

3 Fiona was the only student to pass (the exam). / … the only one to pass (the exam).
4 I was the second customer/person to complain.
5 Neil Armstrong was the first person/man to walk on the moon.

65.6

2 're/are bound to be
3 's/is sure to forget
4 's/is not likely to rain *or* isn't likely to rain
5 's/is likely to be

UNIT 66

66.1

3 I'm afraid of losing it.
4 I was afraid to tell her.
5 We were afraid of missing our train.
6 We were afraid to look.
7 I was afraid of dropping it.
8 a I was afraid to eat it.
   b I was afraid of getting sick.

66.2

2 in starting
3 to read
4 in getting
5 to know
6 in looking

66.3

2 sorry to hear
3 sorry for saying / sorry about saying
4 sorry to disturb
5 sorry for losing / sorry about losing

66.4

1 b to leave
  c from leaving
2 a to solve
  b in solving
3 a of/about going
  b to go
  c to go
  d to going
4 a to buy
  b to buy
  c on buying
  d of buying

UNIT 67

67.1

2 arrive
3 take it / do it
4 it ring
5 him play / him playing
6 you lock it / you do it
7 her fall

67.2

2 We saw Dave and Helen playing tennis.

3 We saw Clare eating in a restaurant. / … having a meal in a restaurant.
4 We heard Bill playing his guitar.
5 We could smell the dinner burning.
6 We saw Linda jogging/ running.

67.3

3 tell
4 crying
5 riding
6 say
7 run … climb
8 explode
9 crawling
10 slam
11 sleeping

UNIT 68

68.1

2 Diane was sitting in an armchair reading a book.
3 Sue opened the door carefully trying not to make a noise.
4 Sarah went out saying she would be back in an hour.
5 Linda was in London for two years working as a tourist guide.
6 Mary walked around the town looking at the sights and taking photographs.

68.2

2 I fell asleep watching television.
3 A friend of mine slipped and fell getting off a bus.
4 I got very wet walking home in the rain.
5 Laura had an accident driving to work yesterday.
6 Two firefighters were overcome by smoke trying to put out the fire.

68.3

2 Having bought our tickets, we went into the theatre.
3 Having had dinner, they continued their journey.
4 Having done the shopping, I went for a cup of coffee.

68.4

2 Thinking they might be hungry, I offered them something to eat.
3 Being a foreigner, she needs a visa to work in this country.
4 Not knowing his phone number, I wasn't able to contact him.
5 Having travelled a lot, Sarah knows a lot about other countries.

6 Not being able to speak the local language, I had trouble communicating.

7 Having spent nearly all our money, we couldn't afford to stay at a hotel.

UNIT 69

69.1

3 We went to a very nice restaurant …

4 *OK*

5 I use a toothbrush …

6 … if there's a bank near here?

7 … for an insurance company

8 *OK*

9 *OK*

10 … we stayed in a big hotel.

11 … I hope we come to a petrol station soon.

12 … I have a problem.

13 … It's a very interesting idea.

14 John has got an interview for a job tomorrow.

15 … It's a good game.

16 *OK*

17 Jane was wearing a beautiful necklace.

69.2

3 a key

4 a coat

5 sugar

6 a biscuit

7 electricity

8 an interview

9 blood

10 a question

11 a moment

12 a decision

69.3

2 days

3 meat

4 a queue

5 letters

6 friends

7 people

8 air

9 patience

10 an umbrella

11 languages

12 space

UNIT 70

70.1

2 a a paper

b paper

3 a a light

b Light

4 a time

b a wonderful time

5 a nice room

6 advice

7 nice weather

8 bad luck

9 job

10 journey

11 total chaos

12 some

13 doesn't

14 Your hair is … it

15 The damage

70.2

2 information

3 chairs

4 furniture

5 hair

6 progress

7 job

8 work

9 permission

10 advice

11 experience

12 experiences

70.3

2 I'd like some information about places to see in the town.

3 Can you give me some advice about which courses to do? / … courses I can do?

4 What time is the news on (TV)?

5 It's a beautiful view, isn't it?

6 What horrible/awful weather!

UNIT 71

71.1

3 It's a vegetable.

4 It's a game. / It's a board game.

5 They're musical instruments.

6 It's a (tall/high) building.

7 They're planets.

8 It's a flower.

9 They're rivers.

10 They're birds.

12 He was a writer / a poet / a playwright / a dramatist.

13 He was a scientist / a physicist.

14 They were U.S. presidents / American presidents / presidents of the U.S.

15 She was an actress / a film actress / a film star.

16 They were singers.

17 They were painters / artists.

71.2

2 He's a waiter.

3 She's a travel agent.

4 He's a surgeon.

5 He's a chef.

6 She's a journalist.

7 He's a plumber.

8 She's an interpreter.

71.3

4 a

5 an

6 – (Do you collect stamps?)

7 a

8 Some

9 – (Do you enjoy going to concerts?)

10 – (I've got sore feet.)

11 a

12 some

13 a … a

14 – (Those are nice shoes.)

15 some

16 You need a visa to visit some countries

17 Jane is a teacher. Her parents were teachers too.

18 He's a liar. He's always telling lies.

UNIT 72

72.1

1 … and a magazine. The newspaper is in my bag, but I can't remember where I put the magazine.

2 I saw an accident this morning. A car crashed into a tree. The driver of the car wasn't hurt, but the car was badly damaged.

3 … a blue one and a grey one. The blue one belongs to my neighbours; I don't know who the owner of the grey one is.

4 My friends live in an old house in a small village. There is a beautiful garden behind the house. I would like to have a garden like that.

72.2

1 a a

b the

c the

2 a a

b a

c the

3 a a

b the

c the

4 a an … The

b the

c the

5 a the

b a

c a

72.3

2 the dentist

3 the door

4 a mistake

5 the bus station

6 a problem

7 the post office

8 the floor

9 the book

10 a job in a bank

11 a small flat in the city centre

12 a supermarket at the end of the street

72.4
Example answers:
3 About once a month.
4 Once or twice a year.
5 50 kilometres an hour.
6 About seven hours a night.
7 Two or three times a week.
8 About two hours a day.

UNIT 73

73.1
2 **a** nice holiday ... **the** best holiday
3 **the** nearest shop ... **the** end of this street
4 listen to **the** radio ... I haven't got **a** radio
5 to travel in space ... go to **the** moon
6 go to **the** cinema ... on television
7 **a** nice day ... by **the** sea
8 for breakfast ... eat breakfast
9 where is Room 25 ... on **the** second floor
10 **the** most expensive hotel ... **a** cheaper hotel

73.2
2 **the** ground ... **the** sky
3 watching television
4 **The** television
5 **the** same time
6 had dinner
7 **the** information ... **the** top of page 15
8 **the** capital

73.3
2 in **a** small village in **the** country
3 **The** moon goes round **the** earth every 27 days.
4 **the** same thing
5 **a** very hot day ... **the** hottest day of **the** year
6 usually have lunch ... eat **a** good breakfast
7 live in **a** foreign country ... learn **the** language
8 on **the** wrong platform
9 **The** next train ... from Platform 3

73.4
2 **the** sea
3 question 8
4 **the** cinema
5 breakfast
6 **the** gate
7 Gate 21

UNIT 74

74.1
2 to school
3 at home
4 to work
5 in hospital
6 at university
7 in bed
8 to prison

74.2
1 c school
  d school
  e ... get home **from school** ... **The school** isn't very far.
  f school
  g the school
2 a university
  b university
  c the university
3 a hospital
  b the hospital ... the hospital
  c hospital
4 a church
  b church
  c the church
5 a prison
  b the prison
  c prison
6 a bed
  b home
  c work
  d bed
  e work
  f work
7 a the sea
  b sea
  c the sea

UNIT 75

75.1
Example answers:
2–5 I like cats.
  I don't like zoos.
  I don't mind fast food restaurants.
  I'm not interested in football.

75.2
3 spiders
4 meat
5 the questions
6 the people
7 History
8 lies
9 the shops
10 The water
11 the grass
12 patience

75.3
3 Apples
4 the apples
5 Women ... men
6 tea
7 The vegetables
8 Life
9 skiing
10 the people

11 people ... aggression
12 All the books
13 the beds
14 war
15 The First World War
16 the Pyramids
17 the history of modern art
18 the marriage
19 Most people ... marriage ... family life ... society

UNIT 76

76.1
1 b the cheetah
  c the kangaroo (and the rabbit)
2 a the swan
  b the penguin
  c the owl
3 a the wheel
  b the laser
  c the telescope
4 a the rupee
  b the (Canadian) dollar
  c the ...

76.2
2 a
3 the
4 a
5 the
6 the
7 a
8 The

76.3
2 the injured
3 the unemployed
4 the sick
5 the rich ... the poor

76.4
2 a German Germans
3 a Frenchman/Frenchwoman the French
4 a Russian Russians
5 a Chinese the Chinese
6 a Brazilian Brazilians
7 an Englishman/Englishwoman the English
8 ...

UNIT 77

77.1
2 the
3 the ... the
4 – (President Kennedy was assassinated in 1963.)
5 the
6 – (Do you know Professor Brown's phone number?)

77.2
3 *OK*
4 **the** United States
5 **The** south of England ... **the** north

6 *OK*
7 the Channel
8 the Middle East
9 *OK*
10 the Swiss Alps
11 The UK
12 The Seychelles ... the Indian Ocean
13 *OK*
14 The river Volga ... the Caspian Sea

77.3
2 (in) South America
3 the Nile
4 Sweden
5 the United States
6 the Rockies
7 the Mediterranean
8 Australia
9 the Pacific
10 the Indian Ocean
11 the Thames
12 the Danube
13 Thailand
14 the Panama Canal
15 the Amazon

UNIT 78

78.1
2 Turner's in Carter Road
3 the Crown (Hotel) in Park Road
4 St Peter's in Market Street
5 the City Museum in George Street
6 Blackstone's in Forest Avenue
7 Victoria Park at the end of Market Street
8 The China House in Carter Road or Mario's Diner in George Street

78.2
2 The Eiffel Tower
3 Buckingham Palace
4 The White House
5 The Kremlin
6 Broadway
7 The Acropolis
8 Gatwick Airport

78.3
2 Hyde Park
3 St James's Park
4 The Grand Hotel ... Baker Street
5 Dublin Airport
6 Liverpool University
7 Harrison's
8 the Ship Inn
9 The Statue of Liberty ... New York Harbour
10 the Science Museum
11 IBM ... British Telecom
12 The Classic
13 the Great Wall

14 The Herald.
15 Cambridge University Press

UNIT 79

79.1
3 shorts
4 a means
5 means
6 some scissors *or* a pair of scissors
7 a series
8 series
9 species

79.2
2 politics
3 economics
4 athletics
5 physics
6 gymnastics
7 electronics

79.3
2 don't
3 want
4 was
5 aren't
6 wasn't
7 does *or* do
8 isn't
9 they are
10 are
11 Do
12 is

79.4
3 ... wearing black jeans.
4 *OK* (Brazil is playing *is also correct*)
5 ... very nice **people**.
6 Ten pounds **isn't**
7 ... buy **some** new pyjamas. *or* ... buy **a** new **pair of** pyjamas.
8 *OK* (The committee hasn't *is also correct*)
9 There was **a police officer / a policeman / a policewoman** ...
10 What **are** the police ...
11 **These** scissors **aren't** ...

UNIT 80

80.1
3 a computer magazine
4 (your) holiday photographs
5 milk chocolate
6 a factory inspector
7 a race horse
8 a horse race
9 a central London hotel
10 (your) exam results
11 the dining room carpet
12 an oil company scandal
13 car factory workers
14 a road improvement scheme
15 a five-day course
16 a two-part question
17 a seven-year-old girl

80.2
2 room number
3 seat belt
4 credit card
5 weather forecast
6 newspaper editor
7 shop window

80.3
3 20-pound
4 15-minute
5 60 minutes
6 two-hour
7 five courses
8 two-year
9 500-year-old
10 five days
11 six miles
12 six-mile

UNIT 81

81.1
3 your friend's umbrella
4 *OK*
5 Charles's daughter
6 Mary and Dan's son
7 *OK*
8 yesterday's newspaper
9 *OK*
10 *OK*
11 Your children's friends
12 Our neighbours' garden
13 *OK*
14 Bill's hair
15 Catherine's party
16 *OK*
17 Mike's parents' car
18 *OK*
19 *OK* (the government's economic policy *is also correct*)

81.2
2 a boy's name
3 children's clothes
4 a girls' school
5 a bird's nest
6 a women's magazine

81.3
2 Last week's storm caused a lot of damage.
3 The town's only cinema has closed down.
4 Britain's weather is very changeable.
5 The region's main industry is tourism.

81.4
2 twenty minutes' walk
3 two weeks' holiday / fourteen days' holiday / a fortnight's holiday
4 an/one hour's sleep

UNIT 82

82.1
2 hurt himself
3 blame herself
4 Put yourself
5 enjoyed themselves
6 burn yourself
7 express myself

82.2
2 me
3 myself
4 us
5 yourself
6 you
7 ourselves
8 themselves
9 them

82.3
2 feel
3 dried myself
4 concentrate
5 defend yourself
6 meeting
7 relax
8 wash

82.4
2 themselves
3 each other
4 each other
5 themselves
6 each other
7 ourselves
8 each other
9 introduced **ourselves** to **each other**

82.5
2 He cuts it himself.
3 No, I'll post/do it myself.
4 Linda told me herself. / Linda herself told me. / Linda did herself.
5 Why can't you phone him yourself? / ... do it yourself?

UNIT 83

83.1
2 We met a relative of yours.
3 Henry borrowed a book of mine.
4 Liz invited some friends of hers to her flat.
5 We had dinner with a neighbour of ours.
6 I went on holiday with two friends of mine.
7 Is that man a friend of yours?
8 I met a friend of Jane's at the party.

83.2
2 his own opinions
3 her own business
4 its own (private) beach
5 our own words

83.3
2 your own fault
3 her own ideas
4 your own problems
5 his own decisions

83.4
2 makes her own clothes
3 bake/make our own bread
4 writes his own songs

83.5
2 my own
3 myself
4 himself
5 themselves
6 herself
7 their own
8 yourself
9 our own
10 her own

UNIT 84

84.1
3 Is there ... there's / there is
4 there was ... It was
5 It was
6 There was
7 is it
8 It was
9 It's / It is
10 there wasn't
11 Is it ... it's / it is
12 there was ... There was
13 It was
14 There wasn't
15 There was ... it wasn't

84.2
2 There is a lot of salt in the soup.
3 There was nothing in the box.
4 There was a lot of violence in the film. / There was a lot of fighting ...
5 There were a lot of people in the shops.
6 There is a lot to do in this town. / There is a lot happening in this town.

84.3
2 There may be
3 there will be / there'll be or there are going to be
4 There's going to be / There is going to be
5 There used to be
6 there should be
7 there wouldn't be

84.4
2 and **there** was a lot of snow
3 **There** used to be a church here
4 **There** must have been a reason.
5 OK
6 **There's** sure to be a car park somewhere.

7 **there** will be an opportunity
8 OK
9 **there** would be somebody ... but **there** wasn't anybody.
10 **There** has been no change.
11 OK

UNIT 85

85.1
2 some
3 any
4 any ... some
5 some
6 any
7 any
8 some
9 any
10 any

85.2
2 somebody/someone
3 anybody/anyone
4 anything
5 something
6 somebody/someone ... anybody/anyone
7 something ... anybody/anyone
8 Anybody/Anyone
9 anybody/anyone
10 anywhere
11 somewhere
12 anywhere
13 anybody/anyone
14 something
15 anybody/anyone
16 something
17 anybody/anyone ... anything

85.3
2 Any day
3 Anything
4 anywhere
5 Any job *or* Anything
6 Any time
7 Anybody/Anyone
8 Any newspaper *or* Any one

UNIT 86

86.1
3 no
4 any
5 None
6 none
7 No
8 any
9 any
10 none
11 no

86.2
2 Nobody/No-one.
3 None.
4 Nowhere.
5 None.
6 Nothing.
8 I wasn't talking to anybody/anyone.

9 I haven't got any luggage.
10 I'm not going anywhere.
11 I didn't make any mistakes.
12 I didn't pay anything.

86.3
2 nobody/no-one
3 Nowhere
4 anything
5 **Nothing**. I couldn't find **anything** …
6 Nothing
7 anywhere
8 **Nobody/No-one** said **anything**.

86.4
2 nobody
3 anyone
4 Anybody
5 Nothing
6 Anything
7 anything

UNIT 87

87.1
3 a lot of salt
4 *OK*
5 It cost a lot
6 *OK*
7 many people *or* a lot of people
8 I use the phone a lot
9 *OK*
10 a lot of money

87.2
2 He's got plenty of money.
3 There's plenty of room.
4 … she still has plenty to learn.
5 There are plenty of things to see.
6 There are plenty of hotels.

87.3
2 little
3 many
4 much
5 few
6 little
7 many

87.4
3 a few dollars
4 *OK*
5 a little time
6 *OK*
7 only a few words
8 a few months

87.5
2 a little
3 a few
4 few
5 little
6 a little
7 little
8 a few

UNIT 88

88.1
3 –
4 of
5 –
6 –
7 of
8 of
9 – (of *is also correct*)
10 –

88.2
3 of my spare time
4 accidents
5 of the buildings
6 of her friends
7 of the population
8 birds
9 of the players
10 of her opinions
11 European countries
12 (of) my dinner

88.3
Example answers:
2 the time
3 my friends
4 (of) the questions
5 the photos / the photographs / the pictures
6 (of) the money

88.4
2 All of them
3 none of us
4 some of it
5 none of them
6 None of it
7 Some of them
8 all of it

UNIT 89

89.1
2 Neither
3 both
4 Either
5 Neither

89.2
2 either
3 both
4 Neither of
5 **neither** driver … **both / both the / both of the** cars
6 both / both of

89.3
2 either of them
3 both of them
4 neither of us
5 neither of them

89.4
3 Both Joe and Sam are on holiday.
4 Neither Joe nor Sam has (got) a car.
5 Brian neither watches TV nor reads newspapers.

6 The film was both boring and long.
7 That man's name is either Richard or Robert.
8 I've got neither the time nor the money to go on holiday.
9 We can leave either today or tomorrow.

89.5
2 either
3 any
4 none
5 any
6 either
7 neither

UNIT 90

90.1
3 Everybody/Everyone
4 Everything
5 all
6 everybody/everyone
7 everything
8 All
9 everybody/everyone
10 All
11 everything/all
12 Everybody/Everyone
13 All
14 everything

90.2
2 The whole team played well.
3 He ate the whole box (of chocolates).
4 They searched the whole house.
5 The whole family play/plays tennis.
6 Ann/She worked the whole day.
7 It rained the whole week.
8 Ann worked all day.
9 It rained all week.

90.3
2 every four hours
3 every four years
4 every five minutes
5 every six months

90.4
2 every day
3 all day
4 The whole building
5 every time
6 all the time
7 all my luggage

UNIT 91

91.1
3 Each
4 Every
5 Each
6 every
7 each
8 every

91.2
3 Every
4 Each
5 every
6 every
7 each
8 every
9 every
10 each
11 Every
12 each

91.3
2 Sonia and I had ten pounds each. / Sonia and I each had ten pounds.
3 Those postcards cost 80 pence each. / Those postcards are 80 pence each.
4 We paid £120 each. / We each paid £120.

91.4
2 everyone
3 every one
4 Everyone
5 every one

UNIT 92

92.1
2 A burglar is someone who breaks into a house to steal things.
3 A customer is someone who buys something from a shop.
4 A shoplifter is someone who steals from a shop.
5 A coward is someone who is not brave.
6 An atheist is someone who doesn't believe in God.
7 A pessimist is someone who expects the worst to happen.
8 A tenant is someone who pays rent to live in a house or flat.

92.2
2 The waitress who/that served us was impolite and impatient.
3 The building that/which was destroyed in the fire has now been rebuilt.
4 The people who/that were arrested have now been released.
5 The bus that/which goes to the airport runs every half hour.

92.3
2 who/that runs away from home
3 that/which were on the wall
4 that/which cannot be explained
5 who/that stole my car

6 that/which gives you the meaning of words
7 who/that invented the telephone
8 that/which can support life

92.4
3 that/which sells
4 who/that caused
5 OK (who took is also correct)
6 that/which is changing
7 OK (which were is also correct)
8 that/which won

UNIT 93

93.1
3 OK (the people who/that we met is also correct)
4 The people who work in the office
5 OK (the people who/that I work with is also correct)
6 OK (the money that/which I gave you is also correct)
7 the money that/which was on the table
8 OK (the worst film that/which you've ever seen is also correct)
9 the best thing that/which has ever happened to you

93.2
2 you're wearing or that/which you're wearing
3 you're going to see or that/which you're going to see
4 I/we wanted to visit or that/which I/we wanted to visit
5 I/we invited to the party or who/whom/that we invited …
6 you had to do or that/which you had to do
7 I/we hired or that/which I/we hired
8 Tom had recommended to us or that/which Tom had recommended …

93.3
2 we were invited to or that/which we were invited to
3 I work with or who/that I work with
4 you told me about or that/which you told me about
5 we went to last night or that/which we went to …
6 I applied for or that/which I applied for
7 you can rely on or who/that you can rely on
8 I saw you with or who/that I saw you with

93.4
3 – (that is also correct)
4 what
5 that
6 what
7 – (that is also correct)
8 what
9 – (that is also correct)

UNIT 94

94.1
2 whose wife is an English teacher
3 who owns a restaurant
4 whose ambition is to climb Everest
5 who have just got married
6 whose parents used to work in a circus

94.2
2 where I can buy some postcards
3 where I work
4 where Sue is staying
5 where I/we play football

94.3
2 where
3 who
4 whose
5 whom
6 where
7 whose
8 whom

94.4
Example answers:
2 I'll never forget the time we got stuck in a lift.
3 The reason I didn't write to you was that I didn't know your address.
4 Unfortunately I wasn't at home the evening you phoned.
5 The reason they don't have a car is that they don't need one.
6 1996 was the year Amanda got married.

UNIT 95

95.1
3 We often go to visit our friends in Bristol, which is not very far away.
4 I went to see the doctor, who told me to rest for a few days.
5 John, who/whom I've known for a very long time, is one of my closest friends.
6 Sheila, whose job involves a lot of travelling, is away from home a lot.
7 The new stadium, which can hold 90,000 people, will be opened next month.

8 Glasgow, where my brother lives, is the largest city in Scotland.

9 A friend of mine, whose father is the manager of a company, helped me to get a job.

95.2

3 The strike at the car factory, which began ten days ago, is now over.

4 I've found the book I was looking for this morning. *or* … the book that/which I was looking for.

5 The population of London, which was once the largest city in the world, is now falling.

6 Few of the people who/that applied for the job had the necessary qualifications.

7 Amy showed me a photograph of her son, who is a policeman.

95.3

2 My office, which is on the second floor, is very small.

3 *OK* (The office that/which I'm using … *is also correct*)

4 Ben's father, who used to be a teacher, now works for a TV company.

5 *OK* (The doctor who examined me … *is also correct*)

6 The sun, which is one of millions of stars in the universe, provides us with heat and light.

UNIT 96

96.1

2 of which he's very proud

3 with whom we went on holiday

4 to which only members of the family were invited

96.2

2 most of which was useless

3 neither of which she has received

4 none of whom was suitable

5 one of which she hardly ever uses

6 half of which he gave to his parents

7 both of whom are teachers

8 only a few of whom I knew

9 (the) sides of which were lined with trees

10 the aim of which is to save money

96.3

2 Jane doesn't have a phone, which makes it difficult to contact her.

3 Neil has passed his exams, which is good news.

4 Our flight was delayed, which meant we had to wait three hours at the airport.

5 Kate offered to let me stay at her house, which was very kind of her.

6 The street I live in is very noisy at night, which makes it difficult to sleep sometimes.

7 Our car has broken down, which means we can't go away tomorrow.

UNIT 97

97.1

2 the man sitting next to me on the plane

3 The taxi taking us to the airport

4 a path leading to the river

5 A factory employing 500 people

6 a brochure containing the information I needed

97.2

2 damaged in the storm

3 Most of the suggestions made at the meeting

4 The paintings stolen from the museum

5 the man arrested by the police

97.3

3 living

4 offering

5 called

6 blown

7 sitting … reading

8 working … studying

97.4

3 There's somebody coming.

4 There were a lot of people travelling.

5 There was nobody else staying there.

6 There was nothing written on it.

7 There's a course beginning next Monday.

UNIT 98

98.1

2 a exhausting
  b exhausted

3 a depressing
  b depressed
  c depressed

4 a exciting
  b exciting
  c excited

98.2

2 interested

3 exciting

4 embarrassing

5 embarrassed

6 amazed

7 astonishing

8 amused

9 terrifying … shocked

10 bored … boring

11 boring … interesting

98.3

2 bored

3 confusing

4 disgusting

5 interested

6 annoyed

7 boring

8 exhausted

9 excited

10 amusing

11 interesting

UNIT 99

99.1

2 an unusual gold ring

3 a beautiful old house

4 black leather gloves

5 an old American film

6 a long thin face

7 big black clouds

8 a lovely sunny day

9 an ugly yellow dress

10 a long wide avenue

11 a little old red car

12 a nice new green sweater

13 a small black metal box

14 a big fat black cat

15 a lovely little old village

16 beautiful long black hair

17 an interesting old French painting

18 an enormous red and yellow umbrella

99.2

2 tastes/tasted awful

3 feel fine

4 smell nice

5 look wet

6 sounds/sounded interesting

99.3

2 happy

3 happily

4 violent

5 terrible

6 properly

7 good

8 slow

99.4

3 the last two days

4 the first two weeks of May

5 the next few days
6 the first three questions (in the exam)
7 the next two years
8 the last three days of our holiday

UNIT 100

100.1
2 badly
3 easily
4 patiently
5 unexpectedly
6 regularly
7 perfectly ... slowly ... clearly

100.2
3 selfishly
4 terribly
5 sudden
6 colourfully
7 colourful
8 badly
9 badly
10 safe

100.3
2 careful
3 continuously
4 happily
5 fluent
6 specially
7 complete
8 perfectly
9 nervous
10 financially *or* completely

100.4
2 seriously ill
3 absolutely enormous
4 slightly damaged
5 unusually quiet
6 completely changed
7 unnecessarily long
8 badly planned

UNIT 101

101.1
2 good
3 well
4 good
5 well
6 well (good *is also possible here*)
7 well
8 good
9 well
10 good
11 well

101.2
2 well-known
3 well-kept
4 well-written
5 well-informed
6 well-dressed
7 well-paid

101.3
2 *OK*
3 *OK*
4 hard
5 *OK*
6 slowly

101.4
2 hardly hear
3 hardly slept
4 hardly speak
5 hardly said
6 hardly changed
7 hardly recognised

101.5
2 hardly any
3 hardly anything
4 hardly anybody/anyone
5 hardly ever
6 Hardly anybody/anyone
7 hardly anywhere
8 hardly *or* hardly ever
9 hardly any
10 hardly anything ... hardly anywhere

UNIT 102

102.1
4 so
5 so
6 such a
7 so
8 such
9 such a
10 such a
11 so
12 so ... such
13 so
14 such a
15 such a

102.2
3 I was so tired (that) I couldn't keep my eyes open.
4 We had such a good time on holiday (that) we didn't want to come home.
5 She speaks English so well (that) you would think it was her native language. *or* She speaks such good English (that) ...
6 I've got such a lot to do (that) I don't know where to begin. *or* I've got so much to do (that) ...
7 The music was so loud (that) you could hear it from miles away.
8 I had such a big breakfast (that) I didn't eat anything else for the rest of the day.
9 It was such horrible weather (that) we spent the whole day indoors.
10 I was so surprised (that) I didn't know what to say.

102.3
Example answers:
2 a She's so friendly.
 b She's such a nice person.
3 a It's so lively.
 b It's such an exciting place.
4 a It's so exhausting.
 b It's such a difficult job.
5 a I haven't seen you for so long.
 b I haven't seen you for such a long time.

UNIT 103

103.1
3 enough money
4 enough milk
5 warm enough
6 enough room
7 well enough
8 enough time
9 enough qualifications
10 big enough
11 enough cups

103.2
2 too busy to talk
3 too late to go
4 warm enough to sit
5 too shy to be
6 enough patience to be
7 too far away to hear
8 enough English to read

103.3
2 This coffee is too hot to drink.
3 The piano was too heavy to move.
4 These apples aren't / are not ripe enough to eat.
5 The situation is too complicated to explain.
6 The wall was too high to climb over.
7 This sofa isn't / is not big enough for three people (to sit on).
8 Some things are too small to see without a microscope.

UNIT 104

104.1
2 quite hungry
3 Quite good
4 quite often
5 quite noisy
6 quite surprised
7 quite late
8 quite old

104.2
2 quite a good voice
3 quite a long way
4 quite a strong wind
5 quite a lot of traffic
6 quite a busy day
7 quite a nice time

104.3
Example answers:
2 rather long
3 rather disappointed
4 rather strange
5 rather impatient

104.4
3 more than a little …
4 completely
5 more than a little …
6 more than a little …
7 completely

104.5
2 quite safe
3 quite impossible
4 quite right
5 quite different
6 quite unnecessary
7 quite sure

UNIT 105

105.1
2 stronger
3 smaller
4 more expensive
5 warmer/hotter
6 more interesting / more exciting
7 nearer
8 more difficult / more complicated
9 better
10 worse
11 longer
12 more quietly
13 more often
14 further/farther
15 happier / more cheerful

105.2
3 more serious than
4 thinner
5 bigger
6 more interested
7 more important than
8 simpler / more simple
9 more crowded than
10 more peaceful than
11 more easily
12 higher than

105.3
2 It takes longer by train than by car.
3 I ran further/farther than Dave.
4 Joe did worse than Chris (in the test).
5 My friends arrived earlier than I expected.
6 The buses run more often than the trains. *or* The buses run more frequently than … *or* The buses are more frequent than …

7 We were busier than usual (at work today). *or* We were busier at work today than usual.

UNIT 106

106.1
2 much bigger
3 much more complicated than
4 a bit cooler
5 far more interesting than
6 a bit more slowly
7 a lot easier
8 slightly older

106.2
2 any sooner / any earlier
3 no higher than / no more expensive than
4 any further/farther
5 no worse than

106.3
2 bigger and bigger
3 heavier and heavier
4 more and more nervous
5 worse and worse
6 more and more expensive
7 better and better
8 more and more talkative

106.4
2 the more I liked him *or* the more I got to like him
3 the more profit you (will) make *or* the higher your profit (will be) *or* the more your profit (will be)
4 the harder it is to concentrate
5 the more impatient she became

106.5
2 older
3 older *or* elder
4 older

UNIT 107

107.1
2 My salary isn't as high as yours.
3 You don't know as much about cars as me. *or* … as I do.
4 It isn't as cold as it was yesterday.
5 I don't feel as tired as I did yesterday. *or* … as I felt yesterday.
6 Our neighbours haven't lived here as long as us. *or* … as we have.
7 I wasn't as nervous (before the interview) as I usually am. *or* … as usual.

107.2
3 The station wasn't as far as I thought.

4 The meal cost less than I expected.
5 I don't go out as much as I used to. *or* … as often as I used to.
6 Karen used to have longer hair.
7 You don't know them as well as me. *or* … as I do.
8 There aren't as many people at this meeting as at the last one.

107.3
2 as well as
3 as long as
4 as soon as
5 as often as
6 as quietly as
7 just as comfortable as
8 just as well-qualified as
9 just as bad as

107.4
2 Your hair is the same colour as mine.
3 I arrived at the same time as you (did).
4 My birthday is the same day as Tom's. *or* My birthday is the same as Tom's.

107.5
2 than him / than he does
3 as me / as I do
4 than us / than we were
5 than her / than she is
6 as them / as they have been

UNIT 108

108.1
2 It's the cheapest restaurant in the town.
3 It was the happiest day of my life.
4 She's the most intelligent student in the class.
5 It's the most valuable painting in the gallery.
6 It's the busiest time of the year.
8 He's one of the richest men in the world.
9 It's one of the biggest castles in Britain.
10 She's one of the best players in the team. (on the team *is also possible*)
11 It was one of the worst experiences of my life.
12 He's one of the most dangerous criminals in the country.

108.2

3 larger
4 the smallest
5 better
6 the worst
7 the most popular
8 … the highest mountain in the world … It is higher than …
9 the most enjoyable
10 more comfortable
11 the quickest
12 The oldest *or* The eldest

108.3

2 That's the funniest joke I've ever heard.
3 This is the best coffee I've ever tasted.
4 She's the most generous person I've ever met.
5 That's the furthest/farthest I've ever run.
6 It's the worst mistake I've ever made. *or* It was the worst …
7 Who's the most famous person you've ever met?

UNIT 109

109.1

3 Joe doesn't like football very much.
4 *OK*
5 I ate my breakfast quickly and …
6 … a lot of people to the party?
7 *OK*
8 Did you go to bed late last night?
9 *OK*
10 I met a friend of mine on my way home.

109.2

2 We won the game easily.
3 I closed the door quietly.
4 Diane speaks German quite well.
5 Sam watches TV all the time.
6 Please don't ask that question again.
7 Does Kevin play football every weekend?
8 I borrowed some money from a friend of mine.

109.3

2 I go to the supermarket every Friday.
3 Why did you come home so late?
4 Sarah takes her children to school every day.
5 I haven't been to the cinema recently.
6 Please write your name at the top of the page.

7 I remembered her name after a few minutes.
8 We walked around the town all morning.
9 I didn't see you at the party on Saturday night.
10 We found some interesting books in the library.
11 Jackie left her umbrella in a restaurant last night.
12 They are building a new hotel opposite the park.

UNIT 110

110.1

3 I usually have …
4 *OK*
5 Steve hardly ever gets angry.
6 … and I also went to the bank.
7 Jane always has to hurry …
8 We were all tired, so …
9 *OK*

110.2

2 a We were all on holiday in Spain.
   b We were all staying at the same hotel.
   c We all enjoyed ourselves.
3 Catherine is always very generous.
4 I don't usually have to work on Saturdays.
5 Do you always watch TV in the evenings?
6 … he is also learning Italian.
7 a The new hotel is probably very expensive.
   b It probably costs a lot to stay there.
8 a I can probably help you.
   b I probably can't help you.

110.3

2 usually take
3 am usually
4 has probably gone
5 were both born
6 can also sing
7 often sleeps
8 have never spoken
9 always have to wait
10 can only read
11 will probably be leaving
12 probably won't be
13 is hardly ever
14 are still living
15 would never have met
16 always am

UNIT 111

111.1

3 He doesn't write poems any more.
4 He still wants to be a teacher.

5 He isn't / He's not interested in politics any more.
6 He's still single.
7 He doesn't go fishing any more.
8 He hasn't got a beard any more. *or* He doesn't have …

10–12
He no longer writes poems.
He is / He's no longer interested in politics.
He no longer goes fishing.
He's no longer got a beard. / He no longer has a beard.

111.2

2 He hasn't gone yet.
3 They haven't finished (repairing the road) yet.
4 They haven't woken up yet.
5 Has she found a place to live yet?
6 I haven't decided (what to do) yet.
7 It hasn't taken off yet.

111.3

5 I don't want to go out yet.
6 she doesn't work there any more
7 I still have a lot of friends there. *or* I've still got …
8 We've already met.
9 Do you still live in the same place
10 have you already eaten
11 He's not here yet.
12 he still isn't here (he isn't here yet *is also possible*)
13 are you already a member
14 I can still remember it very clearly
15 These trousers don't fit me any more.
16 'Have you finished with the paper yet?' 'No, I'm still reading it.'

UNIT 112

112.1

2 even Amanda
3 not even Julie
4 even Amanda
5 even Sarah
6 not even Amanda

112.2

2 We even painted the floor.
3 She's even met the prime minister.
4 You could even hear it from the next street. *or* You could even hear the noise from …
6 I can't even remember her name.
7 There isn't even a cinema.

8 He didn't even tell his wife (where he was going).

9 I don't even know the people next door.

112.3
2 even older
3 even better
4 even more difficult
5 even worse
6 even less

112.4
2 if
3 even if
4 even
5 even though
6 Even
7 even though
8 even if
9 Even though

UNIT 113

113.1
2 Although I had never seen her before
3 although it was quite cold
4 although we don't like them very much
5 Although I didn't speak the language
6 Although the heating was on
7 although I'd met her twice before
8 although we've known each other a long time

113.2
2 a In spite of (or Despite)
  b Although
3 a because
  b although
4 a because of
  b in spite of (or despite)
5 a although
  b because of
Example answers:
6 a he hadn't studied very hard
  b he had studied very hard
7 a I was hungry
  b being hungry / my hunger / the fact (that) I was hungry

113.3
2 In spite of having very little money, they are happy. *or* In spite of the fact (that) they have very little money …
3 Although my foot was injured, I managed to walk to the nearest village. *or* I managed to walk to the nearest village although my …

4 I enjoyed the film in spite of the silly story. / … in spite of the story being silly. / … in spite of the fact (that) the story was silly. *or* In spite of … , I enjoyed the film.
5 Despite living in the same street, we hardly ever see each other. *or* Despite the fact (that) we live in … *or* We hardly ever see each other despite …
6 Even though I was only out for five minutes, I got very wet in the rain. *or* I got very wet in the rain even though I was …

113.4
2 It's very windy though.
3 We ate it though.
4 I don't like her husband though.

UNIT 114

114.1
2–5 Take a map with you in case you get lost.
Take an anorak with you in case it rains.
Take a camera with you in case you want to take some photographs.
Take some water with you in case you're thirsty. *or* … you get thirsty.

114.2
2 I'll say goodbye now in case I don't see you again (before you go).
3 Can you check the list in case we've forgotten something? *or* … forgotten anything?
4 You should back up your files in case the computer crashes.

114.3
2 He wrote down the name (of the book) in case he forgot it.
3 I phoned my parents in case they were worried (about me).
4 I sent (Liz) another email in case she hadn't received the first one.
5 I gave them my address in case they came to London (one day).

114.4
3 If
4 if
5 in case
6 if
7 if
8 in case
9 in case

UNIT 115

115.1
2 You won't know what to do unless you listen carefully.
3 I'll never speak to her again unless she apologises to me. *or* Unless she apologises to me, I'll …
4 He won't be able to understand you unless you speak very slowly. *or* Unless you speak very slowly, he …
5 The company will have to close unless business improves soon. *or* Unless business improves soon, the company …

115.2
2 I'm not going (to the party) unless you go too.
3 The dog won't attack you unless you move suddenly.
4 Ben won't speak to you unless you ask him something.
5 The doctor won't see you unless it's an emergency.

115.3
2 unless
3 providing
4 as long as
5 unless
6 unless
7 provided
8 Unless
9 unless
10 as long as

115.4
Example answers:
2 it's not too hot
3 there isn't too much traffic
4 it isn't raining
5 I'm in a hurry
6 you have something else to do
7 you pay it back next week
8 you take risks

UNIT 116

116.1
2 We all smiled as we posed for the photograph.
3 I burnt myself as I was taking a hot dish out of the oven.
4 The crowd cheered as the two teams ran onto the field.
5 A dog ran out in front of the car as we were driving along the road.

116.2
2 As it was a nice day, we went for a walk by the sea.
3 As we didn't want to wake anybody up, we came in very quietly.

4 As the door was open, I went in.

5 As none of us had a watch, we didn't know what time it was.

116.3
3 because
4 at the same time as
5 at the same time as
6 because
7 because

116.4
3 *OK*
4 when I was asleep on the beach
5 When I left school
6 *OK*
7 when I was a child

116.5
Example answers:
1 I saw you as you were getting into your car.
2 It started to rain just as we started playing tennis.
3 As I didn't have enough money for a taxi, I had to walk home.
4 Just as I took the photograph, somebody walked in front of the camera.

UNIT 117

117.1
3 like her mother
4 people like him
5 *OK*
6 like most of his friends
7 like talking to the wall
8 *OK*
9 *OK*
10 *OK*
11 like a bomb exploding
12 like a fish

117.2
2 like blocks of ice
3 like a beginner
4 as a tourist guide
5 like a church
6 as a birthday present
7 like winter
8 like a child

117.3
2 like
3 as
4 like
5 like
6 as (like *is also possible*)
7 like
8 as
9 as
10 like
11 like
12 as
13 as

14 Like
15 as
16 As
17 like
18 as (like *is also possible*)

UNIT 118

118.1
2 You look as if you've seen a ghost.
3 You sound as if you're enjoying yourself.
4 I feel as if I've (just) run a marathon.

118.2
2 It looks as if it's going to rain.
3 It sounds as if they're having an argument.
4 It looks as if there's been an accident.
5 It looks as if we'll have to walk.
6 It sounds as if you should see a doctor.

118.3
2 as if he meant what he said
3 as if she's hurt her leg / as if she hurt her leg
4 as if he hadn't eaten for a week
5 as if she was enjoying it
6 as if I'm going to be sick
7 as if she didn't want to come
8 as if I didn't exist

118.4
2 as if I was/were
3 as if she was/were
4 as if it was/were

UNIT 119

119.1
3 during
4 for
5 during
6 for
7 for
8 for
9 during
10 for
11 for
12 for
13 during
14 for

119.2
3 while
4 While
5 During
6 while
7 during
8 During
9 while
10 during
11 while

12 during
13 while
14 while

119.3
Example answers:
3 I hurt my arm while I was doing the housework.
4 Can you wait here while I make a quick phone call?
5 Most of the students looked bored during the lesson.
6 I was asked a lot of questions during the interview.
7 Don't open the car door while the car is moving.
8 The lights suddenly went out while we were having dinner.
9 It started to rain during the game.
10 It started to rain while we were walking home.

UNIT 120

120.1
2 I have to be at the airport by 8.30.
3 Let me know by Saturday whether you can come to the party.
4 Please make sure that you're here by 2 o'clock.
5 If we leave now, we should arrive by lunchtime.

120.2
2 by
3 by
4 until
5 until 5.30 ... by now
6 by
7 until
8 by
9 by
10 until
11 By
12 by

120.3
Example answers:
3 until I come back
4 by 5 o'clock
5 by next Friday
6 until midnight

120.4
2 By the time I got to the station / By the time I'd got to the station
3 By the time I finished (my work) / By the time I'd finished (my work)
4 By the time the police arrived / By the time the police had arrived
5 By the time we got to the top / By the time we'd got to the top

UNIT 121

121.1
2 at night
3 in the evening
4 on 21 July 1969
5 at the same time
6 in the 1920s
7 in about 20 minutes
8 at the moment
9 in the Middle Ages
10 in 11 seconds
11 (on) Saturdays

121.2
2 I last saw her **on** Tuesday. *or*
  I last saw her Tuesday.
3 in
4 At
5 on
6 in
7 in
8 at
9 on
10 at
11 in
12 at
13 on
14 in
15 **On** Saturday night *or*
  Saturday night ... **at** midnight
16 **at** 5 o'clock **in** the morning
17 **on** 7 January ... **in** April
18 at home **on** Tuesday morning
  or at home Tuesday morning
  ... **in** the afternoon

121.3
3 a
4 *both*
5 b
6 b
7 *both*
8 a
9 b
10 a

UNIT 122

122.1
2 on time
3 in time
4 on time
5 in time
6 on time
7 in time
8 in time
9 on time

122.2
2 I got home just in time.
3 I stopped him just in time.
4 I got to the cinema just in
  time for the beginning of the
  film.

122.3
2 at the end of the month
3 at the end of the course
4 at the end of the race
5 at the end of the interview

122.4
2 In the end she resigned (from
  her job).
3 In the end I gave up (trying to
  learn German).
4 In the end we decided not to
  go (to the party). *or*
  In the end we didn't go (to the
  party).

122.5
2 In
3 at ... at
4 in
5 in
6 at
7 in
8 at
9 in

UNIT 123

123.1
2 On his arm. *or*
  On the man's arm.
3 At the traffic lights.
4 a On the door.
  b In the door.
5 On the wall.
6 In Paris.
7 a At the gate.
  b On the gate.
8 On the beach.

123.2
2 on my guitar
3 at the next garage
4 in your coffee
5 on that tree
6 in the mountains
7 on the island
8 at the window

123.3
2 on
3 at
4 on
5 in
6 on
7 at
8 **in** a small village **in** the south-
  west
9 on
10 in
11 **on** the wall **in** the kitchen
12 at

UNIT 124

124.1
2 On the second floor.
3 At/On the corner.
4 In the corner.
5 At the top of the stairs.
6 In the back of the car.
7 At the front.
8 On the left.
9 In the back row.
10 On a farm.

124.2
2 on the right
3 in the world
4 on the way to work
5 on the west coast
6 in the front row
7 at the back of the class
6 on the back of this card

124.3
2 in
3 in
4 at
5 in
6 on
7 At
8 in
9 in
10 on
11 in
12 on
13 in
14 on ... on

UNIT 125

125.1
2 on a train
3 at a conference
4 in hospital
5 at the hairdresser's
6 on his bike
7 in New York
8 at the Savoy Theatre

125.2
2 in a taxi
3 at the cinema
4 in prison
5 at school
6 at the sports centre
7 in hospital
8 at the airport
9 on the plane
10 at sea

125.3
2 at
3 in
4 at
5 **at/in** a very nice hotel ... **in**
  Amsterdam
6 in
7 on
8 at
9 in
10 at
11 in
12 at ... at
13 in
14 **in** Birmingham ... **at**
  Birmingham University

UNIT 126

126.1
3 at
4 to
5 to
6 into
7 at
8 to
9 into
10 to
11 at
12 to
13 into
14 to
15 get home ... going **to** bed
16 returned **to** France ... two years **in** Brazil
17 born **in** Chicago ... moved **to** New York ... lives **in** New York

126.2
Example answers:
2–4 I've been to Sweden once.
I've never been to the United States.
I've been to Paris a few times.

126.3
2 in
3 –
4 at
5 to
6 –

126.4
2 I got on the bus.
3 I got out of the car.
4 I got off the train.
5 I got into the taxi. *or* I got in the taxi.
6 I got off the plane.

UNIT 127

127.1
2 in cold weather
3 in pencil
4 in love
5 in block capitals
6 in the shade
7 in my opinion

127.2
2 on strike
3 on a tour
4 on television
5 on purpose
6 on a diet
7 on business
8 on holiday
9 on the phone
10 on the whole

127.3
2 on
3 on
4 at

5 in
6 on
7 for *or* on
8 on
9 at
10 at
11 on
12 **In my opinion ... on** television
13 on
14 on
15 on
16 at
17 on
18 in

UNIT 128

128.1
2 by mistake
3 by hand
4 by credit card
5 by satellite

128.2
2 on
3 by
4 **by** car ... **on** my bike
5 in
6 on
7 by

128.3
Example answers:
3–5 *Ulysses* is a novel by James Joyce.
Yesterday is a song by Paul McCartney.
Guernica is a painting by Pablo Picasso.

128.4
2 by
3 with
4 by
5 by
6 **by** car ... **in** your car
7 **by** the bed **with** a lamp and a clock **on** it

128.5
2 travelling **by** bus *or* travelling **on the** bus *or* travelling **on buses**
3 taken **with** a very good camera
4 this music is **by** Beethoven
5 **pay cash** *or* pay **in** cash
6 a mistake **by** one of our players

128.6
2 The price has gone up by ten pence.
3 Helen won by two votes.
4 I missed her/Kate by five minutes.

UNIT 129

129.1
2 to the problem
3 with her brother
4 in the cost of living
5 to your question
6 for a new road
7 in/to working at home
8 in the number of people without jobs
9 for shoes like these any more
10 between your job and mine

129.2
2 invitation to
3 contact with
4 key to
5 cause of
6 reply to
7 connection between
8 pictures of
9 reason for
10 damage to

129.3
2 to
3 in
4 for
5 of
6 in *or* to
7 for
8 to *or* towards
9 with
10 in
11 to
12 of
13 **for** a rise **in** pay
14 to
15 with

UNIT 130

130.1
2 That was nice of her.
3 That was generous of him.
4 That wasn't very nice of them.
5 That's very kind of you.
6 That wasn't very polite of him.
7 That's a bit childish of them.

130.2
2 kind to
3 sorry for
4 annoyed with
5 annoyed about
6 impressed by/with
7 bored with (or bored by)
8 astonished at/by

130.3
2 of
3 to ... to
4 of
5 of
6 with
7 to
8 with

9 at/by
10 with
11 about
12 about
13 sorry **for/about** ... angry **with**
14 furious **with** us **for** making
15 about
16 about
17 at/by
18 by/with
19 about
20 about
21 for

UNIT 131

131.1
2 of furniture
3 on sport
4 of time
5 at tennis
6 to a Russian (man)
7 of him / of Robert
8 from yours / to yours

131.2
2 similar to
3 afraid of
4 interested in
5 responsible for
6 proud of
7 different from/to

131.3
2 for
3 of
4 of
5 in
6 to
7 of ... of
8 on
9 of
10 with
11 of
12 of
13 in
14 of
15 of
16 at
17 of
18 on
19 of

131.4
Example answers:
2 I'm hopeless at telling jokes.
3 I'm not very good at
   mathematics.
4 I'm quite good at
   remembering names.

UNIT 132

132.1
3 Can you explain this question
   to me? / Can you explain it to
   me?
4 Can you explain the problem to
   me? / Can you explain it to me?

5 Can you explain to me how
   this machine works?
6 Can you explain to me what I
   have to do?

132.2
3 to
4 –
5 to
6 to
7 –
8 –
9 to
10 –

132.3
3 speaking to
4 point them at
5 glanced at
6 listen to
7 throw stones at
8 throw it to

132.4
2 at
3 at
4 to
5 to
6 at
7 at
8 to
9 at
10 at
11 to

UNIT 133

133.1
2 for
3 for
4 to
5 for
6 about
7 –
8 about
9 –
10 for
11 for
12 about
13 for
14 for

133.2
2 waiting for
3 talk about
4 asked the waiter for
5 applied for
6 do something about
7 looks after *or* has looked
   after
8 left Boston for

133.3
2 for
3 about
4 of
5 for
6 of
7 about
8 –

133.4
2 looking for
3 looked after
4 looking for
5 look for
6 looks after

UNIT 134

134.1
2 about
3 **to us about**
4 of
5 of
6 about ... about ... about ...
   about
7 of
8 about
9 about/of

134.2
2 complaining about
3 think about
4 warn you about
5 heard of
6 dream of
7 reminded me about
8 remind you of

134.3
2 hear about
3 heard from
4 heard of
5 hear from
6 hear about
7 heard of

134.4
2 think about
3 think of
4 think of
5 thinking of/about
6 think of
7 thought about
8 think much of
9 thinking about/of

UNIT 135

135.1
2 for the misunderstanding
3 on winning the tournament
4 from/against his enemies
5 of eleven players
6 on bread and eggs

135.2
2 for everything
3 for the economic crisis
4 on television
5 is to blame for the economic
   crisis
6 television is to blame for the
   increase in violent crime

135.3
2 paid for
3 accused of
4 depends on

5 live on
6 congratulated him on
7 apologise to

135.4
2 from
3 on
4 of/from
5 for
6 for
7 –
8 on
9 on
10 – *or* on
11 from/against
12 of

UNIT 136

136.1
2 I prefer small towns to big cities.
3 Jane provided me with all the information I needed.
4 This morning I spent £70 on a pair of shoes.

136.2
2 happened to
3 invited to
4 divided into
5 believe in
6 fill it with
7 drove into
8 Concentrate on
9 succeeded in

136.3
2 to
3 on
4 in
5 to
6 in
7 with
8 into
9 in
10 on
11 into
12 to
13 –
14 into
15 on
16 **from** one language **into** another
17 happened **to** ... spend it **on**
18 into
19 with

136.4
Example answers:
2 on CDs
3 into a wall
4 to volleyball
5 into many languages

UNIT 137

137.1
2 sit down

3 flew away
4 get out
5 speak up
6 get by
7 gone up
8 looked round

137.2
2 back at
3 up to
4 forward to
5 away with
6 up at
7 in through

137.3
2 wake me up
3 get it out
4 give them back
5 switch it on
6 take them off

137.4
3 I have to take **them back**
4 We can turn **the television off** *or* We can turn **off the television**
5 I knocked **it over**
6 I don't want to wake **her up**.
7 (*example answer*) You should put **your coat on** *or* You should put **on your coat**.
8 I was able to put **it out**
9 (*example answer*) they've put **the price(s) up** *or* they've put **up the price(s)**
10 Shall I turn **the light(s) on?** *or* Shall I turn **on the light(s)?**

UNIT 138

138.1
2 eats
3 moved
4 drop/call
5 checked
6 cut
7 plug
8 filling / to fill
9 left
10 dive
11 rub
12 dropped

138.2
2 into
3 in
4 out
5 into
6 out of

138.3
2 dropped out
3 moved in
4 left out
5 joined in
6 eating out *or* to eat out
7 taken in

8 dropped in / called in
9 get out of

138.4
2 Fill them in *or* Fill them out
3 cross it out
4 took me in
5 let us in

UNIT 139

139.1
2 a mistake
3 a candle
4 an order
5 a cigarette / a candle
6 a new product
7 a mess

139.2
2 works out
3 carried out
4 ran out
5 sort out
6 find out
7 tried out
8 pointed out
9 work out
10 went out
11 turned out
12 works out
13 find out
14 put out

139.3
2 giving/handing out
3 turned out nice/fine/sunny
4 fallen out
5 to sort out / sorting out the post / the mail
6 work out how to use the camera / her new camera

139.4
2 try it out
3 work it out
4 sorted it out

UNIT 140

140.1
2 put the heating on
3 put the oven on
4 put the kettle on
5 put a CD on

140.2
2 going on
3 take off
4 switched off / turned off
5 drove off / went off
6 put on
7 set off / be off
8 put off
9 called off
10 put on
11 see me off

140.3

2 took off
3 tried on a/the hat *or*
  tried a/the hat on
4 was called off
5 see him off
6 put them on

UNIT 141

141.1

2 went on / carried on
3 walked on / carried on /
  carried on walking
4 dozed off / dropped off /
  nodded off
5 go on / carry on
6 went off
7 keeps on phoning me

141.2

2 went off
3 finish off
4 drive on / carry on
5 ripped off
6 getting on
7 dozed off / dropped off /
  nodded off
8 told off
9 get on
10 going off
11 keep on
12 get on
13 showing off
14 put off

141.3

2 finish it off
3 were ripped off
4 go off
5 did you get on
6 carried on (playing) / went on
  (playing)
7 tell them off
8 doesn't get on (well) with

UNIT 142

142.1

2 turn it down
3 calm him down
4 put them up
5 let her down
6 turned it down

142.2

2 took them down
3 stand up
4 turned it up
5 put their bags down
6 were blown down / fell down
7 wrote it down
8 bent down and picked them
  up

142.3

2 calm down
3 slowed down
4 was turned down
5 broken down
6 cut down
7 let down
8 (has) closed down
9 be knocked down (*or* be
  pulled down *or* be torn down)
10 turned down
11 was knocked down
12 broke down

UNIT 143

143.1

2 went up to / walked up to
3 catch up with
4 keep up with

143.2

2 used up
3 washed up
4 grow up
5 turn up
6 gave up
7 taking up
8 give up
9 ended up
10 takes up
11 make up

143.3

3 tidy it up / tidy up
4 fixed it up
5 keep up with
6 was brought up
7 keep it up
8 went up to
9 was made up of
10 set it up / fix it up

UNIT 144

144.1

2 D
3 E
4 C
5 G
6 A
7 B

144.2

2 held up
3 did it up
4 cheer him up

144.3

2 blew up
3 beaten up
4 broken up / split up
5 did up
6 clears up
7 mixed up

144.4

2 look it up
3 put up with
4 made it up
5 come up with
6 tear it up
7 saving up for

UNIT 145

145.1

2 Pay
3 throw
4 gets
5 be
6 look
7 gave
8 get

145.2

2 be away / have gone away
3 be back
4 ran away
5 smile back
6 get away
7 Keep away

145.3

2 blew away
3 put it back
4 walked away
5 threw it back (to her)
6 threw them away

145.4

2 throw it away
3 take them back
4 pay you back / pay it back
5 gave them away
6 call back / call me back

Key to Additional exercises *(see page 302)*

1
3 'm getting / am getting
4 do you do
5 arrived … was raining
6 phones … didn't phone
7 were thinking … decided
8 are you looking
9 doesn't rain
10 rang … were having
11 went … was preparing … didn't want … didn't stay
12 told … didn't believe … thought … was joking

2
2 didn't go
3 is wearing
4 has grown
5 haven't decided
6 is being
7 wasn't reading
8 didn't have
9 It's beginning
10 got
11 wasn't
12 you've been
13 I've been doing
14 did she go
15 I've been playing
16 do you come
17 since I saw her
18 for 20 years

3
3 are you going
4 Do you watch
5 have you lived / have you been living / have you been
6 Did you have
7 Have you seen
8 was she wearing
9 Have you been waiting / Have you been here
10 does it take
11 Have you finished
12 Have you (ever) been

4
2 've known each other / have known each other *or* 've been friends / have been friends
3 I've ever had / I've ever been on / I've had for ages (*etc.*)
4 He went / He went home / He went out / He left
5 I've worn it
6 I was playing
7 been swimming for
8 since I've been / since I (last) went
9 did you buy / did you get

5
1 got … was already waiting … had arrived

2 was lying … wasn't watching … 'd fallen / had fallen … was snoring … turned … woke
3 'd just gone / had just gone … was reading … heard … got … didn't see … went
4 missed … was standing … realised … 'd left / had left … had … got
5 met … was walking … 'd been / had been … 'd been playing / had been playing … were going … invited … 'd arranged / had arranged … didn't have

6
2 Somebody has taken it.
3 They'd only known / They had only known each other (for) a few weeks.
4 It's been raining / It has been raining all day. *or* It's rained / It has rained all day.
5 I'd been dreaming. / I had been dreaming.
6 I'd had / I had had a big breakfast.
7 They've been going / They have been going there for years.
8 I've had it / I have had it since I got up.
9 He's been training / He has been training very hard for it.

7
1 I haven't seen
2 You look / You're looking
3 are you going
4 are you meeting
5 I'm going
6 Do you often go
7 are you going
8 I'm meeting
9 has been
10 I've been waiting
11 has just started
12 is she getting
13 Does she like
14 she thinks
15 Are you working
16 spoke
17 you were working
18 went
19 I started / I had started
20 I lost
21 you haven't had
22 I've had
23 have you seen
24 has he been
25 I saw
26 he went
27 He'd been
28 he decided / he'd decided

29 He was really looking forward
30 is he doing
31 I haven't heard
32 he left

8
1 invented
2 it's gone / it has gone
3 had gone … left
4 did you do … Did you go
5 have you had
6 was looking
7 She's been teaching / She has been teaching
8 I bought … I haven't worn
9 I saw … was … I'd seen / I had seen … I remembered … it was
10 Have you heard … She was … died … She wrote … Have you read
11 does this word mean … I've never seen
12 Did you get … it had already begun
13 knocked … was … she'd gone / she had gone … she didn't want
14 He'd never used / He had never used … he didn't know
15 went … she needed … she'd been sitting / she had been sitting

9
3 used to drive
4 was driving
5 were working
6 used to have
7 was living
8 was playing
9 used to play
10 was wearing

10
2 I'm going to the dentist.
3 No, we're going to hire a car.
4 I'll look after the children.
5 I'm having lunch with Sue.
6 What are you going to have?
7 I'll turn on the light.
8 I'm going to turn on the light.

11
2 I'll come
3 shall we meet
4 begins
5 I'll meet
6 I'm seeing
7 Shall I ask
8 I'll see
9 are going
10 does the film begin
11 Are you meeting
12 I'll be

12
1 (2) Are you going to do
  (3) it starts
  (4) you'll enjoy
  (5) it will / it's going to be
2 (1) you're going
  (2) We're going
  (3) you have
  (4) I'll send
  (5) I'll get
  (6) I get
3 (1) I'm having / I'm going to
      have
  (2) are coming
  (3) they'll have gone
  (4) they're
  (5) I won't be
  (6) you know
  (7) I'll phone
4 (1) shall we meet
  (2) I'll be waiting
  (3) you arrive
  (4) I'll be sitting
  (5) I'll be wearing
  (6) Is Agent 307 coming / Is
      Agent 307 going to come /
      Will Agent 307 be coming
  (7) Shall I bring
  (8) I'll explain
  (9) I see
  (10) I'll try

13
1 I'll have
2 Are you going
3 shall I phone
4 It's going to land
5 it's / it is
6 I'll miss / I'm going to miss …
  you go (or you've gone)
7 Shall I give … I give … will
  you send
8 does it end
9 I'm going … is getting
10 I'll tell … I'm … I won't be
11 I'm going to have / I'm having
12 she apologises
13 we'll be living
14 you finish

14
2 I've had
3 I bought *or* I got
4 I'll come
5 I've been *or* I've eaten
6 I used to play
7 I haven't been waiting *or*
  I haven't been here
8 I'd been
9 I'm going
10 I haven't seen *or* I haven't
   heard from
11 I'll have gone *or* I'll have
   left

15
2 I've been travelling

3 I'm beginning
4 I've seen
5 has been
6 I've met
7 I left
8 I stayed *or* I was staying
9 I'd planned *or* I was
  planning
10 I ended up
11 I enjoyed
12 I took
13 met
14 I'm staying *or* I'm going to
   stay *or* I'll be staying *or*
   I'll stay
15 I continue
16 I'll get
17 I'm
18 I'll let
19 I know
20 I'm staying
21 we're going to visit *or*
   we're visiting
22 are building *or* have been
   building
23 it will be
24 I'll be

16
2 A
3 C
4 B *or* C
5 B
6 A *or* C
7 A *or* C
8 C
9 B *or* C
10 A *or* B
11 A
12 C
13 A *or* B
14 B *or* C
15 B

17
3 He must have forgotten.
4 You needn't have gone home
  so early.
5 It can't be changed now.
6 She may be watching
  television.
7 She must have been waiting
  for somebody.
8 He couldn't have done it.
9 You ought to have been here
  earlier.
10 I would have helped you.
11 You should have been warned
   about it.
12 He might not have been
   feeling very well. *or*
   He might not have felt …

18
3 could rain / might rain
4 might have gone / could have
  gone
5 couldn't go

6 couldn't have seen / can't have
  seen
7 should get
8 wouldn't recognise / might not
  recognise
9 must have heard
10 should have turned

19
4 rings
5 were
6 's / is
7 was/were
8 had been
9 had
10 hadn't had
11 'd driven / had driven *or*
   'd been driving / had been
   driving
12 didn't read

20
2 I'd be surprised if Sarah came
  (to see us now).
3 If I'd known you were busy, I
  wouldn't have disturbed you.
4 They'd be upset if I told them
  what happened.
5 If you hadn't frightened the
  dog, it wouldn't have attacked
  you.
6 I wouldn't have got (so) wet if
  I'd had an umbrella. *or*
  … if I had had an umbrella.
7 If he hadn't been (so) nervous,
  he wouldn't have failed (his
  driving test).

21
Example answers:
1 I wasn't feeling so tired
2 I hadn't had so much to do
3 I would have forgotten Jane's
  birthday
4 you hadn't taken so long to
  get ready
5 I would have gone to the
  concert
6 you were in trouble
7 there was less traffic
8 people would go out more

22
3 was cancelled
4 has been repaired
5 is being restored
6 's believed / is believed
7 'd be sacked / would be
  sacked
8 might have been thrown
9 was taught
10 being arrested / having been
   arrested
11 Have you ever been arrested
12 are reported … have been
   injured

23
3 've sold / have sold
4 's been sold / has been sold

5 are made
6 might be stolen
7 must have been stolen
8 must have taken
9 can be solved
10 should have left
11 is delayed
12 is being built ... is expected

24
Castle Fire
2 was discovered
3 was injured
4 be rescued
5 are believed to have been destroyed
6 is not known

Shop robbery
1 was forced
2 being threatened
3 had been stolen
4 was later found
5 had been abandoned
6 has been arrested / was arrested
7 is still being questioned

Road delays
1 is being resurfaced
2 are asked / are being asked / have been asked
3 is expected
4 will be closed
5 will be diverted

Accident
1 was taken
2 was allowed
3 was blocked
4 be diverted
5 have been killed

25
1 I told **her (that) Paul had gone out** and **I didn't know when he'd be back.** I asked (her) **if/whether she wanted to leave a message,** but she said (that) **she'd try again** later.
2 I had reserved a hotel room, but when I got to the hotel they told **me (that) they had no record of any reservation in my name.** When I asked (them) **if/whether they had any rooms free anyway,** they said (that) **they were sorry,** but **the hotel was full.**
3 The immigration official asked us **why we were visiting the country,** and we told **him (that) we were on holiday.** Then he wanted to know **how long we intended to stay** and **where we would be staying during our visit.**
4 She said (that) **she'd phone us from the airport when she arrived.** *or* She said (that)

she'll phone us from the airport when she arrives.
No, she said **not to come to the airport.** She said (that) **she'd take the bus.** *or* She said (that) **she'll take the bus.**
5 He wanted to know **what my job was** and asked (me) **how much I earned.** *or*
He wanted to know **what my job is** and asked (me) **how much I earn.**
... so I told **him to mind his own business** and I put the phone down.
6 He said (that) **he'd be at the restaurant at 7.30.**
He said (that) **he knew where the restaurant was.** And I told **him to phone me if there was any problem.**
7 You just said (that) **you weren't hungry.**
But you said (that) **you didn't like bananas.** You told **me not to buy any.**

26
3 changing
4 to change
5 change
6 being
7 saying
8 to phone
9 drinking
10 to be
11 to see
12 to be
13 to think ... making
14 living ... to move
15 to be ... playing
16 being stopped ... stealing ... driving
17 work ... pressing

27
3 I don't fancy going out.
4 He tends to forget things.
5 Would you mind helping me? / Do you mind helping me?
6 Everybody seems to have gone out.
7 We're thinking of moving.
8 I was afraid to touch it.
9 He's / He is afraid of being robbed.
10 It's not worth seeing.
11 I'm not used to walking so far.
12 She seems to be enjoying herself.
13 He insisted on showing them to me.
14 I'd rather somebody else did it.

28
3 I've given up reading newspapers.

4 I'd rather not go out tonight / ... stay at home tonight.
5 He has difficulty walking / ... difficulty in walking.
6 Do you want me to phone you this evening?
7 I came in without anybody seeing me / ... without being seen.
8 I was accused of being a cheat / ... of cheating.
9 I'm looking forward to seeing them again.
10 What do you advise me to do?
11 I'd like to have gone out with you.
12 I regret not taking your advice / ... that I didn't take your advice.

29
2 Tennis ... twice a week ... a very good player
3 for dinner ... after work ... to the cinema
4 Unemployment ... for people ... find work
5 an accident ... going home ... taken to hospital ... I think most accidents ... by people driving
6 an economist ... in the investment department of Lloyds Bank ... for an American bank ... in the United States
7 the name of the hotel ... The Imperial ... in Queen Street in the city centre ... near the station
8 The older one ... a pilot with British Airways ... The younger one ... at school ... he leaves school ... go to university ... study law

30
2 B
3 C
4 A *or* B
5 C
6 B
7 A *or* C
8 A
9 C
10 B *or* C
11 B
12 A
13 A *or* B
14 B

31
3 It's the most polluted place ...
4 I was disappointed that ...
5 OK
6 Joe works hard, but ...
7 ... in a large modern building.
8 OK (as fast as he can *is also correct*)

9 I missed the last three days ...
10 *OK*
11 The weather has been unusually cold ...
12 The water in the pool was too dirty to swim in.
13 ... to wait such a long time. (so long *is also correct*)
14 *OK*
15 ... I got up earlier than usual.

32
2 If
3 when
4 if
5 when
6 if
7 if
8 unless
9 if
10 as long as
11 in case
12 in case
13 if
14 even if
15 Although
16 Although
17 When
18 when

33
2 on
3 **at** 9.30 **on** Tuesday
4 at
5 on
6 at
7 In
8 at
9 during
10 **on** Friday... **since** then
11 for
12 at
13 **at** the moment ... **until** Friday
14 by
15 in

34
1 in
2 by
3 at
4 on
5 in
6 on
7 **to** a party **at** Linda's house
8 on
9 on
10 to ... to
11 **in** Vienna ... **at** the age of 35
12 **in** this photograph ... **on** the left
13 **to** the theatre ... **in** the front row

14 **on** the wall **by** the door
15 at
16 on
17 **in** a tower block ... **on** the fifteenth floor
18 on
19 by
20 **On** the bus ... **by** car
21 on ... on
22 in
23 **in** London ... **to** Italy
24 to
25 on

35
1 for
2 at
3 to
4 to
5 in
6 with
7 of
8 to
9 of
10 at/by
11 of
12 about

36
1 of
2 after
3 – *(no preposition)*
4 about
5 to
6 – *(no preposition)*
7 into
8 of
9 to
10 – *(no preposition)*
11 on
12 of
13 of
14 – *(no preposition)*
15 in
16 at (about *is also possible*)
17 on
18 If Kevin asks you **for** money
19 I apologised **to** Sarah **for** keeping ...
20 I thanked her **for** everything

37
2 h
3 e
4 g
5 a
6 k
7 c
8 j
9 b
10 f
11 i

38
2 D
3 B
4 B
5 A
6 A
7 D
8 C
9 C
10 B
11 A
12 D

39
2 out to
3 up with
4 forward to
5 up with
6 out of
7 on with
8 out with
9 up with
10 back on
11 out about
12 on with

40
3 went off
4 turned up / showed up
5 fill it in / fill it out
6 knocked down / pulled down / torn down
7 sorted out
8 give up
9 dozed off / dropped off / nodded off
10 split up / break up
11 put up with it
12 get by
13 went on
14 put it off

41
2 put
3 moving
4 put
5 done
6 turned / turns
7 find
8 Calm
9 set
10 held
11 left *or* 've left / have left
12 works
13 join
14 works
15 drop / call
16 sort / work
17 **went** off ... **woke** me up

Key to Study guide

Present and past

1.1	A
1.2	B
1.3	C
1.4	B, C
1.5	C
1.6	A

Present perfect and past

2.1	B
2.2	C
2.3	A
2.4	C
2.5	A
2.6	B
2.7	A
2.8	D
2.9	A
2.10	A
2.11	C
2.12	A
2.13	C
2.14	C
2.15	D
2.16	C

Future

3.1	B
3.2	A
3.3	C
3.4	A, C
3.5	B
3.6	C
3.7	A

Modals

4.1	A, B
4.2	B
4.3	A, C, D
4.4	C
4.5	B
4.6	C, D
4.7	B
4.8	A, C
4.9	B, C
4.10	A, B, D
4.11	A
4.12	D, E
4.13	A

If and wish

5.1	B
5.2	C
5.3	B
5.4	D
5.5	A

Passive

6.1	C
6.2	B
6.3	D
6.4	A
6.5	A, B
6.6	C
6.7	D

Reported speech

7.1	A
7.2	B
7.3	A

Questions and auxiliary verbs

8.1	C
8.2	A
8.3	D
8.4	A
8.5	B

–ing and the infinitive

9.1	A
9.2	B, D
9.3	B
9.4	A
9.5	A
9.6	A
9.7	C
9.8	D
9.9	C
9.10	C
9.11	B
9.12	C
9.13	B, D
9.14	B
9.15	A, B
9.16	A
9.17	A
9.18	B, C

Articles and nouns

10.1	B
10.2	A
10.3	B, C
10.4	B
10.5	C
10.6	A
10.7	A
10.8	A
10.9	D
10.10	C
10.11	C
10.12	A
10.13	C
10.14	B

Pronouns and determiners

11.1	A
11.2	B
11.3	D
11.4	B
11.5	B
11.6	C
11.7	A, C
11.8	C
11.9	D
11.10	A, C
11.11	B

Relative clauses

12.1	A, C
12.2	A, B
12.3	C
12.4	B
12.5	D
12.6	B, C

Adjectives and adverbs

13.1	B
13.2	C
13.3	B, C
13.4	A
13.5	A, D
13.6	B
13.7	B, C
13.8	C
13.9	C
13.10	B, C
13.11	D
13.12	A, B
13.13	B
13.14	D
13.15	D

Conjunctions and prepositions

14.1	A, D
14.2	C
14.3	B, C
14.4	B, D
14.5	B
14.6	C, D
14.7	B, C
14.8	A

Prepositions

15.1	B, D
15.2	A
15.3	C
15.4	B
15.5	A
15.6	B, D
15.7	B
15.8	B
15.9	C
15.10	C
15.11	C
15.12	A
15.13	C
15.14	B
15.15	D
15.16	D
15.17	A

Phrasal verbs

16.1	B
16.2	A
16.3	D
16.4	C
16.5	C
16.6	B
16.7	A
16.8	A, D
16.9	B

Index

The numbers in the index are unit numbers, not page numbers.

Index

0208 574
0208 574.
4293

– Hillingdon Motor Company
11 New Broadway Oxbridge Road
UB10 OLJ – 0844477587